LET'S GO

## PAGES PACKED WITH ESSENTIAL INFOR...

"Value-packed, unbeatable, accurate, and comprehensive."

**—The Los Angeles Times**

"The guides are aimed not only at young budget travelers but at the independent traveler; a sort of streetwise cookbook for traveling alone."

**—The New York Times**

"Unbeatable; good sight-seeing advice; up-to-date info on restaurants, hotels, and inns; a commitment to money-saving travel; and a wry style that brightens nearly every page."

**—The Washington Post**

## THE BEST TRAVEL BARGAINS IN YOUR BUDGET

"All the dirt, dirt cheap."

**—People**

"Let's Go follows the creed that you don't have to toss your life's savings to the wind to travel—unless you want to."

**—The Salt Lake Tribune**

## REAL ADVICE FOR REAL EXPERIENCES

"The writers seem to have experienced every rooster-packed bus and lunar-surfaced mattress about which they write."

**—The New York Times**

"[Let's Go's] devoted updaters really walk the walk (and thumb the ride, and trek the trail). Learn how to fish, haggle, find work—anywhere."

**—Food & Wine**

"A world-wise traveling companion—always ready with friendly advice and helpful hints, all sprinkled with a bit of wit."

**—The Philadelphia Inquirer**

## A GUIDE WITH A SPIRIT AND A SOCIAL CONSCIENCE

"Lighthearted and sophisticated, informative and fun to read. [Let's Go] helps the novice traveler navigate like a knowledgeable old hand."

**—Atlanta Journal-Constitution**

"The serious mission at the book's core reveals itself in exhortations to respect the culture and the environment—and, if possible, to visit as a volunteer, a student, or a teacher rather than a tourist."

**—San Francisco Chronicle**

# LET'S GO PUBLICATIONS

## TRAVEL GUIDES

Australia
Austria & Switzerland
Brazil
Britain
California
Central America
Chile
China
Costa Rica
Costa Rica, Nicaragua & Panama
Eastern Europe
Ecuador
Egypt
Europe
France
Germany
Greece
Guatemala & Belize
Hawaii
India & Nepal
Ireland
Israel
Italy
Japan
Mexico
New Zealand
Peru
Puerto Rico
Southeast Asia
Spain & Portugal with Morocco
Thailand
USA
Vietnam
Western Europe
Yucatán Peninsula

## ROADTRIP GUIDE

Roadtripping USA

## ADVENTURE GUIDES

Alaska
Pacific Northwest
Southwest USA

## CITY GUIDES

Amsterdam
Barcelona
Berlin, Prague & Budapest
Boston
Buenos Aires
Florence
London
London, Oxford, Cambridge & Edinburgh
New York City
Paris
Rome
San Francisco
Washington, DC

## POCKET CITY GUIDES

Amsterdam
Berlin
Boston
Chicago
London
New York City
Paris
San Francisco
Venice
Washington, DC

# LET'S GO

# YUCATÁN PENINSULA

RESEARCHERS
**DANIEL HERTZ**
**NATALIE SHERMAN**

**ASHLEY LAPORTE** MANAGING EDITOR
**NADAV GREENBERG** RESEARCH MANAGER
**CLAIRE SHEPRO** RESEARCH MANAGER

EDITORS
**COURTNEY A. FISKE**    **RUSSELL FORD RENNIE**
**CHARLIE E. RIGGS**       **SARA PLANA**
**OLGA I. ZHULINA**

# HOW TO USE THIS BOOK

**COVERAGE LAYOUT.** *Let's Go Yucatán Peninsula* begins in the state of **Campeche,** where you can get your bearings in the smallest and least-touristed state on the peninsula before moving on to the historically rich **Yucatán,** home to some of the most magnificent Mayan ruins in the country. Move on to tourist-mobbed **Quintana Roo** and relax on the beaches of Cancún or go scuba diving off Isla Mujeres. We then leave the peninsula and take you to **Tabasco and Chiapas,** venturing into beautiful, less touristed cities like San Cristóbal de las Casas and Villahermosa, as well as thousands of miles of jungle and national parks. Our final stop is **Oaxaca**—make sure to leave time to explore the city as well as the numerous small towns and sites surrounding it in Oaxaca Valley.

**TRANSPORTATION INFO.** For connections between destinations, information is generally listed under both the arrival and departure cities. Parentheticals usually provide the trip duration followed by frequency, then the price. For more general information on travel, consult **Essentials** (p. 6).

**COVERING THE BASICS.** The first chapter, **Discover the Yucatán Peninsula** (p. 1), contains highlights of the country, complete with **Suggested Itineraries.** The **Essentials** (p. 6) section contains practical information on planning your trip, as well as useful tips for traveling throughout the region. Take some time to peruse the **Life and Times** section (p. 38) and brush up on your Mayan history. The **Appendix** (p. 265) features climate information, a list of national holidays, measurement conversions, and a glossary. For study abroad, volunteer, and work opportunities throughout the region, **Beyond Tourism** (p. 52) has all the resources you need.

**RANKINGS, TIP BOXES, AND FEATURES.** Our researchers list establishments in order of value from best to worst, with absolute favorites denoted by the *Let's Go* thumbpick (🔑). Since the lowest price does not always mean the best value, we've incorporated a system of price ranges (❶-❺) for food and accommodations. Tip boxes come in a variety of flavors: warnings (⚠), helpful hints and resources (📖), inside scoops (📷), and a variety of other things you should know. When you want a break from transportation info and listings, check out our features for unique opportunities, surprising insights, and fascinating stories.

**PHONE CODES AND TELEPHONE NUMBERS.** Area codes for each region appear opposite the name of the region and are denoted by the ☎ icon. Phone numbers in text are likewise preceded by the ☎ icon.

> **A NOTE TO OUR READERS.** The information for this book was gathered by Let's Go researchers from May through August of 2009. Each listing is based on one research-er's opinion, formed during his or her visit at a particular time. Those traveling at other times may have different experiences as prices, dates, hours, and conditions are always subject to change. You are urged to check the facts presented in this book beforehand to avoid any inconveniences or surprises.

# CONTENTS

# RESEARCHERS

**Daniel Hertz** *Western Yucatán Peninsula, Tabasco & Chiapas, Oaxaca*

Armed with reliably unreliable directions and a keen eye for delicious, refreshing *licuados*, this Chicago-born Government major blazed a trail from Mérida to Oaxaca, churning out pages and pages of consistently refined, subtly tongue-in-cheek writing. What will we remember most about him? His mouth-watering descriptions of the chocolate cafes in Oaxaca. Oh, and the time at the beginning of the summer when he told us he thought he might have swine flu. Not funny, but he more than made up for it with his delightful marginalia and beautiful photos, which left us staring at our computer screens green with envy.

**Natalie Sherman** *Eastern Yucatán Peninsula*

After spending her sophomore summer working at Let's Go headquarters for Mexico '08, followed by a summer of trailblazing in Argentina for Buenos Aires '09, Natalie returned to the Spanish-speaking world this year to shake things up on the Yucatán Peninsula. From Cancún to Campeche (with a few stops in between), this LG All-Star scoured sidestreets, mused over menus, and climbed lots (and lots) of ruins in some of the Peninsula's most gorgeous historical cities, as well as a few of her more notorious destinations. Never one to skimp on facts, Natalie infused her coverage with a history of Mexico's most storied region, and her editors couldn't have been happier to be working with such an enthusiastic traveler and dedicated Let's Go veteran.

# STAFF WRITERS

Megan Lee Amram
Allison Averill
Meagan Anne Michelson
Daniel C. Barbero

# CONTRIBUTING WRITERS

**Laura Ann Schoenherr** was a member of the Class of 2008 at Harvard University. She graduated with an A.B. in chemistry, a certificate in health policy, and a citation in Spanish.

# ACKNOWLEDGMENTS

# LET'S GO

**CLAIRE THANKS:** The Yucatán Peninsula for staying swine-flu free, Let's Go's 9-5 work day for helping me maintain a normal sleep schedule for the first time since middle school, Daniel for his impeccable writing, my fellow Research Managers for all the bonding and fun times in the pod, Kavita for the swine flu piglet that sat on my desk all summer, Molly for being my aloe buddy and putting up with my many whackings of the snooze button in the morning, my family (and little brother) for their guidance with my various cooking experiments, and my friends for an adventure-packed and fun-filled summer.

**EDITORS THANK:** The Ed Team would first and foremost like to thank our lord (Jay-C) and savior (Starbucks, Terry's Chocolate Orange). We also owe gratitude to Barack Obama (peace be upon Him), the Oxford comma, the water cooler, bagel/payday Fridays, the HSA "SummerFun" team for being so inclusive, Rotio (wherefore art thou Rotio?), the real Robinson Crusoe, the Cambridge weather and defective umbrellas, BoltBus, Henry Louis Gates, Jr. (sorry 'bout the phone call), the office blog, gratuitous nudity, the 20-20-20 rule and bananas (no more eye twitches), the Portuguese flag, trips to the beach (ha!), sunbathing recently-married Mormon final club alums, non-existent free food in the square, dog-star puns, and last but not least, America. The local time in Tehran is 1:21am.

But seriously, to the MEs and RMs, our researchers (and all their wisdom on table-cloths and hipsters), LGHQ, HSA, our significant others (future, Canadian, and otherwise), and families (thanks Mom).

**Publishing Director**
Laura M. Gordon
**Editorial Director**
Dwight Livingstone Curtis
**Publicity and Marketing Director**
Vanessa J. Dube
**Production and Design Director**
Rebecca Lieberman
**Cartography Director**
Anthony Rotio
**Website Director**
Lukáš Tóth
**Managing Editors**
Ashley Laporte, Iya Megre,
Mary Potter, Nathaniel Rakich
**Technology Project Manager**
C. Alexander Tremblay
**Director of IT**
David Fulton-Howard
**Financial Associates**
Catherine Humphreville, Jun Li

**Managing Editor**
Ashley Laporte
**Research Managers**
Nadav Greenberg, Claire Shepro
**Editors**
Courtney A. Fiske, Sara Plana, Russell Ford Rennie,
Charlie E. Riggs, Olga I. Zhulina
**Typesetter**
C. Alexander Tremblay

**President**
Daniel Lee
**General Manager**
Jim McKellar

Our researchers list establishments in order of value from best to worst, honoring our favorites with the Let's Go thumbpick (🖐). Because the cheapest *price* is not always the best *value*, we have incorporated a system of price ranges based on a rough expectation of what you will spend. For **accommodations,** we base our range on the cheapest price for which a single traveler can stay for one night. For **restaurants,** we estimate the average amount one traveler will spend in one sitting. The table below tells you what you'll *typically* find in the Yucatán Peninsula at the corresponding price range, but keep in mind that no system can accommodate the quirks of individual establishments.

| ACCOMMODATIONS | RANGE | WHAT YOU'RE *LIKELY* TO FIND |
|---|---|---|
| ① | Under 170 pesos (Under US$13) | Campgrounds and dorm rooms, both in hostels and actual universities. You're getting cozy in bunk beds and washing in a communal bath. |
| ② | 170-220 pesos (US$13-16) | Upper-end hostels or lower-end hotels. Perhaps a private bathroom, or there may be a sink in your room and a communal shower in the hall. |
| ③ | 221-270 pesos (US$16-20) | A small room with a private bath. Should have decent amenities, such as a phone and TV. Breakfast may be included. |
| ④ | 271-325 pesos (US$20-24) | Should have bigger rooms than a ③, with more amenities or in a more convenient location. Breakfast probably included. |
| ⑤ | Over 326 pesos (Over US$24) | Large hotels or upscale chains. If it's a ⑤ and it doesn't have the perks you want, you've paid too much. |

| FOOD | RANGE | WHAT YOU'RE *LIKELY* TO FIND |
|---|---|---|
| ① | Under 30 pesos (under US$2.50) | Mostly street-corner stands, *taquerías*, or fast-food joints. Much better than McDonalds, these eateries usually serve yummy tacos or *quesadillas*. |
| ② | 31-50 pesos (US$2.50-4) | Smaller restaurants and cafes with a basic appetizer, entree, and drink menu. |
| ③ | 51-70 pesos (US$4-5) | More formal restaurants with wait staffs; larger plates and meals, usually with sides. |
| ④ | 71-100 pesos (US$6-8) | Nicer eateries serving full meals; elaborate entrees and creative ambiance; fresh seafood plates. |
| ⑤ | Over 100 pesos (Over US$8) | High-class establishments with elegant versions of traditional staples. You might have to dress the part. |

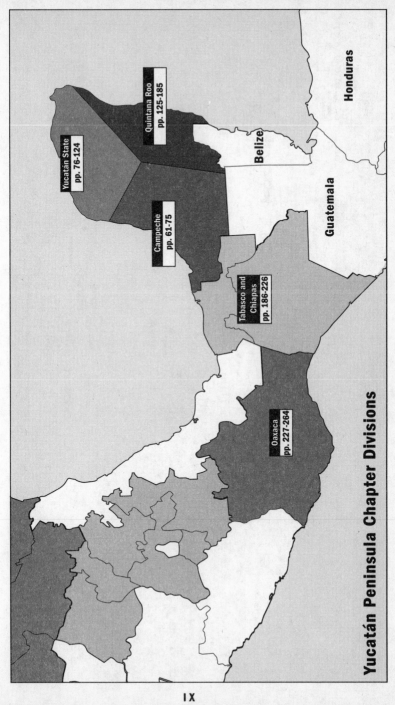

# Yucatán Peninsula Chapter Divisions

Honduras

Belize

Guatemala

Quintana Roo
pp. 125-185

Yucatán State
pp. 76-124

Campeche
pp. 61-75

Tabasco and
Chiapas
pp. 186-226

Oaxaca
pp. 227-264

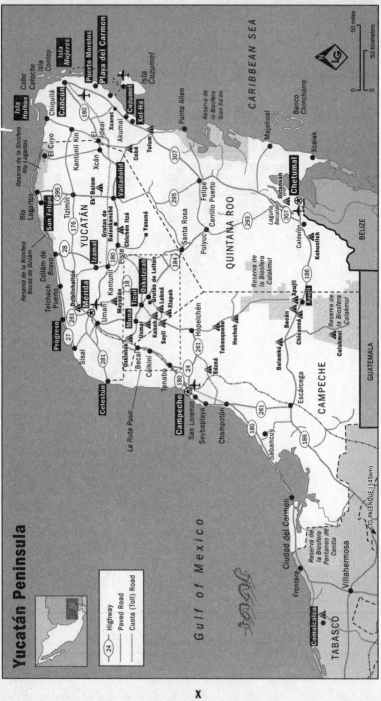

# Yucatán Peninsula

# DISCOVER THE YUCATÁN PENINSULA

We know what you're thinking. Mexico's Yucatán Peninsula? Tequila shots, sweaty nightclubs, and beach volleyball here we come. Think again. *Let's Go*'s intrepid Researchers once again dove headlong off the beaten path to bring you the best of the best in one of the continent's cultural capitals. And while we haven't yet given up the tequila shots, we have come up with the peninsula's most exciting and inspiring destinations, all safe from the mayhem of the beach resort scene.

In this region, at the extreme southeastern edge of Mexico, tucked between the Gulf of Mexico and the Caribbean, imagination meets reality. Legends of Mayan civilizations, pirates, and Spanish *conquistadors* surround steamy jungles, centers of modern trade, and sultry pleasures to create the ultimate travel experience. Quiet Campeche inspires romantic images of history and legend, while Yucatán state overflows with cross-cultural treasures. Meanwhile, Quintana Roo boasts incredible barrier reef exploration and an abundance of natural wonders.

Sleep on the ocean in one of Celestún's tiny hotels, or camp among Mayan ruins in La Ruta Puuc. We've found the best chimichangas and enchiladas, the coolest fish markets, and raging beachside bars along the entire peninsula. Whether you are looking to get that perfect tan on a quiet beach or to plunge into the jungle, the Yucatán Peninsula is the perfect setting for an unforgettable adventure.

## FACTS AND FIGURES

**MEXICO, DEFINED:** Náhuatl word meaning "Bellybutton of the World."

**POPULATION:** 108 million

**LAND MASS:** 1,972,550 sq. km

**GDP PER PERSON:** US$10,700

**ANNUAL TORTILLA CONSUMPTION PER PERSON:** 270 lbs.

**ANNUAL BEER PRODUCTION:** Over 6 million liters of brew—the world's fifth largest exporter.

**REGULAR CHURCHGOERS:** 45 million

**REGULAR SOCCER FANS:** 31 million

**MEXICO CITY METRO:** Built for 1968 Olympics, used daily by 9 million riders.

**CHICHÉN ITZÁ:** Mayan city named one of the "New Seven Wonders of the World" in 2007.

**RED SAVINA HABANERO:** World's hottest pepper, measuring a scorching 577,000 Scoville units.

# WHEN TO GO

Mexico's lush jungles, gleaming beaches, and textured highlands entice visitors year-round. Winters tend to be mild, while summers vary from warm to excruciatingly hot, as temperatures soar to upwards of 42°C (108°F). High-altitude regions, such as the Oaxaca Valley, remain temperate year-round. During the **rainy season** (May-Sept.), the south receives an average of 2-3hr. of rain every afternoon. The best time to hit the beach is during the **dry season** (Oct.-Apr.), when afternoons are sunny, evenings balmy, and nights relatively mosquito-free.

The **peak tourist season** (high season) encompasses December, *Semana Santa* (the week before Easter), and mid-summer. In March and the early part of April—the traditional US spring break—resort towns like Cancún fill with boozing college students. If you travel to the Yucatán during any of these times, expect to pay slightly higher prices at hotels and restaurants.

# WHAT TO DO

Whether climbing age-old Mayan temples, haggling for silver trinkets in colonial open-air markets, diving near coral reefs, or dancing with a margarita in hand, visitors head to the Yucatán Peninsula for its individual cultural allure. Step out of the resort mayhem and you'll land in any of a number of the region's adventures. We've highlighted just a few of them here. See the individual **Sights** sections throughout the guide for more information about all the region has to offer.

## RUNNING TO THE RUINS

A journey through the Yucatán Peninsula is like a whirlwind tour through time. While you might have to fight the crowds at some of the more popular Mayan ruins, the effort is worth it: there is no better place to get a sense of Mexico's rich history. In the lowland jungles of the Yucatán Peninsula, the Maya built grand cities like **Palenque** (p. 212), where distinct architecture rests surrounded by lush green jungle. The region is also home to the once warring Mayan trio of **Chichén Itzá** (p. 111), **Mayapán** (p. 91), and **Uxmal** (p. 101). These religious and political centers of Mayan civilization are not to be missed.

## BEACH BUMMING

Mexico's infinite stretches of sparkling golden and white beaches will please even the most discriminating beachgoer. Those who like an audience can strut their stuff in front of the millions of bronzed bodies in **Cancún** (p. 125). If the glam tourist scene isn't your style, ramble down the turquoise coast toward **Tulum** (p. 161), to cavort in the beachside ruins. Likewise, the shores of **Isla Mujeres** (p. 136) offer a quiet respite from the insanity, as does **Isla Cozumel** (p. 153). In **Celestún (p. 91)** umbrellas and frisbees are replaced with quiet fishermen and conch shells. No matter your preference, if you're looking to be a beach bum, the Yucatán Peninsula is the place to be.

## UNDER AND ABOVE THE SEA

Snorkeling? Deep sea diving? You find both off the coast of **Isla Cozumel (p. 153)**. Whether you're an old pro or putting on goggles for the first time, the Caribbean Sea promises underwater adventure. If you'd rather stay above the waves, try windsurfing, jetskiing, or parasailing along the shores of **Playa del Carmen (p. 146)**. Explore lagoons in a *lancha* in **Bacalar** (p. 183), or swim with whale sharks with guides from **Isla Holbox (p. 142)**. Eat all the quesadillas, burritos, and queso dips you want; with all the activities western Mexico has to offer, you'll have no problem working off the calories.

## WALK ON THE WILD SIDE

If you are looking to see your first bonefish, snap a photo of a Mayflower Orchid, or paddle through lush lagoons, a visit to the Yucatán's National Parks or nature reserves will not disappoint. Take time away from the beachside bar, and support Mexico's environmental conservation efforts. In Cozumel, **Punta Sur Ecological Reserve (p. 159)** wows visitors with boat rides through crocodile-infested lagoons. **Ria Celestún Biosphere** along the Gulf of Mexico is home to some 200 species of migratory birds, including the loudmouth cormorant and the flaming pink flamingo. If visiting Tulum, a daytrip to **Sian Ka'an Biosphere Reserve (p. 173)** is well worth the trip. This reserve is Mexico's largest coastal wetland reserve and is a UNESCO Natural Heritage Site. From birds to barracuda, lakes to lagoons, western Mexico is full of exciting wildlife.

## ☑ LET'S GO PICKS

**BEST WAY TO WAY TO CURE A HANGOVER:** By eating cow brains and intestines?

**BEST PLACE TO LOSE YOURSELF IN THE CROWD:** In **Mérida** (p. 76) where throngs of tourists mingle among the 1 million Mexicans that call the city home.

**BEST THIGH-MASTER SUBSTITUTE:** Climbing up massive pyramids in the ancient city of **Chichén Itzá** (p. 111).

**BEST ONLY-IN-MEXICO ICE CREAM FLAVORS: Chicharrón** (pork rind), **elote** (corn meal), **aguacate** (avocado), and **cerveza** (beer).

**BEST ROUTE TO THE UNDERWORLD:** Through the longest set of underground caverns in the world, at **Cenote Dos Ojos** (p. 166).

**BEST PLACE TO HEED THE CALL OF THE WILD:** Outside Tulum at **Sian Ka'an Biosphere Reserve** (p. 172), where 1200 species of flora, 336 species of birds, and 103 species of animals hang out.

**BEST PLACE TO SPIT SOME GAME:** On the tranquil beaches of **Isle Mujures** (p. 136).

**BEST DEATH:** By chocolate; in **Oaxaca** (p. 244), the Mexican cocoa capital.

**BEST PLACE TO PROPOSE:** On the shores of **Isla Holbox** (p. 142), while watching the sunset, dressed in palm fronds, drunk.

**BEST PIPELINE:** Off the coast of **Isla Cozumel** (p. 152), where massive waves draw hundreds of surfers each year.

**BEST HEAD:** The 33 enormous Olmec sculptures at **Parque-Museo La Venta** in **Villahermosa** (p. 191).

**BEST FEAST FOR CULTURE VULTURES: Campeche City** (p. 61), where beautiful colonial churches and foreboding stone embattlements lurk around every corner.

**BEST PLACE TO SEE THE WRITING ON THE WALL:** At the ruins of **Edzná (p. 69)**, where 65 stairs are adorned with 1300-year-old hieroglyphics.

DISCOVER

# RUNNING AROUND THE RUINS

**Dzibilchaltún**

This site, which means "place where there is writing on stones" in Maya, sprawls over 19 sq. km of jungle. Be sure to leave time for El Museo del Pueblo Maya, the site's museum, which displays intricate Mayan sculptures and ceramics (p. 90).

**Uxmal**

Around AD 900 Uxmal was the most influential and impressive city in the Ruta Puuc region. Today, the site remains the most spectacular in the region with massive palaces and other striking architecture set against a vibrant green hillside (p. 101).

**Mayapán**

While these ruins south of Mérida are less impressive than Uxmal and other sites in the peninsula, the incredible paintings of here make the ruin well worth the visit. Plus, this site has a pretty remarkable history (p. 91).

**Chichén Itzá**

You may have to throw up a few elbows to see anything at this Disney World of Mayan ruins, but it's well worth it. Be sure to find El Tzompantli, the site where the heads of prisoners and enemies were put on display, and the impressive steambath El Baño de Vapor (p. 111).

**Tulum**

This site, also known as Záma, boasts striking architecture and spectacular views of the Caribbean Sea (p. 160).

**Cobá**

An impressive 70 sq. km, these tranquil ruins are surrounded by lakes and rubber trees. Giving some 6500 buildings at this site remain unexcavated, but this number dwindles each year, so be sure to visit and be one of the first to see a newly uncovered structure (p. 169).

# BEST OF THE BEACHES (1-2 WEEKS)

**START**

**END**

## Cancún (as long as it takes you to realize this isn't where you want to be)

We're not actually suggesting you stay here; this should function more as a warning. This spring break capital of the world promises hangovers, regrets, and sunburn. If you can handle the craziness, stick around. If not, grab a bus heading to bigger and better things (p. 125).

## Isla Cozumel (3 days)

This diving mecca once shared its waters with greedy pirates. Today pro and novice divers alike flock to Cozumel looking to explore beneath the surface. If deep sea diving is not for you, take a boat ride through the island's lush lagoons (p. 153).

## Celestún (3 days)

Quiet Celestún is the perfect destination for those looking to escape cities and towns filled with cruise ship tourists. Enjoy scrumptious seafood, meet friendly fishermen, and visit the Ria Celestún Biosphere, where hundreds of birds flock among the greenery (p. 91).

## Playa del Carmen (2 days)

Quieter, but with the same white-sand beaches as its more touristed neighbors, Playa del Carmen has become a tourist destination in its own right in recent years. Hang out here before heading to nearby Isla Cozumel (p. 146).

# ESSENTIALS

## PLANNING YOUR TRIP

**BEFORE YOU GO**
**Passport** (see opposite page). Required for citizens of all countries except the US and Canada. Note that a passport is required to return to the US from Mexico.
**Tourist Card** (p. 8). Required for citizens of all countries who plan to venture past border towns and/or stay for more than 3 days. Available at airports and points of entry. Good for anywhere from 30 to 180 days depending on country of origin. Included in price of plane ticket or US$20 at the border.
**Visa (p. 8)**. Required for visitors from most countries outside of the Americas and Europe. Must be obtained through a Mexican consulate before arrival.
**Under 18?** Any non-Mexican under the age of 18 departing for Mexico must carry notarized written permission from parent or guardian not traveling with the child.
**Work Permit (p. 8)**. Business visas and proof of employment required for all foreigners planning to work in Mexico.
**Recommended Vaccinations (p. 16)** Hepatitis A, Hepatitis B, Typhoid.
**Other Health Concerns:** Malaria pills are recommended for those traveling to malaria risk areas: Mexico's southern borders and in Sinaloa, Durango, Chihuahua, and Sonora states (p. 18).

## EMBASSIES AND CONSULATES

### MEXICAN CONSULAR SERVICES ABROAD

**Australia:** 14 Perth Ave., Yarralumla, Canberra, ACT 2600 (☎+61 02 62 73 39 63; www.mexico.org.au).

**Canada:** 45 O'Connor St., Ste. 1000, Ottawa, ON K1P 1A4 (☎+1-613-233-8988; www.sre.gob.mx/canada). **Consulates:** Commerce Court West, 199 Bay St., Ste. 4440, Toronto ON M5L 1E9 (☎+1 416 368 2875; www.consulmex.com); 411-1177 W. Hastings St., Vancouver BC V6E 2K3 (☎+1-604-684-3547; www.consulmexvan.com).

**Ireland:** 19 Raglan Road, Ballsbridge, Dublin 4 (☎+353 166 73105; www.sre.gob.mx/irlanda).

**New Zealand:** 111 Customhouse Quay, Level 8, Wellington (☎+64 44 72 05 55). **Consulate:** 88 Shortland St, Private Bag 92 518, Wellesley St, Auckland (☎+64 99 77 50 41; portal.sre.gob.mx/nuevazelandia).

**UK:** 16 St. George St., Hanover Sq., London W1S 1LX (☎+440 207 499 8586; portal.sre.gob.mx/reinounidoeng). **Consulate:** 8 Halkin St., London SW1X 7DW (☎+440 207 235 6393).

**US:** 1911 Pennsylvania Ave., Washington, DC 20006 (☎+1-202-728-1600; portal.sre.gob.mx/eua). **Consulates:** 20 Park Plaza, Ste. 506 Boston, MA 02116 (☎+1-617-

426-4181; http://www.sre.gob.mx/boston); 2401 W. Sixth St., Los Angeles, CA 90057 (☎+1-213-351-6800; fax 389-9249; portal.sre.gob.mx/losangeles); 5975 SW 72nd St. Ste. 301-303 Miami, Fl. 33143 (☎+1-786-268-4900; portal.sre.gob.mx/miami); 27 E. 39th St., New York, NY 10016 (☎+1-212-217-6400; fax 217-6493; portal.sre.gob.mx/nuevayork).

## CONSULAR SERVICES IN MEXICO

**Australia:** Ruben Dario 55, Col. Polanco, Mexico, D.F., 11580 (☎55 1101 2200; fax 1101 2201; www.mexico.embassy.gov.au).

**Canada:** Schiller 529, Col. Polanco Del. Miguel Hidalgo, Mexico, D.F., 11560 (☎55 5724 7900; www.dfait-maeci.gc.ca/mexico-city).

**Ireland:** Cda. Blvr. Avila Camacho 76-3, Col. Lomas de Chapultepec, Mexico, D.F., 11000 (☎55 5520 5803; www.irishembassy.com.mx).

**New Zealand:** Jaime Balmes No. 8, 4to piso, Los Morales, Polanco, Mexico, D.F. 11510. (☎55 5283 9460; fkiwimexico@prodigy.net.mx).

**UK:** Río Lerma 71, Col. Cuauhtémoc, Mexico, D.F. 06500 (☎55 5242 8500; www.embajadabritanica.com.mx).

**US:** Paseo de la Reforma 305, Col. Cuauhtémoc, Mexico, D.F., 06500 (☎55 5080 2000; mexico.usembassy.gov).

## TOURIST OFFICES

Mexico's **Tourism Board and Ministry of Tourism (SECTUR)** is dedicated to promoting Mexico as a tourist destination. Most official tourism offices outside North America have consolidated with local consulates while some in Canada and the US remain independent. For more information on tourism, visit the nearest consulate or www.sectur.gob.mx.

# DOCUMENTS AND FORMALITIES

## PASSPORTS

### REQUIREMENTS
Citizens of Australia, Canada, Ireland, New Zealand, the UK, and the US need valid passports to enter Mexico and to re-enter their home countries. You may also be asked for evidence of a return ticket and sufficient funds. A recent paycheck stub, bank statement, or credit card information will suffice. Returning home with an expired passport is illegal and may result in a fine.

### NEW PASSPORTS
Citizens of Australia, Canada, Ireland, New Zealand, the UK, and the US can apply for a passport at any passport office or at selected post offices and courts of law. Citizens of these countries may also download passport applications from the official website of their country's government or passport office. All new passports and renewal applications must be filed well in advance of the departure date, though most passport offices offer rush services for a steep fee. Note, however, that "rushed" passports still take up to two weeks to arrive.

ESSENTIALS

ESSENTIALS

## PASSPORT MAINTENANCE

Photocopy the page of your passport with your photo as well as your visas, traveler's check serial numbers, and any other important documents. Carry one set of copies in a safe place, apart from the originals, and leave another set at home. Carry an expired passport or an official copy of your birth certificate in a part of your baggage separate from other documents.

If you lose your passport, immediately notify the local police and your home country's nearest embassy or consulate. To expedite its replacement, you must show ID and proof of citizenship; it also helps to know all information previously recorded in the passport. In some cases, a replacement may take weeks to process, and it may be valid only for a limited time. Consulates in Mexico can issue replacements within seven business days. Any visas stamped in your old passport will be lost forever. In an emergency, ask for temporary traveling papers that will permit you to re-enter your home country.

# TOURIST CARDS, VISAS, AND WORK PERMITS

## TOURIST CARD (FOLLETO DE MIGRACIÓN TURÍSTICA)

All persons, regardless of nationality, must carry a tourist card **(FMT)** in addition to proof of citizenship. Most tourist cards are good for up to 180 days; some, however, are only good for 30 days, and some for even fewer. If you need to leave and re-enter Mexico during your trip, make sure your tourist card will enable you to do so; you might have to ask for a multiple-entry permit. Canadian and US citizens do not need an FMT if they are staying in Mexico for less than 72hr. or intend to stay within the 20-30km US-Mexico Border Zone. If you are traveling into Mexico by plane, the FMT fee is included in the airline ticket price, and the tourist card will be given to you to fill out during your flight. If driving into Mexico, you will be charged US$20 at your point of entry. You can avoid any delays by obtaining a card from a Mexican consulate or tourist office before you leave.

## VISAS

Tourist visas are not necessary for citizens of Australia, Canada, New Zealand, the UK, the US, most EU countries, and Latin American countries for visits under 180 days. Individuals with African, Asian, Eastern European, or Middle Eastern citizenship must procure a tourist visa from a Mexican consulate in their home country before traveling. In order to do so, a valid passport, a valid visa application, three passport photographs, proof of sufficient funds, and evidence of a round-trip ticket are necessary. The consular fee is around US$40, depending on your country of origin. Non-Mexicans under 18 who wish to exit the country must have written permission from their legal guardian(s) in the form of a notarized letter. Double-check entrance requirements at a Mexican embassy or consulate in your home country (listed under **Mexican Consular Services Abroad,** p. 6) for up-to-date info before departure. US citizens can also consult http://travel.state.gov. Entering Mexico to study for longer than six months requires a special visa. For more information, see **Beyond Tourism,** p. 52.

## WORK PERMITS

Admittance to a country as a traveler does not include the right to work, which is authorized only by a work permit. For more information, see **Beyond Tourism,** p. 52.

# IDENTIFICATION

When you travel, always carry at least two forms of identification on your person, including a photo ID. A passport and a driver's license will usually suffice. Never carry all of your IDs together; instead, split them up in case of theft or loss, and keep photocopies in your luggage and at home.

## STUDENT AND YOUTH IDENTIFICATION

The **International Student Identity Card (ISIC)**, the most widely accepted form of student ID, provides discounts on some sights, accommodations, food, and transportation, access to a 24hr. emergency help line, and insurance benefits for US cardholders (see **Insurance**, p. 16). Applicants must be full-time secondary or post-secondary school students at least 12 years old. Because of the proliferation of fake ISICs, some services (particularly airlines) require additional proof of student identity. For travelers who are under 26 years old but are not students, the **International Youth Travel Card (IYTC)** offers many of the same benefits as the ISIC.

Each of these identity cards costs US$22. ISICs and IYTCs are valid for one year from the date of issue. To learn more about ISICs and IYTCs, visit www.myisic.com. Many student travel agencies (p. 21) sell the cards; for a list of issuing agencies or more information, see the **International Student Travel Confederation (ISTC)** website (www.istc.org).

The **International Student Exchange Card (ISE Card)** is a similar identification card available to students, faculty, and children ages 12 to 26. The card provides discounts, medical benefits, access to a 24hr. emergency help-line, and the ability to purchase student airfares. An ISE Card costs US$25; call ☎800-255-8000 (in North America) or ☎480 951 1177 (from all other countries) for more info or visit www.isecard.com.

## CUSTOMS

Upon entering Mexico you must declare certain items from abroad. Mexican regulations limit the value of goods brought into Mexico by US citizens arriving by air or sea to US$300 per person; by land the limit is US$50 per person. Amounts exceeding the duty-free limit are subject to a 15% tax. Note that goods and gifts purchased at duty-free shops abroad are not exempt from duty or sales tax; "duty-free" merely means that you need not pay a tax in the country of purchase. Upon returning home, you must likewise declare all articles acquired abroad. If the items you acquired are in excess of your home country's allowance you will be required to pay another tax. In order to expedite your return, make a list of any valuables brought from home and register them with customs before traveling; also be sure to keep receipts for all goods acquired abroad.

# MONEY

## CURRENCY AND EXCHANGE

The currency chart on the next page is based on August 2009 exchange rates. Check the currency converter on websites like www.xe.com or www.bloomberg.com for the latest exchange rates.

| PESO | | |
|---|---|---|
| AUS$1 = 10.58 PESOS | 1 PESO = AUS$0.095 | |
| CDN$1 = 11.85 PESOS | 1 PESO = CDN$0.084 | |
| EUR€1 = 18.57 PESOS | 1 PESO = EUR€0.054 | |
| NZ$1 = 8.34 PESOS | 1 PESO = NZ$0.12 | |
| UK£1 = 21.22 PESOS | 1 PESO = UK£0.047 | |
| US$1 = 13.30 PESOS | 1 PESO = US$0.075 | |

As a general rule, it's cheaper to convert money in Mexico than at home. While currency exchange will probably be available in your arrival airport, it's wise to bring enough foreign currency to last for the first 24-72hr. of your trip. When changing money abroad, try to go only to banks or *casas de cambio* that have at most a 5% margin between their buy and sell prices. Since you

ESSENTIALS

lose money with every transaction, convert large sums (unless the currency is depreciating rapidly), but no more than you'll need. Keep in mind that banks tend to have better exchange rates than *casas de cambio*.

Store your money in a variety of forms; ideally, at any given time you will be carrying some cash, some traveler's checks, and an ATM or credit card. All travelers should also consider carrying some US dollars (about US$50 worth), which are often preferred by local tellers to the peso or other currencies.

## TRAVELER'S CHECKS

Traveler's checks are one of the safest and most convenient means of carrying funds. **American Express** and **Visa** are the best-recognized brands. Many banks and agencies sell them for a small commission. Check issuers provide refunds if the checks are lost or stolen, and many provide additional services, such as toll-free refund hotlines abroad, emergency message services, and assistance with lost and stolen credit cards or passports. Traveler's checks are readily accepted in large commercial and urban areas. Purchase checks in US dollars; many *casas de cambio* refuse to exchange other currencies. Ask about toll-free refund hotlines and the location of refund centers when purchasing checks. Remember to always carry emergency cash.

**American Express:** Checks available (with commission fee) at AmEx offices and select banks (www.americanexpress.com). AmEx cardholders can also purchase checks by phone (☎+1-800-528-4800). Cheques for Two are available for two people traveling together; either person may use the check. For purchase locations or more information, contact AmEx's service centers: in Australia ☎+61 2 9271 8666, in Canada and the US ☎+1-800-528-4800, in New Zealand ☎+64 9 583 8300, in the UK ☎+44 1273 571 600. Within Mexico, call ☎01 866 247 6878 for assistance; this line also accepts collect calls.

**Visa:** Checks available at banks worldwide. For the location of the nearest office, call the Visa Travelers Cheque Global Refund and Assistance Center: in the UK ☎+44 800 895 078, in the US ☎+1-800-227-6811; elsewhere, call the UK collect at ☎+44 2079 378 091. Checks available in American, British, Canadian, European, and Japanese currencies, among others. Visa also offers TravelMoney, a prepaid debit card that can be refilled online or by phone. For more information on Visa travel services, see http://usa.visa.com/personal/using_visa/travel_with_visa.html.

## CREDIT, DEBIT, AND ATM CARDS

Where they are accepted, credit cards often offer superior exchange rates—up to 5% better than the retail rate used by banks and other currency-exchange establishments. Credit cards may also offer services such as insurance or emergency help and are sometimes required to reserve hotel rooms or rental cars. **MasterCard** (a.k.a. **Cirrus in Mexico**) and **Visa** (a.k.a. **PLUS**) are the most frequently accepted; **American Express** cards work at some ATMs and at AmEx offices and major airports. **Debit cards** are as convenient as credit cards and can be used wherever the associated credit card company (usually MasterCard or Visa) is accepted.

The use of **ATM cards** is widespread in Mexico. Depending on the system that your bank at home uses, you can most likely access your personal bank account from abroad. ATMs get the same wholesale exchange rate as credit cards, but there is often a limit on the amount of money you can withdraw per day (usually around US$500). There is also typically a surcharge of 7.50 pesos to withdraw; it costs three pesos to check your balance.

The two major international money networks are **MasterCard/Maestro/Cirrus** (for ATM locations call ☎+1-800-424-7787 or visit www.mastercard.com) and **Visa/PLUS** (for ATM locations visit http://visa.via.infonow.net/locator/

global/). Contact your bank or credit-card company before going abroad; frequent charges in a foreign country can sometimes prompt a fraud alert, which will freeze your account.

# GETTING MONEY FROM HOME

If you run out of money while traveling, the easiest and cheapest solution is to have someone back home make a deposit to your bank account. Otherwise, consider one of the following options.

## WIRING MONEY

It is possible to arrange a **bank money transfer,** which means asking a bank at home to wire money to a bank in Mexico. This is the cheapest way to transfer cash, but it's also the slowest, usually taking several days or more. Note that some banks may only release your funds in pesos, potentially sticking you with a poor exchange rate; inquire about this in advance. Expect transactions to take between one and three days to complete. Money transfer services like **Western Union** are faster and more convenient than bank transfers—but also much pricier. Western Union has many locations worldwide and works with **Dinero en Minutos** in Mexico for wire transfers. To find a Western Union near you, visit www.westernunion.com or call the appropriate number: in Australia ☎800 173 833, in Canada and the US 800-325-6000, in the UK 0800 735 1815, or in Mexico 800 325 4045. To wire money using a credit card in Canada and the US call ☎800-CALL-CASH, in the UK 0800 833 833. In Mexico, call 800 325 4045 for assistance. Money transfer services are also available to **American Express** cardholders and at selected **Thomas Cook** offices. In Mexico, money transfer services can also be found at **Banamex** and **Bancomer** banks nationwide.

## US STATE DEPARTMENT (US CITIZENS ONLY)

In serious emergencies only, the US State Department will forward money within hours to the nearest consular office, which will then disburse the money according to your instructions for a US$30 fee. If you wish to use this service, contact the **Overseas Citizens Services** division of the US State Department (☎+1-202-501-4444, from the US 888-407-4747).

# COSTS

The cost of your trip will vary considerably depending on where you visit, how you travel, and where you stay. The most significant expense will probably be your round-trip airfare (see **Getting to the Yucatán: By Plane,** p. 20) and a railpass or bus pass.

## STAYING ON A BUDGET

To give you a general idea, a bare-bones day in Mexico (camping or sleeping in hostels or guesthouses, buying food at supermarkets) would cost about US$15-25 (160-370 pesos). A slightly more comfortable day (sleeping in hostels/guesthouses and the occasional budget hotel, eating one meal per day at a restaurant, going out at night) would cost US$30-40 (375 pesos). For a luxurious day, the sky's the limit. Don't forget to factor in emergency reserve funds (at least US$200) when planning how much money you'll need.

## TIPPING AND BARGAINING

The age-old question: to tip or not to tip? In Mexico, it can be hard to know what to do. Overly eager tipping can be offensive (never, for example, throw a couple of pesos at someone you just asked for directions), but many people make their

ESSENTIALS

livings assisting tourists in exchange for tips. In general, anyone who offers a service and then awkwardly waits around afterward is expecting a tip.

In a restaurant, waiters are tipped based on the quality of service; good service deserves at least 15%. Taxi drivers are generally not tipped, as they do not run on meters—when hailing a taxi, settle the price of the ride beforehand to avoid exorbitant charges. Regardless of the quality of service, never leave without saying *gracias*. In Mexico, skillful bargaining separates the savvy budget traveler from the timid tourist. If you're unsure whether bargaining is appropriate, observe locals and follow their lead.

## PACKING

**Pack lightly:** lay out only what you think you absolutely need, then pack half of the clothes and twice the money. If you plan to do a lot of hiking, consult **The Great Outdoors,** p. 32.

> **Converters and Adapters:** In Mexico, electricity is 127V AC. 220/240V electrical appliances won't work with a 120/127V current, which will work for any 120V North American appliance. The electrical outlets in Mexico are shaped the same as those in Canada and the US. Visitors from the UK, Australia, and New Zealand should buy an **adapter** (which changes the shape of the plug; US$5) as well as a **converter** (which changes the voltage; US$10-30).

> **Important documents:** Don't forget your passport, traveler's checks, ATM and/or credit cards, adequate ID, and photocopies of all of the aforementioned in case these documents are lost or stolen. Also check that you have any of the following that might apply to you: a hostelling international membership card (p. 31), driver's license, travel insurance forms, ISIC (p. 9), and/or railpass or bus pass.

# SAFETY AND HEALTH

## GENERAL ADVICE

In any type of crisis, the most important thing to do is **stay calm.** Your home country's embassy abroad is usually your best resource in an emergency; registering with your embassy upon arrival in the country is a good idea. The government offices listed in the **Travel Advisories** box (p. 14) can provide information on the services each government office offer their citizens in case of emergencies abroad.

## LOCAL LAWS AND POLICE

Travelers are advised to comply with the Mexican legal codes detailed below. Although the Mexican government is working hard to strengthen its police force, police officers remain infamous for corruption. Remember to exercise caution when approached by individuals identifying themselves as police officers. Some tourists have fallen victim to mistreatment, including harassment and extortion, by local officials. Some may seek bribes from tourists, generally asking for about US$5; most stop when asked for permission to speak to higher authorities. Several larger urban areas maintain a separate **tourist police force;** contact the local tourist office for more information. Visitors should be aware that under the Mexican judicial system offenders are presumed guilty until proven innocent.

# DRUGS AND ALCOHOL

**DRUGS.** Contrary to international opinion, Mexico rigorously prosecutes drug cases. Jail sentence awaits anyone found guilty of possessing an illegal drug. Beware: Mexican law does not distinguish between marijuana and other narcotics. Even if you aren't convicted, getting arrested and tried will be a long and incredibly unpleasant process, and it is not uncommon to be detained for a year before a verdict is reached. Foreigners and suspected drug traffickers are never released on bail. Ignorance of Mexican law is no excuse, and a flimsy "I didn't know it was illegal" won't get you out of jail. If you are arrested, there is little your embassy can do other than inform your relatives and bring care packages to you in jail. (For information on how to address those packages, see **Keeping in Touch,** p. 27.)

Travelers should also exercise caution with **prescription drugs.** The US State Department cautions against bringing large amounts of prescription drugs into the country. Mexican police can arrest you if they feel that your drugs are being abused or exceed the amount needed for personal use. It may be helpful to bring a doctor's letter certifying the drugs' legitimacy.

**ALCOHOL.** Mexicans get annoyed with foreigners who cross the border for nights of debauchery, so avoid public drunkenness—it is against the law and could land you in jail. The US State Department reports cases of tourists—almost always traveling alone—who have been drugged or intoxicated at night-clubs or bars and then beaten, robbed, abducted, or raped

# SPECIFIC CONCERNS

## NATURAL DISASTERS

**EARTHQUAKES.** Mexico is prone to seismic activity, often with devastating consequences. Should an earthquake occur, take cover under a heavy piece of furniture, such as a table or sturdy doorway, and protect your head. If outside, avoid standing near buildings or walls, as debris may begin to fall. Do not stand near windows. Listen for radio or television announcements for developing information. Beware of aftershocks.

**HURRICANES.** Mexico's Gulf and Pacific coasts often fall victim to hurricanes. Tourists should take the hurricane season (July-Nov.) into consideration when traveling. In the event of a hurricane, stay indoors and away from windows. Be wary of drinking the local water supply after the storm.

## DEMONSTRATIONS AND POLITICAL GATHERINGS

Mexican presidential elections (most recently in 2006) tend to be quite turbulent. During election years, expect widespread political protests. It is illegal for foreigners to participate in demonstrations deemed political by officials. Such actions violate tourist cards and visas and can result in arrest, fines, or deportation. Travelers are advised to avoid mass gatherings and keep close tabs on current political conditions.

## TERRORISM

The Yucatán Peninsula has not suffered the same degree of escalating violence seen in other parts of Mexico. However, in 2008, several high profile criminal acts served as a reminder that the Yucatán is part of the nationwide narco-conflict underway in Mexico. The Mexican Drug War is an armed conflict taking place

ESSENTIALS

between rival drug groups and the Mexican government. The crackdown has resulted in the arrest of some high-level figures in the drug trade, but as the gangs are dismantled, violent power struggles erupt over who will take their places. Criminals select victims based on appearance, vulnerability, and inattentiveness.

## KIDNAPPING

Kidnapping, including the kidnapping of non-Mexicans, continues to occur at alarming rates. Express kidnappings, attempts to get quick cash in exchange for the release of an individual, have occurred in almost all the large cities in Mexico. Travelers may want to contact their country's embassy or consulate in Mexico to discuss precautions they should take.

**TRAVEL ADVISORIES.** The following government offices provide travel information and advisories by telephone, by fax, or via the web:

**Australian Department of Foreign Affairs and Trade:** ☎+61 2 6261 1111; www.dfat.gov.au.

**Canadian Department of Foreign Affairs and International Trade (DFAIT):** ☎+1-800-267-8376; www.dfait-maeci.gc.ca. Call or visit the website for the free booklet *Bon Voyage...But.*

**New Zealand Ministry of Foreign Affairs:** ☎+64 4 439 8000; www.mfat.govt.nz.

**United Kingdom Foreign and Commonwealth Office:** ☎+44 20 7008 1500; www.fco.gov.uk.

**US Department of State:** ☎+1-888-407-4747, 202-501-4444 from abroad; http://travel.state.gov.

# OTHER AREAS OF CONCERN

## BEACHES

Crime has infiltrated even the most beautiful and pristine parts of the country, and tourists have not escaped the onslaught. **Avoid hidden or secluded beaches** unless they are known to be especially safe. If you are going to the beach, it's a good idea to go during daylight hours. Do not leave your belongings on your towel if you expect to find them when you come back after swimming. Several tourists have been killed while walking alone on beaches; some of these attacks happened during the morning hours. Avoid beaches that have been black-flagged and always exercise caution.

## CANCÚN

This international tourist mecca draws pickpockets and petty thieves from all over the country. Muggings, purse-snatchings, and hotel-room burglaries are on the rise. Use common sense and protect your valuables. Sexual assaults and rapes are known to occur during evening or early morning hours in the **Zona Hotelera,** Cancún's tourist hub. Intoxicated clubbers separated from friends are at higher risk of being attacked.

# PERSONAL SAFETY

## EXPLORING AND TRAVELING

To avoid unwanted attention, try to blend in as much as possible. Respecting local customs (in many cases, dressing more conservatively than you would at home) may ward off would-be hecklers. Familiarize yourself with your surroundings before setting out and carry yourself with confidence. Check maps in shops and restaurants rather than on the street. If you are traveling alone, be sure someone at home knows your itinerary and never tell anyone you meet that you're by yourself. When walking at night, stick to busy, well-lit streets and avoid dark alleyways. If you ever feel uncomfortable, leave the area as quickly and directly as you can. There is no sure-fire way to avoid all the threatening situations that you might encounter while traveling, but a good self-defense course will give you concrete ways to react to unwanted advances. **Impact, Prepare,** and **Model Mugging** (www.modelmugging.org) can refer you to local self-defense courses in Australia, Canada, Switzerland, and the US.

Travelers in Mexico should hail **taxis** from a *sitio* (regulated taxi stand) or telephone a reputable organization ahead of time and make note of the drivers' name and license plate number.

## POSSESSIONS AND VALUABLES

Never leave your belongings unattended; crime can occur in even the most safe-looking hostel or hotel. Bring your own padlock for hostel lockers and don't ever store valuables in a locker. Be particularly careful on **buses** and **trains;** horror stories abound about determined thieves who wait for travelers to fall asleep. Carry your bag or purse in front of you where you can see it. When traveling with others, sleep in alternate shifts. When alone, be careful in selecting a train compartment; never stay in an empty one and always use a lock to secure your pack to the luggage rack. Use extra caution if traveling at night or on overnight trains. Try to sleep on top bunks with your luggage stored above you (if not in bed with you) and keep important documents and other valuables on you at all times.

There are a few steps you can take to minimize the financial risk associated with traveling. First, **bring as little with you as possible.** Second, buy a few combination **padlocks** to secure your belongings either in your pack or in a hostel or train-station locker. Third, **carry as little cash as possible.** Keep your traveler's checks and ATM/credit cards in a **money belt**—not a "fanny pack"—along with your passport and ID cards. Fourth, **keep a small cash reserve separate from your primary stash.** This should be about US$50 (US dollars or euro are best) sewn into or stored in the depths of your pack, along with your traveler's check numbers and photocopies of your important documents.

In large cities, con artists often work in groups and may involve children. Beware of certain classics: sob stories that require money, rolls of bills "found" on the street, mustard spilled (or saliva spit) onto your shoulder to distract you while they snatch your bag. **Never let your passport or your bags out of your sight.** Hostel workers will sometimes stand at bus and train arrival points to recruit tired and disoriented travelers to their hostel; never believe strangers who tell you that theirs is the only hostel open. Beware of **pickpockets** in city crowds, especially on public transportation. Also, be alert in public telephone booths.

If you must say your calling-card number, do so very quietly; if you punch it in, make sure no one can look over your shoulder.

Travelers in Mexico are reminded to be especially vigilant when using ATMs. Both Mexicans and non-Mexicans alike are sometimes subjected to express kidnappings or are forced to withdraw large sums of cash. Avoid street-side ATM machines in favor of protected ones inside commercial buildings.

If you will be traveling with electronic devices, such as a laptop computer, check whether or not your homeowner's insurance covers loss, theft, or damage when you travel. If not, you might consider purchasing a low-cost separate

ESSENTIALS

insurance policy. **Safeware** (☎+1-800-800-1492; www.safeware.com) specializes in covering computers and charges US$90 for 90-day comprehensive international travel coverage up to US$4000. Using iPods or wearing expensive jewelry and prominently labeled designer clothes in Mexico will make it clear that you are in fact a tourist and therefore a target for theft.

# PRE-DEPARTURE HEALTH

In your **passport,** write the names of people you wish to be contacted in case of a medical emergency and list any allergies or medical conditions. If you take **prescription drugs,** carry up-to-date prescriptions or a statement from your doctor stating the medications' trade names, manufacturers, chemical names, and dosages. While traveling, be sure to keep all medication with you in your carry-on luggage. The names in Mexico for common drugs are: *acetaminofén* (acetaminophen), *aspirina* (aspirin), *ibuprofén* (ibuprofen), *antihistimíno* (antihistamine) and *penicilina* (penicillin).

## IMMUNIZATIONS AND PRECAUTIONS

Travelers over two years old should make sure that the following vaccines are up to date: **MMR** (for measles, mumps, and rubella); **DTaP** or **Td** (for diphtheria, tetanus, and pertussis); **IPV** (for polio); **Hib** (for *Haemophilus influenzae* B); and **HepB** (for Hepatitis B). Adults traveling to the developing world on trips longer than four weeks should consider the following additional immunizations: **Hepatitis A vaccine and/or immune globulin (IG), typhoid and cholera vaccines,** particularly if traveling off the beaten path, a **rabies vaccine,** and yearly **influenza vaccines.** For recommendations on immunizations and preventions, consult the **Centers for Disease Control and Prevention (CDC;** below) in the US or the equivalent in your home country and ask a doctor for guidance.

## INSURANCE

Travel insurance covers four basic areas: medical and health problems, property loss, trip cancellation and interruption, and emergency evacuation. Though regular insurance policies may well extend to travel-related accidents, you may consider purchasing separate travel insurance if the cost of potential trip cancellation, interruption, or emergency medical evacuation is greater than you can afford. Prices for travel insurance purchased separately generally run about US$50 per week for full coverage, while trip cancellation or interruption may be purchased separately at a rate of US$3-5 per day, depending on length of stay.

**Medical insurance** often covers costs incurred abroad; check with your provider. **Homeowners' insurance** (or your family's coverage) often covers up to US$500 in case of theft during travel and/or loss of travel documents. **American Express** (☎+1-800-528-4800) grants most cardholders automatic collision and theft car-rental insurance on rentals made with the card.

## USEFUL ORGANIZATIONS AND PUBLICATIONS

The American **Center for Disease Control and Prevention (CDC;** ☎+1-800-CDC-INFO/232-4636; www.cdc.gov/travel) maintains an international travelers' hotline and an informative website. Consult the appropriate government agency of your home country for consular information sheets on health, entry requirements, and other issues for various countries (see the listings in the box on **Travel Advisories,** p. 14). For quick information on health and other travel warnings, call the **Overseas Citizens Services** (☎+1-202-647-5225) or contact a passport agency, embassy, or consulate abroad. For information on medical evacuation services and travel insurance firms, see the US government's website at http://travel.state.gov/travel/abroad_health.html or the **British Foreign and Commonwealth Office** (www.fco.gov.uk). For general health information, contact the **American Red Cross** (☎+1-202-303-5000; www.redcross.org).

# STAYING HEALTHY

Common sense is the simplest prescription for good health while you travel. Drink lots of fluids to prevent dehydration and constipation and wear sturdy, broken-in shoes and clean socks.

## ONCE IN THE YUCATÁN

### ENVIRONMENTAL HAZARDS

**Heat exhaustion and dehydration:** Heat exhaustion leads to nausea, excessive thirst, headaches, and dizziness. Avoid all this by drinking plenty of fluids, eating salty foods, abstaining from dehydrating beverages (e.g., alcohol and caffeinated beverages), and wearing sunscreen. Continuous heat stress can eventually lead to heatstroke, characterized by a rising temperature, severe headache, delirium and cessation of sweating. Victims should be cooled off with wet towels and taken to a doctor.

**High Altitude:** The Yucatán Peninsula's mountains are high enough for altitude sickness to be a concern. Symptoms may include headaches, nausea, dizziness, and sleep disruption. To minimize possible symptoms, avoid rapid increases in elevation, stay well hydrated, and allow your body a couple of days to adjust to less oxygen before exerting yourself. Note that alcohol is more potent and UV rays are stronger at high elevations.

### INSECT-BORNE DISEASES

Many diseases are transmitted by insects—mainly mosquitoes, fleas, ticks, and lice. Be aware of insects in wet or forested areas, especially while hiking and camping. Wear long pants and long sleeves, tuck your pants into your socks, and use a mosquito net. Use insect repellents with DEET and soak or spray your gear with permethrin (licensed in the US only for use on clothing). **Mosquitoes**—responsible for malaria, dengue fever, and yellow fever—can be particularly abundant in humid, coastal areas.

**Dengue fever:** A viral infection transmitted by *Aedes* mosquitoes, which bite during the day rather than at night. The incubation period is 3-14 days, usually 4-7 days. Early symptoms include a high fever, severe headaches, swollen lymph nodes, and muscle aches. Many patients also suffer from nausea, vomiting, and a pink rash. If you experience these symptoms, see a doctor immediately, drink plenty of liquids, and take fever-reducing medication such as acetaminophen (Tylenol®). Never take aspirin to treat dengue fever. There is no vaccine available for dengue fever.

**Lyme disease:** A bacterial infection carried by ticks and marked by a circular bull's-eye rash of 2 in. or more. Later symptoms include fever, headache, fatigue, and aches and pains. Antibiotics are effective if administered early. Left untreated, Lyme can cause problems in joints, the heart, and the nervous system. If you find a tick attached to your skin, grasp the head with tweezers as close to your skin as possible and apply slow, steady traction. Removing a tick within 24hr. greatly reduces the risk of infection. Do not try to remove ticks with petroleum jelly, nail polish remover, or a hot match. Ticks usually inhabit moist, shaded environments and heavily wooded areas. If you are going to be hiking in these areas, wear long clothes and insect repellent with DEET.

**ESSENTIALS**

**Malaria:** Transmitted by *Anopheles* mosquitoes that bite at night. The incubation period varies anywhere between 10 days and 4 weeks. Early symptoms include fever, chills, aches, and fatigue, followed by high fever and sweating, sometimes with vomiting and diarrhea. See a doctor for any flu-like sickness that occurs after travel in a risk area. To reduce the risk of contracting malaria, use mosquito repellent, particularly in the evenings and when visiting forested areas. See a doctor at least 4-6 weeks before a trip to a high-risk area to get up-to-date malaria prescriptions and recommendations. A doctor may prescribe oral prophylactics, like mefloquine or doxycycline. Know that mefloquine can have serious side effects, including paranoia and psychosis.

## FOOD- AND WATER-BORNE DISEASES

Prevention is the best cure: be sure that your food is properly cooked and that the water you drink is clean. Do not ingest tap water. Watch out for food from markets or street vendors that may have been cooked in unhygienic conditions. Other culprits are raw shellfish, unpasteurized milk, and sauces containing raw eggs. Buy bottled water, or purify your own water by bringing it to a rolling boil or treating it with **iodine tablets;** note, however, that some parasites such as giardia have exteriors that resist iodine treatment, so boiling is more reliable.

**Cholera:** An intestinal disease caused by bacteria in contaminated food. Symptoms include diarrhea, dehydration, vomiting, and muscle cramps. See a doctor immediately; if left untreated, cholera can be lethal within hours. Antibiotics are available, but the most important treatment is rehydration. No vaccine is available in the US.

**Dysentery:** Results from an intestinal infection caused by bacteria in contaminated food or water. Common symptoms include bloody diarrhea, fever, and abdominal pain and tenderness. The most common type of dysentery generally only lasts a week, but it is highly contagious. Seek medical help immediately. Dysentery can be treated with the drugs norfloxacin or ciprofloxacin (commonly known as Cipro). If you are traveling in high-risk (especially rural) regions, consider obtaining a prescription before you leave.

**Giardiasis:** Transmitted through parasites and acquired by drinking untreated water from streams or lakes. Symptoms include diarrhea, cramps, bloating, fatigue, weight loss, and nausea. If untreated, Giardiasis can lead to severe dehydration.

**Hepatitis A:** A viral infection of the liver acquired through contaminated water or shellfish from contaminated water. Symptoms include fatigue, fever, loss of appetite, nausea, dark urine, jaundice, vomiting, aches and pains, and light stools. The risk is highest in rural areas and the countryside, but it is also present in urban areas. Ask your doctor about the Hepatitis A vaccine or an injection of immune globulin.

**Traveler's diarrhea:** Results from drinking fecally contaminated water or eating uncooked and contaminated foods. Symptoms include nausea, bloating, and urgency. Try quick-energy, non-sugary foods with protein and carbohydrates to keep your strength up. Over-the-counter anti-diarrheals (e.g., Imodium®) may counteract the problem. The most dangerous side effect is dehydration; drink 8 oz. of water with ½ tsp. of sugar or honey and a pinch of salt, try uncaffeinated soft drinks, or eat salted crackers. If you develop a fever or your symptoms don't go away after 4-5 days, consult a doctor. Consult a doctor immediately for treatment of diarrhea in children.

**Typhoid fever:** Caused by the salmonella bacteria; common in villages and rural areas in Mexico. Mostly transmitted through contaminated food and water, it may also be acquired by direct contact with another person. Early symptoms include high fever, headaches, fatigue, appetite loss, constipation, and a rash on the abdomen or chest. Antibiotics can treat typhoid, but a vaccination (70-90% effective) is recommended.

## OTHER INFECTIOUS DISEASES

The following diseases exist all over the world. Travelers should know how to recognize them and what to do if they suspect they have been infected.

**AIDS and HIV:** For detailed information on Acquired Immune Deficiency Syndrome (AIDS) in Mexico, call the CDC's 24hr. National AIDS Hotline at ☎+1-800-232-4636.

**Hepatitis B:** A viral liver infection transmitted via blood or other bodily fluids. Symptoms, which may not surface until years after infection, include jaundice, appetite loss, fever, and joint pain. It is transmitted through unprotected sex and unclean needles. A 3-shot vaccination sequence is recommended for sexually active travelers and anyone planning to seek medical treatment abroad; it must begin 6 months before traveling.

**Sexually transmitted infections (STIs):** Gonorrhea, chlamydia, genital warts, syphilis, herpes, HPV, and other STIs are easier to catch than HIV and can be just as serious. Though condoms may protect you from some STIs, oral or even tactile contact can lead to transmission. If you think you may have contracted an STI, see a doctor immediately.

**Swine influenza:** "Swine flu," also known by its subtype H1N1, is a highly infectious strain of flu that originated in Mexico in 2009. Athough there have been some reports of individuals coming down with it after visiting Cancún and other destinations in the peninsula, the Yucatán has been relatively free from swine flu. Symptoms include fever, fatigue, chills, muscle pain, and congestion. Hand washing, good hygienic practices, and avoiding areas where Swine Flu is prevalent are the best way to minimize the rist of contracting it. Seek immediate medical attention if you notice symptoms. There is currently no vaccine.

# OTHER HEALTH CONCERNS

## MEDICAL CARE ON THE ROAD

The quality of medical care in Mexico varies with the size of the city or town. The same applies to the availability of English-speaking medical practitioners. Medical care in heavily touristed areas of the Yucatán is first-class, while care in more rural parts can be limited. Local pharmacies can be invaluable sources for medical help. Most pharmacists are knowledgeable about mild illnesses—particularly those that plague tourists—and can recommend shots or medicines. Wherever possible, *Let's Go* lists 24hr. and late-night pharmacies.

If you are concerned about obtaining medical assistance while traveling, you may wish to employ special support services. The **International Association for Medical Assistance to Travelers** (IAMAT; US ☎+1-716-754-4883, Canada +1-416-652-0137; www.iamat.org) has free membership, lists English-speaking doctors worldwide, and offers details on immunization requirements and sanitation. For those whose insurance doesn't apply abroad, you can purchase additional coverage.

Those with medical conditions (such as diabetes, allergies to antibiotics, epilepsy, or heart conditions) may want to obtain a **MedicAlert** membership (US$40 per year), which includes, among other things, a stainless-steel ID tag and a 24hr. collect-call number. Contact the MedicAlert Foundation International (from US ☎888-633-4298, outside US +1-209-668-3333; www.medicalert.org).

## WOMEN'S HEALTH

**Tampons** are hard to find in Mexico and, if available at all, come only in regular sizes. It might be wise to bring a supply along, especially if you are traveling to smaller cities. Condoms can be found in most large pharmacies, but other contraceptive devices are difficult to find.

ESSENTIALS

# GETTING TO
# THE YUCATÁN PENINSULA

## BY PLANE

When it comes to flying on a budget the key is to hunt around, be flexible, and ask about discounts. Students, seniors, and those under 26 should never have to pay full price for a ticket.

### AIRFARES

Airfares to Mexico peak in late March and early April, and mid-June through August. Holidays are also expensive. Midweek (M-Th morning) round-trip flights run US$40-50 cheaper than weekend flights, but they are generally more crowded and less likely to permit frequent-flier upgrades. Not fixing a return date ("open return") or arriving in and departing from different cities ("open-jaw") can be pricier than round-trip flights. Patching one-way flights together is the most expensive way to travel. Flights between Mexico's capitals or regional hubs—Mexico City, Guadalajara, and Cancún—tend to be cheaper.

Fares for round-trip flights to Cancún from the US or Canada's east coast cost US$200-400, US$85 in the low season; from the US or Canada's west coast US$450/250; from the UK, UK£900/750; from Australia AUS$4000/3700; from New Zealand NZ$3300/2700.

---

**FLIGHT PLANNING ON THE INTERNET.** The internet may be the budget traveler's dream when it comes to finding and booking bargain fares, but the array of options can be overwhelming. Many airline sites offer special last-minute deals on the web. Popular Mexican carriers include **Aeroméxico** (www.aeromexico.com), which flies to practically every Mexican city with an airport, and **Mexicana** (www.mexicana.com).

**STA** (www.statravel.com) and **StudentUniverse** (www.studentuniverse.com) provide quotes on student tickets, while **Orbitz** (www.orbitz.com), **Expedia** (www.expedia.com), and **Travelocity** (www.travelocity.com) offer full travel services. **Priceline** (www.priceline.com) lets you specify a price and obligates you to buy any ticket that meets or beats it; **Hotwire** (www.hotwire.com) offers bargain fares but won't reveal the airline or flight times until you buy. Other sites that compile deals include www.bestfares.com, www.flights.com, www.lowestfare.com, www.onetravel.com, and www.travelzoo.com.

**Cheapflights** (www.cheapflights.co.uk) is a useful search engine for finding—you guessed it—cheap flights. **Booking Buddy** (www.bookingbuddy.com), **Kayak** (www.kayak.com), and **SideStep** (www.sidestep.com) are online tools that let you enter your trip information and search multiple sites at once. *Let's Go* does not endorse any of these websites. As always, be cautious and research companies before you hand over your credit card number.

---

## BUDGET AND STUDENT TRAVEL AGENCIES

**STA Travel,** 2871 Broadway, New York City, NY 10025, USA (24hr. reservations and info ☎+1-800-781-4040; www.statravel.com). A student and youth travel organization with offices worldwide, including US offices in Los Angeles, New York City, Seattle, Washington, DC, and a number of other college towns. Ticket booking, travel insurance, rail-passes, and more. Walk-in offices are located throughout Australia (☎+61 134 782), New Zealand (☎+0800 474 400), and the UK (☎+44 8712 230 0040).

# COMMERCIAL AIRLINES

### TRAVELING FROM NORTH AMERICA

Basic round-trip fares to Mexico cost roughly US$500-600, US$400 in the low season. Standard commercial carriers like **American** (☎+1-800-433-7300; www.aa.com) and **United** (☎+1-800-538-2929; www.ual.com) will probably offer the most convenient flights to Mexico, but they may not be the cheapest, unless you snag a special promotion or airfare-war ticket. You will probably find flying one of the following "discount" airlines a better deal, if any of their limited departure points is convenient for you.

**JetBlue Airways** (☎+1-800-538-2583; www.jetblue.com). Cheap flights to a few Mexican cities, including Cancún.

**US Airways,** 4000 E. Sky Harbor Blvd., Phoenix, AZ 85034 (☎+1-800-428-4322 for 24hr. reservations; www.usairways.com). Discount fares to Cancún and Mérida.

### TRAVELING FROM IRELAND AND THE UK

Basic round-trip fares to Mexico cost roughly US$900-1200, US$800 in the low season. Standard international carriers like American and Continental will probably offer the most convenient flights.

**American Airlines** (☎207 365 0777 from London, 8457 789 789 from the UK outside London, 1602 0550 from Ireland; www.aa.com). International flights to a large number of Mexican cities.

**Continental Airlines** (☎0845 607 6760 from the UK, 1890 925 252 from Ireland; www.continental.com). Services similar to American Airlines.

### TRAVELING FROM AUSTRALIA AND NEW ZEALAND

Basic round-trip fares to Mexico cost roughly US$1900-2200, US$1800 in the low season. Most likely, this trip will require multiple carriers.

**Air New Zealand** (NZ☎+64 0800 737 000, US☎+01-800-262-1234; www.airnewzealand.co.nz).

**Mexicana** (☎US+01-800-380-8781, www.mexicana.com).

# BY BUS

**Greyhound** (☎+1-800-231-2222, from outside the US +1-214-849-8100; www.greyhound.com) serves many US-Mexico border towns, including El Paso (Juárez) and Brownsville (Matamoros) in Texas and San Ysidro in California. Schedule information is available at any Greyhound terminal, on their website, or by calling their toll-free number. Smaller lines serve other destinations.

In the past, US buses did not cross the US-Mexico and Guatemala-Mexico borders; travelers had to switch to Mexican bus lines at the border. Many bus tours now cross the border, though you can still pick up Mexican bus lines (among them **Estrella de Oro, Estrella Blanca, ADO,** and **Transportes Del Norte**) on the other side. Guatemalan bus lines operate at Guatemala-Mexico border towns, including **Talismán** and **La Mesilla.** Buses usually stop just short of the border. You can walk across to Guatemala and pick up a local bus to the nearest town. For more information on **Border Crossing**, see p. 22. Buses also operate between Chetumal, Mexico, and Belize City.

ESSENTIALS

# BORDER CROSSINGS

There are 24 overland border crossings to Mexico from **Arizona, California, New Mexico,** and **Texas.** The busiest point of entry by far is between **San Ysidro, CA** and **Tijuana.** Though it is done, it is best not to drive into Mexico, as US car insurance is not valid in Mexico. The larger border towns have parking lots from which travelers can walk or be bused across the border.

There are three land crossings between Guatemala and Mexico. In the highlands, **Ciudad Cuauhtémoc** and **La Mesilla,** 90km west of Huehuetenango, have buses to **San Cristóbal de las Casas,** Mexico. Buses from Huehue, Guatemala City, and other towns go to La Mesilla. **El Carmen** and **Talismán** are west of Quetzaltenango and Retalhuleu, near Tapachula, Mexico. **Tecun Umán** and **Ciudad Hidalgo** on the Pacific coast are 75km west of Retalhuleu. Buses head there from Quetzaltenango, Retalhuleu, and Tapachula, Mexico. There are several land and river crossings from Flores toward Palenque, Mexico.

**CROSSING THE BORDER.** Before leaving Mexico, travelers must pay an exit fee of around US$20. If you flew into Mexico, this fee was included in your airfare. If you didn't fly in, go to any bank and ask to pay the DNE fee, and they will stamp your immigration papers, which you must then present, along with your passport, at the border immigration office. Citizens of the EU, Canada, and the US visiting Guatemala do not need a visa for visits of 90 days or less. Citizens from other countries need to get a visa from a Guatemalan consulate, such as the one in Tapachula. If you plan on staying longer than 90 days, check with an immigration office in Guatemala; otherwise, you might have to pay a fee when you leave. The easiest, safest, and most practical way to cross into Guatemala is to take a direct bus from Tapachula to Guatemala City. Unión y Progreso buses leave Tapachula from C. 5 Pte., between Av. 12 and 14 Nte., for Talismán, passing by the ADO station on their way out of town (30min., every 15min., 15 pesos). They drop passengers a few blocks from the Mexican emigration office; follow the stream of tricicleros (passenger carts; 10 pesos). Present your passport and papers at the office and follow the crowd across the bridge. On the Guatemalan side, get your passport stamped at a small blue building on the left. Beware of those who offer "help" getting your passport stamped, or anyone who asks for an entrance fee at this checkpoint—there is no fee to enter Guatemala here. It's best to change only a little bit of money with the men with credentials who are holding wads of quetzales. If you choose to brave the crossing on foot, the closest crossing point from Tapachula is Talismán (16km), which has considerably less traffic than Ciudad Hidalgo (37km).

# GETTING AROUND THE YUCATÁN PENINSULA

When traveling around the Peninsula, fares are either **one-way** or **round-trip.** "Period returns" require you to return within a specific number of days; "day return" means you must return on the same day. Unless stated otherwise, *Let's Go* lists single one-way fares, and round-trip fares on trains and buses are simply double the one-way fare.

# BY PLANE

Flying within Mexican borders is a method of transportation typically beyond the reach of budget travelers. That said, time is money. You may want to consider flying when long bus rides (e.g., over 24hr.) cost about the same or are only marginally cheaper than flying. In July 2005, **Mexicana** launched its budget airline, **Click** (www.click.com.mx), which offers low fares to 16 domestic destinations. For other deals, you can visit one of the ubiquitous travel agencies in Mexico. Students and senior citizens should ask about the possibility of discounts or standby seats. You can also check with Mexican airlines directly.

> **AIRCRAFT SAFETY.** The airlines of developing-world nations do not always meet safety standards. The **Official Airline Guide** (www.oag.com) and many travel agencies can tell you the type and age of aircraft on a particular route. This can be especially useful in Mexico, where less reliable equipment is often used for internal flights. The **International Airline Passengers Association** (www.iapa.com) provides region-specific safety information to its members. The **Federal Aviation Administration** (www.faa.gov/passengers/international_travel) reviews the airline authorities for countries whose airlines enter the US. **US State Department** travel advisories (www.travel.state.gov) sometimes involve foreign carriers, especially when terrorist bombings or hijackings may be a threat.

# BY BUS

From most large cities, it is possible to get almost anywhere in the Peninsula by by bus. Several companies provide cheap and efficient service. **Autotransportes del Oriente** (**ADO**; www.ado.com.mx) services Chiapas, the Gulf Coast, Mexico City, Oaxaca state, Puebla, Veracruz state, and the Yucatán. Many tickets can be purchased online. Check www.ticketbus.com.mx for schedules.

There are several types of bus services. **Servicio ejecutivo** (executive service), also called **de lujo** (deluxe), is fairly rare but provides royal treatment: plush reclining seats, sometimes too-frigid air-conditioning, sandwiches and soda, and movies galore. These buses are also known as **directo** (no stops). Less fancy are **primera clase** (first-class) buses, which usually feature second-rate movies and air-conditioning. The *primera clase* are also called **express** buses because they have few stops. For both executive and first-class buses, tickets should be purchased in advance at the bus station. **Segunda clase** (second-class) buses are lower-quality. They are usually converted school buses or some variation thereof, and are often overcrowded and uncomfortable. The drivers will stop along the road many times to pick up people. Tickets for *segunda clase* buses can often be purchased on board. When traveling between small towns, *segunda clase* buses may be the only available option.

> **THE ROAD LESS TRAVELED.** First-class buses are more likely to take toll *(cuota)* roads, while second-class buses often take free *(libre)* highways, which have more reports of hijacking and other crime.

Buses are categorized as either *local* or *de paso*. **Locales** originate at the station from which you leave. **De paso** (in passing) buses originate elsewhere and pass through

E S S E N T I A L S

ESSENTIALS

your station. Because *de paso* buses depend on the seating availability when the bus arrives, tickets are not available in advance. Be on the watch for when tickets do go on sale, as buses do not stay in the station long and may fill quickly.

# BY CAR

Mexicans tend to be rowdy on the road. It's not unusual to hear drivers exchange such greetings as *"¡Baboso!"* (Drooling fool!), *"¡Eh, estúpido!"* (Hey, stupid!), and, of course, the ubiquitous *"¿Dónde aprendiste a manejar, menso?"* (Where did you learn how to drive, dummy?). With enough practice, you'll be able to curse with the best Mexican drivers. It's also not unusual for Mexican drivers to overuse their car horns; drive down any busy street and you'll be serenaded by a cacophony of honks. In such a climate, it's best to drive defensively.

Be sure to learn local driving signals and wear a seat belt. Study route maps before you hit the road and, if you plan on spending a lot of time driving, consider bringing spare parts. For long drives in desolate areas, invest in a cell phone and a roadside assistance program. Park your vehicle in a garage or well-traveled area and use a steering-wheel locking device in larger cities. Sleeping in your car is the most dangerous way to get your rest, and it's also illegal.

In general, avoid freeways *(libres)* and driving at night, when there is a greater chance of hijacking and other criminal acts. Driving on unpaved side roads can be unsafe and difficult; if you plan to do a lot of driving off major highways, a four-wheel-drive vehicle is recommended. **The Association for Safe International Road Travel** (www.asirt.org) is a good resource to learn more about safe car travel while abroad.

## DRIVING PERMITS AND CAR INSURANCE

### INTERNATIONAL DRIVING PERMIT (IDP)

If you plan to drive a car while in the Yucatán, you must have a valid **International Driving Permit (IDP),** American license, or Canadian license. It may be a good idea to get an IDP anyway, in case you're in a situation (e.g., an accident or stranding in a small town) where the police do not know English; information on the IDP is printed in 11 languages, including Spanish.

Your IDP, valid for one year, must be issued in your home country before you depart. For an IDP application, you'll need one or two passport photos, a current local license, an additional form of identification with a photo, and a fee. To apply, contact your home country's automobile association. Be vigilant when purchasing an IDP online or anywhere other than your home automobile association. Many vendors sell permits of questionable legitimacy for higher prices.

### CAR INSURANCE

Most credit cards cover standard insurance. If you rent, lease, or borrow a car in Mexico, you will need a **green card,** or **International Insurance Certificate,** to certify that you have liability insurance and that it applies abroad. Green cards can be obtained from your domestic insurer who issued your motor insurance. To avoid being taken into police custody in the event of an accident (as your international liability insurance is most likely invalid in Mexico), purchase Mexican insurance through your car rental agency, at a point of entry, or online at www.drivemex.com or www.bajabound.com.

# RENTING

Having a car certainly has its advantages: some of the most beautiful parts of the Yucatán are off the major highways and bus stations can be inconveniently spread out. As many roads are not paved, having a car whose undercarraige is far from the ground (e.g., a pick-up truck) is helpful. A four-wheel-drive is not necessary, but is certainly recommended if available. You can drive in Mexico with a regular economy car, but keep in mind that cheaper cars tend to be less reliable and harder to handle on difficult terrain. Also note that less expensive four-wheel-drive vehicles tend to be more top-heavy, and are more dangerous when navigating particularly bumpy roads.

## RENTAL AGENCIES

You can generally make reservations in advance by calling major international offices in your home country. However, sometimes the price and availability information they give doesn't jive with what the local offices in Mexico will tell you. Try checking with both numbers to make sure you get the best price and the most accurate information possible. For home-country numbers, call your toll-free directory.

To rent a car from most establishments in Mexico, you need to be at least 21 years old. Some agencies require renters to be 25, and most charge those under 25 an additional insurance fee of around US$20 per day. Keep in mind that policies and prices can vary considerably between agencies. Small local operations occasionally rent to people under 21, but be sure to ask about the insurance coverage and deductible, and always check the fine print. The **Mexico Car Rental Guide** (www.mexicocar.net) compares the prices of numerous companies and helps make online bookings. Rental agencies in the Peninsula include:

**Avis:** ☎+1-800-288-8888, in Cancún (airport) +52 998-886-0221; www.avis.com.mx.

**Budget:** ☎+1-800-700-1700, in Cancún +52 984 873 1875; www.budget.com.mx.

**Hertz:** ☎+1-800-654 3001, in Cancún +52 55 5566 0099; www.hertz.com.mx.

## COSTS AND INSURANCE

Rental car prices start at around US$45 per day. Expect to pay more for larger cars. Cars with **automatic transmission are harder to come by;** if available, expect to pay up to US$20 more per day.

Many rental packages offer unlimited kilometers, while others offer a limited number of kilometers per day with a surcharge per kilometer after that. Return the car with a full tank of gasoline to avoid high fuel charges upon return. Be sure to ask whether the rental price includes **insurance** against theft and collision. Remember that if you are driving a conventional rental vehicle on an **unpaved road,** you are almost never covered by insurance; ask about this before leaving the rental agency.

# ON THE ROAD

If possible, avoid driving during the rainy season (June-Oct.) when road conditions deteriorate. If you plan on driving extensively between cities, check with local authorities or with your nearest consulate for updates on potential dangers. Unless otherwise posted, the speed limit on Mexican highways is 100km per hr. (62 mph), but, like most other traffic regulations, it is often ignored. The speed limit in cities and towns is generally 40km per hr. (25 mph). Gasoline prices vary, but they average about US$2.95 per gallon in cities and around US$2.40 per gallon in outlying areas

E S S E N T I A L S

## CAR ASSISTANCE

If you're unlucky enough to have a car break down on a major toll road between 8am and 8pm, pull completely off the road, raise the hood, stay with your car, and call for the **Ángeles Verdes** (Green Angels; ☎01-800-903-9200). You can also reach them by calling the **Ministry of Tourism's hotline** (☎078). These green-and-white emergency trucks, dispatched by radio and staffed by English-speaking mechanics, are equipped to perform common repair jobs, tow cars, change tires, and address minor medical problems. Your green saviors may take a while to show up, but the service— provided by the government—is free (except for gas, parts, and oil). Tipping is optional but a good idea.

 **LET'S NOT GO.** *Let's Go* urges you to consider the risks before you choose to hitchhike. We do not recommend hitching as a safe means of transportation, and none of the information presented here is intended to do so.

# KEEPING IN TOUCH

## BY EMAIL AND INTERNET

Although in some places it's possible to forge a remote link with your home server, in most cases this is a much slower (and thus more expensive) option than taking advantage of free **web-based email accounts** (e.g., www.gmail.com and www.hotmail.com). **Internet cafes** are listed in the **Practical Information** sections of major cities. These cybercafes can even be found in some of the smaller Mexican towns, with varying quality and speed. Expect to pay US$1-8 per hour for access. For lists of additional cybercafes in Mexico, check out cybercaptive.com.

Increasingly, travelers find that taking their **laptops** on the road with them can be a convenient option for staying connected. Laptop users can occasionally find internet cafes that will allow them to connect their laptops to the internet. Travelers with wireless-enabled computers may be able to take advantage of an increasing number of internet "hot spots," where they can get online for free or for a small fee. Newer computers can detect these hot spots automatically; otherwise, websites like www.jiwire.com, www.wififreespot.com, and www.wi-fihotspotlist.com can help you find them. For information on insuring your laptop while traveling, see p. 16.

 **WARY WI-FI.** Wireless hot spots make internet access possible in public and remote places. Unfortunately, they also pose **security risks.** Hot spots are public, open networks that use unencrypted, unsecured connections. They are susceptible to hacks and "packet sniffing"—the theft of passwords and other private information. To prevent problems, disable "ad hoc" mode, turn off file sharing and network discovery, encrypt your email, turn on your firewall, beware of phony networks, and watch for over-the-shoulder creeps.

# BY TELEPHONE

## CALLING HOME FROM THE YUCATÁN PENINSULA

You can usually make direct international calls from pay phones, but if you aren't using a phone card, you may need to feed the machine regularly. **Prepaid phone cards** are a common and relatively inexpensive means of calling abroad. To purchase prepaid phone cards, check online for the best rates; www.callingcards.com is a good place to start. Online providers generally send your access number and PIN via email, with no actual "card" involved. You can also call home with prepaid phone cards purchased in Mexico (see **Calling Within the Yucatán** below). Another option is to purchase a **calling card,** linked to a major national telecommunications service in your home country. Calls are billed collect or to your account.

Many travelers rely on **Skype**, a software application that allows users to make telephone calls over the internet. Calls to other users of the service, and to free-of-charge numbers are free, while calls to other landlines and mobile phones can be made for a fee. If you do not have internet there are many cafes in Mexico that rent computers and you can ask them to install Skype in their machines if they do not have it already.

Placing a collect call through an international operator can be an expensive but necessary last resort in case of an emergency.

## CALLING WITHIN THE YUCATÁN PENINSULA

The **LADATEL phones** that have popped up all over the country have revolutionized Mexico's phone card system. To operate one, you'll need a colorful **pre-paid phone card**, available at most *papelerías* (stationery stores) or *tiendas de abarrotes* (general stores)—look for the *De venta aquí LADATEL* signs posted in store windows. You may purchase 30, 50, or 100 peso cards. Using a card will usually save you time, if not money, in the long run. The computerized LADATEL phone will tell you how much time, in units, you have left on your card. Phone rates typically tend to be highest in the morning, lower in the evening, and lowest late at night and on Sundays.

---

 **PLACING INTERNATIONAL CALLS.** To call Mexico from home or to call home from Mexico, dial:

1. The **international dialing prefix.** To call from **Australia,** dial ☎0011; **Canada** or the **US,** ☎011; **Ireland, New Zealand,** or the **UK,** ☎00; **Mexico,** ☎00.
2. The **country code** of the country you want to call. To call **Australia,** dial ☎61; **Canada** or the **US,** ☎1; **Ireland,** ☎353; **New Zealand,** ☎64; the **UK,** ☎44; **Mexico,** ☎52.
3. The **city/area code.** *Let's Go* lists the city/area codes for cities and towns in Mexico opposite the city or town name, next to a ☎, as well as in every phone number. If the first digit is a zero (e.g., ☎0998 Cancun), omit the zero when calling from abroad (e.g., dial ☎998 from Canada to reach Cancun).
4. The **local number.**

---

## CELLULAR PHONES

The international standard for cell phones is **Global System for Mobile Communication (GSM).** To make and receive calls in Mexico, you will need a GSM-compatible phone and a **SIM (Subscriber Identity Module) card,** a country-specific,

ESSENTIALS

thumbnail-size chip that gives you a local phone number and plugs you into the local network. Many SIM cards are prepaid, and incoming calls are frequently free. For more information on GSM phones, check out www.telestial.com. Companies like **Cellular Abroad** (www.cellularabroad.com) rent cell phones that work in a variety of destinations around the world.

**GSM PHONES.** Just having a GSM phone doesn't mean you're necessarily good to go when you travel abroad. The majority of GSM phones sold in the US operate on a different frequency (1900) than international phones (900/1800) and will not work abroad. Tri-band phones work on all three frequencies (900/1800/1900) and will operate through most of the world. Additionally, some GSM phones are SIM-locked and will only accept SIM cards from a single carrier. You'll need a SIM-unlocked phone to use a SIM card from a local carrier when you travel.

# TIME DIFFERENCES

The Yucatán is 6 hours behind Greenwich Mean Time (GMT) and observes Daylight Saving Time.

# BY MAIL

## SENDING MAIL HOME FROM THE YUCATÁN

Keep in mind that Mexican postal service can be painfully slow, even for domestic mail. Airmail from major cities in Mexico to Canada and the US takes anywhere from 10 days to six weeks; to Australia or New Zealand, one month; to Ireland or the UK, three weeks to one month. Add another one or two weeks for mail sent from more rural areas within Mexico. Sending postcards and letters to the United States via air mail costs approximately 11 pesos.

Outgoing mail is picked up infrequently, but the bright plastic orange boxes labeled *Express* that have appeared in large cities are quite reliable and are picked up every morning. Anything important should be sent *registrado* (registered mail) or taken directly to the post office, at the very least.

Packages cannot weigh more than 25kg. Keep in mind that all packages are opened and inspected by customs at border crossings; closing boxes with string, instead of tape, is recommended. Sometimes you may have to provide certain information: your tourist card data, the contents, value, and nature of the package ("gift" works best), and your address and return address.

**Mexpost,** a more expensive, but more reliable, mailing system, advertises two-day delivery out of state and three-day delivery to major international cities. Despite the promises, expect at least a week for delivery. Mexpost offices are usually found next to regular post offices; if not, the post office staff can usually give you directions to the nearest Mexpost office. Mexpost may not be available in smaller towns.

## SENDING MAIL TO THE YUCATÁN

To ensure timely delivery, mark envelopes "airmail," *"par avion,"* or *"por avión"* and use Spanish abbreviations of countries' names (e.g. E.U. for the US). In addition to the standard postage system whose rates are listed

ESSENTIALS

below, **Federal Express** (☎+1-800-463-3339; www.fedex.com) handles express mail services from most countries to Mexico. There are several ways to arrange pickup of letters sent to you while you are abroad. Mail can be sent via **Poste Restante** (General Delivery; *Lista de Correos* in Spanish) to almost any city or town in Mexico with a post office, but it is not very reliable. Address *Poste Restante* letters like so:

Mato LAGATOR

Lista de Correos

Street address of post office

Cancún, the Yucatán, 77500

MEXICO

The mail will go to a special desk in the central post office, unless you specify a post office by street address or postal code. It's best to use the largest post office, since mail may be sent there regardless. It is usually safer and quicker, though more expensive, to send mail express or registered. Letters should be marked *Favor de retener hasta la llegada* (Please hold until arrival); they will be held for up to 15 days. Bring your passport (or other photo ID) for pick up; there may be a small fee. If the clerks insist that there is nothing for you, ask them to check under your first name as well. *Let's Go* lists post offices in the Practical Information section for each city and most towns.

# ACCOMMODATIONS

Budget accommodations are not hard to find in Mexico, though your options are pricier in resort towns. All hotels are controlled by the government's **Secretaría de Turismo (SECTUR)**. This organization ensures that hotels of similar quality charge similar prices; you should always ask to see an up-to-date official tariff sheet if you doubt the quoted price. Many hotels post their official tariffs somewhere near the reception area.

## HOSTELS

Many hostels are laid out dorm-style, often with large single-sex rooms and bunk beds, although more private rooms that sleep from two to four are becoming more common. Hostels sometimes have kitchens and utensils for your use, breakfast and other meals, storage areas, laundry facilities, internet, transportation to airports, and bike or moped rentals. However, there can be drawbacks: some hostels impose a maximum stay, close during certain daytime "lockout" hours, have a curfew, don't accept reservations, or, less frequently, require that you do chores.

In the Yucatán, a dorm bed in a hostel will average around 130 pesos (under US$12) and a private room around 170-220 pesos (US$16-21). Hostels are often located within a block or two of a city's *zócalo* (the main square of a Mexican town) and have hot water and private bathrooms, but rarely provide amenities such as air-conditioning. For more information about Mexican hostels, contact **Hostelling Mexico, A.C.,** Guatemala 4, Colonia Centro, Mexico D.F. (☎+52 55 5518 1726; www.hostellingmexico.com), which is affiliated with Hostelling International (see p. 31).

**A HOSTELER'S BILL OF RIGHTS.** There are certain standard features that we do not include in our hostel listings. Unless we state otherwise, you can expect that every hostel has no lockout, no curfew, free hot showers, some system of secure luggage storage, and no key deposit.

## HOSTELLING INTERNATIONAL

Joining the youth hostel association in your own country (listed below) automatically grants you membership privileges in **Hostelling International (HI)**, a federation of national hostelling associations. Non-HI members may be allowed to stay in some hostels, but they will have to pay extra to do so. HI hostels are scattered throughout Mexico and are typically less expensive than private hostels. HI's umbrella organization's website (www.hihostels.com), which lists the web addresses and phone numbers of all national associations, can be a great place to begin researching hostelling in a specific region. Other hostelling websites include www.hostels.com and www.hostelplanet.com.

Most HI hostels also honor **guest memberships**—you'll get a blank card with space for six validation stamps. Each night you'll pay a nonmember supplement and earn one guest stamp; six stamps make you a member. This system works well most of the time, but in some cases you may need to remind the hostel reception to stamp your card. Most student travel agencies (p. 21) sell HI cards, as do all of the national hostelling organizations listed below.

**Australian Youth Hostels Association (AYHA),** 422 Kent St., Sydney, NSW 2000 (☎+61 2 9261 1111; www.yha.com.au). AUS$42, under 26 AUS$32.

**Hostelling International-Canada (HI-C),** 205 Catherine St., Ste. 400, Ottawa, ON K2P 1C3 (☎+1-613-237-7884; www.hihostels.ca). CDN$35, under 18 free.

**Hostelling International Northern Ireland (HINI),** 22-32 Donegall Rd., Belfast BT12 5JN (☎+44 28 9032 4733; www.hini.org.uk). UK£15, under 25 UK£10.

**Youth Hostels Association—England and Wales,** Trevelyan House, Dimple Rd., Matlock, Derbyshire DE4 3YH (☎+44 1629 592 600; www.yha.org.uk). UK£16, under 26 UK£10.

**Youth Hostels Association of New Zealand Inc. (YHANZ),** Level 1, 166 Moorhouse Ave., P.O. Box 436, Christchurch (☎+64 3 379 9970, in NZ 0800 278 299; www.yha.org.nz). NZ$40, under 18 free.

**Hostelling International—USA,** 8401 Colesville Rd., Ste. 600, Silver Spring, MD 20910 (☎+1-301-495-1240; www.hiayh.org). US$28, under 18 free.

## OTHER TYPES OF ACCOMMODATIONS

### HOTELS, GUESTHOUSES, AND PENSIONS

Single hotel rooms in the Yucatán Peninsula cost about US$16-20 (170-250 pesos) per night, doubles US$20-55 (200-600 pesos) per night. You'll typically share a hall bathroom; a private bathroom will cost extra, as may hot showers. Some hotels offer "full pension" (all meals) or "half pension" (no lunch). Smaller guesthouses are often cheaper than hotels. It is often easiest to make reservations over the phone with a credit card.

## CAMPING

Travelers accustomed to clean and well-maintained campgrounds may be in for a few surprises in the Yucatán. By and large, Mexican national parks exist only in theory. The "protected lands" are often indistinguishable from the surrounding countryside or city and may be dirty, unappealing, and overrun with amorous teenagers. Privately owned **trailer parks** are relatively common on major routes—look for signs with a picture of a trailer, or the words *parque de trailer*, *campamento*, or *remolques*. These places often allow campers to pitch tents or sling up a hammock.

For those budget-minded individuals traveling along the coast, the **hammock** is the way to go. Most beach towns in Mexico are dotted with **palapas** (palm-tree huts). For a small fee, open-air restaurants double as places to hang your hat and hammock when the sun sets. At beaches and some inland towns frequented by backpackers, **cabañas** (cabins, usually simple thatch-roof huts) are common. For the truly hard-core, camping on the beach can sometimes be an option. Lax permit laws and beach accessibility—every meter of beach in Mexico is public property—offer campers many options. For more information on outdoor activities in Mexico see **The Great Outdoors**, below.

# THE GREAT OUTDOORS

The **Great Outdoor Recreation Page** (www.gorp.com) provides excellent general information for travelers planning on camping or enjoying the outdoors.

 **LEAVE NO TRACE.** *Let's Go* encourages travelers to embrace the "leave no trace" ethic, minimizing their impact on natural environments and protecting them for future generations. Trekkers and wilderness enthusiasts should set up camp on durable surfaces, use cookstoves instead of campfires, bury human waste away from water supplies, bag trash and carry it out with them, and respect wildlife. For more detailed information, contact the **Leave No Trace Center for Outdoor Ethics**, P.O. Box 997, Boulder, CO 80306, USA (☎+1-800-332-4100 or 303-442-8222; www.lnt.org).

# NATIONAL PARKS AND RESERVES

Many of Mexico's lands are classified as national parks and biosphere reserves. There are 93 protected areas (encompassing about 6% of the country) controlled by **La Sistema Nacional de Areas Naturales Protegidas** (**SINAP**; The National System of Protected Natural Areas) and protected by the **Instituto Nacional de Ecología** (**INE**; National Institute of Ecology). National parks can range from small urban parks to large expanses of land. Volcanoes and most architectural ruins are considered national parks. Conservation and sustainable development are two important goals of the reserves. For more information on conservation efforts in Mexico, including how you can help, see **Beyond Tourism, p. 52**.

In general, it is difficult to explore Mexico's lush wilderness by yourself. Aside from highly visited ruins and parks found in cities, most sights do not have organized trails. In many places, the safest and most common way to see some of Mexico's beautiful natural areas is to hire a guide.

# WILDLIFE

**MOSQUITOES WILL CONSUME YOU.** Protect yourself from **mosquito bites,** which may transmit diseases like malaria (p. 18). Thick materials and **100% DEET** are useful in forested areas.

**TICKS.** To prevent **tick bites,** exercise the same caution as you would for mosquitoes. When camping, check your site for ticks. Ticks usually bite between your toes, behind your knees or neck, on your head, in your armpits, or around your groin. Damage from ticks can be minimized by removing them as quickly as possible with a pair of tweezers. Ticks are known to transmit **Lyme disease** (p. 18). If bitten, seek medical attention immediately.

**WHY DID IT HAVE TO BE SNAKES?** The Yucatán is home to several venomous snakes, including the **pit viper,** the **fer-de-lance,** and the **rattlesnake.** If you are bitten by one, go to a hospital immediately. Do not ice or otherwise irritate the wound, as this may lead to the need for amputation. Do not try to suck out the venom on your own! Instead, leave the bite untouched and elevate the limb.

**LIZARDS.** Mexico is home to some poisonous lizards. The **Gila Monster** has dark skin with pink coloration and is 35-45cm long. The **Mexican Beaded Lizard** looks like the Gila and is also poisonous. Never try to touch or pick up one of these lizards. If bitten, seek medical help immediately.

**WILD CATTLE AND NON-DOMESTIC ANIMALS.** Wild cattle have been known to attack people. This should not be a concern in most tourist areas, but those spending time in remote places should be aware of the possibility. Note that non-domestic animals may have rabies.

# CAMPING AND HIKING EQUIPMENT

## WHAT TO BUY

Good camping equipment is both sturdy and light.

**Sleeping bags:** Temperature ratings can be misleading; err on the side of being too warm by choosing a bag for the highest altitude and the coldest night of your trip. Bags are made of **down** (durable, warm, and light, but expensive and miserable when wet) or of **synthetic** material (heavy, durable, and warm when wet).

**Tents:** The best tents are freestanding (with their own frames and suspension systems), set up quickly, and only require staking in high winds. A-frame and dome tents are the best all around. Make sure yours has a rain fly and seal its seams with waterproofer. Other useful accessories include a **battery-operated lantern,** a plastic **ground cloth,** and a nylon **tarp.**

**Backpacks: Internal-frame** packs mold well to your back, keep a lower center of gravity, and flex adequately to allow you to hike difficult trails, while **external-frame** packs are more comfortable for long hikes over even terrain, as they carry weight higher and distribute it more evenly. Make sure your pack has a strong, padded hip belt to transfer weight to your legs. There are models designed specifically for women.

**Boots:** Be sure to wear hiking boots with good **ankle support.** They should fit snugly and comfortably over 1-2 pairs of **wool socks** and a pair of thin **liner socks.** Break in boots over several weeks before you go to spare yourself blisters.

**Other necessities: Synthetic layers,** like those made of polypropylene or polyester, will keep you warm even when wet. A **space blanket** will help you to retain body heat and doubles as a **ground cloth.** Water bottles are vital; look for metal ones that are shatter- and leak-resistant. Carry **water-purification tablets** for when you can't boil water. Although most campgrounds provide campfire sites, you may want to bring a small **metal grate** or **grill**. Also bring a **first-aid kit, pocketknife, insect repellent,** and **waterproof matches** or a **lighter.**

# SPECIFIC CONCERNS

## SUSTAINABLE TRAVEL

As the number of travelers on the road rises, the detrimental effect they can have on natural environments is an increasing concern. With this in mind, *Let's Go* promotes the philosophy of **sustainable travel**. Through a sensitivity to issues of ecology and sustainability, today's travelers can be a powerful force in preserving and restoring the places they visit.

**Ecotourism,** a rising trend in sustainable travel, focuses on the conservation of natural habitats—mainly, on how to use them to build up the economy without exploitation or overdevelopment. Travelers make a difference by doing advance research and by supporting organizations and establishments that pay attention to their carbon. For Mexico-specific information on ecotourism, see **Beyond Tourism, p. 52**.

**ECOTOURISM RESOURCES.** For more information on environmentally responsible tourism, contact one of the organizations below:

**Conservation International,** 2011 Crystal Dr., Ste. 500, Arlington, VA 22202, USA (☎+1-800-429-5660 or 703-341-2400; www.conservation.org).

**Green Globe 21,** Green Globe vof, Verbenalaan 1, 2111 ZL Aerdenhout, the Netherlands (☎+31 23 544 0306; www.greenglobe.com).

**International Ecotourism Society,** 1301 Clifton St. NW, Ste. 200, Washington, DC 20009, USA (☎+1-202-506-5033; www.ecotourism.org).

**United Nations Environment Program (UNEP;** www.unep.org).

## RESPONSIBLE TRAVEL

Your tourist pesos can make a big impact on the destinations you visit. The choices you make during your trip can have powerful effects on local communities—for better or for worse. Travelers who care about the destinations and environments they explore should make themselves aware of the social and cultural implications of their choices. Simple decisions such as buying local products, paying fair prices for products or services, and attempting to speak the local language can have a strong, positive effect on the community.

**Community-based tourism** aims to channel tourist pesos into the local economy by emphasizing tours and cultural programs that are run by members of the host community. This type of tourism also benefits the tourists themselves, as it often takes them beyond the traditional tours of the region. *The Ethical Travel Guide* (UK£13), a project of **Tourism Concern** (☎+44 020 7133 3330; www.tourismconcern.org.uk), is an excellent resource for information on community-based travel with a directory of 300 establishments in 60 countries.

Mexico's inhabitants have been impacted by travel in a variety of ways. Adaptation of Mexican culture to tourist demands, loss of authenticity and commodification of Mexican traditions, and economic inequality between tourists and locals are some of the issues that have been exacerbated by tourism. When visiting Mexico, show respect for local traditions and culture.

# WOMEN TRAVELERS

Women exploring on their own inevitably face some additional safety concerns. Single women should consider staying in hostels that offer single rooms that lock from the inside. It's a good idea to stick to centrally located accommodations and to avoid solitary late-night treks or metro rides. Always carry extra cash for a phone call, bus, or taxi. **Hitchhiking** is never safe for lone women or even for two women traveling together. Look as if you know where you're going and approach older women or couples for directions if you're lost or feeling uncomfortable in your surroundings.

Generally, the less you look like a tourist, the better off you'll be. Mexican women seldom travel without the company of men; foreign women who do so often draw attention. Moreover, Mexican men are notorious for their *machismo*, a brand of Latin-American chauvinism accompanied by whistles, catcalls, and stares. Persistent men may insist on joining you and "showing you the sights." If you're fair-skinned or have light-colored hair, you might hear *"güera, güera"* (blonde, blonde). Regardless of your hair color, expect to hear the typical come-on, *"¿Adónde vas, mamacita?"* (Where are you going, babe?). The best answer to verbal harassment is often none at all; feigning deafness, sitting motionless, and staring straight ahead at nothing in particular will do more than reacting to taunts. *Machismo* is usually more annoying than dangerous, but in real emergencies, a firm, loud, and very public "Go away!" *("¡Vete!")* or a yell for help *("¡Socorro!")* might fend off unwanted attention. Be aware, however, that many police officers and uniformed officials are the biggest *machistas* of all.

Awareness of Mexican social standards and dress codes may help to minimize unwanted attention. Outside of urban areas, Mexican women seldom wear shorts, short skirts, tank tops, or halter tops. In many regions, doing so may draw harassment or stares. Shorts and tank tops are appropriate only at beach and resort areas or in towns with a large number of foreign students and tourists. More traditional areas of the country generally require conservative dress; wear a long skirt and sleeved blouses in churches or very religious towns. If you are traveling with a male friend, it may help to pose as a couple; this will make it easier to share rooms and will also chill the blood of Mexican Romeos. Wearing a **wedding band** on your left hand or a **crucifix** around your neck may further help discourage unwanted attention. In addition to talking loudly and frequently about their muscular boyfriend *(novio muy fuerte)* or easily angered husband *(esposo muy enojón)*, some savvy women even carry pictures of these "boyfriends" and "husbands," gladly displaying them to prospective suitors. Most importantly, act confidently in potentially dangerous situations.

Memorize the emergency numbers in Mexico (☎**060**). A self-defense course will both prepare you for a potential attack and raise your level of awareness of your surroundings (see **Personal Safety**, p. 15). Talk with your doctor about the health concerns that women face when traveling (p. 35).

# GLBT TRAVELERS

Discrimination by sexual orientation is illegal in Mexico. Despite its legal status, homosexuality is frowned upon at best, and intolerance is especially rampant in rural areas of the country where displays of affection may attract harassment. The best rule of thumb is to avoid public displays of affection until you know that you are in a safe and accepting environment, such as one housing gay-friendly clubs and establishments. These types of establishments are particularly prevalent in Cancún. Whenever possible, *Let's Go* lists gay- and lesbian-friendly establishments; the best way to find out about the many others that we do not list is to consult organizations, mail-order bookstores, and publishers that offer materials addressing gay and lesbian concerns. **Out and About** (www.planetout. com) is a comprehensive site that offers a weekly newsletter addressing travel concerns. The online newspaper **365gay.com** also has a travel section. Listed below are contact organizations, mail-order catalogs, and publishers that offer materials addressing some specific concerns.

**Giovanni's Room,** 345 S. 12th St., Philadelphia, PA 19107, USA (☎+1-215-923-2960; www.giovannisroom.com). An international lesbian and gay bookstore with mail-order service (carries many of the publications listed below).

**Ser Gay,** www.sergay.com.mx. A Mexico City-based site with chat forums and event listings around the country.

**ADDITIONAL GLBT RESOURCES**

*Damron Men's Travel Guide, Damron Women's Traveller, Damron Accommodations Guide,* and *Damron City Guide.* Published annually by Damron Travel Guides. For info, call ☎+1-415-255-0404 or visit www.damron.com.

*The Gay Vacation Guide: The Best Trips and How to Plan Them,* by Mark Chesnut. Kensington Books.

*Gayellow Pages USA/Canada,* by Frances Green. Also publishes regional editions. Visit Gayellow pages online at http://gayellowpages.com.

*Spartacus International Gay Guide 2009,* by Bruno Gmunder Verlag.

# TRAVELERS WITH DISABILITIES

Mexico is increasingly accessible to travelers with disabilities, noticeably in popular resort towns like Cancún. Generally, the more you are willing to spend, the less difficult it is to find wheelchair-accessible facilities. Keep in mind, however, that most public and long-distance modes of transportation (e.g., buses) and most of the non-luxury hotels cannot accommodate wheelchairs. Though more archaeological sites are becoming wheelchair-accessible, many public bathrooms, ruins, parks, historic buildings, and museums are relatively inaccessible. Those with disabilities should inform airlines and hotels when making reservations. Call ahead to restaurants, museums, and other facilities to find out if they are wheelchair-accessible.

## USEFUL ORGANIZATIONS

**The Guided Tour, Inc.,** 7900 Old York Rd., Ste. 111B, Elkins Park, PA 19027, USA (☎+1-800-783-5841; www.guidedtour.com). Organizes travel programs for persons with developmental and physical challenges in Mexico.

**Mobility International USA (MIUSA),** 132 E. Broadway, Ste. 343, Eugene, OR 97401, USA (☎+1-541-343-1284; www.miusa.org). Provides a variety of books and other publications containing information for travelers with disabilities.

**Society for Accessible Travel and Hospitality (SATH),** 347 5th Ave., Ste. 605, New York City, NY 10016, USA (☎+1-212-447-7284; www.sath.org). An advocacy group that publishes free online travel information. Annual membership US$49, students and seniors US$29.

ESSENTIALS

# MINORITY TRAVELERS

Most of Mexico's population is white, *indígena* (of indigenous descent), or a combination of the two. This means that many travelers are bound to stick out, particularly when traveling in rural or less touristed areas. In general, the whiter your skin, the better treatment you'll receive. Unfortunately, light-skinned travelers are also viewed as wealthier and therefore are more likely to be the targets of crime. Travelers of African or Asian ancestry will likely attract attention for their perceived exoticism. East Asians may find themselves called *chinos*, South Asians might be referred to as *índus* or *árabes*, while those of African descent are often called *morenos* or *negros*. None of these words are considered derogatory in Mexico; they are simply descriptive terms. In many rural areas, non-Spanish speakers may also be viewed as a threat. Note that most of Mexico is Catholic—non-Catholics are also considered a minority.

# DIETARY CONCERNS

Vegetarians are rare in Mexico, and vegans are almost unheard of. Expect incredulous stares in many places. *"Soy vegetariano,"* means "I'm vegetarian"; *"Sin carne/puerco/pollo/pescado/animal"* is "Without meat/pork/chicken/fish/animal." If you just ask for your meal "without meat," your waiter may assume that you eat chicken or fish, so be sure to specify what you cannot eat. When pressed, allergies or illness (*"Soy alérgico; voy a vomitar si como mucha carne.* "I'm allergic; I will vomit if I eat lots of meat") make better alibis.

That said, the carnivorous culture of Mexico can make it difficult for **vegetarian tourists,** as almost all meals are prepared using animal products. Some popular vegetarian dishes available in most restaurants include quesadillas (melted cheese between tortillas), *chilaquiles* (strips of fried tortillas baked in tomato sauce with cheese and fresh cream), *molletes* (french bread smothered with refried beans and cheese), and *frijoles* (beans). Be aware that nearly all flour tortillas and many types of beans are prepared with *manteca* (lard). **Vegan tourists** will have a harder time finding edible dishes and may have to subsist on the old standbys of corn tortillas and rice.

The travel section of the **The Vegetarian Resource Group's** website, at www.vrg.org/travel, has a comprehensive list of organizations and websites geared toward helping vegetarians and vegans traveling abroad. Some good resources on the web include www.vegdining.com, www.happycow.net, and www.vegetariansabroad.com.

Despite the increasing number of Jews in Mexico, keeping **kosher** can be difficult. Many large supermarkets sell kosher foods, but travelers will have less luck in restaurants and smaller towns. Those who keep kosher should contact Mexican synagogues for information on kosher restaurants. Your own synagogue or college Hillel should have access to lists of Jewish institutions across Mexico. If you are strict in your observance, you may have to prepare your own food on the road. A good resource is the *Jewish Travel Guide*, edited by Michael Zaidner (Vallentine Mitchell; US$18). Travelers looking for **halal** restaurants may find www.zabihah.com a useful resource.

**LET'S GO ONLINE.** Plan your next trip on our newly redesigned website, **www.letsgo.com.** It features the latest travel info on your favorite destinations as well as tons of interactive features: make your own itinerary, read blogs from our trusty Researchers, browse our photo library, watch exclusive videos, check out our newsletter, find travel deals, and buy new guides. We're always updating and adding new features, so check back often!

READY. SET.

LET'S GO

www.letsgo.com

THE STUDENT TRAVEL GUIDE

# LIFE AND TIMES

## HISTORY

**1300 BC:** A stable Mayan culture begins to develop, heavily influenced by the Olmecs.

**PRECLASSIC PREPARATIONS (2000 BC-AD 250).** Around 1300 BC, Mayan tribes in the Yucatán developed a sedentary culture heavily influenced by the Olmecs. The Mayan civilization built cities with massive public works, sophisticated agriculture, and a hieroglyphic writing system and calendar. In the Yucatán, however, trade was still limited and the spread of Olmec influence slow. At the edge of the Yucatán area, in the Mirador Basin of what is now Petén, Guatemala, rich Mayan societies began to form civilizations, but the emergence of a written language would have to wait for the coming glory days.

**AD 250:** The Maya dominate everything from astronomy to trade.

**MAYAN MAJESTY (AD 250-900).** Mayan civilization reached its peak by the second century AD, when Mayan peoples established centers such as Bonampak, Tikal, Palenque, Copán, and Chunchucmil. Mayan astronomers also predicted the movements of planets and stars as well as the dates of solar eclipses with startling accuracy, all based on their sophisticated calendar. These advances coexisted with the common Mesoamerican practice of human sacrifice, often at the sacred *cenotes* of the rainforest. Piety could also be less violently displayed through the elaborate Mayan ball game. During the Yucatán's glory days, stone scabé roads crisscrossed the peninsula, providing an artery for trade from the Zapotec to Teotihuacan, the majestic city of the Pyramids of Sun and Moon.

**1450:** A general revolt erupts, resulting in the defeat of Mayapán and the fragmentation of the Yucatán Peninsula.

**POSTCLASSIC PAINS (900-1511).** The cities of the southern Yucatán declined around the 9th century, leaving the Postclassical period dominated by the northern cities of Chichén Itzá, Uxmal, and Mayapán. Scholars still debate about the causes of this swift decline; some propose disease, crop failures, and overhunting, while others postulate that invasions or peasant revolts were the cause. Nevertheless, the northern cities persisted for centuries despite the mysterious collapse of the south, though fewer and fewer wielded the old glory until only one remained. Mayapán reigned over the entire Mayan civilization for two hundred years. A general revolt in 1450 left the peninsula divided, just in time for the Spanish Conquest.

**1512:** Spaniards get all up in the Yucatán's grill. In other words, they invade and conquer.

**YUCATÁN YOKED (1512-1810).** The Spanish arrival in the Yucatán was unusual to say the least, with a ship bound for Santo Domingo landing near Belize and the crew going native: either as slaves or warriors. Two men, who became so integrated in native culture that they were dubbed nobles of Mayan chiefdoms, **Gonzalo Guerrero** and **Gerónimo de Aguilar**, took very different paths when **Hernan Cortés** and later Spanish invad-

**1519:** Hernán Cortés arrives on the peninsula.

ers arrived. The first stuck by his new loyalties and became a master tactician of the Maya against his Spaniard kin, while the second became Cortés's translator. His choice portended the future of the Yucatán, which lay in Spanish subjugation.

One surprising advantage of the Yucatán locals, as opposed to the Aztec or the Incas, was their lack of a capital or central leadership, which prevented anyone from surrendering the entire civilization to the Spaniards. However, various expeditions largely finished the conquest of the Yucatán within twenty years. The Viceroyalty of New Spain appointed a governor for the region, roughly corresponding in size to modern Mexico. Because of the peninsula's unruly conduct, however, this governor was promoted to a more autonomous Captaincy-General in 1617. The later Bourbon dynasty of Spain tried to modernize the area by granting it even more autonomy as an Intendency in 1786.

As in the rest of the Americas, the population suffered from the introduction of foreign diseases such as smallpox and typhoid, as well as from *encomiendas*. Tensions between creoles and Maya were so high that Mérida, the principal city of the Yucatán, was built with walls to protect it from native rebellions.

## BRAVE NEW YUCATÁN (1811-46).

In 1835, the central government, by now the military dictatorship of President **Santa Anna**, assumed unprecedented authority over the actions of states, and the local elite's discontent came to a boil in an 1838 insurrection. The local Congress approved a declaration of independence and pronounced a Republic of Yucatán. Various negotiations with Santa Anna proved fruitless, and by 1841, the cities, ships, and soldiers of the peninsula were under the striped banner of the Republic. A Mexican invasion failed but prompted reconciliation in 1843, which spoiled when Mexico reneged on its promises of autonomy. The Yucatán thus declared neutrality in the war between America and Mexico in 1846.

## DON'T CROSS THE MAYA (1847-1901).

The local government suddenly faced bigger problems than Mexican meddling, however— a massive rebellion broke out within the native population, beginning with the execution of three Mayan conspirators at Valladolid. The Caste War, named for its starkly racial nature, spread like wildfire, nearly clearing the peninsula of Europeans. In 1848 the Maya nearly breached the walls of Mérida, the center of creole resistance, and were only stopped by the appearance of the flying ant, signifying the start of planting season and causing the dissolution of the peasant army.

The Republic didn't bank on such luck again, so it sent identical missives to Mexico, Spain, the United States, and Britain, offering its submission to whoever would quash the rebellion. Mexico, cash-rich after its indemnities from the Mexican-American War, elected to bring Yucatán into the fold, and joint Mexican-Yucateco forces made some headway against the Maya. But the Maya for their part still had a secret weapon—the Talking Cross. A series of apparitions

**1617:** A Captaincy General is instituted to bring more autonomy to the region.

**1786:** The Bourbons go easy on the Yucatán and establish an Intendency, which grants greater administrative powers to local elites.

**1838:** Local elite need to blow off some steam. They head an insurrection against President Santa Anna and his military dictatorship.

**1841:** The Republic of Yucatán is born.

**1846:** The Yucatán declares a neutral position in the war between the United States and Mexico.

**1847:** The Caste War, a racial brawl among the natives, erupts and lasts until 1851.

**1901:** Chan Santa Cruz surrenders to the Mexican forces

**1902:** Though lacking its own military, the state of Quintana Roo is established. Only the Maya are allowed to live in the new state.

LIFE AND TIMES

**1930s:** Mexican President Lázaro Cárdenas and the Institutional Revolutionary Party thank the people, giving land and resources to Mayan peasants.

**1950s:** The Yucatán Railroad is completed. Chugga-chugga, choo-choo.

**1970:** The extremely profitable tourist city of Cancún is founded. Please, keep your shirts on.

**1975:** Queen Elizabeth II and other foreign dignitaries are caught in a typical Mexican downpour in Uxmal during—what else?—a prayer to Chaac, the Mayan god of rain.

**1976:** The Controversial Francisco Luna Kan—a Mayan—is elected governor of the state of Yucatán. Yes we Kan.

**1980s:** Ominously called the "lost decade," this was an era of widespread economic depression in Latin America.

**2007:** Oscar Rivera of the Leones de Yucatán pitches a perfect game. Baller.

to Mayan priests generated a new syncretistic Church of the Talking Cross in the city-state of Chan Santa Cruz. Known as the *Cruzobs*, the re-energized Maya of Chan Santa Cruz led the alliance against Mexico, which also included traditional Catholic rebels such as the Ixcanha Maya. Mexican pressure slowed the resistance, and in 1883 Chan Santa Cruz briefly accepted submission. A return to rebellion in 1884 was short-lived; Mexican dictator **Porfirio Diaz** was friendly to British business, and in return the British closed the Belizean border to trade with the Maya, cutting them off from arms and ammunition. The *Cruzobs* held out until 1901, when Chan Santa Cruz was occupied.

**BECOMING MEXICAN (1902-70).** The Yucatán remained unstable as it entered the 20th century; the new state of **Quintana Roo** was established in 1902, but it remained off-limits for non-Maya without military protection for decades. In central and western areas of the peninsula, however, the cultivation of *sisal* and *henequen*, plants used in ropes and fibers, were bringing riches to the area, with old Mérida suddenly transforming into an electrified city of paved roads, streetcars, and more millionaires than any other city in Mexico. These exports dropped off after WWI and the development of synthetic fibers, but Yucatán was no longer the uneasy, violent frontier of centuries past. Under the powerful PRI government, Mexican policies began to reshape the peninsula, especially **President Lázaro Cárdenas's** seizure and redistribution of land and resources to the Mayan peasantry in the 1930s. Two decades later, a railroad was finally completed connecting the Yucatán to the rest of Mexico.

**TIME IN THE SUN (1971-2009).** As the rest of Mexico reeled from the economic downturn of the 1970s, something exciting was happening in the Yucatán—local officials and the Bank of Mexico began to entice foreign tourism by financing resort construction and laying the foundations for the future super-city of Cancún in 1970. Over the next decades, international tourism grew to a trickle and then a torrent, reshaping the nature of the peninsula, which had controversially elected a Maya governor, **Francisco Luna Kan,** in 1976. Yucatán proved an unnaturally bright spot amid the general flight of foreign capital from Mexico during the *década perdida* (lost decade) of the 1980s. Tourism continued to grow at a less spectacular rate in the next decades, and the Yucatán today is an international destination.

# TODAY

# GOVERNMENT

The Mexican portion of the Yucatán Peninsula is split between three states: Campeche, Yucatán, and Quintana

Roo. Each of these states has its own full government. Mexico's official name is the United Mexican States, and, particularly since the democratization of the 1990s, state governments exert considerable authority.

The largest by population, with approximately 1.8 million residents, is the state of Yucatán. Merída, the venerable colonial capital and urban center of the peninsula since the Spanish arrival, is its main city. The governor of Yucatán is Ivonne Ortega Pacheco, the fifth woman governor of a Mexican state, and a member of the Institutional Revolutionary Party (PRI), the old establishment party of Mexico.

Quintana Roo lies to the southeast of the state of Yucatán and has a smaller population of 1.1 million. The center of economic activity is the notorious resort city of Cancún, while the capital lies in the sleepier but growing city of Chetumal to the south. Its PRI government is headed by Félix González Canto, who replaced the infamously corrupt Mario Villanueva Madrid after he fled the country two weeks before the end of his term.

Most sparsely settled is the state of Campeche—Mayan for the "Place of the Boa Serpent"—in the western part of the peninsula. Populated by a mere half million residents, the ownership of considerable portions of the territory of Campeche is still disputed with neighboring Quintana Roo.

## ECONOMY

The most salient feature of the Yucatán's economy is its tourism industry, which began to take off in the 1970s after new highways and airports expedited travel. This influx of cash from around the globe accounts for nearly the entirety of state income in Quintana Roo, home to the boomtown of Cancún. Apart from the attractions of Spring Break, Mayan ruins and the rainforest of the interior also draw crowds of tourists, a phenomenon that has prompted the large-scale construction of resorts and infrastructure penetrating deep into the interior of the territory.

Manufacturing and agriculture are still responsible for the bulk of the economy, however, especially in less-visited areas like Campeche. In those western areas, most residents make their living in the petroleum and commercial fishing industries, while in the east, logging is the predominant vocation. In addition, large numbers of rural farmers still rely on traditional agriculture to put tortillas on the table.

## PEOPLE

## DEMOGRAPHICS

The land now occupied by Mexico's Yucatán Peninsula was originally part of the vast Mayan Empire and remained exclusively populated by Mayan populations until the Spanish conquest. Today, the peninsula's three states—Yucatán, Campeche, and Quintana Roo—are home to large native populations: though definitions of "native" vary, statistics counting only native language speakers show that indigenous people constitute 37% of the population of Yucatán, 23% of the population of Quintana Roo, and 15% of the population of Campeche; by contrast, indigenous peoples make up 6.2% of the population of Mexico. The remaining inhabitants of the Yucatan are indigenous non-speakers, *mestizos*, and to a much lesser extent, white Europeans.

# LANGUAGE

Although Spanish is the official language of Mexico, more than 30 indigenous Mayan languages are spoken on the Yucatán penninsula, including Maya (or Yucatec), Itza', and Mopan. Locally, indigenous languages have had considerable influence on the colloquial Spanish, incorporating Mayan sounds into traditional Spanish pronunciations and even importing some Mayan words into the lexicon. English is not spoken very widely on the peninsula. Non-Spanish speakers need not worry—there are plenty of English speakers in areas frequented by Western travelers.

# RELIGION

Roman Catholics constitute the vast majority of Mexicans both on and off the Yucatán Peninsula. Many indigenous people have adopted the Catholic faith while maintaining some of the beliefs and practices of the pre-Colombian Mayan religion. Often they merge the Catholic Holy Trinity and Saints with traditional Mayan gods, which number over 100. Mayas still seek the help of shamans for spiritual healing and guidance, find comfort in ancient rituals, and believe in the power of sacrifice.

# LAND

## GEOGRAPHY AND GEOLOGY

The Yucatán Peninsula is a landmass of approximately 197,600 sq. km dividing the northern and western shores of the Gulf of Mexico from the Caribbean Sea. The peninsula lies mostly within the three Mexican states of Quintana Roo, Yucatán, and Campeche, but parts of the peninsula's southern highlands are governed by Guatemala and Belize. From the mountainous south to the lowland north, the land is thickly forested with thin, dry trees. The northern and western coasts are mostly barren. The peninsula's few ports, beaches, and bays are on the eastern side facing the Caribbean. Several small islands lie off the eastern shore; the largest are Cozumel and the Isla Mujeres.

The land is an exposed portion of the Yucatán Platform, a large limestone shelf riddled with the Yucatán's characteristic *cenotes*, or sinkholes, and a plethora of caves. The shelf is characterized by karst topography, a term that refers to the multiple layers of porous rock that prevent rivers from forming. Most unusual, however, is the peninsula's greatest geologic mystery, the Chicxulub crater. At 180km in diameter, it is one of the largest craters on the planet and is considered by many scientists to be the location of an impact that may have caused the extinction of the dinosaurs.

## CLIMATE AND WEATHER

The climate is hot and humid throughout the Yucatán, but with important regional variations: the north is hotter and drier, with limited rainfall of about 460mm annually, while in the south, moisture reaches 2,000mm annually. In both regions, the dry season lasts from December to May, with temperatures peaking in May and June. Hurricane season, running from June to November, is the most anxiety-inspiring time of year. The few that touch land are usually sensational: Hurricane Dean, in 2007, wreaked billions of dollars of damage across the Yucatán.

# FLORA AND FAUNA

The Yucatán peninsula is home to a broad spectrum of tropical animal life, with about 500 species of birds—over half of all the bird species of Mexico. The only band of American flamingo in Mexico, of which there are 40,000, is perhaps the most boisterous of all. Pelicans, ibis, and heron migrate to the Yucatán in the summer. These migratory birds, as well as those that stay year-round, transform the peninsula into a raucous display of color. Mammals include the elegant jaguar, coati, agouti, and pig-like tapir. Various species of monkeys can be found in the Yucatán, including the black howler monkey and the Central American spider monkey. Innumerable fish, small sharks, sea turtles, dolphins, and whales swim in the Yucatán's coastal waters. In the inland waters, travelers often happen upon cave-dwellers such as the blind eel and blind white dama.

Green dominates the Yucatán. Much of the north is overgrown with low scrub forest, while thickets of mahogany, vanilla, sapodilla, and logwood grow in the south. The region running along the border between Quintana Roo, Campeche, western Belize, and northern Guatemala contains one of the largest uninterrupted tracts of rainforest in all of Central America. The Yucatán Peninsula is also known for its flowering plants, including almost 300 varieties of orchids, some of which are very rare.

# CULTURE

# VISUAL ARTS AND ARCHITECTURE

The art and architecture of the Yucatán Peninsula can be divided into three periods: **Pre-Hispanic** (prior to AD 1521), **Colonial** (1522-1810), and **Contemporary** (1810-present). The Olmecs, Toltecs, and Mayans have contributed significantly to the region's indigenous artistic tradition, while the presence of a strong Hispanic aesthetic influence recalls the colonial era.

## THE PRE-HISPANIC ERA

Pre-Hispanic artistic traditions can be further divided into three categories: **Preclassic** or **Formative** (BC 2000-AD 250), **Classic** (AD 250-AD 900), and **Postclassic** (900-1521). Heavily influenced by religion and politics, Pre-Hispanic paintings, sculpture, and architecture offer a glimpse into the culture of the time.

### STEP BY STEP

Perhaps the most splendid Mayan architectural site in the region—**Chichén Itzá** (p. 111)—is located in the north-central part of Yucatán Peninsula. A complex network of roads connects the various buildings on the site, including several temples, a steam bath, and the Temple of Kukulcan, also known as **"El Castillo"** (p. 115). This 75 ft. pyramid was recently declared one of the Seven Wonders of the World. During the spring and fall equinoxes, the corner of this structure casts the Kukulcan's serpentine shadow upon the western side of the north staircase. Another popular Mayan site is **Tulum** (p. 161), on the northeastern

LIFE AND TIMES

coast of Quintana Roo. While much of Tulum appears to be a small-scale version of Chichén Itzá, the mural and stucco figurines paying tribute to the Mayan diving god are truly unique. The Mayan city of **Uxmal** (p. 101), a UNESCO World Heritage site, exhibits Puuc architecture, a style characterized by buildings with concrete cores, developed in the hilly areas of the southern Yucatán.

### LEGENDS OF THE HIDDEN TEMPLE

This Olmec head represents the definitive art form of the Olmec people who populated southern Central America in the Preclassic era. These enormous, helmet-clad sculptures are believed to depict rulers of the period; the majority of them have been uncovered in **San Lorenzo** (p. 210) and **La Venta** (p. 191).

## THE COLONIAL ERA

When the Spanish infiltrated the New World, a juggernaut conversion followed. Newly introduced Christianity inevitably affected the artistic and architectural practices of the region. As natives were baptized in increasingly large numbers, for example, the *capilla abierta* (open-air chapel) was developed as a new facility for worship.

### CHECKMATE

**Campeche City** (p. 61), the first Yucatán city settled by the Spanish, was designed in the pattern of a chessboard in the Renaissance tradition. The city center, called the Plaza de la Independencia (Square of Independence), still boasts multiple fortresses and much of its 17th-century defensive wall, and was recently declared a UNESCO World Heritage Site. Within the city center is the **Templo de Nuestra Señora De La Purísima Concepción** (p. 68), built in 1540, the oldest cathedral on the Yucatán Peninsula.

### IT'S ALL MAYAN

Vestiges of the extraordinary Mayan culture are scattered all over the Yucatán Peninsula. For instance, **El Meco,** in northern Cancún, was used by the Mayans as a point of departure to Isla Mujeres, and still contains many Postclassic ruins, including temples and pyramids. The capital of the state of Yucatán, **Mérida** (p. 76), contains many postcolonial structures that provide a gateway into the Mayan civilization. **La Iglesia de Jesús** (Church of Jesus), erected in 1618, was built using the stones of Mayan temples that had been destroyed by the Spanish. In fact, Mayan carvings are still visible on some of the stones. Also built out of the stones of Mayan temples, Mérida's cathedral, **La Catedral de San Ildefonso** (p. 85), is the largest building of its kind on the Yucatán Peninsula. Another colonial town bursting with a distinct artistic style is **Valladolid** (p. 118). The Church of San Bernardino and Convent of Sisal, built in 1552, compose what is reputedly the Yucatán's oldest Christian structure.

### CALL ME IZAMAL

The Franciscan convent of **San Antonio de Padua** (p. 110) in the city of **Izamal** (p. 108) was founded in the mid-16th century. Its enormous atrium is surrounded by an impressive arcade, said to be second in dimensions only to Saint Peter's Basilica in Vatican City. If that's not enough to draw you in, the city is painted almost completely in yellow, as it was in colonial times.

## THE CONTEMPORARY ERA

To this day, the flavor of the Mayan people is embodied in the artistic practices of the Yucatán Peninsula. The unique quality of art in the region by no means

LIFE AND TIMES

died out in the postcolonial era. In fact, some of the Yucatán's most definitive artists emerged in the 20th century. In the Governor's Palace in Mérida, you can see the colorful murals painted by Fernando Castro Pacheco in the 1970s, which have such names as *Social Evolution of Man in the Yucatán* and *Mexico's Eternal Struggle.* Rafael Gonzalez y Gonzalez is usually regarded as the originator of the distinctly Mayan Tz'utujil style of painting, which illustrates Mayan life, tradition, and persecution in robust colors. Several of his family members, including Pedro Rafael Gonzalez Chavajay and Mario Gonzalez Chavajay, have followed in his artistic footsteps.

# CRAFTS

Many people who visit the Yucatán Peninsula like to take a piece of the indigenous cultures home with them. Popular merchandise includes woods carvings, Mayan masks, hammocks, and gold. Mérida's central *mercado* is the heart of the Yucatán shopping scene, although most of the major cities in the region have craft shops and outdoor vendors. Playa del Carmen (p. 146) in Quintana Roo, for one, is chock-full of promising shops.

### SNAZZY

One traditional craft that lives on in the Yucatán is embroidery, which adorns the characteristic clothing of the region. Mayan women wear cotton dresses called *huipiles*, while men usually don pleated shirts called *guayaberas*. If you'd like to cover your head but still let it breathe, you should purchase a Panama hat, made in Campeche (p. 61) out of the fibers of palm trees. Alternatively, if you prefer bling to garb, gold and silver filigree jewelry is available in the region for relatively low prices.

### SNOOZY

Catch some ZZZs like the Mayans and pick up a hand-woven hammock in **Tixkokob,** a city to the east of Mérida. Although the industry is now booming, hammocks weren't always a Mayan tradition. It is believed that they only began popping up on the peninsula in the years shortly before the invasion of the Spanish. Today, hammocks serve as the "beds" of young and old across the Yucatán Peninsula.

# MUSIC

### CAN YOU DO THE FANDANGO?

If you answered "yes," then you can probably do the traditional *danza jarana* of the Yucatán. This dance, which means "merry chatter" in the Mayan language, is performed in pairs, and is accompanied by a small ensemble comprising a clarinet, trumpet, trombone, and saxophone. Much of the music of the Yucatán is an amalgamation of Spanish, Caribbean, and native influences. Without a doubt, the most definitive element of the peninsula's musical legacy is the *trova yucateca*. In the early 20th century, before the heyday of the radio, troubadours traveled throughout the region sharing poetic songs with sensual rhythms (like that of the Caribbean bolero). It is this music of the troubadours that came to be known as the *trova*. If Mexican mariachi flare is more your thing, you are sure to find, in cities like Cancún, small ensembles in silver-studded clothes and wide-brimmed hats wielding trumpets and string instruments.

# MAYAN CULTURE

## WRITING AND 'RITHMETIC

By 100 BC—perhaps even earlier—the Mayans had begun using a highly complex writing system consisting of over a thousand "block glyphs." They usually carved their writing into stone monuments, but sometimes used paper made of tree bark. Fortunately, some Mayan inscriptions still exist on buildings and stelae. The process of deciphering the enigmatic language has been long and difficult, but major strides were made in the last century, and now most of the language is understood by scholars. As if their writing system were not impressive enough, the Mayans also developed a form of mathematics based on units of 20. They established the idea of zero, which was represented by a half-shell symbol. Beyond that, their "number" system consisted only of dots and dashes—and yet they performed calculations complex enough to develop a calendar and a conception of the solar system. And they say we need calculus? Pshaw.

## STAR SEARCH

In the Mayan civilization, priests were responsible for recording astronomical phenomena. One of the most important heavenly events they scrutinized was the zenial passage—that is, the moment when the sun passed directly overhead, a solar position represented by the Mayan Diving God. As a result of their observations, the Mayans were able to develop a calendar that, astonishingly, had only one incorrect day every 6000 years.

# CUSTOMS AND ETIQUETTE

### MACHO MACHO MAN

Mexican men take great pride in their machismo and tend to flaunt this virility by catcalling ladies on the street. While this is meant as a compliment, chances are it will make you feel uncomfortable. While most displays of machismo are harmless, be aware of your surroundings.

### ALLOW ME TO INTRODUCE... MYSELF

Ladies: shaking your booty might be a given in Cancún, but shaking hands isn't. When meeting other women, Mexican ladies pat each other on the right forearm or shoulder instead of shaking hands. Also, don't refer to a Mexican by his first name until you're explicitly invited to do so. What's in a name? Apparently, a lot.

### FLOWER POWER

If invited over to a Yucatec home, it is customary to give a gift of flowers (or candy). However, not just any petaled posy will do. Marigolds symbolize death (who knew that a cheery yellow plant could be so morbid?), and red flowers have negative associations (blood, devil, red speeding tickets...). White flowers are your best bet.

### MIND YOUR MANNERS

Table manners in the Yucatán are almost as important as margaritas in Cancún. Rule one: keep your hands in full sight when eating. Who knows what you could be doing with them under the table? Don't begin eating until the host or hostess does. Everyone in the Yucatán chews with their

LIFE AND TIMES

mouth closed. Women don't even think about giving a toast: only men in the Yucatán do the honors at the table.

## TIME FLIES WHEN YOU'RE ARRIVING LATE

The early bird may catch the worm, but the early Yucatán tourist might just be slapped on the wrist. It's considered inappropriate to arrive earlier than a half an hour late to any given event. Check with other attendees to see if you should arrive even later than that.

# FOOD AND DRINK

## THE STAPLES

Although regional cuisine varies widely, **tortillas** are popular throughout the country. This millennia-old classic is a flat, round, thin pancake made from either *harina* (wheat flour) or *maíz* (corn flour). In the North, flour tortillas are the norm, while corn rules the South. **Arroz** (rice) and **frijoles** (beans) round out the triumvirate of Mexican staples. *Arroz*, either of the yellow Spanish or white Mexican variety, is prepared with oil, tomato sauce, onions, and garlic. *Frijoles* range from a soupy "baked" variety to a thick "refried" paste. Expect to see this trio accompanying most restaurant meals.

Mexican culinary experts enjoy spicing up a meal with **chiles,** or peppers. Most meals come with red and green hot sauce, and sometimes *chiles curtidos*—jalapeño peppers fermented in vinegar with sliced carrots and onions. Be careful when attempting to bite into any sort of pepper: keep in mind your own tolerance toward spicy food, and don't be fooled by size. A small chile can pack a dangerous punch: measuring less than 6cm, Mexico's native **habanero** pepper is the world's hottest.

**Salsas** and **moles** (sauces) add zest and flavor to most Mexican dishes. The classic salsa Mexicana blends *jitomate* (red tomato), *cilantro* (coriander), and *tomatillo* (green tomato) with copious amounts of onion, garlic, and *chiles*. **Mole poblano** is a thick, simmered-down sauce made with three to four types of chiles, garlic, tomato, cocoa, and a variety of nuts and spices.

## DESAYUNO (BREAKFAST)

Breakfast can range from a simple snack to a grand feast rivaling the midday meal. **Huevos** (eggs), prepared in one of countless ways, are the mainstay of most Mexican breakfasts, often served with a side of **café con leche** (coffee with milk) and **pan dulce** (sweetened bread). *Huevos revueltos* (scrambled eggs) are usually prepared with *jamón* (ham), *tocino* (bacon), *machaca* (dried, shredded beef), or *nopales* (cactus). *Huevos rancheros* (fried eggs served on corn tortillas and covered with chunky tomato salsa), *huevos albañil* (scrambled eggs cooked in a spicy sauce), *huevos motuleños* (eggs served on a fried corn tortilla, topped with green sauce and sour cream), *huevos ahogados* (eggs cooked in simmering red sauce), and *huevos borrachos* (fried eggs cooked in beer and served with beans) are other common preparations. In more expensive restaurants, omelettes are offered with any of the common meats or with *camarones* (shrimp) or *langosta* (lobster).

## COMIDA (MIDDAY MEAL)

Mexicans eat their main meal of the day—**la comida**—between 2 and 4pm. Both parents and children come home for an hour or two to eat, relax, and perhaps indulge in a *siesta*. Restaurants often offer **comida corrida** (sometimes called *la comida* or *el menú*), a fixed-price meal including **sopa** (soup), ensalada (salad), **té** (tea) or **agua fresca** (cold, fresh fruit juice), a **plato fuerte** (main dish), and a **postre** (dessert).

One of the most popular *caldos* (warm soups) is *sopa de tortilla* (or *sopa azteca*), a chicken broth-based soup with strips of fried tortilla, chunks of avocado, and chipotle peppers. Other favorites are caldo *tlalpeño*, a smoky blend of chicken broth and vegetables, and sopa de mariscos, featuring fish and shellfish. Mexico's strong national pride is evident in *pozole*, a chunky soup with red, white, or green broth. Served with tostadas (fried tortillas) and lime wedges, pozole is made with large hominy kernels, radishes, lettuce, and meat (usually pork).

The main dish of any *comida* will usually feature some sort of **carne** (meat) platter —usually beef in the country's interior or fish along the coasts—with sides of *frijoles*, tortillas, and *arroz*. Choose from *carne barbacoa* (barbequed), *parrillada* (grilled), or *milanesa* (breaded and fried).

## CENA (SUPPER)

Mexicans tend to snack lightly around 9 or 10pm. Dominating nearly every Mexican menu, **antojitos** (little cravings) are equivalent to a large snack or a small meal. Tacos consist of grilled pieces of meat folded in a warm corn tortilla and topped with a row of condiments. **Burritos,** which are especially popular in northern Mexico, are thin flour tortillas usually filled with beans, meat, and cooked vegetables. **Enchiladas** are rolled corn tortillas, filled with cheese and usually meat, baked in a red or green sauce. **Quesadillas** are flat tortillas with cheese melted between them; *quesadillas sincronizadas* (sometimes called gringas) are filled with ham or pork. **Tostadas** are crispy, fried tortillas usually topped with meat and vegetables. **Chimichangas** are burritos that have been deep-fried for a rich, crunchy shell. **Flautas** are similar to chimichangas but are rolled thin (like a cigar) before being deep-fried, and resemble small flutes, for which they are named. Adventurous eaters can look out for the fried **jumiles** (stinkbugs) or **chapulines** (grasshoppers) sold at roadside snack stands.

## DULCES (SWEETS)

Mexicans have an incurable sweet tooth. Beyond the ubiquitous chocolates (often flavored with chili powder) and pastries, traditional desserts include **flan,** a vanilla custard cake with a toasted sugar shell, **nieve** (ice cream), and **arroz con leche** (rice pudding). Many of the more traditional Mexican candies rely on fruits and produce, such as coconut, bananas, and sweet potatoes for sweetness, rather than sugar. Puebla (located north of Oaxaca), the country's candy capital, is full of shops selling **dulce de leche** (a milk-based sweet) and **camotes** (candied sweet potatoes). Morelia and Michoacán specialize in ates, sticky sweet blocks of ground and candied fruit concentrate. San Cristóbal de las Casas (p. 201) and parts of Chiapas are renowned for their **cajetas** (fruit pastes) and coconut candies and cookies, while the Yucatán boasts tasty pumpkin marzipan.

## BEBIDAS (DRINKS)

Along with the table staples of tortillas, beans, and rice, **cerveza** (beer) ranks high in Mexican specialties. It is impossible to drive through any Mexican town without coming across numerous Tecate and Corona billboards, painted buildings, or roadside beer stands proudly advertising their products. Popular beers in Mexico (listed roughly in order of quality) are **Bohemia** (a world-class lager), **Negra Modelo** (a fine dark beer), **Dos Equis** (a light, smooth lager), **Pacífico, Modelo, Carta Blanca, Superior, Corona Extra,** and **Sol** (watery and light). Mexicans share their love for bargain beer with the world, as demonstrated by Corona Extra's status

LIFE AND TIMES

as a leading export and international chart topper in Australia, Canada, France, Italy, New Zealand, Spain, and many other European markets.

**Tequila** is the king of Mexican liquor. A more refined version of **mezcal,** tequila is distilled from the maguey cactus, a large, sprawling plant often seen along Mexican highways. **Herradura, Tres Generaciones, Hornitos,** and **Cuervo 1800** are among the more famous, expensive, and quality brands of tequila. *Mezcal,* coarser than tequila, is sometimes served with the worm native to the plant— upon downing the shot, you are expected to ingest the worm. **Pulque,** the fermented juice of the maguey, was the sacred drink of the Aztec nobility. **Ron** (rum), while originally manufactured in the Caribbean, is incredibly popular in Mexico and is manufactured in parts of the Valley of Mexico. Coffee-flavored **Kahlúa** is Mexico's most exported liqueur, but well-made **piña coladas** (pineapple juice, cream of coconut, and light rum), **cocos locos** (coconut milk and tequila served in a coconut), and the ever-popular **margarita** (tequila blended with ice and fruity mix) are just as tasty. A **michelada**—lemon juice, tabasco sauce and light beer—is a popular way to perk up after overindulging.

Non-alcoholic favorites include **licuados** (fresh fruit smoothies or milk shakes) and **horchata** (a milky, rice-based beverage loaded with cinnamon and sugar). **Atole** is a thick drink made from cornmeal, water, cane sugar and vanilla; the cocoa-based version is known as **champurrado.**

# SPORTS AND RECREATION

## PROFESSIONAL SPORTS

### LIONS AND SLIDERS AND CHAMPS, OH MY!

The 2006 Mexican League Champions, Los Leones de Yucatán, have become a sports phenomenon in the region. The Yucatán Lions are a AAA-level baseball team, and boast arguably the most valuable pitcher in the Mexican League, Oscar Rivera. Visit the home field of the team, Kukulcán Stadium in Mérida.

### HAVE A BALL

Intact ball courts in cities like Chichén Itzá are evidence of ancient Mayan ballgames, which were likely a combination of soccer and basketball—two activities still going strong in the region. The state of Yucatán has its own team in the Liga Nacional de Baloncesto Profesional de México (National Professional Basketball League of Mexico). Not surprisingly, the team is called the Mayas de Yucatán. The Mérida Football Club, or simply Mérida F.C., was founded in 2003 by Arturo and Mauricio Millet Reyes, though the duo has since sold the team. The club, which has enjoyed recent success, currently plays in Primera División A, and their home stadium is Estadio Carlos Iturralde (Carlos Iturralde Stadium) in Mérida.

## FOR THE LAND-DWELLING TOURIST

### CYCLING

There are many ways for the lusty traveler to get in on the athletic action of the Yucatán Peninsula. Cycling is one popular way to explore the ruins from days of yore. Of course, one should exercise extreme caution when cycling in busy

LIFE AND TIMES

city centers and along highways. Also, be sure to research your route before you head out to avoid ending up in a steep, dangerous, un-bikeable area. One safe cycling option is to ride along La Bici Ruta in Mérida on Sunday mornings. From 8am-12:30pm, many roads in the city are closed off from cars, specifically for the benefit of cyclists. You'll even fit in with the locals, as many residents of the Yucatán use bicycles and motorbikes for regular transportation.

# FOR THE AQUATIC TOURIST

Along the Caribbean coast of Quintana Roo, the Riviera Maya—formerly called the Cancún-Tulum Corridor—is the Yucatán's hotspot for water sports. Off the coast of the Riviera Maya, The Great Mayan Reef, also called the Mesoamerican Barrier Reef System, stretches from Cancún to Belize and is second in size only to Australia's Great Barrier Reef. Among the countless marine options for the adventurous tourist in the Yucatán are scuba diving, parasailing, kayaking, and fishing. You can often find equipment for water activities at local tour companies. One of the most popular activities in the region is snorkeling off the coast of **Playa del Carmen** (p. 146).

# FOR THE GREEN AND AMPHIBIOUS TOURIST

So you want to escape the debauched bustle of cities like Cancún and venture deep into the jungles of the Yucatán. Luckily, for nature-lovers looking for something both educational and outdoorsy, there are many eco-friendly tourist organizations that offer land and water activities in the Yucatán. Such companies as **EcoEcolors** (www.ecotravelmexico.com/index.php) and **Ecotourismo Yucatán** (www.ecoyuc.com/tours.html) lead excursions to many of the region's environmental treasures, from coral reefs to nature reserves. You may even discover a rare type of bird in your travels, as the Yucatán is a veritable mecca for birdwatchers, with some of the most unique species in the world. For more information on ecotourism in the Yucatán Peninsula, see the **Volunteering** section of **Beyond Tourism** (p. 52).

# HOLIDAYS AND FESTIVALS

Mexico loves to celebrate its rich history, and nearly every month boasts a national holiday. In addition to these official *fiestas*, cities and towns across the country host smaller-scale but lively events to honor patron saints or local traditions. Further information about these frequent celebrations can be found in individual city listings. Sundays are always special; "daily" schedules frequently refer only to Monday through Saturday.

Most Mexican businesses close to observe national holidays, and hotels and sights flood with vacationing families. Advance reservations are absolutely necessary when planning travel during *Semana Santa* and the Christmas holidays. Dates listed below are for 2010 and 2011.

| DATE | NAME | DESCRIPTION |
|---|---|---|
| Jan. 1 | Año Nuevo | New Year's Day. |
| Dec. 31-Jan. 10 | Feria de Los Tres Reyes Tiziman, Yucatán | Three Kings Fair. |
| Jan. 6 | Día de los Reyes | Epiphany, the feast celebrating the journey of the Three Wise Men. |
| Jan. 17 | Día de San Antonio de Abad | Feast of the Blessing of the Animals. |

| Feb. 2 | Día de la Candelaria | Candlemas, commemorating Mary's purification after the birth of Jesus. |
|---|---|---|
| Feb. 5 | Día de la Constitución | Constitution Day. |
| Feb. 19 | Día del Ejército | Army Day. |
| Feb. 24 | Día de la Bandera | Flag Day. |
| Feb. 11-16, 2010; Mar. 3-9, 2011 | Carnival | A week-long festival of indulgences leading up to Ash Wednesday and the somber Lenten period. |
| Mar. 21 | Día del Nacimiento de Benito Juárez | Birthday of former President Benito Juárez. |
| Mar. 26-Apr. 4, 2010; Apr. 15-Apr. 24, 2011 | Semana Santa | Holy Week, culminating in Easter. |
| Apr. 30 | Día de los Niños | Children's Day. |
| May 1 | Día del Trabajo | Labor Day. |
| May 5 | Cinco de Mayo | Commemorates the Mexican victory at the Battle of Puebla, 1862. |
| June 1 | Día de la Marina | Navy Day. |
| Aug. 15 | La Asunción | Feast of the Assumption of Mary. |
| Sept. 16 | Día de la Independencia | Anniversary of the Cry of Dolores, 1810. |
| Sept. 21-29 | Fiesta de San Miguel Arcángel | Celebration of Cozumel's patron saint. |
| Oct. 12 | Día de la Raza | Day of Race, commemorates the arrival of Columbus in the "New World." |
| Nov. 1-2 | Día de Todos Santos and Día de los Muertos | Families honor the souls of their ancestors by visiting cemeteries and creating elaborate shrines. |
| Nov. 20 | Día de la Revolución | Anniversary of the Revolution, 1910. |
| Dec. 12 | Día de Nuestra Señora de Guadalupe | Feast Day of Mexico's Patron Saint. |
| Dec. 16-24 | Posadas | Processions reenacting the journey of Mary and Joseph to Bethlehem. |
| Dec. 24 | Noche Buena | Christmas Eve. |
| Dec. 25 | Navidad | Christmas Day. |

LIFE AND TIMES

# BEYOND TOURISM

## A PHILOSOPHY FOR TRAVELERS

**HIGHLIGHTS OF BEYOND TOURISM IN THE YUCATÁN**

**TEACH ENGLISH** to children in **Oaxaca** (p. 55).

**RESCUE** sea turtles and their habitat in **Quintana Roo** (p. 54).

**LEARN** Spanish on the shores of the Gulf of Mexico in **Cancún** (p. 59).

As a tourist, you are always a foreigner. Sure, hostel-hopping and sightseeing can be great fun, but connecting with a foreign country through studying, volunteering, or working can extend your travels beyond tourist traps. We don't like to brag, but this is what's different about a *Let's Go* traveler. Instead of feeling like a stranger in a strange land, you can understand the Yucatán Peninsula like a local. Instead of being that tourist asking for directions, you can be the one who gives them (and correctly!). All the while, you get the satisfaction of leaving the Yucatán Peninsula in better shape than you found it. It's not wishful thinking—it's Beyond Tourism.

As a **volunteer** in the Yucatán Peninsula, Tabasco, Chiapas, or Oaxaca, you can roll up your sleeves, cinch down your Captain Planet belt, and get your hands dirty doing anything from tracking endangered turtles to working alongside doctors in poverty-stricken areas. This chapter is chock-full of ideas for how to get involved, whether you're looking to pitch in for a day or to run away from home for a whole new life in Mexico.

Ahh, to **study** abroad! It's a student's dream, and when you find yourself actually getting to visit the Mayan ruins you're learning about in your art history class, it actually makes you feel sorry for those poor tourists who don't get to do any homework while they're here. Many programs are centered around these ancient Mexican ruins, offering the chance to participate in archaeological digs. If ruins aren't your thing, opportunities to engage in environmental conservation abound along the coast.

**SHARE YOUR EXPERIENCE.** Have you had a particularly enjoyable volunteer, study, or work experience that you'd like to share with other travelers? Post it to our website, www.letsgo.com!

# VOLUNTEERING

Feel like saving the world this week? Volunteering can be a powerful and fulfilling experience, especially when combined with the thrill of traveling in a new place. Mexico is currently facing significant challenges in terms of education, public safety, the environment, public health (what up, swine

# Face to Face

The summer after my junior year of college, I spent eight weeks in Oaxaca with Child Family Health International (CFHI; p. 55), a nonprofit that sends pre-medical and medical students abroad for service-learning experiences and language study. My experience in Mexico dramatically improved my Spanish, and, more significantly, deepened my understanding of the sociology of medicine, and the problems currently facing Mexico's health care system.

My first rotation was at a government-run neighborhood clinic, where the majority of the patients are diabetic, pregnant, suffering from high blood pressure, or seeking contraceptives. My first day of work took me out of the clinic, as I joined doctors and nurses going door to door in the countryside, teaching residents ways to prevent the spread of dengue fever.

In recent years, dengue infection rates in Mexico have swelled to epidemic proportions. The virus is primarily transmitted by mosquitoes (Aedes aegypti), which thrive in the humid climate. Many of the homes I visited were glorified lean-tos, with dirt floors and fireplaces for stoves. Chickens lived alongside humans, and families collected rainwater in jugs for laundry and dishwashing. These open containers of water are prime breeding grounds for deadly mosquitoes.

In one particularly dilapidated house, I saw mosquito larvae as large as tadpoles swimming through the fetid rainwater. Although the nurse accompanying me warned the family of the potential danger and instructed them to throw the water out, she confessed to me she thought it unlikely they would comply. Without this water, there would be none until the next rain. Although families seemed to pay close attention to our

well-rehearsed speeches, the doctors and nurses conducting the campaigns rarely notice any improvement. There is only so much medicine can do in the face of the extreme poverty affecting the majority of Mexicans.

Economic disparity permeates every aspect of Mexico's medical services. Upon returning to the clinic, I watched a pregnant woman—already 2cm dilated—experience rapid contractions as she waited to receive the paperwork necessary for a hospital delivery. A colleague of mine described how local pediatricians unnecessarily prescribe penicillin, for fear of being thought bad doctors for letting patients leave untreated. An emergency room intern watched a boy die from cardiac arrest after eating poisonous mushrooms because it took too long to obtain a defibrillator. The highest-ranking professional on duty in the emergency room at the time was a resident medical student. Meanwhile, I was shadowing a surgeon in a private clinic as he provided a client with breast implants.

From my perspective, the problem with Mexican health care is not

## "I went door to door, teaching residents ways to prevent dengue fever."

a lack of resources; rather, it's that these resources are not currently being used or distributed effectively. With care and attention, this phenomenon can change. If you can devote a month or two to understanding the problems with modern health care, try an internship with CFHI.

*Laura Ann Schoenherr was a member of the Class of 2008 at Harvard University. She graduated with an A.B. in chemistry, a certificate in health policy, and a citation in Spanish.*

flu?), and rural development. Be aware that volunteering in this region may mean sacrificing many of the comforts you're accustomed to, particularly in rural areas, and carries with it the risks of disease and less accessible health care. It's easy to minimize these risks by doing background research on the organization you're working with and the region to which you are traveling so that you can be appropriately prepared.

Most people who volunteer in these regions do so on a short-term basis at organizations that make use of drop-in or once-a-week volunteers. The best way to find opportunities that match your interests and schedule may be to check with local or national volunteer centers, some of which are listed below. Unsurprisingly, due to the problems Mexico is currently facing, many of the volunteer opportunities in these regions are related to economic development, environmental conservation, and public health. As always, read up before heading out.

Those looking for longer, more intensive volunteer opportunities usually choose to go through a parent organization that takes care of logistical details and often provides a group environment and support system—for a fee. There are two main types of organizations—religious and secular—although there are rarely restrictions on participation for either. Websites like **www.volunteerabroad.com, www.servenet.org,** and **www.idealist.org** allow you to search for volunteer openings both in your country and abroad.

**I HAVE TO PAY TO VOLUNTEER?** Many volunteers are surprised to learn that some organizations require large fees or "donations," but don't go calling them scams just yet. While such fees may seem ridiculous at first, they often keep the organization afloat, covering airfare, room, board, and administrative expenses for the volunteers. (Other organizations must rely on private donations and government subsidies.) If you're concerned about how a program spends its fees, request an annual report or finance account. A reputable organization won't refuse to inform you of how volunteer money is spent. Pay-to-volunteer programs might be a good idea for young travelers who are looking for more support and structure (such as pre-arranged transportation and housing) or anyone who would rather not deal with the uncertainty of creating a volunteer experience from scratch.

# ENVIRONMENTAL CONSERVATION

The quest for sustainable development is a crucial one throughout Mexico, but particularly in Yucatán and Chiapas, where the exploitation of abundant natural resources has resulted in widespread environmental degradation. Of particular concern are the disappearing rainforests.

**Centro Ecológico Akumal (CEA),** Apartado Postal 2, Akumal, Quintana Roo, 77730 México (☎984 875 9095; ceakumal.org). CEA conducts ecological research and offers several different volunteer programs, including a Sea Turtle Protection Program and an Environmental Education and Communication Program.

**Mérida Yucatán Conservation Program,** AmeriSpan, 1334 Walnut Street, 6th Floor, Philadelphia, PA 19107 (☎800-879-6640; www.amerispan.com). Although AmeriSpan itself is an American-run study abroad company, this volunteer program sets you up with a government organization in the Yucatán that works for the promotion and conservation of wildlife and the environment throughout the peninsula. Must be 21+, minimum time commitment 4 weeks. Must be proficient in Spanish. US$1095 for 4 weeks, US$190 for each additional week.

# MEDICAL OUTREACH

Mexico offers universal health care to its citizens, but despite this provision, good medical services can be hard to find, particularly in the more rural areas of the Yucatán Peninsula, Tabasco, and Chiapas that house vast numbers of the indigenous population; better care is available in larger cities. Dealing with any area of medical outreach, you will probably encounter vestiges of last year's swine flu outbreak (see **Essentials,** p. 6). Corruption within the health industry continues to be a problem. The organizations listed below aim to give aid to the Yucatán's disadvantaged.

**Child Family Health International (CFHI),** 995 Market Street, Suite 1104, San Francisco, CA 94103 (☎415-957-9000; www.cfhi.org).Provides pre-med and medical students with an opportunity to work with physicians in the developing world. In Mexico, CFHI has a variety of programs throughout Oaxaca state. Programs last between 4 and 8 weeks. Knowledge of Spanish not required but encouraged; volunteers encouraged to participate in Spanish language classes and homestays. Program fees US$2195-2235 for 4 weeks, not including airfare.

**Amigos de las Américas,** 5618 Star Lane, Houston, Texas 77057 (☎800-231-7796; www.amigoslink.org). An international non-profit organization, Amigos has a Community Nutrition Program in Oaxaca that gives volunteers the opportunity to work with community members, educating them about nutrition issues. High level of Spanish proficiency required. Open to high school students. Participation fee US$4400 (includes airfare and insurance).

**Global Medical Training (GMT),** 2701 E. Hill Drive, Rock Falls, Illinois 61071 (☎815-622-1605; www.gmtonline.org). This international humanitarian organization (which is not, incidentally, on Green Mountain Time, but on Central Time), provides healthcare students with the opportunity to learn about medicine and dentistry in the Yucatán, working side-by-side with doctors in the clinic. Trips last from a week to two weeks and range from US$1250 to US$1850, not including airfare.

# SOCIAL ACTIVISM

Mexico has long been dominated by huge disparities between the country's rich and poor. Although economic growth in the postwar period has resulted in some parts of the country reaching standards of living comparable to parts of Europe, the bottom 40% of the population as of 2008 were considered to live below the poverty line, and share only 11% of the country's wealth. The organizations listed below provide volunteer opportunities intended to reduce this disparity and the problems associated with it.

**AmeriSpan,** 1334 Walnut Street, 6th Floor, Philadelphia, PA 19107 (☎800-879-6640; www.amerispan.com). American-run study abroad company which also offers volunteer placement in Mérida and Oaxaca in a variety of different programs, ranging from cancer prevention education to social work in woman's crisis centers or orphanages to language schools. Must be proficient in Spanish. $1095 for 4 weeks, $190 for each additional week.

**Visions in Action,** 2710 Ontario Rd. NW, Washington, D.C. 20009 (☎202-625-7402; www.visioninaction.org). This nonprofit aims to promote social and economic justice by working with grassroots programs and communities of independent volunteers throughout the developing world. The Mexico Classic Volunteer Program in Oaxaca sets volunteers up with organizations in a variety of areas, including reproductive health, human rights, education, and agriculture. 6- or 12-month commitment beginning in January or July (US$4700 or US$5900), 1-month summer program during June (US$2800). Program fee does not include airfare. Must be 20 years old, proficient in Spanish, and have college degree. US$900 3-week pre-orientation for those with only basic Spanish.

**www.idealist.org.** A comprehensive search engine run by Action Without Borders. Lists domestic and international job and volunteer opportunities, but focuses on the non-profit sector. Search by region and area of interest.

# ARCHAEOLOGICAL RESEARCH

The Yucatán Peninsula's rich history is manifest in over 10,000 Mayan ruins. The following programs provide volunteers a chance to delve into the region's past.

**Foundation for Latin American Anthropological Research (FLAAR;** ☎419-823-9218; www.maya-art-books.org/volunteer.php). This non-profit education organization aims to disseminate information about Mesoamerican culture. FLAAR accepts students and others as volunteers on field trips and expeditions. Cost for students is typically US$1000-2000, for non-students US$1500-5000 (average US$2500), not including airfare.

**Maya Research Program,** 209 W. 2nd St. #295, Fort Worth, TX 76102 (☎817-257-5943; www.mayaresearchprogram.org). This US-based non-profit sponsors archaeological research in Latin America, including the opportunity to live and volunteer in the Mayan village of Yaxunah. Programs run for 2, 3, or 4 weeks. Required donation of US$1500 for 2 week session (US$1200 for students), $500 for each subsequent week.

# RURAL DEVELOPMENT

Though Mexico's countryside constitutes more than 80% of Mexico's land and houses nearly 36% of the country's population, it represents a just a small share of the country's economy. Rural areas tend to be poor, with few jobs and less access to government services. A series of organizations, including those listed below, are attempting to bridge the divide between city and country.

**Habitat for Humanity Mexico,** Soria No. 47 Colonia Alamos, Del Benito Juárez, Mexico D.F. 03400, Mexico (☎55 5519 0113; www.habitat.org). 1-week stays in Oaxaca for those interested in building houses in a host community. Costs range from US$1300-2500, not including airfare.

**United Planet,** 11 Arlington Street, Boston, MA 02116 USA (☎617-267-7763; www.unitedplanet.org). Provides 6- or 12-month volunteer opportunities in Chiapas. Participate in community projects. Must be at least 18 years old. Program Fee US$5252 for 6 months, US$7965 for 12 months.

**Pro World Service Corps,** P.O. Box 21121, Billings, MT 59104 USA (☎877-733-7378; www.myproworld.org). Organization that offers study abroad and unpaid internships to Latin America with the goal of promoting social and economic development throughout the world. Offers the opportunity to work in Oaxaca with an NGO on a wide variety of issues, including health, the environment, and social and economic development. US$1895 for 2 weeks, US$2665 for 4, US$3050 for 5; US$385 for each subsequent week.

BEYOND TOURISM

# STUDYING

> **VISA INFORMATION.** If you're planning to study in Mexico for 6 months or less, there's no need to apply for a visa. If your stay will be longer, you should head to the consulate nearest you well before you leave. In addition to other documents, you will need the acceptance letter from your school in Mexico to receive a visa. Some countries may be charged US$29 for consular fees.

It's completely natural to want to play hooky on the first day of school when it's raining and first period Trigonometry is meeting in the old cafeteria, but when your campus is San Cristóbal de las Casas and your meal plan revolves around authentic enchiladas and tortillas, what could be better than the student life?

A growing number of students report that studying abroad is the highlight of their learning careers. If you've never studied abroad, you don't know what you're missing—and, if you have studied abroad, you know not to miss it.

Study-abroad programs range from basic language and culture courses to university-level classes, often for college credit (sweet, right?). In order to choose a program that best fits your needs, research as much as you can before making your decision—determine costs and duration as well as what kinds of students participate in the program and what sorts of accommodations are provided.

In programs that have large groups of students who speak English, there is a trade-off. You may feel more comfortable in the community, but you will not have the same opportunity to practice a foreign language or to befriend other international students. For accommodations, dorm life provides a better opportunity to mingle with fellow students, but there is less of a chance to experience the local scene. If you live with a family, you could potentially build lifelong friendships with natives and experience day-to-day life in greater depth, but you might also get stuck sharing a room with their pet iguana. Conditions can vary greatly from family to family.

## UNIVERSITIES

Most university-level study-abroad programs are conducted in Spanish, although many programs offer classes in English as well as lower-level language courses. Savvy linguists may find it cheaper to enroll directly in a university abroad, although getting college credit may be more difficult. You can search **www.studyabroad.com** for various semester-abroad programs that meet your criteria, including your desired location and focus of study. If you're a college student, your friendly neighborhood study-abroad office is often the best place to start.

### AMERICAN PROGRAMS

**Central College Abroad,** Office of International Education, 812 University, Pella, Iowa 50219, USA (☎800-831-3629; www.central.edu/abroad). Offers internships and study-abroad programs in Mérida, the latter through Marista University, Modelo University, and the Autonous University of the Yucatán. Courses in English and Spanish. All-inclusive semester-long tuition US$13,200, year-long US$26,400, not including airfare.

**Council on International Educational Exchange (CIEE),** 300 Fore St., Portland, ME 04101, USA (☎207-553-4000 or 800-40-STUDY/407-8839; www.ciee.org). One of

BEYOND TOURISM

the most comprehensive resources for work, academic, and internship programs around the world, including in Mexico.

**International Association for the Exchange of Students for Technical Experience (IAESTE),** 10400 Little Patuxent Parkway, Suite 250, Columbia, MD, 21044, USA (☎410-997-3069; iaeste.amipp.org). Offers internships in Mexico for college students who have completed 2 years of technical study (minimum 8 weeks).

**School for International Training (SIT) Study Abroad,** 1 Kipling Rd., P.O. Box 676, Brattleboro, VT 05302, USA (☎888-272-7881 or 802-258-3212; www.sit.edu/studyabroad). Semester-long programs in Oaxaca cost around US$13,770 for tuition (an additional US$2486 for room and board). Also runs **The Experiment in International Living** (☎800-345-2929; www.experimentinternational.org), which offers 3- to 5-week summer programs for high-school students looking to participate in cross-cultural homestays, community service, ecological adventure, and language training in Mexico City (US$4100-4300).

## MEXICAN PROGRAMS

Short-term study in Mexico is relatively easy, especially since no visa is required for stays of up to six months. Mexican universities are generally open to accepting foreign students for study abroad, but do not have a formalized program for doing so. *Let's Go* suggests that you contact universities you are interested in individually and inquire as to the process for enrolling as a temporary foreign student. Mexican universities also often have flourishing exchange programs with many countries around the world. Applications are usually due in early spring. Below are two universities that accept study abroad students.

**Universidad Autónoma de Yucatán,** C. 60 No. 491-A por 57, Mérida, Yucatán, México (☎999 930 0900; www.uady.mx). Ranked as the top public university in Mexico, UADY's top departments are anthropology, archaeology, education, literature, Latin American studies, and psychology. Apply through the Institute for Study Abroad at Butler University (www.ifsa-butler.org/universidad-autonoma-de-yucatan.html). Tuition US$7735, housing $2640.

**Universidad Autónoma Benito Juárez de Oaxaca**, Av. Universidad S/N, Ex - Hacienda de 5 Señores, Oaxaca, México (☎951 516 6979 or 5644 or 5844; www.uabjo.mx). Located in the heart of the city of Oaxaca, this public university, founded in 1827, is the alma mater of two former presidents of Mexico (Benito Pablo Juárez García and José de la Cruz Porfirio Díaz Mori). The university is very open to foreign students; contact them directly for details.

## LANGUAGE SCHOOLS

Old lady making snarky comments to you in the plaza? Imprudent cashier at the taquería? Cute moped girl that is totally into you? To communicate is to be human, and without the local language in your toolbelt, you're up a creek without a *pala*. Fear not! Language school here to help.

While language school courses rarely count for college credit, they do offer a unique way to get acquainted with the culture and language of Mexico. Schools can be independently run or university affiliated, local or international, youth-oriented or full of old people—the opportunities are endless. Some worthwhile organizations include:

**Becari Language School,** M. Bravo #210, Plaza San Cristóbal, Oaxaca, Mexico, 68000 (☎951 514 6076; www.mexonline.com/becari.htm). Offers classes on a weekly basis, with new classes starting each Monday. Program can also arrange a homestay or other forms of housing. Regular program (15 hr. per week) US$120 per week, Intensive (20 hr. per week) US$160 per week, Super Intensive (30 hr. per week) US$240 per week. Super Intensive workshop (30 hrs) $260. Private lessons also available.

**El Bosque del Caribe,** Av. Nader #52 SM. 3, Cancún, Mexico (☎998 884 1065; www.cancunlanguage.com). With a maximum of 6 students per class, this language course offers options ranging from a mini-course (3 hr. per day, US$150 ), to an Executive Program (6 hr. per day, $255). You may also choose the Spanish-dive program, where you take Spanish courses in the morning and learn to SCUBA-dive in the afternoon. Private classes are also available (20 hr. per week, US$340). Dive program US$435. Accommodations available either with host family or in student residences; prices range from US$14 to US$28 per night.

**Instituto Cultural Oaxaca,** Avenida Juarez #909, Oaxaca de Juarez, Mexico (☎951 515 3404 or 1323). This language school offers a plethora of classes. Cultural workshops offered year-round. Will arrange homestays or accommodations in *posadas* (inns), hotels, or apartments. 1 week US$115-160; 3 weeks US$315-380; 5 weeks US$480-540 depending on the program. After the 5th week, the cost per week is US$100, but students must purchase the first 5 weeks at the same time to receive this discount. Homestays range US$13-24 per night.

**Language Courses Abroad,** 67 Ashby Road, Loughborough, England (☎01509 211612; www.languagesabroad.co.uk). This British  program runs language courses throughout the world, and has programs in Oaxaca and in Playa del Carmen. Both programs offer standard courses, intensive courses, and private lessons, and can arrange housing if desired. The schools also organize a variety of cultural activities to help students integrate themselves into the regions' cultures and practice their language skills. And while you're at it, you can also take Salsa and Merengue dance classes. Max. of 5 students per class. US$360-420 for group classes depending on intensity level, US$620 for private lessons. If you wish to live with a host family, add about US$200-220 per week.

**Languages in Action** (www.languagesinaction.com). Programs available in Cancún, Mérida, Oaxaca, and San Cristóbal, as well as other locations in Mexico. Max. 5-10 students per class depending on location. Homestays and other accommodations can be arranged through the program. One week US$195. Some locations give a discount for multiple weeks.

# WORKING

Due to high unemployment in Mexico, short-term employment opportunities are few and far between. *Let's Go* urges you to leave short-term work opportunities to the Mexican citizens who need them most. For those looking to work long-term in Mexico, teaching English is the way to go. In general, you should try to make your work arrangements before you leave for Mexico, as working abroad often requires a special work visa, which can be difficult to obtain (see below for more information about visas). **Transitions Abroad** (www.transitionsabroad.com) also offers updated online listings for work over any time period.

**MORE VISA INFORMATION.** It is difficult to obtain a general work visa for Mexico, and the government reserves the right to restrict permits to sectors experiencing labor shortages. In order to work, you must be authorized by the **National Immigration Institute** (Instituto Nacional de Migración), which will require proof of employment as well as a letter (written in Spanish) requesting entry and detailing your intended activities, estimated time, and pay while in Mexico. You will also need to declare your prospective employee. See website for further details. Homero 1832, Col. Los Morales Polanco, Delegación Miguel Hidalgo; C.P. 11510, México, D.F. (☎555 387 2400; www.inm.gob.mx).

## TEACHING ENGLISH

Suffice it to say that teaching jobs abroad pay more in personal satisfaction and emotional fulfillment than in actual cash. Nevertheless, even volunteer teachers often receive some sort of a daily stipend to help with living expenses; expect your salary to match the low cost of living in Mexico. In almost all cases, you must have at least a bachelor's degree to be a full-fledged teacher, although college undergraduates can often get summer positions teaching or tutoring. Many schools require teachers to have a **Teaching English as a Foreign Language (TEFL)** certificate. You may still be able to find a teaching job without one, but certified teachers often find higher-paying jobs.

The Spanish-impaired don't have to give up their dream of teaching, either. Private schools usually hire native English speakers for English-immersion classrooms where no Spanish is spoken. (Teachers in public schools will more likely work in both English and Spanish.) Placement agencies or university fellowship programs are the best resources for finding teaching jobs. The alternatives are to contact schools directly or try your luck once you arrive in Mexico. In the latter case, the best time to look is several weeks before the start of the school year. The following organizations are helpful in placing teachers in the Yucatán Peninsula, Tabasco, Chiapas, and Oaxaca.

**International Schools Services (ISS),** 15 Roszel Rd., P.O. Box 5910, Princeton, NJ 08543, USA (☎609-452-0990; www.iss.edu). Hires teachers for more than 200 overseas schools, some in Mexico. Candidates should have teaching experience and a bachelor's degree. 2-year commitment is the norm.

**Office of Overseas Schools,** US Department of State, Room H328, SA-1, Washington, D.C. 20522, USA (☎202-261-8200; www.state.gov/m/a/os). Keeps a list of schools abroad and agencies that arrange placement for Americans to teach abroad, including in Mexico.

**Teachers Latin America,** Avenida Cuahtemoc 793, Col. Navarte, Del. Miguel Hidalgo, Mexico City D.F., Mexico (☎555 256 4108; www.innovative-english.com). TESS-EFL and TEFL certification, language courses, internships, and job placement services. US $200-1200 depending on the service (see website for more details). TEFL course fees include accommodations (or homestay). Typical certification program 9-12 weeks for minimum 6-month position.

# CAMPECHE

The smallest state in the Yucatán Peninsula, Campeche is also the region most blissfully free of the tourist mobs you're likely to find in Cancún or Playa del Carmen. The capital, the city of **Campeche** (see below), is the highlight of region –in 1999, UNESCO named its *centro histórico* a World Heritage Site. Today, you can still see many of the fortresses built in the 17th century to protect against the pirates that plagued the region. Although the region does boast several significant (and significantly less crowded) Mayan ruins, Campeche is better known for its rollicking buccaneers.

Fortunately, the pirates didn't make it inland, and the impressive Mayan ruins of **Edzná** (p. 69), **Xpujil** (p. 70) and **Calakmul** (p. 72) remain sites well worth visiting. The **Edificio de Cinco Pisos** (Building of the Five Floors) in Edzná is striking and well worth the visit, while Calakmul, located in the heart of the vast and largely unexplored **Reserva de la Biosfera Calakmul,** boasts marvelous pyramids—try climbing one to get a sense of just how extensive the surrounding rainforest really is.

## CAMPECHE ☎981

Campeche (pop. 220,000) is full of buried treasures. Around practically every corner are beautiful colonial churches, foreboding stone embattlements, and hole-in-the-wall local establishments. Old wood, stone, and stucco frame one of the peninsula's most scenic central parks, where shoe shiners and candy vendors find comfort in the shade. Pirates once thought Campeche to be full of treasure—their relentless raids on the commercial center prompted the construction of the city's most prominent features: a 17th-century cannon-lined wall and two hilltop fortresses. Campeche has fewer late-night parties than other Yucatán hot spots, but this peaceful city is still worth a longer stay.

## ▐ TRANSPORTATION

**Flights:** *Ingeniero* (Engineer) **Alberto Acuña Ongay** (CPE; ☎816 5678), on Porfirio, 13km from the centro. Taxis to the *centro* 80 pesos. Served by **Aeroméxico** (☎816 6656).

**Buses:** Taxis run from both bus stations to the *Parque Principal* (30 pesos). A confusing network of local buses links Campeche's distant sectors to the old city (4.50 pesos). The market, where Gobernadores becomes the Circuito, is the hub for local routes. Buses can be flagged down along the Circuito, but do not regularly stop in the *centro*. Blue signs and crowds of people huddled in the shade mark the bus stops.

**1st-class station:** (☎981 9910), on Av. Central at Av. Colosio, 5km from the city center. ADO buses to: **Cancún** (7hr., 7 daily 8:40am-11:50pm, 372 pesos); **Chetumal** (7hr., noon, 282 pesos); **Ciudad del Carmen** (3hr., 27 daily, 154 pesos); **Mérida** (2hr., every hr. 1:35am-11:50pm, 136 pesos); **Mexico City** (16hr.; 12:26, 10:26, 11:40pm; 966 pesos); **Oaxaca** (F 12:30, 9:50pm; 754 pesos); **Palenque** (6hr.; midnight, 2:35am, 11:10pm; 242 pesos); **San Cristóbal de las Casas** (9-10hr., 9:40pm, 354 pesos); **Veracruz** (12hr., 10:15pm, 736 pesos); **Villahermosa** (7hr., 15 daily 12:55am-11:40pm, 298 pesos); **Xpujil** (5hr., noon, 198 pesos).

**2nd-class station:** At Gobernadores and Chile, 500m from the old city. To reach the *parque principal* from this station, catch a Gobernadores bus (4.50 pesos) across from the station and ask to be let

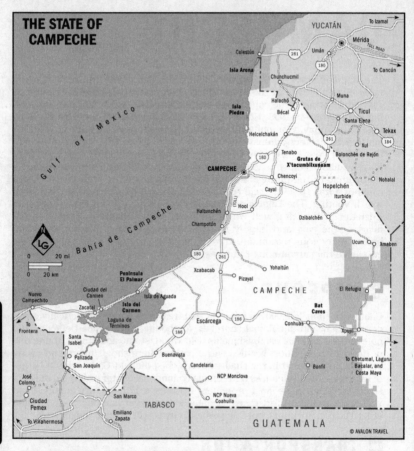

## THE STATE OF CAMPECHE

© AVALON TRAVEL

CAMPECHE

off at the Baluarte de San Francisco. Turn right into the old city and walk 4 blocks on C. 57 to the park. **ATS** and **Sur** buses to: **Ciudad del Carmen** (3hr., 6 per day, 113 pesos); **Champotón** (every 30-60min., 33 pesos); **Mérida** (4hr., every 30min., 94 pesos); and **Uxmal and Santa Elena** (3hr., 5 per day 6am-5pm, 83-90 pesos), stopping at every town on the way. **Unión de Transportistas de Camino Real** heads to destinations within the state of Campeche every 30min. **Combis** to **Edzná** (30 pesos) stop in the lot between Parque Alameda and the market. *Combis* to **Seyba Playa** and **Sabancuy** (17 pesos) leave from the other side of the Parque Alameda on República.

> **TIP** **EASY RIDER.** Worried about booking that 18hr. bus trip? Worry no more. For peace of mind, all ADO tickets can be purchased online ahead of time at www.ticketbus.com.mx. For *de lujo* (luxury) tickets, check out www.adogl.com.mx.

**Taxis:** (☎816 1113 or 6666). Taxis operate out of 4 stands: on C. 8 at C. 51, across from the post office; on C. 55 at *Circuito*, near the market; and at both bus stations. Local travel usually costs 25-30 pesos (30-35 pesos after dark).

**Car Rental: Europcar** (☎152 1163), in the airport. To reserve a car, simply call before you arrive; they can have one waiting for you at your hotel. Phone available 24hr. Office open 9am-1pm and 4:30pm-6pm. MC/V.

# ▣ ⚡ ORIENTATION AND PRACTICAL INFORMATION

Campeche's historic **centro**, the old city, is based on an easy-to-follow numbered grid. North-south streets have odd numbers that increase to the west. East-west streets are even numbered and increase as they get farther from the coast. The *centro* is surrounded by a hexagonal series of roads known collectively as the **Circuito de Baluartes,** marked by seven lookout towers. Within this area and the surrounding neighborhoods of **San Francisco, Guadalupe,** and **San Ramón** is some of Campeche's most beautiful colonial architecture. The **malecón** stretches along the Gulf of Mexico coastline. Locals refer to the main square as the **parque principal,** or main park, instead of the *zócalo*, which is more common in the rest of Mexico.

**Tourist Office:** C. 55 3 (☎811 3989 or 811 3990), between C. 8 and 10, next to the Cathedral. Houses a diorama of the old walled city and hands out pamphlets on area sights. Open daily 9am-9pm.

**Banks: Santander Serfín** (☎816 1055), on C. 57 between C. 10 and 12, just off the *zócalo*. Open M-F 9am-4pm, Sa 10am-2pm. **Banamex** (☎816 5252), at the corner of C. 53 and 10. Open M-F 9am-4pm. Both have **24hr. ATMs.**

**Luggage Storage: Guarda Plus,** at the ADO station. 5-12 pesos per hr. Open 6am-10pm.

**Bookstore:** C. 57 6 (☎816 1350), in the Casa de Cultura, across from the *parque principal*. A good selection of coffee table books in Spanish as well as maps and music from the area. Open daily 9am-9pm.

**Laundromat: Lavandería y Tintorería Antigua,** C. 57 28 (☎811 6900), between C. 12 and 14. Same-day service 15 pesos per kg. Open M-Sa 8am-4pm.

**Police:** (☎812 7133, emergencies ☎060), on Av. López Portillo at Prolongación Pedro Moreno Sascalum.

**Red Cross:** (☎815 2378), on Av. Las Palmas at Ah Kin Pech, 1km up the coast from the old city.

**Pharmacy: Farmacia Canto,** Av. López Mateos 365 (☎816 6204), at Lazareto. Another location (☎816 4100) at C. 59 and 10, closer to the *parque principal*. Free delivery to nearby hotels. Open M-Sa 8am-10pm, Su 8am-3pm.

**Medical Services: Hospital General** (☎811 9580), on Central at Circuito Baluartes.

**Fax Office: Telecomm** (☎816 5210), in the Palacio Federal, opposite Mexpost. Open M-F 8am-7:30pm, Sa-Su 9am-1pm.

**Internet Access: Cyber VIP,** at the corner of C. 51 and 14. 10 pesos per hr. Open daily 7am-9:30pm. **Intertel,** C. 57 1 (☎816 7334), between C. 10 and 12. 10 pesos per hr. Open M-Sa 9am-10pm, Su 9am-8pm.

**Post Office:** (☎816 2134), on 16 de Septiembre at C. 53, in the Palacio Federal. Open M-F 8am-7:30pm, Sa 9am-1pm. Mexpost (☎811 1730) inside. **Postal Code:** 24001.

# ⌂ ACCOMMODATIONS

Campeche offers ample opportunities to stay in colonial buildings, complete with soaring ceilings, old archways, and pastel facades, all without going broke. Most quality budget accommodations are located in the *centro*. During

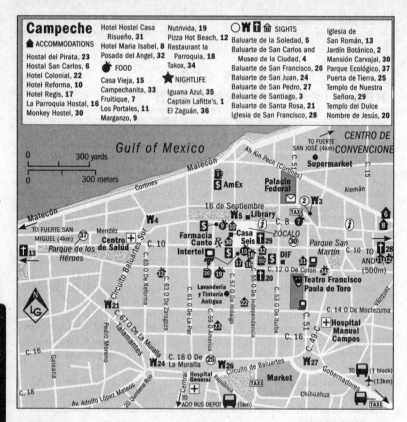

**Campeche**

**ACCOMMODATIONS**

Hostal del Pirata, **23**
Hostal San Carlos, **6**
Hotel Colonial, **22**
Hotel Reforma, **10**
Hotel Regis, **17**
La Parroquia Hostal, **16**
Monkey Hostel, **30**

Hotel Hostel Casa
   Risueño, **31**
Hotel Maria Isabel, **8**
Posada del Angel, **32**

**FOOD**

Casa Vieja, **15**
Campechanita, **33**
Fruitique, **7**
Los Portales, **11**
Marganzo, **9**

Nutrivida, **19**
Pizza Hot Beach, **12**
Restaurant la
   Parroquia, **18**
Takox, **34**

**NIGHTLIFE**

Iguana Azul, **35**
Captain Lafitte's, **1**
El Zaguán, **36**

**SIGHTS**

Baluarte de la Soledad, **5**
Baluarte de San Carlos and
   Museo de la Ciudad, **4**
Baluarte de San Francisco, **26**
Baluarte de San Juan, **24**
Baluarte de San Pedro, **27**
Baluarte de Santiago, **3**
Baluarte de Santa Rosa, **21**
Iglesia de San Francisco, **28**

Iglesia de
   San Román, **13**
Jardín Botánico, **2**
Mansión Carvajal, **30**
Parque Ecológico, **37**
Puerta de Tierra, **25**
Templo de Nuestra
   Señora, **29**
Templo del Dulce
   Nombre de Jesús, **20**

July, August, and *Semana Santa*, hostels and hotels often fill up before sunset with tourists; call ahead for reservations.

**Monkey Hostel** (☎811 6605 or 800-CAMPECHE/2267-3243; www.hostalcampeche. com), at C. 57 and 10, in the *centro*. The best location in town, with an unpretentious and friendly atmosphere that invites long visits and rooftop parties. Stay includes breakfast, kitchen access, linens, purified water, and a splendid view of the cathedral. Helpful staff can arrange tours to nearby sights. Bike rental 20 pesos for 2hr., each additional hr. 5 pesos. Laundry 40 pesos. Internet 5 pesos per 30min. Reception 24hr. Check-out noon. Dorms 100 pesos; singles 260 pesos. Cash only. ❶

**Hostal del Pirata**, C. 59 47 (☎811 1757), between C. 14 and 16. This hostel sticks to its theme with pirate paraphernalia in every nook of the ex-mansion. Quiet, fan-cooled dorms are spacious and sparkling clean. Outdoor kitchen and cafeteria on the roof with complimentary beer and soda. Dorms 100 pesos; partitioned doubles 240 pesos; private rooms 270 pesos. Cash only. ❷

**La Parroquia Hostal**, C. 55 8 (☎816 2530; www.hostalparroquia.com), between C. 10 and 12. This clean, attractive hostel in a colonial building is full-service, offering currency exchange, kitchen use, continental breakfast, lockers, and a great terrace overlooking the city—there's even table tennis in the common room. Discounts at the lively 24hr. restaurant of the same name next door and at the upscale Marganzo (p. 66). Bike rental 20 pesos per hr. Internet 12 pesos per hr. Reception 24hr. Dorms 90 pesos; doubles 210 pesos; quads 320 pesos. Cash only. ❶

**Hotel Hostel Casa Risueño,** C. 10 224 (☎816 8231), between C. 53 and 51. Walk up a winding staircase to reach the rooms, which are well kept and have free Wi-Fi. If you need some air, Casa Risueño has a terrace that looks out on a park. Reception 24hr. Dorms 100 pesos; singles 304 pesos, with A/C 386 pesos; doubles 339/421 pesos. ❶

**Hotel Colonial,** C. 14 122 (☎816 2222), between C. 55 and 57. Green rooms with bath, fan, and a retro look and feel. Common area has cable TV and a few lounge chairs as well as purified water. Singles 175 pesos; doubles 240 pesos; triples 280 pesos; each additional person 35 pesos; A/C 90 pesos extra. Cash only. ❷

**Hostal San Carlos,** C. 10 255 (☎816 5158), at the intersection with C. 49-B. Removed from the *centro* in the Barrio Guadalupe, this impeccably restored colonial house has period-style furniture and lighting, in a common area with TV. Free continental breakfast and Wi-Fi. Reception 24hr. Dorms 100 pesos. Cash only. ❶

**Hotel María Isabel** (☎811 3559), on C. 49-B between C. 10 and 12. Right around the corner from cheap and delicious food at the Portales de San Martín, Hotel María Isabel is a snug place to lay your head. Floral decor and cable TV in all rooms. Singles 350 pesos, with A/C 400 pesos; doubles 500/550 pesos. Cash only. ❺

**Hotel Regis** (☎816 3175), on C. 12 between C. 55 and 57. Large, warmly lit orange rooms all have A/C, comfy beds, fans, checkered floors, and TVs; some with balcony. The lobby courtyard has a small fridge and purified water. Singles 320 pesos; doubles 385 pesos; triples 440 pesos. Cash only. ❹

**Hotel Reforma,** C. 8 257 (☎816 4464), between C. 57 and 59. Conveniently located 1 block off the *parque principal,* Hotel Reforma's tile floor patterns might make you feel like a king. Big rooms with TVs. Free Wi-Fi. Reception 24hr. Check-out 1pm. Singles 175 pesos, with A/C 292 pesos; doubles 292/351 pesos. Cash only. ❷

**Posada del Angel** (☎816 7718), on C. 10 between C. 53 and 55. Posada del Angel rents simple, clean rooms less than a block from the main park, but lacks the charming colonial courtyard and backpacker scene you might get elsewhere. Singles 304 pesos, with A/C 386 pesos; doubles 339/421 pesos. Cash only. ❺

# 🍴 FOOD

Campechan cuisine is known for combining Yucatec specialties with European flavors and seafood. Sample *pan de cazón* (stacked tortillas filled with baby

## TOP 10 WAYS TO SAVE IN THE YUCATÁN

Tourism opportunities abound in the Yucatán—be a savvy spender and get the most for each peso with these tried-and-true budget tips.

1. Visit museums on weekends when some offer free admission (usually on Sundays).

2. Listen to time-share hawkers at mega resorts like Cancún; most offer coupons on meals and attractions just for listening to their pitch.

3. Use public transportation during the day. Most towns will have routes to major attractions.

4. Buy your souvenirs from smaller towns to avoid inflated tourist prices.

5. When appropriate, bargain! It's more accepted than most major credit cards.

6. Stock up on beer, bread, fresh fruit, liquor, and vegetables from local markets.

7. Visit during the low season (usually any time but Semana Santa, mid-summer, or December), when prices are lower.

8. Add more outdoors experiences to your itinerary—beachfront camping is often free, and Mexico's countless natural wonders offer plenty of budget-friendly adventure.

9. Stay at hostels and hotels that offer free breakfast.

10. Round up hostelmates and fellow tourists when visiting local attractions to get group rate discounts.

shark and refried beans, covered with onion, tomato, and chile sauce) and *pámpano en escabeche* (fish broiled in olive oil and flavored with onion, garlic, chile, and orange juice). Don't be sucked into the overpriced restaurants in the *parque principal;* delicious, inexpensive food (9-38 pesos) can be found under the red *portales* (archways) in **Parque San Martín,** where you'll find several extremely popular restaurants. Campeche also has a **market,** on Circuito Baluartes, between C. 53 and 55, near Baluarte de San Pedro (open M-Sa sunrise-sunset, Su sunrise-3pm). There is also a supermarket, **San Francisco de Asís,** in Plaza Comercial Ah Kin Pech, behind the post office. (☎816 7977. Open daily 7am-10pm.)

**Marganzo** (☎811 3898), on C. 8 between C. 57 and C. 59. An ambience as fresh and colorful as its food. Caesar salad (56 pesos), fish parmesan (126 pesos), and a trio of guitarists (Tu-Sa 8-10pm, Su afternoons) contribute to one of the best dining experiences in town. All meals come with tasty crab salad *bocatas* (sandwiches). Open daily 7am-11pm. MC/V. ❹

**Los Portales** (☎811 1491), on C. 10 between Arista and Gómez Farías, off Parque San Francisco. Your reward for making the walk through Barrio Guadalupe is cheap Campechan food in a beautiful cobbled plaza. Traditional and vegetarian entrees 9-40 pesos. Open daily 6pm-1am. Cash only. ❶

**Restaurant La Parroquia,** C. 55 8 (☎816 2530), between C. 10 and 12. Fills up with diners and the sounds of street life from nearby shoppers and revelers. Serves large portions of *chilaquiles* (56 pesos), shish kebabs (88 pesos), and stuffed fish with bacon (112 pesos). Home to the most delicious beverage in Campeche, *horchata* with coconut milk (18 pesos). Open 24hr. Cash only. ❹

**Frutique** (☎811 7062), on C. 8 between C. 51 and 53. Another member of Campeche's surprisingly robust vegetarian-friendly restaurant scene. Come at the right time and the owner's kids might be munching at the table next to you. Vegetarian sandwiches for 18 pesos; delicious fruit *licuados* for 19 pesos. Open M-Sa 7:30am-4pm. Cash only. ❶

**Takox,** C. 49 22, across from Parque San Martín. Campeche's go-to place to satisfying your late-night cravings with just the change in your pocket. Enjoy tacos (from 7 pesos) or split an *alambre* (a plate of meat, onion and spices served with tortillas; feeds 3 for 60 pesos) outside while you watch the activity in the park across the street. Open daily 7pm-2am. Cash only. ❶

**Pizza Hot Beach** (☎811 3131), on C. 10 just past Parque San Francisco, near Los Portales. This well-known local chain serves up huge, delicious pizzas (70-125 pesos), plus Italian/American-style pastas (from 95 pesos) and sandwiches (from 70 pesos). Free delivery. Small pizza serves 2. Open daily 9am-midnight. Cash only. ❷

**Nutrivida,** C. 12 167 (☎816 1221), between C. 57 and 59. Nutrivida serves mostly vegetarian food deep behind enemy lines in meat-loving Mexico. Delicious, healthy dishes, such as soy burgers (27 pesos), *chaya* (a native Yucatán plant, similar to spinach) tamales stuffed with soy (9 pesos), and homemade yogurt (11 pesos). Chicken or tuna salads 8-16 pesos. In front of the seating area—a small bar near the kitchen and some tables in the building's open courtyards—there are a few racks of health food and supplements. Open M-F 8am-8:30pm, Sa 8am-2pm. Cash only. ❶

**Campechanita,** at C. 12 and 63. The dishes at this self-described "fast food" establishment aren't delivered particularly quickly, but neither are they the soggy, pre-wrapped affair Americans usually associate with the phrase. The white walls and plastic, bolted chairs and tables might fit the bill better. The food is cheap and decent, including *enchiladas* (22 pesos), caesar salad (17 pesos), and the *comida del día* (35 pesos). Open M-F 7:30am-5pm, Sa-Su 7:30am-2pm. ❷

**Casa Vieja,** C. 10 319, 2nd fl. (☎811 8016), between C. 55 and 57. The view overlooking the *parque principal* and the collection of local folk art are worth the visit, even if the pricey food is hit or miss. *Fajitas al mole* 132 pesos. Pasta dishes from 95 pesos. Open daily 10am-11pm. MC/V. ❹

# 🔾 🔾 SIGHTS AND BEACHES

Campeche's colonial streets are lovely enough during the day, but it's when the sun sets that the city becomes truly magical. The air cools and the centuries-old stone churches and painted homes are softly illuminated by street lamps and moonlight. Though the only standing walls of the fortress are at **Puerta de Tierra** and **Baluarte de la Soledad,** which both have museums and allow you to walk along their terraces, there are still seven *baluartes* (bulwarks), visible along **Circuito Baluartes.**Don't make the mistake of staying within the boundaries of the old walled city. Many of the surrounding neighborhoods are equally beautiful, especially **Barrio Guadalupe** to the north.

The city has a popular **trolley** system, which tours the major sights and historic neighborhoods. The red **Tranvía** tours the *centro* and *malecón*, departing from *parque principal* (45min., every hr. 9am-1pm and 5-9pm). The green **El Guapo** and **Superguapo** (40min.) make short stops at either the **Fuerte de San José** (9am, 5pm; 70 pesos) or the **Fuerte de San Miguel** (every hr. 9am-1pm and 5-9pm, 70 pesos). Schedules and destinations are erratic, and trolleys often leave when they have the minimum 10 passengers; it's best to inquire with the driver about the route. Attendants ring a brass bell from the green kiosk in *parque principal* when they are about to depart. Tours are also available in English. Nearly all of Campeche's historical sights are within walking distance of the *centro*.

**FUERTE DE SAN JOSÉ EL ALTO.** Built in 1792, Campeche's smaller fort stands guard to the northeast of the city. The path leading to the operating drawbridge is full of turns, a deliberate attempt to prevent attacking pirates from using battering rams on the gate. Inside, you can see various weapons—including a particularly impractical-looking giant sword—and models of the rogue pirate ships that used to torment the city. Exhibits are in Spanish only. *(4km from the centro on the northern hills overlooking town. The Bellavista or San José el Alto buses, which pass in front of the post office, come within a few blocks of the fort. Get off at a small park with a basketball court and white, rectangular water tower; walk uphill 2-3 minutes. Alternatively, the 4km walk is scenic and breezy. Head north along the malecón about 2½km, then turn right at the PEMEX station and head up the steep hill another 1½km. Open Tu-Su 9:30am-5:30pm. 31 pesos.)*

**FUERTE DE SAN MIGUEL.** Completed in 1801, this fort used to stand guard against naval threats coming from the Gulf. Today, there's something a bit wistful about the way it looks down on the modern mansions at the bottom of the hill. Today, the structure hosts the impressive **Museo Arqueológico de Campeche,** which has intriguing exhibits on the state's ruins and ancient Mayan city life, religion, war, power, trade, and beliefs about death and the afterlife. Objects of particular interest include jade masks, Mayan glyphs, and the contents of royal tombs found in nearby ruins. On the top level, 20 cannons still stand guard. *(5km south of town, just before the town of Lerma. Take a 4.50-peso Lerma or Playa Bonita bus, both of which stop in front of the post office and will drop you off at the bottom of the steep, 600m hill leading to the fort. Look for the signs on the left. Open Tu-Sa 9am-5:30pm, Su 9am-noon. 37 pesos.)*

**IGLESIA DE SAN ROMÁN.** The church houses **El Cristo Negro** (The Black Christ), a 6 ft. ebony statue that arrived from Italy in 1575. The church, completed in 1570, was built for future protection and good luck after a locust plague struck the city. *(A few blocks southwest of the centro on C. 10, past the long, narrow Parque de los Héroes. Open M-Sa 6am-noon, Su 6am-9pm. Su mass 7am, 1, 6pm.)*

**JARDÍN BOTÁNICO XMUCH'HALTUN.** Something about this small, tightly packed collection of flowers and greenery, tucked inside the walls of the Baluarte de Santiago, suggests fairies. Even if you don't see any, it's a beautiful refuge from the honks and fumes of the nearby Circuito de Baluartes. *(At C. 8 and 51. Open M-Sa 9am-9pm, Su 9am-4pm. 20 pesos, Mexican citizens 10 pesos.)*

**CASA SEIS.** Right on the main park, opposite the Cathedral, Casa Seis is a beautifully restored 16th-century mansion with period-appropriate tiled floors and furniture. There's also a library, focused mostly on Yucatec history. The staff rents walking audio tours of the historic *centro* for 100 pesos. *(C. 57 6. ☎816 1782; www.campechetravel.com. Open daily 9am-9pm. 5 pesos.)*

**IGLESIA DE SAN FRANCISCO Y ANTIGUO CONVENTO.** This church, built in 1546 on an ancient Mayan foundation, marks the site of the first Mesoamerican Catholic mass in 1517 and the site of the baptism of Hernán Cortés's grandson. The three differently sized bells atop the Renaissance-style church toll for humility, obedience, and chastity—though it's not clear which is for which. Ask the caretaker to open the gate to the roof for a view. *(On Alemán, about 1km northwest of the centro. Open daily 8am-noon. Free.)*

**TEMPLO DE NUESTRA SEÑORA DE LA PURÍSIMA CONCEPCIÓN.** Francisco de Montejo initially ordered the construction of Campeche's cathedral in 1540, but the massive structure was not completed until 1705. The marble altar, stained-glass windows around the vaulted chapel, and Renaissance paintings are worth a look. The cathedral is at its best at night, when the towers are lit. *(In the central park. Open daily 6am-9pm. Daily mass 7pm. Free.)*

**PARQUE ECOLÓGICO.** This city park houses a zoo with native animals (crocodiles, turtles, monkeys, snakes) and picnic space. If you want a break from the city for an afternoon, this is the place to do it. *(Tours of the wildlife leave M-F 9:30am and 11:30am, Sa-Su 10:30, 11:30am, 12:30pm. From Fuerte de San Miguel, turn right at the top of the hill. Open Tu-F 9am-1pm and Sa-Su 10am-4pm. 10 pesos.)*

**MANSIÓN CARVAJAL.** Perhaps the most extravagant building in all of Campeche, this mansion stands as a striking reminder of the city's rich past as a center of commerce. Built in the 18th century by Rafael Carvajal Yturralde, who owned the most prosperous *hacienda* in the area, it features Moorish arches, Tuscan columns, wrought iron window coverings, and traditional black-and-white marble floors. Today, the government agency **DIF** (Integral Family Development) is based here. *(C. 10 14, between C. 53 and 51. Open M-F 8am-3pm. Free.)*

**BEACHES.** Downtown Campeche lacks a conventional beach. To get closer to the water, flag down a bus in front of the post office and head to **Playa Bonita** (30min., every 20min., 5 pesos). Maintained by a wall with stairs leading to the water, the hard-packed, dirty sand fills up quickly in the summer. Several artificial sand bars allow you to lounge around in the water. Entrance to the *balneario* of the same name is 5 pesos. *(Palapa rental 20 pesos. Open daily 9am-5pm.)* For a more beautiful beach without services, try **Seyba Playa,** 29km away.

**ECO-ADVENTURES.** Campeche's upstart tourist industry has created a few eco-adventure options near town. For information on tours and directions, call tour operators directly. **Turtlecamp Xpicob** offers interactive tours in turtle-rich mangrove swamps. *(Highway Mex. 180 at km 185. ☎812 5887 and 152 1800.)* **Campamento Ecotouristico Yax-Ha** offers kayak and walking tours into the Yucatán bush. *(☎819 3470.)* **Expediciones Ecoturísticos de Campeche** has mangrove tours by kayak. *(☎111 2179.)*

# ♫ ❀ ENTERTAINMENT AND FESTIVALS

Traditional music fills the air of Campeche almost every night. The city sponsors various outdoor events, such as the **sound-and-light show** at **Puerta de Tierra,** which tells the story of the *campechanos* staving off foolhardy pirates. Weather permitting, documentary film clips and eight actors keep the 80-minute show exciting. (On C. 59 and 18. 8:30pm; July to mid-Aug. and during *Semana Santa* M-Sa, the rest of the year Tu and F-Sa. 50 pesos.) The state band, local trios, and dance groups perform in the *parque principal.* (Sa-Su 6pm-11pm.) The **Casa de Cultura Seis,** off the main park, hosts Bingo. (Sa-Su 5-9pm. 1 peso per board.) More events are scheduled during the high season (July-Aug. and Dec.); ask for a program at the tourist information center (p. 63). On quieter nights, families, couples, and kids jog and ride bikes along the *malecón.* Admire the musical fountain (daily performances at 7, 8, 9pm) next to the main park on C. 8 by C. 53.

*Campechanos* celebrate the **feast of San Francisco,** the city's patron saint, beginning on October 4. Another popular festival, the **Feria de San Román** (Sept. 14-31), has been celebrated for over 400 years in the neighborhood of the same name.

## ◪ NIGHTLIFE

Bars are few and far between in the *centro.*

**Iguana Azul,** C. 55 11 x 10 y 12 (☎816 3979). Billiards and live music. Serves huge specialty drinks for 35 pesos. Beer 16 pesos. Open Th 5pm-2am, F-Sa 7pm-2am.

**Captain Lafitte's** (☎816 2233), inside Hotel del Mar at C. 59 and the shore. For a full night and a lively crowd, try Captain Lafitte's, complete with costumed waiters, indoor moats, and wooden boat decor. Music and dancing kick off late in the evening. Live DJ Sa. Open Su-Th 7pm-2am, F-Sa 7pm-3am.

**El Zaguán,** on C. 59 between C. 10 and 12. Benches, tables, walls and ceiling all made out of the same dark red wood. A big, flashing jukebox helps lighten the mood. Most patrons are men. Beer 20 pesos. Open daily mid-evening to 2am.

## ◪ DAYTRIPS FROM CAMPECHE

### EDZNÁ

*Catch a combi in the lot between the park and the market. Combis run from Campeche to Pich (50min., 13 per day, 30 pesos). Be sure to ask the driver when he will return (last bus 4pm). An ADO bus also makes the trip from Campeche (Tu-Su 7am, 12:30pm; round-trip 100 pesos). Site open daily 8am-5pm. 41 pesos. Bring bug repellent and water. Allow a minimum of 1-2hr. to visit the site. Pack a lunch, as there are no on-site food vendors.*

Once the most important city in western Campeche, Edzná provided a vital link between the Puuc region and other sights to the north. The word "Edzná" may relate to the Itzáes, a surname that now refers to a group of people native to southwestern Campeche, who spread throughout the Yucatán during the late Classic and post-Classic periods. The site, settled in the middle of the pre-Classic period, covers 25 sq. km. Edzná once had a unique rainwater distribution system composed of an elaborate network of 29 canals, 27 reservoirs, and more than 70 *chultunes* (manmade water cisterns that channeled, drained, and stored rainwater). The crown jewel of the ruins is the **Edificio de Cinco Pisos** (Building of the Five Floors), which towers over the surrounding valley from atop the magnificent **Gran Acrópolis** (31m), a large base that supports several structures. Built in five stages, the Edificio's 65 stairs—some adorned with hieroglyphics over 1300 years old—lead to tiers of columns crowned by a five-room temple. This temple once housed a stela with an engraving of the corn god. The sun illuminated the stela twice yearly, signaling planting (May 2-3) and harvesting (August 9). From its heights, you can observe a dense, green jungle and a few small green mounds on the horizon, which are actually unexcavated ruins. Next to the Edificio is the architecturally intriguing **Templo del Norte**, remodeled at least four times over 1100 years. The east side of the Gran Acrópolis faces the 135m wide stairway of **Nohoch-Ná** (Large House), which functioned as an administrative center as well as a stadium for events. Be sure to see the remains of the **ball court**—although the hoops are now gone, the narrow space between the sloped sides allows you to imagine the scene from the participants' point of view centuries ago. Nearby, under a *palapa*, the **Temple of Masks** has two painted stucco reliefs of the sun god, representing sunrise and sunset. The crossed or squinted eyes and flattened foreheads on the incredibly well-preserved masks are typical of the Maya and were considered a sign of beauty. The **Small Acropolis** is the oldest group of buildings at the site, but the **Patio de los Embajadores** near its entrance is a modern addition. It takes its name from the many ambassadors who have visited the site since it began employing Guatemalan refugees to help with the reconstruction in 1986. The path to the right of the entrance provides a nice walk but ends in a small group of ruins that look minuscule by comparison.

# XPUJIL ☎983

Blink as you cruise down Mex. 186 and you might miss Xpujil (pop. 3000). A pit stop on the Chetumal-Campeche trucking route, it is not one of the prettiest towns in Mexico, and makes the guidebooks primarily because it's the only town of any size in the Rio Bec region, providing access to the numerous sites in the area. The forests here are riddled with ruins, many of which are just starting to be excavated and remain inaccessible to tourists. The ones that are open are among the most stunning in the Yucatán, huge cities set in dense forest, where the elites waged war on rivals Palenque and Tikal and impressed their neighbors with lavishly decorated palaces. The experience is enhanced thanks to bumpy roads and a lack of public transport, which leave the stones largely untrammeled by tourists. The only reason to visit Xpujil is to hire taxis or stock up on supplies before hitting the ruins. Travelers with their own transport would do best to camp in the Reserva Calakmul, 2 hours west, or at one of the accommodations further along the highway.

## ◼ TRANSPORTATION

Xpujil's **ADO bus station** (☎871 6027; www.ado.com.mx), inside the restaurant La Victoria, marks the center of town and the crossroads of highways 186 and 261. Buses here service **Campeche** (4hr; 4, 6, 10:30am, 1:45, 1:55, 4:05pm; 198 pesos); **Cancún** (10am, 10:30pm; 324 pesos); **Chetumal** (2hr; 11:10am, 2, 2:50, 4:05pm; 84 pesos); **Escarcega** (1hr; 10 daily, mostly in the early evening; 102 pesos); and **Mexico City** (1:15, 6:15, 9:45pm; 962 pesos).

**Taxi:** The ruins are not accessible by public transport. Travelers who do not want to take a tour or rent a car must hire a taxi. (871 6101.) Drivers charge 100 pesos per hr for waiting. 3hr. roundtrip to Calakmul and Balamkú 800 pesos. One way to Becán 36 pesos. One way to Chicanná 45 pesos. 3hr. roundtrip to Dzibanché and Kohunlich 800 pesos.

The gas stations just east of Xpujil are the last drivers will see for quite some kilometers. Those with dwindling supplies of gasoline should fill up.

**EARLY BIRD CATCHES THE WORM.** Even the most efficient traveler cannot see all the ruins in one day without starting at the crack of dawn from Xpujil or the Reserva. Prepare to spend at least one night in the region. The most practical routes combine Calakmul and Balamkú, or Becán, Chicanná, el Hormiguero, and Xpujil.

## ORIENTATION AND PRACTICAL INFORMATION

**Tourist Office:** Located about 2km west of Xpujil, this deserted-looking "parador turistico" has helpful maps of the area. 104 9641; www.calakmul.gob.mx. Open daily 11am-6pm.

**Police:** ☎871 6105.

**Red Cross:** ☎132 2788. Open M-Th 7am-3pm.

**Pharmacy:** Across from the taxis. ☎891 6254. Open daily 7am-10pm.

**Supermarket: Super Willy's** (☎871 6245), a short walk west of the bus station. Open daily 7am-10pm.

**Laundry: Lavandería Calakmul,** close to the Xpujil ruins. Open M-Sa 7am-3pm. 15 pesos per kg.

**Internet: Mundo Maya,** just east of the bus station. Open M-Th and Su 7am-10:30pm, F 7am-6pm, Sa 6-10:30pm. 10 pesos per hr.

**Post Office:** Open M-F 6am-3pm. **Postal Code:** 240624.

## ACCOMMODATIONS AND FOOD

The best accommodations in town can be found at the **Hotel-Restaurant Calakmul ❸,** a 10min. walk west from the bus stop on the highway. Clean rooms in a modern building surround a grassy courtyard; for fewer pesos, there are cramped *cabañas* with dubious beds. (☎871 6029. *Cabañas* 250 pesos; rooms 470 pesos, with TV 600 pesos.)

Those who want a cheaper, more picturesque base should try **Zoh Laguna,** a quiet village 10km north void of telephone lines and full of sedate oak trees. To get to Zoh Laguna,pay 10 pesos for a communal taxi on 50 pesos for a private one. Driving, it's 10km north; look for the intersection just past the bus station. **El Viajero ❷,** on the town's main road, just before Hotel del Bosque, has simple rooms with private bath, hot water, and TV. There is a small restaurant attached. (☎114 9779. Doubles 150 pesos, with A/C 250 pesos.)

The cheapest rooms can be found in the bright red **Cabañas "Don Jorgito" ❶,**Carreterra Escarcega-Chetumal km 153, just across from the Xpujil ruins. You get what you pay for–small double beds with slimy, synthetic bedding. (☎871 6128. No hot water. Reception 7am-11pm. 100 pesos per cabaña.)

For food, the highway strip has a number of 24hr. places with heaping, trucker-size portions. The **Mirador Maya ❷,** Av. Calakmul No. 94, close to the ruins, has an extensive and affordable menu. Your meal may come cheap here, but the internet costs, 20 pesos. (Breakfast 30-40 pesos; *antojitos* 12-60 pesos. Open daily 7am-10pm. MC/V.)

The best way to see all the ruins and sleep comfortably is to book a room at ▧**Rio Bec Dreams ❸,** Carretera 186 Escarcega-Chetumal km142. Large *cabañas* with private bath have nice beds with comforter, crisp sheets, and mosquito netting. The shared bathroom comes with plush towels and bathmats. (*Cabañas* 950-1100 pesos. Cash only.) The hotel also organizes tours to local sites. (Chicanná 250 pesos, Becán 450 pesos, Calakmul 1500 pesos.) The hotel res-

**taurant** has appetizing international food. (Entrees 95-150 pesos. Open daily 8am-9pm, but mostly for breakfast and dinner.)

## 👁 ⚠ SIGHTS AND ACTIVITIES

**XPUJIL RUINS.** Estructuras IV and II preview the lavish residential decoration on display in Chicanná. Look for details like the small niches in **Estructura IV**, evidence of rods that used to hang cotton drapes, or the red paint to the left of the label on **Estructura II**, the last vestige of former grandeur. The largest building on the site is **Estructura I**, recognizable by the signature Rio Bec towers shooting from its base. Local high schoolers routinely clamber to the top; less-intrepid visitors will probably keep two feet on the ground. *(The ruins are an easy, walk west on the highway from the bus station. Open daily 8am-5pm. 37 pesos.)*

**EL HORMIGUERO.** The ruins at El Hormiguero date from Classical period and were at their height between AD 600 and 800. Discovered 1933, El Horminguero became known as "the anthill." This reference concerns the insects that cut busily across the grounds. The site contains two buildings. The first, **Estructura II,** is notable for its giant snake-mouth door (similar to the one found at Chicanná) and the restored stucco around the back. A bit farther from the entrance, **Estructura V** is the site of an old temple. The access road has fallen into disrepair, making this a spot reserved for ruin enthusiasts. *(The ruins lie about 1hr. outside of Xpujil, 14km south from the Xpujil intersection, and another 8km west down a pothole-ridden road. Open daily 8am-5pm. 24 pesos.)*

## 📰 THE RESERVA DE LA BIOSFERA CALAKMUL

Calakmul's two **pyramids** climb high above the forest canopy. Literally, "adjacent mounds" in Maya, the site's most famous landmarks will leave knees trembling, whether its due to a fear of heights or the sheer effort it takes to make it to the top. Though the chicle adventurer Cyrus Longworth Lundell first spotted the place in 1931 (it's hard to imagine the pyramid's "hiding" for even that long), large scale excavations did not begin until the 1980s. Excavations have unearthed more than 120 stelae, many of which have been deciphered by archeologists. These huge stone slabs tell the history of one of the capital city of the **Kingdom of the Serpent Head** (Cabeza de Serpiente), which fought with Palenque and Tikal for control of southern Yucatán. Calakmul was first inhabited in the sixth century BC, with its highest populations recorded during the AD seventh century under the reign of **Yukom the Great** and his son, **Jaguar Claw.** Jaguar Claw's name appears on stelae found at Tikal and Palenque (p. 212); his eventual defeat at Tikal in 695 is depicted in a frieze there. In addition to the stelae and buildings, archeologists have recovered a number of valuables—jade masks, pearls, conches, murals—many of which are on display in Campeche.

From the entrance, it's a 1km walk to the ruins. They lie in five groups: **Grupo Suroeste, Gran Acropolis, Acropolis Norte, Pequeña Acropolis,** and **Grupo Noreste.** Each of these show the influence of the Chenes and Peten styles. A short route heads directly to the impressive **Gran Plaza,** with the grand **Estructura II.** The long tour winds east along the back wall, through a residential compound, reaching its climax at the pyramids. Allow 3-4hr. to explore the grounds thoroughly.

The **Reserva de la Biosfera Calakmul,** created in 1989, is a remote, tropical jungle. Its 180,000 acres encompass savannah, forest, and swamp; it is second in size only to Sian Ka'an (p. 172). The territory supports a rich array of plant and animal species, a large number of which are endangered. In addition to spider and howler monkeys, tapirs, and more than 235 different kinds of birds, South America's giant cats prowl the territory, a fact that should make solo travelers

CAMPECHE

think twice before exploring on their own. There are some short trails accessible through the campsite. At km 27, a 1km path leads to a lake where it is possible to observe alligators. Km 28 marks a "*Sendero interpretivo*" from which you can observe spider monkeys and other wildlife.

**Camping is forbidden inside the ruins.** People with camping gear can set up tents at km 20, near the park service station. Inside the park, **Hospedaje Ecologico,** at km 7 offers accommodations. (☎983 871 6064. Tent space 70 pesos per person; rental tents 200 pesos. Bike rental 150 pesos per day.) The Hospedaje also runs the **Restaurant Oxte'tun ●,** which charges double what you can find outside the park. (Soda 20 pesos; quesadillas 65 pesos, eggs and *comida del día* 75 pesos. Open daily 7am-9pm. Cash only.)

*(The ruins lie 56km west of Xpujil on Carreterra 186 and 60km south into the Reserva de Calakmul. From the highway, a winding road leads south to the ruins; the trip will take at least two hours. Ruins open daily 8am-5pm. The only way to visit these ruins is though a tour company, or by private car or taxi (800 pesos from Xpujil). Guides can be organized through the Servidores Turísticos o Guías Locales. ☎987 0684. 2hr. tour 300 pesos for two people; longer tours 400-500 pesos. Vehicles that enter the park are registered, and charged a fee of 40 pesos per car and 40 pesos per passenger. Hold onto the ticket, as it will permit you to exit and re-enter should you want to explore the park for longer than a day. 51 pesos.)*

 **TWO HANDS ON THE WHEEL.** Drive slowly in this area. Pheasants and other wildlife are known to burst onto the road without warning from the dense jungle.

## BALAMKÚ

Most visitors to Balamkú, the "Jaguar Temple," make a beeline for the last building. The door on the left provides access to a beautifully preserved panel with iconography representing fertility and the life cycle. Two kings, cloaked in animal skins, sit astride rotund amphibious figures that represent the connection between the world of the living and the world of the dead. To each side, a jaguar, the symbol of the sun and war, writhes. The room must be unlocked by a park attendant. The reliefs, which date from the early classic period (250-600 AD), were only discovered in 1990; many of the site's other buildings have yet to be excavated. *(Just 2km past Calakmul on highway 186. The turn off is badly marked. Turn just before the Restaurant-Hospedaje La Selva. Open daily 8am-5pm. 31 pesos.)*

## BECÁN

Becán's grounds, 25 hectares surrounded by a moat, resemble a medieval town. Discovered in 1934, its name means "Ravine formed by water," and the grounds are rife with staircases and narrow passageways. The first buildings at Becán date from 550 BC; the site was not abandoned until AD 1200. The tops of the pyramids provide views of rolling farmland and forest; you'll definitely hear cows bellow in the background. A well-labeled path, which takes about 1½hr. to complete, takes visitors to the main buildings. *(8km west of Xpujil and 500m north of the highway. Open daily 8am-5pm. 41 pesos.)*

## CHICANNÁ

Discovered in 1969, Chicanná served as the tiny suburb for Becán's elite families, who displayed their wealth in lavish home decoration. The mansions here incorporate styles from around the region. The first building, **Estructura XX,** is adorned with many Chaac masks. The mask of Itzamná is an example of the Chenes style.

A path leads toward the **main plaza.** The two tall towers on **Estructura I** to the west, are an example of Rio Bec architecture. Across the plaza lies Chicanná's most famous building, ▨ **Estructura II,** the source of the site's name, which means "House of the Serpent Mouth." Stone jaws the size of a human head guard the door, a representation of Itzamná, who according to Mayan mythology, was a priest and the creator of mankind. Some of the original red paint is still visible inside. *(11km west of Xpujil, and a 400m jog south from the carretera. Open daily 8am-5pm. 37 pesos.)*

## DZIBANCHÉ

Dzibanché's large structures date from the Mayan Classic Period (300-900 AD). Its main attractions are the many **temple-topped pyramids,** which provide one of the best workouts on the peninsula.

Edificio VI, **The Palace of the Lintels,** is the structure that gave Dzibanché its name. The temple at the top of this large pyramid has two rooms, the ceilings of which are supported by wooden beams (the eponymous lintels). A sharp-eyed climber, undaunted by the temple's thriving community of bees, can glimpse a calendrical inscription from 733 AD on the right (south) side.

From Edificio VI, the path swings left, past the **Palacio de los Tucanes** (Tucan Palace) to the **Plaza Gann.** The site is named for Thomas Gann, the British archeologist who explored the site in the 1920s. The most interesting building here is Edificio XIII, the **Templo de los Cautivos,** identifiable by the thatched roof partway up the stairs. The hut protects friezes depicting prisoners of war in various degrees of torment; these carvings have led archeologists to believe that Dzibanché's society was very militaristic. Archeologists also believe Dzibanche was possibly the direct predecessor to Calakmul in Campeche. **Edificio II,** the tallest structure at Dzibanché, lies straight ahead. This is the burial grounds of the the Lord of Dzibanché (el Señor de Dzibanché). A path up the side leads to the elevated **Plaza Xibalbá,** "Plaza of the Underworld", which is named for the burial monuments that ring its sides. Edificio I, **Templo de Buho** (Temple of the Owl), is the massive pyramid crowned by two columns. During its excavation, archeologists found a staircase leading to an inner chamber believed to be the tomb of a wealthy woman.

To get to **Kinich-ná,** the final pyramid at Dzibanché, you drive back toward the park entrance. The turn-off is on the right; the ruins lie 2km north. Trees sprout from the massive steps of this equally massive acropolis, marked by five temples and tombs. Once richly painted and decorated with stucco representations of Mayan gods, the pyramid's name comes from a sculpture of the sun god once found at the top. Scaling the summit affords a view of the surrounding farmland. *(Located 72km from Chetumal, Dzibanché cannot be reached by public transportation. Taxis from Chetumal charge 800 pesos round-trip; this includes the wait. Taxis from Xpujil also cost 800 pesos. If you are driving from Chetumal, head west on Carreterra 186 for 44km, turning north after the sign. It's another bumpy 24km, the last five of which proceed on unpaved, suspension-busting terrain. The ticket center is located 1km before the ruins themselves; after registering, continue straight to the parking lot. You'll pass the turn-off to Kinich-na on your left. Set aside at least 1hr. to tour the well-labeled site. Open daily 8am-5pm. 41 pesos.)*

## KOHUNLICH

Kohunlich receives more visitors than nearby Dzibanché, as much because of its well-maintained access road as for the impressive masks that adorn one of its main temples. Many of the buildings here reveal the influence of the Rio Bec style. Based on a mural found at the site, archeologists believe that Kohunlich was governed by a cadre of elites; they speculate that this may explain the absence of one giant temple. The cause of Kohunlich's decline remains a mystery, but the end came suddenly and was accompanied by an unusual amount of ritualistic activity, recorded in offerings and human sacrifice. These rituals and offerings were performed in temples and private homes. Nature has taken a toll on Kohunlich's ruins. The ruins, which encompass nearly 21 acres, still contain unexcavated mounds.

Most of what is known about the site comes from the excavation of the **Plaza de las Estelas,** the large plot of green visible at the entrance. A stagnant pool of water is a reminder of the once impressive irrigation system. On the left lie the remains of the northwest residential complex, with some traces of the original paint; the **Acropolis,** straight ahead, is Kohunlich's largest building. Veering right leads to **Plaza Merwin,** named for the explorer who originally discovered the site. Majestic Cohune palms, valued for their oil-rich nuts shade the plaza, and are the source of Kohunlich's name.

Continue through the **ball court** to the **27 Escalones.** This was once a palace for the Kohunlich nobility. The steps are carpeted with a lush moss layer and lead to rooms. The circular stone pits were once wells, another reminder of the impressive irrigation system that once functioned here.

From the 27 *Escalones*, follow signs through the jungle to the ▧**Templo de los Mascarones.** The masks, which represent a dazzling 8-foot tall Kinich Ahau (the sun god), date from AD 500 and are in the Peten style. Five masks have been fully restored; the sixth was stolen by looters. *(From Chetumal, Kohunlich is 3km past the Dzibanché turn-off, then another 8.5km south. The site, which lies a short walk through the jungle from the ticket office, takes about an hour to see properly. Taxis from Xpujíl or Chetumal charge about 800 pesos round trip. Tours from Chetumal run about US$80 per person. Open daily 8am-5pm. 49 pesos.)*

# YUCATÁN STATE

While Quintana Roo has surpassed the Yucatán State as the economic center of the region, Yucatán still takes the cake in terms of historical and cultural richness. At the forefront of this abundance is **Chichén Itzá** (p. 111), the most heavily-touristed Mayan ruin in the peninsula, and for good reason. It is here that the brilliance and creativity of the Maya is best displayed. The jam-packed streets of **Mérida** (p. 76), the state's capital, remind you that the Yucatán is a modern state keeping up with the hustle and bustle of the twentieth century. Still, Mérida is anything but devoid of historical significance. Named after the city by the same name in Extremadura, Spain, the city represents an amalgamation of Mayan and Spanish colonial culture. The Spanish built the city on the site of the Mayan city of T'hó; they reused some of the city's ruins to build Mérida.

Big cities are not all the Yucatán has to offer. The small fishing village of **Celestún** (p. 91), is a must-see. Chill on its estuary **Isla de Pájaros** with thousands of flamingos. In **Izamal** (p. 108), visit the enormous ochre Convento de San Antonio de Padua. If you're looking for some Mayan ruins, but want to avoid the crowds of Chichén Itzá, pay a visit to **La Ruta Puuc** (p. 96). **Uxmal** (p. 101), a breathtaking site in the midst of jungle, is a UNESCO World Heritage site and is the perfect place to discover the rich history of the local Maya

## MÉRIDA                                              ☎999

A teeming center of food and culture, Mérida (pop. 1.7 million) is the hub of the Yucatán Peninsula. With a rich blend of indigenous history, colonial influence, and modern international flavor, the city is the oldest continuously settled place on the peninsula, known to the Maya as T'ho ("Place of the Fifth Point" in Mayan), then to the Spanish as the "The Very Noble and Very Loyal City of Mérida." The modern city was built in 1542 by Francisco de Montejo. During the nineteenth century, a boom in *henequén* (a hemp-like fiber) fueled city growth, and an aristocracy began to settle here. Mérida earned the title of Ciudad Blanca (the white city) for the white splendor of its stucco center. Modern Mérida continues to serve as an important center of culture and business. The city strikes a balance between old and new, the international influences and tourists side by side with locals and traditional customs. Mérida's commercial centers burst with *jipis* (Panama hats) shipped from Campeche, hammocks from Tixcocob, and *henequén* from all over the peninsula. The ever-crowded *zócalo* is the hub of the city and the site of frequent public *fiestas*, especially on Sundays, when families, musicians, dancers, and food vendors come out to enjoy the city. For independent travelers, Mérida serves as a comfortable, cosmopolitan, and budget-friendly base to explore Mayan ruins, inland *cenotes*, and the coast.

**CROSSTOWN TRAFFIC.** Addresses in Mérida are given using an "x" to separate the main street from the cross streets, and "y" ("and" in Spanish) to separate the two cross streets if the address falls in the middle of the block. Thus "54 509 x 61 y 63" reads "C. 54 509, between C. 61 and C. 63."

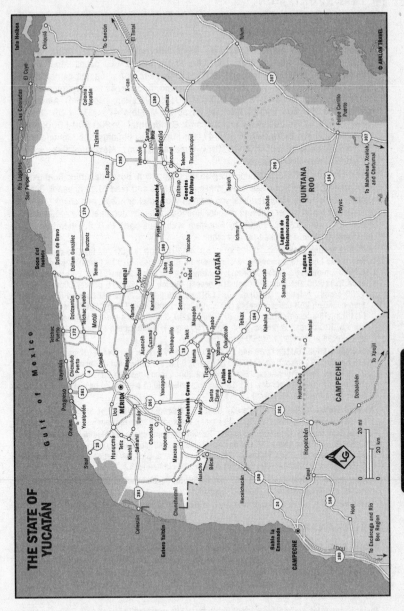

THE STATE OF YUCATÁN

YUCATÁN STATE

© AVALON TRAVEL

## ▐ TRANSPORTATION

### INTERCITY TRANSPORTATION

**Flights: Licenciado Manuel Crecencio Rejon International Airport (MID;** ☎946 1530), 7km southwest on Mex. 180. Taxis to the *centro* 110 pesos. Most airline offices are on Paseo Montejo and in Plaza Americana, the shopping center in the Hotel Fiesta Americana. MID services: **Aeroméxico,** C. 56 N. 451 at Av. Colón, in the Plaza Americana (☎964 1780 or 800 021 4010; www.aeromexico.com); **American Airlines** (☎800 904 6000); **Aviacsa,** Paseo de Montejo 475 x 37 y 39 (☎925 6890 or 800 006 2200; www.aviacsa.com); **Continental** (☎800 900 5000; www. continental.com); **Delta** (☎800 123 4710); **Mexicana,** Prolongación Montejo 91 X 17 (☎924 6633 or 800 801 2010; www.mexicana.com); **MexicanaClick** (☎800 112 5425; www.click.com.mx).

**Buses:** Leave from 5 stations depending on the destination. Buses departing from terminals other than the first-class CAME make more stops and tend to be cheaper. Before setting out, confirm which terminal you want at your hotel or hostel, and check to see if a *colectivo* would better suit your purpose. Mérida's 2 largest terminals are southwest of the *centro.* The *zócalo* is 15min. by foot from both. Walk north to C. 63, then turn right and walk another 4 blocks from the other.

**1st-class station (CAME):** C. 70 555 x 71 (☎924 8391). **ADO** (☎800 702 8000; www.ado.com. mx) sends buses to **Campeche** (2½hr., every hr. 6am-11:45pm, 136 pesos); **Cancún** (every hr. 6:30am-midnight, 300-350pesos); **Chetumal** (4 per day 7:30am-11pm, 280 pesos); **Chichén Itzá** (6:30, 9:15am, 12:40pm; 100 pesos); **Mexico City** (22hr., 6 per day 10am-9:15pm, 1200 pesos); **Palenque** (8:30am, 10, 11:50pm; 364 pesos); **Playa del Carmen** (10 per day, 5am-midnight, 258 pesos); **Puebla** (20hr., 4:30pm, 1000 pesos); **San Cristóbal de las Casas** (7:15pm, 434 pesos); **Tulum** (6:30, 10:40am, 12:40, 5:45pm; 194 pesos); **Valladolid** (2hr., 11 per day, 120 pesos); **Veracruz** (15hr., 9pm, 730 pesos); **Villahermosa** (10hr.; 14 per day, most in late night or evening; 426-500 pesos).

**2nd-class station (TAME):** C. 69 544 x 68 y 70 (☎923 2287). To: **Campeche** (92 pesos); **Cancún** (35 per day, 194 pesos); **Chichén Itzá** (6 per day, 54 pesos); **Playa del Carmen** (7 per day, 160-214 pesos); **Ruta Puuc** (leaves 8am, returns 2:30pm; round-trip with 30min. stop at each ruin; 140 pesos); **Tulum** (8 per day, 121-186 pesos); **Valladolid** (6 per day, 74 pesos) **Uxmal** (1¼hr., 5 per day 8am-5pm, 40 pesos).

**Noreste Station:** C. 50 531 x 67 (☎924 6355). To: **Celestún** (2hr., every hr. 5:15am-8:30pm, 41 pesos); **Izamal** (every hr. 7am-9pm, 30 pesos); **Mayapán** (1½hr., 8:30am and 4pm, 15 pesos); **Piste** (2hr., every hr. 6am-8pm, 55 pesos); **Tizimín** with connections to **Chiquilá** (Isla Holbox); **Río Lagartos,** and **San Felipe** (16 per day, 65-83 pesos); **Valladolid** (3hr., every hr. 6am-midnight, 90 pesos) and other smaller towns. *Colectivos* wait just outside the station and run to **Cuzama** (1½hr., every 30min. 8am-6pm, 14 pesos) with stops in **Acanceh.**

**Autoprogreso Station:** C. 62 x 65 y 67 (☎928 3965). Sends buses to **Dzibilchaltun** (30min., 7 pesos) and **Progreso** (every 20min., 13 pesos).

**San Juan:** Sends buses and *colectivos* south to **Ticul** and towns along the Ruta Puuc.

### LOCAL TRANSPORTATION

**Public Transportation: Municipal buses** run daily (6am-midnight, 5 pesos). Buses usually drop you within a few blocks of your destination. The destinations listed on the windshield provide an approximate route. *Taxis colectivos* (also known as *combis* or *camiones*) charge 5 pesos for any destination in the city; drop-offs are on a first-come, first-serve basis.

**Taxis:** Some taxis are metered, identifiable by the **"taximetro"** sign on top. Others charge by zone, charging about 30-40 pesos for a trip within the *centro.* They do not generally roam the streets. **Taximetro** (☎928 3031 or 945 7500.) For a shorter wait, call one of

YUCATÁN STATE

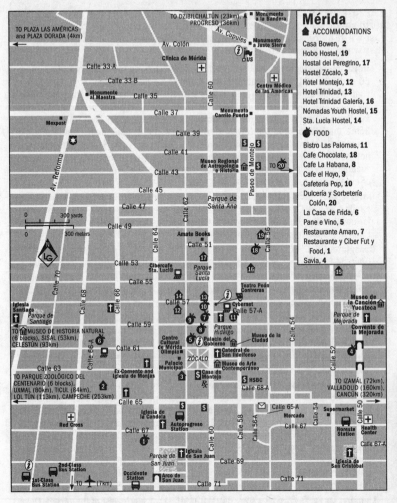

**Mérida**

**ACCOMMODATIONS**

Casa Bowen, 2
Hobo Hostel, 19
Hostal del Peregrino, 17
Hostel Zócalo, 3
Hotel Montejo, 12
Hotel Trinidad, 13
Hotel Trinidad Galería, 16
Nómadas Youth Hostel, 15
Sta. Lucia Hostel, 14

**FOOD**

Bistro Las Palomas, 11
Cafe Chocolate, 18
Cafe La Habana, 8
Cafe el Hoyo, 9
Cafetería Pop, 10
Dulcería y Sorbetería
  Colón, 20
La Casa de Frida, 6
Pane e Vino, 5
Restaurante Amaro, 7
Restaurante y Ciber Fut y
  Food, 1
Savia, 4

the others at **Radio Taxis Grupo** (☎982 1504 or 1171). Stands are located around the *parques*, along Paseo de Montejo, at the airport, and in the *zócalo*.

**Car Rental:** Mérida has a proliferation of car agencies, including the standard international agencies. *Yucatán Today* sometimes offers coupons.

## ORIENTATION AND PRACTICAL INFORMATION

Mérida sits on the west side of Yucatán state, 30km south of the Gulf of Mexico. The *zócalo* (also known as the Plaza Grande), bordered by C. 60, 61, 62, and 63, anchors the historic center, splitting the city in half. Recent growth has fueled increasing urban sprawl. Traditionally wealthy areas stretch north along a series of bank-lined roads, culminating at the Yucatán Country Club. In the south, government housing projects fill impoverished neighborhoods such as

San Jose Tecoh, home of the municipal prison. Even-numbered streets run north-south, with numbers increasing to the west; odd-numbered streets run east-west, increasing to the south. Most attractions and services are within easy walking distance from the *zócalo*.

**Tourist Information:** ☎942 0000. On the Plaza Grande, in the **Palacio Municipal,** C. 60 (☎930 3101; www.yucatan.travel). Open M-Sa 8am-8pm, Su 8am-2pm. Offers guided tours of the *zócalo* (1½hr., daily 9:30am, free). Rents audio tours with walking tour maps of the *centro histórico*. (4hr. 80 pesos, 20 pesos per extra hr.) Other locations include **Palacio del Gobierno,** C. 61. (open M-Sa 8am-9pm, Su 8am-8pm), the **Teatro Peón Contreras,** C. 62 (☎924 3954; open daily 8am-9pm), and near the US consulate (open daily 8am-8pm). The tourist offices, most museums and hotels, and many restaurants distribute copies of the invaluable *Yucatán Today* (www.yucatantoday.com), a bilingual city guide that provides detailed city maps, schedules of events, and coupons for ✂free margaritas.

**Travel Agency: Yucatán Trails,** C. 62 482 x 57 y 59 (☎928 2582 or 5913; www.yucatantrails.com.mx). Canadian owner Denis Lafoy is a great source for info and hosts parties for travelers the 1st F of every month. Check the agency or *Yucatán Today* for details. Open M-F 9am-7pm, Sa 9am-1pm.

**Consulate: US,** C. 60 330 x 29 y 31 (☎942 5759, emergency switchboard 942 5700). Open M-F 9:30am-1:30pm. Emergency hours for American citizens M-F 7:30am-4:30pm. Closed Mexican and American holidays, and the 2nd and 4th W every month.

**Banks: Banamex** (☎924 1011), in Casa de Montejo on the Plaza Grande. Has a **24hr. ATM.** through the courtyard. Open M-Sa 9am-4pm. Other banks cluster on Paseo de Montejo and C. 65.

**American Express:** Paseo de Montejo 492 x 41 y 43 (☎942 8200 or 8210 ext. 42201). Open M-F 9am-6pm, Sa 9am-1pm. Money exchange closes 1hr. earlier.

**Luggage Storage: GuardaPlus,** on C. 70 x 69 y 71, at the TAME terminal. Serves 1st-and 2nd-class bus stations. 5-12 pesos per hr. Open 6am-10pm.

**English-Language Bookstores:** ✂**Amate Books,** C. 60 453A x 51 (☎924 2222; www.amatebooks.com). An excellent selection of Mexican classics, travel books, and translations of Latin American novels. Also offers a secondhand book section. Open Tu-Su 10:30am-1:30pm and 3:30-8:30pm. **English Language Library,** C. 53 524 x 66 y 68 (☎924 8401; www.meridaenglishlibrary.com) is a good stop for those in town for a bit longer. Open M 9am-1pm and 6:30-9pm, Tu-F 9am-1pm, Sa 10am-1pm. Those looking to read in Spanish should head for **Librerías Educal,** C. 60 499 x 59 y 61 (☎930 9485), inside the Teatro Daniel Ayala Pérez. A range of Spanish literature and nonfiction, from classics to contemporary works. Open daily 9am-9pm.

**Laundry: La Fe,** C. 61 518 x 62 y 64 (☎924 4531), 1 block west of the *zócalo*. Open M-F 8am-7pm, Sa 8am-5pm. Another on C. 64 x 57 y 55 (☎252 0702). 50 pesos per 3kg. Open M-F 8am-6pm, Sa 8am-3pm.

**Emergency:** ☎066.

**Police:** Reforma x 39 y 41 (☎925 2034 or 942 0070; tourist police ☎942 0060), accessible by the Reforma bus.

**Red Cross:** C. 68 533 x 65 y 67 (☎065 or 924 9813).

**24hr. Pharmacy: Farmacia YZA,** C. 62 and 63 (☎924 1490), on the *zócalo*. MC/V.

**Medical Services: Centro Médico de las Américas,** C. 54 365 x C. 33A (☎927 3199, ☎926 2111), for serious illnesses. **Clínica de Mérida,** C. 32 242 x 27 y 29 (☎942 1800).

**Internet Access:** Internet cafes are plentiful throughout the city, as is Wi-Fi. **Cibercafe Sta. Luci@,** at C. 62 and 55. 12 pesos per hr. Open daily 8am-midnight.

**Post Office:** C. 53 469 x 52 y 54 (☎928 5404). Open M-F 8am-5pm, Sa 8am-1pm. Mexpost inside. **Postal Code:** 97000.

# ACCOMMODATIONS

For those who love bargains and colonial architecture, accommodations in Mérida will be a treat. What were once elaborate, turn-of-the-century private mansions now offer affordable lodging near the main bus station and the Plaza Grande. The hotels right outside the second-class bus station and a few blocks south of the Plaza have tempting offers, but the neighborhood is something of a red-light district and is not recommended for nocturnal meandering. That said, crime against tourists here is very rare.

**Nómadas Youth Hostel,** C. 62 433 x 51 (☎924 5223; www.nomadastravel.com). Mérida's oldest and most well-known hostel offers clean dorms with soaring ceilings, an outdoor kitchen, patios, live *trova* performances, and free weekday salsa lessons. Trips to *cenotes*, Celestún, and other attractions can be arranged. Ask for a spot toward the back (away from the noisy street) and near a fan. Continental breakfast included. Laundry sinks available. Separate girls' bunk. Bunks 98 pesos. Private en suite doubles start at US$25. Lights out policy at 11pm. Cash only. ❶

**Sta. Lucía Hostel (HI),** C. 55 512 x 62 y 64 (☎928 9070; www.hostelstalucia.com). Mérida's newest hostel joins the already crowded scene with the HI stamp of approval. Separate male and female rooms and a few private A/C-equipped rooms share an immaculate bathroom and a pleasant kitchen/patio space. Private rooms entered through the dorms. Breakfast with eggs and fruit, lockers, and internet included. On-site tourist agent can help set up daytrips to nearby beaches and ruins. Dorm 90 pesos; private rooms 220 pesos. 10% HI discount. Cash only. ❶

**Hostal Zócalo,** C. 63 x 60 y 62 (☎930 9562). One of the best locations in town. Housed in an annex of the Montejo mansion next door. Small dorms with large, soft beds. Cheery communal kitchen. Some rooms have balconies overlooking the busy *zócalo*. The abundance of private rooms accounts for a slightly older clientele. Breakfast and lockers included. Reception 24hr. Check-out noon. Beds 135 pesos; private rooms 280-500 pesos. Cash only. ❶

**Hotel del Peregrino,** C. 51 488 x 54 y 56 (☎924 5491; www.hoteldelperegrino.com), in a bright blue colonial mansion a few blocks from the city center. Former hostel turned upscale, with clean private rooms. Leafy patio, kitchen, and upstairs terrace. Price includes breakfast and Wi-Fi. 1-2 people 490 pesos; 3-4 people 590 pesos; each additional person 120 pesos. ❻

**Hotel Trinidad,** C. 62 464 x 55 y 57 (☎923 2033; www.hotelestrinidad.com). Choose from colonial- or modern-style rooms at this hotel that once appeared in *Art Forum* magazine. Rooftop hot tub, enormous TV with DVD and digital cable, outdoor kitchen, and pool access at a neighboring hotel. Breakfast included. Singles and doubles with fan and shared bath 250 pesos, with private bath 380 pesos, with A/C 400 pesos. 50 pesos per extra person. MC/V. ❸

**Hotel Trinidad Galería,** C. 60 456 x 51 (☎923 2463; www.hotelestrinidad.com). Dusty artwork decorates every nook and cranny of this quirky, overgrown colonial mansion. Clean rooms, each devoted to a different art movement. 2nd fl. rooms have much better light and breeze. Couches and fountain with live turtles in the lobby. Large outdoor pool and Wi-Fi. Reception 8am-9pm. Singles and doubles 350 pesos, with A/C 450 pesos; triples 520 pesos. V. ❺

**Hotel Montejo,** C. 57 507 x 62 y 64 (☎928 0390; www.hotelmontejo.com), 2 blocks north of the *zócalo*. Large wooden doors open into rooms with baths, A/C, TVs, window porticos, and high ceilings with wooden beams. 2nd fl. rooms get more air and light.

YUCATÁN STATE

Lush garden patio and restaurant downstairs. Breakfast included. Free Wi-Fi. Singles 490 pesos; doubles 590 pesos; each additional person 100 pesos. MC/V. ❺

**Casa del Tio Dach,** C. 61 446 x 50 y 52, (☎924 5931; www.lacasadeltiodach.com.mx) Slightly farther from the *zócalo* than other options, Tio Dach doubles as an art gallery, offering small rooms with no windows. Travelers who prefer privacy will like the rooms, which fit 2 people at dorm prices. Breakfast included. Free Wi-Fi. 150 pesos per bed. Cash only. ❶

**Casa Bowen,** C. 66 521B x 65 y 67 (☎928 6109), between the main bus station and the *zócalo*. Slightly aging colonial mansion. Rooms have fans and firm beds. Rooms in the adjoining building are not as attractive, but still comfortable. Parking available. Reservations recommended July-Aug. Singles 180 pesos; doubles 270 pesos, with A/C 400 pesos; each additional person 50 pesos. Cash only. ❷

## ◐ FOOD

As the cultural and political capital of the Yucatán, Mérida's chefs work overtime introducing the uninitiated to the distinctive flavors of the area's Cuban-influenced Yucatec cuisine. Try *sopa de lima* (soup with freshly squeezed lime, chicken, and tortilla), *pollo pibil* (chicken with sour orange and herbs baked in banana leaves), *poc-chuc* (pork steak with pickled onions, doused in sour orange juice), *papadzules* (chopped hard-boiled eggs wrapped in corn tortillas served with pumpkin and tomato sauce), or *huevos motuleños* (refried beans, fried egg, chopped ham, and cheese on a crispy tortilla, garnished with tomato sauce, peas, and fried plantains). The cheapest food is at the **mercado**, particularly on the second floor of the restaurant complex on C. 56A at C. 67. (Open M-Sa 6am-7pm, Su 6am-5pm.) The **Mercado de Santa Ana** at C. 60 and 47 is smaller and much cleaner—the cleanest stalls will be the busiest. (Open M-Sa 6am-8pm, Su 8am-2pm.) A supermarket, **San Francisco de Asís,** C. 65 x 54 y 52, is across from the market in a huge gray building. (☎924 3011. Open M-Sa 7am-9pm, Su 7am-5pm.)

 **TIP**

**THE BIGGER THE SOMBRERO...** Though the streets of Mérida tend to be free of tourist gimmicks, the restaurants don't follow this rule. In Mérida, the bigger and more extravagant the costume of the waiters, the bigger the prices are on the menu.

▨ **La Casa de Frida,** C. 61 526A x 66 y 66-A (☎928 2311). This beautiful addition to Mérida's restaurant scene is host to Mexican specialties like *chile en nogada* (poblano stuffed with ground meat and fruits, covered in a pecan cream sauce and pomegranate; 105 pesos) and creative vegetarian dishes (80 pesos). An attentive staff will make you feel relaxed among the cacti, twinkling lights, and Frida Kahlo reproductions. Entrees 65-130 pesos. Open Tu-Sa 6pm-midnight. Cash only. ❹

**Cafe la Habana,** C. 59 511 x 62 (☎928 6502). This large cafe with A/C and a giant coffee-roasting machine is at the heart of Mérida's vibrant scene. Always busy, it is a great place for coffee (from 14 pesos), people-watching, and checking email (12 pesos per hr.). Breakfast specials from 35 pesos. Open 24hr. MC/V. ❷

**Savia,** C. 59 x 52 y 54 (☎134 5414). A little bit of Berkeley in Mérida, Savia offers a friendly respite for vegetarians. Thumb through National Geographics® *(en español)* or chat with the waiter over daily specials like vegetarian *chilaquiles* (30 pesos, with juice) and fruit salad (18 pesos, 21 pesos with yogurt). Open daily 7:30am to 4pm. Cash only. ❷

**Cafe Chocolate,** corner of C. 60 and 49 (☎928 5153). Cafe Chocolate is half student hangout, half unpretentious art gallery. Your waitress, when she becomes bored of her conversation on her laptop, will weave past sculptures and paintings to bring you deli-

YUCATÁN STATE

cious smoothies (19-29 pesos), a caprese salad (49 pesos), or *pollo al mole* (65 pesos). Bilingual poetry readings Sa 6-8pm. Open M-Sa 7am-midnight. Cash only. ❸

**Dulcería y Sorbetería Colón,** Paseo Montejo x 39 y 41 (☎927 6443). At some point on the Paseo Montejo, you will realize that the sun has destroyed any desire to continue moving. Instead of lying prostrate on the sidewalk, come here, sit in the ample and shady outdoor seating area, and have a generously sized portion of sorbet (25 pesos). Flavors run from chocolate to lime to *guanabana*. Pastries 6 pesos. Open daily 9am to midnight. Cash only. ❷

**Restaurante Amaro,** C. 59 507 x 60 y 62 (☎928 2451). Popular with tourists seeking a night out in a calm setting. Attentive service and intimate candlelit tables in a quiet courtyard with live music and a variety of healthful Mexican meals. Great vegetarian dishes like eggplant curry (62 pesos), *chaya* (leafy vegetable similar to spinach) crepes (69 pesos), and apple pie with wheat crust (30 pesos). Live regional trova guitar 9pm. Tango show F 8:30pm, cover 100 pesos. Open daily 11am-2am. MC/V. ❹

**Cafetería Pop,** C. 57 501 x 60 y 62 (☎928 6163). Mérida's oldest cafe, this spotless, retro diner recently celebrated its 36th anniversary. Cheap, well-prepared food served by attentive waiters. Superior coffee (15 pesos) and banana splits (45 pesos). Breakfast specials (28-48 pesos) served until noon. Entrees 28-65 pesos. Open M-Sa 7am-midnight, Su 8am-midnight. MC/V. ❸

**Pane e Vino,** C. 62 496 x 59 y 61 (☎928 6228), in the center of town just across from Teatro Mérida. The slow service at this dimly lit restaurant caters to romantic vacationing couples looking for Italian treats and hearty salads (50 pesos). Homemade gnocchi with fresh pesto 75 pesos. 10% service charge included on all meals. Open daily 9am-9pm. MC/V. ❹

**Los Almendros** (☎928 5459) and **Los Gran Almendros** (☎923 8135), both at C. 50 493 x 57 y 59. Upscale, world-famous Yucatec food with picture menus make these the ideal places to splurge on local delicacies. *Poc-chuc* (grilled pork steak) or *pavo en relleno negro* (turkey with dark sauce; 90 pesos). Live trova at Los Almendros and instrumental music at Gran Almendros. Los Almendros open daily 10am-11pm. Gran Almendros open daily 1-5pm. MC/V. ❹

**Restaurante y Clber Fut & Food,** C. 69 524 x 62 y 64 (☎928 3854). Fut & Food's menu and prices mirror those of dozens of holes-in-the-wall in Mérida. It is this restaurant's ample, airy space looking out on the charming neighborhood park that makes it stand out from the rest. Tacos 5 pesos. Open daily 7am to 7pm. Cash only. ❶

**Cafe el Hoyo,** C. 62 487 x 57 y 59 (☎928 1531). Catch up with Mérida's hip youth at the high tables in the red-painted courtyard. Game room off the side contains classics like Clue®. Waffles all day starting at 50 pesos. Coffee frappes from 30 pesos. Also serves local beer (20 pesos) making it a popular Friday afternoon stop. Open M-Sa 9am-11:30pm. MC/V. ❸

**Bistro Las Palomas,** C. 60 488 x 55 y 57 (☎924 8824), inside Hotel Casa del Balam. A quiet, elegant restaurant with a number of Yucatec specialties for 110 pesos. For the indecisive, the Combinación Maya comes with *pibil, poc-chuc, longaniza* and *queso relleno* for 130 pesos. Open daily 7am-10pm. MC/V. ❺

**Vito Corleone,** C. 59 508 x 60 y 62 (☎928 5777). Vito Corleone is the Don of pizza in Mérida's downtown scene, making offers you can't refuse. Look for the huge, hanging antique bicycle, the giant, wood-fired oven, and the swarms of people spilling onto the street with steaming slices of favorites like margarita (25 pesos for a small). Takeout and delivery also available. Open daily 10am-10:30pm. Cash only. ❶

**Restaurante Mérida,** C. 62 498 x 59 y 61 (☎116 3489). Recommended by locals for cheap, dependable Yucatec cuisine. Entrees, like *cochinita pibil* (slow-roasted pork in citrus juice) and *pollo en escabeche* (marinated chicken), are a bargain at 35 pesos. Open daily 7:30am-1am. Cash only. ❷

YUCATÁN STATE

## ON THE MENU

## MÉRIDA AND THE ᴿTISTS THAT LOVE HER

Mérida supports a flourishing ᵃrt scene. Yucatán Living (www.ʸucatanliving.com), an online ᵐagazine run by American ex-pats, ᵖroduces a useful guide to galler-ᵉs and artist studios. We've listed ᵗhree of our favorites below:

**Arte, Puros, y Cafe.** A newly ᵒpened gallery with works by ᴄuban artists. After perusing the ᵈisplays, backpackers can stock up ᵒn more portable mementos, like ᶜoffee and "puros" cigars straight ᶠrom Havana. (C. 62 449 x 53 y ⁵1. ☎999 923 2130; www.arte-ᶜubaonline.com. Open M-F 2-7pm, ʷeekends by appointment.)

**SoHo Galleries.** SoHo show-ᶜases a mix of photographs and ᵖaintings, devoting two galleries ᵗo local artists. (Calle 60 400A x ³3 y 41. ☎999 928 5710; www.ˢohogalleriesmx.com. Open T-F 11am-2pm and 5-7pm, Sa-Su 11am-3pm.)

**Casa Frederick Catherwood.** ᵗhis small museum displays ᵒriginal lithographs of Maya ruins ᵈrawn by the artist-explorer Fred-ᵉrick Catherwood, who traveled ᵗhe Yucatán in 1839. He accom-ᵖanied American diplomat John ˢtephens, who later documented ᵗheir adventures in his 1841 Inci-ᵈents of Travel, a Yucatán classic, ʷhich was illustrated by Cather-ʷood. (C. 59 572 x 72 y 74. www.ᶜasa-catherwood.com. Open M-Sa ⁹am-2pm and 5-7pm. 43 pesos.)

**Mc. Taco,** C. 56 520 x 63 y 65 (☎928 6989). If you don't think your stomach can handle the food from the stalls in the market next door, Mc. Taco is a nearby alternative. Small but clean and air-conditioned. You can get standard Mexican enchiladas with a Coke (45 pesos), or *kibi frito* (*kibbe*, a spiced Lebanese meat patty; 28 pesos). Open M-Sat 8am-8pm, Su 10am-5pm. Cash only. ❸

## ⑥ SIGHTS

Mérida stands as a testament to the lengthy and often tumultuous history of the Yucatán. Rimmed by historic palaces, modern Oxxo stores, and a towering cathedral, the busy *zócalo* is the capital's social center. On Sundays, the surrounding streets are closed to traffic as vendors cram into stalls. Yucatec folk dancers perform in front of Palacio Municipal while crowds of people stroll along the cobblestone streets. If you can't make the Sunday festivities, don't fret. Mérida has daily cultural activities in the many plazas, as well as a host of markets, theaters, and museums to explore. Free 1½hr. walking tours of the *zócalo* begin at 9:30am in the information office at the Palacio Municipal.

## ON THE ZÓCALO

**◪PALACIO DE GOBIERNO.** Built between 1879 and 1892, the green Palacio fuses two architectural styles—Tuscan (on the main floor) and Dorian (on the upper floor). Giant murals by the famous *meri-deño* muralist Fernando Castro Pacheco line the courtyard as well as the giant Versailles-like salon on the upper level. The muted murals depict the violent history of the conquest and the subsequent *indigenismo* revival on the peninsula. Begun in the early 1970s, the murals took more than a decade to complete, yet are remarkably coherent in their style and story and offer one of the more dramatic and poetic retellings of Yucatec history. *(On the north side of the zócalo. Open daily 8am-9pm. Free.)*

**CASA DE MONTEJO.** Built in 1549 by Francisco de Montejo el Mozo ("Francisco the Younger"), then the highest authority in Yucatán, the house was occupied by his descendents until the 1970s, when they sold out (literally) to Banamex. Built with stones from the Mayan temple T'ho, the 17th-century facade portrays warriors standing on the heads of their victims. An open patch in the stucco, visible from the path leading into the bank, shows how the walls were originally constructed. Inside, some of the rooms have been restored and are occasionally open to the public. *(On the south side of the zócalo. Open M-Sa 9am-4pm. Free.)*

**CATEDRAL DE SAN ILDEFONSO.** Begun in 1561 and finished in 1598, Mérida's cathedral is the oldest on the continent. It towers 40m over the city, about the height of the Mayan pyramids whose stones were used to construct it. Statues of St. Peter and St. Paul flank the door. The upper levels contain slits, suggesting that the early *conquistadors* also used the cathedral as a fortress. The cathedral was intended solely for use of the Spanish elite, but despite its exclusivity, some Chinese names can be found among the gravestones on the left, a testament to the city's diverse heritage. During the Mexican Revolution, the rebel army, led by Salvador Avarado, looted the Church. Today it holds the world's largest indoor crucifix (20m). In a chapel on the left, the **Cristo de Ampollas** (Blister Christ, also known as the Black Christ) is venerated for ending a drought in the 19th century. *(On the east side of the zócalo. Open daily 6-11am and 4-8pm. Free.)*

**CENTRO CULTURAL DE MÉRIDA OLIMPIA.** This giant glass and steel building stands out from the other colonial buildings around the *zócalo*. A recently renovated exhibition hall with four galleries, the center hosts work by well-known local and international artists. The theater in the complex also has free performances: *trova*, the Yucatán's signature musical style, on Tuesdays; live bands on Wednesdays; classical music and movies on Thursdays; and plays and dances on weekends. The downstairs planetarium is a popular spot for school children. A cinema shows international films nearly every day. Check the bulletin board near the entrance for a full schedule of events. *(C. 62 y 61, just north of the municipal building. ☎ 942 0000; www.merida.gob.mex/capitalcultural. Open Tu-Su 10am-8pm. Free; planetarium 30 pesos.)*

**TEATRO PEÓN CONTRERAS.** Named for the *merideño* poet José Peón Contreras (1843-1907), this beautiful turn-of-the-century building is notable for its marble Rococo interior. The theater has frequent concerts and shows; see the box office and the *Divertimento* booklet, found at the tourist office, for more information. *(C. 57 x 60. ☎ 923 7354; www.culturayucatan.com.)*

**UNIVERSIDAD AUTÓNOMA DE YUCATÁN.** Located in a Hispano-Moorish complex dating from 1938, the headquarters of the state's national university has screening rooms on the ground floor and a gallery with works by local artists and students. *(On C. 57 x 60. Galería open M-F 9am-1pm and 5-9pm, Sa 10am-1pm, Su 10am-2pm. Movie schedule varies. Free.)*

**PASEO DE MONTEJO.** Aging French-style mansions, a large and impressive sculpture garden, and boutiques line the Paseo's brick sidewalks, culminating in the **Monumento a la Patria.** In faux-Mayan style, the stone monument—built by the Colombian artist Rómulo Rozo from 1945 to 1956—depicts Cinco de Mayo, scenes from the Mexican Revolution, and interpretations of the founding fathers of Mexico's constitution. On the other side of the monument, the *ceiba* (the Mayan tree of life) stretches above a pool of water, surrounded by *conquistadores*, the national symbol of an eagle devouring a snake, Mexican states' coats of arms, and butterflies in the four cardinal directions. For an interesting detour from the Paseo, veer left onto Colón to see historic mansions in varying stages of decay. During the week, the Paseo, lined with banks and fast food chains, feels like any busy suburban thoroughfare; on Sunday, the city closes the street to cars, making for a pleasant bike ride to the wealthy part of town. Bike rentals are available at the Monumento a la Patria or in the *zócalo*. *(10 pesos per hr.)*

## MUSEUMS

**▨MUSEO REGIONAL DE ANTROPOLOGÍA E HISTORIA.** Mérida's most impressive museum is housed in the **Palacio Cantón**, a magnificent Beaux Art mansion. The collection includes Mayan head-flattening devices, jade tooth inserts, sacrificial offerings recovered from the *cenote sagrado* of Chichén Itzá, and a Chichén Itzá *chac-mool* (p. 115). You can also view intriguing exhibits on Mayan science, language, and distinctive ideals of beauty. Most exhibits are in Spanish and English. *(Paseo Montejo y C. 43. ☎923 0557. Open Tu-Su 8am-5pm. 41 pesos, Su Mexican citizens free.)*

**MUSEO DE LA CIUDAD.** Reopened in the Palacio Federal, where the post office used to be, this small history museum provides well-labeled history of the Yucatán and Mérida's central role in it. Exhibits begin with the Maya and end around the 1950s. The upstairs galleries host rotating exhibits with local art. *(C. 56 x 65 and 65A, in the heart of the shopping district. ☎923 6869. Open Tu-F 9am-8pm, Sa-Su 9am-2pm. Free.)*

**MUSEO DE ARTE CONTEMPORÁNEO (MACAY).** MACAY is renowned for its large collection of Mexican sculpture as well as a few late murals by Fernando Castro Pacheco. Much of the permanent collection is found in the nooks and crannies of the sunny central courtyard. Rotating exhibits with pieces by well-known Mexican painters are in the air-conditioned galleries on the upper level. The outside sculpture garden on the **Callejón del Congreso** (also known as the "Pasaje de la Revolución" after the army quartered its horses there during the revolution) is worth a quick peek. *(Paseo Revolución x 58 y 60, on the east side of the zócalo, south of the Cathedral. ☎928 3191; www.macay.org. Open M-Th 10am-5:15pm, F-Sa 10am-7:15pm. Free.)*

**MUSEO DE LA CANCIÓN YUCATECA.** This small museum is home to sheet music, instruments, trophies, and portraits of the area's best singers and musicians. The center also hosts free concerts the last Wednesday of every month at 9pm. *(C. 57 464 x 48. ☎923 7224. All exhibits in Spanish. Open Tu-F 9am-5pm, Sa-Su 9am-3pm. 20 pesos.)*

**MUSEO DE ARTE POPULAR DE YUCATÁN.** This collection displays *artesanía* from around Mexico. Just as interesting is the building, the **Casa Molina,** built in 1900 as a wedding gift for the daughter of Olegario Molina Solis, who was a wealthy *henequén* hacienda owner, governor of Yucatán, and a member of the cabinet of Porfirio Díaz. *(At the corner of C. 57 and 59, on the Plaza Mejorada. ☎928 5263. Labels in English and Spanish. Open Tu-Sa 9:30am-6:30pm, Su 9am-2pm. 20 pesos, Su free. Students with ID free. Cash only.)*

**PARQUE ZOOLÓGICO DEL CENTENARIO.** Check out tigers, bears, and hippos in a large park, complete with rides for kids, walking paths, and food stands. The zoo features a large aviary and fountains that visitors can walk through. The creatures make for a good show while wandering or riding the miniature train (10 pesos) that makes circuits of the park. The Museo de Historia Natural is right next door. *(On C. 84 x 61 y 59, or at C. 59 and C. 86, Itzáces. Snag an El Centenario bus at C. 64 x 61 y 63 and ask to be let off at the park; 5 pesos. Park and zoo open Tu-Su 6am-6pm. Both free. Museum open 9am-3pm.)*

**OTHER SIGHTS.** The many churches, statues, and parks scattered throughout Mérida's *centro* invite exploration. Mérida has several remaining arches, built in the latter part of the 17th century, which used to mark the roads connect-

YUCATÁN STATE

ing the city with the rest of the state. These arches established boundaries between European and indigenous peoples. The oldest is **San Juan,** C. 64 x 71. **Iglesia Santiago,** on C. 59 x 72, one of the oldest churches in Mexico, is worth a visit, as are **Iglesia de San Juan de Dios,** on C. 64 x 69, and the Franciscan **Convento de la Mejorada,** at C. 50 x 57 y 59. The cloisters of the Convento have now been turned into the Department of Architecture for MACAY University.

## ◪ ◪ MARKETS AND SHOPPING

South of the *zócalo*, the sidewalks narrow, while the number of people multiplies. This is Mérida's shopping district, where locals bus in by the thousands to stock up on cheap vegetables and clothing. Each neighborhood has its own market. Stock up on white *huipiles* (traditional dresses and blouses; 250-350 pesos), *rebozos* (shawls; 220 pesos), and *guayaberas* (men's shirts; 150-250 pesos). Cheaper goods, such as *huaraches* (sandals), are sold on the first floor. While shopping in the crowded market, don't carry any valuables and keep your money in a safe place, like an under-the-shirt money belt. Mérida offers the best shopping in the Yucatán, but aggressive vendors and high-pressure salespeople are inescapable.

If you're worried about the prospect of hard-core bargaining or if you just want to get a feel for prices, you can try the government-run **Casa de las Artesanías del Estado de Yucatán,** C. 63 503A x 64 y 66, where every item has a fixed price. (☎928 6676; www.casadelasartesaniasdeyucatan.com. Open M-F 9am-9:45pm, Sa 9am-6:45pm, Su 9am-1:45pm.) While shopping, don't be fooled by imitations; look for the logo with two hands. Some of the boutiques around the *centro* offer slightly steeper prices than those you can bargain for in the *mercado*, but they are also air-conditioned, less stressful, and sometimes offer goods of a higher quality. Although jewelry stores line the streets, the best prices are in the market or at the *zócalo* every Sunday. You're more likely to get what you're paying for at more established stores. All genuine silver has a ".925" stamp. **El Centro Joyero** (C. 75 x 70 y 72) also sells jewelry.

**LUCAS DE GALVEZ.** The main *mercado*, established in 1903, occupies the block southeast of the pink Palacio Federal, spreading outward from the corner of C. 65 and 58. People from the surrounding villages pour into Mérida to load up on produce and cheap clothes. The second-floor artisans' market, part of the modern building behind and to the right of the Palacio Federal, sells *artesanías*, regional clothing, and the omnipresent hammock.

**ARTESANÍAS BAZAR GARCÍA REJÓN.** This spot is popular with tourists for its concentration of *artesanía*, local clothing, and hammocks. The food stalls are less frenzied than those at the main market; they're toward the back, heading south. (*Open daily 6am-6pm. Food stalls close earlier.*)

**MERCADO DE SANTIAGO.** Food dominates the Mercado de Santiago, around C. 59 and 72, close to the Iglesia Santiago. Two stand-out stalls include **Santa Cecilia,** near the back, where chef Marcos Vera cooks vats of *cochinita pibil* for restaurants around town (☎928 2657; open daily 7am-1pm), and **Helado Polito,** close to the church (see **Food,** p. 82).

**MERCADO DE SANTA ANA.** Much smaller and cleaner than the other markets—the cleanest stalls will be the busiest. (*C. 60 and 47. Most stalls open M-Sa 6am-8pm, Su 8am-2pm.*)

**CONSUMER BEWARE.** Though Mérida is one of the safest cities in Mexico, it's important to be on the defensive against assaults on your wallet. In particular, be wary of the friendly, crafty polyglots hanging out in the *zócalo* and in the market who claim to work for the tourist office. They will likely be passing out tourist information and will offer to lead you to an "official" artisan market, where you will be charged two to three times the fair price for souvenirs. Always ask for a receipt with the name and address of the store. Report fraud to the consumer protection agency (☎923 2323, C. 59 x 54 y 56) or the government tourist office in the Palacio del Gobierno.

## NIGHTLIFE AND ENTERTAINMENT

Though Mérida is full of relaxing, culturally interesting nightlife options, clubbing is better saved for another port. Mérida's nightlife happens in the streets where the city hosts almost-nightly free music and cultural shows in its many *zócalos* and parks, each of which offers the chance to dance, drink, eat, and get a true taste of the *sabor* of the Yucatán. You can find listings for events and shows in the free *Yucatan Today* magazine, available at the tourist office, and at www.yucatanliving.com. For a chilled out evening in a bar, try one of Mérida's many delicious, hard-to-find local beers, like the distinctive Montejo León and the darker Negra León. Local establishments give out free snacks with the purchase of a few beers.

 **THE GREAT BOTANA TOUR.** Mérida's tradition of *botanas*—beer accompanied by free appetizers—is great news for the budget traveler. The plates of *papadzules*, tacos stuffed with *cochinita pibil*, *panuchos*, *salbutes*, and other regional comfort foods easily make a meal. Unfortunately, these complimentary goodies are also typically set to earsplitting band music and tend to end early in the evening. Visitors with a low tolerance for trumpets can still partake during one of the country's soccer games.

**Outdoor Concerts:** Yucatec dancing in the Palacio Municipal M 9pm. 1940s-style big-band concerts in Plaza de Santiago, at C. 59 x 72 Tu 8:30pm.

**Miércoles de Espectáculo:** A show in the **Centro Cultural**, on the *zócalo*. W 9pm.

**The Serenade:** At C. 60 x 55, in Parque de Santa Lucía. The most historical event in Mérida, with well-known Mexican music, poetry, and folklore. Th 9pm.

**University Serenade:** At C. 60 X 57, in the main university building. Theatrical performances at the **Centro Cultural.** F 8pm.

**Noche Mexicana:** On Paseo Montejo between C. 47 and 49. A night of national food, dance performances, and arts and crafts. Sa 7pm. During **Fiesta el Corazón de Mérida,** at the *zócalo* and at C. 60 x 53 y 61, restaurants in the historic center move their tables into the streets under the stars.

**Mérida en Domingo:** Art vendors, food stalls, and live music fight for space in the *zócalo* and surrounding streets. Paseo de Montejo closed for bicycle route. Su 9am-9pm.

### BARS AND CLUBS

**El Nuevo Tucho,** C. 60 482 x 55 y 57 (☎924 2323). One of the oldest of Mérida's family bars, "El Nuevo Tucho" entertains mostly local customers with slapstick com-

YUCATÁN STATE

edy and live music. Beer 33 pesos. Entrees 60-80 pesos. *Comida rapida* 30-50 pesos. Open daily 12:30-7pm. MC/V.

**Eladio's,** C. 59 425 at 44 (923 1087; www.eladios.com.mx); 5 other locations around the city. Eladio's is large and casual, with wooden tables facing a stage. Beer 30-35 pesos. Open daily 11am-9pm.

**Cielo,** Prolongación Paseo de Montejo and C. 25 (☎944 5127). A smooth black-lit box that bops electronica. Only gets going late. Cover includes open bar. Th women free; men cover 100 pesos. F cover 50 pesos, Sa cover 50 pesos before 10:30pm, 100 after.

**KY60,** C. 60 x 55 y 57 (☎924 2289). Part of the cluster of clubs on the same block, catering mostly to young locals looking for alternative music and late-night romance. The scene picks up around midnight. Cover men 130 pesos, women 70 pesos. Open F-Sa 10pm-3am.

**La Parranda,** C. 60 x 59 y 57, across from Parque Hidalgo. One of the central fixtures of Sa night festivals, La Parranda is a tourist attraction in itself. Beer is sold by the "yarda" and early 90s salsa music is the house standard. Beer 33 pesos. Open daily 7am-2am. MC/V.

## ❄ FESTIVALS

Mérida is known throughout the peninsula for the vibrancy of its *fiestas.* The city celebrates its anniversary with a two-week festival every January 6, coinciding with the **Festival de los Reyes.** The city has also begun to amp up its **Carnaval** festivities, which generally start in February. Other large holidays include **Semana Santa,** the last week of Lent before Easter Sunday.

## ▶ DAYTRIPS FROM MÉRIDA

### ACANCEH

*Ruins open daily 9am-5pm, last entry 4:30pm. No labels. 31 pesos. Buses and colectivos to Acanceh, continuing on to Cuzamá, can be found outside the Noreste station, in Mérida. (45min., every 30min., 10-14 pesos.) Buses and colectivos return to Mérida every 20-30min. Buses to Mérida head away from the Church. Buses heading on to Cuzamá drive toward the Church.*

Acanceh, a small city just 21km south east of Mérida, conceals three Maya pyramids within the town limits, one of which boasts the ▉largest stucco masks in the Yucatán state. The ruins, restored and opened to the public in 2000, which date from the Early Classic period, are the remains of a small settlement dedicated to ceremonial activities. *Akankeh* means "dying deer" in Maya—historians maintain that no human sacrifices were practiced at the site. A pyramid with the masks borders the town plaza. Most of the masks have decayed past identification, but traces of the red paint that used to cover the structure are still visible. Archeologists have managed to identify one of the masks as the Maya sun god Kim, recognizable by his square eyes. They speculate that the others represent different incarnations of the god. There are two other pyramids; the one located behind the pyramid with masks offers a view of the town. The other pyramid is the **Palace of the Stuccos,** where nobles and priests lived. It's a zig-zagging walk behind the church (the ruin guard will direct you). Scrambling up the rocks brings you to friezes showing anthropomorphic figures, like man-monkeys and man-eagles, with terrestrial creatures positioned closer to the ground.

Travelers returning from Cuzamá may want to stop for a meal at Acanceh. On the corner by the bus stop, **La Dulcita** , at C. 21 and 22, serves a *menú del día* of juicy fried chicken breast served with rice, beans, and a small salad for 40 pesos. (Open daily 8am-5pm. Cash only.)

YUCATÁN STATE

## CUZAMÁ

*Colectivos depart for Cuzamá, stopping in Acanceh, from near the Terminal Noreste about every 30min. 6am-6pm. 14 pesos. From Cuzamá, visitors can walk 4km to the cenotes or hire a bicycle taxi or moped taxi (20 pesos). If you plan to hire a bicycle, walk across the town square away from the bus stop for a better deal. (An enterprising villager has a sign welcoming tourists to a cenote halfway there. Don't be fooled! This mosquito infested pit, accessed by a rickety ladder, is far less impressive than the cenotes farther on.) Changing facilities available at the site. Cenotes open 8am-5pm. 3hr., 200 pesos for the ride, max. 4 people.*

Cuzamá, about 50km south east of Mérida, boasts three spectacularly blue *cenotes* buried in the Yucatán brush. Located in the middle of former *henequén* plantations, they are accessible from the village of Chunkanan via a bone-rattling ride in a horse-drawn carriage. The best time to visit the *cenotes* is in the morning, when the sun illuminates the caverns, which are dripping with stalactites and hanging roots. At this time of day, the iridescent light plays on the brilliant turquoise water. **Chekeltun,** the first and largest *cenote*, used to serve as the private pool for the owners of the nearby *hacienda*. **Chac Cinik Che,** 15-20m deep, is prominent in tourist promotional materials. To access the ▨**final cenote,** visitors must descend a ladder. The *cenotes* are all about 3km apart.

## DZIBILCHALTÚN

*Buses leave from the Autoprogreso station (every 2hr. 7:20am-1:20pm, 7 pesos) and drop you off at the access road to the ruins, a 5-10min. walk from the entrance. Return buses depart 2hr. later than the departure time in a given location. Combis also run on an irregular schedule past the access road to the ruins (9 pesos). Taxis charge 400 pesos for a round-trip ride and 2hr. wait. Parking 15 pesos. English language labels. Site and museum open daily 8am-5pm. 79 pesos, Mexican citizens under 13 free, Mexican students with ID free, Su free for Mexican citizens.*

These ruins are worth it just to see ▨**El Museo del Pueblo Maya.** Situated 20km north of Mérida en route to the Gulf coast, Dzibilchaltún ("place where there is writing on stones" in Mayan) sprawls over 19 sq. km of jungle brush. The site flourished as a ceremonial and administrative center, with 40,000 inhabitants at one point, from approximately 500 BC until after the arrival of the Spanish in the 1540s, making it one of the longest continuously inhabited Mayan settlements. The carefully preserved site now houses a 300m "ecological path," with nearly 100 different species of birds and labeled plants. The museum displays sculptures and ceramics from Dzibilchaltún and other Mayan sites, as well as more recent Catholic altars and contemporary Mayan handiwork. The museum is the first building to the left of the entrance. The path leading to the museum is lined with an all-star gallery of Mayan stelae with original sculptures from Chichén Itzá ( p. 111) and Uxmal (p. 101).

From the museum, follow the path to *sacbé* no. 1, the raised causeway, and turn left. At the end of this road lies Dzibilchaltún's showpiece, the fully restored 5th-century **Templo de las Siete Muñecas** (Temple of the Seven Dolls), which covers 24,300 sq. m. The seven phallically enhanced clay "dolls" discovered in this temple at the four cardinal directions are on display in the museum. Shortly after sunrise during the spring and autumn equinoxes, a huge shadow mask of the rain god Chaac appears as the sun's rays pierce the temple. The other end of the *sacbé* leads to a seemingly out-of-place chapel with a rounded roof that was a Mayan temple before being rebuilt by Franciscan missionaries. Just beyond the eastern edge of the quadrangle is **Cenote Xlacah** (Old People Cave), which served as a sacrificial well and water source, and is now a lily pad garden and mosquito breeding ground. Divers have recovered ceremonial artifacts and human bones from the depths of the 44m deep *cenote*, where you can now take a non-sacrificial dip. A path to the south leads past several

YUCATÁN STATE

smaller structures to the site's exit. Peace, quiet, and the fact that the bus won't come for 2hr. make for an ideal picnic spot.

## MAYAPÁN

*Mayapán is 43km southeast of Mérida on Mex. 18 and 6km northwest of Tekit on the same road. It's the only site north of Mex. 184 and is not officially part of the Ruta Puuc; Ticul (p. 105) is the nearest base, a 1hr. drive away. The closest village is Telchaquillo, a 1½km walk along the highway. Buses leave from the station in Mérida every hr. (1½hr., 15 pesos). Buses also pass by every hr. from Mérida on their way to Oxkutzcab (31 pesos). Open daily 8am-5pm. 31 pesos.*

The ruins of Mayapán themselves are less impressive than their revered history as a central part of the late, great Mayapán alliance. Still, the on-site paintings are unique to the ruins circuit and worth the trip. From AD 1000 to 1200, the city was dominated by Chichén Itzá, which then controlled the Mayapán League. After AD 1200, the beginning of its golden age, the 12,000 people of Mayapán overthrew Chichén Itzá and came to control the league. The small city was destroyed in 1441, when Ah Xupan of Uxmal rebelled against the Cocom dynasty in a fight to retrieve his daughter, a princess captured by Chichén Itzá's prince. Restoration began in 1948, producing several impressive structures. The principal pyramid is the **Pyramid of Kukulcán,** with straight lines and little detail. The peak affords a view of the rest of the compact site. To the west are three stucco models with painted warriors; the round shape of the **Templo Redondo** stands out. **El Templo de Pescadores** has nicely preserved murals. Within the site are 32 *cenotes*, one of which is near the Caracol. With the lack of crowds at this site, the ruins are easily seen in an hour.

# CELESTÚN      ☎998

On one side of this small village, fishermen and tourists share a beach unspoiled by the cruise ship bustle of Progreso; on the other, flamingos and spider monkeys share a mangrove forest in the Ria Celestún Biosphere. Take a tour of the Biosphere to see flamingos and mangroves, *"bosques muertos"* (dead forests), and an abandoned salt mining town. Afterwards, have some fresh *jaiba* (blue crab) at one of many seaside restaurants. The only downside to this tiny town are the mosquitoes, which are striped like (and bite almost as hard as) tigers.

**🖃🔁 TRANSPORTATION AND PRACTICAL INFORMATION.** Celestún lies 93km southwest of Mérida on the Gulf Coast. To get there by **bus,** go to the Noreste bus station in Mérida on C. 67 x 50 y 52 (2hr., every hr., 41 pesos). By **car,** take Mex. 281 into town where it becomes C. 11, the main east-west street. C. 11 passes the *zócalo* and hits the shore two blocks later. Odd numbers increase to the south, while even numbers increase to the west, toward the beach. The *zócalo* is bounded by C. 8, 10, 11, and 13. **Oriente** sends buses from a small booth at the corner of C. 8 and 13 to Mérida (2hr., every hr. 5am-8pm, 47 pesos).

Other services include: **police,** on C. 13 in the *zócalo* (☎998 957 0200; open 24hr.); **Farmacia Celestún,** C. 11 94 x 8 y 10 (☎998 916 2106; open daily 8am-11pm); **Centro de Salud,** C. 5 x 8 y 10 (open M-F 8am-4pm, Sa-Su 8am-8pm; emergencies 24hr.); **Telecomm,** on C. 11 at the *zócalo* (☎998 916 2053; open M-F 9am-3pm); and **internet** at **Hostel Ría Celestún** (20 pesos per hr.) and **Ciberline,** right next to the police station on C. 13 in the *zócalo* (open 10am-11pm). Bring a pocketful of cash as there is no bank, ATM, or traveler's check exchange. Most services accept cash only.

**ACCOMMODATIONS.** Mexican tourists and biologists flock to Celestún from mid-July through August, sending prices through the roof. Call ahead to make sure there's room. Most accommodations are on C. 12. **Hostel Ría Celestún ❶**, C. 12 104A x 13, has cool, simple, concrete facilities with few windows and saggy beds, but a lovely garden. Hammocks, kitchen, snorkel gear, towels, TV/VCR, internet (20 pesos per hr.), and bike rental (20 pesos per hr.) are all available. (☎998 916 2170. Dorms 80 pesos, private doubles 200 pesos. Prices rise about 50 pesos during the high season. Cash only.) Right on the beach, **Hotel María del Carmen ❷**, C. 12 111 x 13 y 15, is a 14-room complex. Spartan, golden-toned rooms have ocean views, balconies, and immaculate baths. Try to get a room on the third level where sea breezes help out the struggling overhead fans. (☎998 916 2170. Parking available. Singles and doubles 200-250 pesos, with A/C 300-350; each additional person 50 pesos. Cash only.) **Hotel Sol y Mar ❸**, C. 12 104 x 11 y 13, is one block from the beach. Vacationing *merideños* love the spotless rooms with TVs and fans. The colorful common area boasts a private bar and a working fountain. (☎998 916 2166. Singles and doubles 250 pesos, with A/C 350 pesos; 2-bed suites with kitchen, refrigerator, and A/C 350 pesos; 4-bed suites 350 pesos, with A/C 450 pesos. Cash only.) Marco and the gang at **Restaurant and Camping El Muelle ❶**, on C. 12 x 17 near the town pier, are hard at work transforming this popular nightlife spot into a backpacker's beach paradise. So far, three private *cabañas* and a shady camping area have been built. (Clean, communal baths and kayak rental. Camping 80 pesos; *cabañas* start at 300 pesos. Cash only.)

**FOOD.** The seafood in Celestún is as much a draw as the Biosphere's flamingos. Specialties include *jaiba* (blue crab), *pulpo* (octopus), and *caracol* (small conch) served fried, battered, or in a simple *ceviche*. Restaurants line C. 12 and the beach, and *loncherías* cluster in the *zócalo* (most stalls open daily 6-11am and 6pm-10pm). **Restaurant la Playita ❹**, C. 12 99 x 9 y 11, is a good place to lay down your towel and spend the day. This restaurant is fully equipped for beach fun with clean bathrooms and showers as well as a light seafood menu. Flavorful *jaiba frita* (fried blue crab) costs 80 pesos and ice cold beer runs 20 pesos. (☎998 916 2052. Open daily 10am-6pm. Cash only.) Popular dutch-owned **El Lobo ❷**, on the corner of the *zócalo* between C. 10 and 13, serves hot waffles with fresh fruit (37 pesos), pancakes (25 pesos), pizza (from 35 pesos), and assorted coffees from a second floor open-air balcony. (Open Tu-Su 8am-11am and 7pm-midnight. Cash only.) For true decadence, head to **La Palapa ❸**, C. 12 105 x 11 y 13, and try the outstanding and elegantly presented seafood (80-130 pesos) and *botanas* (snacks; 25-35 pesos) on the beach. (☎998 916 2063; www.hotelmanglares.com. Open daily 11am-6:30pm. AmEx/MC/V.)

**SIGHTS.** Celestún's **estuary** is a major winter stop on a central migratory route for birds. The best tour takes you south along the coast to **La Ría,** where you'll wind through a river tunnel of intertwining tree branches. After viewing the petrified forests of **Tampetén,** visit the abandoned village of **Real de Salinas** for a breathtaking view of the salt fields. Heading north through La Ría, you'll reach the **Isla de Pájaros** (Island of Birds), an avian playground with hundreds of flamingos. The tour ends with a visit to a cold, freshwater *cenote*. To see some fascinating ruins, ask your boat captain to enter the inlet at **Punta Ninum.** Past the inlet, walk into the jungle and you will come to **Can Balam.** Two main tour operators offer different packages. Tours given by the co-op of fishermen on the beach at the end of C. 11 leave right from the beach and allow you to see more of La Ría. (2hr.; rates depend on size of group. Full boat 200 pesos per person; alone 800. Request sights before paying. Tours daily 8am-4pm.)

YUCATÁN STATE

Tours given by **CULTUR** (the state government's tourist agency) leave from their center on Mex. 281, 2km before the town of Celestún. They offer two options, including a tour that stops at a flamingo colony, mangroves, and a freshwater spring. (1hr. 600 pesos; 2hr. 1200 pesos; 6-person max. Entrance 41 pesos per person. Tours daily 8am-6pm.)

If boating isn't your thing, a bike ride through the key is equally stunning. Rent a **bike** and get advice on various routes from Marcos at Hostel Ría Celestún (p. 92). Follow Av. al Puerto Abrigo south until you hit the entrance to the Charcos del Sal. Take a right at the small harbor. Head 4km down the dirt road (past a landfill) to **Real de Salinas,** an abandoned town that survived on the salt industry until the Revolution. Through the ruins and 2.8km farther down the road at **Punta Lastre** is a freshwater spring. On the way back, follow the trails on the west to find a private beach perfect for cooling off. A bike ride in the opposite direction, north along the shore, will take you to the tallest lighthouse on the peninsula, **Palmar Faro** (20km from the Celestún center), and to the peaceful **Maya Playa.** Bike rental (20 pesos per hr.) is available at Hostal Ría Celestún (p. 92).

Finally, between the town and the CULTUR office is **Jaltún Parque Recreativo,** which has crocodile shows, an orchid garden, and kayak rentals. You can get more information in **Celestún at Hospedaje Celestún,** C. 9 x 10 y 12. (☎998 916 2095).

# PROGRESO ☎969

Something about Progreso lets you know you're near the beach before you see or even smell the Gulf of Mexico. That may be why this town of 35,000, just 30km north of Mérida on the northwestern Yucatec coast, attracts so many vacationers from the state's landlocked capital. The two main streets feel like big, open-air markets; few shops have normal doors, most just roll down a metal covering when it's time to close. At the beach, you'll notice Progreso's 6km-long pier stretching into the distance. In the past, the primary export was *henequén*, a hemp-like fiber. Today, the *henequén* has been replaced with a stream of cruise-ship tourists who come for fresh seafood and endless beaches.

## ◼ TRANSPORTATION

**Autoprogreso buses** travel to **Mérida** (☎969 955 3024; 50min., every 15 min. 5:20am-10pm, one-way 14 pesos, round trip 25 pesos). To get to the *zócalo* from the station (on C. 29 between C. 80 and C. 82), take a left on C. 29 and a right on C. 80 and walk a block. To get to the beach, follow C. 80 the opposite direction. *Colectivos* to nearby beaches and towns leave from the west side of the *zócalo* and a depot at C. 82 and C. 29 (8am-9pm).

## ◼◼ ORIENTATION AND PRACTICAL INFORMATION

Calle 19, Progreso's brick **malecón,** runs east-west along the beach. Odd-numbered roads run parallel to the *malecón,* increasing as you move the south. Even-numbered streets run north-south and increase as you move the west. Progreso's **zócalo** is bounded by C. 31 and C. 33 on the north and south and bisected by the main street, **C. 80.**

**Tourist Office:** (☎935 0104), on C. 80 between C. 25 and C. 27. To the right side of Progreso's **Casa de la Cultura,** north of the lighthouse. Provides helpful maps of town and useful beach suggestions. Open M-F 8:30am-8pm, Sa 9am-4pm.

**Bank: HSBC** (☎935 0856), on C. 80 between C. 29 and C. 31. **24hr. ATM.** Open M-F 9am-7pm, Sa 9am-3pm.

YUCATÁN STATE

**Laundromat:** C. 29 132 (☎935 0856), between C. 76 and C. 78. Next-day service. Wash and dry 10 pesos per kg, 3kg minimum. Open M-Sa 8am-7pm.

**Police:** (☎935 0026), in the Palacio Municipal on the west side of the *zócalo*. Open 24hr.

**Pharmacy: Farmacia Canto** (☎935 1549), at C. 29 and C. 80. Open daily 7:30am-midnight.

**Medical Services: Centro Médico Americano** (☎935 1549), at C. 33 and C. 82. Open 24hr.

**Internet Access: Cyber Progreso** (☎935 0772), on C. 78 between C. 29 and C. 31. 12 pesos per hr. Open daily 8am-midnight.

**Fax Office: Telecomm,** next door to the post office. Western Union inside. Open M-F 8am-7pm, Sa-Su 9am-noon.

**Post Office:** C. 31 150 (☎935 0565), between C. 78 and the *zócalo*. Open M-F 8am-4pm, Sa 8am-3pm. **Postal Code:** 97320.

## ▐ ACCOMMODATIONS

Progreso, unlike Mérida, does not have any hostels, and finding a bed for less than 200 pesos per night is a challenge. In addition, prices tend to soar in July and August—sometimes doubling on weekends—and vacancies may be hard to find. Plan ahead during the Easter rush as well. All hotels listed have hot water and fans. Camping on the beach, with several bath houses along the *malecón*, is also permitted and generally safe, though you should check in with the police beforehand. Be aware that you may be kept up by late-night drinking near the pier.

**Hotel Miralmar,** C. 27 124 (☎935 0552), between C. 74 and 76. This is one of the oldest hotels in Progreso. Despite looks, Miralmar contains relatively comfortable beds and clean (if small) bathrooms. Singles 170 pesos; 1-bed doubles 230 pesos, 2-bed 260 pesos; rooms with A/C 310 pesos; each additional person 50 pesos. Prices rise 10% July-Aug. Cash only. ❷

**Hotel Progreso,** C. 29 142 (☎935 0039), at C. 78. Mainly distinguished by an attractively tiled lobby and A/C in all the rooms. You can also expect cleanliness and a TV. If you're used to a hard bunk next to a snoring Australian, this may feel surprisingly close to luxury. Singles 200 pesos; 50 pesos per additional person, up to 4 people. Cash only. ❷

**Hotel San Miguel,** C. 78 148 (☎935 1357), between C. 29 and 31. Your room may be painted Fanta orange. One of the only cheap-ish hotels in Progreso. Free Wi-Fi. Singles with fan 250 pesos; doubles with A/C 280 pesos. Cash only. ❸

**Hotel Vialmar** (☎935 5879), at C. 70 and 21. Only a block from the ocean and out of reach of the tourist bustle along C. 80 and the main stretch of the *malecón*. Rooms are without frills, but with a private bath and a small balcony. Up to 2 people 250 pesos; triples 350 pesos; suites for up to 5 people 600 pesos. Cash only. ❸

## ▐ FOOD

Most restaurants in Progreso fit into three distinct categories. Along the *malecón* are seafood-heavy establishments, specializing in *pescado frito* (fried fish) and with signs featuring large, brightly-colored animal mascots to lure in tourists. The fare on C. 80 is a bit more diverse, mixing Mexican with international. C. 80 also tends to be somewhat less expensive than places on the beach. If you're looking for something really cheap and local, go to a *lonchería* on the side streets off C. 80. Vegetarians may want to check out the supermarket **San Francisco de Asis** at C. 80 144 between C. 29 and 31. (☎955 3760. Open daily 7am-10pm.) The **Plaza del Mar shopping center,** on C. 27 between C. 76 and 78, also hosts an air-conditioned food court with a couple of affordable options, including pizza and Greek cuisine.

YUCATÁN STATE

**Restaurant los Cocos,** between C. 76 and 78, on the *malecón.* Choose your own fish from the day's catch and they'll fry it to golden-brown salty perfection (70 pesos per kg). Entrees 90 pesos. Open daily 8am-7pm. Cash only. ❹

**El Cordobés,** C. 80 150 (☎955 2621), at C. 31. A local gathering place on one of the main streets with a great view of the park and the lovely Palacio Municipal. In contrast to the mostly impersonal, touristy places on the *malecón,* the owner here gives you a pat on the back as you order. Get a heaping fruit salad for 40 pesos. Fish dishes from 76 pesos. Open daily 6am-midnight. Cash only. ❹

**Flamingos** (☎935 2122), on the *malecón* near C. 72. A choice of seafood special-ties, Chinese food, pastas, and salads, though you can get most of the same thing (and cheaper) elsewhere. Access to clean bathrooms and showers, however, may make it worth the extra expense. In an ode to the touristy atmosphere, local entrepreneurs attempt to sell you chirping plastic birds as you enjoy your beach-side meal. Open M-F 7:30am-2am, Sa-Su 7:30-midnight. Cash only. ❸

## 🖼️ 👁️ BEACHES AND SIGHTS

Progreso's shallow waters, beach boardwalks, and *palapas* attract hordes of visitors in August, but manage to remain calm the rest of the year (except when cruise ships dock). The **Puerto de Altura muelle,** Mexico's longest pier, appears to extend infinitely from the beach west of the malecón. The beach east of the pier along the *malecón* is prime territory for food and art vendors as well as large families frolicking in the gentle surf.

For a more remote beach experience, try the beaches at one of the many nearby fishing villages. **Chelem,** 9km west of town, or the even less inhabited **Chuburná,** 13km beyond Chelem, have plenty of clean sand with few services and no strolling vendors. From Chuburná, you can also arrange for a bird-watching tour or rent a kayak to explore the north end of the **Celestún Biosphere Reserve's lagoon,** though tours are easier to arrange from Celestún. **Combis** leave for Chelem and Chuburná in front of the parking lot of the supermarket San Francisco on C. 80. (Every 15min. or when full, until 8pm. 7 pesos.) *Combis* to Chuburná leave when full from the opposite side of the street, in front of HSBC (7 pesos). The wider, cleaner, closer beaches 3km to the east of town in **Chicxulub** are lined with the summer homes of Mérida's and Mexico City's well-to-do and provide for nice walks. Chicxulub also happens to be the source of the name of the asteroid that killed the dinosaurs. (5min. *combi* ride from the northwest corner of C. 82 and 29, near the bus station. 4 pesos.) Before heading to the beach, stop at **Uaymitun Reserve,** where a three-story observation tower allows you to look out over blue-green marshes, home to thousands of pink flamingos. Before dawn and in the evening the flamingos come right up to the lookout to nest; they spend the rest of the day farther out on **Laguna Ciénega.** Binoculars are available for rent for 11 pesos. (Take a 4-peso *combi* to Chicxu-lub. At the zócalo in Chicxulub, find a Uaymitun-bound *combi* to continue to the observatory; 5 pesos. Open daily 8am-6pm.)

The largely unexplored Mayan city and salt distribution center of **X'cambó** ("Heavenly Crocodile" or "Trading Place") lies 10km east of Uaymitun and 26km east of Progreso, at the end of a 2km road that intersects the road to Telchac Puerto. The only way to get to X'cambó from Progreso is by taxi (round-trip 300 pesos). The small, recently restored site consists of several structures and two pyramids—one of which supports two large, unidentified stucco masks. A Catholic church, still a place of pilgrimage and offering, was built into the side of one of the pyramids 50 years ago in honor of the Virgin of X'cambó. Small paths branch from the site to unexcavated ruins and tiny villages. (Open daily 9am-5pm. Free.)

# LA RUTA PUUC AND ENVIRONS

Between Mérida and Campeche lies the hilly and fertile Puuc ("hills" in Mayan) region. In the heart of this remote area lie dozens of Mayan ruins, collectively known as La Ruta Puuc (The Puuc Route). In ancient times, between 300 BC and AD 1200, the Mayan cities along La Ruta Puuc were linked by regular trade, a north-south *sacbé* (raised roadway), and a collective population of over 25,000. Today, the ruins are more visibly united by the salmon-pink limestone and the strikingly similar geometric patterns. Though La Ruta Puuc refers to a very specific set of ruins (Uxmal, Kabah, Sayil, and Labná), the small farming towns and a few other nearby sights make worthwhile stopovers and are included in this section of our guide. The towns of Muna, Ticul, Oxkutzcab, and Santa Elena offer shelter, food, and friendly advice. Two to three days should provide ample time for exploration.

# ⊟ TRANSPORTATION

### GETTING THERE

Visitors from Mérida or Campeche take **Mex. 180** to **Mex. 184,** which run east and form the northern border of much of Puuc; together with **Mex. 261,** these routes frame most of the ruins. The sites **Oxkintok** and **Las Grutas de Calcehtok,** not properly part of the Ruta, are 20km northwest of Muna, while the ruins of **Mayapán** lie 30km northeast of Muna.

### GETTING AROUND

Because of the large number of sights scattered about the area, renting a car in Mérida is the easiest and most flexible way to see what you came for. The roads are generally safe and well-marked, and will bring you through jungle and indigenous villages on your way between sites. Travel agencies in both Mérida and Campeche offer organized tours, which are frequently whirlwind affairs. Alternatively, **Autotransportes del Sur** sends a "Ruta Puuc" bus from Mérida at 8am that will whisk you through **Kabah, Sayil, Xlapak, Labná,** and **Uxmal**—quickly enough to return by 4pm. The bus spends 30min. at the sites and 2hr. at Uxmal, and costs 87 pesos. Admission to sites is not included. No other buses travel the Sayil-Oxkutzkub road. Disorganized public transportation can be difficult and will undoubtedly lead to frustrating waits. **Buses** are most frequent in the mornings, but return trips are never

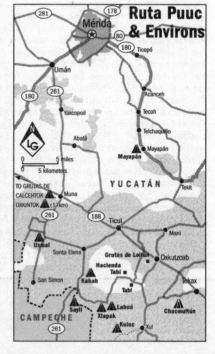

Ruta Puuc & Environs

YUCATÁN STATE

guaranteed. **Second-class buses** do travel Mex. 261 frequently and will stop when flagged down. **Combis** run frequently between Oxkutzcab, Ticul, Santa Elena, and Muna, and will make any trip for the right price. To pursue this option, it is best, though not easiest, to catch *combis* from the *zócalo* in Muna. Although *Let's Go* does not recommend hitchhiking, many travelers are successful at finding rides along the Sayil-Oxkutzkub road.

# ◉ SIGHTS IN LA RUTA PUUC

## KABAH

*Located 23km southeast of Uxmal, Kabah is bisected by Mex. 261 and is reachable by any 2nd-class bus between Mérida and Campeche; travel is easiest by the Ruta Puuc bus. Buses will only stop by request. Open daily 9am-5pm. 37 pesos. Video camera use 30 pesos.*

Kabah boasts what is arguably the single most psychedelic piece of architecture in the Yucatán Peninsula, the **▨Codz-Poop Temple** (Wall of Masks). Two-hundred and fifty faces of Chaac, the rain god, stare out fearsomely from the temple's western facade. The effect is diluted slightly because nearly all the noses are broken, but the spectacle is nonetheless alarming. The temple was built by slaves during the Classic period (AD 700-1000), when kabah was the second largest city in northern Yucatán. Unlike other Puuc structures and often characterized by plain columns and a superior decorative frieze, Codz-Poop stands out as an extreme example of the more ornate Puuc Classic Mosaic style. Chaac's prominence relates to the importance of rain for the inhabitants of Kabah, where there is little to no rainfall for half of the year. Standing proudly behind the temple are two impressive statues whose facial scarring and claw-like hands indicate noble lineage. Continue east and you will come across the two-story **Palacio,** which contains 14 *chultunes* (cisterns), suggesting its use as a residence for the elite. The palace's groups of small columns, separated by simple panels, are characteristic of the early Classic style. A path beginning at the rear left corner of the Palacio will take you to **Las Columnas.** The site is thought to have served as a court where justices settled disputes while gods made up the jury. Across the street by the parking lot, a short dirt road leads to rubble (right), more rubble (left), and the famous **Kabah Arch** (straight). The arch marks the beginning of the ancient *sacbé* (paved road) that ended with a twin arch in Uxmal. The archway is perfectly aligned with the north and south, testifying to the Maya's astronomical prowess.

 **STYLE NUMBER TWO.** The Codz-Poop style was developed late in the Classic Puuc period (AD 770-950). The exterior decorations, carved from thousands of pre-cut stones, were larger, more elaborate, and more durable than their stucco predecessors. New cement techniques were developed to secure stones to the building. The name Codz-Poop, which means "rolled-up mat" in Mayan, is derived from the peculiar appearance of the repeated stone pattern.

## SAYIL

*Sayil lies 5km off Mex. 261 on the Sayil-Oxkutzcab road, and is a stop on the Ruta Puuc bus. A bus between Mérida and Campeche passes by the crossroads (5km from the site) on the hour. Site open daily 8am-5pm. 34 pesos.*

Sayil, located in a small fertile valley, once controlled over 70 sq. km of territory (possibly taking advantage of rich earth) and had a population of about

YUCATÁN STATE

7000-8000. The site is a favorite of archaeologists for its long history and various styles of architecture. The **Palace of Sayil** stands out among the region's ruins as one of the only asymmetrical buildings. The unique three-story structure was constructed in several stages from around AD 650 to 900. Its facade remains a great example of the Classic Colonette style. The palace harbors 98 rooms, which once served as housing, storage, and administrative space for 350 people. In the foundation are eight underground **chultunes.** Crowning the otherwise unadorned second level are friezes of Chaac and the "Diving God" flanked by stylized serpents. The symbolism of these friezes is still being researched. Seven large human figures wearing ornate headdresses once decorated the third level of the Palace. The *sacbé* across from the Palace leads to **El Mirador,** a lofty pyramidal temple topped by a once-painted and plastered roof-comb, typical of early Puuc architecture. To the left, a 100m path leads through the jungle to the **Estela del Falo (Stela of the Phallus),** a tribute to Yum Keep, a Mayan fertility god. The peaceful feminine figure with the large phallus is worth a look, if only to lighten the mood. Among the buildings lying in pieces is **El Templo de las Cabezas (The Temple of Heads),** which is across the street and up a dirt path. The steep hike through a thriving colony of mosquitoes leads to a view of the top of Sayil's palace, which is best seen during the dry season.

## HACIENDA TABI

*The hacienda is accessible only in the dry season with a reliable car. The way is well-marked heading south from the Grutas de Loltún; take the road that branches off to the right and follow the signs. From Labná heading north, turn at the sign for the hacienda and go straight, passing 3 roads. Take a right at the 4th road through the orchards. At the end, turn left and continue straight for 1km until you reach the gate. The final 4km are unpaved. The hacienda is now run by the state government's Secretaría de Desarollo Urbano y Medio Ambiente (SEDUMA), but there are no regularly stationed employees. To stay in the building or at the campground, you must call ahead and make a reservation. SEDUMA can also arrange bird-watching tours, bicycle tours, or historical tours in the area if requested in advance. (☎999 164 8454).*

A break from the Ruta Puuc ruins, this hacienda, built among waving grasses and rabbles of yellow butterflies, is a monument to a less glorious part of Mexico's history. The building was once a sugar-producing facility that relied on Mayan and Chinese slave labor. A fire after the Caste War (1847-1901) destroyed a large part of the fields and the church, which was rebuilt in 1896. The **Casa Principal** was built in stages and finished in 1895 by its then-owner, Elogio Duarte Troncoso, a native of the Canary Islands. In 1910, the hacienda had 433 residents who lived in huts near the processing facility. During the Revolution, the slaves were set free; most either moved to another plantation or dispersed to surrounding towns. Since 1993, the beautifully restored hacienda has been part of a state government reserve. Lumbering has been prohibited, allowing for uninhibited growth of trees native to the area.

## GRUTAS DE LOLTÚN

*Loltún is accessible by car on the Sayil-Oxkutzcab road. Alternatively, snag a combi to Oxkutzcab from C. 25A between C. 24 and 26 in Ticul (every 20min., 12 pesos). You'll be let off at C. 23 and 26. Combis and colectivos leave across from Oxkutzcab's market for Loltún, on 20 de Noviembre. Ask to be dropped off at the caves (10min., 10 pesos). The caves are lit only during tours; you are not allowed to enter without a guide. Tours in English and Spanish daily at 9:30, 11am, 12:30, 2, 3, 4pm. 67 pesos; guides expect tips of around 30 pesos per person. Parking 20 pesos.*

The Grutas de Loltún make up what is believed to be the largest cave system in the Yucatán state. The word *loltún* ("stone flower" in Mayan) refers to the fascinating natural formations in the caves. The enormous caverns hold the earliest evidence of humans on the Yucatán, as well as fossils of extinct mastodons and saber-toothed tigers from the Ice Age. Around 2000 BC, ancient indigenous people settled here to take advantage of the water and clay, leaving behind pottery, marine shells, carvings, and cave paintings. Thousands of years later, Mayan *campesinos* returned, seeking refuge from the Caste War. Important caverns include the **Galería de las Manos Negras** (known as the "Room of Inscriptions"), full of black-painted handprint murals representing the Mayan underworld; the **Na Cab** ("House of the Bees"), named for the many niches in the cavern wall that host beehives; and the **Maya Gallery,** which once contained an Olmec sculpture known as "La Cabeza de Loltún."

# MUNA

A mere 15km northeast of Uxmal, Muna (pop. 3,500) is the best place for getting an early start at the ruins if you're coming from Mérida. Muna has recently grown into a convenient stop for tourists, with internet access above the PEMEX gas station in the town center (open daily 7am-10pm; 10 pesos per hr.), many *loncherías* (most open daily 6am-noon), *combis* (7 pesos to Uxmal), a Copercaja currency exchange booth, and basic services all located on the *zócalo*.

Two kilometers west of Muna on the Muna-Opichen highway you'll find **Conjunto Ecoturístico Mun-Ha Uxmal ❸,** which offers palapa huts with fans, cool concrete floors, and a large kitchen. A small museum covers the history of the area and the Puuc Maya. (☎997 979 9205; www.munha.org. 331 pesos per night.) **Hotel GL ❶,** C. 26 200, is right before the *zócalo,* just off the highway on your right as you approach from Uxmal. This simple inn allows you to park outside your room, take a hot shower, and sleep under a fan or A/C. (☎997 971 0095. 1 person 150 pesos, with A/C 200 pesos; 2 people with fan 250 pesos; 3 people with A/C 300 pesos. Hammock space free. 10% student discount.) The best restaurant, **Lol-Pich ❸,** is 1km north on Mex. 261. A shady courtyard and small swimming pools as well as a forest of pich trees surround a small palapa-roofed seating area. Try the traditional entrees like *pollo pibil* (chicken marinated in bitter orange juice and baked in banana leaves) for 50 pesos. (Open daily 10am-5pm. Cash only.)

# XLAPAK

*Xlapak is about 14km east of Mex. 261. As no public buses travel there, you'll have to either take a "Ruta Puuc" bus or rent a car. Site open daily 8am-5pm. Free.*

Xlapak, which means "old walls," is one of the smallest and least fussed-over ruins along the Ruta Puuc. The ruin consists of a few small jungle clearings connected by stone and dirt paths off of an underused road. Archaeologists are still in the process of excavating and analyzing much of the area. Without the tourist bustle or soaring grandeur of places like Uxmal, Xlapak invites you to spend time examining the beautiful, sometimes frightening artistic details that can be overshadowed elsewhere. At the first clearing, you are confronted with **El Palacio,** whose front facade is the most well-preserved in the site. The corners of the building are adorned with the glowering face and protruding nose of **Chaac,** the rain god. In the back, only a small section of the facade and a couple doorways remain, but above them is one of the most striking images in the Ruta Puuc: two enormous faces of Chaac, teeth bared, eyes wide. Take time to properly scrutinize the intricate little curves composing his eye sockets and nose. Behind the building is what appears to be a simple pile of rubble. If you look closely, though, a small section of wall sits under the the twisted, tentacle-like roots of a nearby tree. To the right, a stone path leads to the next clearing, which hosts a somewhat larger building, of which little is intelligible other than a few series of small columns. The last area is reachable through a narrow dirt path to the right; as you walk along it, you'll see more unexcavated buildings in the jungle on both sides. The final ruin consists of little more than an archway. Walk through the archway to find a small *cenote*. The path marked *"Salida"* will return you to the ruin's entrance.

## OXKINTOK

*Oxkintok is 5km off Mex. 180, near the town of Maxcanú. Coming from Mérida, it is the first sight. Follow the well-marked road about 2km. Go right at the fork. The ruins lie about 3km farther. The last kilometer is unpaved. Ruins open daily 8am-5pm. 37 pesos.*

Oxkintok (osh-kin-TOHK) is one of the most remote Ruta Puuc ruins. Its entrance consists of little more than a man sitting under a *palapa* at the end of a dirt road. The site contains several artificially raised squares of what was once the largest city in the Puuc region during the early Classic period. At first, you might think that the main attractions here are the views of the lonely jungle that surrounds it. There are, however, at least two must-do activities before you leave. First, stand face-to-face with the statue in front of the **Templo del Diablo (Temple of the Devil).** This wild-eyed figure carved into a stone column has his arms raised over his head, and two mysterious holes where one might expect horns. Next, bring along your flashlight and ask the guard to open up the three-story **Laberinto** (Labyrinth), where a tomb was found. Workers take you through the narrow corridors and subterranean rows that were likely once a prison, an observatory, or a training camp for priests. Most of the ruins were constructed between AD 400 and 600, and were abandoned by 1050. The architectural elements, symbolism, and materials have a Teotihuacán influence.

## GRUTAS DE CALCEHTOK

*Follow the signs marked "Grutas" (the left fork) when approaching Oxkintok; the caves are 2km southwest of the ruins at the end of the paved road.*

From above, the cavern looks like it opens into a jungle, with a tropical ecosystem characterized by honeybees, parrots, and leafy plants. It's a different story once you descend the ladder. The view from inside the cavern looking up, as light and jungle vines stream down, is breathtaking. A guide can take you deep inside the 10km long pitch-black caverns. Guide lamps illuminate thousands of unharmed and still growing stalactites, stalagmites, ancient pottery shards, and rock formations. A central stone slab is said to have been used for human sacrifice. During the Caste Wars, a group of 60 Maya survived for months in the darkness of the *grutas* as a Spanish army waited outside. The last person to live in the cave left in 1895; she had remained there since the time of the Caste Wars, having lost her parents inside. A Mayan priest was then brought to cleanse the cave of its *malos vientos* (bad spirits). (Prices of longer tours negotiable. Open 8am-5pm.)

A family from the *ejido* (cooperative) mans the entrance and will take you on a tour. The paseo turístico (150 pesos per person) lasts less than 1hr. and goes to the **Salón de Ceremonias.** The adventure tour (2hr.) includes the **Tumba del Rey (king's tomb)** and a Mayan cemetery. The extreme tour (5hr.) takes you shimmying down ropes and crawling through spaces just big enough to squeeze into. You will also see a room of glowing quartz and Mayan pottery. Wear old clothes and boots, as you will get filthy. Shoes with good traction are recommended, as the cave is extremely slippery. Be careful about going in alone; it is easy to get lost in the cave system. Bring a flashlight.

## LABNÁ

*17km east of Mex. 261. No public buses make the trip; the Ruta Puuc bus or a private car are the best options. Site open daily 8am-5pm. 34 pesos.*

The last of the Ruta Puuc ruins, Labná, the best example of the Puuc style, was constructed toward the end of the Late Classic period (AD 700-1000) when the Puuc cities were connected by *sacbé*. A short, reconstructed section of the *sacbé* runs between Labná's most impressive sights: the **palace** and the **Arch of Labná**. The partially restored palace stretches along the northern side of Labná, to the left as you enter the site. Built in 12 stages, its 67 rooms, seven patios, and two levels lack architectural unity. On the second tier of the eastern portion is the image of **Itzamná,** the creator god, represented by a lizard, whose belly is filled with a human head. What Labná is famous for, though, is the picturesque Arch of Labná, which still has hints of its original red and green colors as well as ancient handprints on the inner walls. Archaeologists believe that the arch could have served either as a ceremonial entry point for victorious returning warriors, as a vaulted passageway linking two ceremonial patios, or as an entrance for the upper class. The lattice and upper mosaic designs (in the form of two thatched houses) are considered a classic example of the Puuc style. They are also reminiscent of Maya-Toltec sites like Chichén Itzá (p. 111), whose residents conquered Puuc territories around AD 900. The observatory, **El Mirador,** stands atop a rocky pyramid, beyond the arch. The roof-comb of El Mirador was once magnificently decorated with stucco-modeled figurines of Mayan nobility. Back toward the palace, **El Templo de las Columnas** is off the *sacbé* to the right. The columns on the upper face, the middle layer, and the molding all exemplify the Classic Colonette style.

## ◼ UXMAL

The first thing you see when you enter Uxmal (oosh-MAL; "thrice built" or "region of fruitful harvests" in Mayan) is the towering and curvy *pirámide del mago*. It is the courtyards behind it that envelop tourists in their massive, ornately carved walls and arches. These are the most breathtaking parts of the ruins. The site is surrounded by jungle, which have swallowed up Uxmal's buildings for centuries. In fact, several buildings have yet to be excavated and are visible only as large mounds covered with vegetation, adding to Uxmal's sense of mystery. The jungle is also home to the region's 2 ft. long iguanas and singing birds, which seem to emerge from every crevice and doorway.

◼ **TRANSPORTATION.** Uxmal sits just off Mex. 261. **Autotransportes del Sur** runs from **Mérida** (1hr., 6 per day, 45 pesos). The "Ruta Puuc" **bus** also stops here. From Campeche, take a **"Camioneros de Campeche"** bus to **Mérida** (3hr., 5 per day, 55 pesos) and ask to be dropped off at the ruins' access road. The last bus returns at 6pm. You may be able to catch a **combi** back to Santa Elena and surrounding villages with the hotel workers, but departure times are unpredictable. Due to the complications of transportation in Ruta Puuc, it is usually best to take a **car** to Uxmal.

◼ **ACCOMMODATIONS AND FOOD.** Uxmal is the only site on the Ruta Puuc with accommodations and food, but all the convenient rooms are in luxurious, multi-star hotels. On the access road, you'll see **The Lodge at Uxmal ❺,** a hotel and restaurant complex owned by a suave Mexican polyglot. The hotel features two pools and wooden doors with Maya-style engravings. The restaurant, next door under a giant *palapa*, has upscale takes on traditional *comida yucateca* starting at about 70 pesos and ending near 400. (☎976 2032. Doubles 700 pesos, with A/C 1200 pesos. AmEx/MC/V.) Five kilometers north of the ruins on Mex. 261, **Rancho Uxmal ❸** has pink rooms and a swimming pool. (Rooms 250 pesos, with A/C 300 pesos.) The attached, *palapa*-covered **bar-restaurant ❺** serves breakfast for 30-50 pesos and Yucatec favorites for 40-100 pesos. (☎977 6254. Open daily 8am-6pm.) Next door is **Cana Nah Restaurant ❹**, which has a relatively modern-looking semi-enclosed dining room and serves traditional Mexican food. Cana-Nah also offers the cheapest lodging in the area, with camping available nearby for 60 pesos per person. (☎109 7513. Entrees 80-90 pesos. Open daily 10am-7pm.) At the ruins, the air-conditioned **Restaurant Yax-beh ❸** makes sandwiches (45-50 pesos), spaghetti (80 pesos), and *comida típica*. All are unexciting and pricey. (Entrees 55-115 pesos. Open daily 10am-7pm. Cash only.)

**◨ SIGHTS.** In AD 200, Uxmal was a mere village with a system of *chultunes* (cisterns) used to collect water for the dry months. Soon thereafter, Uxmal became the most prominent of the Ruta Puuc sites and its influence extended across the region. By AD 900, Uxmal had grown into a sizable town of 20,000 and dominated the fertile Santa Elena Valley. The Xius, an immigrant group who probably came from Tikal or central Mexico, brought the cult of Quetzal-cóatl in the 10th century. Some evidence indicates an alliance with Chichén Itzá, but a wall built later around the inner city implies that Uxmal went on the defensive, possibly because the city's relationship with Chichén Itzá had turned ugly. The city depopulated around the same time as the rest of the Puuc region—many archaeologists believe a series of droughts rendered the area uninhabitable. *Chilam Balam*, Mayan texts from after the Spanish Conquest that include both mythology and local history, seem to support this theory. *(Sight and museum open daily 8am-5pm; shops close in winter at 8pm, in summer at 9pm. Light-and-sound show in summer 8pm, in winter 7pm. Show 30 pesos; English and French audio translations 25 pesos. Sight, museum, and show combo 95 pesos. Parking 10 pesos. Spanish guides 400 pesos, other languages 450 pesos for 1-20 people. Video camera use 35 pesos. Free luggage storage. ATM in the museum complex.)*

**CHULTUNE.** On the walkway as you enter Uxmal is an example of a Puuc region *chultune*. This cistern, typical of the area, collected water for the city. Many Mayan sites depended on *cenotes* for collecting water, but groundwater in the Puuc region runs much deeper than in the rest of the peninsula. This forced residents to use *aguadas*, limestone-lined depressions, as reservoirs.

**PIRAMIDE DEL MAGO.** According to legend, the 35m **"Pyramid of the Magician"** was built overnight by a dwarf who hatched from a witch's egg and grew to maturity in a year. In response to a challenge by the king, who was angry over a previous defeat, the dwarf agreed to build the structure overnight. He completed the building and was named "Magician of the Land." The pyramid contains five temples and was actually built in five stages between AD 600 and 900; the multiple stages of construction are apparent in the mix of stonework used.

**CUADRANGULO DE LOS PAJAROS.** Immediately west of the pyramid lies the **"Quadrangle of the Birds,"** named for the bird sculptures adorning the western side and the palm leaves (or feathers) on the roof. Buildings erected at different times enclose the north and south sides and center on an altar.

**CUADRANGULO DE LAS MONJAS.** Continuing to the west, you'll find Uxmal's famed nunnery and the large **"Quadrangle of the Nuns."** Around AD 900, the Spanish, who thought the many rooms resembled those of a convent, misnamed the site. Each of the four buildings was built on a different level with distinctive decor. Some say the buildings represent the Mayan vision of the cosmos: the southern building is the lowest and symbolizes the underworld; the northernmost is highest, the house of heaven; and the east and west buildings are on the same level, representing the middle world where the sun sets and rises daily. A column in the center stands as a symbolic ceiba tree, the center of the universe in Mayan cosmology. To the south of the site lies the 34m long ball court. The court runs from north to south; the eastern side represents good and light, while the western side symbolizes evil and darkness.

**EL CEMENTERIO.** Emerging from the ball court, a path leads to a small, leafy plaza bounded by a pyramid to the north and a temple to the west. Stones that were once platforms at the foot of the pyramid bear haunting reliefs of skulls. The platforms, known as *tzompantles*, likely had to do with Uxmal's military victories and undertakings. To the west, **El Palomar** (Pigeon House), with a plain facade and cornice typical of older Puuc constructions, has three doors leading to the central patio.

**PALACIO DEL GOBERNADOR.** From the ball court, head south to the enormous **Governor's Palace.** Replete with strikingly well-preserved engravings and arches, it was one of the last buildings constructed (around AD 900). The attention to detail has led many to consider it the finest example of architecture at Uxmal. Intertwined stylized snakes, representing Quetzalcóatl, along with Chaac masks that create their own serpentine illusions, cover much of the frieze. The center features the rain god Chaac on his throne. The building is thought to have served as the royal dwelling, as well as the meeting place for the town council.

**CASA DE LAS TORTUGAS.** Realistic turtle sculptures adorn the upper frieze of the outwardly simple, two-story House of the Turtles. These sculptures may symbolize rain, suggesting that the building was used for the worship of water.

**GRAN PIRAMIDE.** Also known as "The Dwarf's House," the Great Pyramid consists of nine square levels stretching 80m long and 30m high. According to legend, the spiteful ruler tried to undermine the dwarf-magician's less-traditional pyramid by complaining that its base was oval. The king suggested settling their quarrel by seeing who could break a *cocoyol* (a small, hard-shelled fruit) on his head. The dwarf-magician cleverly slipped a turtle shell over his head and easily cracked the *cocoyol*, while the unfortunate king bashed in his own head. Atop the pyramid sits the **Macaw Temple,** with many engravings of a bird on its facade. The masks and artwork here have a more rounded look than other Uxmal art; they represent the eighth-century Codz-Poop ("rolled-up mat") style (p. 97).

**EL PALOMAR DOVECOTES.** Just west of the Great Pyramid, these structures were designed in the same style as the nunnery. Their name is derived from a series of roof-combs, which look like nesting sites, on the northern building. The protruding stones once supported stucco and stone figures now guarded in museums.

**CASA DE LA VIEJA.** To reach the "House of the Old Woman" from the entrance, follow the trail south to five buildings surrounding a small patio. Among these is the Casa, one of the oldest constructions in Uxmal, dating from between AD 670 and 770. The House supposedly belonged to the witch who gave birth to the famed dwarf. **El Templo de los Falos** (the Temple of the Phalli), 500m farther south, was once adorned with phallic structures symbolizing earthly and human fertility.

THE LOCAL STORY

## MAGICAL (SUR)REALISM

Santa Elena is a village of about 5000 people, largely indigenous, about 2½hr. south of Mérida. If it weren't on the heavily-trafficked road from Mérida to the ruins on the Ruta Puuc, there's pretty much no chance it would make it into even the most comprehensive guidebook. But it is on that road, so on an early Saturday evening, I stepped off a bus from the ruins in Santa Elena and started to look around for a ride home. Usually that ride would come in the form of a combi, or any one of dozens of vans that shuttle about a dozen people at a time between the small towns in the area. But there were none waiting in the usual place, so I asked a man sitting in a nearby park where I might find one. He said they would probably be at the town fair a few blocks away.

The town fair, which I found after winding my way through a few blocks of huts with roofs made of dried leaves was one of the more surreal scenes of my trip so far. Across the street from the huts, the people of Santa Elena had built a stadium of what appeared to be large sticks and rope. When I arrived, the stadium was packed with people watching what turned out—upon closer inspection—to be bullfighting. Around the stadium were dozens of vendors selling hot dogs, Cokes, and various other snacks. One husband and wife

# SANTA ELENA ☎997

This town, with 4300 Mayan residents, has the basics and then some, including a park and an 18th-century church (once the site of a Mayan pyramid) that boasts magnificent views from its roof. The small local museum, on the top of the hill beside the church, showcases recently unearthed infant mummies dubbed "The Dwarves of Santa Elena" by the local newspaper, along with explanations of ancient Mayan funeral practices. You can also see some small but well-preserved examples of Mayan stone carvings.

**TRANSPORTATION AND PRACTICAL INFORMATION. Buses** bound for **Palenque** via **Campeche** (7 per day 7:30am-7:30pm) stop on C. 20 in front of the *zócalo*, as do buses from **Mérida** (7 per day 6am-8pm). The **Ruta Puuc buses** pass Santa Elena on the highway at C. 20, across from the school. They then proceed to the area's ruins, ending up at **Uxmal**, but you'll need a lift or a **combi** to return to Santa Elena. Be aware that the Ruta Puuc buses are unreliable, since insufficiently full buses are often canceled. **Combis** from the *zócalo* go to **Ticul** as they fill up until 8pm. To reach **Grutas de Loltún,** take a series of *combis* going to Ticul, through **Oxkutzcab,** and finally on to **Loltún.** Basic services include: **police** (☎978 5244), at the north end of the *zócalo;* **Farmacia Mirna,** one block south of the *zócalo* on C. 20 (☎978 5048; open daily 8:30am-1:30pm and 5:30pm-9:30pm); and **Consultorio Médico** next door. **Internet** is available at **@.com**, on the corner of C. 19 and 18, uphill from the *zócalo.* (Open M-F 10am-1pm and 3pm-9:30pm, Sa-Su 10am-1pm and 3pm-9pm.) **Laundry** and **Internet** also available at **The Pickled Onion** (see opposite page).

**ACCOMMODATIONS AND FOOD.** Santa Elena has a few appealing accommodations for travelers along Mex. 261. Be aware that American and Mexican student groups often fill up all the beds in town in late June and early July. **Sacbé Bungalows ❶,** km 127, offers travelers a near-jungle experience with well-marked gardens as well as tidy *cabañas* with solar-heated showers, toilets, outdoor grills, and on-site breakfast for 50 pesos per night. (☎985 858 1281 or 978 5158; www.sacbe-bungalows.com.mx. 2-bed bungalows 250-350 pesos.) Slightly closer to town, the **Flycatcher B&B ❺,** across highway 261 from the school, has four large suites with private baths and A/C. There's also a cabin with its own 10 hectare grounds, which can accommodate up to 5 people for between 55 and 85 pesos a day, depending on the length of the stay. A 1500m trail leading from the hotel gives you a chance to spot wetland deer and jungle birds. (www.flycatcherinn.com. Rooms 550-750 pesos. Cash only.) Across the road and only 150m from Sacbé Bungalows is **Hotel/Restaurant El Chac-Mool** ❶, which has hammock space in private *cabañas* (35 pesos) and several well kept rooms. (Doubles 300 pesos, with A/C 400; triples 400/500 pesos.) The adjacent **restaurant** ❷ is the best in town, serving large helpings of eggs, tacos, chicken, sandwiches, and veggie options for 35-60 pesos. (☎978 5117. Open daily 10am-10pm, though guests can have breakfast beginning at 7am. Cash only.) **La Central** ❷, off the *zócalo*, has traditional Yucatec meals for 50 pesos and also sells ice cream for 6-11 pesos. (Open daily 11am-8pm.) **The Pickled Onion** ❸, 500m from town on the road to Kabah, is the last food stop before delving into the heart of La Ruta Puuc. Valerie, the friendly British-Canadian owner, is rapidly expanding her two-year-old business, having recently added a pool, a massage parlor, a hand-washed laundry service, and internet access (20 pesos per hr.). The menu includes vegetarian treats like *chaya soufflé*, traditional Yucatec cuisine, and North American-style salads and sandwiches (52-86 pesos). For 100 pesos, you can also spend the night in the hammock in the massage *cabaña*. (☎999 223 0708. Open daily 7:30-8:30. 15% discount to anyone who shows Valerie a *Let's Go* book. Cash only.) There are also **food stands** in the *zócalo* across from the Palacio Municipal.

# TICUL ☎997

Ticul (pop. 35,000) is a convenient, lively, and inexpensive base for exploring the Ruta Puuc sites of Uxmal, Kabah, Sayil, and Labná, as well as the Grutas de Loltún and the ruins of Mayapán (p. 91). In the streets around the large, bustling *zócalo*, you'll notice an excessive number of *zapaterías* (shoe stores)—Ticul is the shoe-producing capital of southern Mexico. The town is home to the 17th-century Templo de San Antonio. Ticul hosts shoe fairs several times a year, where you'll see men carting tremendous stacks of shoeboxes tied together with twine. On the outskirts of town, large *alfererías* (kilns) turn out enormous earthenware pots by the thousands for international distribution.

**⊏ TRANSPORTATION.** Ticul's **bus station** (☎997 972 0162) is on C. 24 x 25 y 25A, behind the church. Buses go to **Mérida** (every hr. 4:30am-9pm, 45 pesos), **Cancún** (16 per day 1:30am-11:30pm, 200

team had pieces of fresh meat hanging from hooks and split vending duties: the woman would take the slabs down and grill them, while the man spent most of his time on the ground, cutting the copious intestines of whatever animal he had just killed. No more than 15 ft. from the intestines was a stage covered in advertisements for Sol, the Mexican beer company. On the stage there was a live band and two women in bikinis.

"Ladies and gentlemen!" the band's leader called out. "Let's hear it for these two lovely ladies, straight from the capital, the White City, Mérida, Yucatán!" The women began to dance, turning to shake their tushes at the audience. The man with the intestines stopped cutting for a moment, looked up, and smiled.

—*Daniel Hertz*

pesos), **Tulum** (7am and 2:50pm, 155 pesos), and a few other destinations. **Combis** leave from Hotel San Miguel for **Muna** (12 pesos) and **Santa Elena** (10 pesos) from C. 30, between C. 25 and 25A, and for **Oxkutzcab** (every 20min., 10 pesos) from C. 25A, between C. 24 and 26.

**■ ⊠ ORIENTATION AND PRACTICAL INFORMATION.** The main road, **Calle 23**, runs east-west, with odd-numbered streets increasing to the south. Even-numbered streets run north-south, increasing to the west. The **zócalo** is east of C. 26 between C. 23 and 25.

There is a **Banamex** on C. 26 199, between C. 23 and 25, which exchanges currency and has a **24hr. ATM.** (☎972 1120; open M-F 9am-4pm). Other services include: **police** on C. 23, at the northeast corner of the *zócalo* (☎972 0210); **Farmacias Bazar,** C. 25 201, at the corner of C. 26A (☎972 1934; open M-Sa 7am-10pm, Su 7am-8pm); **Centro de Salud,** C. 27 226, between C. 30 and 32 (open M-F 7am-2pm; 24hr. for emergencies); fax at **Telecomm,** on C. 24A between C. 21 and 23, northeast of the *zócalo* (☎972 0146; open M-F 9am-3pm, Sa 9am-1pm); **internet** at **CamHeros,** on C. 25 between 26 and 26A on the second floor (10 pesos per hr.; open daily 9am-10pm), and **Ciber Hobie,** on the eastern end of the *zócalo* (10 pesos per hr.; open daily 9am-2am); and the **post office,** in the Palacio Municipal, on the northeastern side of the *zócalo*. (☎972 1120; open M-F 8am-4:30pm). **Postal Code:** 97861.

**⚑ ACCOMMODATIONS.** During the shoe fairs and in mid-July cheaper hotels fill up, so it is a good idea to reserve ahead before visiting Ticul. **Hotel Sierra Sosa ❷,** C. 26 199A, between C. 21 and 23 near the northwest corner of the *zócalo*, has clean baths, strong fans, cable TV, and free purified water. The small lobby is a meeting place for locals. (☎972 0008. Reception 8am-10pm. Check-out 1pm. Singles 190 pesos, with A/C 250 pesos; doubles 220/280 pesos; each additional person 50 pesos. Cash only.) **Hotel San Miguel ❶,** on C. 28 half a block north of C. 23, has clean rooms but the relatively small fans might not be able to keep you from sweating through the night. (☎972 0051. Reception 24hr. Singles 100 pesos; 1-bed doubles 150 pesos, with 2 beds 180 pesos. Cash only.) The nicest hotel in town, **Hotel Plaza ❺,** C. 23 202 between C. 26 and 26A, has rooms with large beds, private bath, and powerful A/C. Rooms overlooking the *zócalo* tend to be noisy. The pleasant garden patio restaurant serves breakfast 7-10am for 40 pesos. (☎972 0484; www.hotelplazayucatan. com. Doubles 360 pesos; triples 460 pesos. MC/V.) **El Jardín Posada ❹,** C. 27 216 between C. 28 and 30, is set back from the street amid lush vegetation. Four attractive, spacious cabins each come with A/C, living room, kitchenette, porch, and hammock. El Jardín also has a pool. (☎972 0401; www.posada-jardin.com. Breakfast 40 pesos. Cabins 300-350 pesos. Cash only.) **Hotel San Antonio ❸,** C. 25A 202 between C. 26 and 26A, rents immaculate rooms with A/C, phone, and TV. (☎972 1893. Reception 24hr. Check-out 1pm. Singles 245 pesos; doubles 368 pesos.)

**◻ FOOD.** After a hot day on the Ruta Puuc, Ticul is a great place to refuel and rehydrate. **Los Almendros ❷,** 1km from the centro off the Ticul-Chetumal highway (C. 22B), was the first in a chain of restaurants now in Mérida (p. 76) and the birthplace of *poc-chuc* (pork cooked with onions, beans, tomatoes, and spicy habanero peppers; 70 pesos). It serves popular Yucatec cuisine, with dishes like *pollo pibil* (chicken marinated in bitter orange juice and baked in banana leaves; 60 pesos). The restaurant also has a pool. (☎972 0021. Open daily 9am-9pm. Cash only.) **Cocina Económica D'Rubí ❷,** C. 25 216A between C. 30 and 32, offers tourists two delicious, home-cooked daily specials that come

YUCATÁN STATE

with soup, side, and tortillas for 30 pesos. (☎972 0509. Open daily 9am-5pm. Cash only.) **Cafe Trovadores ❷**, on C. 26 on the *zócalo*, lacks the down-home feel of the *cocinas económicas*, but you can get good enchiladas for 30 pesos and check your email while you're at it. (Open daily 8am-10pm. Cash only.) If you're tired of *poc-chuc*, **Pizzeria la Gondola ❹**, C. 23 208 at C. 26A, offers a taste of Italy with large pizzas for 80-110 pesos. (☎972 0112. Free delivery. Open daily 8am-1pm and 5:30pm-midnight. Cash only.) The **market,** off C. 23, between C. 28 and 30, has food stands, produce, and more. (Open daily 6am-2pm; busiest Tu, Th, and Sa.) **Súper Che,** behind the market on C. 21 x 28 and 30, has standard groceries. (☎997 972 1619. Open M-F and Su 7am-10pm, Sa 7am-11pm. MC/V.) *Loncherías* along C. 23 between C. 26 and 30 serve up Ticul's cheapest food.

# OXKUTZCAB                                                   ☎997

Oxkutzcab (osh-kootz-KAB; pop. 30,000) lies farthest east along the Ruta. Less touristed than Ticul or the ruins, Oxkutzcab is a convenient jumping-off point for the Grutas de Loltún, and has cheap lodging and food. Oxkutzcab is known as the "Orchard of the State," and its central market is appropriately overflowing with fruits and vegetables. Climb the hill on C. 54 to the Santa Isabel Church for a view of the entire city, or stop by the old railroad station, now the Casa de Cultura. The city isn't a great entertainment hub, but sometimes the cantinas play host to traditional dance parties.

**⬛ TRANSPORTATION.** The Mayab **bus station** is on C. 51 x 54 y 56, two blocks north of the centro. Buses go to: **Campeche** (6pm, 85 pesos); **Cancún** (13 per day, 195 pesos); **Chetumal** (6 per day 1:15am-10:30pm, 169 pesos); **Mérida** (26 per day 1am-11:30pm, 48 pesos); **Muna** (26 per day 1am-11:30pm, 19 pesos); **Playa del Carmen** (13 per day, 178 pesos); **Ticul** (26 per day 1am-11:30pm, 10 pesos); **Tulum** (13 per day, 148 pesos). **Combis** across from the market leave for the **Grutas de Loltún** (10 pesos). The *zócalo* is bordered by C. 48, 50, 51, and 53.

**⬛ PRACTICAL INFORMATION.** Local services include: **Banamex,** C. 50 x 51 y 53 (**24hr. ATM;** open M-F 9am-4pm); **police** (☎975 0615); **Farmacia María del Carmen,** C. 51 106 x 52 (☎975 0165; open 7am-11pm); **Hospital IMSS,** C. 64 x 49 y 51 (☎975 0332; 24hr. emergency service); fax at **Telecomm,** in the municipal building (☎975 0079; open M-F 9am-3pm, Sa 9am-noon); **internet** at **Interc@fe,** C. 52, one block north of the *zócalo* (12 pesos per hr.; open M-Sa 8am-9pm, Su 9:30am-4:30pm), and **Ciber-Ox,** on C. 48 across from the *zócalo* (18 pesos per hr.; open daily 8am-4pm); and the **post office,** on C. 48 x 53 y 55. **Postal Code:** 97880.

**⬛⬛ ACCOMMODATIONS AND FOOD.** All accommodations are within walking distance of public transportation. **Hotel Rosalía ❶**, C. 54 101 x 51 y 53, is a favorite among traveling vendors. Well-kept rooms with private bath, fan, and TV are 50m from the bus station and 100m from the *centro*. (☎975 0167. Singles 130 pesos; doubles with fan 160 pesos, with A/C 200 pesos; triples with A/C 300 pesos.) **Hospedaje Dorán ❶**, on the walkway behind the *loncherías* across from the market, is cheap and very basic. (☎975 1648. Singles and 1-bed doubles 130 pesos; 2-bed doubles with TV 160 pesos.) One block south of the *zócalo* is **Hotel Las Palmeras ❶**, C. 53 x 46 y 48, which has breezy open-air corridors that lead to air-conditioned rooms with queen beds. A balcony on the second floor allows you to look down the street over the central square. (☎979 9963. Singles 150 pesos; doubles 190 pesos.) The nicest place is town is the **Hotel Puuc ❷**, at C. 55 and 44, which has beautiful rooms adorned with paintings and photographs of Mayan ruins. (☎975

YUCATÁN STATE

0103; hotelpuuc.com.mx. Free internet and parking. Singles 220 pesos, with A/C 270; doubles 300/350 pesos; triples 370/420 pesos.)

Oxkutzcab doesn't have a lot of restaurant options, but what it has is cheap and delicious. At **Cafetería La Guadalupana ❷**, on C. 50 diagonally opposite the church, you can get enchiladas or tortas with a drink for 33 pesos. (Open M-Sa 5am-4pm, Su 5am-1pm.) **Cocina Económica Los Danis ❷**, next to Hospedaje Dorán on the walkway across from the market, has daily Yucatec menus for 42 pesos. It also has a few outdoor seats, from which you can watch locals shopping in the stalls a few feet away. (Open daily 7am-9pm.) If you're missing take-out from home, go a few blocks north of the *zócalo* to **Carolina's Pizza ❶**, C. 51 x 54 y 56. (Open 4pm-10pm. Large pizza 90 pesos; burrito with a drink 28 pesos.)

# IZAMAL ☎988

Izamal (pop. 13,500), Mayan for "dew that falls from heaven," has been a site of spiritual pilgrimage for over a millennium and a half. Originally home to Zamná, a legendary Mayan demigod, the site is the resting place of the statue of the Virgen de Izamal. Over the years, the town has sported a variety of nicknames. The name "City of the Hills" refers to the town's many Mayan pyramids, remnants of a time when Izamal was the principal religious center of the Yucatec Maya. Izamal is also known as "The Yellow City" for the rich egg-yolk color and white trim of its main buildings and world-famous convent. "The City of Three Cultures," yet another nickname, refers to the harmonious blend of Mayan pyramids, Spanish architecture, and *mestizo* character that defines Izamal.

## ▐ TRANSPORTATION

The **bus station** (☎954 0107) is on C. 32 between C. 31 and 31A, behind the Palacio Municipal. (Open daily 4:30am-8pm.) **Oriente** and **Autocentro** buses go to **Cancún** (5hr.; 6:15, 11:30am; 12:30, 4:30pm; 124 pesos), **Mérida** (1hr., every hr. 5:30am-7:30pm, 25 pesos), and **Valladolid** (2hr., 9 per day 6am-8pm, 44 pesos). For smaller towns in the area, catch one of the **combis** that leave from the streets outside the bus station (6am-9pm). There are a few **taxis** in town near the market; a **horse-drawn carriage** is the more setting-appropriate option. Carriages line up in front of the convent and take passengers to local hotels and sights (10-15 pesos).

## ◆ ▐ ORIENTATION AND PRACTICAL INFORMATION

The road from Mérida, 72km to the west via Hoctún, becomes **Calle 31,** which runs east-west like the other odd-numbered streets. C. 31 runs past the Convento de San Antonio, passing even-numbered north-south streets. C. 30, 31, 31A, and the Palacio Municipal frame **Parque 5 de Mayo,** the town's *zócalo*. The larger **Parque Itzamná** is surrounded by buildings with arched entryways.

**Tourist Information:** Palacio Municipal (☎954 0009; www.izamal.travel), just west of the *zócalo* across from the Convento de San Antonio. The main office offers an invaluable walking map of the city. Tours of they city can be arranged from the office or near the convent. Guides work for tips. Open daily 9am-9pm.

**Bank:** Banorte (☎954 0425), at C. 31 and 28, just north of the *convento*. **Exchanges currency** and has a **24hr. ATM.** Open M-F 9am-4pm. Other ATMs can be found at **Super Willy's** (open daily 7am-11pm) and **Farmacias Bazar** (open M-Sa 7am-10pm, Su 8am-8pm.)

**Police:** C. 32 (☎954 0505), at the end of the street where it hits C. 19.

**24hr. Pharmacy:** Farmacia YZA (☎954 0600), on the corner of C. 31 and 28.

**Internet Access: DirecWay** (☎954 0950), at C. 31 and 28, half a block east of Parque Itzamná. 10 pesos per hr. Open daily 9am-10pm. With more sporadic hours, but cheaper service, the **Centro Computacional de Yucatán** (☎954 0378) also has internet. Open M-Th 8am-8pm, F 8am-8pm, Sa 4-6pm, Su 2-4pm. 7 pesos per hr.

**Bike Rental: The Izamal Centro de Arte Folklórico y Cultura,** C. 31 (☎954 1012) rents 2-wheelers for an astronomical 50 pesos per 2hr. Open M-Sa 10am-8pm, Su 10am-5pm.

**Laundry: Lavandería Maria Jose,** C. 32 No. 253 (☎954 0037), between C. 21 and 23. 8 pesos per kg., minimum 3kg. Open M-Sa 7am-8pm.

**Post Office:** (☎954 0390), at C. 31 and 30A. Has a card-operated **LADATEL** phone out front. Open M-F 8am-4:30pm, Sa 8am-noon. **Postal Code:** 97540.

# ACCOMMODATIONS

Most travelers visit Izamal as a quick daytrip from one of the larger towns nearby, but the town is attempting to refashion itself as a low-key homebase for Yucatán explorers.

**Macan Ché Bed and Breakfast,** C. 22 305 (☎954 0287; www.macanche.com), between C. 33 and 35, 8 blocks southeast of the *zócalo*. Take a carriage from the north side of the *convento* (5-10min., 10-15 pesos) or walk 4 blocks south on C. 33 and turn right on C. 22. The hotel is 200m behind a bougainvillea-covered wall. A private retreat with individually decorated rooms. A hectare of cool gardens, a steam bath, and a natural rock-bottom pool are relaxing. Breakfast included. Wi-Fi available under the *palapa*. Reception until 9pm. Check-out noon. Suites 350-700 pesos. A six-person house for 1716 pesos (US$130) puts Macan Ché within reach of budget travelers. 132 pesos (US$10) per extra person. ❺

**Posada Flory** (☎954 0562), on C. 27 at C. 30. Clean, well-priced and uniquely decorated rooms close to the center of town. Each has private bath, fan, and TV. A/C optional. Guests are welcome to use the living room and kitchen. Rooms 180-280 pesos. Cash only. ❷

**Hotel San Miguel Arcangel,** C. 31A 308 (☎954 0109; www.sanmiguelhotel.com.mx), between C. 30 and 30A. In the center of town, Hotel San Miguel is the most noticeable hotel in the area, with its own private pyramid ruin. Elegant dark wood furniture and jacuzzi suite for those looking for deluxe treatment. Rooms with a view of the plaza and convent cost a bit extra. Breakfast included. Free Wi-Fi. Doubles with A/C 540 pesos; triples 740; 50 pesos for additional person. AmEx/MC/V. ❺

**Posada Los Arcos,** C. 30 260 (☎ 954 0261), between C. 21 and 23. Despite the less than enchanting reception area, Izamal's newest budget option offers spacious, serviceable rooms. Farther from the *centro* than other options. Rooms starting at 220 pesos fit up to 4. ❷

# FOOD

Don't plan on late-night wining and dining in the Yellow City: most restaurants close by early evening. For cheap eats, head to the Izamal **market,** on the corner of C. 30 and 33, which offers up big portions of *tacos de venado* (deer tacos) and other regional specialties. (Open daily 6am-2pm and 5-8pm.) **Super Willy's,** C. 33 300B between 30 and 32, is a good place to go for groceries. (☎954 0944. Open daily 7am-11pm. MC/V.)

**El Toro** (☎967 3340), on C. 33 between C. 30 and 32. El Toro serves generous helpings of regional food. Meals begin with a flavorful *puré de pepita* (puréed squash seeds with roasted tomato and cilantro), continue with regional dishes (65-90 pesos), and finish up with an enormous glass of *horchata* (12 pesos). Tasty, handmade tortillas. Open daily 8am-11pm, F-Su 11am-1am. Cash only. ❸

**Los Portales** (☎954 0302), at the corner of C. 30 and 31A next to the market. Kandi and company will fix you a plate of home-cooked local specialties for rock-bottom prices in a super clean diner setting. Breakfast 20-30 pesos. Lunch and dinner entrees 35-50 pesos. Open daily 7am-6pm. Cash only. ❷

**Kinich,** C. 27 299 (☎954 0489; sabordeizamal.com), between C. 28 and 30. Serves Yucatec favorites (75 pesos) as well as the yummy, if meagerly portioned, vegetarian *papa dul* (squash salsa and hard boiled egg in handmade rolled tortillas, topped with 2 sauces; 55 pesos). Open daily noon-7:30pm. MC/V. ❸

**Cafe Boglio** (☎988 103 0100), at the corner of C. 30 and 31A. A basic pizzeria offering cheap pies. Individual pizza 12 pesos, large 65 pesos. Open daily 6-11:30pm. Cash only. ❶

## 👁 SIGHTS

In addition to the sites listed below, Izamal offers a series of workshops, where visitors work alongside local artisans to produce crafts or learn about local medicine. The **tourist office** (p. 108) provides more information on these authentic activities.

**CONVENTO DE SAN ANTONIO DE PADUA.** This huge yellow convent consists of three main sections: **the church,** completed in 1554; **the convent,** completed in 1561; and **the atrium,** completed in 1618. The open-air atrium has 75 arches and is said to be second in size only to the Vatican. Several original 16th-century frescoes are painted on the facade and roof. These frescoes depict the Virgin Mary, the arrival of the Spanish and the first missionaries, Franciscan priests, and a Spanish shield with the symbols of Castilla and León. Inside the Baroque church is an ornate wooden gold-leafed altar built in 1949 by Tlaxcalan artisans. Through an opening in the altar, Izamal's famed statue of the Immaculate Conception, commissioned in 1558, is wheeled out for daily mass. Devotees make the pilgrimage to Izamal in her honor, as she is said to have the power to bestow miracles. When not on display, she resides with her dresses and crowns in a room behind the altar. There were originally two statues, called Las Dos Hermanas; one was sent to Mérida and the other to Izamal. In 1829, Izamal's *hermana* was apparently destroyed in a fire, and Mérida's statue was brought here. Legend has it that the Izamal original was saved and taken to the nearby pyramid of Kinich-Kakmó (see below). People say that every December 8, at the beginning of the town's 15-day *fiesta*, the two statues switch places in El Paso de las Dos Hermanas. You can visit Izamal's prized possession in Mexico's oldest *camarín* (alcove or resting place) by going through the door to the left of the main entrance to the church, passing the sacristy, and climbing the stairs.

On your way down, visit the convent's small **museum,** which exhibits pictures and mementos of the Pope's visit to Izamal in August of 1993, when he held a mass and meeting specifically for the indigenous people in the area. The Pope also bestowed upon the Virgin a necklace of pearls. *(Mass daily 7am, 1, 7pm. Camarín open 8am-6:30pm. Convent museum open Tu-Sa 10am-1pm and 3-5pm, Su 9am-4pm. All exhibits in Spanish. 5 pesos.)*

Four times a week, the convent is illuminated during the **Light of the Maya light-and-sound show,** which projects images onto the convent portico while recounting Mayan history. The show somehow manages to combine a celebration of Mayan heritage with the more recent colonial architecture and Christian themes. *(Light show Tu and Th-Sa 8:30pm. Spanish only. Free.)*

Izamal's small **community museum,** on C. 31 on the north side of the Convent, details Izamal's three historical phases and has a model of Izamal in 500 BC. *(Community museum open Tu-W and F-Su 10am-1pm and 4:30-8:30pm. Free.)*

YUCATÁN STATE

**PYRAMIDS KINICH KAKMO.** Five of the pyramids in Izamal are open to visitors and are all within walking distance of the plaza. The most impressive is Kinich-Kakmó (dedicated to the fire and sun god, whose name means "fire parrot" or "sun face" in Mayan). At 34m, it is Izamal's most dominating structure. The massive pyramid, measuring 200m by 180m, is the fifth largest in the country and the second largest in the Yucatán Peninsula. Kinich-Kakmó was built during the Early Classic period (AD 400-600) and formed the northern border of the ancient city's central plaza. From the top, visitors can look out over the entire city. *(Entrance with restored steps on C. 27 between C. 28 and 26. Open daily 8am-5pm. Free.)*

**LIQUOR HENEKUN.** A 20min. walk or short bike ride outside of town, the local distillery produces a tequila-like liquor using the juice of *henequen*, the cactus which lines the driveway. The distillery kicks into high gear during the summer, when just under 30 workers process 20 tons of juice, which amount to some 12,000kg of alcohol. The juice spends anywhere between three months and several years fermenting in barrels, emerging with a 34 percent alcohol content. Free guided visits with an explanation of the distillation process culminate in a tasting of the tequila-like liquor and *xtabentum*. *(Head south on C. 32. When you hit Av. Zamná, the 2-lane C. 39, make a right. Turn left at the sign for the distillery. It will be on your right. Open daily 8am-3pm. For tours, arrive around 11am.)*

**CENTRO CULTURAL Y ARTESANAL.** This new, slightly overpriced museum, opened with funds from Banamex, showcases contemporary folk Mexican art. Similar work can be found in most *mercados* in the region, making this feel a bit like an air-conditioned tourist trap. *(C. 31 on the Parque 5 de Mayo. ☎ 954 1012. Open M-Sa 10am-8pm, Su 10am-5pm. 20 pesos. Facilities include cafe and spa. Bike rental also available.)*

**OTHER PYRAMIDS.** Other pyramids dot Izamal, blending in with the modern cityscape. At one time, **Pap-Hol-Chac** ("Thunder House" or "Castle") beat out Kunch-Kakmó as the largest pyramid in ancient Izamal. Pap-Hol-Chac was home to Mayan priests before its ruin. El Convento de San Antonio was constructed with its stones. **Itzamatul** ("He Who Receives or Possesses the Grace of the Sky") looms 22m high to the east and is today the second largest pyramid in Izamal, offering excellent views of the city. *(Entrance on C. 26 between C. 29 and 31).* **Habuc** ("Dress of Water") is the most removed from the city center, on C. 28, between C. 35 and 37. **Chal Tun Ha** ("Water of the Flat Stone"), behind the Green River hotel on C. 41, was recently restored. **El Conejo** ("The Rabbit"), on C. 22 between C. 31 and 33, is also open to the public, though El Conejo appears to the untrained eye to be little more than a pile of rocks. The most centrally located pyramid, **Kabul** ("House of the Miraculous Hand"), is just north of the *zócalo* and is where the mask of Zamná was found. Unfortunately, surrounding homes and businesses make it almost impossible to reach, though there are plans to reopen the site in the future. *(All pyramids open daily 8am-5pm. No guides available at entrances. Free.)*

# CHICHÉN ITZÁ ☎ 985

Gracing hundreds of glossy brochures and suffering the footfalls of thousands of tourists, the post-Classic Mayan ruins at Chichén Itzá seem like the equivalent of a Mayan Disney World. The hype is understandable. Here lies the religious and political center of ancient Mayan civilization. With a pyramid that was once the site of human sacrifice and stunningly accurate astronomical calculations, Chichén Itzá is truly a thing to behold. The town of Piste (pop. 3100), 2.5km away, offers a range of services. Piste offers budget accommodations generally nicer than in nearby Valladolid, but it lacks the charm of other nearby colonial towns. The main reason to stay for a night in Piste would be to catch Chichén Itzá's light-and-sound show. In the morning, scout for spider monkeys amidst the rubble. Avoid visiting the ruins around noon, when the sun beats down and the tour buses roll in.

## ▐ TRANSPORTATION

The ruins of Chichén Itzá lie 1.5km from **Mex. 180** and 2.5km from the town of **Piste**. Mex. 180 runs west to Mérida (119km away) and east through Valladolid (42km) and Cancún (200km). Mex. 180 becomes **Calle 15,** the main drag in Piste. The main road leading to the ruins is the well-marked cobblestone road that runs from the eastern edge of Piste.

**Buses:** The main bus station (☎851 0052) in Piste is on the eastern edge of town on C. 15 next to the Piramide Inn. **ADO** sends buses to: **Cancún** (2hr., 4:15pm, 162 pesos); **Mérida** (1hr.; 2:15, 5pm; 90 pesos); **Playa del Carmen** (3hr.; 2:20, 4:15pm; 202 pesos); **Tulum** via **Valladolid** (2hr.; 8:10am, 2:20, 4:15pm; 120 pesos). Second-class **Oriente** buses run to **Cancún** (every 30min. 8:30am-6:30pm, 94 pesos) and **Mérida** (every 45min. 7am-5:30pm, 54 pesos), stopping at all the towns in between. For **Valladolid,** take the second-class eastbound **Cancún bus** (1hr., every hr. 9am-5:30pm, 20 pesos) or hop on one of the faster red and white **combis** (45min., 20 pesos).

## ▐ PRACTICAL INFORMATION

All services in Chichén Itzá are at the site's western entrance (open daily 8am-10pm), but you'll have to visit Piste for most services.

**Tours:** In Chichén Itzá, guides available at a table across from the ticket counter.

**Currency Exchange: ATM** at Chichén Itzá. This is the only ATM in the Chichén Itzá/Piste area.

**Luggage Storage:** Past the ticket booth in Chichén Itzá. Free. Open daily 8am-5pm.

**Police:** (☎985 10365). At the Camandancia in Piste, on the east side of the *zócalo*. Open daily 6am-6pm.

**Telephones: LADATEL** phones along Mex. 180.

**Internet Access: Grupo Informatico del Caribe.** 10 pesos per hr. Long distance phone service to the US for 3.50 pesos per min. Open daily 9am-10pm.

## ▐ ACCOMMODATIONS

Although finding a bed in Piste is not difficult, finding lodging that is both economical and appealing can be a challenge. Beware of taxi drivers who steer you to particular hotels, as they are likely doing this to get a commission from the owner.

**Posada Olalde** (☎851 0086), on C. 6 and off C. 15, across from Restaurant Carrousel (p. 113) down the dirt road. The best place to stay in Piste. Great value with large, spotless rooms in the main house and well-kept bungalows off the intimate courtyard. Bungalows for 2 from 250 pesos; each additional person 60 pesos. Cash only. ❸

**Posada Chac Mool** (☎851 0270), on C. 15, 500m east of the town square. Clean but dark rooms near the bus station. For larger groups, the rooms on the 2nd floor have significantly more light than those below. The friendly owner who lives in the 1st room loves to give travelers the scoop on local happenings. Singles with fan and private bath 220 pesos; doubles 300 pesos; triples 400 pesos; each additional person 100 pesos. Cash only. ❷

**Pirámide Inn,** C. 15 30 (☎851 0115; www.chichen.com). Next to the bus station and closest to the ruins. Offers bathrooms, electricity, and spacious, shady gardens in addition to a pool. Some rental hammocks available. Private rooms have fans, TVs, and

YUCATÁN STATE

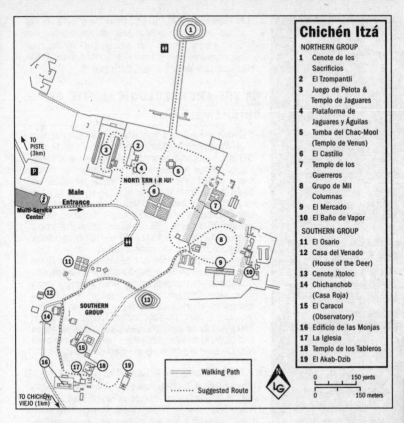

**Chichén Itzá**

NORTHERN GROUP

1 Cenote de los
   Sacrificios
2 El Tzompantli
3 Juego de Pelota &
   Templo de Jaguares
4 Plataforma de
   Jaguares y Águilas
5 Tumba del Chac-Mool
   (Templo de Venus)
6 El Castillo
7 Templo de los
   Guerreros
8 Grupo de Mil
   Columnas
9 El Mercado
10 El Baño de Vapor

SOUTHERN GROUP

11 El Osario
12 Casa del Venado
   (House of the Deer)
13 Cenote Xtoloc
14 Chichanchob
   (Casa Roja)
15 El Caracol
   (Observatory)
16 Edificio de las Monjas
17 La Iglesia
18 Templo de los Tableros
19 El Akab-Dzib

········ Walking Path

········ Suggested Route

0          150 yards
0          150 meters

TO PISTE (3km)

Main Entrance

Multi-Service Center

NORTHERN GROUP

SOUTHERN GROUP

TO CHICHÉN VIEJO (1km)

private baths. Camp space 60 pesos per person. Doubles from 450 pesos; each additional person 100 pesos. MC/V with 5% charge. ❶

## 🍴 FOOD

Those too engrossed with the ruins to think about eating should consider themselves extremely lucky—pickings are slim in Chichén Itzá. The on-site **restaurant ❸** specializes in *comida non-típica*: high prices and small servings. (☎851 0111. Entrees 50-100 pesos. Open daily 9:30am-6:30pm. MC/V.) You can save a few pesos by packing a lunch from one of the small grocers lining C. 15 in Piste, near the *zócalo*.

**Las Mestizas** (☎851 0069), in Piste across from Hotel Chichén Itzá. Caters to busloads of tourists; the enormous space has capacity for you and a couple hundred of your closest pyramid-bound friends. Also serves good breakfasts (25-50 pesos) and *comida regional*, like *cochinita pibel* (pork in red sauce wrapped in banana leaves; 70 pesos). Open Tu-Su 8am-10pm. Cash only. ❷

**Restaurant Carrousel**, C. 15 41 (☎808 0628), in the *posada* of the same name. Tasty and inexpensive regional food abounds at this *palapa*-covered joint. *Enchiladas con pollo* (tortilla casserole with cheese, onions, and chicken) 35 pesos. Open daily 11am-9:30pm. Cash only. ❷

YUCATÁN STATE

## TOP 10 MAYAN GODS

Most knowledge of the Mayan gods comes from the Popul Vuh, a compilation of creation myths penned by an anonymous Quiché in 1550. The original text was lost, but an 18th century translation survived, and now resides in the Newberry Library in Chicago.

**1. Itzamná:** the god of creation, agriculture, writing, and healing.

**2. Chaac:** god of rain and harvest. Depicted with catfish whiskers, scales, and lightning bolts.

**3. The Hero Twins:** Hunahpu, identified by the black spot on his cheek, and Xbanalque, who sports jaguar pelts. Pro-ballplayers who battled the underworld gods to avenge their father's death.

**4. Ah Puch:** "the flatulent one." Also the god of death. Associated with owls and depicted with rotting skin and popped eyeballs.

**5. Ix-Chel:** the moon and fertility goddess. Her fling with Itzamná produced the Bacabs, who hold up the four corners of the sky.

**6. Vacub Caquix:** a deluded bird deity who thinks he's the sun god.

**7. Ek Chuah:** god of merchants and war.

**8. Backlum Chaam:** the male sex god. Also one of the bacabs.

**9. Acan:** patron of intoxication and the honey brew, Balche.

**10. Zipacna:** Vacub Caquix's giant demon son. Kills 400 warriors in one sitting. Actually.

**Los Pájaros** (☎808 0628), across the street from Carrousel and 100m west. Good, cheap regional food under a small, smoke-filled *palapa*. Look for the roasting chickens and onions out front. Entrees 35-40 pesos. Open daily 1-10pm. Cash only. ❷

## ⬡ THE ARCHAEOLOGICAL SITE OF CHICHÉN ITZÁ

*The ruins are a 20min. walk or a 30-peso taxi ride from Piste. Alternatively, take an eastbound bus (every hr. until 5:30pm, 5 pesos). To return to Piste, wait in the bus parking lot outside the Mercado de Artesanías (by the big tree to the left as you exit) until a taxi, van, or bus swings by on its way to Mérida or Valladolid (every 30min.). Site open daily 8am-5pm. 111 pesos, Mexican students with valid ID 45 pesos, Su free for Mexican citizens. Video camera use 35 pesos. A light-and-sound show attempts to recreate the color and feel of Chichén Itzá in its heyday. During the summer, the show takes place daily at 8pm, in winter 7pm. 40 pesos, or free with admission to the site; headphones with English translation 35 pesos. Also available in other languages. For those seeking in-depth information, 2hr. guided tours begin at the entrance and cost 600 pesos for languages other than Spanish, including English, German, Italian, French, and Dutch; 500 pesos for Spanish; 100 pesos per person for groups of 8-10. Make sure to specify if you want the tour to cover "Old Chichén" in addition to the main courtyard.*

**HISTORY.** During the height of its power in the AD 12th century, Chichén Itzá ("by the mouth of Itzá's well" in Mayan) was a huge political and religious center with nearly 80,000 inhabitants. The center of the powerful Mayapán League, however, was not built in a day. Settlement of Chichén Itzá took place in three stages. The first two are known as the **Maya Phase** and are still visible today in the mostly unexcavated ruins of **Chichén Viejo.** The third phase, which began around AD 1000, is known as the **Toltec-Maya Phase,** and it left the most lasting constructions still visible today in **Chichén Nuevo.** It is believed that Puuc and Maya from Chiapas and Guatemala first settled the area around AD 700, building structures in the Chichén Viejo as well as smattering of smaller structures in the Chichén Nuevo area. By AD 900, Chichén Itzá had become a larger and more powerful center of trade. Central construction in the Chichén Nuevo in the post-Classic style saw the construction of the inner pyramid of **El Castillo** and the original **Temple of Chac-mool.** By AD 1100, Chichén Itzá was a major crossroads of trade and culture, including the ever-expanding influence of the Toltecs from central Mexico. The **Toltecs** brought with them their own gods, including **Quetzalcóatl** (the serpent-god) and religious practices like human sacrifice. It also saw the largest growth of the settlement and the construction of major structures like **El Castillo** and the ball court. However, by the mid-15th century, Chichén Itzá was abandoned—torn apart by constant warring with surrounding city-states and stripped of any potential for agricultural expansion by the huge stress of supporting its large population. The site was finally abandoned in 1461. Although climbing on any of the structures is now prohibited, walking among the ruins of this old city is an exciting experience.

**JUEGO DE PELOTA (BALL COURT).** Just northwest of El Castillo, immediately on your left as you enter the site, the **ball court** rises as a monument to the great sport of the Maya. Though Chichén Itzá is home to more than seven ball courts of varying sizes, this playing field, bounded by high walls and impressive temples to the god of fertility, and measuring 146m by 37m, is the largest in Mesoamerica. The surround sound effect of the court makes a few clapping tourists sound like a packed stadium. Check out the life-size reliefs on the southern wall showing the consequences (or honor) of winning—a man kneeling as blood-red serpents erupt from his neck. The elaborate game played here fascinated Cortés so much that he took two teams back to Europe in 1528 to perform before the royal court. The ball court continues to amaze, reputedly having served as the model for Harry Potter's famous Quidditch hoops.

**EL TZOMPANTLI.** A short distance from the ball court, underneath the shady trees to the south, is El Tzompantli (the Platform of the Skulls), which once exhibited the shrunken heads of prisoners and enemies. The eerie columns of bas-relief skulls lined up like gravestones on the lower platform walls serve as reminders of the Mayan practice of stringing skulls together to strike fear in the hearts of enemy prisoners. Nine skeletons were found beneath the mound that was once used to perform ceremonies and cremations.

**PLATAFORMA DE JAGUARES Y ÁGUILAS.** Next to Tzompantli, the "Platform of Jaguars and Eagles" pays homage to the warriors, represented by jaguars and eagles, whose job it was to kidnap members of other tribes. These hostages were then sacrificed to the gods. On either side of the feathered serpent heads, reliefs of jaguars and eagles with human features clutch human hearts in their claws. Originally brightly colored with beeswax paints, these are some of the best carvings at the site.

**EL CASTILLO.** Chichén's trademark, El Castillo (also known as Pyramid of Kukulcán) stands as tangible evidence of the astronomical mastery of the ancient Maya. The 91 steps on each of the four faces, in addition to those on the the upper platform, total 365; 52 panels on nine terraced levels equal the number of years in a Mayan calendar cycle. A staircase divides each face of the nine terraces, yielding 18 sections representing the 18 Mayan *uinal* (months) in each turn of the Long Count dating system. The most impressive feature is the precise alignment of El Castillo's axes, which produces a biannual optical illusion. At sunrise during the spring and fall equinoxes, the rounded terraces cast a serpentine shadow down the side of the northern staircase. A lunar serpent-god, identical to that of the equinoxes, creeps down the pyramid at the dawn of the full moon following each equinox.

**PLATAFORMA DE VENUS.** Directly north of El Castillo is the Plataforma de Venus (Temple of Venus), a square platform decorated with a feathered serpent holding a human head in its mouth. The temple's reliefs symbolize the planet Venus, as well as other stars and planets, and give information on their motions. The platform was most likely used for ceremonies. A statue of Chaac reclining characteristically with his offering dish was found here.

**CENOTE DE LOS SACRIFICIOS.** This 60m wide subterranean pool, 300m north of El Castillo and connected via a *sacbé*, was Chichén Itzá's most important religious symbol. The rain god Chaac was believed to dwell beneath the surface and request frequent gifts of virgin royal daughters in exchange for good rains; hence the name, "Cenote of Sacrifices." Elaborate rituals, beginning atop El Castillo and culminating in the sacrificial victim's 25m plunge to death, appeased the god during times of severe drought. Since 1907, over 30,000 sacrificial remains—including skulls, teeth, and jewelry—have been dredged from the 14m deep water, thanks to the work of American anthropologist and diplomat Edward H. Thompson (1856-1935), who at one time owned the entirety of the ruins. Unfortunately, much of the archaeological evidence was lost due to inexpert dredging; for example, mud extracted from the *cenote* was used for the foundation of a neighboring *hacienda*.

**TEMPLO DE LOS GUERREROS.** On the left as you return from the *cenote*, northeast of El Castillo, the "Temple of the Warriors" presents an array of carved columns. These columns once supported a massive wood and thatch roof. On the temple itself, before two great feathered serpents and several sculpted animal gods, is one of Chichén's best-preserved *chac-mools* and a table where human hearts were ritually extracted. This building's ornamentation shows heavy Toltec influence: a nearly identical structure stands in Tula, the former Toltec capital to the west. The temple was built over the former Temple of Chac-mool.

**GRUPO DE MIL COLUMNAS.** Extending to the southeast of the Templo de los Guerreros, this "Group of a Thousand Columns" contains an elaborate drainage system that channeled rainfall away from what is believed to have been a civic or religious center. The columns bear inscriptions and carvings. To continue the tour from this point, you have two options. The path that appears in the break in the columns leads to the Mercado and Baño de Vapor. You can also swing around the Castillo to another vendor-lined path heading for the "Old Chichén" collection of ruins.

**EL BAÑO DE VAPOR.** All the way past the columns, the steambath is divided into three sections. In the interior, water was poured over hot rocks, creating steam to purify those in poor health or those involved with religious ceremonies. The steam-bath ritual is an extremely old tradition. Travelers headed to the mountainous Mayan regions to the south can experience this ritual with locals from the area.

**EL MERCADO.** The final ruin before entering the older, central zone has taller, rounded columns and wider vaults that show the advances in architecture made over time. The markets here operated largely on the barter system, often using cocoa beans as money. To access the other ruins, you must retrace your steps back to the main courtyard and head down the path behind the Castillo.

**CENOTE XTOLOC.** To the east, off the first left from the main trail, in a hollow beyond the ruined temple of the lizard-god Xtoloc, is a *cenote*. There is no path leading down the slope, and swimming is prohibited due to dangerous currents. The secular counterpart to the holy waters of the Cenote de los Sacrificios, this pool once provided all of Chichén with drinking water. To get behind the observatory, follow *sacbé* No. 5, which becomes a winding trail.

**TUMBA DEL GRAN SACERDOTE AND EL OSARIO.** The High Priest's Grave is the first structure to the right of the path leading to the southern or central zones of Chichén. The distinctive serpent heads mimic El Castillo. Human bones and votive offerings of gold, silver, and jewels were found in a natural cave, which extends from the pyramid 15m into the earth. These objects are believed to have belonged to the ancient high priests and members of seven distinct dynasties of Chichén Itzá.

**EL OBSERVATORIO AND EL CARACOL.** Just beyond the **Casa del Venado** (House of the Deer) and **Chichanchob** (Red House) lies the ancient observatory. One of the few circular structures built by the Maya, the observatory consists of two rectangular platforms with large, west-facing staircases. Two circular towers with spiral staircases earned the building the name El Caracol (The Snail). The slits in the dome, functioning much like a sundial, can be aligned with the major celestial bodies and cardinal directions. The red handprints above the doorway were supposedly made by the hands of sun god Kinich Ahau. Six protruding snake heads were used for burning incense. Some believe that astronomers used the observatory when designing and constructing the impressive El Castillo.

**EDIFICIO DE LAS MONJAS.** Built in six phases, these buildings were probably the residence of the nobility or a high priest. To the Spanish, however, the stone rooms looked something like a convent—hence the ruins' name. Notches in the sides of the structure served as altars to various gods, but the predominant image is the face of Chaac. Mayan glyphs are still visible above the entrance on the east side of the building. Also on the east side is the annex, which predates the rest of the convent. Above the doorway facing the small courtyard is a well preserved bas-relief of a seated royal or divine figure. Many rooms in the convent have doorways that lead to dark corridors, which are home to bats, poisonous snakes, and frogs.

**LA IGLESIA.** This elaborate building, one of the oldest at the site, lies diagonally to the convent and is similarly misnamed. Its top-heavy walls are encrusted with intricate, hook-nosed masks of Chaac. The "church" incorporates a variety of architectural styles: over the doorway are Mayan stone lintels, while the use of wood and inclined edges indicate a Toltec influence. Above the door, a crab, a turtle, an armadillo, and a snail represent the four Bacabs—brothers who, according to Mayan mythology, were placed at the four corners of the universe (the four cardinal directions) to hold up the sky.

**TEMPLO DE LOS TABLEROS AND TABLEROS ESCULPIDOS.** Just south of El Caracol, the "Temple of the Panels" has rows of columns and carved panels. Though difficult to decipher, the panels on the exterior walls contain emblems of warriors—jaguars, eagles, and serpents—in three rows. The upper part of the structure is believed to have been a site for fire-related ceremonies.

**EL AKAB-DZIB.** This complex, 60m east of the convent, earned its name for the "dark writing" found in its 17 rooms. The older parts of this structure are believed to be Chichén's most ancient buildings—the two central rooms date to the second or third century, while the annexes on either side and to the east were added later.

## ⯈ DAYTRIP FROM CHICHÉN ITZÁ

### GRUTAS DE BALANKANCHÉ
*6km east of Chichén Itzá. The caves are easily reached from Chichén or Piste by any eastbound bus (the ones headed in the direction of Valladolid) on Mex. 180 (10 pesos).*

*When boarding, be sure to tell the driver where you are headed. You can also take a taxi (60 pesos). To get back, catch any westbound bus or colectivo, but be prepared to wait a while. If you get impatient, do not start walking in the direction you want to go, as buses will only pick you up at designated stops. Mandatory guided tours (30-45min.) in English daily 11am, 1, 3pm; in Spanish 9am, noon, 2, 4pm. 67 pesos; 2-person min., 6-person max. Open daily 9am-4pm. Small museum free.*

Descend into the ultra-humid corridors of the Mayan underworld at the inner caves of Balankanché, which were discovered in 1959 when a local tour guide noticed the passageway blocked with stones. Archaeologists believe the cave was a center for Maya-Toltec worship of the rain god Chaac (Tlaloc) and the serpent-god Kukulcán (Quetzalcóatl) during the 10th and 11th centuries. For unknown reasons, subterranean worship in Balankanché stopped at the end of this period. Afterwards, the offerings of pottery and sculpture rested undisturbed for nine centuries. Explorations have opened 450m of caves that are 25m deep. One could easily get lost in here if not for the light show that entertains and guides visitors. Pass by stalactites carved to resemble leaves, a huge column representing the sacred *ceiba* tree (the tree of life), and three groups of ancient ceramic vessels and stone sculptures. Hidden speakers tell the garbled story of the cave's past. The impressive stalactites and ceramics merit a visit, even if you have only a few extra hours on hand.

# VALLADOLID                                    ☎985

Tourists seem somewhat more scarce in the subdued town of Valladolid (pop. 46,000), despite its location on the Mérida-Cancún route, its proximity to Chichén Itzá, and its numerous colonial churches and natural *cenotes*. The town is a quiet stop on the way to many of the major tourist attractions of the Yucatán and a blossoming center of modern Mayan culture. In 1543, Spaniard Francisco de Montejo attacked the city, then the Mayan city of Zací (sah-KEY; "white falcon" in Mayan), which held out for several years before succumbing. Despite the imposing churches and grid-like streets that serve as reminders of Spanish dominion, the Maya were not so easily forgotten. In 1848, they rose up and took the city hostage for several months in what is now known as the Caste War. The Maya hold on to their past today: their language is still heard among *indígena* women weaving *huipiles*, between vendors on street corners selling locally made *huaraches*, and on the city's most colonial street, the Paseo de los Frailes (Street of the Friars).

## ▐ TRANSPORTATION

**Buses:** All buses leave from a **station** (☎856 3448) in the *centro*, at C. 39 and 46. To get to the *zócalo* from the station, take a left out of the main entrance and walk a block and a half east on C. 39 and look for the *centro's* huge church bell towers. **Buses** go to: **Cancún** (2hr., 20 per day, 42-74 pesos); **Chichén Itzá** (1hr., every 45 min. 7:15am-5:30pm, 20 pesos); **Chiquilá** (2hr., 2:45am, 78 pesos); **Izamal** (1hr., 12:45 and 3:50pm, 44 pesos); **Mérida** (2hr., every hr. from 12:15am, 74-112 pesos); **Playa del Carmen** (2hr., 9 per day, 88-136 pesos); **Tizimín** (1¼hr., every hr. 5:30am-5:30pm, 19 pesos); and **Tulum** (2hr., 9 per day 9:15am-8:30pm, 54-70 pesos). The best way to reach **Chichén Itzá** from Valladolid is by **combi**. The red-and-white vans depart from the parking lot on C. 39, just before the bus station (45min., 20 pesos).

**Bike Rentals: Refaccionaria de Bicicletas Silva** and **Antonio "Negro" Aguilar** (☎856 2125), both on C. 44 between C. 39 and 41. 10 pesos per hr. Both open M-Sa 8:30am-8pm, Su 9am-2pm. **Rudolfo,** on C. 40 across from the Bazar, between C. 37 and 39, also rents bikes and conducts tours out to local sites and villages, including San Felipe and Río Lagartos. Open daily 8am-7pm.

## ⚔ 🔓 ORIENTATION AND PRACTICAL INFORMATION

Even-numbered streets in Valladolid run north-south, increasing to the west. Odd-numbered streets run east-west, increasing to the south. The one notable exception is the **Paseo de los Frailes,** which runs diagonally northeast to south-west, beginning at the intersection of C. 41 and 46. Except for **Cenote X'keken** and the **Ek' Balam ruins,** everything lies within walking distance of the *zócalo,* circumscribed by C. 39, 40, 41, and 42. Blocks are spaced out, so what appears to be a short jaunt might really be a long haul.

**Tourist Office:** (☎856 2063 ext. 114) in the Palacio Municipal, on the corner of C. 40 and 41. Provides helpful maps and pamphlets. Open daily 9am-9pm.

**Currency Exchange: Bancomer** (☎856 2150), on the C. 40 side of the *zócalo.* **24hr. ATM** next door. Open M-F 8:30am-4pm. **Banamex** (open M-F 9am-4pm) and **HSBC** (open M-F 8am-7pm), on C. 41 between C. 42 and 44, offer the same services. HSBC also offers cash advances on credit cards.

**Luggage Storage:** At the bus station (p. 118). Free with bus ticket. Open 6am-9pm.

**Laundromat: Lavandería Teresita,** on the corner of C. 42 and 33. Wash and dry 10 pesos per kg. Open M-Sa 7:30am-8pm, Su 8am-2pm. **Lavandería Progreso,** C. 42 165, between C. 29 and 31. Full service 10 pesos per kg. Open M-Sa 8am-8pm, Su 9am-2pm.

**Emergency:** ☎066.

**Police:** ☎060. On C. 41, 10 blocks east of the *zócalo.*

**Red Cross:** ☎856 2413.

**24hr. Pharmacy: Farmacia Todo** (☎856 5353), on the corner of C. 42 and 39 on the *zócalo.* Several other locations on the streets off the *zócalo.*

**Hospital:** (☎856 2883), on the corner of C. 51 and C. 52.

**Internet Access: Phonet,** C. 42 No. 197 (☎856 5884), between C. 39 and 41 on the *zócalo.* Fax available. Internet 10 pesos per hr. Open daily 7am-midnight.

**Post Office:** (☎856 2623), on C. 40, in the *zócalo.* Open M-F 8am-4:30pm, Sa 8am-1pm. **Postal Code:** 97780.

## 🏠 ACCOMMODATIONS

Despite the city's charm, Valladolid's lack of comfortable budget accommodations means that it will likely remain a brief stop-over for budget travelers until the hotels in the area get their acts together. Penny-pinchers will want to stay away from the pricey hotels bordering the *zócalo.* Better bargains can be found one block west, especially on C. 44.

**Hotel María Guadalupe,** C. 44 198 (☎856 2068), between C. 39 and 41. Rooms with clean bath, ceiling fan, and dark wood furniture. Rooms 220 pesos; each additional person 50 pesos. Cash only. ❷

**Hotel Zací,** C. 44 191 (☎856 2167; www.hotelzaci.com), between C. 37 and 39. Rooms include 1 double bed and 1 twin and come with phones, pools, and cable TVs. There is also an on-site restaurant. 1 person 260 pesos, with A/C 390 pesos; 2 people 350/385 pesos. Cash only. ❸

**Hotel Lili,** C. 44 192 (☎856 2163), between C. 37 and 39, across from Hotel Zací. Private rooms in garish colors with private bath off of a small interior courtyard. Singles 190 pesos; doubles 220 pesos; each additional person 40 pesos. Cash only. ❷

## ■ FOOD

*Comida yucateca*, which blends European and Mexican flavors, tops every menu in Valladolid. Some favorites include *poc-chuc* (tender slices of pork marinated in a Yucatec sauce and covered with pickled onions), *panuchos* (tortillas filled with beans and topped with either chicken or pork, lettuce, tomato, and hot sauce), and *escabeche oriental de pavo* (a hearty turkey soup with pasta). *Xtabentún* is a delectable liqueur of anise and honey. Grab a *pibihua* (maize and bean rolls filled with beef and tomato salsa) from one of the many street vendors. Valladolid has a **municipal market,** four blocks northeast of the *zócalo*, bordered by C. 30, 32, 35, and 37, which offers fresh fruit, meat, and vegetables for cheap. (Open daily 6am-1pm.) A supermarket, **Soriana,** is on C. 39 between C. 48 and 50. (☎856 2630. Open daily 7am-10pm.)

■ **Bazar Municipal,** on C. 39 at C. 40, on the southeastern corner of the *zócalo*. A narrow courtyard crowded with cafes serving *comida típica*, pizza, and juice. *Comida corrida* (25 pesos) includes meat, beans, rice, tortillas, and a drink. Breakfast 20-30 pesos. Hours vary by restaurant, but most open daily 6am-midnight. Cash only. ❶

■ **Cafe Itali@,** C. 35 202 (☎ 856 5539), on the Parque Candelaria. A small, family-run restaurant. Just like eating at home, if home happens to house a professional SoHo-trained Italian chef with a handbuilt, woodfired pizza oven. Try the *fusilli* with mushrooms and prosciutto. Free Wi-Fi. Fresh pasta with pesto 50 pesos. Woodfired pizzas 90-100 pesos. Open M-Sa 6:30-11:30pm. Cash only. ❸

**Las Campanas,** C. 42 199 (☎856 2365), on the southwestern corner of the *zócalo*. Another larger location on C. de los Frailes. Though it might be the biggest tourist trap in town, the stellar view of the cathedral and tasty *comida yucateca*, like *queso relleno* (tortilla stuffed with meat, egg, and salsa and drenched in a creamy cheese sauce; 65 pesos), make it a worthwhile pit stop to escape Valladolid's heat. Live music daily 9pm. Open daily 8am-1am. Cash only. ❸

**Restaurante María de la Luz** (☎856 2071), at the corner of C. 42 and 39 on the west side of the *zócalo*, in the Hotel María de la Luz. Take in the life of the *zócalo* through the breezy French bay doors. Vegetarian and American dishes available in a relatively upscale setting. Breakfast buffet and *comida corrida* 60 pesos. Open daily 7am-9:45pm. MC/V. ❸

## ♫ ▣ ENTERTAINMENT AND FESTIVALS

For a raving party scene, look elsewhere—Valladolid is a small, quiet city with few nightlife options. The *zócalo* is beautifully illuminated at night, and fills with strolling families, Mayan vendors, lively small-time political ranters, and guitar-strumming teens. Later at night, **Santos y Pecadores,** C. 39 between C. 38 and 40, is the only club in town that attracts a crowd. A young set parties to *reggaetón*, salsa, and Spanish rock, romancing into the wee hours. (Open Th-Sa 10pm-late.) The only disco in town is **Xalaquia,** C. 37 210A (☎856 4920; www.xalaquia.com), between C. 50 and 52. Xalaquia is a self-described lounge bar within walking distance from the center. (Open Th-Sa 10pm-late.) Valladolid hosts a number of cultural celebrations and parties in addition to the standard weekend activities. From January 22 to February 2, the **Virgen de la Candelaria** celebration brings bull-fights and traditional music and dance to the fairgrounds.

## ◉ SIGHTS

While most visitors move on to Mérida or Chichén Itzá, those seeking a dose of history, *cenotes*, and cathedrals should give Valladolid a chance. The city mixes the rural charm and authenticity of the small towns and countryside surrounding it with the colonial elegance of the compact city center.

YUCATÁN STATE

**CATEDRAL DE SAN SERVASIO.** According to legend, two criminals were pulled from the church and murdered by an angry mob. When the bishop found out, he had the church destroyed. It was rebuilt from 1720 to 1730 and is the only cathedral on the peninsula facing north instead of east. Legend holds that the few cathedrals in Mexico not built east-west were so constructed because priests wanted to mark former sites of human sacrifice. The massive colonial twin towers make it an unmistakable physical landmark. *(Over the zócalo on C. 41. Open M-Sa 7:30am-12:30pm and 4-8pm, Su 6am-2pm and 4-9pm. Mass M-Sa 7pm; Su 7am, 1, 7pm. Free.)*

**MUSEO DE SAN ROQUE.** This humble museum, founded in 1998, offers well-presented exhibits about local history. A relaxing courtyard and detailed information on Ek' Balam make it a good pre-ruins stop. Avid craft shoppers can pick up tips on how to spot a fake. *(On C. 41, between C. 40 and 38. All exhibits in Spanish. Open M-Sa 9am-8pm, Su 9am-6pm. Free.)*

**EL PASEO DE LOS FRAILES.** This picturesque, colonial street with colorful, flat-front houses stands out in the otherwise plain city. The "Street of the Friars," dominated by pedestrians, provides the perfect setting for a morning or evening stroll. Many residents leave their doors open. *(C. 41A between Las Cinco Calles and San Bernardino.)*

**SAN BERNARDINO DE SIENA.** Affiliated with the Ex-Convento de Sisal, the church was built over a *cenote* (now visible inside the circular tower) in 1552 with stones from the main Mayan temple. It is the oldest ecclesiastical building in the Yucatán and bears a peculiar square pattern. A large image of the Virgen de Guadalupe hangs on the altar in the back. The frescoes on either side of the altar are unique to the church. *(On C. 41A, at the end of Paseo de los Frailes. Open daily 8am-noon and 5-8pm. 10 pesos.)*

**CENOTE ZACÍ.** In the middle of the city, Cenote Zací is a cavernous hollow full of protruding stalagmites, tropical gardens, and serene green-blue water. *(3 blocks east of the zócalo, on C. 36 between C. 37 and 39. Free view from the palapa restaurant on the edge. Open daily 8am-5pm. 15 pesos, children 10 pesos.)*

**CASA DE LA CULTURA.** This building, now the city's cultural center, was originally home to diplomats and later functioned as a school. Art exhibits are on display inside, and an attendant in the front office can fill you in on upcoming traditional dance performances. If there is no show, you may be able to join a class (20-50 pesos per month). The region's traditional dance, the *jarana*, has several varieties, one involving braiding ribbons about a pole. Classes range from guitar and ballet to dances from Jalisco and Veracruz. *(☎856 1866. Next to the municipal building on the eastern side of the zócalo. Dance classes mostly in the late afternoon or evening. Free.)*

## 🔳 DAYTRIPS FROM VALLADOLID

**▨CENOTE DZITNUP** (X'KEKÉN). The gorgeous *cenote*, ironically named "dirty" in Mayan, allows you to escape underground in its refreshingly cool water. Visit before midday to catch a beam of light slicing through a circular hole in the roof, bathing the cavern in blue light. **Cenote Sambula** (25 pesos, under 8 15 pesos) is only 200m away and offers beauty on a smaller scale. The well-lit Sambula has been used to film a number of commercials. *(6km west of town. To get there by car or bike, take busy C. 39 to the highway toward Mérida. At the roundabout near the gas station, cross the street and get on the bike path that runs along the highway. Make a left at the sign for Dzitnup and continue to the entrance plaza on your left. 20min. Alternatively, catch a dark blue colectivo taxi (15 pesos) on C. 38 between C. 37 and 39. Open daily 8am-5pm. 25 pesos, children and students with ID 15 pesos.)*

YUCATÁN STATE

**EK' BALAM.** Ek' Balam ("Black Jaguar") was a Mayan city that flourished in the late Classical period, around AD 700-1000. The site covers 12 sq. k. Excavations, which began in 1984, are still very much in progress. Ek' Balam contains several temples, a rare circular observatory, a ball court, and a *chac-mool* stone sacrificial table. Everything is organized around two plazas and divided by the ball court. Two walls surround the city for added defense. The pyramid itself is one of the biggest in the Yucatán and one of the last that tourists are still able to climb. It is believed to have been the tomb of a king. At 303m high, it's not quite as tall as other Mayan pyramids, but its base is an astonishing 160m long. Note the two giant unexcavated mounds flanking the pyramid—archaeologists expect to find more pyramids reaching 20-25m in height somewhere in the rubble. The ruins are generally uncrowded and, as reconstruction continues, are definitely worth a visit. Don't forget bug repellent! *(The ruins are 25km northeast of Valladolid. The Oriente bus (40 pesos) leaves from the C. 40 side of the main plaza at 9am and returns at 1pm. Taxis run 200-225 pesos round-trip, and the driver will generally wait up to 2hr. Taxis colectivos are a better deal at 40 pesos, although you should go early to make sure one will stop by to pick you up on the way back. They leave from the stand on C. 44, at the corner with C. 31. Open daily 8am-5pm, last entry 4:30pm. 31 pesos. Guided tours available 350 pesos.)*

Down a 1.5km path from the Ek Balam parking lot, **Cenote Xcache** has been turned into a tourist attraction. *(30 pesos to walk, 60 pesos to rent a bicycle. 200 pesos for the complete package with kayak and zip line. Open daily 8am-5pm. Cash only.)*

# RÍO LAGARTOS
☎986

A small fishing village on the Yucatán Peninsula's northern coast, Río Lagartos (pop. 7000) is home to one of the largest concentrations of flamingos in the world. The sea has inched its way inland here, with mangrove forests creating a buffer from the Gulf and providing shelter to more than 350 bird species. Río Lagartos teems with wildlife—crocodiles (the mistakenly identified alligators that have given the town its name), snowy egrets perched like Christmas ornaments in the treetops, and a massive colony of pink flamingos call this village home. Wind-whipped Río is located inside the Reserva de la Biósfera Río Lagartos. Apart from Las Coloradas, the salt mine outside of town, the tourism industry provides employment for most locals, resulting in intense competition between tour companies.

**▐▐ TRANSPORTATION AND PRACTICAL INFORMATION.** Río is small and easily walkable. The **bus terminal** is located on C. 10, just a few blocks from the water. There is **no bank or ATM,** so bring cash. From **Tizimín,** buses head to Río Lagartos, continuing on to **San Felipe** (1hr.; 6:30, 9:15am, 2:15, 4:15pm; 30 pesos). From Río, buses leave for **Tizimín,** with quick connections to **Mérida** (5:30, 7, 11am, 12:30, 2:30, 5:30pm). The **police** can be reached at ☎105 3144. There's **internet** at **Cyber Nayo,** on the plaza at the end of C. 11 and 12. (10 pesos per hr. Open daily 3-10pm.)

**▐▐ ACCOMMODATIONS AND FOOD. Cabañas Las Escondidas ❶,** on C. 19, next to Restaurant Isla Contoy, is the cheapest accommodation in town. These basic flamingo-themed *cabañas* have thatched roofs, beds, private baths, and deck chairs close to the Isla Contoy restaurant. The Cabañas Las Escondidas also has guides. Signs at the bus station point the way. (☎862 0121. Check-out 1pm. Single 150 pesos; doubles 200. Cash only.) **Posada las Gaviotas ❹,** at the corner of C. 12 and 13, in front of the water, has basic rooms that fit three. Rooms have private baths, but they're something of a squeeze with the sink in the shower. Ask for a view, as rooms all cost the same. From the bus station door, exit right and walk

YUCATÁN STATE

until you hit the water. Make a left. The Posada will be on your left, close to the Restaurant La Torreja. (☎862 0116. Rooms 300 pesos. Cash only.)

The open-air **Bar el Bandolón ❶**, on C. 9 (☎862 0090), serves cold beer and fresh whole fish, eyeballs and whiskers included. (Open daily 11am-7pm.) The festive dining room at **Macumba ❸**, C. 16 102 (☎862 0092), between 9 and 11, is decorated with seashell handicrafts made by the owner. (Seafood 55-85 pesos. Open daily 8am-midnight. Cash only.)

**FLAMINGO TOURS AND WATER ACTIVITIES.** The best time to see the birds is at sunrise, especially in the months of May and July. Tours stop running around 3:30pm, typically last 2½hr., and cost between 500-600 pesos for a six-person boat. Tours include visits to the flamingos, a stop at a beach for a mud bath, and a trip to a fresh water spring. Haggling can sometimes bring the price down. For the best trip, ask for a certified guide (with larger operators, usually only the top guys are fully licensed). The flamingos tend to be the highlight of the trip, but you'll want a guide that takes his time getting there, allowing you to appreciate all the other wildlife Río Lagartos has to offer. Some operators offer night tours to watch the crocodiles. You can also hire boats to take you to the beach for 150 pesos.

It's easy to find someone to take you to the flamingos—you'll be approached by one of the tour companies as soon as you step off the bus. Many restaurants in town double as the headquarters for tour companies; walking along the waterfront will allow you to compare all the options. Some respected operators include **Flamingos Tour** (☎862 0158), **Ismael Navarro** (☎862 0000; www.riolagartos-ecotours.com), who works out of the Restaurant Isla Contoy, and **Diego Nuñez,** who arranges tours from his restaurant **Las Palapas de la Torreja,** C. 9 105 (☎862 0452; www.riolagartosexpeditions.com/diego). Diego also rents equipment. Bikes 50 pesos per hr., 80 pesos per ½ day. Kayak 100 pesos per 2hr.

**FESTIVALS.** In mid-July, Río Lagartos hosts the **Fería de Santiago.** During this festival, a bullring is constructed in town, and townspeople take turns taunting the animals.

## SAN FELIPE

Pelican-ridden boats bob quietly in San Felipe's town harbor, which is fronted by a picturesque yellow boardwalk. Even smaller than its neighbor, San Felipe (pop. 2500) remains largely untouched by tourists, though its access to the Reserva de la Biósfera Ría Lagartos and nearby beaches draws groups of sport fishermen and some summer traffic. Río Lagartos and San Felipe are only 20min. apart, but infrequent buses mean that the town might be best enjoyed as a daytrip from Río Lagartos. Unless you rent a car, it's difficult to visit both Río and San Felipe in a day from larger cities like Mérida.

**TRANSPORTATION AND PRACTICAL INFORMATION. Buses** leave San Felipe for **Tizimín,** stopping daily in **Río Lagartos** (8:30, 10:30, 11:45am, 2, 3:30, 5:30pm). For buses to San Felipe, see Río Lagartos **Transportation** (opposite page). **Calle 10** is the main road leading into town. C. 10 hits the beach, which is flanked by **Calle 9** along the coast. The town cooperative has a stand with **tourist information,** including boat tours and hotels. The stand is located at the end of the *malecón*, on C. 9. (☎862 2045. Ask for Luciano Figueroa Salamanca. Open 7am-6pm.)

**ACCOMMODATIONS AND FOOD. Hotel San Felipe de Jesus ❻,** C. 9A 59, between 14 and 16, just a few blocks from the beach, has a range of rooms with views of the water. Suites with purified water, plush towels, and king size beds host groups in for sport fishing. (☎862 2027. Doubles 486-503 pesos, triples 500-574 pesos; 40 pesos per additional person. Cash only.)

In the morning, **Alvaro's Lonchería** ❸, across from the bus station, prepares hearty breakfast *tortas*. From a plastic table, patrons can watch Mexican game shows play on an ancient television set. (Open daily 6-10am. Cash only.) An overgrown beach shack, **Restaurant Vaselina** ❷, C. 9 52, looks out to the sea. It's the biggest franchise in town, with a *palapa*-covered dining room and small dance club next door. Tart *ceviches* and *pescado frito* cost 50-150 pesos. (☎100 3831. Open daily 8am-7pm. Disco open Sa 10pm-3am. MC/V.)

**🎏 OUTDOOR ACTIVITIES.** San Felipe offers commissioned boat tours, but without a stop to see the flamingos in the Reserva. Trips go to **Isla Cerritos,** a port once used by the Maya to exchange salt, meat, and corn. (400 pesos for five people, including beach time. Round-trip tour to the beach 100 pesos. Longer trips 700 pesos per boat.)

YUCATÁN STATE

# QUINTANA ROO

If it's beautiful beaches, snorkeling, scuba diving, and wild nightlife you seek, look no further than Quintana Roo. Home to **Isla Cozumel** (p. 152), a diving mecca which attracts over 2 million visitors every year, it should come as no surprise that Quintana Roo's booming tourist industry also makes it the economic powerhouse of the peninsula. But if being packed like sardines on the shores of the Gulf of Mexico sounds less than appealing, have no fear—you can find your own patch of uncrowded sand if you venture far enough away from these hot spring break hubs. Head out to **Isla Mujeres** (p. 136), easily accessible by ferry from Cancún. Still touristy, its beaches are less crowded than its neighbors, and as a bonus, it provides easy access to the Mayan ruins of Ixchel. Those with more time on their hands should make the longer trip to **Isla Holbox** (p. 142). You can also escape the crowds by making your way down the Riviera Maya toward destinations like **Tulum** (p. 160), a quickly developing backpacker destination with some impressive Mayan ruins to boot. Or, make the trek to the **Sian Ka'an Biosphere Reserve** (p. 172), which occupies approximately 10% of Quintana Roo.

Founded in 1974, Quintana Roo is Mexico's youngest state. Originally part of Yucatán State, Quintana Roo separated in the 1840s during the Caste War and was renamed Chan Santa Cruz—an independent Mayan nation. In the following years the Mexican government struggled to reassert its power over the region. Quintana Roo remained a territory until 1974, when it attained statehood. Among the reasons for this eventual shift was Cancún's growing popularity. Today, while Cancún continues to steal the headlines, other destinations in Quintana Roo are quietly making a name for themselves among those looking for a relaxing getaway.

## CANCÚN                                                          ☎998

Built along the sparkling Caribbean coast, the once modest city of Cancún (pop. 600,000) has transformed into a resort behemoth whose alcohol-soaked, disco-shaken, sex-stirred insanity surpasses that of any other party destination in the Western Hemisphere. In the "Zona Hotelera," Vegas-style monster hotels crowd the beach, while buses and rental SUVs whiz by on the nearby highway. Ask university students who have "done" spring break Cancún and their eyes will invariably glass over as they recall—or wish they could recall—night after night of drunken debauchery. Upside-down tequila shots and bikini contests, however, are not the only way to enjoy this former Mayan fishing village. In the city proper, a few scattered parks provide respite from the madness, while still keeping nightlife accessible. Cheap airfare and Cancún's central location on the peninsula make it a great starting point for excursions up and down the Mayan Riviera. Still, most travelers—regardless of budget—will want to make their stay here brief.

## ▞ TRANSPORTATION

### INTERCITY TRANSPORTATION

**Flights: Aeropuerto Internacional de Cancún (CUN;** ☎886 0028), south of the city on Mex. 307. Airlines include: **AeroCaribe** (☎884 2000); **Aeroméxico** (☎884 3571); **American** (☎+1-800-904-6000); **Continental** (☎886 0006); **Delta** (☎+1-800-123-4710); **Lan Chile** (☎883 0361); **LACSA** (☎887 3101); **Martinair** (☎886 0070);

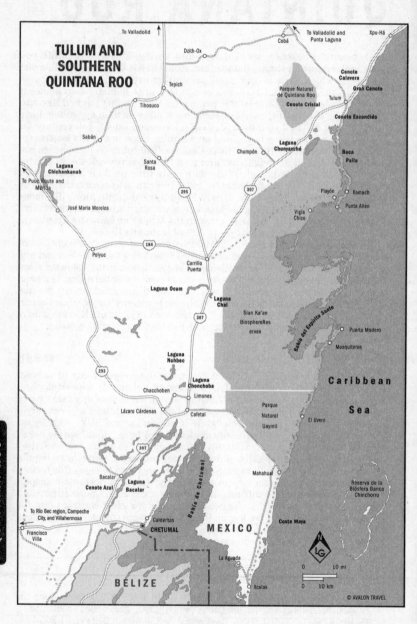

TULUM AND
SOUTHERN
QUINTANA ROO

To Valladolid

Dzith-Ox

Cobá

To Valladolid and
Punta Laguna

Xpu-Há

Tepich

Cenote
Calavera

Gran Cenote

Parque Natural
de Quintana Roo

Tulum

Tihosuco

Cenote Cristal

Cenote Escondido

Sabán

Chumpón

Laguna
Chunyaxché

Boca
Paila

Santa
Rosa

Laguna
Chichankanah

295

Playón

Xamach

To Puuc Route and
Mérida

Vigía
Chico

Punta Allen

José María Morelos

184

Polyuc

Carrillo
Puerto

Laguna Ocum

Laguna
Chal

Sian Ka'an
BiosphereRes
ervae

Bahía del Espíritu Santo

307

Puerto Madero

Mosquiteros

Laguna
Nohbec

Caribbean

293

Laguna
Chonchoba

Sea

Chacchoben

Limones

Parque
Natural
Uaymil

Lázaro Cárdenas

Cafetal

El Uvero

307

Mahahual

Reserva de la
Biósfera Banco
Chinchorro

Bacalar

Laguna
Bacalar

Cenote Azul

Bahía de Chetumal

To Río Bec region, Campeche
City, and Villahermosa

Calderitas

Francisco
Villa

CHETUMAL

MEXICO

Costa Maya

La Aguada

N

BÉLIZE

Xcalak

0       10 mi

0       10 km

© AVALON TRAVEL

QUINTANA ROO

**Mexicana** (☎881 9090); and **United Airlines** (☎+1-800-003-0777). **ADO** runs a bus to the bus station (30min., 40 pesos) from the domestic terminal. Private shuttles, SUVs, and taxis wait just outside customs (158-740 pesos/US$12-56).

**WAIT!** Before leaving the airport, make sure to grab a copy of *Cancún Tips*. The magazine and accompanying coupon book is full of deals on bars, restaurants, and tours, and can help save a few pesos in Mexico's most expensive city. Available at the tourist office, airport, Plaza Caracol, and most hotels.

**Buses:** (☎884 1378, reservations +1-800-702-8000), on the corner of Uxmal and Tulum facing Plaza Caribe. The 4 major companies are **ADO, Norte, Oriente,** and **Mayab.** Destinations include: **Campeche** (7hr., 5 per day 7:45am-10:30pm, 372 pesos); **Chetumal** (6hr., every hr. 5am-11pm, 244 pesos); **Chichén Itzá** (3hr., several per day, 85-126 pesos); **Chiquilá** (5hr.; 7:15am, 12:15pm; 64 pesos); **Mérida** (4hr., every hr. 5:15am-12pm, 256 pesos); **Mexico City** (26hr.; 7:45, 11am, 6, 8pm; 1252 pesos); **Palenque** (13hr.; 7:30, 8:30pm; 562 pesos); **Playa del Carmen** (1hr., every 15min., 36 pesos); **Puerto Morelos** (30min., every 10min. 4:30am-11pm, 10 pesos); **Tulum** (2hr., every hr. 7am-11pm, 82 pesos); **Valladolid** (2hr., 8 per day 5am-8pm, 128 pesos).

**Ferries:** To get to Isla Mujeres, take a bus marked "Pto. Juárez" to any of the 3 ferry depots north of town (**Punta Sam** for cars, **Gran Puerto** and **Puerto Juárez** for passengers; 15min.). Tour companies in the Zona Hotelera provide ferry service starting at 300 pesos.

## LOCAL TRANSPORTATION

**Public Transportation: Buses** marked **"Hoteles R1"** (6.50 pesos) run every 5min. during the day and every 10-20min. at night between the bus station downtown and the end of the Zona at Club Med. They stop at blue bus signs along Tulum and Kukulcán; there is often live music, and buses can become mobile parties at night. Blue buses marked **"Bus One"** (with A/C and light jazz; 11 pesos) follow the same route as the Hoteles R1 buses. To get off either bus in the Zona Hotelera, give a hearty shout of *"¡Señor!"*

**Taxis:** Within the **Zona Hotelera** (ask at hotels for rates to specific destinations), downtown (around 20 pesos), and between (100-150 pesos). Set a price before getting in.

**Car Rental: Alamo,** at km 9.5 (☎886 0168). Summer high season 925 pesos (US$70) per day not including insurance; summer low season 594 pesos (US$45) including insurance. **Avicar,** Tulum 3 (☎887 2389; www.avicar.com.mx). Cars with A/C and insurance. See website for rates and discounts. Open daily 8am-7pm. Other rental options are located along the Zona Hotelera, in the *centro*, and at the airport. Prices range 462-725 pesos (US$35-55) per day, with A/C 660-1055 pesos (US$50-80). Look for coupons in *Cancún Tips* magazine.

**Moped Rental:** Vendors between km 3 and 5. 100 pesos per hr., 500 pesos per day. **Bicycles** and **in-line skates** 70 pesos per hr., 160 pesos per day.

## ■ 🔢 ORIENTATION AND PRACTICAL INFORMATION

Perched on the northeastern tip of the Yucatán Peninsula, Cancún lies 285km east of Mérida via Mex. 180, and 382km north of Chetumal and the Belize border via Mex. 307. Cancún is divided into two areas: **downtown,** or the *centro*, where you'll find bargains but no beaches, and the **Zona Hotelera,** with fewer bargains but plenty of beaches, though many of them were severely eaten away by Hurricane Wilma in 2005. The Zona is a slender "7"-shaped strip of land; addresses along its one main highway are given by kilometer number. Kilometer numbers increase from one to 20 beginning at the outskirts of the *centro*.

QUINTANA ROO

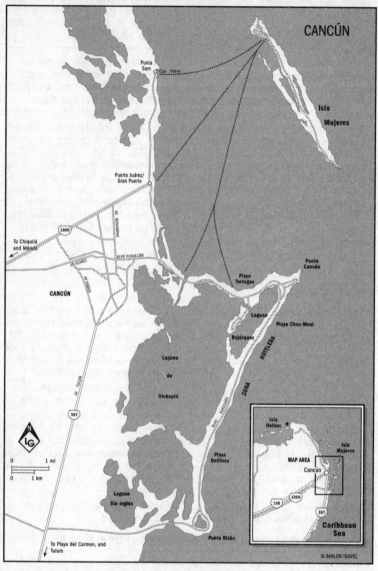

CANCÚN

Punta Sam
Car Ferry

Isla Mujeres

Puerto Juárez/
Gran Puerto

AV. BONAMPAK

To Chiquilá
and Mérida

1800

BLVD KUKULCÁN

AV. XCARET

AV. YAXIL

CANCÚN

Punta Cancún

Playa Tortugas

Laguna

Playa Chac-Mool

Bojórquez

ZONA HOTELERA

Laguna

de

Nichupté

AV. TULUM

307

N

0        1 mi

0      1 km

Playa Delfines

Isla Holbox

Isla Mujeres

MAP AREA

Cancún

180    1800

307

Caribbean Sea

Laguna Río Inglés

Punta Nizúc

To Playa del Carmen, and Tulum

© AVALON TRAVEL

QUINTANA ROO

**Tourist Offices:** (☎881 2800; www.cancun.gob.mx), on Av. Cobá, between Tulum and Nader. Ask for *Cancún Tips*, a free English-language magazine with information, coupons, and maps. Also available at the airport, Plaza Caracol, and hotels. Open M-F 9am-7pm, Sa 9am-2pm.

**Consulates: Canada,** km 8.5, Plaza Caracol, 3rd fl. (☎883 3360 or 3361, fax 883 3232). Open M-F 9am-3:30pm. **UK,** in Royal Sands Hotel (☎881 0100, ext. 65898;

fax 848 8244). Open M-F 9am-3pm. **US,** km 8.5, Plaza Caracol, 3rd fl. (☎883 0272, emergency line for U.S. citizens 845 4364). Open M-F 9am-2pm.

**Currency Exchange and Banks: Bancomer,** Tulum 20 (☎881 6207), at C. Claveles. Open M-F 8:30am-4pm, Sa 9am-3pm. **Banamex,** Tulum 19 (☎881 6474). Open M-F 9am-4pm, Sa 10am-2pm. Both give cash advances and have **24hr. ATMs.** Independent **exchange booths** are plentiful in the *centro* and give better rates than vendors accepting dollars.

**American Express:** Tulum 208 (☎881 4000), 3 blocks south of Cobá. Open M-F 9am-6pm, Sa 9am-1pm. Another in the Zona Hotelera on the 1st fl. of Plaza Kukulcán at km 13 (☎885 3905). Open daily 10am-5pm.

**Luggage Storage:** Bus station (p. 127), near the snack bar. 5-12 pesos per hr. Open daily 6am-10pm.

**Bookstores: Fama,** Tulum 105 (☎884 6541), between Claveles and Tulipanes. Small selection of English-language beach reading. Open daily 9am-9pm.

**Laundromat: Lavandería Alborada,** Náder 5 (☎884 2669), behind the Ayuntamiento Benito Juárez. Self-service wash and dry 36 pesos. Open M-Sa 9am-8pm, Su 9am-5pm.

**Emergency:** ☎066.

**Police:** ☎884 1913, in city hall.

**Red Cross:** Yaxchilán 2 (☎884 1616).

**24hr. Pharmacy: Farmacia YZA,** C. Diagonal Pino (☎887 3738), across from the bus station.

**Medical Services: Hospital Americano,** Viento 15 (☎884 6133), 5 blocks south on Tulum after Cobá. For an ambulance, call **Total Assist,** Claveles 5 (☎884 1092), near Tulum.

**Fax Office: Telecomm** (☎884 1529), on Xel-Ha at Sunyaxchén, next to the post office. Telegram service. Open M-F 8am-7:30pm, Sa 9am-12:30pm.

**Internet Access:** Internet cafes are not hard to find, especially near the bus station on Tulum and Uxmal. Most hostels include free internet or offer lower prices than independent cafes. **La Taberna,** Yaxchilán 23 (☎887 5433), is a sports bar, pool hall, cafe, and internet cafe all rolled into one. 12 pesos per hr. Open daily 1pm-5am.

**Post Office:** (☎884 1418), on Xel-Ha at Sunyaxchén. Open M-F 8am-6pm, Sa-Su 9am-1pm. **Postal Code:** 77500.

# ACCOMMODATIONS

Trying to find cheap accommodations in the Zona Hotelera is not for the faint of heart. Budget travelers looking to have all the fun at a fraction of the cost will do better staying in the much calmer downtown area and partying in the Zona Hotelera. Public transportation between the two is cheap and frequent. Generally, the hotels on the lagoon side of the road and those before km 5 are cheapest. Buses run less frequently during the early morning hours, however; it is advisable to travel in groups, especially post-clubbing. If you don't mind dipping into your retirement fund, any tourist agency can set you up at one of the behemoths in the Zona. Prices generally rise during mid-summer and in the winter by 25%. Reservations are a good idea any time of the year.

■ **Hostel Quetzal,** Orquídeas 10 (www.hostelquetzal.com), entry from the park. Farther from the bus station than other hostels, but well worth the walk. Travelers up for one last hurrah before the end of their adventures congregate in the common areas, which include a lounge, patio, and upstairs terrace. Clean and comfortable, despite the clientele. Young, English-speaking staff. Breakfast, locker, and linens included. Free internet. 14-bed dorm 150 pesos. Cash only. ❶

■ **Haina Hostal,** Orquídeas 13 (☎898 2081; www.hainahostal.com). Just around the corner from Quetzal and less social than its neighbor, Haina has spotless dorms with

QUINTANA ROO

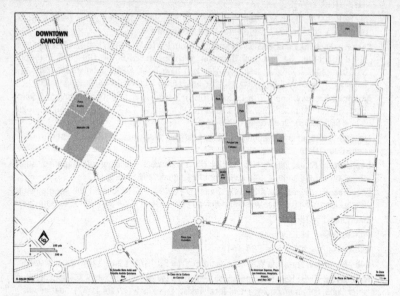

sturdy wooden bunks. A great value and better alternative for travelers who want to sleep. Breakfast, lockers, and Wi-Fi included. 50 peso deposit for linens, towels, and keys. Reception 24hr. 6- or 8-bed ensuite dorms 110 pesos. Cash only. ❶

**The Weary Traveler: Mexico Hostel,** Palmera 30 (☎887 0191), 4 blocks west of the bus station. Entry on Uxmal. This HI-approved hostel has a kitchen and a large common area for lounging. Breakfast, basic dinner, linens, and private lockers included. Lock deposit 50 pesos. Laundry 30 pesos. Free internet and Wi-Fi. Reception 24hr. Check-out noon. 4- and 6-bed dorms 125 pesos; doubles 250 pesos. 10% discount for HI members. Cash only. ❶

**The Nest,** Alcatraces 49 (☎884 8967), at Claveles. This small hostel on a quiet, shady street is worlds removed from the glitter of the disco circuit. 1 large dorm with powerful fans and private lockers. Gated garden with tables is a good escape from the heat. Full kitchen and small lounge. Breakfast with fresh fruit and internet included. Laundry 30 pesos. Dorms 115 pesos. Cash only. ❶

**Hostal Chacmool Hostel Cancún,** Gladiolas 18 (☎887 5873; www.chacmool.com.mx), on the Parque de las Palapas. There isn't much common space to hang out in, but the large dorm rooms with A/C and the lovely Parque de las Palapas more than make up for the deficit. Breakfast included. Laundry 30 pesos. 1hr. free internet per day. Dorms 130 pesos; singles 320 pesos, with bath 350 pesos. Cash only. ❶

**Soberanis Hostal,** Cobá 5 (☎884 4564; www.soberanis.com.mx), next to the supermarket at Tulum and Cobá. This well-maintained, 78-room hostel has dorms and private rooms to accommodate a wide range of budgets. 4-bed dorms have sturdy wooden bunks, private lockers, A/C, and in-room baths. Guests flock to the restaurant and open-air bar downstairs. 10% discount on tours booked through the tourist agency in the lobby. Breakfast included. Internet 15 pesos per hr. Reception 24hr. Dorms 120 pesos; rooms from 590 pesos. 20% discount with ISIC. MC/V. ❶

**Hostal Las Palmas,** Palmera 43 (☎884 2513), 3 blocks from the bus station on a quiet side street. A good deal in a convenient location. Dorms and private rooms with A/C and large, wooden bunks. The lack of common space and internet are drawbacks. Continental breakfast included. Dorms 100 pesos; private rooms 300-360 pesos. Cash only. ❶

QUINTANA ROO

**Hotel Los Girasoles,** Piña 20 (☎887 3990; www.losgirasolescancun.com), on a small side street. This sunny family-run hotel offers clean rooms with A/C, kitchenettes, cable TV, and wrought iron bed stands. Free Wi-Fi. Doubles 380 pesos, for 4 people 460 pesos. Discounts in low season. Cash only. ❺

**Mayan Hostel,** Margaritas 17 (☎892 0103; www.amigohostelgroup.com), 1 block from the bus station. Unremarkable dorm rooms show their years of use, but a pleasant rooftop patio decorated with ceramics and tropical plants overlooking a quiet park makes this an acceptable option for those who want to stay close to the bus station. Breakfast and dinner included. Kitchen available. Locker and linens included. Free internet and Wi-Fi. Reception 24hr. 10-bed dorms 120 pesos, with A/C 140; 6-bed dorms 130 pesos; 4-bed dorms 150 pesos; doubles 370 pesos; triples 170 pesos. 100 peso deposit. Cash only. ❶

**Hotel Colonial,** Tulipanes 22 (☎884 1535; www.hotelcolonialcancun.com), off Tulum on the pedestrian mall. The Colonial's convenient *centro* location makes it a favorite with vacationers. Cramped rooms with TV face a lovely Spanish courtyard complete with tiled fountain. Internet 10 pesos per hr. Free parking. Doubles 450 pesos, with A/C 550 pesos. MC/V. ❺

## 🍴 FOOD

Though the resort-heavy Zona Hotelera has a surprising number of affordable places serving tasty Mexican cuisine, chances of a good meal and good prices are better in the *centro*. The uninitiated should avoid the street vendors, who may or may not follow health codes. Those with stomachs of steel can eat with the locals at one of the countless stands in the **Parque de las Palapas,** three blocks from the bus station on Alcatraces. Two-course meals usually include *sopa* (soup) and fruit juice (35-50 pesos). A huge supermarket, *Comercial Mexicana*, is across from the ADO bus station on Tulum. (☎880 3330. Open daily 7am-midnight.) Smaller but more centrally located is **Chedaui,** Tulum 22, at the intersection with Cobá. (☎884 1155. Open daily 7am-11pm.)

🔲 **Restaurante Los Huaraches de Alcatraces,** Alcatraces 31 (☎884 2528), near El Parque de las Palapas. Locals love this cafeteria-style restaurant for its cheap and delicious regional food served in the fan-filled dining room. Special quesadilla fillings, such as zucchini blossoms, change daily (20-28 pesos). *Mole* made from scratch 55 pesos. Delivery available. Open Tu-Su 8am-6:30pm. Cash only. ❸

**El Tapatío,** Uxmal 30 (☎887 8317), at the corner of Uxmal and Palmera. Despite the somewhat noisy setting, the Camacho-Zepeda family has been indoctrinating backpackers into the wonders of traditional Jalisco-style *pozole* (a chunky soup made with hominy kernels, radishes, lettuce, and meat; 65-75 pesos) since 1981. Daily specials 60 pesos. Fruit smoothies 32-45 pesos. Open M-Sa 8am-1:30am, Su 9am-11pm. MC/V. ❸

**100% Natural** (☎884 3617; www.100natural.com.mx), near Yaxchilán and Sunyaxchén. The cook selects produce from beneath a central fountain at this open-air restaurant, where eclectic fare from *nopales* (vegetables made from the stems of prickly pears) to grilled salmon in fruit sauce (141 pesos) is followed by freshly baked goodies. Enjoy a fresh apple, honey, and carrot *licuado* for 29 pesos. Salads 50-100 pesos. Live music weekend mornings. Delivery available. Open daily 7am-11pm. MC/V. ❹

**El Tacolote,** Cobá 19 (☎887 3045; eltacolete.com). Good local fare served in a typical Mexican setting. Look for the sombrero-sporting chicken logo out front. Tacos 8-67 pesos. Quesadillas 23-30 pesos. Entrees 90-200 pesos. Roving *mariachis* frequently stop by during dinner hours. For dessert, don't miss the mangos in tequila (60 pesos), which involve caramel and ice cream pyrotechnics carried out right before your eyes. Open daily 11am-2am. AmEx/D/MC/V. ❹

**Los Arcos** (☎887 6673; www.losarcoscancun.com), at the corner of Yaxchilán and Rosas. A safe bet for filling meals and a stiff drink. The bar gets going on F nights when locals come to jam out to the classic rock DJ. Try the pasta with shrimp and marinara sauce for 89 pesos. 2-for-1 happy hour daily 7-9pm. Open daily noon-4am. AmEx/MC/V. ❹

**Tacos Rigo** (☎884 0638; www.tacosrigo.com.mx), at Av. Palenque and Playas, near Mercado 28. This informal, open-air taco joint gets traffic that rivals the busy *avenida* out front. Tacos 16-30 pesos. Open daily 8am-midnight. Cash only.

**Taco Factory,** km 9.5, Plaza Party Center, Local 14 (☎883 1651; www.taco-factory.com), down a passageway between the Congo and Dady'O (p. 135) night clubs in the Punta Cancún area. Good for cheap, late-night munchies and people-watching in the Zona. Tacos made with fresh tortillas 15-30 pesos. Open daily 11am-7am. Cash only. ❶

# 🔆 SIGHTS

Other than the packs of tourists at the beach or the bar, Cancún has little to offer by way of sights. For those eager to remind themselves they are indeed in Mexico, head to El Embarcadero at km 4. The massive port building is home to the local theater, **Teatro de Cancún,** and a small craft museum, **La Casa del Arte Popular Mexicano.** The theater has a rotating calendar of shows with something playing almost every night, mostly in Spanish. (☎849 4848; www.elteatrodecancun.com.) La Casa del Arte focuses primarily on Mexico's rich history of polychromatic folk art. The detailed displays make it well worth the trip. Especially striking are the intricately crafted "trees of life" (clay sculptures interpreting man's fall from the Garden of Eden) and the enormous snake-shaped rain stick. The gift shop is brimming with crafts bought directly from artisans all over Mexico. (☎849 4332 or 5583; www.museoartepopularmexicano.org. Open M-F 9am-6pm, Sa-Su 11am-6pm. 55 pesos, includes 20min. audio tour.) The small archaeological site of **Ruinas del Rey,** on the lagoon at km 18, provides a glimpse into local history. The ruins were once part of a Mayan fishing community that inhabited what is now the Zona Hotelera from AD 150 to 1200. The centerpiece of the site is the king's pyramid, though it will only impress those who have yet to see any of the other spectacular Mayan ruins scattered throughout the country. Hundreds of iguanas that now find sanctuary here will keep you on your toes. (Open daily 8am-5pm; last entry 4:30pm. 37 pesos.)

# 🏖 BEACHES

The world-famous beaches of Cancún are the city's biggest attraction. Multihued waters caress the Caribbean coastline and gentle sea breezes stave off the heat of the day. Although you'll usually have plenty of sunburned company on the sands, Cancún's beaches are long enough (22km) to accommodate meditating, napping, reading, swimming, and even a game of volleyball or soccer. Don't fret about the wall of luxury hotels standing between you and the glorious surf—all **beaches** in Mexico are public property. There are regular public access points to the beaches along Kukulcán—you can also walk confidently through any of the hotel lobbies. Recent hurricanes have washed out much of the sand in the Zona, so those who don't want to crowd together with the sunburned gringos on resort chairs would do best to seek out beaches further south, where the hotels are less imposing.

Stealing the show on the north side of the Zona Hotelera are **Playa Langosta** (at km 5) and **Playa Tortugas** (at km 6.5). The gradually sloping shores, small hotels, and clear waters make for better swimming than at the beaches farther south. Less spectacular and also less crowded are **Playa las Perlas** (at km 2.5) and **Playa Linda** (at km 3.8) to the west. On the east side of the Zona Hotelera,

QUINTANA ROO

**Playa Chac-Mool** starts just south of **Punta Cancún.** For those who don't mind a bit of a longer trek, **Playa Marlín** (at km 12.8) and **Playa Delfines** (at km 17.8), farther south, are normally quiet and less commercial, attracting throngs of locals on the weekends. Delfines and Marlín have the largest waves and also the highest salt content, which makes underwater vision more difficult. At Delfines, umbrellas (100 pesos) and chairs (25 pesos) can be rented from the small shack near the lifeguard stand.

**TAKE A HINT.** When swimming at any of the beaches along the Zona Hotelera, look for flags that indicate water conditions. Green and yellow flags mean "swim with caution." Black flags mean "do not enter."

Watersports enthusiasts are in luck: Cancún offers opportunities to participate in all the aquatic sports you've ever heard of and some you haven't. As in most resort areas, prices in Cancún are much higher than those in lower-profile neighboring communities. Many organized recreational activities can be arranged through the luxury hotels that line the beaches, or through private companies and tour guides. It is a good idea to have a sense of what you want to do and how much money you want to spend before starting to bargain with vendors. Expect to pay at least 400 pesos (US$30) for the most basic snorkeling tours.

**Aqua World,** km 15.2 (☎848 8300; www.aquaworld.com.mx). A popular choice for exploring Cancún's aquatic paradise. Glass-bottom boat tours of Laguna Nichuplé (every hr. 9am-3pm, 588 pesos/US$44) and jungle tours (last tour 2:30pm, 725 pesos/US$55). Call to reserve in advance. Open daily 7am-10pm. MC/V.

**Scuba Cancún,** km 5 (☎849 7508; www.scubacancun.com.mx). Well-established dive and watersport center offers 2hr. scuba diving lessons (1160 pesos/US$88). 2-tank dive for certified divers 900 pesos (US$68). Wetsuit rental 105 pesos (US$8). Daily snorkeling tours at 2 and 4:30pm 383 pesos (US$29). *Cenote* tours on Tu, Th, and Sa at 8am 1042 pesos (US$79). Open daily 8:30am-8pm. MC/V.

## ♪ 🎭 ENTERTAINMENT AND SHOPPING

As night descends, Cancún morphs from a beachgoer's playground into the home of some of the biggest, hottest clubs in the Western Hemisphere. In the Zona, expect to see tipsy tourists parading, drink in hand, down **Kukulcán.** Crowds vary according to time and season. April hosts US college students, June welcomes high-school and college graduates, and late nights belong year-round to a stream of wealthy international tourists. Locals favor bars and discos in the *centro,* at the south end of Tulum near **Cobá,** and at the north end of **Yaxchilán** near **Sunyaxchén.** Unlike much of Mexico, Cancún boasts a gay nightlife that is well incorporated into the large disco scene in the Zona, with a few gay clubs in the *centro* as well. In the small parks in the *centro,* there are often live musicians and impromptu dance parties. Most establishments in Cancún open at 9pm, get going after midnight, and close when the crowds wane around dawn.

Cancún also has options for more relaxing entertainment. Movie theaters show many of the same films you would find in the US. Downtown, the **Plaza Kukulcán** and **Plaza las Américas** are two options; see www.cinepolis.com.mx for details.

## SPORTS

Death comes every Wednesday at 3:30pm to the **Plaza de Toros** (☎884 8372 or 882 8248), on Bonampak at Sayil. Tickets for the bullfights (2hr.) are available at travel agencies on Tulum (300 pesos, under 5 free; group discounts available) or at the bullring on a fight day. Catch your favorite sports teams at the sports

QUINTANA ROO

bar **Caliente,** in the Forum by the Sea in the Zona Hotelera, where you can enjoy drinks and snacks on red velvet seats. The huge screens broadcast coverage of every imaginable sporting event, from the college level on up. The bookies will happily help you place your bets. (☎883 4761; www.caliente.com.mx. Open M-F 11am-1am, Sa-Su 10am-1am. Cash only.)

## SHOPPING

Cancún is best enjoyed on a loose budget. Popular international luxury brands on sale in Plazas Terramar, Caracol, Flamingo, Islas, and Kukulcán will swallow your dollars whole. Ravenous for crafts, dazed vacationers pour into the *centro* daily to shop at the tourist market, **Mercado 28,** on Av. Xel-Ha. Be ready to bargain, as the *mercado* has the heaviest concentration of doodads in Cancún. Popular items include *sombreros*, blankets, pottery, and leather goods. To get there from the Zona, take the R-2 bus marked "Mercado 28" or the R-1 bus to the ADO terminal, from which the *mercado* is a short 10min. walk. Parking available. (Open daily 9am-8pm.)

## █ NIGHTLIFE

Most bars in the *centro* are along **Yaxchilán,** near **Uxmal,** and on **Tulipanes,** off **Tulum.** In the Zona Hotelera, don't bother seeking out local bars—the party is at clubs and chains like Carlos'n Charlie's, T.G.I. Friday's, and Señor Frog's. Hotel **happy hours** are usually between 5 and 7pm. Most of the glitziest clubs and discos are near the Zona's **Punta Cancún,** near Playa Caracol and Forum by the Sea. Cancún's glam clubs attract American youth eager for sinful pleasures. The dress code for discos is simple: less is more and tight is right. Bikini tops often get women in for free; use your judgment in more laid-back clubs. Note that US dollars rule in the Zona. In this section we have listed prices in US$ where it is best to pay in this currency.

 **MORE THAN A PINT, LESS THAN A 40.** A good way to save a few pesos when out for a night at the bar or just kicking back with friends is to buy a *caguama* instead of a lone beer bottle. All major Mexican beer companies bottle *caguamas*, which contain a liter of beer and sell for around 40 pesos.

**⊠ Coco Bongo,** km 9.5 (☎883 5061; www.cocobongo.com.mx), in Forum by the Sea. Steamy, exhilarating, unstoppable. Vegas-style shows come to this always-popular club, where dancing to the eclectic rock, pop, and trance music is secondary to the main show. Last call is at 3am, even though the club won't close for another 3hr. Cover M-Th US$40, F-Sa US$50; includes open bar. Shows 11:30pm. Open daily 10:30pm-late. AmEx/MC/V.

**Roots,** Tulipanes 26 (☎884 2437), off Tulum. Caribbean-themed walls and eclectic artwork set the stage in this superior jazz 'n' blues joint that opens to the pedestrian walkway. Live regional musicians Tu-Sa 10:30pm. Cover F-Sa 50 pesos; no cover if you loiter on the patio. Open Tu-Sa 6pm-1am; kitchen closes at midnight. MC/V.

**Carlos'n Charlie's,** km 9.5 (☎883 1862), in the Forum by the Sea. Smaller than some of its locations in other Mexican cities, the Cancún Carlos'n Charlie's leaves the all-night dance parties to the big clubs. Sip drinks, nibble snacks, and watch the insanity pass on by. Beer 45 pesos. Margaritas 69 pesos. Open daily midnight-3am. AmEx/MC/V.

**Señor Frog's,** Blvr. Kukulcan, km 9.5 (☎883 1092; www.senorfrogs.com), across from Playa Chac Mool. Owned by the same company as Carlos'n Charlie's, Señor Frog's is a long-time

QUINTANA ROO

Mexican chain and a popular mid-week hangout for tourists. Cover US$6, with open bar $36. Beer 45 pesos. Open midnight-3am. Cash only.

**Mambo Cafe,** Plaza las Avenidas (☎887 8761; www.mambocafe.com.mx), the best place for true salsa nightlife. Frequented by locals and curious visitors eager to live out their dancing dreams. Come dressed for success or embarrassing failure (glitter and spangles are recommended for the latter). Free salsa classes Th-F 9-10pm. Th ladies night. Cover F-Su men 100 pesos, women 50 pesos. Open Th-Sa 10pm-5am. Cash only.

**Dady'O,** km 9.5 (☎883 3333; www.dadyo.com.mx), in Forum by the Sea. The cave-like entrance lets you know you're headed into a disco inferno. The club opens onto a stage and dance floor streaked with lasers and pulsating with strobes, promising plenty of fun. Piercing booth upstairs. Bikini contests held regularly. Snacks 30-60 pesos. Cover US$15, with open bar US$35. Open daily 10pm-late. Cash only.

**Dady Rock** (☎883 3333). *Ayyyy papi*—another Dady club, brought to you by the same conglomerate that owns Dady'O and 7 other clubs in Punta Cancún. This club is distinctive for the variety of its music—anyone for techno pan pipes? Cover US$30, includes open bar. Open daily 6pm-late. Cash only.

**Bulldog Cafe,** km 8 (☎849 9800; www.bulldogcafe.com), near Forum by the Sea. Originally founded in Mexico City, the Bulldog Cafe attracts a mostly Mexican crowd with its *rock en español* and live performances by some of Latin America's biggest acts. Ladies drink for free. Cover varies depending on event. Open daily 10pm-5am. Cash only.

## GLBT NIGHTLIFE

Though many of the clubs in the Zona combine straight and gay nightlife, the only explicitly gay nightlife is in the *centro*.

 **SAFETY FIRST.** While the brave may leave the club at 5am feeling buzzed and ready for the bus ride back to the *centro,* the wise will travel in a groups. Safety in numbers.

**Karamba,** Tulum 5 (☎884 0032; www.karambabar.com), on the corner of Azucenas. A spacious, multi-level gay bar and disco with pop-art murals and a wide variety of dance music. Nightly theme shows or contests at 1:30am. Cover 60 pesos. Open Tu-Su 10:30pm-6am. Cash only.

## ON THE MENU

### TAKE ATOLE ON YOU

When you think of traditional Mexican beverages, you probably have visions of downing tequila in crowded bars until the wee hours of the mañana. However, Mexican refreshments don't have to include headaches, hangovers, and hazy memories of last night. Locals teetotal in style with atole, a hot, cornstarch-based drink served throughout Mexico and Central America as a street food. Atole is a combination of cooked cornmeal (masa), water, and cane sugar blocks (piloncillo), creating a drink with a consistency ranging from thin and watery to porridge-like. Traditional flavorings include cinnamon, vanilla, fruit, and that ubiquitous Mexican indulgence, chocolate. Other cereal grains may be substituted for cornmeal.

Atole is imbibed most frequently during the Mexican holiday season. Chocolate atole, called champurrado, is commonly enjoyed on Christmas and the Day of the Dead (November 2nd). Whatever the time of year, grab a cup of atole, unwrap a tamale, and enjoy a beautiful hangover-free day in the Yucatán.

# ISLA MUJERES ☎ 998

In 1517, Francisco Hernández de Córdoba happened upon this tiny island and found hundreds of small female statuettes scattered on the beaches. He promptly named the island Isla Mujeres. Hernández had stumbled upon a sanctuary for Ixchel, the Mayan goddess of fertility, weaving, happiness, medicine, and the moon. For years, Isla Mujeres (pop. 14,000) was a small fishing village with few visitors. It wasn't until the 1950s that vacationing Mexicans discovered the remote island. Americans, Australians, Canadians, and Europeans soon followed, transforming it into a tourist hotspot. While some locals still fish for a living, most now cater to daytrippers and those who use the island as a base for exploring the pristine waters around Isla Mujeres and Isla Contoy. Although the *centro* has become a full-fledged tourist haven, buildings do not crowd the beaches as they do in Cancún, and the Caribbean life in the quiet southern *colonias* has a different feel altogether.

## ▐ TRANSPORTATION

**Ferries** are the only way to reach Isla Mujeres. They leave from **Gran Puerto** (3km north of downtown Cancún) and **Puerto Juárez** (200m beyond Gran Puerto), and are accessible by a **Puerto Juárez** bus (8 pesos), **microbús**, (15min., 6 pesos), or **taxi** (from 16 pesos). Two companies run express ferries: **Maritimos Magaña** (☎877 0382; 20min., from Puerto Juárez every 30min. 5:30am-10pm; 35 pesos) and **UltraMar** (☎843 2011; 15min., every 30min. from Gran Puerto 5am-midnight, 35 pesos). Arrive early—ferries are notorious for leaving ahead of schedule when full. A **car ferry** runs to the island from **Punta Sam** (5km north of Puerto Juárez; 5 per day; 15 pesos per person, 185 pesos and up per car; arrive 30min. early).

Walking is the best way to navigate the island's compact, cobblestone *centro*. For longer trips, red **taxis** (☎877 0066; 20-80 pesos) line up at the stand directly to the right as you come off the passenger dock. They zip to **Playa Paraíso, Playa Lancheros, Tortugranja, Garrafón**, and the Mayan sanctuary **Ixchel**. Prices to common destinations are listed at the taxi stand between the two ferry docks. You should have no problem catching one elsewhere. **Public buses** pick up passengers from the ferry docks and only go as far as the **Playa Lancheros** roundabout, close to the Isla Mujeres Palace (roughly every 15-30min. 6am-7pm, 4 pesos).

To explore the ends of the island, rent a moped, bike, or golf cart, which are all more common than cars. **Moped and golf cart** rentals available at **Pepe's Rentals,** Hidalgo 19, between Matamoros and Abasolo (☎ 877 0019; mopeds 80 pesos per hr., 300 pesos per day; golf carts 180/600 pesos, includes gasoline; open daily 9am-5pm; MC/V). **Bicycles** can be rented from a number of vendors along Rueda Medina (30 pesos per hr., 100 per day; cash only). Be sure to check the tire pressure and durability of the bike before handing over your cash.

## ▦ ▐ ORIENTATION AND PRACTICAL INFORMATION

Isla Mujeres is a narrow landmass (7.5km by 1km) 11km northeast of Cancún. The *centro* is laid out in a rough grid at the northwest corner of the island. Perpendicular to the dock is **Rueda Medina,** which runs the length of the island along the coastline, past the **lagoon, Playa Paraíso, Playa Lancheros,** and the **Garrafón Reef.** On the northeast coast, the **Sea Wall Walk** runs the length of the island, though as of August 2009 the route was under construction.

**Tourist Office:** (☎877 0307), on Rueda Medina. Across the street and to the left from the port. Open daily 9am-5pm. **Cooperativo Isla Mujeres** (☎877 1363), on Rueda

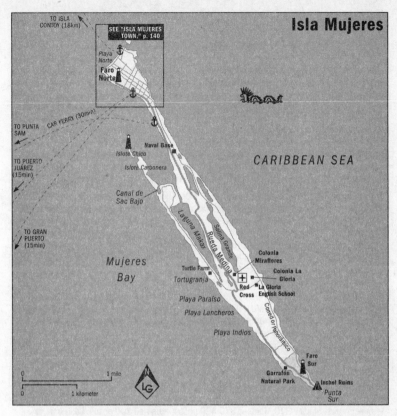

# Isla Mujeres

Medina in the *palapa* near the PEMEX station, has a wealth of information about tours and local happenings. Open daily 8am-8pm.

**Currency Exchange: HSBC** (☎877 0005), on Rueda Medina, across from the port. Has **24hr. ATMs.** Open M-F 9am-7pm, Sa 9am-3pm. Another ATM is at Súper Xpress (p. 138).

**Bookstore: Cosmic Cosas,** Guerrero 70 (☎877 0555), inside the restaurant Mañana (p. 139). Buy, sell, and exchange books in various languages while snacking on delicious vegetarian-friendly foods. Open M-Sa 8:30am-6pm. Another on Juárez (☎144 9138), between Madero and and Matamoros. Also carries old English-language magazines. Open daily 1-10pm.

**Laundromat: Lavandería Tim Phó,** Juárez 94 (☎877 0529), at Abasolo. Full service (2hr.) 55 pesos per 4kg. Open M-Sa 7am-9pm, Su 8am-2pm.

**Police:** (☎999 0051), in Colonia La Salina, outside of town. Open 24hr.

**Red Cross:** (☎877 0280), at the Colonia La Gloria, 3½km south of town just before the Playa Lancheros roundabout.

**Pharmacy: La Mejor,** Madero 17 (☎877 0116), between Hidalgo and Juárez. Open daily 9am-10pm.

**Medical Services: Centro de Salud,** Guerrero 5 (☎877 0117), at Morelos. The white building at the northwest corner of the *zócalo*. Open 24hr. **Doctor Antonio E. Salas**

(☎877 0477), at the **Clínica del ISSSTE** on the corner of López Mateos and Carlos Lazo, speaks English and will make house calls. Clinic open M-F 8am-3pm.

**Fax Office: Telecomm and Western Union,** Guerrero 13 (☎877 0113), next to the post office. Open M-F 8am-7:30pm.

**Internet Access: Cafe Internet y Tours** (☎877 1676), on the plaza is the go-to place for those with computer problems. Internet 20 pesos per hr. Open daily 8am-11pm.

**Post Office:** (☎877 0085) Guerrero and López Mateos, at the northwest corner of town, 1 block from Playa Norte. Open M-F 9am-5:30pm, Sa 9am-1pm. **Postal Code:** 77400.

# ACCOMMODATIONS

During high season (July-Aug. and Dec.-Apr.), prices increase by about 100 pesos. You should inquire ahead and make reservations. Free camping is permitted on the beach, but for safety reasons, it's best to check in with the police first.

**Poc-Na Youth Hostel,** Matamoros 15 (☎877 0090; www.pocna.com), near Playa Panchalo. An all-inclusive resort masquerading as a hostel, Poc-Na is legendary on the backpacker circuit. Chill under the giant *palapas,* tan on the private beach, fill up on cheap grub, then party all night. Also has 2 bars, a volleyball court, soccer fields, and ping pong tables. Can arrange snorkel tours. Restaurant open daily 8am-10:30pm. Breakfast included. Free lockers; you provide the lock. 30min. of internet daily. Tent site 70 pesos; bunk beds 100-120 pesos; dorms with A/C 125 pesos; private rooms 270-375 pesos. Work opportunities available in exchange for room and board. Cash only. ❶

**Hotel Xul-Ha,** Hidalgo 23 (☎877 0075), between Matamoros and López Mateos. Set around a jungle-like courtyard. All rooms have 1 double bed and 1 single. Large rooms have ceiling fans and mirrors; some have balconies and refrigerators. TV in the small lobby. Rooms 300 pesos, with A/C and TV 400 pesos. Cash only. ❹

**Roca Teliz Hotel,** Hidalgo 93 (☎877 0407 or 0804). Centrally located behind a gift shop on a pedestrian-only street, this 9-room inn with a courtyard and fountain offers peace and quiet. High-season singles 280 pesos, with A/C 400 pesos; doubles 380/500 pesos. MC/V. ❸

**Hotel Marcianito,** Abasolo 10 (☎877 0111). Recently remodeled, with spotless rooms, colorful bedspreads, lockboxes for valuables, and overhead fans. Rooms on the 3rd fl. have ocean views. Singles 370; doubles 370-430 pesos; extra bed 100 pesos. Cash only. ❺

**Hotel Carmelina,** Guerrero 4 (☎877 0006), between Abasolo and Madero. Carmelina has lively owners and bright colors to make up for hot nights. The breezy 3rd fl. is the coolest. Parking available. Reserve ahead Dec.-Jan. Doubles with fan 350 pesos, with refrigerator 400 pesos; triples with fan 540 pesos. Cash only. ❺

**Sol Caribe,** Abasolo 6 (☎877 1698). Those looking to save money on food will be pleased with the super clean, complete kitchens included in every room. Rooms have private baths, TVs, and A/C. Free Wi-Fi. Singles and doubles 550-750 pesos. Cash only. ❻

# FOOD

Seafood abounds in Isla Mujeres, as do, strangely, crepes and waffles. *Ceviche de pulpo* (octopus) is a local delicacy. Restaurants along **Hidalgo** cater to tourists with extensive menus and perks like roving mariachis. These tend to be of the best quality; however, many of the menus are nearly identical and prices are gringo-adjusted. Plan ahead—many restaurant owners close between lunch and dinner for *siesta.* For cheap eats, head to the **municipal market,** on Guerrero between Matamoros and López Mateos, which is lined with food stalls. (Most stalls open daily 8am-4pm; open longer during high season.) A supermarket, **Súper Xpress,** is at Morelos 5, on the plaza. (☎887 1094 or 1092. Open M-Sa 7am-10pm, Su 7am-9pm.)

QUINTANA ROO

**Mañana,** Guerrero 70 (☎877 0555), on the corner of Matamoros and Guerrero. Handpainted tables, indoor and outdoor seating, chill tunes, and friendly international owners make this a tourist favorite. Vegetarian-friendly meals like fiery falafel (65 pesos) or hand-pressed veggie burger (70 pesos) come with a fresh salad. After lunch, grab a beach read from Cosmic Cosas (p. 137). Open M-Sa 8:30am-6pm. Cash only. ❸

**Aquí Estoy** (☎877 1777), on Matamoros between Guerrero and Hidalgo. No seating. Pizzas with tasty toppings like goat cheese and pesto. Slices and Mexican pizzas (tortillas with melted cheese and toppings) 20-35 pesos. Whole pizzas 120-160 pesos. Open M-Sa 1-9pm. Cash only. ❶

**El Poc-Chuc Lonchería,** Juárez 5, on the corner of Abasolo. Colorful murals of sharks and Mayan temples watch over as you dine on traditional Quintana Roo fare. 2 beers 35 pesos. Entrees 30-90 pesos. *Tacos de camarón* 50 pesos. Open daily 8am-10pm. Cash only. ❸

**French Bistro Francais,** Matamoros 29, at Hidalgo. Hand-painted tiles and a parrot named Petey keep the place lively. Hearty French meals are each served with 3 vegetable sides. French toast (67 pesos) and crepe specials (50-59 pesos) are popular morning picks, but the specialty is *coq au vin* (chicken in red wine; 135 pesos). Open daily Jan.-May and July-Dec. 8am-noon and 6-10pm. Cash only. ❹

**Chiles Locos,** Av. Hidalgo Local B-1 (☎877 1219), between López Mateos and Matamoros. A stand-out Mexican place along restaurant-packed Hidalgo. Chef Ziggy and wife Donna fill customers with their signature *poblanos* stuffed with shrimp and cheese (115 pesos). Happy hour with 2-for-1 drinks every evening. Open M-Sa 11am-11pm. Cash only. ❺

**Cafe Cito,** Matamoros 42 (☎877 1470), at Juárez. Sand and shells under the see-through tabletops let patrons pretend they never left the beach. Replenish body and soul with Mexican breakfasts (37-45 pesos), freshly made crepes (31-61 pesos), sandwiches (30-40 pesos), and fruit salads (25-40 pesos). Portions are small. Open M-Sa 7am-2pm, Su 7am-1pm. Cash only. ❸

# ⓖ SIGHTS

The Mayan ruins of **Ixchel**—a pilgrimage destination for women who sought help from the goddess of fertility—are on the southern tip of the island, accessible by taxi (71 pesos). Most of the site was reduced to rubble by Hurricane Gilbert in 1988, but a partially reconstructed one-room building and an awesome panorama of the Yucatán and the Caribbean await those who make the journey. You must enter the **sculpture park** for access (open daily

## TEACH TO TOTS

The sound of happy chatter greets visitors to La Gloria English School on Isla Mujeres. Kids of all ages flock to this American school for daily English lessons that emphasize oral communication. The school addresses a pressing need in the island's changing social climate: as tourism increases, the ability to speak English is not simply a convenience, but a matter of economic survival for the predominantly Mayan population.

Built and managed by the Washa family of Middleton, WI, La Gloria opened its doors in 2004, offering classes to all and acting as an impromptu library. Today, La Gloria also serves the community as an active volunteer program. Visitors to the island are welcomed to assist in classes (one week minimum commitment), where they will act as secondary teachers, lending an extra ear, correcting mistakes, and interacting with the students in English. You can also help out by donating school supplies, as La Gloria gets much of its materials through the kindness of tourists.

For information on volunteering, visit www.folges.org. La Gloria English School is at the top of the hill in Colonia La Gloria, about 3½km south of town. Buses and taxis service the area. ☎888 0666. Mza. 156 Lote 20 Mujeres, Quintana Roo, Mexico, 77400.

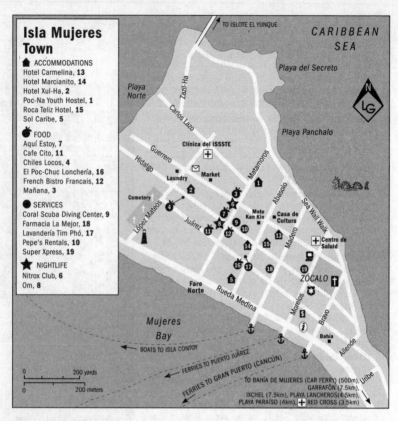

## Isla Mujeres Town

**ACCOMMODATIONS**
Hotel Carmelina, **13**
Hotel Marcianito, **14**
Hotel Xul-Ha, **2**
Poc-Na Youth Hostel, **1**
Roca Teliz Hotel, **15**
Sol Caribe, **5**

**FOOD**
Aquí Estoy, **7**
Cafe Cito, **11**
Chiles Locos, **4**
El Poc-Chuc Lonchería, **16**
French Bistro Francais, **12**
Mañana, **3**

**SERVICES**
Coral Scuba Diving Center, **9**
Farmacia La Mejor, **18**
Lavandería Tim Phó, **17**
Pepe's Rentals, **10**
Super Xpress, **19**

**NIGHTLIFE**
Nitrox Club, **6**
Om, **8**

QUINTANA ROO

9am-5pm; 30 pesos). Visitors can climb the small white lighthouse for free. **Hacienda Mundaca,** a small 19th-century home with landscaped grounds, lies close to the Playa Lancheros roundabout. (Open daily 9am-4pm. 20 pesos.) **La Casa de Cultura,** Av. Guerrero and Abasolo, offers afternoon courses (mostly for kids) in folkloric dance and music. It also houses the island's library and a few glass-encased Mayan artifacts. (☎877 0639. Open M-F 9am-9pm.)

## BEACHES AND OUTDOOR ACTIVITIES

### BEACHES

The Caribbean beaches of Isla Mujeres offer more tranquility than the beaches in Cancún and are much easier to access. Hotels on the north end of the island tend to be hidden behind trees and far from the shore, leaving plenty of space for play or rest. The most popular and accessible beach is **Playa Norte,** on the north shore, where gentle breezes and waves lull sunbathers to sleep. The water is shallow, and you can wade out far from shore. Recline under the *palapas* in the hammocks owned by **La Barra de Kin,** a bar on the north side of the beach. On the southwest side of the island, **Playa Lancheros** and **Playa Paraíso** open onto Mujeres Bay, where many of the island's snorkeling and diving trips go. The south end of the island is now the property of **Garrafón,** an adventure park similar to and with the same management as Xcaret and Xel-ha (p. 171). The eastern shores of the island are much rockier and currents can be dangerous—these beaches are not for swimming.

### SNORKELING AND DIVING

The beautiful **Isla Contoy** (www.islacontoy.org), a wildlife sanctuary reef with over 100 bird species, lies 18km north of Isla Mujeres. Opportunities to commune with nature are abundant and include birdwatching tours, diving, snorkeling, and boat tours. Divers should ask to see the diving certificates of those they hire; if they don't ask for yours as well, think again. Local captains with the **Cooperativo Isla Mujeres,** on Rueda Medina in the *palapa* near the PEMEX station, take visitors snorkeling around Isla Mujeres (4hr.; tours daily 11am; 220 pesos, includes equipment, lunch, and park fees), snorkeling and birding at Isla Contoy (5hr.; tours daily 8 and 9am; 600 pesos, includes equipment, breakfast and lunch, and park fees), or fishing (5000 pesos for full-day private *lancha*, lunch, and equipment). Most tours require a minimum of six people and are far less frequent during the low season. (☎877 1363. Open M-Su 8am-8pm. Cash only.) **The Coral Scuba Diving Center,** at the intersection of Matamoros and Rueda Medina, is the oldest dive operation on the island and has cheap scuba diving packages. Trips include visits to the **Cave of Sleeping Sharks,** 70 ft. below the surface and 3 mi. northeast of the island, where you can catch a glimpse of the carnivores in their most vulnerable state. (☎877 0763; www.coralscubadivecenter.com. 1-tank dive 382 pesos/US$29. Discover SCUBA lesson 779 pesos/US$59. Open daily 9am-9pm. MC/V.) **Bahía,** to the right of the dock on Rueda Medina, sells fishing, snorkeling, and diving gear. (☎877 0340. Open daily 9am-9pm.)

### OTHER WILDLIFE

Like turtles? Head over to the **Tortugranja** (Turtle Farm), to the right at the Playa Lancheros roundabout, less than 1km down the Playa Paraíso road. This biological research station breeds three species of sea turtles: Green, Hawksbill, and Loggerhead. Female turtles lay their eggs in the safety of the station's beach during the summer. After the eggs hatch, around August and September, the young are reared for a year before being released. You can see the adolescent turtles and native tropical fish in two tanks. The center welcomes volunteers for any amount of time to help monitor the beaches, tag turtles, and collect eggs at night from May to October. For volunteer information, speak to the director Irma Moguel. (☎888 0705. Open daily 9am-5pm. 30 pesos.) Other aquatic treats include swimming with dolphins at **Dolphin Discovery,** at the end of the Playa Paraíso road. To get there, turn right at the Playa Lancheros roundabout and head 3km down the paved road. (☎849 4748 or +1-800-713-8862; www.dolphindiscovery.com. Dolphin swims 911-1716 pesos/US$69-130. Reserve ahead. AmEx/MC/V.) If you prefer your adventures in a strictly controlled environment, head to **Garrafón Park** on Punta Sur, where you'll fork over 779 pesos (US$59) for access to a reef, climbing tower, hammocks, zip line, kayaks, a seaside pool, and much more. (☎877 1101; www.garrafon.com. Open daily 10am-5pm. AmEx/MC/V.)

## ◪ NIGHTLIFE

Isla Mujeres offers a relaxing nightlife for those who want to escape the megaclubs and throngs of drunken American teens in Cancún. The best nighttime activity is concentrated at the north end of Hidalgo. Around sunset, tourists and locals bounce from one bar to the next toasting with two-for-one happy hour drinks. Backpackers hang all night long at the indoor and beach bars at

**Poc-Na Youth Hostel** (p. 138). The indoor bar is open daily 8-11:30pm, and the beach bar gets going around midnight with two-for-one drink specials (40 pesos) and a DJ who spins an eclectic mix of Latin, hip hop, and electronica to suit the international crowd. Music shuts down around 4am. **Om,** on Matamoros, stands out for its trendy Indian decor and live music. The kitchen serves Japanese food (45-150 pesos) and giant salads (75 pesos) big enough for two. (Live music 10:30pm-midnight. No cover. Open Tu-Su 1pm-3am.) **Nitrox Club,** the bright red, unmarked building on the corner of Matamoros and Guerrero, is the local *discoteca*, suitable for all who feel the need to get down. Attracts a mostly local crowd with a few intrepid tourists thrown in the mix. (Sa cover 36 pesos. Open F-Su 11pm-4am. Cash only.)

# ISLA HOLBOX                                        ☎984

A barrier island marking the start of the Caribbean Sea and the end of the Gulf of Mexico, quiet Isla Holbox (hohl-BOSH; pop. 1600) is the Yucatán's alternative to the glitter of Cancún. Holbox stretches along nearly 40km of white sand beach, and despite the golf carts that serve as its primary mode of transport, remains largely untouched by tourist traffic. A hectic backpacker itinerary has no place here; the island, which is located inside the small Reserva Yum Balam, is best enjoyed as a retreat for birdwatching or beach walks. For those into a little more action, the island is home to a host of seafaring outdoor activities ranging from catching the waves on a kiteboard to swimming with the famous whale sharks. Come with cash if you intend to partake in any of the island's activities, as credit cards are rarely accepted and there is no bank.

## ▐ TRANSPORTATION

To get to Isla Holbox, take the **bus** to **Chiquilá** (3hr., 74 pesos) from Cancún, then take the **Hermanos ferry** #9 (☎875 2067; 30min., every 2hr. on the hr. 6am-6pm; 60 pesos). From **Chiquilá, buses** run to **Cancún** (daily 5:30,7:30am, and 1:30pm with additional service Sa-Su at 4:40pm), **Mérida** (daily 5:30am, with stops in Valladolid and Chichán Itzá), and **Tizimín** (M-F and Su 4:30pm, Sa 3:30pm). Ferries and fast boats leave with ample time to catch the bus. On Holbox itself, golf cart **"taxis"** cart suitcases to and from the dock (20 pesos). The rest of the island is small enough for walking. **Bicycles** can be rented at **Abarrotes,** one block to the right of the plaza, across the street from Cyber@Shark (see opposite page). (10 pesos per hr., 80 pesos per day. Open 8am-10pm. Cash only.)

## ✈ ❓ ORIENTATION AND PRACTICAL INFORMATION

Arriving ferries dock on the southern side of the island, a short walk from the town center. Any of the roads leading away from the water will take you to the plaza and the beach. The **Zona Hotelera** swings away from town to the island's eastern tip, and contains quite a few fancy resorts; unlike in ostentatious Cancún, the villas here are shrouded in palm fronds. Isla Holbox (literally "black hole") is off the grid as far as local services go. There is **no bank, no ATM,** and **no hospital.** For general emergencies, try the **mayor's office** (☎875 2162). If you need to connect to the outside world, head to **Cyber@ Shark,** one block to the right of the plaza, for fast internet. (☎875 2044. 15 pesos per hr. Open daily 10:30am-11pm.)

QUINTANA ROO

# ACCOMMODATIONS

Most foreigners ship in for the day to swim with the whale sharks, but some new budget options are opening the island to a younger crowd looking for an overnight stay.

**Ida y Vuelta Camping and Hostel,** C. Plutarco Elias (☎875 2358), next to Posada Aquario. About a 20min. walk from the ferry. From the ferry dock, turn right and take the first road leading away from the water on your left. At Posada Laury turn right. Take a left just before the tall white Posada Aquario. Holbox's best budget option. A romantic hippie utopia close to the beach, complete with thatched *palapa* bungalows, hammocks, and barbecue. Reception is all the way at the back of the compound. 100 peso deposit for lock. Limited locker space, sporadic hot water. Campsite 80 pesos; dorms 110 pesos; private room 350 pesos. Discounts on stays longer than 3 days. Cash only. ●

**Casa Maya,** C. Guaya 33 (☎875 2428; www.casamayadejoselimaholbox.com), by the beach. Rents tents to travelers in a more rustic, less landscaped setting. No hot water or kitchen. Tents 132 pesos (US$10). Rooms with bathrooms, TVs, A/C, and complimentary breakfast 750 pesos. AmEx/MC/V. ●

**Posada "Laury"** (☎875 2133). From the ferry dock exit right and take your first left. This road leads to the hotel. Killer value for a group of 4, with tidy double beds, kitchen, and bathroom close to town. 500 pesos per room for up to 4 people, 660 pesos during *Semana Santa*. Cash only. ●

**Casa Las Tortugas** (☎975 2129; www.holboxcasalastortugas.com). With plush white towels and its own private bar, this is an affordable option that feels deluxe. Romantic lighting sets the tone. Las Tortugas also organizes kite surfing lessons (660-1056 pesos/US$50-80 depending on private or group) and horseback rides. Beds start at 475 pesos (US$36). ●

# FOOD

Good seafood comes easily to this fishing village. Every morning fishermen sell their catch on the beach close to the town square.

**Doña Rosy,** underneath the covered market. Acts as the town *taquería,* dishing out tacos stuffed with chicken, onion, and potato for 12 pesos each. Open daily 5pm-midnight. Cash only. ●

**Carlucas,** next to the Casa de las Tortugas. Picturesque bar perfect for a cold beer or beachside *ceviche.* 2 beers for 25 pesos 5-7pm. Lobster with a drink 250 pesos. Open Tu-Su 11am-8pm. Cash only. ●

**Edelín Pizzeria** (☎875 2024), on the plaza. Thin crust pies with lobster to give them island flavor. Pizza 50-180 pesos. Open daily 11am-midnight. Cash only. ●

**La Isla de Colibrí** (☎875 2162), across the street from Edelín. This funky joint serves massive dishes amid folk art and Christmas lights. Try *camarones en salsa mango* (shrimp in mango salsa; 140 pesos) or a fresh fruit and yogurt bowl (55 pesos). Open daily 8am-1:30pm and 6-10pm. MC/V. ●

**Restaurant Villa Mar** (☎2736 5989), just past the *zócalo.* Dishes up seafood on *palapa*-covered plastic tables. *Ceviche* 80-120 pesos. Beer 25 pesos. Open 10am-late. Cash only. ●

# OUTDOOR ACTIVITIES

Holbox's claim to fame is the chance to swim with *tiburón ballenas,* or **whale sharks** (May 15-Sept. 15; 700-900 pesos). During the low season, companies offer **birdwatching tours,** which typically depart early in the morning, stopping at **Isla Pájaros** for birdwatching, **Isla Pasión** for photos, and **Yalahau,** a freshwater spring once sacred to Maya chiefs (3hr., 200-300 pesos). More extended boat trips include **snorkeling** with the turtles at **Cabo Catoche** (June-Aug., 5hr., 800 pesos),

**birdwatching** in the mangrove forests (6hr., 700 pesos), and **sport fishing** for your own *ceviche* (1500-3000 pesos). Tours, which leave at 7am and return around lunchtime, include all the necessary equipment and typically provide a small breakfast and lunch. For **kite fishing,** inquire at resorts like Casa de las Tortugas.

**Turística Miguel** (☎875 2028; www.holboxislandtours.com), on the corner of the *zócalo*. The largest excursion company on the island. Arranges tours and rents out golf carts. (100 pesos per hr.; full day 550 pesos.)

**Holbox Monkeys** (☎ 875 2442; www.holboxmonekys.com.mx), just one block from the town square, offers services similar to Turística Miguel.

**Hotel La Palapa** (☎875 2003). A host of airborne activities available. Laser sailing (half-day 600 pesos, full-day 1000 pesos) and 3-day kitesurfing courses (1800 pesos) are taught by Lino (as in Adrenalino), an Italian expat with 21 years on the island and an intense passion for the wind. Windsurfing is available upon request. Paypal or cash only.

# PUERTO MORELOS ☎998

Nestled between a mangrove swamp and the azure Riviera coastline, tiny Puerto Morelos (pop. 4500) is a relaxing beach escape for tourists tired of the city life. The nearby ecological reserve has prevented over-development and sprawl, and waterskiing is forbidden, as are resort hotels and Cancún-style hedonism. The town's tranquility pulls in families and wealthy Americans who rent private villas by the week. Just off-shore, a world-class reef provides opportunities for snorkeling and diving. Travelers who prefer privacy on the beach will be able to find their own patch of sand.

## TRANSPORTATION

**Buses** from **Cancún** to **Playa del Carmen** stop on the highway 2km west of Puerto Morelos (30min., every 10min. 5am-11pm, 17 pesos). To get into town, take one of the **buses** or **colectivos** that wait near the bus stop (4 pesos). **Taxis** are also available (20 pesos). Buses back to the highway leave from the central plaza. **Bike rental** (50 pesos per day) is through **Puerto Morelos Travel Agency,** on the southwest corner of the plaza, in front of Oxxo. This agency also arranges tours to *cenotes* and ruins. (☎871 0332; www.puertomorelostravelagency.com. MC/V.)



## ORIENTATION AND PRACTICAL INFORMATION

Puerto Morelos extends three blocks back from the beach. The road leading into town heads straight for the dock, and is crossed by **Avenida Javier Rojo Gomez** running north-south at the **plaza.** To the north sit private villas and a long stretches of sandy beach. There is a **24hr. ATM** in the plaza. **Alma Libre Bookstore,** Plaza Morelos 3, at Av. Tulum, sells English-language books. (☎871 0713; www.almalibrebooks.com. Open M-Sa 10am-3pm and 6-9pm, Su 4-9pm.)

## ACCOMMODATIONS

There are no hostels in Puerto Morelos. If you have a group of four and don't mind sharing, there are some moderately priced rooms available. Reservations are recommended. Discounts are often negotiable for longer stays.

**Hotel Inglaterra** (☎206 9081; www.hotelinglaterra.com), on Av. Niños Heroes. Turn left 1 block before the plaza. Equipped with patio and pool, Hotel Inglaterra has larger rooms upstairs with kitchenettes and smaller (less expensive) suites downstairs. Doubles from 462 pesos (US$35) in low season, high season from 727 pesos (US$55); suites 648/912 pesos (US$49/69). MC/V. ⑤

**Posada Amor** (☎871 0033), on Av. Javier Rojo Gomez. Reception through the restaurant in front. The cheapest place in town, with a good reputation for housing budget travelers. Doubles 336 pesos, with bath 392-560 pesos. Cash only. ⑤

**Posada el Moro** (☎871 0159; www.posadaelmoro.com), on Av. Javier Rojo Gómez 1 block north of the central square. Basic rooms with fridge and a small pool. At the time of publication, construction was underway for a tower addition. Singles 660 pesos (US$50), 4-person room 1060 pesos (US$80). Paypal or cash. ⑥

## ◼ FOOD

Eating is a major event in this sleepy town. The infusion of American dollars has resulted in some creative offerings.

**David Lau** (☎251 2531), on the south side of the plaza. Ever popular, Lau's serves Chinese-Mexican fusion in a casual *palapa* setting. Open Tu-Sa 3-11pm, Su 1-10pm. Cash only. ④

**Rosy's Pizza N Love** (☎871 0777), on the northwestern spoke of the plaza. A cosmopolitan menu, topping soft crusts with jalapeños for the Mexicana, or stuffing them with sweet onion and mozzarella to create the Argentine favorite *la fugazzetta*. Free Wi-Fi. Pizza 25-120 pesos. Open daily 6-11pm. Cash only. ①

**Cantino Habanera,** farther down the block. Black-lit and blasting Texas country music. Acts as the local gringo bar. Guacamole 45 pesos. Beer 15 pesos. Mojitos 35 pesos. Open M and W 3pm-midnight, Tu and Th-Su noon-midnight. Cash only. ②

## ◼ ACTIVITIES

The most popular activity in Puerto Morelos (besides soaking up the rays) is heading out in a *lancha* to **snorkel** or **scuba dive**. Trips can be arranged at **Dive In Puerto Morelos,** Rojo Gómez 14, two blocks north of the plaza. The company also offers a full range of PADI certification courses. (☎206 9084; www.diveinpuertomorelos.com. 2hr. snorkeling trip 396 pesos (US$30), including 10min. boat ride, equipment rental, and marine park entrance fee; 4-person min. 2-tank dive 925 pesos (US$70), including equipment rental and park fee; 2-person min. Open M-Sa 8am-6pm. MC/V.)

 **HEADS UP.** The reef around the town dock is neither as clean nor as safe as the reefs farther to the north. Avoid swimming in the wake of the fishing boats and make sure you're visible while in the water.

For those interested in keeping two feet on the ground, the Riviera's 150 acre **Jardín Botánico,** where spider monkeys scramble through 150 species of exotic flora, is located 2km south of town. Paths afford lovely opportunities for bird-watching. (☎206 9233. Open daily 8am-4pm. 93 pesos/US$7.) There are also **ATV tours** through Puerto Morelos Travel Agency (see **Bike Rentals,** p. 144).

# PLAYA DEL CARMEN ☎984

The quiet tourist should steer clear: the party in Playa never stops. Smack in the middle of the legendary Mayan Riviera, Playa del Carmen (pop. 150,000) ranks as one of the fastest-growing resort areas in Latin America, tempting travelers with pristine reef diving, white sand beaches, inland Mayan ruins, and fiery nightlife. Unlike Cancún and Tulum, Playa del Carmen has developed

QUINTANA ROO

without automobiles in mind (or sight), and the beach, stretching kilometers in either direction (it's no coincidence that the city often simply goes by "Playa") is easily accessible. On Quinta, the town's main street, a never-ending parade of holiday revelers struts around in various states of undress and sunburn, and new, slick storefronts go up every day as the avenue pushes northward. Despite the glitz, the city remains affordable, full of budget accommodations and cheap eats away from the central *paseo*.

## ▐ TRANSPORTATION

**Buses: Bus station** (☎873 0109 or 878 0309), at the corner of Quinta and Juárez. **ADO** (www.ado.com.mx) sends 1st-class buses to: **Chetumal** (30min., 17 per day, 204 pesos); **Chichén Itzá** (4½hr., 8am, 420 pesos); **Mérida** (5hr., 14 per day, 286-344 pesos); **Mexico City** (25hr.; 12:30, 7:30, 9:30pm; 1220 pesos); **Orizaba** (20hr., 7:30pm, 1006 pesos); **Palenque** (11½hr., 7pm); **Puebla** (21½hr., 6:25pm, 1128 pesos); **San Andrés** (17½hr.; 3:40, 10:15pm; 788 pesos); **San Cristóbal de las Casas** (16½hr., 7pm, 776 pesos); **Veracruz** (20hr.; 3:40, 6:45, 10:15pm; 890-1068 pesos). Many lines offer service to **Tulum** (1hr., 22 per day, 48 pesos) with stops in **Xcaret, Xel-Ha,** and **Cobá.** Daily service to the **Cancún airport** (1hr., every hr. 7am-7pm, 90 pesos).

**Ferries: UltraMar** (☎803 5581) and **Mexico Waterjets** (☎872 1508 or 1588; www.mexicowaterjets.com.mx) offer similar ferry service to **Isla Cozumel** (30-40min., every hr. 5am-2pm and 4-11pm, 140 pesos). Tickets can be purchased from booths in front of the ferry terminal or bus station.

**Public Transportation: Taxis colectivos** leave from C. 2 Nte, just north of the park. **White vans** leave every 15-20min. for **Cancún** and **Tulum** (15-25 pesos), hitting up the fancy hotels in between. A bit cheaper and faster than a bus.

**Taxis:** Taxis (☎873 0414) line up on Juárez in front of the bus station and run to sights around Playa (40-60 pesos). Prices are negotiable; be sure to set a price before getting in the car.

**Bike Rental: Agencia Ruta Maya** (☎803 0840), on C. 2 between 10 and 15. 150 pesos per day.

## ✈ ❷ ORIENTATION AND PRACTICAL INFORMATION

Playa is located on the Mayan Riviera, 68km south of Cancún and 63km north of Tulum. The ferry to Cozumel docks below the town's *zócalo*, a block south and a block west of the bus station. The heart of the tourist industry lies on the pedestrian walk, **Quinta Avenida,** to the north when exiting the bus station. A large shoping mall filled with chain stores anchors the southern end of the road. The newer area north of **Avenida Constituyentes** goes by "Little Italy" in honor of the Italians who have settled there. **Juárez,** the town's other main drag, runs west from the beach to the **Cancún-Chetumal Road** (Highway 307), 1½km away. East-west *calles* are even-numbered north of Juárez, odd-numbered south from it. North-south *avenidas* increase by fives from the beach.

**Tourist Office:** (☎873 2804), on the corner of Juárez and Av. 15. English, French, and Italian spoken. Open M-F 9am-7:30pm, Sa-Su 9am-1pm.

**Consulates: US,** C. 1 Sur (☎873 0303; emergency line 807 8355), in "The Palapa" between Av. 15 and 20. Open M-F 10am-1pm.

**Currency Exchange: HSBC** (☎873 0272), on Juárez, 1 block west of the *zócalo*, has a **24hr. ATM.** Open M-F 9am-7pm, Sa 9am-3pm. Traveler's checks must be exchanged at *casas de cambio.*

**Luggage Storage:** In the bus station. 5-11 pesos per hr. Open daily 6am-9pm. Minimal storage at the docks on Playa and Cozumel.

QUINTA ROO

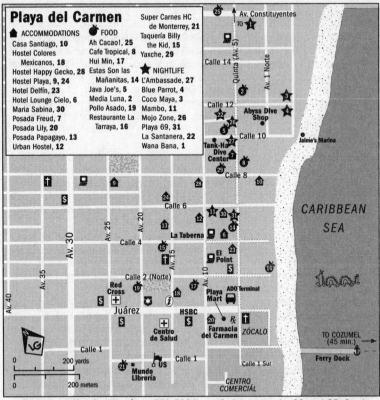

**Playa del Carmen**

🏠 ACCOMMODATIONS
Casa Santiago, **10**
Hostel Colores
Mexicanos, **18**
Hostel Happy Gecko, **28**
Hostel Playa, **9, 24**
Hotel Delfín, **23**
Hotel Lounge Cielo, **6**
Maria Sabina, **30**
Posada Freud, **7**
Posada Lily, **20**
Posada Papagayo, **13**
Urban Hostel, **12**

🍴 FOOD
Ah Cacao!, **25**
Cafe Tropical, **8**
Hui Min, **17**
Estas Son las
Mañanitas, **14**
Java Joe's, **5**
Media Luna, **2**
Pollo Asado, **19**
Restaurante La
Tarraya, **16**

Super Carnes HC
de Monterrey, **21**
Taquería Billy
the Kid, **15**
Yaxche, **29**

⭐ NIGHTLIFE
L'Ambassade, **27**
Blue Parrot, **4**
Coco Maya, **3**
Mambo, **11**
Mojo Zone, **26**
Playa 69, **31**
La Santanera, **22**
Wana Bana, **1**

Av. Constituyentes
Quinta (Av. 5)
Av. 1 Norte
Calle 14
Calle 12
Abyss Dive Shop
Calle 10
Jaime's Marina
Tank-Ha Dive Center
Calle 8
CARIBBEAN SEA
Av. 30
Av. 35
Av. 40
Av. 25
Av. 20
Av. 15
Av. 10
Calle 6
Calle 4
La Taberna
El Point
Calle 2 (Norte)
Red Cross
Juárez
HSBC
Playa Mart
ADO Terminal
Centro de Salud
Farmacia del Carmen
ZÓCALO
Calle 1
Mundo Librería
US
Calle 1
Calle 1 Sur
CENTRO COMERCIAL
TO COZUMEL (45 min.)
Ferry Dock

0 ____ 200 yards
0 ____ 200 meters

**Bookstore: Mundo Librería** (☎879 3004), on C. 1 between Av. 20 and 25. Stocks a wide selection of new and used beach reads, atlases, and academic treatises in English, German, and Spanish. Exchange available for used books. Open M-F 9am-8pm, Sa 10am-6pm. Another location in Plaza las Americas. Open M-Sa 9:30am-9:30pm, Su 2-9:30pm. MC/V.

**Laundromat: GigaLav,** on C. 2 between Av. 10 and 15. 15 pesos per kg. 35 peso minimum. Self-service 30 pesos. Internet cafe attached (10 pesos per hr). Open daily 8am-11pm.

**Emergency:** ☎066.

**Police:** (☎066), on Juárez, 2 blocks from the plaza between Av. 15 and 20.

**Red Cross:** (☎873 1233), on Av. 25 at Juárez.

**Pharmacy: Farmacia del Carmen** (☎873 2330), on Juárez, opposite the bus station. Open daily 7am-11pm. AmEx/MC/V.

**Medical Services: Centro de Salud** (☎873 0314), on Juárez and Av. 15.

**Internet Access: La Taberna Internet Cafe** (☎803 0448), on the corner of C. 4 and Av. 10. Internet 16 pesos per hr. Open daily 10am-5am. **Phonet** (104 1699), on Av. 10 between C. 2 and 4. Open daily 8am-11pm. 12 pesos per hr.

**Post Office:** (☎873 0300), at C. 2 and Av. 20. Open M-F 9am-4pm, Sa 9am-1pm. **Postal Code:** 77710.

QUINTANA ROO

# ACCOMMODATIONS

With Playa's recent rapid growth, both luxury and budget accommodations are proliferating. Hostels are the way to go if you're looking to spend less than 400 pesos per night. Compared to other hostels in Mexico, hostels in Playa del Carmen are toward the high end of the price spectrum, and often come without the amenities you might expect elsewhere. During high season (Dec. 21-Apr. 15 and July 15-Sept. 15), prices are especially high and reservations are necessary. Most establishments lie along Quinta or Juárez, within walking distance of the beach.

## HOSTELS

**Hostel Playa** (☎803 3277; www.hostelplaya.com), on the corner of C. 8 and Av. 25. One of Playa's biggest and most popular hostels, especially among the backpacker crowd. Years of use have made their mark. A bit far from the beach, but good fans, a large common room, and a well-stocked kitchen make this hostel worth a look. Separate men's and women's dorms encircle a spacious living area with books, games, hammocks, full kitchen, TV/DVD, and purified water. Dorms 140 pesos; doubles 380 pesos. Cash only. ❶

**Hostel Rio Playa** (☎803 0145; www.hostelrioplaya.com), on C. 8 between Av. 5 and 10. The center of the party. Packs beds into the noisy main dorm room. The bunks are sturdy, but people looking for quiet or privacy will want to pay the extra pesos for smaller rooms. Includes sunny rooftop pool and bar. Free Wi-Fi. 14-bed dorms 150 pesos; 6-bed dorms 160 pesos; 4-bed dorms 170 pesos. Cash only. ❶

**Casa Santiago** (☎873 0492, www.casasantiago.com.mx), on C. 10 between Av. 5 and Av. 1. As close to the beach as you can get. Formerly just a small hotel, Santiago has a cheery yellow finish and well-sized rooms. Limited common space inhibits the hostel atmosphere, and low thread count sheets mean less bang for your buck. Creaky fans. Wi-Fi in lobby. Dorms 185 pesos; private rooms 350 pesos. Cash only. ❷

**Hostel Colores Mexicanos** (☎873 0065), on Av. 15 between Juárez and C. 2. A good option for those seeking a quieter dorm atmosphere or a place for small groups. The well-lit courtyard has plenty of chairs and tables for impromptu picnics. Minimalist rooms have ceiling fans, lockers, private baths, and plenty of soap. Linens included. Reception 9am-9pm. Check-out noon. 4-bed dorms 150 pesos; singles 300 pesos; doubles 400 pesos; each additional person 50 pesos. Cash only. ❶

**Maria Sabina, Hotel and Backpackers Hostel**, C. 6 796 (☎873 0113; www.mariasabinahotel.com), between Av. 5 and 10. Named for the "Mother of the Sacred Mushroom," a 20th-century *indígena* shaman. Small, dark rooms have balconies over the noisy street. Bronzed travelers lounge in the common areas nursing beers before a night out. Breakfast included. Free Wi-Fi. Beds 150 pesos. Cash only. ❶

**Urban Hostel** (☎879 9342; www.urbanhostel.com.mx), on Av. 10 between C. 4 and 6. 2 blocks from the beach. The cheapest hostel in Playa, Urban distills the bohemian vibe with bunk beds under a giant *palapa* and ceiling fans. Kitchen available. Continental breakfast and Wi-Fi included. Small lockers; bring your own lock. Ring the bell for reception. Check-out noon. Dorms 120 pesos; private rooms with shared bath 200 pesos. Cash only. ❶

**Hostel Happy Gecko** (☎147 0692), on Av. 10 between C. 6 and 8. Dorms have private bath and kitchen. Good for groups, potentially noisy for solo travelers. Linens and Wi-Fi included. Dorms 150 pesos. Cash only. ❶

**Cabañas Popul Vuh** (☎803 2149), on C. 2 between Av. 5 and the beach. Close to the beach and the bus station. Basic rooms in rustic conditions. Double with fan 400 pesos, with A/C 620 pesos; each additional person 100 pesos. MC/V. ❺

## BUDGET HOTELS

▨ **Posada Freud** (☎873 0601; www.posadafreud.com), on Quinta between C. 8 and 10. Palm trees and colorful hammocks draw travelers to Freud's unique abodes, which boast a clean, beachy decor. The small on-site bar is perfectly situated for people-watching. Reception 24hr. Check-out noon. Reservations recommended. Rooms 530-1850 pesos (US$40-140) depending on the season. MC/V. ❺

**Posada Papagayo,** Av. 15 154 (☎873 2497), between C. 4 and 6. A good option for those seeking more privacy than dorms offer. The breezy lounge area and green interior garden make up for the slightly sunless rooms. Reception 24hr. Check-out noon. Singles and doubles 300 pesos; triples 400 pesos; 4 people 500 pesos. Prices rise by up to 100 pesos in high season. Cash only. ❹

**Hotel Delfin** (☎987 30176, from the US ☎831 425 1669; www.hoteldelfin.com). Clean, simple rooms close to the action. Every room gets a window and a private bath. Doubles from 660 pesos (US$50) in low season, in high season from 925 pesos (US$70). MC/V with 5% added. ❺

**Hotel Lounge Cielo** (☎873 1227, from the US ☎718 710 4773; www.hotelcielo. com), on C. 4 between Quinta and Av. 10. Colorful bedspreads and a trough to wash sandy feet make this trendy hotel-lounge a good option for travelers looking to scale it up. Pay more for rooms with balconies. Free Wi-Fi. Rooms 700-1600 pesos; 800 pesos for 3 people. Cash only. ❺

**Posada Lily** (☎871 3016), on Juárez, 1 block west of the plaza. The flaming pink building set back behind a parking lot. Noisy but convenient location near the bus station. Houses small, cushy beds in clean rooms with powerful fans. Parking available. Reception 8am-9pm. Check-out 1pm. Singles with double bed 250 pesos; 2 double beds 300 pesos. Cash only. ❸

## ◨ FOOD

It's easy to eat well in Playa. It's harder to do so on a budget. Bargains are difficult to find among Quinta's flashy French and Italian restaurants that cater to a growing tourist population. For a sampling of the finest Playa has to offer, check out the Little Italy district, north of Av. Constituyentes near the beach. While Quinta is the place to splurge on a meal, inexpensive regional cuisine at the *loncherías* west of Av. 10 near C. 6 will fill your belly without emptying your pockets. Breakfast vendors flood the *zócalo* in the early morning. For essential grocery goods, head to **Wal-Mart,** at Av. 30 and C. 8. (Open daily 8am-1am.)

▨**Restaurant La Tarraya** (☎873 2040; www.tarraya.com.mx), on the beach at the end of C. 2. This budget-friendly bar-restaurant is perfect if you're in the mood for seafood but don't want to leave the beach. *Palapas* shade plastic tables with vistas looking out to Cozumel. Fish filet *tikin xic* (freshly barbecued) 95 pesos per kg. Open daily noon-9pm. Cash only. ❹

▨ **Ah Cacao Chocolate Cafe** (☎984 803 5748; www.ahcacao.com), at Quinta Av. and Constituyentes, with another location (☎984 879 4179) at Quinta Av. and C. 30. Offering exquisite chocolate and Wi-Fi, Ah Cacao knows how to keep a budget traveler happy. Light and creamy chocolate mousse (39 pesos) and fresh-churned ice cream (29 pesos). Both locations open 7:15am-11:30pm. MC/V. ❷

**Media Luna** (☎873 0526), on Quinta between C. 12 and 14. This upstairs eatery with spacious seating has found its niche experimenting with international fusion. Romantic lighting, with a menu varied enough to satisfy even vegetarians. Open daily 4-11pm. MC/V. ❹

**Taquería Billy the Kid,** on the corner of Av. 15 and C. 4. Famous throughout the Mayan Riviera for incredibly cheap tacos, Billy the Kid has a well-earned reputation and a devoted local following. Make sure to request the *cebolla cocida* (cooked onions) on your steak taco (5 pesos). Drinks 10 pesos. Open daily 24hr. Cash only. ❶

**Java Joe's** (☎876 2694; www.javajoes.net), on C. 10 between Av. 5 and 10. A favorite of Playa's burgeoning expat community. Pick up tips from Java Joe himself while enjoying the famous coffee (20 pesos) and bagel sandwiches (40-65 pesos) at tables that spill out into the street. Open daily 6:30am-11pm. Cash only. ❷

**Super Carnes HC de Monterrey/La Raza,** C. 1 190 (☎803 4227), between Av. 20 and 25. For the best *arracheras* (steak fajitas) in town, locals head to this restaurant and butcher shop with enormous portions and a casual atmosphere. Full meals (100 pesos) include potatoes, guacamole, and drink. Meals for 3 people 150 pesos. Open daily noon-8:30pm. Cash only. ❹

**Pollos Asado al Carbon,** Av. 20 at C. 2. The budget option for fowl. 45 pesos buys a quarter chicken, tortillas, rice, onions, and a soda. Open daily 10am-6pm. Cash only. ❷

**La Hora Feliz** (☎803 3436), Quinta at C. 26. A small cafe in Playa's Little Italy. Wi-Fi available. Martini Hour begins at 5. Sandwiches 50 pesos. Pasta 70-110 pesos. Open daily 8am-2am. Cash only. ❷

**Estas Son las Mañanitas** (☎873 0114), on Quinta between C. 4 and C. 6. Even picky locals recommend this blend of Mexican and Italian cuisine. Pizza from 119 pesos. Traditional Mexican dishes 69-175 pesos. Open daily 7am-midnight. AmEx/MC/V. ❸

**Cafe Tropical** (☎873 2111), on Quinta between C. 8 and 10. Enjoy the generous portions of falafel, hummus, chicken, and seafood beneath a giant *palapa*. Street-side tables are perfectly situated to watch the Quinta traffic. Smoothies 27 pesos. Omelets with a rich variety of fillings 78 pesos. Big falafel sandwiches 78 pesos. Pad thai 105 pesos. Wi-Fi available. Open daily 7am-midnight. MC/V. ❹

**Hui Min** (☎113 3263), on C. 2 between Av. 10 and 15. You can't beat the prices at this family-owned Chinese restaurant. Heaping spoonful of any rice or noodle dish for only 12 pesos. Spring rolls 10 pesos. Plentiful platters 30 pesos. Open daily 11am-11pm. Cash only. ❷

**Yaxche** (☎873 2502; www.mayacuisine.com), on C. 8 between Av. 5 and 10. A large, elegant restaurant serving upscale Yucatec cuisine. The menu is a refresher course in Mayan history. The Kukulkan lobster is sized (and priced) for a king. Open daily noon-11:30pm. MC/V. ❺

## ⌐ DIVING

Despite the damage from Hurricane Wilma in 2005, Playa's off-shore reefs have become a hot spot, entrancing divers with bright coral reefs, ancient underwater formations, and plentiful schools of fish. Snorkeling is best at Coco Beach, the point north of Mamita's.

**Abyss Dive Shop** (☎873 2164; www.abyssdiveshop.com), on Av. 1 between C. 10 and 12. Services 13 different dive sites and caters to all skill levels. "Discover" scuba trips 1190 pesos (US$90). Open-water courses 5220 pesos (US$395). 2-tank dive 925 pesos (US$70), equipment 200 pesos (US$15). Trips leave at 9am and 2pm; 2-person min. Open M-Sa 8am-7pm, Su 8am-6pm. MC/V.

**Tank-Ha Dive Center** (☎873 0302 or 879 3427; www.tankha.com), on C. 10 between Quinta and Av. 10. Another reputable diving company. Tank-Ha owns a fleet of seven boats, offers the full range of PADI courses, and conducts dives in Dutch, English, German, Italian, and Spanish. 1-tank dive 595 pesos (US$45). 2-tank dive 990 pesos (US$75). Trips leave at 9am and 2pm; 2-person min. Multi-day dive packages receive 10-15% discount. 2-tank *cenote* dive 1585 pesos (US$120); 4 person max.; includes lunch and transportation to *cenotes*. Popular 2hr. snorkel tour visits 2 reefs. 9:30am and 1:30pm. 4-person min. 530 pesos (US$40). Open M-Sa 8am-9pm, Su 8am-5pm. MC/V.

QUINTANA ROO

## 🌴🏄 BEACHES AND WATERSPORTS

Lined with palm trees and skirted by the turquoise waters of the Caribbean, Playa's beaches are sandy, white, and oh-so-cool. Relatively free of seaweed and coral, the beaches here are instead strewn with scantily-clad tourists and a small forest of umbrellas. The water off the coast of Playa is calmer than in Tulum, making it a better spot for snorkeling. In the center, restaurants with sunbeds take up much of the space. Walking north brings you to a wider beach. **Mamita's Beach Club,** at C. 28 (www.mamitasbeachclub.com), attracts the young and the restless, who soak up rays to the thump thump of a disco bass. For a more private beach experience, hike north toward the point.

In search of an aquatic escape? Vendors near the *zócalo* have a "special offer just for you"—which may involve snorkeling, scuba diving, fishing, jetskiing, parasailing, or windsurfing. Some of the fancier hotels just south of the pier rent equipment, as do shacks a few hundred meters north. One reliable stand is **Jaime's Marina,** at C. 10 on the beach in front of El Faro Hotel. (☎130 2034; www.jaimesmarina.bravehost.com. 2hr. sail or snorkel tours 436 pesos/US$33 per person; 2-person min. Full-day private windsurfing lesson 990 pesos/US$75. Kayak rentals 185 pesos/US$14. Open 10am-6pm, last trip 4pm. Cash only.)

## 🎵🎭 NIGHTLIFE AND ENTERTAINMENT

Come nightfall, Quinta transforms from a busy commercial thoroughfare into a glitzy nightspot. Sun-lovers recuperate from the day's rays by swaying in hammocks and jiving to live jazz and salsa. Though chains such as Carlos'n Charlie's and Señor Frogs near the ferry dock are popular with American teens grinding to hip hop, Playa has plenty of alternatives with a more international flavor. Most of the action occurs between C. 8 and 14, C. 12, and on the streets between Quinta and the beach. The Carmen crowds follow Ladies' Nights around the city. Though things don't really start to happen until after midnight, budget travelers should arrive early to avoid cover charges.

**THE REAL DEAL.** Though Cancún claims to have cornered the market on nightlife, Playa del Carmen is now nipping at its heels. Though you won't find the same smoke and light shows, Playa offers more budget-conscious night owls plenty of beachside options to dance until dawn.

**Blue Parrot Inn** (☎206 3360), on C. 12 at the beach. Once on the list of the 10 best beach bars in the world, the Blue Parrot hasn't lost its tropical touch. Swings replace the conventional bar stools and the nightly fireshow is the best attraction in town. The show can also be viewed for free from the beach, though a small donation is requested for the dancers. Mix of US hip hop, pop, and reggaeton. M and Th 9-midnight women drink free. Cover 100-150 pesos. Kitchen open 5-11pm. Dance club open 9pm-4am. AmEx/MC/V.

**Coco Maya** (☎863 5687; www.cocomayabeachclub.com), on C. 12 next to the Blue Parrot Inn. A slightly cheaper alternative to Blue Parrot, its neighbor, for partying into the wee hours. Nightly DJ spins hip hop and electronica while music videos project onto the surrounding walls. Women drink free daily 9pm-midnight. Cover 50 pesos. Open daily 9pm-5am. Cash only.

**Mojo Zone** (www.mojozonebar.com), on Quinta between C. 10 and 12. An intimate, incense-infused bar 1 story above the Quinta traffic. Live music and creative drinks, like the "Brainwashing" (Captain Morgan cloaked in lime, raspberries, strawberries, and sugar; 65 pesos). Beer 25 pesos. Mixed drinks 55-90 pesos. Open W-Sa 9:30pm-1:30am. Cash only.

**Mambo** (☎803 2656; www.mambocafe.com.mx), on the corner of C. 6 and Av. 0. Mambo reels in a crowd with its colorful atmosphere and salsa music. Dancers file in at 11:30pm and the band goes on just after midnight. Get prepared with an 80-peso salsa lesson before the club opens at 11pm; details are at the club. Open Th-Sa 10pm-4am. Cover 50 pesos. MC.

**L'Ambassade** (☎745 3788), on C. 10 between Av. 5 and 10. A lively bar pregame spot popular for its budget-friendly drinks. Mixed drinks 60-100 pesos. Beer 20 pesos. Open M 6pm-2am, Tu-Su noon-2am. Cash only.

**La Santanera** (☎803 4771; www.lasantanera.com), on C. 12 between Av. 5 and 10. Santanera's terrace lounge caters to the well-tanned and trendy. Downstairs world-famous DJs spin electronica. Tu ladies night. W alternative music. Cover F-Sa 100 pesos. Open Tu-Su midnight-5am. Terrace open from 11pm. MC/V.

**La Botica,** on Quinta between 22 and 24. A small bar with pulsing techno and 30 types of *mezcal.* Shots 36-46 pesos. Beer 20 pesos. Open daily 2pm-2am. Cash only.

**Playa 69,** up a passageway off Quinta between C. 4 and 6. A gay dance spot just off Quinta. Don't expect any action until after midnight. Open daily 9pm-late. Cash only.

# ISLA COZUMEL                                    ☎987

Mexico's largest Caribbean island, Cozumel, is a diving mecca, drawing more than two million annual visitors to its barrier reef, the second largest in the world. When Cortés stopped in Cozumel on his way to Mexico, he found an island dedicated to the worship of the Maya goddess Ixchel. Cortés suppressed the religion, and gradually the island was abandoned, serving largely as a refuge for pirates. During the Caste Wars, rebels fled here for safety, and economic growth began again in the early 20th century when the island became a hub of the chewing gum trade. Tourism had a foothold as early as the 1930s, but it exploded in 1961 when French diver Jacques Cousteau called attention to the amazing coral formations and colorful marine life of Palancar Reef. These days, the island's name—Mayan for "land of swallows"—might as well refer to the flocks of cruise ship passengers who crowd the main town to drink beer and peruse items in the shops along the main avenue. Despite the throngs, much of the island, protected by Mexican law, remains undeveloped and ripe for

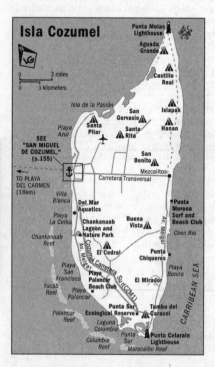

QUINTANA ROO

exploration. Miles of empty white sand beaches, Mayan ruins, and crocodile-filled lagoons encourage travelers to look beyond the island's main city, San Miguel de Cozumel (pop. 80,000).

## ⊏ TRANSPORTATION

**Flights: Cozumel Airport (CML;** ☎872 2081), 2km north of town. Served by **American Airlines** (☎+1 800 904 6000; www.aa.com), **Continental** (☎872 0487; www.continental.com), and **Mexicana** (☎872 2945; www.mexicana.com). Taxis (50 pesos) and shared minivans take passengers into San Miguel.

**Ferries:** The most popular form of transportation to reach the island from **Playa del Carmen. UltraMar** (☎803 5581) and **Mexico Waterjets** (☎872 1508 or 1588; www.mexicowaterjets.com.mx) offer similar ferry service to and from Playa del Carmen. Tickets can be bought from one of the many booths in front of the ferry terminal. (Both companies 30-40min., almost every hr. 6am-10pm, 140 pesos.) **Trans de Caribe** sends car ferries from **Punto Venados** to Cozumel, 20 min. south of Playa del Carmen, on the way to **Tulum** (☎872 7688 or 7671).

**Public Transportation:** San Miguel de Cozumel has a local bus system, but it operates only within the town, and does not take tourists to attractions on other parts of the island.

**Taxis:** (☎872 0041 or 0236). Line up on Av. Melgar. Prices on a sign close to the ferry dock. 50 pesos to the **airport,** 250 to **Punta Moreno.** Set a price before the taxi departs.

**Car Rental:**

**LE$$ Pay,** Melgar 628 (☎872 4744 or 869 0030; www.lesspaycars.com.mx), about 1km south of town. VW Safaris 385 pesos per day. Jeeps 660 pesos per day. Mopeds 360 pesos per day. Discounts for multi-day rentals. Price does not include insurance. Open daily 8am-8pm. AmEx/MC/V.

**Hertz** (☎871 6784), on Av. Juárez between Av. 5 Nte. and 10 Nte. Moped US$25 (330 pesos) per day. 4-door manual transmission US$40 (580 pesos) per day. Automatic US$48 (635 pesos) per day. Open daily 7am-8pm. No cash. AmEx/MC/V.

**Cuarto y Quinto Poder,** Av. Salas 3 (☎869 1328), between Melgar and Av. 5. VW convertible US$40 (580 pesos). Scooters US$25 (330 pesos) per day. Prices include unlimited mileage but not gas. Insurance extra US$5 (65 pesos) per day. MC/V.

**Bike Rental:** Most places that rent mopeds also have bikes, and they cost about the same. **Rentadora Gallo,** Av. 10 25 (☎869 2444), between Juárez and C. 1 Sur. Bikes US$17 (225 pesos). Mopeds US$25 (330 pesos). VW convertibles US$40 (580 pesos). Open daily 8am-7pm. Credit card deposit. Cash only.

 **CRUISE CONTROL.** Renting a car or moped is the best way to see the whole island of Cozumel. Buses are non-existent and taxis are pricey. Split the cost with a buddy to be environmentally and economically conscious. Don't forget that you must show a valid driver's license and an accepted credit card to rent any motorized vehicle on the island.

## ▬▮ ORIENTATION AND PRACTICAL INFORMATION

The island of Cozumel is 18km east of mainland Quintana Roo and 85km south of Isla Mujeres. At 52km long and 14km wide, Cozumel is Mexico's largest Caribbean island. **San Miguel de Cozumel,** the main town and home to the island's ferry docks, sits on the western coast, facing **Playa del Carmen.** Downtown, *avenidas* run parallel to the sea and increase by fives. *Calles* are odd-numbered south of Av. Juárez and even-numbered north of Av. Juárez. The most touristed beaches are also the best for snorkeling and lie south of San Miguel. Beaches

QUINTANA ROO

on the **eastern coast** are much less developed; in fact, most of the interior of the island is unpopulated, creating plenty of opportunities for moped exploration. The perimeter road is a spectacular 75km loop along the sea, with several nice views, beach shacks, and swimming areas. Much of the northern part of the island is inaccessible, with barely-paved roads designed solely to damage rental cars.

**Tourist Office:** Up C. 13 near the Iglesia Corpus Christi, far from the *centro*. Open M-F 9am-5pm. Wooden stands on each corner of the Plaza del Sol can also provide helpful tips and maps of the island, although they may try to sell you a snorkel trip in the process. The free *Blue Guide to Cozumel,* available at tourist locations and hotels, has useful information and coupons.

**Consulates: US** (☎872 4574, emergencies 872 6152), on the 2nd fl. of Plaza Villa Mar shopping mall in the *zócalo,* behind Fat Tuesday's. Open M-F noon-2pm.

**Banks: Banorte** (☎872 0718), on Av. 5 Nte., between Juárez and C. 2. Open M-F 9am-5pm, Sa 9am-2pm. **HSBC** (☎872 0182), in the plaza. Open M-F 9am-7pm, Sa 9am-3pm. Both banks have **24hr. ATMs.**

**Bookstore: Fama** (☎872 5020), on Av. 5 between Juárez and C. 2 Nte. CDs, books, magazines, and maps. Limited English selection. Open daily 9am-10pm.

**Laundromat: Lavandería Margarita** (☎869 1876), on Av. 20 Sur between Salas and C. 3 Sur. Wash 25 pesos, dry 15 pesos per 10min. More for full-service. Open M-Sa 7am-9pm, Su 8am-4pm.

**Emergency:** ☎066.

**Police:** (☎872 0092), on C. 11 Sur in the Palacio Municipal.

**Red Cross:** (☎872 1058), on Av. 20 Sur at Salas. Open daily 7am-11pm.

**24hr. Pharmacy: Farmacia Similares** (☎869 2440), at C. 1 Sur and Av. 15.

**Medical Services: Centro Médico de Cozumel,** 1 Sur 101 (☎872 9400), at Av. 50. Open 24hr. For non-emergencies, there is a small **medical clinic** next to Farmacias Similares, on the corner of C. 1 Sur and Av. 15 Nte. Be prepared for a line. Open M-Sa 9am-3pm and 4-9pm, Su 9am-3pm. For diving or pressure-related emergencies, the island has a hyperbaric-chamber-equipped **DAN referral center,** 21 C. 5 Sur (☎872 1430 or 001 919 684 4326; www.sssnetwork.com). Open 24hr.

**Fax Office: Telecomm** (☎872 0056; fax 872 0376), in the same building as the post office. **Western Union** services available. Open M-F 8am-7:30pm, Sa-Su 9am-12:30pm.

**Internet Access:** Available all over the island. Most cafes charge about 10 pesos per hr. Look for hostels with free internet. **Blau Net,** 233 Av. Salas (☎872 7673), between Av. 10 and Av. 15, has fast service. 10 pesos per hr.

**Post Office:** (☎872 0106), off Melgar, just south of C. 7 Sur along the sea. Open M-F 9am-5pm, Sa 9am-4:30pm. **Postal Code:** 77600.

## ACCOMMODATIONS AND CAMPING

Since hotels cater primarily to foreign divers with cash to burn, they are generally more expensive in Cozumel than on the mainland and hostels are scarce. Sadly, the extra pesos do not guarantee higher quality. Consider asking to see the room before paying—quality may vary considerably by hotel. Try to grab a room before noon during high season. Free **camping,** particularly in secluded spots on the island's east side near Punta Morena, may be the cheapest and most peaceful option, but be sure to check in with police first as camping is not permitted at certain times of year when the sea turtles come ashore.

QUINTANA ROO

**San Miguel de Cozumel**

🏠 ACCOMMODATIONS
Hostelito, 5
Hotel Pepita, 9
Hotel Plaza Cozumel, 8
Hotel Posada Edem, 2
Palma Dorada, 10

🍎 FOOD
Casa Denis, 7
La Candela, 1
Mi Chabelita, 12
Los Otates, 19
Panificadora la
 Cozumeleña, 17
Prima Trattoria, 11
Rock-n-Java Caribbean
 Cafe, 23

⭐ NIGHTLIFE
Carlos'n Charlie's, 21
Neptuno, 25
Señor Frog's, 22

⬤ SERVICES
Aquarius Travel, 15
Aqua Safari, 20
Blau Net, 14
Deep Blue, 13
Fama Bookstore, 3
Hertz, 4
Lavandería Margarita, 18
Le$$ Pay Car Rental, 24
Phonet, 10
Puro Mar, 16

🏨 **Hostelito,** Av. 10 42 (☎869 8157; www.hostelito.com), between Juárez and C. 2 Nte. The only hostel on Cozumel holds up its end of the bargain with an immaculate dorm, spotless bathrooms, and a strict lights-out policy. Private rooms front the open-air kitchen and upstairs patio. Lockers and linens included. Towels 20 pesos. Free Wi-Fi. Some snorkel gear available for rental. Reception 9am-9pm. Check-out noon. Reserve ahead during high season. Dorms 180 pesos; private rooms 400 pesos. Cash only. ❷

**Hotel Pepita,** Av. 15 120 (☎872 0098), between C. 1 Sur and Salas. Costs a little extra, but the A/C, private bath, free coffee, and refrigerator in each room make it worth the price. Clean and spacious with comfy mattresses. Free book exchange. Remote control 100 peso deposit. Reception 24hr. Check-out 1pm. Singles and doubles 350 pesos; each additional person 50 pesos. Cash only. ❺

**Hotel Posada Edem,** C. 2 124 (☎872 1166), between Av. 5 and 10. Fish, turtles, and an energetic dog make good company for hanging out in the lobby. Standard pink rooms with fans surround a tropical jungle courtyard. Purified water in lobby. Free Wi-Fi. Reception 8am-7pm. Check-out noon. Singles 180 pesos, with A/C 280 pesos; doubles 220/280 pesos; each additional person 50 pesos. Prices drop in low season. Cash only. ❷

**Palma Dorada Inn,** Salas 44 (☎872 0330), between Melgar and Av. 5. A large 3-star inn with cheerful paintings of sea creatures and beachy decor. Breakfast included. Check-out 1pm. Rooms from 635 pesos (US$48), with A/C and balcony 846 pesos (US$64), with kitchenette from 1100 pesos (US$83). MC/V with 6% charge. ●

**Hotel Plaza Cozumel,** C. 2 Nte. 3 (☎827 2722; www.hotelplazacozumel.com), between Av. Melgar and Av. 5. A multi-story hotel close to town with functional rooms that smell a bit mildewy. Breakfast included. Free Wi-Fi in lobby. Doubles 727 pesos (US$55); each additional person 154 pesos. ●

**Villa Maya** (☎872 1750; www.villamayacozumel.com), inside Cozumel park by the San Gervasio ruins. Lets travelers put up tents in a rustic, eco-friendly environment. Check-out 12:30pm. Camping 132 pesos (US$10) per person. Tents 132 pesos (US$10). Bicycles 132 pesos (US$10). *Cabaña* with hammock and communal bathroom 330 pesos (US$25). Pricier packages include meals. ●

## 🗂 FOOD

Like most Caribbean islands, Cozumel serves up plenty of seafood. The high-priced eateries along Melgar and surrounding the Plaza del Sol target the resort-vacationer and cruise ship passenger, so skip them. Moderately priced restaurants lie a few blocks from the *centro*, and small cafes offering *comida casera* or *cocina económica* (homemade meals) are hidden on side streets. The **market** on Salas between Av. 20 and 25 Sur has fresh meat, fish, and fruit; the *loncherías* next door are the cheapest. (Open daily 7am-3pm.) The closest supermarket is **San Francisco de Assis**, at Juárez and Av. 35. (Open daily 7am-10pm.) The **Mega**, Av. Melgar 799 at C. 11, is larger but a bit farther away. (☎872 3658. Open daily 7am-10:30pm.)

**Prima Trattoria** (☎872 4242; www.primacozumel.com), on Av. Salas between Av. 5 and 10. Trattoria is the dressed-down version of the similarly-named Italian restaurant in the Wynston Resort. Here, divers come in droves to feast on delicious fresh pasta. Lobster ravioli in tomato cream sauce 150 pesos. Open daily 5-10:30pm. AmEx/MC/V. ●

**La Choza** (☎872 0958), on Av. 10 between Salas and C. 3 Sur. Rumored to have the best *fajitas de camarón* (shrimp fajitas; 165 pesos) on the island, complete with fresh guacamole. All meals come with soup and 2 salsas. Vegetarian options like *sopa azteca* (tomato-based tortilla soup) 44 pesos. Open daily 7am-10:30pm. AmEx/MC/V. ●

**Los Otates** (☎869 1059), on Av. 15 between C. 3 Sur and 5 Sur. The most popular *taquería* on the island. Sit on the open-air patio and watch the taco masters churn out the house specialty, tacos *al pastor* (roasted pork tacos with pineapple and onions; 14 pesos). Open daily noon-4am. Cash only. ●

**Panificadora la Cozumeleña** (☎872 0189), on Av. 3 between Av. 15 and 10. For little more than pocket change, this bakery and coffee shop serves sweet treats (5-10 pesos), coffee brewed from Chiapas-grown and island-roasted beans (15 pesos), and piles of fluffy butter-milk pancakes (30 pesos). Open M-Sa 7am-1pm. Bakery open 7am-9pm. Cash only. ●

**Cafe Optima,** C. 2 Nte. 140 (☎869 2042; www.cafeartesanal.com). No Nescafé here—just walking by provides a caffeine kick. This hole in the wall sells cups o' Joe made from Chiapas beans. Small coffee 12 pesos. Open daily 8am-8pm. Cash only. ●

**Rock-n-Java Caribbean Cafe,** Melgar 602 (☎872 4405), near LE$$ Pay. (p. 153) Enjoy coffee (20 pesos), fruit-topped french toast (75 pesos), and homemade desserts, all with a view of the Caribbean. A port of call for cruise passengers with laptops taking advantage of the free Wi-Fi. Salads 60-90 pesos. Massive sandwiches 65-90 pesos. Open M-F 7am-10pm, Sa 7am-2pm. Cash only. ●

**Mi Chabelita** (☎972 0896) on Av. 10 between C. 1 Sur and Salas. Excellent value on festive tablecloths since 1974. *Menú del día* (50 pesos) comes with soup, fresh juice, tortillas, rice, beans, and a choice of five entrees, like *albondigas con chipotle* (chipotle meatballs), barbecued chicken, or *chile relleno* (stuffed peppers). Open M-Sa 8am-9pm. A la carte entrees 40-90 pesos. Cash only. ❷

**La Candela** (☎878 4471), at Av. 5 and C. 6 Nte. Upscale Mexican set to jazzy music. Small but excellent menu. Each of the 8 delicious daily specials (50-60 pesos) comes with rice, beans, potatoes, soup, and iced tea. Entrees 60-150 pesos. Open M-Sa 8am-6pm. Cash only. ❸

**Casa Denis,** 132 C. 1 (☎872 0067), between Av. 5 and 10, across from the artisan market. Enjoy home-cooked recipes perfected since 1945 beneath photos of the family and prints of Che fishing with Castro. Breakfast 30-50 pesos. Mayan pork 105 pesos. *Comida regional* 100-340 pesos. Buffalo wings 40 pesos. Open daily 7am-11pm. Cash only. ❷

## ◪ DIVING

Many visitors make the trek to Cozumel with one goal: to dive around the island's beautiful coral reefs. Part of the second largest reef system in the world, Cozumel first gained fame when **Palancar Reef** on the south end of the island made French diver Jacques Cousteau's list of the top 10 dive sites in the world. Though Hurricane Wilma inflicted serious damage to many of the reefs in 2005, the delicate coral formations are once again beginning to proliferate, and Cozumel still claims some of the best diving in the Caribbean.

The best way to see the reefs is by organizing a diving trip with one of the many dive shops on the island. Look for shops affiliated with **ANOAAT (Asociación Nacional de Operadores de Actividades Aquaticas Turísticas)** or **IANTD (International Association of Nitrox and Technical Divers).** Never dive with a company that does not require proof of PADI certification. Dive shops should also provide transportation to and from dive sites, as many of the reefs are inaccessible without a boat.

**Deep Blue,** Salas 200 (☎872 5653, from the US ☎214-343-3034; www.deepbluecozumel.com), near Av. 10. Offers a complete range of PADI courses, such as the 4-day open-water course (265 pesos/US$20). Daily 2-tank day and night trips to Palancar, Paradise, and San Francisco reefs 900 pesos (US$68). Full equipment rental 238 pesos (US$18). Open daily 7am-9pm. AmEx/MC/V.

**Aqua Safari** (☎872 0101; www.aquasafari.com), on Melgar at C. 5 Sur. 2-tank dive (925 pesos/US$70) leaves daily at 8:30am and 1:30pm and includes a small snack. Open M-F 7am-8pm, Sa-Su 7am-6:30pm. MC/V.

 **DON'T TOUCH THE CORAL.** One stray kick of the flipper can destroy hundreds of years of growth. Beginners should stay at least 1m away from the coral at all times to prevent contact, and advanced divers should pay careful attention to their buoyancy control.

## ◪ OTHER OUTDOOR ACTIVITIES

**SNORKELING.** Like diving, snorkeling Cozumel's reefs is on every traveler's list of things to do when visiting. Snorkeling can be done from shore or through a guided boat tour. Head to **Chakanaab Natural Park** or the **Punta Sur Ecological Reserve** (p. 159). Alternatively, rent gear from one of the dive shops (50-100 pesos), rent a moped (p. 153), and head to one of the beaches south of town. **Playa San Francisco,** at km 14, and **Playa Palancar,** at km 20, both offer superb snorkeling with sights of barracuda, turtles, and coral reefs from close to the shore, as well as small restaurants and shady *palapas. (Boat tours can be arranged from any* *of the stalls lining the Muelle Fiscal. Most tours are around 2hr., are organized in groups of 12, include equipment rental, and cost around 300 pesos per person. Many dive shops also arrange snorkel tours, but often lump them together with diving. Try to get on a boat with only snorkelers to ensure better guides and more snorkeling-friendly reefs.)*

**SAN MIGUEL BEACHES.** Beachgoers should not be disheartened by the slightly murky waters near San Miguel: calm, clear waters good for snorkeling and swimming can be found south of town. Beaches to the south of San Miguel tend to be more commercial and host beach clubs like Playa Mía, Mr. Sancho's, and Paradise Beach, all popular with the cruise ship crowds who drop anchor in the harbor daily. **Playa Palancar,** 20km south of San Miguel, is a better option. The small **Palancar Beach Club** has a full dive and snorkel center, restaurant, showers, and quiet stretches of white sand. *(At km 20 on the Cozumel Carretera Sur. Open daily 9am-5pm. Food purchase required to use the beach. Beer 33 pesos/US$2.50. Cash only.)*

**EASTERN BEACHES.** The island's true treasures, kilometers of white foam surf and turquoise waters, lie on the eastern coast. **Bonita** (km 38), **Punta Chiqueros, Punta Morena,** and **Mezcalitos** (at the end of the highway) are rougher but virtually undeveloped, leaving miles of sandy shoreline for those who prefer the company of sea gulls to that of tourists. All east coast beaches are accessible from Cozumel's main highway. Given the **strong currents and undertow** in the **Chen Río** and ■**Playa San Martín** areas, swimmers should exercise caution. The road is lined with a series of beach shacks, including the reggae-themed **Freedom in Paradise Restaurant and Beach Bar** ❻, decorated with old t-shirts. (☎869 8300. Shrimp quesadilla 120 pesos/US$9. Open daily 10am-5:30pm. Cash only.)

**SURFING AND KITEBOARDING.** Though Cozumel is a shrine to underwater activity, those wishing to remain on the surface can also enjoy Cozumel's surf and sea breezes. Surfing is an increasingly popular sport on the island. Hard-charging boarders head to **Mezcalitos** for beach breaks, while more adventurous and experienced surfers head to **Punta Morena,** where shallow coral reefs sometimes cause injury. *(Punta Morena Beach and Surf Club. Open M-Sa 9am-5pm.)* **Kiteboarding** also draws crowds from November to April, when winds are the best. At **Puro Mar Bikini Shop,** 298 Av. 5, Adrian is the island's official source of kiteboarding information and gear. He also teaches kiteboarding classes. *(☎872 4483; www.cozumelkiteboarding.com. 3-4hr. lessons US$350; beginners need about 3 days to become self-sufficient. Open M-Sa 10am-7pm.)*

**FISHING.** Even fishermen have a home in Cozumel. Many boats will take fly- or deep-sea fishermen out in groups of two to four people. **Aquarius Travel,** 20 Av. Sur 220, between Salas and C. 3 Sur, leads full day fly-fishing tours for 4000 pesos (US$300). Gear rental is not included. *(☎869 1096; www.aquariusflatsfishing. com. Open daily 8am-1pm and 5-8pm.)*

## ⊙ SIGHTS

The **Federación de Parques y Museos de Cozumel** (☎872 0914; www.cozumelparks. com) operates most of the big attractions on the island.

**CHANKANAAB NATURAL PARK.** Popular with families, this natural amusement park, protects a beautiful bay circled by a well-kept botanical garden, museum, dolphin pen (visitors can pay to swim with the near-domesticated mammals), and restaurants. The abundant fish and stunning coral formations in the bay, open to snorkelers and scuba divers, are the real attractions. *(Carretera Costera Sur km 9.5. Take Av. Melgar south out of town and look for signs. ☎872 0914. Open daily 7am-5pm.*

QUINTANA ROO

*192 pesos, children under 3 free. Snorkel equipment 132 pesos/US$10. For dolphin reservations ☎998 881 7443; www.dophindiscovery.com). MC/V.)*

**PUNTA SUR ECOLOGICAL RESERVE.** South of downtown, this reserve wows visitors with boat rides through crocodile-infested lagoons and snorkeling trips along the turtle-populated Colombia reef. Check out the **Museum of Navigation** and the small ruins of a Mayan tomb. The ⊠**lighthouse** at Punta Celerain presents a spectacular view of the sand dunes on Cozumel's southern shores. *(Carretera Costera Sur km 27. Open daily 8am-4:30pm. 110 pesos. Snorkeling equipment 100 pesos. Lighthouse 66 pesos/US$5.)*

**RUINS.** A former Mayan trading center, Cozumel is sprinkled with dozens of ruins. Unfortunately, none of them have survived the years of hurricanes and the encroaching jungle. The very small **El Cedral,** the oldest of the ruins on the island, dates back to the ninth century and lies in the town square of the small farming community of El Cedral. *(Follow the paved road to the east off the Carretera Sur at km 18 about 2km. Free.)*

The only excavated and reconstructed ruins are at **San Gervasio,** dating from AD 1000-1650. These ruins include the remains of an observatory and several houses, temples, and arches that once made up the most prominent community in Cozumel. *(Take Juárez out of town. After 8km, a sign marked "San Gervasio" points the way to a gravel road branching to the left. Follow the road another 6km. ☎871 4431. Open daily 7am-4pm. 77 pesos.)*

**MUSEO DE LA ISLA DE COZUMEL.** The main museum on the island is small but worth a visit, if only to escape the stifling heat. Its four themed rooms are full of coral, marine and jungle trivia, and one unlucky stuffed flamingo. The Coral and Reefs room, with colorful exhibits and a wealth of information on Cozumel's marine treasures, may especially enrich the underwater experiences of prospective snorkelers and scuba divers. *(On the waterfront between C. 4 and 6. ☎872 1545. Open M-Sa 9am-5pm, Su 9am-4pm. 36 pesos.)*

**HACIENDA ANTIGUA.** An old farmhouse has been restored to look like an *hacienda*, though it functions mainly as a tourist trap. Brief tour includes an explanation of the distillation process and festive dancing. *(Carretera Transversal km 9.8. ☎876 9914; www.cavaantigua.com. Open M-Sa 9am-5pm, Su 10:30am-2pm. 185 pesos (US$14), includes a margarita. MC/V over 264 pesos/US$20.)*

## ▣ NIGHTLIFE

Nights in Cozumel tend to be quiet: cruise ship passengers retreat to their cabins and the soon-to-be-divers forsake alcohol in favor of certification-required reading. Next to the endless revelry of Cancún and Playa del Carmen, Cozumel's nightlife seems a little bush-league. Docked tourists get their jollies at chains like **Señor Frogs** and **Carlos'n Charlie's.**

Fortunately, Cozumel has a host of relaxing and enlightening evening activities to keep you entertained. Live music performances by local salsa and jazz bands take place F-Su in the Plaza del Sol. From 8-10pm, locals and tourists mingle and dance beneath the town gazebo.

**No Name Bar** (☎878 4020), at the Barracuda Hotel. While passengers head for big chains, their crews head here. Run by former cruise ship staff, the food is a fusion of Turkish and Mexican. Patrons have access to a pool and a view of the twinkling lights of Playa del Carmen in the distance. Beer 38 pesos. Open daily 8am-11pm. AmEx/MC/V.

## CARNAVAL IN COZUMEL

The first sign of Carnaval in Cozumel is the enormous, busty female statue that takes the stage in the town's main plaza. As sun sets, people gather in the nearby streets wearing long polyester robes glittering with sequins. The sheen of thier heavily styled hair and makeup is just visible in the twilight. Then, the music starts. Drums, the tinny Latin trumpet, a dose of reggaeton.

Originally, only men could participate in the parade of costumed dancers; today, all genders and ages dress up and dance on the floats parading through the streets, flashing sequins and tossing candy to the crowd. On the first night, the Master of Ceremonies crowns the King and Queen of Carnaval and their consorts the King and Queen of Alegría.

Cozumel's extravaganza dates to 1896, when the city imported the traditions of nearby Cuba. The holiday's name comes from the Latin "carnem levare," to leave off meat, and typically takes places the four days before Lent, acting as a final hurrah before sober days of fasting begin. Timing varies depending on the place. Visitors to the Yucatán in late February and early March can expect to catch at least one festival (if not three or four).

**Los Dorados de Villa,** C. 1 Sur (☎872 3391), on the main plaza. Merits a visit for its good selection of 2-for-1 margaritas and daiquiris (50 pesos) and dollar beers. Open daily 7:30am-11pm.

**Neptuno** (☎872 1537), at C. 11 Sur and Melgar. If you're in desperate need of a night of dancing, this is it. Multi-level dance floors, neon lasers, and throbbing electronic riffs keep locals and tourists happy. Beers 35 pesos. Cover 45 pesos. Open Tu-Sa 9pm-6am.

## ■ FESTIVALS

If you're in town in the spring, don't miss the **Fiesta de Santa Cruz**, held in late April and early May in the inland farming community of El Cedral, southwest of San Miguel. This religious festival traces its roots 150 years back to the Caste Wars, when Don Casimiro Cárdenas fled with his family from the mainland to the relative peace of Cozumel. A pioneer in the El Cedral area, Casimiro promised that he and his descendants would pray devoutly to the Cross in return for divine protection. The event is marked by dances, feasts, and parades. The island also hosts **Carnaval** in February. Festivities begin with the coronation of the king and queen of Carnaval (and a series of lesser royalty), and continue with Corona-soaked parades, costumes, and dancing.

# TULUM      ☎984

Five years ago Tulum (pop. 20,000), 63km south of Playa del Carmen and 131km south of Cancún, was still a small roadside stop, a good base for exploring with a spectacular surf-rimmed beach and nearby Maya ruins. The arrival of the highway has transformed the town into backpacker central, a happening strip lined with hostels, Italian cafes, and trendy boutiques.

For a small town, Tulum attracts an astonishing variety of travelers. Daytrippers from Cancún pass through just long enough to snap a few pictures of the impressive seaside ruins. Diving enthusiasts come from all over the globe to explore the nearby network of over 700km of *cenotes*. Stressed-out city dwellers flock to the beachside *cabañas* to escape electricity, phones, and clothing. Making the most noise is a youthful, bohemian crowd, partying its way up and down the shore come nighttime. Tulum isn't slowing down any time soon. An influx of foreigners, especially Italians, are adding more steam to the developing city. Plans are in the works for an international airport between Cobá and Tulum. A dock for cruise ships might also have a place in the near future.

# ⊫ TRANSPORTATION

Getting around Tulum can be time-consuming and expensive. Although numerous **taxis** are readily available in Pueblo Tulum, along Mex. 307, and at various *cabañas*, fares add up fast. Forty pesos will take you from town to the closest *cabañas*, but fares rise quickly as you travel farther south. The best budget option for those with ambitious plans is to rent a bicycle.

**Bus Stations:** All buses leave from the main **ADO** station (☎871 2122; www.ado.com. mx), on the west side of Mex. 307 between Jupiter and Alfa Sur. Buses head to: **Cancún** (2hr., every hr. 7am-9pm, 82 pesos); **Chetumal** (3½hr., 8 per day 8:25am-10:30pm, 164-192 pesos); **Chichén Itzá** (3hr.; 9:10am, 2:30pm; 118 pesos); **Cobá** (1hr., 5 per day 7am-6pm, 30 pesos); **Felipe Carrillo Puerto** (1¼hr; 8:25, 9:25, 10:05am, 1, 4:55, 10:30pm; 70 pesos); **Mérida** (4hr.; midnight, 1:40, 5am, 12:40, 2:20, 7:40pm; 194 pesos); **Mexico City** (23-25hr.; 1:40, 4:45, 5:25pm; 1202 pesos); **Palenque** (10½hr., 8:15pm, 566 pesos); **Playa del Carmen** (1hr., every hr. 7am-7:30pm, 48 pesos); **San Cristóbal de las Casas** (15½hr.; 8:15pm, 726 pesos); **Valladolid** (2hr.; midnight, 1:40am, 5, 9am, 12:40, 2:30pm; 70 pesos). There is also a bus stop at the Tulum ruins, right next to Hotel El Crucero, where buses stop going to and from **Playa del Carmen** and **Cancún** (every hr. 1-6pm).

**Public Transportation:** Red and white **colectivo vans** run every ½hr. between **Playa del Carmen** (40 pesos) and **Tulum (5 pesos)**, stopping as requested in between. They leave from the east side of the road, heading north, just across from the bus station. The *colectivo* to Punta Allen also leaves from the west side of the highway, several blocks north of the bus station. A **bus** heads to the public beach from behind the Weary Traveler Hostel (p. 162) at 9am and noon. Buses (10 pesos) head back to town at noon and 5pm. **Combis** to **Felipe Carillo Puerto** leave every 45min. from the west side of the highway, just south of the bus station.

**Taxis:** (☎871 2029). Eager taxis cruise Av. Tulum and wait just north of the bus station. 40 pesos to get to the closest beach, 45 for the more expensive places further down the Boca Paila road.

**Car Rental:** Many hotels along the Boca Paila road offer car rental, but be sure to reserve ahead. **Buster Rent a Car** (☎871 2831; www.busterrentacar.com), at Av. Tulum and Juniper Sur. Economy cars start at 655 pesos (US$50) per day; insurance and mileage included. Credit card required for deposit; cash preferred for payment. Look for discounts advertised on the web page. AmEx/MC/V.

**Bike Rental:** Iguana Bike Shop (☎119 0836; www.iguanabike.com), on Satelite Sur, 1 block from Av. Tulum. Ring the bell by the gray door on the left if the shop looks closed. 70 pesos per day includes lock, basket, lights, and insurance. Flyers around town give a 10% discount. Open daily 9am-7pm. Cash only.

# ■✦🛈 ORIENTATION AND PRACTICAL INFORMATION

Located 50km southeast of Cobá and 131km south of Cancún, Tulum is the southernmost tourist attraction on the Caribbean coast of Quintana Roo, and the easternmost of the major Mayan archaeological sites along the Mayan Riviera. Tulum divides into three separate areas: the **zona arqueológica** near the ruin, the **beach cabañas** lining the coastal road Carretera Boca Paila, and **Tulum proper**, concentrated along the **Mex. 307** (Av. Tulum or the Carreterra Federal) strip. Arriving from the north, you'll come first to the *zona arqueológica*, about 3km before town, where several restaurants, hotels, overpriced mini-marts, and a gas station take advantage of traffic to the ruins. One kilometer south is a well-marked turn-off on **Avenida Cobá,** to the left leading to food and accommodations at the beach-side *cabañas.* Tulum itself, another 1½km farther to the south, is the center of the action, lined with restaurants, shops, and hotels. Addresses for places along the beach are listed in terms of their distance from the ruins.

**Tourist Office:** A **tourist kiosk** with free maps and flyers advertising local attractions operates in front of the municipality, at Av. Tulum and Alfa Sur. Open daily 9am-4pm. Frequently closes in the afternoon. Booths in front of the parking lot of the Tulum ruins and in the artisan market provide general info. Open daily 8am-2pm. Additionally, the privately operated www.todotulum.com and www.tulumtravelguide.com websites offer helpful information on sights and hotels in the area.

**Currency Exchange:** HSBC (☎871 2201), on Av. Tulum next to the municipality, between Osiris and Alfa Sur. **24hr. ATM.** Open M-F 9am-7pm, Sa 9am-3pm. Many *casas de cambio* line Av. Tulum.

**Laundromat: Lavandería Barbujas** (☎871 2465), 2 blocks east of Av. Tulum on C. Jupiter Sur. 12 pesos per kg, 3 kg minimum. Open M-F 8am-7pm, Sa 8am-2pm. Cash only. **Lava Easy** (☎115 0684), 5 blocks north of the bus station on Av. Tulum between Satelite and Centauro Nte. Wash and dry 15 pesos per kg. Open M-Sa 8am-8pm.

**Police:** (☎871 2688), Av. Cobá, between Av. Tulum and the beach.

**Red Cross:** Av. Cobá, toward the beach.

**24hr. Pharmacy: Farmacia YZA** (☎116 4048), on the east side of Mex. 307, across from Weary Traveler Hostel (p. 162).

**Medical Services: Centro de Salud** (☎871 2050). Heading south from the bus station, take the 1st 2 lefts. Open daily 8am-8pm; 24hr. for emergencies.

**Internet Access:** Internet cafes cluster around the bus station on Av. Tulum. The bright orange **Praetorian,** a few blocks north of the bus station on Av. Tulum opposite HSBC, has a fast connection. 15 pesos per hr. Open daily 9am-midnight.

**Post Office:** On Av. Tulum, north of the bus station. Follow the signs marked "correos" in pink paint to a small office inside the Tribal Wear passageway. Open M-F 9am-4pm, Sa 9am-1pm. **Postal Code:** 77780.

## ACCOMMODATIONS

Relatively cheap, right on the white beaches, and with little to no electricity (bring a flashlight and some candles), the *cabañas* of Tulum offer a unique experience that shouldn't be missed, though it might require splurging. Tulum is a great place to relax on pristine beaches in hammocks as you perfect your tan, with or without clothing. Bring mosquito netting (though the *cabañas* we list provide netting over beds) and repellent; the bugs can be nasty. Cheaper hostels are located downtown, close to the restaurants and services along the main avenue. The best option for those who want easy access to the ruins and the beach is to stay in the *zona arqueológica,* though you'll miss out on the restaurants and hippie-happy scene downtown. Reservations are essential during the high season (mid-December to April and July-August).

### DOWNTOWN TULUM

**Rancho Tranquilo,** Av. Tulum 86 (☎871 2784; www.ranchotranquilo.com.mx), about 500m south of the bus station. From the bus station, walk south on the same side of the road and cross the bridge. Rancho Tranquilo is another 100m down, marked by two big surfboards. A tropical paradise right off the main highway, Rancho Tranquilo caters to a range of travelers with dorms, private *palapas,* and suites with kitchen, A/C, and pri-

QUINTANA ROO

vate baths. Carefully maintained garden and tiled barbecue pit. Excellent book exchange. Breakfast and kitchen use included. Laundry 15 pesos per kg. Internet and Wi-Fi available. Snorkel gear 40 pesos. 6-bed dorm 150 pesos; *cabañas* from 350 pesos. Prices fall 50-70 pesos in low season. Cash only. ❶

**The Weary Traveler Hostel** (☎871 2389 or 2390; wearytravelerhostel.com), 1 block south of the ADO bus station between Jupiter and Acuario. The largest hostel in town and the closest to the bus station, Weary Traveler is the hub of the backpacker community. Wristbands and long picnic tables lend a summer camp feel. Join the gang for free daily rides to the beach and other sites, barbecues, and a chance to ride the "Party Bus." Do-it-yourself breakfast, lockers (bring your own lock), linens, and Wi-Fi included. Outdoor communal kitchen. Sporadic hot water. On-site bar with beer (16 pesos) and Su barbecue 6pm-midnight (55 pesos). Dorms 130 pesos, with A/C 130 pesos; private rooms 370 pesos. Cash only. ❶

**Casa del Sol Polar,** Pte. 815 (☎129 6426; www.geocities.com/casadelsoltulum), between Saturno and Luna. From the bus station, follow signs south on Av. Tulum. After the bridge, take a right. At the next block, turn left. Smaller than Weary Traveler (above) but caters to a similar clientele. Pancake breakfast served under a giant *palapa.* Upstairs jacuzzi. Sporadic hot water and creaky bunks. Bike rental 50 pesos per day. Breakfast and kitchen included. 10-bed dorms 130 pesos; *cabañas* 300 pesos, with private bath 400 pesos. Cash only. ❶

**Hotel Latino** (☎871 2674 or 108 2684), on Andromeda St.

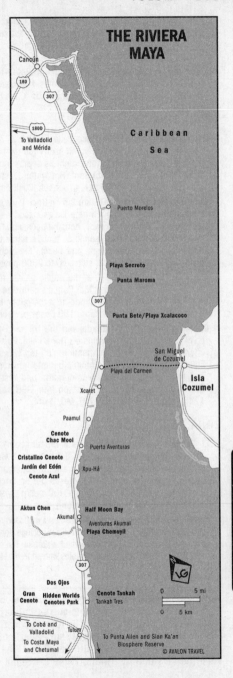

THE RIVIERA MAYA

Cancún
180
307
1800
To Valladolid and Mérida

Caribbean Sea

Puerto Morelos

Playa Secreto
Punta Maroma

307

Punta Bete/Playa Xcalacoco

San Miguel de Cozumel

Playa del Carmen

Isla Cozumel

Xcaret

Paamul

Cenote Chac Mool

Puerto Aventuras

Cristalino Cenote
Jardín del Edén
Cenote Azul

Xpu-Há

Aktun Chen

Akumal

Half Moon Bay

Aventuras Akumal
Playa Chemuyil

307

Dos Ojos

Gran Cenote
Hidden Worlds
Cenotes Park

Cenote Tankah
Tankah Tres

0          5 mi
0     5 km

To Cobá and Valladolid

Tulum

To Costa Maya and Chetumal

To Punta Allen and Sian Ka'an Biosphere Reserve

© AVALON TRAVEL

QUINTANA ROO

between Orion and Beta Sur. Take a right 2 blocks north of the bus station, and then your 1st left. Look up for the sign. A small but sleek little hotel in the center of town. A/C, flat-screen TVs, small pool, and hammocks. Free Wi-Fi. Doubles from 500 pesos, more in high season. Cash only. ❺

**L'Hotelito** (☎136 1240), on Av. Tulum and Beta Nte. Clean but basic rooms in a thatch-roofed 2-story house. Free Wi-Fi. Rooms 400 pesos, with fan 450 pesos, with A/C and TV 500. 100 pesos less during low season. Cash only. ❺

## BEACHSIDE

**Papaya Playa,** km 4.5 on Boca Paila (☎116 3774; www.papayaplaya.com). 45 small *cabañas* on a cliff with the same luxury lounge beds as more expensive resorts down the road. Run by same management as nearby Tribal Village, but with a slightly preppier vibe. On-site bar and restaurant. Hot water. Electricity 5-11:30pm. 2-person *cabañas* from 524 pesos (US$40) in high season. Cash only. ❺

**Hotel Cabañas Diamante K,** km 2.5 on Boca Paila (☎998 185 8300 or 876 2115; www.diamantek.com). The beach here isn't as good as Papaya's, but it's closer to the ruins and to town. Outdoor showers, hanging beds, and "natural A/C" make the transition from beach to *cabaña* almost seamless. At night, garden torches light the area; paths connect the *cabañas*, restaurant, bar, and beach. Electricity 5pm-midnight. *Cabañas* from 300 pesos; doubles 500 pesos; suites up to 2500 pesos. Cash or Paypal only. ❹

**Mar Caribe** (☎114 0422), at the public beach, next to the Mariachi restaurant about 15min. walk from the ruins. Mar Caribe's campsite provides the cheapest place to sleep in Tulum. Pitch tents in the shade near the public beach. Rustic cooking area and bathrooms. 80 pesos per site; tents 180 pesos per person. Cash only. ❶

**Cabañas Copal** (from Canada and the US ☎+1-877-532-6737; www.cabanascopal.com), 5km south of the ruins on Boca Paila. Part of a trio of beachside hotels, Copal offers the ultimate beach vacation: cliff-top views of crashing waves, spa treatments, little electricity, and a clothing-is-optional environment. Hot water, common phones, and Wi-Fi available. Nearby mini-marts and restaurants. High-season *cabañas* from 460 pesos (US$35), in low season from 396 pesos (US$30), with private bath from 1240/920 pesos (US$95/70). MC/V. ❺

## ZONA ARQUEOLÓGICA

**El Crucero** (☎871 2610; www.el-crucero.com), off Mex. 307, across from Hotel Acuario. Just a few paces from the ruins and within walking distance of the beach, El Crucero offers young travelers affordable, clean dorms. No kitchen, but there is an on-site restaurant. Internet 20 pesos per hr. Reception 8am-9pm. Check-out 11am. 4-bed dorms 100 pesos; rooms 400 pesos, with A/C 450 pesos. Prices fall about 100 pesos in low season. Cash only. ❶

**Posada los Mapaches** (☎871 2700; www.posadalosmapaches.com), on Carreterra 307, 5min. south of the entrance to the ruins. Spacious dorms come with shower basket and soap. Has a well-landscaped garden behind a gate on the side of the highway. Breakfast included. Free Wi-Fi. Dorms 180 pesos; doubles with shared bath and bicycles 550 pesos. ❷

## 🔖 FOOD

Pizza and pasta are almost as prevalent as tacos on Tulum's menu. The tourist traffic has resulted in an explosion of culinary offerings, most at mid-range restaurants. Cheaper eats can be found away from the main strip and at cheap *loncherías* in the *pueblo*. The big supermarket in town is **San Francisco de Assisi,** at the intersection of Av. Tulum and Av. Cobá. (Open daily 8am-9pm.) Small supermarkets line Av. Tulum. There is a small supermarket well-stocked with

QUINTANA ROO

suntan lotion just south of Playa Papaya. Most of the *cabañas* have ocean front restaurants open to the public.

**¡Qué Fresco!** (from the US ☎+1-415-387-9806; www.zamas.com), at Hotel Zamas on the Boca Paila road, 6km south of the ruins. A treat for the eye and the stomach— the bright, bold color scheme is complemented by cool, blue-green waves rushing by on both sides. Inventive Mexican options include vegetarian dishes (from 75 pesos). Peanut butter, honey, and banana sandwich 50 pesos. Hearty breakfasts from 65 pesos. Open daily 7:30am-11pm. Cash only. ❹

**Charlie's** (☎871 2573), on Av. Tulum, just south of the bus station. A reminder that sometimes it's worth the upgrade from the *taquería*. Tiled tables in a pretty backyard patio. Vegetarian entrees 80 pesos. Salads 50 pesos. Enchiladas 85 pesos. Live music at 7pm F-Sa. Open Tu-Su 7am-11pm. MC/V. ❹

**Pane, Pizza, e Fantasia,** on Av. Tulum, just south of the bus station. Sidewalk tables catch the morning sun. This small bakery serves enormous sandwiches, pizzas, and mini desserts. Espresso 20 pesos. Sandwiches 35-50 pesos. Yogurt and fruit 40 pesos. Cannoli 15 pesos. Open M-Sa 7am-10pm. Cash only. ❸

**Tacos al Pastor,** on Av. Tulum just south of Weary Traveler Hostel. This small shack with its own spit boasts the cheapest and tastiest grub on the strip. Take your plate inside to load up on cabbage or spicy red sauce. Tacos 7 pesos. Open daily 4pm-1am. Cash only. ❶

**Don Cafeto,** Av. Tulum 64 (☎871 2207), 4 blocks north of the bus station. Always crowded, Don Cafeto serves large plates of local specialties and American standards in a diner-like setting. Walk in and smell the blackened *poblanos* and roasting meat. Breakfasts 35-75 pesos. Mexican specialties 90 pesos. Decadent *licuados* 30 pesos. Open daily 7am-11pm. MC/V. ❸

**Elemental** (☎100 8530), on Centauro Sur, 1 block east of Av. Tulum. Mexican-Italian fusion was bound to come to Tulum. A vegetarian-friendly shop serving luxury salads and sandwiches, like the *nopal* (baguette stuffed with sautéed cactus leaves, onion, refried beans, cheese, lettuce, tomato, avocado, and chipotle mayo; 70 pesos). Salads 55-110 pesos. Sandwiches 50-100 pesos. Open M-Tu and Th-Su 10am-11pm. Cash only. ❸

**La Nave Pizzería,** Av. Tulum 570 (☎871 2592). Thin-crust brick-oven pizzas (50-110 pesos) with fresh ingredients and toppings, and spinach or seafood ravioli (140 pesos) are made daily by the Italian owners. Portions are small, but meals are served with fresh bread and olive oil. Open M-Sa 7:30am-11pm. ❸

**La Palapa del Chino** (☎9745 3294), between Beta and Osiris. Slightly cheaper than some of the other places on the strip. Caters to the gringo palate with complimentary tortilla chips and helpings of guacamole. Chinese and Tex-Mex favorites like chicken quesadillas with guacamole (70 pesos) and a sizeable number of vegetarian dishes (55-90 pesos). Open daily noon-10:30pm. V. ❸

**Casa Díaz,** at Av. Tulum and Oriente Nte. Cheap and crowded. Smoke from the grill wafts across the open-air room as plastic tables and chairs spill onto the sidewalk. *Tacos al pastor* 7 pesos. Drinks 10 pesos. Open daily 6pm-midnight. Cash only. ❶

## ◤ NIGHTLIFE

Tulum is no Cancún. Late at night the bus station is the most crowded place in town, despite the large numbers of backpackers. That said, there's certainly fun to be had in the small number of local clubs.

**Habana Cafe** (☎151 9139), on Av. Tulum between Jupiter Sur and Acuario Sur. Barefoot dancers and Weary Traveler spillovers mingle upstairs at the Skybar, where a picture of Che gives way to a view of the stars. Electronica abounds. Mojito pitcher 300 pesos. Mixed drinks 50-65 pesos. Open Tu-Su 4pm-3am. Cash only.

QUINTANA ROO

**Mezzanine,** km 1.5 on Boca Paila (☎112 3260; www.mezzanine.com.mx). In a town with limited nightlife, their F night scene is as close as you'll get to a dance party in Tulum. The chic wooden deck overlooking the ocean is littered with bean bag chairs, perfect to plop down on with a mixed drink (50-75 pesos). Cover 100 pesos after 9pm. Open M-Th and Sa-Su 8am-10pm, F 8am-2:30am. Cash only.

**Acabar** (☎108 8748), on Av. Tulum between Beta and Orion Nte. The best bet for live music. Rotating acts throughout the week ranging from heavy rock to a roots-reggae night. Mojitos 40 pesos. Beer 20 pesos. Open W-Su 5pm-late. Cash only.

# ⬛ 🏞 SIGHTS AND OUTDOOR ACTIVITIES

## CENOTES

Tulum's hidden treasures are the numerous *cenotes* sunken into the surrounding jungle. Snorkelers can enter independently; divers must be cavern-certified (a rank above open-water) and accompanied by a guide. (To go alone, cave certification is required.) Reservations must be made in advance; arrive early if you want to choose your route. Forty-five minute dives typically visit two of four caves: **Gran Cenote** and **Calaveras** or **Dos Ojos** and **Angelita.** Several free *cenotes,* mainly for those who don't mind the bugs, are hidden across the street from the ranches and hotels at the southern end of Boca Paila right before Sian Ka'an; an especially large one lies behind a wooden gate opposite Rancho San Erik. Ask for a map at Punta Piedra.

**EL GRAN CENOTE.** Regarded as the best spot in the area for snorkeling, El Gran Cenote is part of the second largest underground river in the world, the **Osh-Beh-Ha.** Its unforgettable beauty is like something out of a fairy tale—bats, birds, and butterflies flutter over the cold, clear blue waters filled with friendly fish and green lily pads. *(About 3km west of Tulum on Av. Cobá. Taxis 11 pesos. 80 pesos. Open daily 8am-4pm.)*

**CENOTE CALAVERAS.** Near El Gran, Cenote Calaveras received its official name for its squash-like shape. Insiders call it the Temple of Doom for the 10m plunge it takes to get inside. *(Follow the road to Cobá 1.6km west out of town and look for a path on your right. 50 pesos. Open daily 8am-4pm.)*

**CENOTE DOS OJOS.** Discovered more recently than its neighbor, the often crowded Cenote Dos Ojos was featured in the 1999 IMAX film *Journey Into Amazing Caves.* For those with no diving expertise, this *cenote* offers 450m of cavern to explore with just snorkel gear and a flashlight. The dive center has also installed lights to illuminate the beautiful sights that made it to the IMAX screen. Divers should look for the Barbie being eaten by an alligator at the halfway point. *(Open daily 8am-4pm.)*

**CENOTE ANGELITA.** Though it's not ideal for snorkeling, divers love Angelita for the trippy visual effects created when salt and fresh water mingle. *(Open daily 8am-4pm.)*

**CENOTE ESCONDIDO AND CENOTE CRISTAL.** The closest *cenotes* to town, these mini-lakes are easily reached by bicycle or taxi. Here you'll find fresh-water tropical fish and underwater vegetation in cool, crystal-clear waters. *(Head south on Av. Tulum about 3km. 50 pesos.)*

## OTHER ACTIVITIES

Though it can be a bit rougher than some of the beaches further north, Tulum's surf is exciting and not nearly as rough as many of its neighboring counterparts. Still, choppy seas mean that travelers looking for clear views of

QUINTANA ROO

our marine friends should flipper to other waters. Northernmost is the **public beach,** with closely packed sand and a few fishing boats. Further south, the sand becomes more pillowy, running past expensive foreign-run resorts, like Paraiso, Vita e Bella, and Playa Condesa. Past here you'll hit a rocky, near impassable point before reaching **Playa Papaya** and the nudist **Copal.** Other beaches to the south are accessible primarily through resorts. The popular **Kiteboarding School Tulum** on the beach in front of El Paraiso restaurant offers another way to enjoy Tulum's beaches. (☎ 745 4555; www.extremecontrol.net. Lessons from 970 pesos per hr. Open daily 9am-5pm.)

Tulum has plenty of dive shops in case you want to mingle with the fish or explore the ocean and *cenotes* on your own.

**Cenote Dive Center** (☎876 3285; www.cenotedive.com), on Osiris Nte. across from the HSBC bank. Abyss Tours leave 9am. 2-tank dive 1570 pesos (US$120); snorkel 642 pesos (US$49). Open M-Sa 8:30am-8pm, Su 8am-5pm.

**Kay Op Dive Club,** Av. Tulum 23 (☎144 7323; www.kayopdivers.com), just north of the ADO bus station. 2-tank dive 1310 pesos (US$100). Snorkel trip 590 pesos (US$45). Open M-Sa 8am-9pm.

**Scuba Tulum** (☎745 1490; www.scubatulum.com). 1244 pesos (US$95) 2-tank dive; 590 pesos (US$45) snorkel. Tours leave 9am. Open daily 10am-2pm and 4-8pm. Cash only.

## 🏛 THE ARCHAEOLOGICAL SITE OF TULUM

*The ruins lie a brisk 10min. walk east of Mex. 307 from the zona arqueológica crossing or 20min. north of the public beach. Combis will drop you at the highway. The amusement park-style train pulled by a tractor (20 pesos) covers the distance in slightly less time. Tickets are sold at a booth to the left of the parking lot and at the entrance to the ruins. Open daily 8am-5pm. 51 pesos, video camera use 35 pesos. Guided tours available in several languages (45min.; 1-4 people 500 pesos, 5-8 people 560 pesos, 9-12 people 625 pesos, 13-16 people 750 pesos); inquire at the information or ticket booth. Night tours also available at 8:45 and 9:45pm. 170 pesos, includes audio guide. Reservations required.*

The ruins at Tulum, known as **Záma** to their ancient residents, are famous for their picturesque setting perched above the multi-hued waters of the Caribbean. Tulum was once an important trading port between the interior Yucatán communities and the rest of the Mayan world. One of the last pre-Hispanic Mayan cities, Tulum reached its zenith during the late post-Classic Period (AD 1250-1550). Surrounded by a series of impressively high walls, the fortified and fully functional city was spotted by the Spaniard Juan de Grijalva in 1518 while on a scouting expedition from Cuba; it was promptly given the name Tulum, or "wall." In 1544, the city fell to Spanish conquistadors, but it continued to serve as a fort from which the Spanish fended off English, Dutch, and French pirates. In the early 1840s, the site was rediscovered by archaeologists Frederick Catherwood and John Stephens, though the location had been used infrequently by local Maya. As late as 1847, Tulum provided refuge for Maya rebels fleeing government forces during the Caste Wars. Today, the ruins are infested with mosquitoes and busloads of sunburned tourists from Playa del Carmen, but they remain an impressive and worthwhile excursion into the Mayan world.

**THE WALL.** The impressive wall, made of small rocks wedged together, protected the city's landward sides. Originally 6m thick and 4m high, this wall warded off aggressive neighbors from other Mayan city-states. A smaller inner wall served as a political-religious boundary, preventing everyone except the 150 or so priests and governors of Tulum from entering the inner precinct. The wall is also the oldest standing structure in Tulum, dating back to the Terminal

QUINTANA ROO

Classic Period (AD 800-1000). Every evening, the rays of the setting sun illuminate the representations of the Mayan Descending God that cover the western walls. From the southernmost wall, once a lookout point, you can admire a view of the turquoise sea below.

**LA CASA DEL NOROESTE AND LA CASA DEL CENOTE.** Left of the entrance to La Casa del Noroeste (the House of the Northwest) lie a grave and the remains of the platforms that once supported the thatched-roof houses of important religious figures of Tulum. One step closer to the ocean, up the small hill, is La Casa del Cenote (the House of the Cave). Built atop a small limestone shelf over a deep blue *cenote*, the house feels like part of the encroaching jungle. The western corridor of the home was the final resting ground for many, indicating that the house may have played a role as a family crypt for royal residents.

**TEMPLO DEL DIOS VIENTO.** A few paces to the south of La Casa del Cenote, the Temple of the Wind God is perched precipitously on the northeastern side of the beach. It was ingeniously designed to act as a storm-warning system. Sure enough, before Hurricane Gilbert struck the site in 1988, the temple's cavernous airways dutifully whistled their alarm. Below, you'll see a small beach where turtles lay their eggs.

**EL CASTILLO.** The most prominent structure in the city, the Castle looms to the east over the rocky seaside cliff, commanding a view of the entire walled city. The pyramid, built in three separate stages, may not have been intended as a pyramid at all: the current structure was probably only built around the 12th or 13th century. The two columns separating the three entrances are in the form of serpents. A figure of the Descending God is visible above the center entrance—though it is tough to get close enough to see it. Elsewhere, bee-like imagery stresses the importance of honey in Caribbean trade. More recently, El Castillo served as a lighthouse, guiding returning fishermen through the gap in the barrier reef. In front of the temple is the large sacrificial stone where the Maya held public ceremonies and religious rituals. Behind El Castillo, overheated tourists can scale the steep steps for a refreshing dip in the ocean.

**TEMPLO DEL DIOS DESCENDIENTE.** This structure stands immediately below the castle on the north side of the main religious plaza. A barely visible, fading relief of a feathered and armed divinity diving from the sky gives the temple its name, the Temple of the Descending God. The figure, seen on many buildings in Tulum, is believed to represent the setting sun; an important deity for a city named after the sun itself. The building was once adorned with polychromatic murals depicting events from the life of this winged figure.

**LA CASA DE LAS COLUMNAS AND EL PALACIO REAL.** In the plaza below the El Castillo and the Templo de Dios Descendiente plaza, the Royal Palace and other important residential houses rest with faded majesty. Characterized by the many columns at their entrances and once topped by giant carvings of the serpent-god, these flat-roofed houses were the largest residential homes in Tulum.

**TEMPLO DE LOS FRESCOS.** This temple is Tulum's best example of post-Classic Mayan architecture. Built in three separate stages, the Temple of the Paintings is really one temple on top of a series of older temples. Visible from the north side, 600-year-old murals that depict deities intertwined with serpents, fruits, corncobs, and flowers—all images associated with the gods of agriculture and fertility. The stela outside the temple, dating from AD 546, is the only one ever found at Tulum and the oldest piece at the site.

QUINTANA ROO

# DAYTRIPS FROM TULUM

### COBÁ

*These Mayan ruins are 46km (45min. by bus) northwest of Tulum. Buses drop visitors next to the lake, just outside the parking lot. Return buses leave at 1:30, 3:30, 4, and 5pm. The 4 and 5pm buses leave from the ADO station in town, in the Bocadito restaurant. Other destinations include: Mérida, via Valladolid, and Chichén Itzá (8, 9:30, 10, 10:30am, noon, 1:30pm; 30-114 pesos). Bring a water bottle, hat, and plenty of mosquito repellent. Ruins open daily 8am-5pm. 51 pesos. Parking 40 pesos; bicycle rental inside 30 pesos. Tour guides can be found inside. A 45min. tour for 1-6 people starts at 300 pesos; the 2hr. option will take you to more of the site. Allow at least 2hr. to see most of the site.*

Stretching over 70 sq. km deep within the jungle, the ruins of Cobá recall what was perhaps the largest of all Mayan cities and certainly one of the most important during the Classic Period. Inhabited at various intervals for over a millennium, the city reached its economic, political, and religious climax in the late Classic Period (AD 600-800), when it flourished as a commercial crossroads for the entire Yucatán Peninsula, connecting distant Mayan cities through its vast network of *sacbé*. By the post-Classic Period, around AD 1000, Cobá had mysteriously lost its sway over the nearby cities of Tulum and Xcaret. Still, the city seems to have regained some of its importance between AD 1200 and 1500. When the Spanish arrived, however, they found the city abandoned. It remained in obscurity until John Stephens and Frederick Catherwood happened upon it in the mid-19th century. The government has put less money into the site, leaving an estimated 6500 buildings unexcavated. Nevertheless, work continues at Cobá; each year brings to light new structures. Through the gate, the site's main attractions lie in a Y-shaped formation. Renting a bike restricts exploration, but will reduce stress for travelers on a tight schedule. The site is nearly void of signs; interested visitors may want to spring for a guide.

On your way out, the large lake just outside the ruins has a few crocodiles. Local entrepreneurs have discovered that tourists are willing to pay 5 pesos to watch them being fed. The better (and only) place you should think about swimming after a hot day at the ruins is the *cenote* on the far side, which feeds the lake.

**RUNNING LATE.** The tricitaxis that wait hungrily at the base of the main pyramid aren't just there for wealthy resort goers. Budget your time properly, or you may find yourself hiring one to whisk you back to the bus stop.

**GRUPO COBÁ.** The Grupo Cobá dates from the Early Classic Period (AD 200-600) and is near the entrance, at the base of the "Y." **Templo de la Lluvia** (Temple of the Rain) looms an impressive 28m high. The different levels of each of the seven 52-year periods, each under a new chief priest, are easy to spot. Only the front face of the temple has been excavated, revealing a corbel-vaulted passageway (a passage supported by a stone that sticks out) that you can explore. In front of the structure is a stone table designed for animal offerings to Chaac, the rain god. A second passageway leads farther south and has red plant dye from the fifth century still visible on the walls; it leads visitors to **Plaza del Templo,** where assemblies were once held. Return to the main path for a look at the **ball court** with its intact stone hoops. The ball game was part of a sacred ceremony in which the movement of the round rubber ball (made from native rubber trees) symbolized the sun and moon. It is believed the Maya thought the game maintained cosmic order. As in Mexico's current beloved game, *fútbol*, players could not touch the ball with

QUINTANA ROO

their hands. Varying sources say that either the winners were sacrificed as an honor, or that the losers were sacrificed as punishment.

**GRUPO MACANXOC.** One kilometer farther up the trunk of the "Y," and another kilometer up the right branch of the "Y" brings you to the Grupo Macanxoc and its eight stelae. On the way is a section of the well-engineered Mayan *sacbé*. This particular road is 20m wide and 4m above the jungle floor, made to weather intense tropical rainstorms. Measuring up to 20m wide, the *sacbé* at Cobá range in length from several meters to 100km. Believed by some to serve a ritualistic rather than practical function, some *sacbé* have been built 4m above the ground. The ornately carved stone slabs of the Grupo Macanxoc were memorials above the tombs of Mayan royals. Unfortunately, their pictorial secrets are now barely discernible. The one exception is the first, the impressive and well-preserved **Retrato del Rey,** which portrays a king with quetzal-feather headdress carrying bow and arrow.

Along the left-hand branch of the "Y" is the **Templo de las Pinturas** (Temple of the Paintings), named for the richly colored frescoes that once adorned the building. The group of 20 buildings to which the temple belongs was constructed in the post-Classic period (AD 1250-1550) from reused. Follow an unmarked trail northwest of the temple to the three stelae of **Chumuc Múl.** The first is the tomb of a victorious captain; it depicts a kneeling Mayan ballplayer, forever preserved with his ball. The second stela shows a princess. The third is of a priest, whose seal is stamped on the slab with a jaguar's head, a common Mayan symbol of worship. Two hundred meters farther lies **sacbé No. 1,** a road that led all the way to Chichén Itzá, 101km west. Runners were posted every 5km to deliver messages via a series of quick jogs. Images of the honeybee god around the site are a reminder of when Cobá was an economic hub, as the Maya used honey (along with salt, coconuts, and jade) as a medium of exchange.

**█NOHOCH MÚL.** Several hundred meters farther, toward the pyramid Nohoch Múl, you'll come upon another ball court, **Temple 10,** and the well-preserved **Stela 20.** Finally, you will see towering Nohoch Múl, by some accounts the tallest Mayan structure in all the Yucatán. A climb up this breathtaking 42m high stone pyramid will make the entire visit worth your while. The pyramid's nine levels and 127 steps, where Mayan priests once led processions, display carvings of the diving god similar to those in Tulum.

**PERILOUS PYRAMIDS.** When descending, be especially careful not to lose your footing—several people have slipped and died during the descent. One way to avoid falling is by sitting down and working your way to the ground using your hands for support.

## AKUMAL

*Combis between Tulum and Playa del Carmen drop visitors on the highway, which can be crossed by pedestrian bridge. From here, it's a 5 minute walk east to Akumal. On the road in, one of the big hotels operates a tourist kiosk, with information and maps. ☎875 9060; www.akumalinfo.com. Open 10am-6pm. Police are at ☎802 5459; emergency ☎066. Just to the right of the arches, the small, expensive grocery store, well-stocked with liquor, has an ATM. ☎875 9337. Open 7am-9pm. MC/V with 5% surcharge.*

Akumal, 26km north of Tulum, boasts some of the best and most accessible snorkeling on the Riviera. Swimmers will see giant sea turtles, who seem remarkably unfazed by the all the boats and masked humans crowding their space. The entrance from the highway provides access to three beaches: **Akumal Bay,** where most of the snorkel tours cluster; **Half Moon Bay,** just to the north, past a small conglomeration of hotels and private villas and the secluded **Yal Ku Lagoon.** The bays are sheltered from the open sea, making for calm, clear waters close to shore. It is possible to take a tour, but budget travelers will find it just as easy to swim unobtrusively behind the groups. The best time to snorkel is midday, when the sun is at its peak and filters through the water most directly. **Akumal Dive Center,** on the beach to the right (south) from the arches, rents gear and will store your belongings. (☎875 9625, from the US ☎+1-719-359-9672; www.akumaldivecenter.com. Snorkel set 144 pesos; 1½hr. Snorkel tour 300 pesos. Open daily 8am-5pm. Driver's license required as deposit. Cash only.) To explore less-crowded beaches further north, rent a bike just inside the arches.

If you'd rather forgo the beach for budget-friendly food, **Lonchería Akumalito ❶,** on the right facing the water, just before the arches, is a shady spot serving Mexican classics. (Breakfast 40 pesos. Tacos 50 pesos. *Tortas* 19-30 pesos  Open daily 7am-9pm.).

## OTHER DAYTRIPS

**XEL-HA.** Xel-Ha (SHELL-ha; "Where the Water is Born") was once a Mayan fishing village, but is now an interactive aquarium (read: amusement park) set in the Yucatec jungle. Nestled amid 84 hectares of jungles, caves, and coves, Xel-Ha allows visitors to take in the beauty of the area most conveniently. Float in an inner tube or snorkel down the 4m deep central river that flows from a *cenote.* Admire parrot fish and meter-long jackfish. It's no wonder that an average of 1600 people or more enter the park daily; the scattered rope swings and rock jumps make for fun, spontaneous adrenaline rushes. With dolphin swims (from 1430 pesos/US$109), rocky paths, hidden *cenotes,* beach chairs, and hammocks overlooking the river, it's easy to spend an en tire day here. For relative peace during busy times, cross the inlet and explore the underwater caves, or stay dry and visit the sea turtle nesting camp (Apr.-Nov.) on the beach. Try to come early, as tourists begin to arrive by the busload around noon. Bring insect repellent; the mosquitoes can be ruthless. There is a small archeological site on the highway, 100m south of the park entrance. **El Templo de Los Pájaros** and **El Palacio,** small Classic and post-Classic ruins, are all that remain of the once powerful Mayan community. El Templo de los Pájaros (farther into the jungle) overlooks a peaceful, shady *cenote* where swimming and rope swinging are allowed. *(Xel-Ha lies 15km north of Tulum; ask any northbound bus or colectivo to drop you at Xel-Ha. 30 pesos. Taxis charge 80-100 pesos. To get back at the end of the day, vigorously wave down a bus on its way to Tulum. Locals will usually be able to tell you when the next one is due to pass. ☎998 884 7165; www.xelha.com.mx. Customer service M-F 8am-2pm and 4-7pm, Sa 9am-noon. Park open daily 8:30am-6pm. All-inclusive snorkel gear, lockers, towels, and all-you-can-eat restaurants US$75. 10% discount for tickets purchased online.)*

**BETWEEN PLAYA DEL CARMEN AND TULUM.** The coast between Playa del Carmen and Tulum is lined with beach-side resorts, all easily accessible by *combis* running between the two cities. Some beaches offer public bathrooms (but no cooking areas) for people toting their own tents.

**Xpu-ha,** a long stretch of blustery blue, is less developed than some of the other areas, affording a rare bit of privacy. Like Tulum to the south, the unbroken shoreline is ideal for sandy strolls. Campers can put up tents for 50 pesos per night and will receive access to rustic bathrooms. (☎106 0024; laplayaxpuha.com. The *colectivo* drops you at km 265. From there it's a 10min. walk down the drive.) Gringo RV drivers have colonized the shore by **Paamul,** 49km north of Tulum,

## THE LOCAL STORY

### SEA TURTLES

Only eight species of sea turtles exist in the world: four of them nest in the state of Quintana Roo. At Akumal, snorklers are likely to see two types of turtles. The loggerhead turtle *(tortuga caguama)* has unique orange patterns on its shell. The green turtle *(tortuga verde)* has a rounder and predictably greener shell.

Between April and September, female turtles may nest as many as 6 times, heading on shore and plopping out between 100 and 150 eggs a time. Fifty to sixty days later the eggs hatch. The baby turtles dig themselves out of the sand and scramble to the ocean.

One of the reasons turtles are so rare is that female turtles are picky about where they will lay their eggs. Scientists have observed that female turtles will give nest at the same spot their entire lives. Moreover, if they decide that the conditions aren't right, they will sometimes stop partway through the process. Even if the turtles nest successfully, a turtle faces long odds when it comes to making it out of the egg and into adulthood.

The Centro Ecológico Akumal was founded in 1993 to monitor the Akumal turtle population. During nesting season, staff and volunteers keep track of how many nests appear on the beach and how many successfully produce turtles. For more information visit www.ceakumal.org.

this small, rocky bay has good snorkeling spots. A short walk north on the path leads to **Playa Yantín,** a private beach where you will almost certainly be the lone sun bather. Visitors can pay to put up tents in a small campsite, with access to bathrooms, electricity, volleyball court, pool, and restaurant. (☎925 9422; www.paamul.com.mx. Tents 132 pesos/US$10 per person; RV hook-up 393 pesos/US$30 for two people.) **Casa Willis** rents snorkel gear (☎133 5992; www.scubamex.com. 132 pesos/US$10. V.)

**HIDDEN WORLDS CENOTE PARK.** On Mex. 307 about 12km from Pueblo Tulum, Hidden Worlds is a good way to see a series of spectacular *cenotes* with interactive guides. The privately owned property has more than 25 *cenotes* and has installed lights in many of them to illuminate the dramatic formations. **Cenote Tak Beh Ha** ("place of hidden waters"), which gave the park its name, is a highlight of all the snorkeling tours. The newly opened **Dreamgate cenote** is for advanced cave divers only and has remained virtually untouched by human hands. Tours also include a ride of the jungle on the "Jungle Mobile," a tractor-turned-truck that can leap over rocks. The new skycycle sails from the top of the jungle canopy all the way to a deep *cenote. (To get to Hidden Worlds from Tulum, take a north-bound colectivo on Mex. 307. 20min., every 10min., 30 pesos.* ☎984 115 4514; www.hiddenworlds.com. All inclusive entry 1050 pesos/US$80; packets 1038-1180pesos/US$79-90. Discounts for larger groups if you buy tickets online. Open daily 9am-5pm. MC/V.)

## SIAN KA'AN BIOSPHERE RESERVE

*Follow the coastal road 7km south of Tulum to the Mayan arch at the entrance. The Centro Ecológico Sian Ka'an (☎984 871 2499; www.cesiak.org), next to the zona arqueológica bus station, leads the best tours that depart from Tulum. (boat tour 917 pesos/US$70 per day, kayak tour 590 pesos/US$45 per ½-day.) Open daily 9am-5pm. For those who have transportation to the park, the centro rents kayaks for (singles 262 pesos/US$20, doubles 393 pesos/US$30). It also leads fly fishing tours (for 1 4600 pesos/US$350, for 2 5250 pesos/US$400). The Amigos de Sian Ka'an (☎984 114 0750; www.siankaantours.org.) is a group of ecologists and scientists who work to maintain the reserve. Open M-F 9am-2pm and 4-7pm. 23 pesos.*

Sian Ka'an ("Where the Sky is Born") occupies roughly 10% (over 5200 sq. km) of the state of Quintana Roo and is Mexico's largest coastal wetland reserve, encompassing tropical forests, *cenotes*, savannas, mangrove swamps, lagoons, and 112km of coral reef. Protected by federal decree as of January 20, 1986, the immense reserve was Mexico's first **UNESCO Natural World Heritage** site, though conspicuous "private property" signs attest to ongoing development. The reserve is home to 1200 species of plants, 336 species of birds, 103 species of mammals, and 23 pre-Classic and Classic Mayan archaeological sites. The best way to see the immense reserve is with an organized boat tour through the *lagunas*. Expert guides can point out bonefish, barracuda, snowy egrets, spoonbilled herons, and pink flamingos to those with untrained eyes. Those who like to go it alone could drive or bike down the 57km unpaved road; be prepared to end up staring at a wall of dense jungle. To get an independent peek at all the Reserve has to offer, check out the open-air *cenote* immediately to the right of the Mayan arch at the entrance. The refreshing water is home to many species of fish and a stunning array of orchids.

## PUNTA ALLEN

Tropical and lush Punta Allen (pop. 500) lies 57km down a bumpy road at the tip of a peninsula in the Sian Ka'an Reserve. A longtime haunt of dedicated sport fishermen, the village is no longer as isolated as it once was. Tourists are pushing south along the access road; busloads troop in daily for 3hr. boat tours of the nearby *lagunas*. Still, when the last *colectivo* leaves and the electricity cuts out (which it does, sporadically, sometimes as early as six o'clock), Punta Allen remains a dot on the map where the best—and only—thing to do is admire the Milky Way.

**TRANSPORTATION.** A **colectivo** (200 pesos) leaves Tulum for Punta Allen daily at 2pm, stopping at many *cabañas* and hotels to deliver newspapers and supplies. It returns daily at 5am. Depending on the size of your group, it may be cheaper to hire a **taxi** (450 pesos one-way). Taxis out of Tulum tend to be cheaper. There is a 6am **boat-colectivo** combo to **Felipe Carrillo Puerto** (via Playón) that leaves from the house next to Super Chaamul, several blocks back from the beach. (Follow signs for Las Boyas; 100 pesos.)

**ORIENTATION AND PRACTICAL INFORMATION.** Though not large, Punta Allen can be confusing, especially after dark. Most accommodations and food are on the road that runs along the beach. Other places will be well-signed. There is **no ATM or bank.** Internet can be found at the **Casa de Ascención.** (30 pesos per hr.) **Posada Paraíso** has slightly better rates. (20 pesos per hr. Open 11am-2pm and 6-11pm, if there's electricity.)

**ACCOMMODATIONS AND FOOD.** Blame the gringos: vacationing fishermen keep prices for food and accommodations well above average. The sole exception is **Serenidad Shardon ❶,** south of town on the road parallel to the beach. Camp in comfort. "Dorm tents" come with mattresses and unzip into a small common space. Tents come with towels, hot water, and mattresses. The site also has a kitchen pit and volleyball court. If you have pesos to blow, there are rooms and well-stocked private *cabañas*. (☎876 1827, from the US 248 628 7217; www.shardon.com. Tents 100 pesos. Private tents with 3 beds 150 pesos per person.)

The bright orange **Muelle Viejo ❸** and has fresh seafood with one of the town's best views of the ocean. The *pulpo a la mulle viejo* (octopus in a stew of tomato, onion, sweet pepper, olive, and raisins; 80 pesos) is a savory specialty. (Beer 15 pesos. Open daily 1-7pm.) Local fishermen order Sols by the six pack

QUINTANA ROO

at **Taco Loco,** which cooks up sizable, cheap portions of Mexican staples. (☎801 1290. Open daily 8am-7pm, depending on electricity.) A pun on the famous fishing spot and possibly its rooftop location, **Casa de Ascensión** ❺ is the only place in town with a wine list. Pair your glass with non-Mexican offerings like spaghetti and curry. (☎801 0034; www.casadeascension.com. Breakfast 45-75 pesos. Salads 55-115 pesos. Open daily for breakfast and dinner. Internet 30 pesos per hr. Comfortable rooms starting at 600 pesos.)

🏃 **ACTIVITIES.** Boat tours take visitors out to the *lagunas* and promise sightings of turtles, dolphins, lots of birds, and the occasional manatee. Solo travelers will probably be priced out, but they're doable with a group. A string of *cooperativos* organizes tours and set up along the beach. A 3hr. tour for up to six costs about 1500 pesos and includes snorkeling and swimming.

Often covered in an intimidating quantity of seaweed, Punta Allen's beaches are not ideal. Walking north along the beach leads eventually to the **"Piscina Natural,"** an incredibly clear, aquamarine patch of water. South of town, the young and restless can stretch their legs by walking to the three look-out points near the **Laguna Negro** in the mangrove swamp, or make the 2km jaunt down to the **lighthouse.**

# FELIPE CARRILLO PUERTO ☎983

Felipe Carrillo Puerto (pop. 20,000) is a bustling transportation hub full of busy streets and fruit vendors. This is the Zona Maya, territory that resisted Mexican control well into the 20th century. The town, then called Chan Santa Cruz, sprung up in 1850 during the Caste Wars, when an enterpising ventriloquist united Maya factions under the guise of a "Cruz Parlante" (Talking Cross). This is real Mexico, untouched by tourist development, and with no beach or ancient ruins to lure the tourists in, it is likely to stay that way. The small sanctuary housing the cross today may be a sight of interest for travelers; no less notable is the gas station, the last one you'll see before hitting Chetumal, 157km south. Most travelers will spend little time in Carrillo Puerto, using it as a transportation connection point before moving on.

🚍 **TRANSPORTATION.** The **ADO** bus station is located on the main plaza at the intersection of C. 65 and 66. (☎834 0815; www.ado.com.mx. Open 24hr.) Buses head to: **Bacalar** (58 pesos); **Cancún** (4hr., 116 pesos); **Chetumal** (62 pesos); **Limones** (36 pesos); **Mahahual** (2hr., 3am and 10:45am, 70 pesos); **Mérida** (12 per day midnight-9pm, 150 pesos); **Playa del Carmen** (2½hr., 76 pesos); **Tulum** (1½hr., 48 pesos).

**Combi** vans to and from Tulum stop at the corner of Juarez and C. 73. (1½hr., 50 pesos). From C. 66 and 73, *combis* go to: **Laguna Azul, Señor** (30min., 18 pesos); **Tepich** (40 pesos); **Tihosuco** (1¼hr., 30 pesos); **Valladolid** (50 pesos). Service is frequent during commuter hours, but during the middle of the day expect to wait until the bus is full.

🔖 **ORIENTATION AND PRACTICAL INFORMATION.** Carrillo is arranged on a grid. Even streets run north-south, increasing to the east, while odd-numbered streets run east-west, increasing to the north. Mex 307 becomes **Calle Benito Juárez,** also known as **Calle 70.** The gas station and roundabout *(glorieta)* marked by a statue of the five-time president Juárez, mark the center of town. The plaza is bounded by C. 67, 65, 66 and 68. Services include: **HSBC** (☎834 1241), at the gas station at C. 69 and Juárez (open M-F 9am-5pm); **24hr. pharmacy** at **YZA** (☎267 1475), on Benito Júarez, between 69 and 71.; **Internet at Modeco-vin**

QUINTANA ROO

"S" **Ciber** (☎834 1482) on C. 68 between 61 and 63, just south of the church (8 pesos per. hr.; open daily 7am-10pm); and the **post office** (☎834 0077), at the corner of C. 69 and 66 (open M-F 9am-5:30pm, Sa 9am-1pm). **Postal Code:** 77200.

**⌂ ACCOMMODATIONS AND FOOD.** Felipe Carrillo is void of hostels and has only a handful of very similar budget hotels. **Hotel Maria Isabel ❸**, at Benito Júarez and C. 61, is the cheapest of the lot. It offers clean, if small, rooms with double bed and private bath. (☎136 0933. Singles 240 pesos; doubles 260-300 pesos. Cash only.)

Fruits and vegetables trucked in from the Maya heartland spill from Carrillo storefronts, a striking contrast after restaurant-ridden Tulum. There's a **market** at Juárez and C. 71, close to the *combi* stop. (Most stalls open daily 7am-3pm.) Across from the gas station, **Lonchería 25 Horas ❷** serves Mexican fast food at all hours. (*Comida del día* 40 pesos. *Licuados* 20 pesos. Open 25hr.)

**◙ SIGHTS.** Located on the outskirts of town, the **Sanctuario de la Cruz Parlante** is a small white chapel renowned for the mahogany cross inside. In 1851, the rebel Maya encountered three crosses in the forest. The cross that spoke to the Maya through an interpreter (the skilled ventriloquist Manuel Nahuat). The cross ordered the different rebel factions to unite against the Spanish. The Maya prevailed, and went on to establish pseudo-religious authority (leaders were known as **Cruzoob,** followers of the cross) from the base of Felipe Carrillo Puerto, then known as Chan Santa Cruz. When the Mexican army invaded in 1901, the crosses were hidden away. One went to Veracruz, where it remains to this day. In the 1930s, the most sacred of the crosses was restored to Carrillo, where guards (some former Maya chieftains) watch over it in week-long rotations. Coke bottles and fake flowers litter the altar as offerings. On Wednesday, there is a communal breakfast at 9am, of which the guardians may invite you to partake. (At C. 69 and 60. Be prepared to remove your shoes. Open daily 6am-6pm. Free.)

Many of Carrillo's most important buildings surround the quiet, porticoed **Plaza Central** that holds the *ayuntamiento*, bus station, and the Casa de Cultura. The last was constructed in 1858 by rebel Mayas and converted to its present use in 1974. (☎834 0922. Open M-F 8am-2:30pm, Sa-Su 9am-1pm and 6-9pm.) The Casa de Cultura shares a wall with the plain white **Iglesia Balam Nah.** Larger than the Sanctuario, the Iglesia was built with the labor of several hundred captives during the war.

**▣ DAYTRIP FROM FELIPE CARRILLO PUERTO: TIHOSUCO.** In 1847, Mayan rebels launched an attack against the Mexican army from the villages of Tepich and Tihosuco. This began the half century of struggle known as the Caste Wars. It was hardly the first uprising in the region; local communities had long before taken up arms against the Spanish colonizers. The war, aggravated by increasing land seizures and the sale of *indígenas* to Cuba as slaves, left the Yucatán divided. Mexican power radiated out from Mérida, while the Maya controlled territory from Tulum down to Bacalar. The half-destroyed **Iglesia Católica del Niño Dios,** which presides over Tihosuco's plaza and was used as a fort during the war, bears witness to the carnage. Legend says the church dates from 1560; more likely it was finished in the late 18th or early 19th century, only to be blown up in 1865 in battle. (Entry to the left, near the market.)

The **Museo de la Guerra de Castas** lies a half block north of the plaza. The artifacts—some coins, rifles, and photographs—aren't particularly impressive, but the explanations of the Caste Wars are the best you'll find in the

THE LOCAL STORY

## A REVOLUTION IN LAND DEVELOPMENT

Around 50% of Mexican land is locked up in ejido ownership. The system, under which communities, rather than individuals, own plots of land, draws on the pre-conquest practice of tribal farming and dates back to the final days of the Mexican Revolution and the Law of Agrarian Reform. The goal of this reform was to enable the government to transfer land from wealthy families and businesses to the peasants that actually farmed it; critics say it impeded agricultural productivity.

In 1992, when then-president Carlos Salinas initiated economic liberalization, land politics again took center stage in the debate. Salinas developed a process by which ejido land could be converted into individual parcels—and, therefore, private property.

For the most part, this law has affected change slowly. Nationwide, by 2007, fewer than 10% of the ejidos had undergone the shift to private ownership. In tourist areas, on the other hand, the opportunity to sell land to foreigners—who can often afford to pay more than locals—provides an incentive for cooperatives to take advantage of the conversion.

Proponents of the reform point to Quintana Roo's tourist boom as an example of spurred growth; its critics say that it has allowed foreigners to buy up the region's most valuable land—just as they did before the revolution.

Yucatán. The stairs behind the ticket desk lead to a room used to store arms. This room was once connected to the Church via a secret tunnel. (*Combis from Felipe Carrillo Puerto (1¼hr., 30 pesos) drop off and pick up along the highway 3 blocks west of town. Follow signs for the Museo into town. Museum ☎ 208 9203. Labels in Spanish and Maya. Open Tu-Su 10am-6pm. 50 pesos.*)

**DAYTRIP FROM FELIPE CARRILLO PUERTO: SEÑOR AND THE LAGUNA AZUL.** A small village located 20km outside of Carrillo, Señor's main attraction is the **Laguna Azul**, seven kilometers out of town, this multi-colored shock of turquoise lies in an orchid-filled forest with a *cenote* at one end. The local tourist cooperative, organized in 2002, conducts canoe tours of the lake. The visit includes a hike to an observation tower. A cultural tour is also offered, with story-telling from a former Maya chieftain, *henequén* workshop, and explanations about traditional medicine. Those who are not interested in a tour may still want to stop by to rent a bike (50 pesos per day) or register to use the campsite (200 pesos per person). The office has ornate wooden doors, carved by the leader of the group. If no one is there when you stop by, try the **Tendejón Florencia,** on the corner of the town plaza. (*Combis to and from Felipe Carrillo Puerto drop off and pick up at the highway bus stop. The town plaza is a short walk to the right coming from Carrillo. Laguna ☎ 118 9129; www.xyaat.com. Laguna Azul tour 400 pesos per person; cultural tour 500 pesos per person; 6-person minimum. Reservations required. Cash only.*)

# MAHAHUAL    ☎ 983

227km south of Tulum, Mahahual (pop. 15,000) was nearly obliterated in 2007 by Hurricane Dean. Today, the town is backed by dead mangroves and fronted by a bay broken up with miniature coral reefs, making it an unlikely place for a tourist boom. Still, a palm-lined pedestrian *malecón* and the nearby Mesoamerican reef, with 65 types of coral and 500 species of fish, give the town a laid-back charm. Cruise ships dock Tuesday and Wednesday, releasing passengers in a stream of blue dune buggies. The rest of the week, semi-deserted restaurants and abandoned jet skis give Mahahual an undiscovered, low-season feel.

## ⚡ TRANSPORTATION

The **ADO** (www.ado.com.mx) bus stand is located on the northern end of Huachinango. It's technically open 7am-6:30pm, but is most reliable when buses are due to arrive. Buses head to Mahahual from **Chetumal** (3hr., 5:40am and 4:10pm, 55 pesos) and **Tulum** (3hr., 1:55 and 9:25am, 132 pesos) via **Felipe Carrillo Puerto** (2hr., 3 and 10:45am, 70 pesos). Buses run to **Chetumal** (2hr.; M-Sa 7:30am, 1, 6:30pm; Su 10:30am, 1, 6:30pm; 88 pesos) via **Bacalar** (60 pesos); **Limones** (M-Sa 8:30am and 6:30pm, Su 12:30 and 5pm; 30 pesos); **Cancún** (M-Sa 8:30am and 5:30pm, Su noon and 5:30pm; 206 pesos) via **Carrillo Puerto** (74 pesos), **Tulum** (132 pesos), **Playa del Carmen** (164 pesos), and **Puerto Morelos** (196 pesos). To get to **Xcalak,** you have to catch the bus coming from Chetumal, which passes through on Huachinango at about 9am, give or take 30min. Bright yellow **taxis** linger at the corner of Huachinango and Sierra. Taxis go to **Las Casitas** (20 pesos) and Xcalak (300 pesos).

## ▓ ▞ ORIENTATION AND PRACTICAL INFORMATION

Mahahual is divided into two areas: the 3km stretch of beach, accessible by a long *malecón* and bounded by the cruise ship dock to the north and the fishing dock to the south. **Las Casitas** is 15min. out of town, and is cluttered with tiny, cookie cutter concrete homes. **Avenida Huachinango** runs parallel to the beach. **Calle Sierra** crosses to the beach, near waiting taxis and the ATM.

**Bank:** The lone **ATM** in town is on the beach, just before C. Charna, but it often doesn't work, so it's best to carry cash.

**Laundromat: Lavandería Que Limpio,** 2 blocks south of Loco Ricky's (p. 178) and to the right. Open M-Sa 8am-6pm.

**Emergency:** ☎066.

**Internet: Mobius Cafe** (☎834 5935), in Las Casitas. 30 pesos per hr. Open M-Sa 8am-10pm. A small **cafe** at C. Sardinia and Cherna a few blocks back from the beach has better rates. 20 pesos per hr. Open daily 9am-10pm.

**Postal Code:** 77940.

## ▐ ACCOMMODATIONS

Travelers with cash and cars often stay at one of the hotels that line the coastal road. Budget travelers may want to investigate Mahahual's only hostel, **Macho's,** an orange-trimmed white building on the beach. It was about to open at the time of publication. (About 1.5km south of the bus station, close to the Muelle de Pescadores.)

**Accommodation 1** (☎839 1238), on the northern tip of Av. Huachinango, just a few blocks from the bus station. Small brightly-painted cabins with comfortable beds in a bare-bones setting. Barring further development of the area, porch-sitters can enjoy a view of the Caribbean. No hot water. Singles 300 pesos; doubles 350 pesos. Cash only. ❹

**Las Cabañas del Doctor,** Av. Mahahual 6 (☎832 2102) between C. 2 and 4, 2km south of the bus station. *Cabañas*, rooms, and camping. Rooms have hot water. Camping 50 pesos per person. Doubles 400 pesos; each additional person 50 pesos. *Cabañas* fit up to 4. Cash only. ❺

## ▟ FOOD

Seafood dominates Mahahual menus, which are priced for those with heavy wallets. The local grocery stores carry only the basics. In town, vegetables can be found at a **mini-mart** half a block south of Calle Sierra. (☎119 9778.

QUINTANA ROO

Open daily 7am-10pm.) In Las Casitas, the **Mini Super Bere,** just off the Paseo del Puerto, has a slightly better offering.

**Tienda Chandés,** just across from the bus station. Your best bet for a quick, affordable bite. Serves *tortas,* tamales, and other Mexican fast food. Empanadas 5 pesos. Open Tu-Su 7am-7pm. Cash only. ❶

**Loco Ricky's** (☎834 5724), on the Po. del Puerto In Las Casitas. A gung-ho sports bar all about *fútbol* and *ranchero* music. The place claims a cult following, complete with fan t-shirts. American menu, service, and plate sizes. Free Wi-Fi. Open daily 8am-11pm. Cash only. ❹

**Posada de los 40 Cañones** (☎983 123 8591; www.40canones.com). South of the bus station, in the sleekest hotel in town. Tex-Mex and seafood and access to a clean stretch of beach. Exquisite shrimp fajitas come with guacamole, rice, a crisp salad, and mini-mountain of tortillas. Entrees 120-200 pesos. Free Wi-Fi. Open daily 8am-9pm. MC/V. ❺

**Restaurant Capitán el Mono** (☎123 8254), on the beach in the center of town. Fills up at lunchtime with fish-gobbling families whose kids swim in the ocean out front. Entrees 100-300 pesos. Lobster 250 pesos. Open daily 8am-6pm. Cash only. ❸

## 🏔 OUTDOOR ACTIVITIES

Mahahual's beach is littered with rocks, the source of several sunken ships, countless stubbed toes, and all the breakers rimming the bay. Though not ideal for sunbathers, the terrain is a dream come true for snorkelers and divers. Relatively undiscovered, diving the Mahahual reefs carries a certain cachet in the diving world. Trips go to the **Mahahual reef,** which plunges 40m, and to the **Sea Witch,** popular for its sand chutes and shark sightings. Trips to the sea wrecks at **Banco Chinchorro,** 30km offshore, can be arranged. **Dreamtime,** 2½km down the Mahahual coastal road, is one of the most established and affordable dive shops in the area. (☎700 5824; www.dreamtimediving.com. 2-tank dive 985 pesos (US$75), 3-tank dive 1444 pesos (US$110). Equipment rental 262 pesos (US$20), 197 pesos (US$15) for half-day. Open-water courses 5250 pesos (US$400), including the books.) The **Restaurant Delfín,** in the center of the beach, offers 1¼hr. snorkeling tours (262 pesos/US$20) and boat expeditions to the Banco Chinchorro (1444 pesos/US$110). (☎106 0912. Open daily 8am-6pm.)

## XCALAK                                                          ☎983

Tiny Xcalak (pop. 300), flanked by the Laguna Cementerio and the Caribbean, is no stranger to destruction. When Hurricane Janet tore through the town in 1955, residents abandoned it completely. But the pull of fish-rich waters and spiky palms proved too strong, and families trickled back in. Today, the small community is remaking itself as an eco-friendly tourist spot. In 2000, the town secured protection for the nearly 18,000 hectares surrounding it, successfully petitioning the government to reserve the area as the Parque Nacional Arre-cifes de Xcalak. With a variety of terrain ranging from mangrove swamp to coral reef, the park boasts some of the best dives around, among them La Poza, a trench that runs parallel to shore heavily populated with big fish, and La Chiminea (the Chimney), named for its long ascent.

📧 **TRANSPORTATION. Buses** from Chetumal head daily to **Xcalak** (1½hr.; 5:40am and 4:10pm, return service at 5am and 2pm; 30 pesos) via Mahahual. Buses enter town from the south, driving up the main road, recognizable by the bright orange general store and school decorated with giant colored pencils. Pick-up is near the lighthouse and fishing pier.

**■🖪 ORIENTATION AND PRACTICAL INFORMATION.** Xcalak has **no bank, no ATM, no phone service, no grocery store,** and **no official tourist office.** For good details on the area, visit www.xcalak.info. Services include a **health clinic** (open M-F 8am-4pm) and **telephones** at Telecomm (open M-F 9am-3pm). The best bet for **Internet** is one of the hotels, though most houses in town (and the park service office) get service and have Wi-Fi.

**🖪🖪 ACCOMMODATIONS AND FOOD.** Most tourists stay at one of the North American-owned hotels on the road between Mahahual and Xcalak. In town, **camping ❶** is possible on the land just past the lighthouse, across the bridge. (50 pesos per person.) On the road leading to the beach, **Palapas Tio Bon ❹** has five simple, wooden cabins with private baths, but no hot water. (☎836 6954. Doubles 300 pesos.)

The **Leaky Palapa ❸**, on the main road just past the lighthouse, specializes in "casual fine dining," gringo-style. (Open for dinner Th-Su.) **Lonchería Silvia ❺** serves standard Mexican fare, centered around fish. (☎839 8249. Seafood 120 pesos. Entrees 80 pesos. Open daily 8:30am-10pm. Cash only.)

**🖪 OUTDOOR ACTIVITIES.** The **park office,** on the southern side of town close to the beach, is open daily 9am-2pm and 4-6pm. Independent snorkelers must purchase a bracelet from the park for 46 pesos. For more information on the park, contact the office in Chetumal (see below). (Av. Insurgentes 445. ☎285 4623; www.conanp.gob.mx.) **Bahia Blanca,** in front of the park office, is the local tourist cooperative, operated by the same residents who petitioned for the area to be made into a park. (www.xcalak-ecotours.com. Boat tours of the wetland 460-524 pesos (US$35-40) per person. Snorkel tours 328 pesos (US$25). 2-tank dives 854 pesos (US$65). Open daily 9am-noon and 4-8pm. Cash only.

# CHETUMAL ☎983

The capital city of Quintana Roo, Chetumal (pop. 140,000) is a hub of activity and prosperity in Mexico's youngest state. Founded in 1889 as a naval base, the port's early inhabitants made a living intercepting arms and illegally harvested wood intended for Mayan rebels during the Caste War. The nearby English colony of Belize proved to be a strong influence on the town and many of the early buildings are in the English colonial style—wooden saltbox numbers with stilts and porches. They all came splintering down in 1955 when Hurricane Janet raged through, changing the cityscape for good. Today, you'll find wide boulevards filled with speeding cars, a lively shopping district, and nearby natural wonders like the Laguna de Siete Colores in Bacalar (p. 183).

## 🖪 TRANSPORTATION

**Flights:** Aeropuerto Internacional de Chetumal (CTM), Prolongación Av. Revolución 660 (☎832 0465), 3km west of the city. Serves Fleet Mexicano, including Aerocaribe and Mexicana (☎832 6675) as well as Aviacsa (☎832 7676), on Cárdenas at 5 de Mayo. Taxis to the centro cost 50 pesos.

**Buses: ADO station** (☎832 5110), Insurgentes at Belice. To reach the centro from the station, your best bet is a taxi (15 pesos). 1st-class buses go to: **Belize City** (3hr.; 11:45am, 3, 6pm; 100 pesos); **Campeche** (7hr., noon, 262 pesos); **Cancún** (5hr., 23 per day, 228-274 pesos); **Flores/Tikal** (8hr., 6am, 2pm; 290 pesos); **Mérida** (6-7hr., 4 per day 7:30am-11:30pm, 250 pesos); Mexico City (22hr.; 11:30am, 4:30, 9pm; 962 pesos); **Ocosingo** (5 per day 1:30am-11pm, 378-436 pesos);

Palenque (7hr., 11pm, 356 pesos); **Playa del Carme**n (4hr., 23 per day, 190-228 pesos); **San Cristóbal de las Casa**s (478-568 pesos); **Tulum** (3hr., 11 per day, 152 pesos); **Tuxtla Gutiérrez** (7:45, 9:55, 11pm; 501 pesos); **Villahermosa** (9hr., 8 per day, 259 pesos); **Xpujil** (2hr., 10 per day, 98 pesos). **Caribe lines** leave from the 2nd-class bus station, at Colón and Belice, to **Xcalac** (5:40am, 4:10pm; 56 pesos). **Mayab** goes to: **Bacalar** (1hr., 26 pesos); **Cancún** (7hr., 178 pesos); **Mérida** (8hr., 8, 11:30am, 11pm; 180 pesos); **Playa del Carmen** (6hr., 140 pesos); Ticul (6 per day, 154 pesos); **Tulum** (5hr., 114 pesos).

**Combis:** On Francisco Primo de Verdad, 2 blocks east of Héroes. *Combis* leave for Bacalar (45min., every 40min. 6am-8pm, 15 pesos), La Unión (2hr., every hr. 6am-6pm, 30 pesos), and Santa Elena (every hr., 8 pesos).

**Taxis:** Abundant in the *centro*. Within the *centro,* prices are negotiable (most trips 10-15 pesos).

> **BORDER CROSSING.** To enter Belize for 30 days, Canadian, EU, and US citizens need only a valid passport and a bus ticket. To enter Guatemala, Canadian, EU, and US citizens need a valid passport but not a visa. For those who do need a visa, the process is quick and costs US$15. For more information, contact each country's consulate in Chetumal: Belize, Carranza 562 (☎044 9838 7728; open M-F 9am-2pm and 5-8pm, Sa 9am-2pm); Guatemala, Chapultepec 354 (☎832 3045; open M-F 10am-2pm).

## ORIENTATION AND PRACTICAL INFORMATION

Tucked into the southeastern corner of the Yucatán Peninsula's, Chetumal is just north of Río Hondo, the border between Mexico and Belize. The shopping district lines Héroes, starting at Mercado Viejo and extending 1km south to the bay, and is packed with duty free shops. At the southern end of Héroes lies Bahía, a four-lane avenue that follows the bay for several kilometers, flanked by statues, small plazas, and playgrounds. From here you can see part of Belize—the long, distant piece of land to the south.

**Tourist Offices:** Módulos de Información, in the centro in front of the Museo de la Cultura Maya. Another branch on Bahía between Reforma and Hidalgo near Maqueta de Payo Obisbo. Both open daily 9am-8pm. Secretaria Estatal de Turismo, Centenario 622 (☎835 0860), between Ignacio Somosot and Ciricote, 4km from the centro. Open M-F 8am-6pm.

**Currency Exchange and Bank: Banks line Héroes. Bancomer** (☎832 5300), on Juárez at Obregón. Good rates and **24hr. ATM.** Open M-F 8:30am-4pm, Sa 10am-3pm.

**Laundromat:** Lavandería Juárez, Av. Chapultepec, between Madero and Independencia.

**Luggage storage:** At the ADO bus station. Open 24hr. 10 pesos per hr.

**Emergency:** ☎066.

**Police:** (☎832 1500), on Insurgentes at Belice, next to the bus station.

**Red Cross:** (☎832 0571), on Chapultepec at Independencia.

**Pharmacy: Farmacia Canto,** Héroes 99 (☎832 0483). Open M-Sa 7am-11pm, Su 7am-10pm.

**Hospital: Hospital General,** Quintana Roo 399 (☎832 1932), at Siordia.

**Fax Office: Telecomm** (☎832 0651), by the post office. Open M-F 8am-6pm, Sa-Su **9am-12:30pm.**

**Internet Access: Webcenter Internet** (☎832 8138), on Aguilar between Belice and Héroes. Before 3pm 8 pesos per hr., after 3pm 10 pesos per hr. Open daily 8am-2am.

QUINTANA ROO

**Odissey,** Zaragoza 190 (☎833 0100), between 5 de Mayo and Héroes. 10 pesos per hr. Open daily 9am-10pm.

**Post Office:** C. 2 (☎832 2578), 1 block east of Héroes. Open M-F 9am-4pm, Sa 9am-1pm. **Mexpost** inside. **Postal Code:** 77000.

# ACCOMMODATIONS

Chetumal's budget accommodations are far from fancy, but they score points for location and convenience. A stroll down Héroes, south of the market, will yield many options. Reservations are necessary from mid-July through August. For a more luxurious experience, look into staying at one of the lagoon-side ranches in nearby Bacalar (p. 183).

**Hotel María Dolores,** Obregón 206 (☎832 0508), half a block west of Héroes. A Donald Duck cartoon points the way to aqua-colored rooms with private bath and fan. No A/C. Free purified water. Parking available. Restaurant attached. Check-out 1pm. Singles 215 pesos; doubles 235-270 pesos; triples 305 pesos. Cash only. ❸

**Hotel Ucum,** Gandhi 167 (☎832 0711; www.hotelucumchetumal.com). Dark, clean rooms have tiled floors and modern baths. Coffee after 7am. Parking available. Check-out 1pm. Singles and doubles 200 pesos, with cable TV 230 pesos, with A/C 350 pesos; triples with fan 230 pesos; quads with fan 260 pesos. Cash only. ❸

**COJUDEQ Youth Hostel** (☎832 0525), on Calle Heróica Escuela Naval, half a block from Veracruz, behind the theater. Marked only by the small chac-mool statue lounging in the yard, Chetumal's only hostel is certainly budget. Tidy 4-bed dorms are a bit cramped, but clean. The not-so-private institutional bathrooms could be cleaner. Lockers available. Beds 50 pesos. Cash only. ❶

**Hotel Posada Pantoja,** Lucio Blanco 81 (☎832 1781), 4 blocks from Veracruz. What is lost in location is gained in comfort and service. Spacious, cheerful rooms with A/C, coffee, and cable TV. Rooms on the right, above the reception, are newer and more attractive. Singles 280 pesos; doubles 360 pesos; each additional person 60 pesos. ❹

# FOOD

Chetumal is an international crossroads, and its restaurants serve a spicy blend of Mexican and Belizean cuisine as well as some Chinese buffet-style food and Middle Eastern options. Loncherías, at the Mercado Viejo on Héroes and Aguilar, and at Altamarino, on Obregón, west of Héroes, are the best deals. Try to get a good sense for the sanitation situation in the kitchen before ordering (open daily 6am-6pm). Stock up on vitals at the Super San Francisco de Asís, next to the bus station (open daily 7am-10pm).

**Restaurant El Cocal** (☎832 0882), in Hotel Los Cocos at the corner of Héroes and Héroes de Chapultepec. The terraced seating and neon-blue lighting as well as the strong A/C draws Chetumal's busy businessmen and well-dressed travelers for breakfast and dinner. Fruit and granola 40 pesos. Scrambled eggs with frijoles, tortillas, fruit, and coffee 50 pesos. MC/V. ❸

**Restaurante Pantoja,** Gandhi 181 (☎832 3957). A very popular family restaurant for locals and visitors alike. Delicious comida casera del día (homemade meals that rotate daily; 40 pesos) and great breakfasts (40 pesos) beat market prices. Open M-Sa 7am-7pm. Cash only. ❸

**Nori Sushi Bar** (☎129 2059; www.chetumal.com/sushibar), on Blanco between Héroes and 5 de Mayo. A sleek, small, and very white interior lends a posh vibe to the atmosphere. Maki rolls from 40 pesos. MC/V. ❸

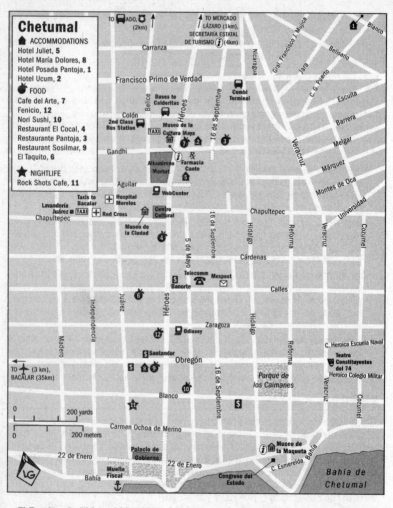

**Chetumal**

🏠 **ACCOMMODATIONS**
Hotel Juliet, **5**
Hotel María Dolores, **8**
Hotel Posada Pantoja, **1**
Hotel Ucum, **2**

🍽 **FOOD**
Cafe del Arte, **7**
Fenicio, **12**
Nori Sushi, **10**
Restaurant El Cocal, **4**
Restaurante Pantoja, **3**
Restaurant Sosilmar, **9**
El Taquito, **6**

⭐ **NIGHTLIFE**
Rock Shots Cafe, **11**

**El Taquito**, C. 220 (☎833 1602). Snack on tacos and antojitos under a fan-cooled palapa while your beef smokes on the spit. Tacos 8 pesos. Quesadillas 10 pesos. Brocheta vegetariana 35 pesos. Open M-Sa noon-5pm and 7pm-midnight. Cash only. ❷

**Restaurant Sosilmar**, Obregón 206 (☎832 6380), in front of the Hotel María Dolores. Tasty fish filets (60 pesos), milanesa de puerco (60 pesos), or comida del día (50 pesos) served amid green decor. Breakfasts 30-50 pesos. Open daily 8am-10:30pm. Cash only. ❹

## 👁 🎵 SIGHTS AND ENTERTAINMENT

At the northern end of the Altamarino market is the **Museo de la Cultura Maya**, on Héroes between Gandhi and Colón. This interactive museum explores the Maya's three-leveled cosmos—the earth, underworld, and heavens—with glyphic text, sculptures, stelae, and models of famous Mayan temples. Though

QUINTANA ROO

the museum only has a small collection of artifacts, digital reproductions and detailed explanations give a cohesive overview of complex Mayan cosmology. (☎832 6838. Open Tu-Th 9am-7pm, F-Sa 9am-8pm, Su 9am-7pm. 50 pesos.) Stop in next door at one of the free art galleries, which showcase the work of regional artists. **The Museo de la Ciudad,** Héroes 68, in the Centro Cultural de las Bellas Artes south of the market, details the history of Chetumal and has art exhibits next door. Check with the office for other cultural events and shows. (Open Tu-Su 9am-7pm. 10 pesos.)

Though Chetumal has long stretches of coastline, none of them are suitable for swimming. The nearest beach is the balneario at **Calderitas.** Buses leave from Colón, between Héroes and Belice. (15min., every 30min. 7am-9pm, 5 pesos.) Although the shores are rocky and the water can be cloudy, the beach draws shoulder-to-shoulder crowds during summer and school holidays. Going left at the fork on Héroes (instead of right, toward Calderitas) and following the signs for 16km will bring you to **Oxtankah,** a set of ruins constructed sporadically over the course of many centuries, beginning in AD 200. In 1531, Spaniards arrived at the site and built a church before being forced to flee two years later. The few remains today showcase an intriguing mix of Mayan and Spanish architecture and history. (There is no public transportation to the site. For jungle adventures and other ecotourism excursions, contact Sacbé Tours, Av. Napoles 399. (☎/fax 833 2080, toll-free 800 036 4892; www.sacbetours.com.)

Chetumal's **nightlife** scene is mostly confined to window shopping at the duty free stores along Héroes. A small, brave, 20-something crowd gets down Cancún-style at **Rock Shots Cafe,** on Juárez between Blanco and Merino. (☎833 4720. Cover 40 pesos; Sa women free before midnight. Open Th-Su 11pm-4am.)

# BACALAR ☎983

Diminutive Bacalar (pop. 10,000) boasts access to the second largest lagoon in all of Mexico, La Laguna de Siete Colores, so named for the seven hues that appear in stripes across the water. This beautiful spot, with its powdery white limestone beaches and warm fresh water, is popular with swimmers, kayakers, campers, and sunbathers.

## ▐ TRANSPORTATION

From Chetumal, the best way to arrive is by **taxi colectivo** (40min., 25 pesos). They line up near the stand just across from the Red Cross at Chapultepec and Independencia. **Combis** also leave (roughly every 45min.) from the bus station at Hidalgo and Verdad (45min., 20 pesos). Both return to Chetumal from the church, one block west of the plaza.

**Buses** also stop at the **ADO** (www.ado.com.mx) station on the highway, at about C. 30, a 20min. walk west of town. Service **to Bacalar** from: **Cancún** (5hr., 7:30am, 220 pesos) via **Playa del Carmen** (3¾hr., 8:55am, 176 pesos); **Tulum** (2½hr., 10am, 111 pesos); and **Chetumal** (50min.; 5, 8:30am, 2:30, 7:30pm; 28 pesos). Buses **from Bacalar** go to **Cancún** (5hr., 12 per day 5:30am-12:45am, 220 pesos); **Mérida** (6hr., 6 per day 6am-11:5pm); **Tizimín** (4½hr.; 7:45am and 2:45pm, with an extra bus at 8:45pm on Su.).

## ▟ ▐ ORIENTATION AND PRACTICAL INFORMATION

From the Laguna, the roads rise in odd numbered *avenidas*, with **Avenida 7** slicing the plaza's west side. Even-numbered streets climb south to north. The **fort,** just east of the plaza, provides the town's most recognizable landmark.

**Currency Exchange:** No bank in town, but **24hr. ATM** on the southwest corner of the plaza.

**Police:** ☎125 6872.

**Pharmacy: Farmacia Similares** (☎834 2843), on Av. 7 between 26 and 28. Open M-Sa 8am-9pm, Su 8am-8pm.

**Internet Access: Internet Infinitum,** on Av. 3, 1 block south of the plaza. 10 pesos per hr. Open M-F 7am-11pm, Sa-Su noon-11pm.

**Post Office:** Open M-F 8am-4:30pm, Sa 8am-noon.

## ▞ ACCOMMODATIONS

Tranquil Bacalar is a good alternative to staying in Chetumal. For camping options, visit the *ejido* (see below).

**Casita Carolina** (☎834 2334; www.casitacarolina.com), just below the fort and to the north. Surprisingly affordable rooms. Outside, there is a very green lawn and a waterfront dock. Inside, rooms are furnished with crisp sheets, a set of drawers, and comfortable mattresses. Book ahead in high season. Doubles 300-400 pesos; 4-person *palapa* 500 pesos. Cash only. ❹

**Accommodation 2,** on Av. 3 between 30 and 32, to the northeast of town. Only hostel in town feels a bit bleak and desolate. Seven non-bunked beds and a kitchen. Bathroom lacks hot water and a shower curtain. Linens included. Contact the upscale **Eco Villas** (☎834 2516; www.villasecotucan.info), 3km out of town, for info. Dorms 70 pesos. Cash only. ❶

## ▞ FOOD

**Orizaba's** (☎834 2069), on Av. 7 between 24 and 26, under the giant, red-rimmed *palapa*. Caters to locals who come for a late lunch. Half-pitcher of *licuado* 15 pesos. Breakfast 27 pesos. *Menú del día* 40 pesos. Open daily 8am-4pm. Cash only. ❷

**Taquería Christian's** (☎114 9094), on Av. 7, 1 block south of the plaza. The most happening place in town after the sun goes down. Tacos *al pastor* from 8 pesos. Open daily 6:30-10pm. Cash only. ❶

## ◉ ▞ SIGHTS AND ACTIVITIES

In 1733, the Spanish built Bacalar's dominating stone **fort** to defend the town against pirates. It was used as a base during the Caste Wars and now houses the fascinating **Museo de la Pirateria.** The look-out tower makes for a Kodak moment. (☎125 1231. Open Tu-Th and Su 9m-7pm, F-Sa 9am-8pm. 50 pesos.)

Behind the fort and 250m to the left lies the **Balneario Ejidal,** a complex of *palapas* and restaurants on an *ejido* (communal farm) that acts as the local swimming pool. (Open daily 7am-7pm. Restaurant 9am-6pm. Entrance 5 pesos. Parking 10 pesos. *Palapas* 30 pesos. Camping 50 pesos.) A little farther north there is free and equally picturesque access to the lake, albeit without bathrooms or a bar. Across the narrow stretch of water from Balneario Ejidal is **Playa de las Piratas** and the channels where the buccaneers supposedly entered the lagoon. If you decide to paddle to Playa de las Piratas, be aware that the current goes toward the Playa, making for a hard return trip. The **Club de Vela,** just below the fort and to the north, rents kayaks and jet skis by the hour. (☎834 2474. Kayaks 100 pesos. Jet skis 900 pesos. Open daily 8:30am-6pm. Cash only.) At the bright yellow **Hotelito Paraíso,** 200m farther south down the lake road, non-guests can rent kayaks for just 50 pesos, but there are only two. (☎834 2787; www.hotelitoparaiso.com.) South of town, the large **Cenote Azul** offers another bathing option.

QUINTANA ROO

The artist **Gilberto Silva** (☎834 2657) has a workshop and modest gallery in town next to the Casa de Cultura. It's worth a stop, even if just for a chat with the friendly local. In the studio, he makes exquisite carvings of Mayan monuments in limestone and then casts them in a mixture of local clay and minerals. His works are distributed as far as the Museum of Natural History in New York City, but he'll sell them to you for surprisingly affordable wholesale prices, starting at 250 pesos. (On C. 26, between C. 5 and 7.)

# TABASCO AND CHIAPAS

The Yucatán Peninsula technically ends at Campeche, but the peninsula's culture and history extend past its boarders, into Tabasco and on to Chiapas. Just visit the ruins at **Palenque** (p. 212) and you'll see that Mayan culture and brilliance is well and alive in this part of the country. Head to **Villahermosa** (p. 186), Tabasco's capital, to get away from your fellow tourists and enjoy a cup of *pozol* with the locals.

If Villahermosa's noise and bustle are beginning to wear on you, visit Chiapas' charming **San Cristóbal de las Casas** (p. 200), a significant city in its own right, with excellent dining, friendly locals, and plenty of backpackers and budget accommodations. Chiapas is the poorest state in Mexico, and has been wrought with political turmoil since 1994 when the **Ejército Zapatista de Liberación Nacional** (Zapatista National Liberation Army) rebelled against the Mexican government on New Year's Day. The Mexican government restrained them, but in 2000 they renewed their resistance and declared their territory an independent and autonomous government from Mexico. The region now is fairly stable: the zapatistas' actions are primarily nonviolent—they often focus on building schools and health facilities in the area—and they have lost much of their local support. Even with this unrest, the region as a whole remains a cultural capital.

## VILLAHERMOSA
☎993

Villahermosa (pop. 1.6 million) is neither a *villa* (small village), nor is it *hermosa* (beautiful). The capital of Tabasco state is a loud, bustling conglomeration of people, food, and concrete, sprinkled liberally with satellite dishes and fast food joints. What holds this lovely concoction together? Crude oil, of course. The city has capitalized on oil discoveries and its strategic location along the Río Grijalva, one of the few navigable rivers in the Republic of Mexico. Nevertheless, the city is far from crude. Studded with lagoons, parks, and pedestrian walkways, Villahermosa is actually quite conducive to daytime rambling. If your aim is to explore a large Mexican city while escaping the typical tourist circuit, Villahermosa is the place. While it's often frequented by those connected to the oil industry, gringos remain few and far between.

## ⌐ TRANSPORTATION

**Flights: Aeropuerto Capitán Carlos Pérez** (VSA; ☎356 0156), on the Villahermosa-Macupana Hwy., 13km from downtown. Taxis shuttle between the airport and the *centro* (*especial* 150 pesos, *colectivo* 100 pesos). Major airlines have offices in Tabasco 2000, including: **Aeroméxico,** Cámara 511 Locale 2 (☎356 0005); **Aviacsa,** Via 3 120 Locale 8 (☎993 356 0131); **Mexicana,** Via 3 120 Locale 5-6D (☎316 3132).

**Buses:** There are 2 main bus terminals in Villahermosa. *Saetas* (public buses) and *combis* (5 pesos) run 6am-10pm.

**1st-class terminal:** on Mina at Merino. To reach downtown from the station, walk 2 blocks to your right on Mina to Méndez Magaña. From there, take a *combi* to Parque Juárez (5 pesos). Or, take a left at Méndez Magaña and walk 5 blocks until Madero. 3 blocks to the right will bring you to the Parque (15-20min.). **ADO** (☎312 7692 or 314 5818) runs to: **Cancún** (11hr., 8pm, 614 pesos); **Campeche** (5hr., 4 per day 12:50pm-10:50pm, 298 pesos); **Mexico City** (11hr., 7 per day 12:10-10:25pm, 728 pesos); **Oaxaca** (11hr., 9:25pm, 480 pesos); **Palenque** (2hr., 5 per day 7:35am-9:15pm, 102 pesos); **Puebla** (8hr.; 12:10pm, 8:40pm; 566 pesos); **San Andrés**

TABASCO AND CHIAPAS

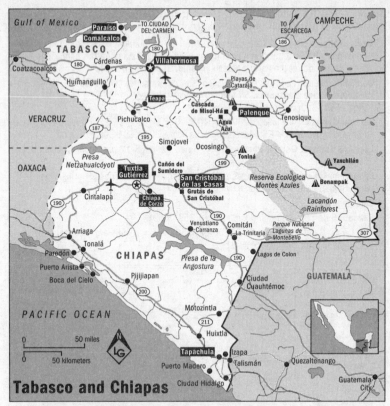

**Tabasco and Chiapas**

**Tuxtla** (4hr.; 9:30am, 11am, 7:25pm; 224 pesos); **Tuxtla Gutiérrez** (7hr.; 3:35pm, 7:55pm; 280 pesos). **OCC, ATS,** and **TRT** also serve the station.

**2nd-class terminal:** on Ruiz Cortines, 2 blocks left of Mina. To reach downtown from the terminal, cross the highway on the pedestrian bridge left of the station and hop on an Indeco Centro bus (5 pesos) to Parque Juárez on Madero. Get off the bus, cross the bridge, and walk toward the Best Western for 2 blocks. Go left on Mina and continue south for 3 blocks until you reach the ADO station. Taxi to the *centro* 15 pesos. 2nd-class service reaches many regional destinations such as **Paraíso, Tacotalpa,** and **Teapa.**

**Taxis: Radio Taxi** (in the *centro* ☎314 3456; in Tabasco 2000, 316 6421) is slightly more expensive than the *taxis colectivos* (20 pesos within the *centro*). Available 24hr. Minimum charge for roaming yellow taxis 15 pesos. Between neighborhoods 20 pesos.

**Car Rental: Europcar** (☎352 4510), in Plaza Farole in Tabasco 2000. Reserve ahead during July and Aug. Open daily 8am-6pm. MC/V.

## ◼🄱 ORIENTATION AND PRACTICAL INFORMATION

Villahermosa is 20km from the Chiapas border and 71km from the Gulf of Mexico. Unlike its more orderly neighbors to the east and north, Villahermosa's streets sprout at seemingly random intervals and angles, and lack numbers for easy navigation. **Paseo Tabasco** links the *centro* to **Tabasco 2000,** a complex of newer buildings with a shopping mall and government offices. Tabasco, **Bulevar Cortines,** and the **Río**

**Grijalva** enclose the main downtown tourist area. At the heart of it all is the **Zona Luz,** a small grid of perpetually buzzing pedestrian streets next to **Parque Juárez.**

**Tourist Office:** (☎316 8271), in Tabasco 2000, in the building across from the Palacio Municipal. Walk into the open-air corridor; take the first stairs on the right. Open M-F 8am-5pm. Booth at the Parque Museo la Venta. Open daily 8am-4pm.

**Banks:** Throughout Zona Luz and on Paseo Tabasco. **Banamex** (☎312 0011), on Madero at Reforma, and **Santander,** on Madero between Zaragoza and Lerdo de Tejada, have **24hr. ATMs.** Both open M-F 9am-4pm.

**American Express:** 1404 Tabasco 2000 (☎310 9900), in the office of Turismo Creativo. Exchanges traveler's checks. Open M-F 8:30am-8:30pm, Sa 9am-8:30pm, Su 9:30am-2:30pm.

**Luggage Storage: Guarda Plus,** at the ADO bus station. 5-12 pesos per hr. Open daily 6am-10pm.

**Laundromat: Lavandería El Angel,** on Mina at Magallanes. 12 pesos per kg. Open M-F 8am-8pm, Sa 8am-4pm. Cash only.

**Emergency:** ☎066.

**Police:** 16 de Septiembre and Periférico (☎352 0659).

**Red Cross:** Sandino 716 (☎315 5600 or 5555), in Col. 1 de Mayo. Reachable by taxi (15 pesos). 24hr. ambulance service.

### Villahermosa

**ACCOMMODATIONS**
Hotel del Centro, **3, 15**
Hostel La Chonita II, **2**
Hotel Hacienda Garau, **1**
Hotel Madero, **11**
Hotel Oriente, **6**
Hotel Palma de
  Mallorca, **5**
Hotel del Río, **16**

**FOOD**
Cafe La Cabaña, **10**
Las Choquitas, **17**
Cockteleria Rock
  and Roll, **9**
Paletería y Nevería
  La Michoacana, **18**
Restaurant Bar
  Impala, **7**
Restaurant Madan, **8**
Restaurant Los
  Tulipanes, **14**
Tacolandia, **4**

**ENTERTAINMENT**
Galería El Jaguar
  Despertado, **19**
Galería de Arte
  Siempreviva, **20**

**NIGHTLIFE**
Bfore, **12**
La Bohemia, **13**
Salsa, **21**

TABASCO AND CHIAPAS

**Pharmacy: Farmacias del Ahorro,** Méndez 1405 (☎314 0603, delivery 315 6606). Also in the Zona Luz, on Reforma near Aldama. Both branches open M-Sa 6am-11pm, Su 7am-10pm.

**Medical Services: IMSS,** Carretera Villahermosa km 205 (☎993 315 1845). **ISSSTE,** Av. 27 de Febrero 1803, Colonial Atasta (☎315 0142).

**Fax Office:** Telecomm, Lerdo 601 (☎314 2525), at Sáenz around the corner from the post office. Open M-F 8am-7:30pm, Sa-Su 9am-12:30pm.

**Internet Access:** Several options near Zaragoza and Aldama. **Multiservicios Computacional,** Aldama 621 (☎312 8334). 10 pesos per hr. Open daily 10am-9pm. **G&G,** Zaragoza 405-A (☎131 0915), in Parque Juárez. 10 pesos per hr. Open daily 8am-1am.

**Post Office:** Sáenz 131, at Lerdo. Mexpost inside. Open M-F 8:30am-6pm, Sa 8am-noon. **Postal Code:** 86000.

> **!** **WATCH YOUR BACK.** Be alert when walking around the Zona Luz, the areas around Parque Canabal, the market, and Tabasco 2000 after lights go out. Robberies and assaults on tourists have been known to occur. Don't wear jewelry or watches, carry only a small amount of cash, and walk in groups.

##  ACCOMMODATIONS

Villahermosa hides its few backpacker-friendly gems in a dense thicket of run-down establishments with flaking plaster walls, and luxury hotels that charge upwards of 1000 pesos a night. Mid-priced options abound in the downtown area, especially on Madero, but quality varies widely. If saving money is the absolute most important thing, you can find a few truly cheap places on the southern stretches of Constitución and Suárez. Be aware, however, that you may be sacrificing a considerable amount of comfort. Call ahead for reservations July-August.

**Hotel Oriente,** Madero 425 (☎312 0121), between Tejada and Reforma. The best of the bunch. Clean rooms and spotless baths in various shades of pale green, all with TV. The staff is friendly and fairly knowledgeable about the Zona Luz. Free purified water in the halls. Reception 24hr. Singles with fan 220 pesos, with A/C 310 pesos; doubles 290/380 pesos; triples 360/480 pesos, each additional person 30 pesos. MC/V. ❷

**Hotel Hacienda Garau,** Merino 604 between Alvarez and Fidencia. This brand new hotel 10min. from the Zona Luz is trying way harder than most other accommodations in the *centro*, and it pays off. Beautiful rooms with paintings and flowers come with big comfy beds, fans, and TVs. Singles 200 pesos, doubles 350 pesos. Cash only. ❷

**Hostel La Chonita II,** Reyes 217 (☎131 2053; www.hostelchonita.com), between Sáenz and C. 1. Walk past the ADO station on Mina; turn left on Reyes and walk 2 blocks. Possibly the only backpacker-style hostel operating in all of Villahermosa. Co-ed and separate men's and women's dorms have a clean, homey feel. There's a reasonably large kitchen for cooking, free continental breakfast, and free internet. Dorms 150 pesos. Cash only. ❶

**Hotel del Centro,** Suárez 209 (☎312 5961), between Sánchez and Mármol. Another branch at Madero 411 (☎312 2565). Large, fairly clean rooms with fan and TV, though the mattresses have seen better days. Reception 24hr. Singles 200 pesos, with A/C 350 pesos; doubles 250/350 pesos; triples 300/450 pesos. Cash only. ❷

**Hotel Madero,** Madero 301 (☎312 0516), near 27 de Febrero. Friendly, family-run hotel with a central location. Light sleepers should ask for a room away from the street. All of the large, clean rooms have A/C, phone, and TV. Free filtered water. Singles 300 pesos; doubles 400 pesos; triples 500 pesos. MC/V. ❹

**Hotel Palma de Mallorca,** Madero 510 (☎312 0144 or 312 0145), near Zaragoza and Madero. Distinguished mainly by its bright green and orange lobby, where locals sometimes sit and watch *la tele.* Singles with fan 160 pesos; doubles with A/C 250 pesos. Each additional person 40 pesos. Cash only. ❶

**Hotel del Río,** Suárez 206 at Reforma. The good news: Hotel del Río will give you a place to stay for 100 pesos. The bad news: that place involves wires hanging from the ceiling (although, happily, they're still insulated), a tiny partitioned shower area, and beds that may or may not be level. Reception 24hr. Singles 100 pesos; with TV, 150 pesos; with A/C, 300 pesos. Cash only. ❶

##  FOOD

Villahermosa, like the rest of Tabasco, specializes in *mariscos* (seafood). A typical *tabasqueño* dish (not for the faint of heart) is tortoise sauteed in green sauce and blood and mixed with pickled armadillo. Crab is often served in chirmol sauce, made from ground squash seeds and burnt tortillas. To wash down your meal, try traditional *pozol,* made from ground cornmeal, cocoa, and water. Downtown, the air is filled with the smell of roasting pork *al pastor,* which is cooked on gyro-style spits. The pork is used for tacos that usually go for about 10 pesos apiece. Most restaurants specializing in seafood are either very expensive or in far-off suburbs. The best places for regional seafood are roadside restaurants and *palapas* along tourist routes, like the **Teapa Comalcalco** route. In the Zona Luz, coffee shops line **Benito Juárez.** Stock up on grocery goods at **Mercado Pino Suárez,** at Pino Suárez and Hermanos Zozaya next to the highway, in the northeastern corner of town (open daily 5am-8pm), and a supermarket, **Soriana Súper,** on Madero at Zaragoza next to Parque Juárez (☎314 0041; open daily 7am-10pm).

---

**TIP** **DEATH IN VENISON.** *Venado,* or venison, is a popular dish throughout the Yucatán peninsula, but those with a flair for conservation may want to think twice before digging into *venado* and radish tacos. The wetland deer are a rare species and the hunting process is often destructive to the animals as well as the marshes they live in.

---

**Restaurant Los Tulipanes** (☎312 9217 or 312 9209), in the CICOM complex. A bounty of *comida tabasqueña,* such as *pan de cazón* (a thick tortilla sandwich filled with refried beans and shark meat, covered in red salsa). In this case, high cost means high quality, not extortion. Breakfast buffet 8am-10am, 108 pesos. Seafood entrees 85-140 pesos. Open M-Sa 8am-9pm, Su 8am-6pm. AmEx/MC/V. ❹

**Tacolandia,** on Aldama in the Zona Luz. Casual and extremely popular, Tacolandia turns out an exorbitant amount of tacos daily. During their busier hours, watching the cooks frantically cut pieces off the roasting pork spits makes you feel like you're getting a free show with dinner. Tacos from 9 pesos. Open M-Sa 8am-10pm. Cash only. ❶

**Cafe la Cabaña,** Juárez 303, near 27 de Febrero. Part of a well-known chain of cafes in town, the Zona Luz location draws out all of Villahermosa's gossiping old men. Cappuccinos 24 pesos. Iced coffees 29-32 pesos. Chocolate malts 34 pesos. Coffee beans 110 pesos per kg. Free Wi-Fi. Open M-Sa 7am-10pm, Su 8:30am-9pm. MC/V. ❷

**Restaurant Bar Impala,** Madero 421 (☎312 0493). One of the many restaurant-bars along Madero, Impala has a wall covered with pictures of local beauty queens and a menu full of Mexican standards. Tasty *tamalitos de chipilín* (10 pesos), *panuchos* (fried tortilla shells stuffed with meat and beans; 20 pesos), and tacos (20 pesos). Open M-Sa 10am-9pm. Cash only. ❶

**Las Choquitas,** on Sáenz at Reforma. Jazz plays in the background at this charming little place, which captures a bit of the bohemian flavor from the art galleries down the street. The *menú*, which comes with soup and a main course, is 40 pesos; entrees like *chilaquiles* are 30 pesos. Open daily 9am-5pm. Cash only. ❷

**Paletería y Nevería La Michoacana**, at Lerdo and Juárez. La Michoacana has nearly 20 flavors of ice cream, from chocolate chip to *guanábana*, to help cool you down on a hot day—around here, that's every day. Ice cream 12-20 pesos. Fruit *licuados* 15-30 pesos. Open daily 9am-10pm. Cash only. ❷

**Restaurant Madan**, inside the Best Western Madan. Madan can feed you all day, from *huevos rancheros* (40 pesos) in the morning, to *enchiladas* (43 pesos) or fish fillets (87 pesos) for lunch and dinner. The *menú del día* comes with salad, soup, an entree, and dessert for 50 pesos. Open daily 7am-11pm. MC/V. ❷

**Coctelería Rock and Roll**, Reforma 307, across from Hotel Miraflores. Specializes in large seafood cocktails (80-100 pesos) and old men guzzling Corona, some of whom might have guitars. The party kicks into high gear when the Mexican National Soccer team plays. Beer 15 pesos. Open daily 9am-11pm. Cash only. ❹

## 👁 SIGHTS

For a city unconcerned with tourism, Villahermosa has a surprising number of worthwhile museums and tourist activities—although recently many of them have been closed for renovations. Still, there's plenty to occupy your time; many of the most tempting options are outdoors, offering a respite from the gritty urbanity of the *centro*.

**◼PARQUE-MUSEO LA VENTA.** Located south of Tabasco 2000, La Venta features 33 Olmec sculptures lifted from their original locations in La Venta, Tabasco, and replanted in Villahermosa by poet and tireless anthropologist Carlos Pellicer Cámara. Immediately beyond the entrance, a small museum details the recovery of the Olmec artifacts by Pellicer Cámara as well as the history of the ancient Olmec people. From the museum, a well-marked 1km jungle walk reveals massive Olmec altars and sculptures, leading eventually to a **zoo, with** all manner of local flora and wild animals. Past the museum, the sprawling **Parque Tomás Garrido Canabal** has a large lagoon, landscaped alcoves, and hidden benches and fountains (which lure plenty of hormonal teenagers). Beware: the *mirador* claims to offer a panoramic view of the city, but the 40m climb yields only an aerial view of blooming trees and the lagoon. *(Take a Tabasco 2000, Carrisal, or Palacio bus for 5 pesos to the Tabasco and Ruiz Cortines intersection and walk 1km through Parque Canabal to the entrance. Taxis 20 pesos. ☎314 1652. Ticket office, archaeological area, wildlife area, and museum open daily 8am-5pm, but ticket sales end at 4pm. 35 pesos. Light-and-sound show Tu-Su 8, 9, 10pm. 100 pesos.)*

**MUSEO DE HISTORIA DE TABASCO.** The small museum displays a series of poorly labeled artifacts and pictures on state history, but the building itself is the most interesting exhibit. A wealthy merchant built the former mansion between 1889 and 1915, and decorated each room with a different pattern of Italian and Spanish Baroque tiles—thus the nickname **Casa de los Azulejos** (House of Tiles). Check out the Egyptian tiles along the ledge of the outside walls. Eleven classical sculptures decorate the roof; the seated female figures are said to be the merchant's family members. The museum is also home to an excellent bookstore. *(At Juárez and 27 de Febrero in Zona Luz. ☎993 314 2172. Exhibits in English and Spanish. Open 9am-5pm July-Aug. daily; Sept.-June Tu-F 9am-5pm. 15 pesos.)*

**CENTRO PARA LA INVESTIGACIÓN DE LAS CULTURAS OLMEC Y MAYA (CIMCOM).** The two biggest draws at CIMCOM, the **Museo Regional de Antropología Carlos Pellicer Cámara** and the **Teatro Esperanza Iris,** are both shuttered for long-term renovations as of August 2009. There are still a few art galleries open. *(From Zona Luz, the museum is a 15min. walk south along Río Grijalva. #1 and CICOM buses (5 pesos) pass frequently. Casa de Artes José Gorostiza ☎314 0202. Open daily 9am-5pm.)*

**YUMKÁ.** A far cry from an African safari, Yumká is nonetheless a good way to escape the stifling heat of downtown. Just 16km from the bustle of Villahermosa, animals run freely throughout the 101 hectare park, which reproduces the four *tabasqueño* ecosystems: jungle, savannah, wetlands, and gift shop. Visitors travel about in boats, by foot, and on trolleys, viewing animals in their natural habitats. *(On Las Barrancas, next to the airport. Buses leave from Parque La Venta; Sa-Su at 9, 10:30am, noon, 1:30pm; 15 pesos. ☎356 0115 or 0119; www.yumka.org. Open daily 9am-5pm; ticket sales end at 4pm. 50 pesos, children 25 pesos.)*

# 🔳 SHOPPING

A few upscale clothing stores are sprinkled around the *centro*, but the only real shopping destination is **Tabasco 2000** (☎316 3641), far from downtown on Paseo Tabasco. The district is made up of monolithic postwar buildings and wide, pedestrian-unfriendly streets that make the car-free walkways of the Zona Luz seem like a dream from another city. The long strip of stucco and concrete facades includes the city's Palacio Municipal, a convention center, several fountains, an upscale shopping mall, most of the larger discos, and a planetarium, which has unfortunately been closed for renovations. To get to Tabasco 2000, take a 5-peso bus from Parque Juárez. (Mall shops open daily 10:30am-8:30pm.)

# 🔳 ENTERTAINMENT

Villahermosa attracts artists and academics with its well established network of lectures and workshops. Travelers should check out the **Centro Cultural Villahermosa,** on Madero at Zaragoza, across from Parque Juárez, for *Travesías*, a monthly program of events around the city and at the Centro, including recitals and screenings. The Centro itself also has an art gallery, mostly for local artists. (Open Tu-Su 10am-8pm.) More down-to-earth entertainment can be found at Parque Juárez in the evenings, when clowns, musicians and dancers perform for whoever's walking by. In early summer, Villahermosa throws a city fair; ask for details at the Cultural Center, or visit expotabasco.com.mx.

**Cafe** (☎314 1244), in the back of Galería el Jaguar Despertado, Sáenz 117, near Reforma in the Zona Luz. Features live classical and jazz performances. A weekly program of cultural events is often hung outside the door; performances are usually at 8pm. Small gallery upstairs featuring local artists with works for sale. Open M-Sa 9am-9pm, Su 10am-3pm.

**Galería de Arte Casa Siemprevíva** Lerdo 602 (☎312 0157), at Sáenz. Hosts various events, including free nightly movie screenings during the week. The people here are also happy to talk about other goings-on around town. Open M-Sa 9am-9pm.

# 🔳 NIGHTLIFE

The Zona Hotelera in and around **Tabasco 2000** (p. 187) is home to a number of discos and clubs. Here, Villahermosa's young and wealthy dress up and get down to a mix of salsa and electronica music. **Taxis are the only safe means of night transportation.**

**Bfore,** Paseo Tabasco (☎352 1191; www.bforelounge.com), at Obrero Mundial, 1 block past the intersection of the Paseo and Magaña. This hip, 2-story club attracts a young crowd with its sleek leather couches, artsy black-and-white photos, and bump-

TABASCO AND CHIAPAS

ing DJs. Beer 50 pesos per L. Mixed drinks 40 pesos. Sa themed parties. Cover 30 pesos. Open Th-Sa 9pm-3am. MC/V.

**La Bohemia de Manrique,** C. Vía 2 (☎316 9224), on Paseo Tabasco. Less hip than Bfore, but no less entertaining. Tasty regional food. The live musical acts enjoy engaging a (somewhat off-color) conversation with their audience. Beer 32 pesos. Mixed drinks 40-70 pesos. *Antojitos* 30-75 pesos. Entrees 75-140 pesos. Cover Tu-Th 30 pesos; F-Sa 50 pesos. Open Tu-Sa 8pm-3am.

**Salsa,** on the *malecón* at 27 de Febrero. A big open-air bar on the banks of the river. Live musical acts (mostly, as the name suggests, playing salsa) give way to a DJ playing danceable pop hits, on weekend nights. Beer 30 pesos. Cover 20 pesos. Open daily 9am-3am.

# 🔁 DAYTRIPS FROM VILLAHERMOSA

As the largest city in the mostly rural state of Tabasco, Villahermosa serves as a base for dozens of daytrips into the state's northern coast and wetlands, southwestern jungle, and southeastern mountains.

## 🟦 TAPIJULAPA AND PARQUE NATURAL DE LA VILLA LUZ

*2 buses serve the town, leaving every hr. from Tacotalpa. To get to Tacotalpa, catch a taxi colectivo (1hr., 37 pesos) from the lot behind and to the right of Villahermosa's Chedraui supermarket. 2nd-class buses leave for Tacotalpa (1hr., every hr. from 5:25am, 26 pesos). Colectivos stop on Tacotalpa's main drag. 1 block farther down, in front of the market, red-and-white buses leave for Tapijulapa (40min., every hr. 5am-6pm, 8 pesos); buses also leave from Teapa. The bus will stop at an archway. To reach the plaza, walk downhill through the arch, keeping right. To reach the Tapijulapa lancha dock, from which you can access the Parque, walk 2 blocks parallel to the river; at the end of the street, turn right and head 1 block downhill. Arrange a pick-up time before disembarking. Return buses to Tacotalpa leave from the same archway, 2 blocks north of the plaza (every hr., last bus 7pm). Buses and colectivos returning to Villahermosa from Tacotalpa stop running around 8pm. Wear shoes appropriate for walking in mud and bring bug repellent for the evening. Returning to the lancha dock will take about 25min.; the entire trek takes approximately 2hr. If you get a guide in Tapijulapa, they will expect a tip of at least 20-25 pesos. Getting to the Parque, 3km from Tapijulapa, requires a lancha (round-trip 20 pesos). Small boys will likely chase you on your way to the lancha dock and offer to be your guide; hiring one of them is not really necessary, as the paths are well marked. Climb the stairs and go through the orange gates on the other side of a field, passing a shack on your right.*

In Tapijulapa, 90km south of Villahermosa, the air smells as fresh as the white-washed houses look. High in the mountains by the Amatán and Oxolotán rivers, this small and relatively untouristed town is a nice change from Villahermosa. The **Parque Natural de la Villa Luz** features pearly-blue sulfuric waters that seem to glow from within. Wandering through the *parque*, you'll likely come across the home of former governor Tomás Garrido Canabal (1891-1943), whose name you might recognize from Villahermosa. The house has been declared a museum, and is outfitted with some token artifacts (including an old sewing machine). There are signs pointing to the *cascadas* (waterfalls with pools popular for bathing; 600m to the left), the *albercas* (mineral pools; 900m to the right), and the **Cueva de las Sardinas Ciegas** (Cave of the Blind Sardines; 900m to the right). The cave's odd name comes from the native sardines that, having adapted to their dark environment, are all blind. Every year on Palm Sunday, residents of Tapijulapa gather at the cave for the **Pesca de la Sardina.** While dancing to the music of the *tamborileros*, celebrants toss *barbasco* (powdered narcotic plants) into the water, which stun the fish and cause them to float to the top of the water for easy harvesting.

## THE RUINS OF COMALCALCO

*The ruins are 3km outside the city of Comalcalco, 56km northwest of Villahermosa. Combis to Comalcalco marked "Comalli" leave from a station on Gil y Sáenz between Reyes and Cortines; walk past the ADO station on Mina and turn left on Reyes, then right on Sáenz (every 20 min., 25 pesos). After arriving in Comalcalco, turn right coming out of the station, and take another right at the corner. Walk two blocks until you get to a wide street; cross it, take a left, and continue until you get to the Soriana supermarket. From there you can catch a Paraíso bus; ask to be let off at "las ruinas" (5 pesos). From the access road, walk 1km, or wait for an infrequent minibus (3 pesos). In Comalcalco, the Comalli station is at Reforma and C. N. Bravo. The last combi back to Villahermosa leaves at 9pm. Site open daily 8am-5pm; last entry 4pm. 41 pesos.*

Unpublicized and generally ignored by backpackers, the Mayan ruins of Comalcalco are surprisingly extensive. Be sure to bring a gallon of repellent: the mosquitoes here are unbelievably persistent. Named after the *comal*—a griddle (originally made of clay) for cooking tortillas—the city was built and rose to its height during the Classic Period (100 BC-AD 800). The Tabasco Maya, known as **Chontals**, used baked clay to construct their temples, making Comalcalco the oldest brick city in all the Americas. In the museum, you will see dozens of these bricks, the surfaces of which have carvings of animals, temples, humans, and hieroglyphics.

The main road, left from the museum entrance, will take you into the main plaza. The 10-level, 20m pyramid left of the site entrance is Comalcalco's most famous structure. Under an awning on the building's north face, the relics of the carvings of a giant, winged toad, and several humans are all that remain of decorations that once covered the structure's surface. Past Temples II and III, a path leads uphill to the **Gran Acrópolis,** a 175m long complex of temples and private residences. Look closely at the dilapidated walls and you can see the insides of Comalcalco's brickwork and oyster-shell mortar. Among the ruins is the precarious-looking **Palacio,** with half a vault cantilevering over its ancient rooms, and what is thought to have been a bathtub and cooling system. From the top of the acropolis, imagine how the jungle might have appeared before deforestation and radio towers. On the way down, watch for sculptural remnants preserved in protected corners. Especially interesting reliefs are on the eastern side in the **Tumba de los Nueve Señores;** the figures are believed to represent the nine night gods of the Mayan pantheon.

## RESERVA DE LA BIOSFERA PANTANOS DE CENTLA

*For information on visiting, contact the on-site Centro de Interpretación Uyutot-Ja, on Carr. Frontera-Jonuta km 12.5. It's also the site of an observation tower, restaurant, and lancha pier. ☎ 310 1422 or 313 9290. Open Tu-Su 9am-5pm. SEMARNAT: ☎ 310 1424. Paseo de la Sierra 613. Open M-F 9am-6pm.*

Though Tabasco's ecotourism industry has been slow to take flight, the state's predominant feature (after its oil reserves) is its natural beauty. One of the best places to explore Tabasco's vast wilderness is the Reserva de la Biosfera Patanos de Centla, a preserve encompassing 302,000 hectares of wetlands. Sediments left behind by the converging Usumacinta and Grijalva rivers create an ideal habitat for mangrove and jungle ecosystems. The reservation is home to over 434 plant species and 365 species of vertebrates, including numerous birds, crocodiles, jaguars, manatees, otters, and turtles. Set aside by the government in 1992, the land is also home to 50,000 people, most of whom live in small fishing villages along the river systems deep inside the Reserve. Unfortunately, the broader economic interests of the indigenous people who live here sometimes pit against the Reserve's ecological goals. Small turtles sell for 100 pesos in the open market, and venison goes for more, giving residents incentive

TABASCO AND CHIAPAS

to hunt protected animals. This hunting is a major concern of workers of the Reserve's station at Tres Brazos.

The best way to see the Reserve is on one of the guided tours organized by **SEMARNAT,** the state agency that runs the Reserve. Tours leave from various stations in Pantanos de Centla, take between two and four hours, and start at 500 pesos. You can get more information at Uyutot-Ja, or at the SEMARNAT office in Villahermosa (p. 186). Going at it alone is possible, but much more expensive; it is difficult to gain access to the more protected areas of the Reserve. You can also find private tour companies in Villahermosa, but they tend to be significantly more expensive.

## PARAÍSO ☎933

Only 71km from Villahermosa, Paraíso and its beaches are the only real spot in the state of Tabasco to enjoy the warm Gulf Coast waters. Public beaches lie east and west of the city. **Varadero, El Paraíso, Pal Mar,** and **Paraíso y Mar** are reachable by the **Playa combi** (20min., every 30min., 5 pesos) that leaves from the second-class bus station. You can also take a **taxi** for 50-60 pesos. All about 500m from the road, these beaches have *palapas* where you can hang a hammock for free. Varadero and El Paraíso are by far the nicest but are often closed during the week; both have restaurants and the latter has hotels and a pool. Alternatively, an eastbound **bus** to **Chiltepec** leaves every 30min. from the second-class bus station. The first stop is **Puerto Ceiba** (15min., every 20min., 5 pesos), a small fishing village on the edge of Laguna Mecoacán, a 51,000-hectare oyster breeding ground. Local fishermen give *lancha* tours of the lagoon (300 pesos; 14-person max.). Ask at any of the docks along the way. Across the bridge from Puerto Ceiba is **El Bellote,** another small fishing town located between the lagoon and the Río Seco. El Bellote has several affordable restaurants. Near the end of the bus route, 27km east of El Paraíso, is the town of **Playa Bruja;** just east is the beach itself, with *palapas* and a restaurant.

The city of Paraíso has several hotel options, though the best bargain is to sleep in a hammock at one of the several *palapa* beach *balnearios.* Make sure to check in with management about beach safety before hanging your hammock. For those interested in a bed, **Hotel Sabina Tabasco,** Ocampo 115 on the plaza, has rooms with air-conditioning, cable TV and free Wi-Fi. (☎333 0016. Singles 325 pesos; doubles 400 pesos. Cash only.) **Hotel Hidalgo,** at the corner of Degollado and 2 de Abril, is another solid option with air-conditioning. (☎333 0007. Singles 270 pesos; doubles 310 pesos. Cash only.)

**Combis** run from Villahermosa to **Paraíso** (1hr., every 30min., 50 pesos) from the blue tarp on Av. Arboledas (Castellanos), next to the Chedraui supermarket. Get off at the first stop, before the traffic circle. From there, catch any passing bus to the station (5 pesos). To reach the 2nd-class bus station from the *zócalo,* walk two and a half blocks away from Juárez to Buenos Aires and continue for nine blocks.

## TEAPA ☎932

Surrounded by banana farms, cacao farms, and cattle ranches, Teapa is a pleasant base for exploring the mountainous southern region of Tabasco. 52km south of Villahermosa, the town itself has several 18th-century churches, including the **Franciscan Temple of Santiago Apostol,** two blocks from the fountain next to the central plaza (mass Su 7am and 1pm) and the **Jesuit Temple of Tecomájica.** The real gems, however, are ◪**Las Grutas Coconá,** 2km outside of the city. Discovered in the late 1800s by two adventurous brothers hunting in the woods, a visit to the caves is like a trip to another planet. A concrete path winds 500m into the hillside as eerie, flute music and dramatic lighting enhance the enormous caverns, underground lagoons, and bizarre geological formations. Guides offer their services, pointing out formations that resemble the Virgin Mary, a moose head, and other objects. The explanations are interesting but, as the caves are lit, your time may be better spent exploring on your own. (Any taxi in town can take you to the caves, 10min., 30 pesos. Open daily 9am-5pm. 30 pesos. Guides 40-60 pesos; 10-person max. Rock and rappel tour 100 pesos. Small on-site museum open daily 10am-5pm; free.)

Teapa also draws tourists with its many riverside *balnearios* and sulfurous thermal spas. The popular mud bath is said to cleanse the spirit and the pores. **Hacienda Los Azufres** ⑥, at km 5.5 along the Teapa-Pichucalco Carretera, offers day services (thermal pools 30 pesos, children 15 pesos) as well as a few rooms. (☎327 5806. Singles 300 pesos; suites with small kitchen 450 pesos. Cash only.)

Other sleeping options in Teapa include the tidy but impersonal **Hotel Los Candiles** ⑤, Carlos Ramos 101 (☎322 0431). All rooms have air-conditioning and TV as well as cheery orange decor. Free purified water. (Singles 250 pesos; doubles 350 pesos. Cash only.)

Teapa has several banks along the main drag. **Banamex**, at the corner of Gregorio Mendez and Bastar, has a **24hr. ATM**. (☎322 0284. Open M-F 9am-4pm.) To get to Teapa from Villahermosa, you can take a **2nd-class bus** (1hr., every hour, 45 pesos).

# TUXTLA GUTIÉRREZ                                    ☎961

The quintessential Tuxtla Gutiérrez (pop. 568,000) experience may be sitting in the crowded, noisy *zócalo* and listening as the modern cathedral across the street rings in a new hour. The central city is an intense collection of honking cars, frenzied sidewalk commerce, and an inexplicably large number of shoe stores, though along its perimeter are a few quieter parks and cultural institutions to get a bit of calm. This isn't the Chiapas of postcards, far from civilization and seasoned with jungle cries and ancient temples: this is the place to get acquainted with modern urban Chiapas, in all its dirty, chaotic, irrepressible charm.

## ▐ TRANSPORTATION

**Flights: Aeropuerto Ángel Albino Corzo** (TGZ), km 12.48 Francisco Sarabia. **Aviacsa**, Av. Central Pte. 160 (☎800 AVIACSA, at the airport 153 6042). **Mexicana**, Plaza Veranda, Loc. 7, 8, and 9 (☎602 5769 and 602 5771). Taxis to town 60 pesos.

**Buses:**

**ADO/Cristóbal Colón Station:** 3km from the city center on 5 Nte. Pte. next to the Gigante Bodega supermarket. **Cristóbal Colón** (☎961 612 5122) goes to: **Cancún** (18hr.; 10:55am, 1:10pm; 738 pesos); **Mexico City** (15hr., 5 per day 5:20-11:40pm, 790 pesos); **Oaxaca** (10hr.; 11:30am, 7:25, 11:55pm; 346 pesos); **Palenque** (6hr., 11 per day 6am-11:55pm, 170-218 pesos); **Puebla** (13hr., 5 per day 5:20-11:40pm, 692 pesos); **Puerto Escondido** (11hr.; 8:25, 11:10pm; 370 pesos); **San Cristóbal de las Casas** (2hr., 24 per day 6am-11:55pm, 38 pesos); **Tapachula** (6hr., 13 per day 6am-11:55pm, 256 pesos); **Veracruz** (12hr., 10:40pm, 536 pesos); **Villahermosa** (7hr.; 11:15am, 4pm; 232 pesos).

**Terminal de Transporte Tuxtla:** at Av. 10 Sur and C. 13 Ote. Various companies send buses to **San Cristóbal** (every 15 min., 2am-9pm), as well as other regional cities like **Comitán, Oaxaca,** and **Tapachula.**

**Transportes Chiapa-Tuxtla Station:** (☎611 2656 or 615 5301), at Av. 1 Sur and C. 5 Ote. To reach Chiapa de Corzo, hop on a Transportes Chiapa-Tuxtla **microbús** at the station (25min., every 2min., 9 pesos) or grab one leaving town on Blvr. Corzo.

**Public Transportation:** VW van colectivos run frequently throughout the city. (R1 6am-10pm; other routes 6am-9pm. 4 pesos.)

**Taxis:** Within the city 20-35 pesos. To the bus station 30 pesos.

**Car Rental: Hertz,** Blvr. Domínguez 1195 (☎617 7777). Child seats available. Open M-Sa 8am-10pm, Su 9am-5pm. Airport location (☎153 6074) open daily 7am-6pm.

## ⚡ 🛈 ORIENTATION AND PRACTICAL INFORMATION

Tuxtla lies 85km west of San Cristóbal and 293km south of Villahermosa. *Avenidas* run east-west and *calles* north-south. The city's central axis, intersecting the *zócalo*, is formed by **Avenida Central** (which becomes **Bulevar Ángel Albino Corzo** to the east and **Bulevar Belisario Domínguez** to the west) and **Calle Central**. Streets are numbered according to their distance from the central axis. For example, C. 2 Sur Ote. lies south of Av. Central and two blocks east of C. Central. Addresses on Av. Central are numbered according to how many blocks from the *centro* they lie (Av. Central Pte. No. 554 is about five blocks west of center). Blvr. Domínguez is dotted with American megastores, chains, shopping malls (Plaza Crystal and Plaza Galería), and many of the city's more expensive restaurants.

**Tourist Office:** The most central location is in front of the Palacio Municipal in the **Secretaría de Desarollo Económico booth**. Open M-Sa 9am-4pm. **Dirección Municipal de Turismo,** Av. Central Pte. 554 (☎613 2099 or 7904, ext. 111 or 112). Open M-F 9am-4pm. **State Tourism Office,** Blvr. Domínguez 950, about 15 blocks west of the *zócalo*. The booth on the *zócalo* has maps and brochures. Open M-Sa 9am-2pm.

**Banks:** The area around the *zócalo* and Av. Central has plenty of banks and ATMs. **Bancomer,** on Av. Central at the corner with C. 2a Pte. exchanges currency and has a **24hr. ATM**. Open M-F 8:30am-4pm. **Scotiabank** (☎612 9562), on Av. Central at the corner with C. 4a Ote. Open M-F 9am-4pm.

**Laundry: Lavandería Automatica,** at the corner of Av. 5 Nte. and C. 2 Ote., offers same-day service at reasonable rates. 12 pesos per kg. Open M-F 8am-8pm, Sa 8am-5pm.

**Emergency:** ☎060.

**Police: Protección Civil,** C. 3a Ote N. 414 (☎615 3646). Another office on Av. 3a Sur. **Tourist police:** (☎800 903 9200).

**Red Cross:** Av. 5a Nte. Pte. 1480 (☎612 0096 or 612 0492).

**Pharmacy: Farmacia del Ahorro** (☎602 6677), at Av. Central and C. Central.

**Medical Services: Sanatorio Rojas,** 2 Av. Sur Pte. 1487 (☎602 5138 or 602 5004). **IMSS** (☎612 3678 or 612 3302), on Calzada Emilio Rabasa.

**Fax Office: Telecomm** (☎613 6547), on Av. 1 Nte. at C. 2 Ote., next to the post office. Open M-F 8am-7:30pm, Sa 9am-3pm.

**Internet Access:** Internet cafes cluster on C. Central past Av. 4 Nte. and on Av. Central east of the *zócalo*. **ProbiNet,** Av. Central Ote. 551 (☎714 7745). Fast connection and A/C. 10 pesos per hr. Open daily 8:30am-11pm.

**Post Office:** (☎612 0416), on Av. 1 Nte. at 2 Ote., on the northeast corner of the *zócalo*, in the corridor to the right of the Palacio Municipal. Mexpost inside. Open M-F 8:30am-4pm, Sa 9am-1pm. **Postal Code:** 29000.

## ▐ ACCOMMODATIONS

Tuxtla has so many hotels north and south of the *zócalo* that you almost wonder how they all stay in business, though if you're a stickler for cleanliness you'll need to be picky. Even then, bathing in these places may be a lukewarm experience at best—the hot water is often unreliable.

**Hotel San Carlos,** C. 2a Nte. Ote. 332 (☎612 5323), 2 blocks from the *zócalo* and across from a sweet-smelling flower market. Large, bright, clean rooms with cushy chairs, TVs, and free Wi-Fi make this possibly the best hotel in town. The new building

TABASCO AND CHIAPAS

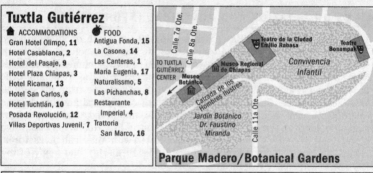

## Tuxtla Gutiérrez

**ACCOMMODATIONS**
Gran Hotel Olimpo, 11
Hotel Casablanca, 2
Hotel del Pasaje, 9
Hotel Plaza Chiapas, 3
Hotel Ricamar, 13
Hotel San Carlos, 6
Hotel Tuchtlán, 10
Posada Revolución, 12
Villas Deportivas Juvenil, 7

**FOOD**
Antigua Fonda, 15
La Casona, 14
Las Canteras, 1
Maria Eugenia, 17
Naturalissmo, 5
Las Pichanchas, 8
Restaurante
Imperial, 4
Trattoria
San Marco, 16

**Parque Madero/Botanical Gardens**

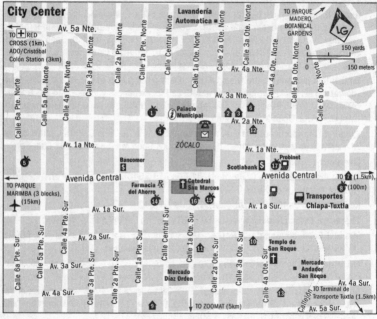

**City Center**

is set back from the street, leaving parking spaces available. Singles 200 pesos, with A/C 280 pesos; doubles 320 pesos. Cash only. ❷

**Hotel Casablanca,** C. 2a Ote. Nte. 334 (☎611 0142 or 611 0305), 1 block from the Palacio Municipal. Definitely one of the better options in town, although if you want amenities like A/C you'll have to shell out a bit more. Clean rooms, gardens, and sitting areas. Rooms are without working outlets and guests may have to request hot water at reception. Free purified water. Reception 24hr. Check-out 1pm. Singles from 154 pesos; doubles from 214 pesos, with A/C and TV 481 pesos; triples 291/467 pesos. Cash only. ❶

**Hotel del Pasaje,** Av. 5 Sur Pte. 140 (☎612 1550), half a block west of C. Central. Enter through a mid-block passageway lined with stores and restaurants. Though a little out of the way, this large hotel has quiet rooms that include private bath, fan,

TABASCO AND CHIAPAS

and purified water. Singles 150 pesos, with A/C 200 pesos; doubles with A/C and TV 260 pesos; triples 290 pesos. V. ❶

**Hotel Plaza Chiapas,** Av. 2a Nte. Ote. 299 (☎613 8365), 1 block east of Palacio Municipal. Clean, basic rooms come with fans and TV. Singles 200 pesos; doubles with fan 230 pesos; triples 320 pesos. Cash only. ❷

**Hotel Tuchtlán,** Av. 2a Sur Ote. 422 (☎611 4461). Wide range of rooms. From no hot water to the works with TV and A/C. Singles with no hot water 140 pesos, with TV and hot water 220 pesos, with TV, A/C, and hot water 330 pesos; doubles 180/280/390 pesos. Cash only. ❶

**Gran Hotel Olimpo,** C. 1 Ote. Sur 381A (☎612 0295). A somewhat overly-grandiose name, but it is indeed one of the largest hotels in Tuxtla Gutiérrez and has its own in-house restaurant. The rooms are small, simple, and clean. Singles 155 pesos; doubles 195 pesos; triples 225 pesos. Cash only. ❶

**Posada Revolución,** Av. 2a Nte. Ote 332 (☎209 1937). Some of the cheapest beds in town are at the end of Posada Revolución's long entrance hallway, lined with maps of Chiapas, Mexico, and the rest of the world. The rooms are basic and not sparkling clean, but for the budget traveler they may be just right. Singles 100 pesos; doubles 160 pesos; triples 240 pesos. Cash only. ❶

**Hotel Ricamar,** Av. 4a Sur Ote 626 (☎612 5873). A more-or-less standard Tuxtla hotel near the bustling shopping district. The chipped tiling contributes to a worn-down atmosphere. Free parking. Singles 190 pesos, 220 with TV; doubles 220/260 pesos; triples 290/315 pesos. Cash only. ❷

**Villas Deportivas Juvenil,** Blvr. Corzo 1800 (☎612 5114), 3km east of the *zócalo*. From any stop on Av. Central, catch an eastbound *combi* and get off at "Índejech" (EEN-deh-hetch). Huge community sports center with dorm-style rooms. Simple and deserted, but clean and cheap. Cafeteria open M-F 7am-9pm. Breakfast 20 pesos. Lunch and dinner 25 pesos each. Dorms 50 pesos. Cash only. ❶

# ▐ FOOD

Tuxtla Gutiérrez is a good place to get to know the region's earthy and delicious cuisine. *Carnes* come prepared in *pepitas de calabaza* (squash seeds) or *hierba santa* (holy herbs). *Tamales* in Tuxtla come with every filling imaginable for only 5-8 pesos. For the adventurous, *nucús* (ants) are plentiful at the start of the rainy season. Tuxtla's bustling **Mercado Díaz Orden,** on C. Central between Av. 3 and 4 Sur, has food and trinket stands. (Open daily 6am-6pm.) **Mercado Andador San Roque,** C. 4 Ote. between Av. 3 and 4 Sur, has the best straw hats in town, oodles of wicker, and several cheap eateries. (Open daily 7am-4pm.) A few more upscale restaurants cluster behind the Cathedral. There is also a supermarket, **Chedraui,** on Blvr. Corzo, on the left just past the military base. To get here, take an eastbound Ruta 1 *combi* from a block west of the *zócalo* on Av. Central.

▨ **Las Pichanchas,** Av. Central Ote. 837 (☎612 5351), between C. 8 and 9 Ote. One of the best for Chiapan food. Waiters ring bells for orders of *pumpo*, the house drink. Marimba music and *ballet folklórico* (9, 10pm) complement the decor. Scrumptious *tamales* (2 for 30 pesos), *cochito* (pieces of pork roasted with a red Chiapan sauce; 100 pesos), and *tascalate* (traditional chocolate drink; 15 pesos). 70-peso minimum after 8pm. Open daily noon-midnight. AmEx/MC/V. ❷

**La Casona,** Av. 1 Sur Pte. 134 (☎612 3976). La Casona is cheaper than the white table cloths and paintings on the walls might suggest, and the food is scrumptious. Breakfasts 32 pesos; regional food and *mariscos* 45-80 pesos. Open daily 7am-11pm. Cash only. ❷

**Antigua Fonda,** C. 2 Ote. Sur 182 (☎612 7663 and 5605). Antigua Fonda's salad bar and free Wi-Fi are enough to set it apart from the crowd of downtown Tuxtla restaurants;

TABASCO AND CHIAPAS

the cherry on top is the friendly and hospitable owner. Breakfasts 30-40 pesos. *Comida corrido* 35-40 pesos. Entrees 40-65 pesos. Open daily 8am-7pm. Cash only. ❷

**Restaurante Imperial,** C. Central Nte. 263 (☎612 0648), 1 block from the *zócalo*. A local favorite with old photos of Tuxtla Gutiérrez on the walls. Excellent breakfasts (24 pesos) and *antojitos* (32-35 pesos). Open M-F 8am-6:20pm. Cash only. ❷

**Naturalissimo,** C. 6 Pte. 124 (☎614 9648), half a block north of Av. Central. The famous health-food chain has by far the widest selection of vegetarian plates in town with meatless tacos (25-35 pesos), delicious *licuados* like the Mango Tango (mango and strawberry; 33 pesos), and vegetarian *comida corrida* (71 pesos). Soy burgers 40 pesos. Delivery available. Open M-Sa 7am-10:30pm, Su 8am-10:30pm. Cash only. ❷

**Trattoria San Marco,** on the plaza behind the Cathedral (☎612 6974). A more upscale option with pleasant outdoor seating. A good option if you want some non-Chiapan food. Crepes 47 pesos. Baked potatoes with cheese and bacon 45 pesos. Pizzas from *chorizo* to Hawaiian (80 pesos). Open M-Sa 8am-10pm. Cash only. ❷

**Las Canteras,** Av. 2a Nte. Pte. 148-A (☎611 4310). Well-known for authentic Chiapan food in a pleasant setting. *Antojitos* 20-45 pesos. Chiapan specialties 55-65 pesos. Open M-Sa 7am-9pm, Su 8am-6pm. Cash only. ❸

**Maria Eugenia** (☎613 3767), at Av. Central Ote. and C. 4 Sur Ote. This Chiapan diner serves regional specialties like *cochito* (82 pesos), plus a variety of Mexican meat dishes (100-120 pesos), and pastas (45-65 pesos). Be careful when you sit down, as the booths are on wheels. Open daily 7am-11pm. Cash only. ❷

# 🔘 SIGHTS

More than 1200 animals live at the **Miguel Álvarez del Toro Zoo (ZOOMAT).** Animals, children, and refreshment stands roam freely. From C. 1 Ote., between Av. 6 and 7 Sur, take the R60 bus (20min., every 30min., 4 pesos). (☎614 4700. Open Tu-Su 8:30-4pm. Foreigners 20 pesos, students 10 pesos. Guided tours in Spanish 20 pesos, in English 40 pesos.)

Many of Tuxtla's attractions are located in **Parque Madero,** in the northeast part of town at C. 6a Ote. and Av. 5 Nte. To reach Parque Madero, walk or take a R3 or R26 *combi* (4 pesos) from Av. 5a Nte. In the middle of the park is **Teatro de la Ciudad Emilio Rabasa.** To the north of the theater is a children's amusement park, **Conviviencia Infantil,** with games, playgrounds, and a mini-train. (Open Tu-Su 9am-7pm.) Down the paved walkway lined with fountains and busts of famous Mexicans is **Museo Regional de Chiapas,** which displays regional archaeological finds along with Olmec and Mayan artifacts. (☎613 4479. Open Tu-Su 9am-6pm. 41 pesos.) To the left is the new **Museo de Paleontología,** which has a small collection of regional fossils and a display of unique Chiapan amber. (☎600 0254. Open Tu-F 10am-5pm, Sa-Su 11am-4pm. 5 pesos.) Down the concourse on the left you'll find the **Jardín Botánico Dr. Faustino Miranda,** a miniature Chiapan jungle. (Open Tu-Su 9am-6pm. Free.) The **Museo Botánico** is right across from the garden.

# SAN CRISTÓBAL DE LAS CASAS ☎967

Most Mexican cities pack their charm into pedestrian walkways lined with museums and cafes, surrounded by diesel-burning trucks with loud horns threatening the cobblestoned peace. San Cristóbal (pop. 142,000), on the other hand, is charming through and through, filled with friendly locals and top-notch dining. Surrounded by a ring of lush green mountains and founded in 1528, the city was named for its mythical patron saint, San Cristóbal, and Bartolomé de las Casas (1484-1566), a crusader for indigenous rights. San

Cristóbal de las Casas sits in the middle of several indigenous villages, on the edge of the politically unstable Lacandón Rainforest. On January 1, 1994, a group of Zapatista insurgents took over parts of the city and surrounding territory. Since 1998, the Zapatistas have become a symbol of rebellion, though they have lost much of their local support. Despite the tensions, San Cristóbal's lovely buildings, Mayan markets, diverse eateries, and happening nightlife make for an inviting city.

>  **INSURRECTION.** On January 1, 1994, over 9000 *indígena* Zapatista insurgents took over parts of San Cristóbal in a 12-day siege. The situation is currently stable; tourists to the city and neighboring villages should not encounter problems as long as they carry their visas and passports at all times. Those who come with political or human rights agendas, however, are unwelcome and could face deportation.

## TRANSPORTATION

**Buses:** 1st- and 2nd-class bus stations are along the Pan-American Highway near Insurgentes. **Cristóbal Colón** (☎678 0291) sends buses to: **Campeche** (6:20pm, 354 pesos); **Cancún** (17hr.; 12:15, 2:30, 4:05pm; 684 pesos); **Comitán** (1hr., 6 per day, 36 pesos); **Mérida** (6:20pm, 506 pesos); **Mexico City** (16hr., 9 per day 4:10-11:30pm, 844 pesos); **Oaxaca** (12hr.; 4:45, 6pm; 385 pesos); **Palenque** (5hr., 7 per day, 132 pesos); **Playa del Carmen** (12:15, 2:30pm; 652 pesos); **Tapachula** (7hr., 7 per day 7:45am-midnight, 222 pesos); **Tuxtla Gutiérrez** (2hr., 18 per day, 22 pesos); **Villahermosa** (11:20am, 11:05pm; 220 pesos). To get downtown, take a right (north) on Insurgentes and walk 7 blocks to the *zócalo*. From the other bus stations, walk east on any cross street and turn left onto Insurgentes. Or, call for a taxi (☎678 9340). 20 pesos to the *centro*.

**Car Rental: Optima Car Rental,** Diego de Mazariegos 39 (☎674 5409), in Mansión del Valle Hotel. Open M-Sa 9am-2pm and 4-7pm, Su 9am-1pm.

**Bike Rental: Los Pingüinos,** Ecuador 4-B (☎678 0202; www.bikemexico.com/pinguinos). Rentals from 131 pesos (US$10) per 4hr., 184 pesos (US$14) per day. Also offers tours (see below). Open M-Sa 10am-2:30pm and 3:30-7pm. Cash only.

## PRACTICAL INFORMATION

**Tourist Office:** (☎678 0665), at the northwestern end of the Palacio Municipal. Helpful maps and tour information. Open daily 8am-8pm.

**Tours:** Tours to the hills or walking tours to indigenous villages are great ways to delve a little deeper into traditional practices and beliefs.

**Los Pingüinos:** Offers a motorcycle tour. Tours pass through the remarkable landscape, including natural limestone bridges and villages with no road access. Leave daily 8:15am, return 1pm, and cover 20-40km on rough dirt paths. From 354 pesos (US$27), 12-person max. Multi-day tours also available. Book 24hr. in advance.

**Alex y Raul** (☎678 3741 or 9141). Offers a popular ½-day tour. 4hr. Departs from the San Cristóbal Cathedral daily 9:30am. 150 pesos.

**Bank: Bancomer,** Plaza 31 de Marzo 10 (☎678 1351), on the south side of the *zócalo*, has a **24hr. ATM.** Open M-F 8:30am-4pm, Sa 10am-2pm.

**English-Language Bookstore: La Pared,** Hidalgo 2 (☎678 6367), ½ a block south of the *zócalo*. Buys and sells new and used books. Open Tu-Sa 10am-2pm and 4-8pm, Su 3pm-7pm.

**Laundromats: Tintoclean Tintorena y Lavandería,** Guadalupe Victoria 20 (☎678 7231), 2 blocks west of the *zócalo*. Full-service: 16 pesos per kg. Open M-Sa 9am-1pm and 4-8pm. **Lavandería Lavamax,** Ejército Nacional 5A. 12 pesos per kg. Open daily 8:30am-2pm and 4-6:30pm.

**Emergency:** ☎066.

**Police:** (☎678 0554), in the Palacio Municipal.

**Red Cross:** Allende 57 (☎678 0772), 3 blocks south of the Pan-American Highway.

**24hr. Pharmacy: Farmacia Esquivar** (☎678 8282), on Mazariegos at Rosas.

**Hospital: Hospital Regional,** Insurgentes 24 (☎678 0770), 4 blocks south of the *zócalo* in Parque Fray Bartolomé.

**Internet Access: Cyber Cafe,** just south of the *zócalo* on Hidalgo. 10 pesos per hr. Open M-Sa 9am-11pm, Su 10am-10pm. **Los Faroles,** Real de Guadalupe 33. 6 pesos per hr. Open daily 9am-10pm.

**Post Office:** Allende 3 (☎678 0765), 2 blocks southwest of the *zócalo*. Mexpost inside. Open M-F 9am-7pm, Sa 9am-1pm. **Postal Code: 29200.**

# ACCOMMODATIONS

An influx of backpackers has created a demand for cheap hotels and hostels. San Cristóbal has responded with a plentiful supply near the *centro*. Camping is available outside town, but temperatures often drop below 10°C (50°F), making heavy blankets or a sleeping bag a must.

**Posada Mexico (HI),** Josefa Ortiz de Domínguez 12 (☎678 0014). A backpacker resort. Spacious gardens with views of the hills, well-appointed common areas, pool table and TV, a huge kitchen, and nightly activities ranging from karaoke to bonfires. Unlimited purified water. Friendly management can arrange any kind of tour. Breakfast included. Laundry 16 pesos per kg. Free internet. Check-out 11am. Hammock 40 pesos; high-season single-sex dorms 100 pesos; singles 220 pesos; doubles 280 pesos. Cash only. ❶

**Backpacker's Hostel,** Real de Mexicanos 16 (☎674 0525; www.backpackershostel. com.mx). All the rooms in this lively hostel face a gorgeous garden courtyard, where the owners host a bonfire every night from 8-10pm. There's also a large kitchen, skylights in the some of the private rooms, and in-house salsa lessons. Laundry 18 pesos per kg. Dorms 99-109 pesos; singles 220 pesos; doubles 280 pesos; triples 350 pesos. 10% discount with HI and ISIC. Cash only. ❶

**Posada la Media Luna,** Hermanos Domínguez 5 (☎631 5590 or 3355; www.hotel-lamedialuna.com.mx), between Hidalgo and Insurgentes. Clean rooms, a beautiful green courtyard, and original artwork in every room. Quieter than other hostels in the area, Media Luna attracts a slightly older crowd. All rooms have Wi-Fi and cable TV. Laundry 15 pesos per kg. Singles 250 pesos; doubles 350 pesos; triples 450 pesos; quads 550 pesos. Cash only. ❸

**Posada Qhia,** Tonala 5 (☎678 0594), near the market in quiet Barrio del Cerrillo. The 2nd-fl. common room has a fireplace, board games, and a guitar, plus unbeatable views of the nearby mountains. Below, cozy rooms surround a lush floral courtyard. Dorms 60 pesos; singles 120 pesos; doubles 130 pesos. Cash only. ❶

**La Casa di Corto Maltese,** Ejército Nacional 12 (☎674 0848). This hostel has a scenic garden, a book collection, and a common room with a guitar for some communal strumming. The Italian owners are exceptionally friendly hosts. Dorms 65 pesos; doubles 200 pesos. Cash only. ❶

**Planet Hostel,** Cintalapa 6 (☎678 5775). A bright, amiable hostel with a steady stream of young travelers entering and exiting daily. Breakfast included. Free internet.

## San Cristóbal de las Casas

### ◆ ACCOMMODATIONS
Backpacker's Hostel, 4
La Casa di Corto Maltese, 5
Casa Tata Intl, 22
Hostel las Palomas, 11
Hotel Posada
Rincón de Cuca, 19
Hotel los Robles, 20
Planet Hostel, 6
Posada la Media Luna, 31
Posada Mexico, 28
Posada Qhia, 1
Rancho San Nicolás, 29
Youth Hostel, 27

### ◆ FOOD
Cafetería del Centro, 16
Cafe Museo, 10
Casa del Pan Papaloti, 15
La Casa del Bagel, 34
Falafel, 36
El Fogón de Jovel, 34
El Gato Gordo, 33
El Manantial Restaurante
Económico, 17
Mayambé, 14
Namandi, 35
El Punto, 2
Restorante Madre Tierra, 32
Ristorante Italiano, 13
Restaurante París México, 18
La Salsa Verde, 9
La Selva Cafe, 30

### ● SERVICES
Farmacia Esquivar, 21
La Pared Bookstore, 25
Pingüinos Bike Rental, 3
Súper Mas, 12
Tintoclean, 15

### ★ NIGHTLIFE
Cafe Bar La Revolución, 7
Cocodrilo, 40
El Domo, 41
Green Pub, 42
Iskra, 39
Latino's, 24
Makia, 26
La Malquerida, 43
La Paloma, 23
La Viña de Bacco, 38
El Zirco, 8

### Map labels
TO TENEJAPA (28km)
TO 29 (1km)
TO TEMPLO DE GUADALUPE (2 blocks)
Isabel la Católica
J.M. Rojas
N. Ruiz
Vicente Guerrero
Na-Bolom
TO MERCADO (2 blocks), MUSEUM OF MAYA MEDICINE (1km), SAN JUAN CHAMULA (8km), ZINACANTÁ
Diagonal Arriaga
D'agonal Arriaga
Iglesia y Ex-convento de Santo Domingo and Centro Cultural de los Altos de Chiapas
Diego Dugelay
Chiapa de Corzo
El Templo del Cerrito
Tonalá
Comitán
Tapachula
Cintelapa
Real de Guadalupe
Francisco Madero
Dr. José Flores
Pantaleon Domínguez
Ramón Corona
María Adelina Flores
Diego Dugelay
Ejto. Nacional
Paniagua
Dr. Navarro
Colón
El Puente
Los Faroles
Francisco León
Julio M. Corzo
Josefa de Domínguez
Domínguez
Escuadrón 201
Artisan's Market
General Utrilla
Lavandería Lavamax
Benito Juárez
Mercado de Dulces y Artesanías
Dr. Moreno
TO CRISTÓBAL COLÓN BUS STATION (50m), GRUTAS DE SAN CRISTÓBAL (9km), COMITÁN (88km)
Iglesia de San Francisco
Insurgentes
Hospital Regional
Catedral
Banamex
ZÓCALO
Palacio Municipal
Teatro Zebadúa
20 de Noviembre
16 de Septiembre
San Jolobil
Miguel Hidalgo
Templo y Arco del Carmen
Miguel Hidalgo
Centro Cultural el Carmen
Crescencio Rosas
Niños Héroes
Hermanos Domínguez
Cyber Cafe
Museo de Ambar
La Palma
5 de Mayo
12 de Octubre
Real de Mexicanos
Venezuela
Ecuador
1 de Marzo
5 de Febrero
Guadalupe Victoria
Diego de Mazariegos
Cuauhtémoc
Ignacio Allende
Álvaro Obregón
San Cristóbal (Mirador)
Cerro de San Cristóbal
TO (15km), TUXTLA GUTIÉRREZ (85km), CHIAPA DE CORZO (80km)
Autotransportes Tuxtla Gutiérrez Station
Transportes Lacandonia and Avisa Station
TUXTLA GUTIÉRREZ (85km), CHIAPA DE CORZO (80km)
Blvd. Juan Sabines Gutiérrez
Moreno

300 yards
300 meters

TABASCO AND CHIAPAS

Dorms 60 pesos per person; private rooms with bath 90 pesos per person, without bath 80 pesos. Cash only. ❶

**Casa Tata Inti (HI),** Dugelay 4 (☎678 0367). Casa Tanta is laid back—the receptionist is literally sprawled out on the couch in the common room watching The Simpsons. The rooms are clean and cozy, and there's an ample kitchen for all your cooking needs. Dorms 40 pesos; private rooms 50 pesos per person. Cash only. ❶

**Hotel Posada Rincón de Cuca,** Ejército Nacional 2A (☎678 4227). The place to go if you want a bit more private space without paying a fortune. Rooms have plush beds, TV, and skylights. Free Wi-Fi. Singles 250 pesos; doubles 375 pesos. Prices rise about 100 pesos in high season. Cash only. ❸

**Youth Hostel,** Juárez 2 (☎678 7655), between Madero and Flores. The name says it all. Cheap, clean, slightly dark rooms, spotless communal baths, kitchen, and common area with TV. Dorms 60-65 pesos; doubles 140 pesos. Cash only. ❶

**Hostel las Palomas,** Guadalupe Victoria 47 (☎674 7034). Las Palomas' common space feels like a friend's living room, with a few cushy sofas and a TV. If there's nothing on (and you don't feel like a movie), have fun looking around at the dozens of butterflies mounted on the wall, collected by one of the owners. The staff is friendly and more than happy to give advice about what to see around town. Free internet and purified water. Dorms 120 pesos; doubles 250 pesos. Cash only. ❶

**Hotel los Robles,** Madero 30 (☎678 0054), 2 blocks from the *zócalo*. Whitewashed walls with soft wooden window frames set this hotel apart; the rooms come with a private bath and TV. Singles 200 pesos; doubles 250 pesos; triples 300 pesos; quads 350 pesos. Discounts may be available for larger groups. Cash only. ❷

**Rancho San Nicolás,** Calz. Ranulfo Tovilla 47 (☎674 5887 or 678 0057), 1km east of town. Take a taxi (15 pesos) or follow León out of town, bear right at the split, and continue until the road reaches a dead end; the ranch is through the gate on your right. A beautiful, quiet spot on the edge of town. Kitchen, common room with fireplace, electricity, and hot water. If no one is around, ring the bell at the *hacienda* across the road. Camping 40 pesos; rooms with shared bath 70 pesos per person. ❶

## ▣ FOOD

San Cristóbal's dazzling array of Mexican and international restaurants is reason enough to prolong your stay. Though there are some high-end eateries, most establishments keep their prices relatively low to attract young backpackers. San Cristóbal also has one of the largest **markets** in Mexico, at Utrilla and Domínguez, seven blocks north of the *zócalo* (open daily 6am-4pm), and a supermarket, **Súper Mas,** on Real de Guadalupe two blocks east of the *zócalo* (☎678 0001; open daily 8am-9:30pm).

**▣ Restaurante Madre Tierra,** Insurgentes 19 (☎678 4297), opposite Iglesia de San Francisco, 2 blocks south of the *zócalo*. All-natural homemade food served in a courtyard or candlelit dining room. Exceptional bakery and bar upstairs. Breakfast 37-49 pesos. Entrees like *spinach cannelloni* and *chiles rellenos* 50-75 pesos. Open daily 8am-10pm. Bar open daily 10:30pm-3am. Cash only. ❷

**▣ El Punto,** Comitán 13 (☎678 7979), on El Cerrillo Plaza. Scrumptious thin-crust Italian pizza with toppings from mozzarella to curry (65-110 pesos). With only 4 tables, it fills up after 8:30pm. Takeout available. Open daily 2-11pm. Cash only. ❸

**Mayambé,** 5 de Mayo 10 (☎674 6278), at 5 de Febrero. You may be suspicious of a restaurant that offers Thai, Indian, and Middle Eastern food, but somehow this place manages to pull it off—though apparently proper Pad Thai noodles are impossible to get in Chiapas. In any case, the prospect of a falafel sandwich with a mango lassi may be too much to resist.

There is also a small collection of books for sale. Thai green curry 52 pesos. Tandoori chicken 75 pesos. Falafel pita 45 pesos. Open W-M 9:30am-11pm. Cash only. ❸

**El Gato Gordo,** Real de Guadalupe 20 (☎678 8313). Fresh, delicious food ideal for budget-friendly face-stuffing. Tacos 27 pesos. Enchiladas 36 pesos. Occasional musical performances at night. Open M and W-Su 1-11pm. Cash only. ❶

**El Fogón de Jovel** (☎678 1153), at 16 de Septiembre and 5 de Febrero. Upscale *chiapaneco* food in a brightly-decorated and covered courtyard, plus live marimba music in the evenings. Delicious *queso fundido* with mushrooms 80 pesos. *Carnes* 130 pesos. Open daily 12:30-11pm. Cash only. ❹

**Ristorante Italiano,** Real de Guadalupe 40C (☎678 4946). A wide and delicious variety of pastas and Italian sauces to choose from, including homemade *tagliatelle* (75-85 pesos). Brick-oven pizza 40-110 pesos. Open Tu-Su 2-11pm. MC/V. ❷

**Namandí,** Mazariegos 16C (☎678 8054). Some of the best breakfast meals in town, including waffles with bacon (37 pesos) or crepes with kiwis and chocolate sauce (45 pesos). Pasta and burgers for later in the day (43-68 pesos). Open daily 8am-10:30pm. MC/V. ❷

**Casa del Pan Papalotl,** Real de Guadalupe 55 (☎678 3723; www.casadelpan.com), inside El Puente language school, 2 blocks from the *zócalo*. This cheerful restaurant gets organic produce direct from local farmers. A back room has cafe-style cushioned chairs and low tables for hanging out. Salads 35-51 pesos. *Chiles rellenos* 65 pesos. Veggie burgers 36-44 pesos. Breakfasts 39 pesos. The lunch buffet (1-5pm; 82 pesos) is often serenaded by roving troubadours. Wi-Fi available. Kitchen open 8am-11pm. 10% student discount with ID. Cash only. ❷

**Falafel,** on Flores just west of Café Museo Café. Listen to Israeli music while you savor every last bit of a big pita sandwich stuffed with hummus, lettuce, tomato, and, of course, falafel (30 pesos). A good place to meet San Cristóbal's significant community of Israeli travelers. Open M-F 1-9pm, Sa-Su 1-7pm. ❶

**La Salsa Verde,** 20 de Noviembre (☎678 7280), 1 block north of the *zócalo*. Large Mexican diner stays busy into the night. Tacos *al pastor* 5 for 35 pesos. Steak and chicken dishes 60-75 pesos. Open daily 8am-midnight. Cash only. ❷

**Restaurante París México,** Madero 20, 1 block east of the *zócalo*. Breakfasts, including crepes with *huevos rancheros*, 17-43 pesos. Later on in the day, you have a choice of five *menús: económico* (30 pesos), *vegetariano* (45 pesos), *mexicano* (50 pesos), *francés* (55 pesos), or francomex (60 pesos). Points for originality. Terrace on 2nd fl. provides great views of the surrounding mountains. Open daily 8am-midnight. Cash only. ❷

**Cafetería del Centro,** Real de Guadalupe 7 and 15B (☎678 3922), near the *zócalo*. Simple Mexican food with great service in a no-frills atmosphere. Breakfast 33-45 pesos. *Comida corrida* 45-70 pesos. Free Wi-Fi. Open daily 7am-10pm. Cash only. ❷

**El Manantial Restaurante Económico,** Francisco Madero 14, ½ a block from the zócalo. Popular hole-in-the-wall restaurant with large portions. The *menú del día* (28 pesos) ranges from *pollo al mole* to *chiles rellenos* to ribs in *salsa verde*. Always includes soup, starch, and entree. Open daily 8am-7pm. Cash only. ❶

**Café Museo Café,** María Flores 10 (☎678 7876), between Utrilla and Domínguez. The name isn't a typo—it translates to "Coffee Museum Café," which is exactly what it is. After you're done with the exhibits, try the *café chiapaneco*, which includes espresso and honey. There's pie and flan too. Organic coffee 12-25 pesos. Live music every night 8pm. Open M-F 7am-10pm, Sa-Su 8am-8pm. Cash only. ❶

**La Selva Cafe,** Rosas 9 (☎678 7243; www.laselvacafe.com.mx), at Cuauhtémoc. A cozy cafe. Watch the rain run down the cobblestone street outside, or in good weather, bask in the sun in the courtyard. Organic coffee and tea 16-32 pesos. Coffee beans 27 pesos per ¼kg. Free Wi-Fi. Open daily 8:30am-11pm. Cash only. ❶

TABASCO AND CHIAPAS

**La Casa del Bagel,** Real de Guadalupe 44A (☎631 6197). Yes, it's true: bagels have reached Chiapas, and surprisingly decent ones at that. Bagel and cream cheese 17 pesos. Bagel pizzas 28 pesos. Bagel sandwiches 45 pesos. Smoothies 20 pesos. Free Wi-Fi. Open daily 7am-11pm. ❷

## 👁 🄼 SIGHTS AND OUTDOOR ACTIVITIES

🄼**NA-BOLOM.** San Cristóbal's most famous attraction is the "House of the Jaguar," a private home that turns into a live-action museum during the day. Guided tours explore the estate of Frans and Trudy Blum, whose name was misinterpreted as *bolom* (jaguar). The Blums worked among the *indígena* communities of the Lacandón Rainforest on the Guatemalan border from 1943 until Trudy's death in 1993. Today, international volunteers continue the Blums' work by conducting tours of their *hacienda* and library. The library's manuscripts focus on Mayan culture, rainforest ecology, and the plight of indigenous refugees. The small chapel (originally intended to be a Catholic seminary) serves as a gallery of religious art. Other rooms are devoted to archaeological finds from the nearby site of **Moxviquil** (mosh-VEE-queel), religious artifacts from the Lacandón Rainforest, and a selection of the 50,000 pictures Trudy took of the jungle and its inhabitants. Na-Bolom also rents rooms furnished by Frans and decorated by Trudy, complete with fireplace, mini-library, antique bath, and original black-and-white photos. *(Guerrero 33, in the northeastern section of the city at the end of Chiapa de Corzo. ☎678 1418; www.nabolom.org. Guided tours in Spanish 11:30am, in English and Spanish 4:30pm. Shop open daily 10am-6pm. Library open M-F 9am-4pm. Breakfast in the old dining room daily at 7:30am; lunch at 1pm; dinner at 7pm; 110 pesos. Reservations are a good idea. Rooms from 500 pesos for 2 people. Museum 35 pesos. Buy your ticket in the garden across the street from the entrance.)*

**MUSEUM OF MAYA MEDICINE.** Also called the Centro de Desarrollo de la Medicina Maya (CEDEMM), this museum features life-size models recreating Mayan healing methods, including strong-smelling herbs, hypnotic shaman prayers, and a display that explains the use of black spiders' teeth to treat inflammation of the testicles. A Spanish-language video at the end documents Mayan midwifery and birthing rituals. *I'lol*, or medicine men, are on hand to dispense advice. *(Blanco 10, 1km north of the market. ☎678 5438. Open M-F 10am-6pm, Sa-Su 10am-4pm. 20 pesos.)*

**ZÓCALO.** Since its construction by Spanish settlers in the 16th century, San Cristóbal's *zócalo* has existed as the geographical and spiritual center of town. The **Palacio Municipal** stands on the west side of the plaza while the yellow **Catedral de San Cristóbal** dominates the northern side. Inside, the cathedral features a splendid wooden pulpit. *(Plaza 31 de Marzo. Cathedral open daily 7am-7pm.)*

**MUSEO DEL AMBAR.** The exhibits in this old monastery are small, but definitely worth a look: they include hundreds of pieces of amber, from unpolished nuggets to sculptures of eagles, children, and dinosaurs. An exhibit downstairs shows you how to identify fake amber, an important skill in the markets of San Cristóbal. *(Plaza de la Merced, in the Ex-Convento de la Merced, at Cuauhtémoc and 12 de Octubre. ☎678 9716; www.museodelambar.com.mx. Open Tu-Sa 10am-2pm and 4-7pm, Su 9am-2pm. 20 pesos.)*

**IGLESIA Y EX-CONVENTO DE SANTO DOMINGO.** The most beautiful church in San Cristóbal, Santo Domingo was built by the Dominicans from 1547 to 1560; it was enlarged to its present size in the 17th century. The elaborate—if poorly maintained—stone facade houses an inner sanctuary covered in gold leaf and dozens of portraits, most of which were painted anonymously in the 18th century. *(Open M-Sa 7am-7pm. Mass Su 7:30, 11am, 1, 7:30pm.)* Inside, the **Centro Cultural de los Altos de Chiapas** features an excellent multimedia exhibit in Spanish on the history of San Cristóbal and Chiapas, with colonial artifacts, photos, and *chiapaneco* textiles. *(Open Tu-Su 9am-6pm. 37 pesos.)* The Ex-Convento's grounds make up the **artisan market.** *(On Utrilla, beyond the Iglesia de la Caridad.)*

**VISTA.** Two hilltop churches overlook San Cristóbal. **El Templo del Cerrito San Cristóbal,** on the west side of town, is accessible by a set of stairs at the intersection of Allende and Domínguez. **El Templo de Guadalupe,** to the east, can be reached by walking west on Real de Guadalupe. Both areas can become deserted at night; El Templo de Guadalupe is closed at night.

**HORSEBACK RIDING.** One of San Cristóbal's most prized recreational activities is horseback riding. Guided rides to San Juan Chamula leave from Cafetería del Centro. *(Real de Guadalupe 7; ☎100 9611; 4hr.; daily 9am, 1pm; 100 pesos.)* Rancho San Nicolás (p. 204) rents horses.

## 🎵 ENTERTAINMENT

**Kinoki,** 1 de Marzo 22 (☎678 0495), at the corner of 5 de Mayo, is both a traditional movie theater and your very own living room away from home. For 30 pesos each, you and up to four friends can rent a small theater and watch any one of the over 1000 movies available. Movie showings daily at 4pm and every hr. 6-9pm. **Cinema el Puente,** Real de Guadalupe 55 (☎678 3723), three blocks from the *zócalo* inside Centro Cultural el Puente, screens American and Mexican films and documentaries (25 pesos; 6 and 8pm daily). During high season, the **park** hosts dances and live marimba music (Th 6pm-midnight). There are also live, intimately scaled concerts just outside the **Palacio Municipal** on the weekends in the early evening.

## 🌿 FESTIVALS

The best way to find out what's happening around town is to pick up a copy of **Arroz,** a free biweekly zine that has an impressively comprehensive list of musical acts, theater, and more. You can find *Arroz* at most hostels. A schedule of events is also posted at the Centro Cultural el Carmen, three blocks south of the *zócalo* on Hidalgo, on the left side of the Arco del Carmen.

**Film Festival,** annually July 28-Aug. 9. In the Sala de Bellas Artes Alberto Domínguez. 20 pesos.

**Feria de la Primavera y de la Paz,** on Easter Sunday. *Semana Santa* gives way to this week-long *feria.* Before riotous revelry begins, a local beauty queen is selected to preside over the festivities, which include concerts, dances, bullfights, cockfights, and baseball games.

**Fiesta de San Cristóbal,** annually July 16-25. The city's saint is vigorously celebrated—particularly by the city's taxi drivers, who claim San Cristóbal as their patron saint—with religious ceremonies, feasts, processions, concerts, and a staggering number of fireworks. In one of the more interesting traditions of the *fiesta,* a procession of cars, trucks, and *combis* from all over Chiapas crawl up the road to Cerro San Cristóbal. At the top, drivers pop their hoods and open their doors so that the engine and controls can be blessed with holy water by a Catholic priest on behalf of San Cristóbal, patron saint of journeys, in hopes of avoiding accidents for another year on the perilous mountain roads.

## 🛍 SHOPPING

San Cristóbal does triple duty as a commercial center for its own residents, its copious number of visitors, and the indigenous peoples of the surrounding Chiapan highlands. As a result, you can get anything from live chickens, to handmade hammocks, to exquisite amber jewelry in its markets and shops. The daily **market** on Utrilla, two blocks past Iglesia y Ex-Convento de Santo Domingo, overflows with fruit, vegetables, and assorted cheap goods. For souvenirs and jewelry, head to the **market** that surrounds Santa Domingo itself (open daily 8am-5pm) or the **Mercado de Artesanías y Dulces** (open daily 8am-7pm), on Insurgentes across from Madre Tierra. Utrilla and Real de Guadalupe, the two streets radiating from the northeastern corner of the *zócalo*, are dotted with colorful shops that sell amber and traditional attire. Tucked into the Ex-Convento is the **San Jolobil,** a cooperative "House of Weaving" made up of 800 weavers from Tzotzil and Tzeltal villages in the *chiapaneco* highlands. Their objective is to preserve and revitalize ancestral weaving techniques. Most top-quality *huipiles* cost more than your flight home, but San Jolobil is a good place to admire them. (☎678 2646. Open M-Sa 9am-2pm and 4-6pm. AmEx/MC/V.)

## NIGHTLIFE

### BARS

▣ **Cafe Bar La Revolución,** on 20 de Noviembre, 2 blocks from the *zócalo*. Che's red star marks this hopping spot that offers politically themed decor and live music. Beer 25 pesos. Mixed drinks 39 pesos. Live music daily 7:30-9:30pm. Open daily noon-midnight.

▣ **La Viña de Bacco,** Real de Guadalupe 7. If you've never tried Mexican wine before, this is the place to do it. The space is small, but the tightly-packed customers have a contagious good humor that makes you feel like you're at a dinner party with 25 new best friends. Squeeze in, get a cup, and join the party! Wine by the cup 18-40 pesos. Tapas 15-30 pesos. Open M-Sa 2pm-midnight; high season open daily.

**Iskra,** Real de Guadalupe 53. Iskra is less packed than some other popular bars in the *centro*, and the friendly people make you want to stay a while. If you've got a late-night food craving, paninis are served until closing (38-65 pesos). Live music. Regular beer 20 pesos; specialty beers 45 pesos. Open M-Sa 4pm-12:30am.

**Cocodrilo,** 31 de Marzo (☎678 1140), on the Plaza Central. Lively but low-key, Cocodrilo is the perfect place for a few drinks while listening to live acoustic guitar. Look out for the giant wooden crocodile. Beer 25 pesos. Mixed drinks 45 pesos. Salsa F and Sa. Open daily 8am-midnight.

**Green Pub,** Rosas 4 (☎678 6666). Ostensibly an Irish bar, Green Pub called itself green, put a leprechaun on the ceiling, and called it a day. The patrons have the right spirit, though. This place gets packed early with 20-something *Cristobaleños* drinking, finding new friends, and happily talking over the live music. Beer 15 pesos. Open Tu-Sa 5pm-3am.

**La Paloma,** Hidalgo 3 (☎678 1547). The place for a sophisticated night out next to art from the in-house gallery. Regulars say not to miss the food, which runs from burgers (38 pesos) to homemade ravioli (60 pesos). Beer 15 pesos. Mixed drinks 40 pesos. Live music M-Tu and Th-Su 9:30-10:30pm. Open daily 9am-11pm.

**Latino's,** Madero 23 (☎678 9927; latinosclub.com), at Juárez. Have a 25-peso beer and some 25-peso guacamole and enjoy the live music after 10:30pm. Ask about salsa lessons during the day. Cover Th-F 25 pesos, Sa 30 pesos. Open M-Sa 8pm-3am. MC/V.

TABASCO AND CHIAPAS

## CLUBS

▨ **Madre Tierra.** When the rest of the town goes home to sleep, the adventurous head to Madre Tierra. Live music (M-Sa after midnight) is as eclectic as the clientele. Beer 25 pesos. Open M-Sa 10pm-3am.

**El Domo,** Rosas 2 (☎631 6933). Though there isn't much of a dance floor, the young Mexicans who come here are happy dancing to salsa or *rock en español* between the tables. Food includes nachos and sushi. Beer 20 pesos. Mixed drinks 45 pesos. Open Th-Sa 7pm-3am, Tu-Su 7pm-3am in the high season.

**La Malquerida Taberna & Tapas,** at 1 de Marzo and 20 de Noviembre. Downstairs, people stand wall-to-wall and dance to the pulsing music; upstairs, you might have a chance to sit down. Beer 30-40 pesos. Mixed drinks 45-50 pesos. Open Tu-Sa 7pm-4am.

**El Zirko,** on 20 de Noviembre 7, 1 block from the *zócalo*. A spirited crowd dances to a variety of music, from live salsa to 80s classics. Cover Th-Sa 35 pesos. Open M-Sa 8pm-3am.

**Makia,** Hidalgo 2 (☎678 2574), on the park. Recently renovated, Makia attracts a young crowd to its 2nd fl., where you can have a few drinks around a high table or get down to an eclectic mix of music. Beer 30 pesos. Mixed drinks 40 pesos. Cover F-Sa 50 pesos. Open Th-Sa 9pm-3am.

## ▶ DAYTRIPS FROM SAN CRISTÓBAL DE LAS CASAS

A host of indigenous villages lie within easy reach of San Cristóbal. Sunday morning is the best time to visit the markets of nearby villages. All buses originate in San Cristóbal, so visiting more than one village in a single morning is difficult, though possible in the case of San Juan Chamula and Zinacantán, especially if you're willing to take a 50 peso taxi ride between them. *Combis* leave from various stands in the vicinity of the market. Destination signs are rarely accurate; always ask drivers where they're going.

### ▨ SAN JUAN CHAMULA

*Combis (15min., every 15min. 5am-6pm, 10 pesos) to Chamula leave 2 blocks north of the market just off Utrilla.*

The town of San Juan Chamula ("the place of adobe houses" in Tzotzil; pop. 9000) is the largest and most touristed village near San Cristóbal. Home to 110 *parajes* (clusters of 15-20 families), San Juan Chamula is known for its colors (black and blue), its *Carnaval*, and its unique indigenous-Catholic church. Chamulans expelled their last Catholic priest in 1867; they are legendary for their resistance to the government's religious and secular authority—the last Catholic mass here was held in 1968. The bishop is allowed into the church only once a month to perform baptisms, and the government's medical clinic is used only after Mayan medicinal methods have failed. Villagers have great faith in the powers of local *ilol*, priests who function as medicine men. Before entering the lively church, which also functions as a hospital, you must obtain a permit (20 pesos) from the tourist office in the city hall in the *zócalo*. As you enter the courtyard in front of the building, be prepared for some aggressive sales practices from girls selling small bracelets and weavings. At the front of the church is a sculpture of St. John the Baptist, who, after the sun, is the second most powerful figure in Chamulan religion. Jesus Christ, who is believed never to have risen, resides in a coffin. Chamulans take their religion seriously, and any unfaithful residents who change religions (to increasingly popular Evangelical varieties, for example) are promptly expelled from the village. Over 38,000 people have been expelled since 1976.

**NO SOUL THEFT, PLEASE.** The local Maya practice a unique fusion of Catholicism and native religion. In this system of faith, it is commonly believed that cameras capture a piece of the spirit. While visiting these villages, do not take pictures in churches while devotees are present. Always ask before taking pictures of individuals; some may request a few pesos in return for a photo.

Multiple shrines in the residence of the current *mayordomo* (superintendent) honor each saint. Look for the leaf arches outside signaling the house's holy function. Generally, the best time to visit is on Sundays, when the mayor and town authorities line up in their white suits and red- and green-ribboned straw hats to listen to villagers' complaints and make rulings. The men in white wool vests who crowd around the mayor are the town's citizen policemen. Homes and chapels are generally not open to the public—join an organized tour for a peek into private Chamulan life.

It's during **Carnaval,** the week before Ash Wednesday, that Chamula is transformed into a once-in-a-lifetime experience. The town hosts about 70,000 *indígenas* and 500 tourists every day during the festival. In addition to *Carnaval*, the city celebrates the *fiestas* of San **Juan Bautista** (June 22-24), **San Sebastián**(Jan. 19-21), **San Mateo** (Sept. 21-22), and the **Virgen de Fátima** (Aug. 28).

 **DRINK AWAY YOUR SINS.** When Coca-Cola first introduced its flagship beverage to the residents of San Juan Chamula, the drink's bubbly aftereffect was said to release a person's sins from the body. The beverage continues to be a staple in Chamulan religious practices.

## SAN LORENZO ZINACANTÁN

*Combis to Zinacantán (20min., 6am-8pm, 12 pesos) leave from the lot on Edgar Robledo, across from the market.*

Eight kilometers over the hill from Chamula lies the colorful community of Zinacantán (pop. 38,000). Zinacatán is composed of a ceremonial center and outlying hamlets. As you enter, you'll probably notice a bunch of long, off-white buildings—these are greenhouses, where flowers are cultivated for international exportation. Removed from the religious tensions of Chamula, the Zinacantecas hold mass on a regular basis. The village's handsome, whitewashed church dates from the 16th century and, along with the small white convent, is used for both Catholic and pre-Hispanic forms of worship. (Admission 15 pesos. Obtain a permit from the *caseta de turismo* in the *zócalo*.) As in Chamula, Jesus Christ is portrayed inside a coffin. Animal sculptures in the interior of the church attest to the pervasive presence of *indígena* religion, in which every family has its own animal soul. Perhaps the most impressive sight in Zinacantán, though, is around the shoulders of nearly every woman and girl in the village: traditional shawls in deep blues and violets, adorned with beautiful stitched flowers. Men wear their own version of the shawl, often in redder hues. Festivals include **Fiesta de San Lorenzo** (Aug. 1-19, peaking on Aug. 10) and **Fiesta de San Sebastián** (Jan. 19-22).

## HUÍTEPEC ECOLOGICAL RESERVE

*The Reserve lies just off the road to Chamula, 3½km from San Cristóbal, and can be reached by any combi headed in that direction. Ask the driver to let you off at the Reserva Huítepec (10min., every 15min., 7 pesos). To return to San Cristóbal, go 500m downhill*

TABASCO AND CHIAPAS

*to a combi stop. Reserve open Tu-Su 9am-3pm. 20 pesos. Birdwatching tour 100 pesos. Plant-specific tours 50 pesos.*

The Huítepec Ecological Reserve, on the east face of the Huítepec Volcano, provides a chance to explore an evergreen cloud-forest ecosystem. Two trails wind around the park, which is home to over 100 species of birds and more than 300 species of plants. Plants with medicinal properties or religious importance are marked by small signs. The short trail is an invigorating 2km hike that rises 240m. The longer 8km hike is led by a guide. For more information on the park and the tours offered, call or visit **ProNatura** (☎678 5000), Pedro Moreno 1 at Benito Juárez, across from the Iglesia de San Francisco.

## ROMERILLO AND TENEJAPA

*Combis and taxis to Romerillo and Tenejapa (45min., 4 person min., 25 pesos) leave 2 blocks north and 2 blocks east of the market, around the corner from the combis to Zinacantán.*

Marked by 32 blue-and-green wooden crosses, the **Cementerio de Romerillo**, on the way to Tenejapa (pop. 5000), sits atop the Chiapan highlands. This local cemetery comes alive during **Día de los Muertos** (Nov. 2). The planks on each mound of dirt are pieces of a relative's bed or door, and old shoes are scattered around for the spirits' use. The town of **Tenejapa**, 28km from San Cristóbal, is surrounded by mountains, canyons, and corn fields. Crosses representing the tree of life stand at crossroads, near adobe homes, and in front of La Iglesia de San Ildefonso. Women's *huipiles* (traditional Mayan textiles) are replete with traditional symbols, such as the sun, earth, frogs, flowers, and butterflies. Men wear black ponchos tied at the waist with a belt, red-and-white trousers, dark boots, and a purse worn diagonally across the chest. Religious and community leaders carry a staff of power and wear a long rosary necklace. Tenejapa's **markets** (open Th and Su mornings), the **Fiesta de San Alonzo** (Jan. 21), and the **Fiesta de Santiago** (July 25) attract crowds from near and far.

## GRUTAS DE SAN CRISTÓBAL

*Combis (10 pesos) to the Grutas leave from Blvr. Sabines Gutiérrez No. 6, ½ a block to the right of the Cristóbal Colón station. Camionetas leave from the same spot (every 5-10min., 7 pesos). To return, hop on any westbound combi or camioneta. From the highway, the entrance is a 5min. walk through the park. Open daily 8am-4:30pm. 10 pesos. Vehicle entrance 10 pesos.*

The *grutas* and the surrounding park are an excellent way to unwind after a few days in the excitement of San Cristóbal. From the small entrance at the base of a steep, wooded hillside, a narrow fissure opens into a chain of caves that leads almost 3km into the heart of the rock. A modern concrete walkway, up to 10m above the cave floor at points, penetrates 750m into the caverns. The dimly lit caves harbor a spectacular array of stalactites, stalagmites, columns, rushing streams, and formations said to resemble certain figures; look out for *Santa Claus*. After you're done with the *grutas*, you may be tempted to hang around in the park itself, which is shady, cool, and sweetly scented by a dense forest of pine trees. Horses are available for rent across from the cave entrance (1 ride around the corral 15 pesos; 30min. rental 45 pesos, 1hr. 70 pesos). There are a few *roticerías* near the entrance to the cave, but if you're planning on spending an afternoon, a picnic is probably the way to go. Numerous free barbecue pits for fires and outdoor cooking are also located here, but overnight camping is not permitted.

**TABASCO AND CHIAPAS**

# PALENQUE ☎916

Honduras has Copán, Guatemala has Tikal; Mexico has Palenque. World-renowned for their expression of beauty, power, and glory of the Mayan Classic Period, the sites that comprise Palenque are some of the most famous in all of Mesoamerica. These impressive ruins straddle a magnificent 300m high natural *palenque* (palisade) in the foothills of the Chiapan highlands. Dense jungle meets the bases of Palenque's pyramids. The sounds of birds, monkeys, and crashing waterfalls echo off the rolling hills. The town of Palenque (pop. 85,500) is not nearly as picturesque as the ruins, but it serves as an important crossroads for the thousands of travelers who come to visit the site. So, come sample the waters of the famous cascadas of Agua Azul and Misol-Ha, make forays into the heart of the Lacandón jungle, and set off on excursions to Mayan sites in Guatemala—the opportunities in and around Palenque are endless.

## TRANSPORTATION

The ADO bus station and several local transportation hubs are all 5-8 blocks west of the park on Juárez. To get to the park from the ADO stations, turn right out of the station and follow Juárez to the left for six blocks.

**Buses: ADO** (☎345 1344) runs first-class buses to: **Campeche** (6hr.; 8am, 9, 10pm; 242 pesos); **Cancún** (12hr., 8pm, 562 pesos); **Chetumal** (7hr., 8pm, 322 pesos); **Mexico City** (12hr.; 6:30, 9pm; 756 pesos); **Oaxaca** (13hr., 5:30pm, 550 pesos); **Playa del Carmen** (11hr., 8pm, 514 pesos); **Puebla** (10hr., 7pm, 660 pesos); **Villahermosa** (2hr., 8 per day 7am-9pm, 102 pesos). One block east on Juárez, **Autobuses Express Azul** sends buses to **Ocosingo** (50 pesos), **San Cristóbal** (80 pesos) and **Tuxtla Gutiérrez** (115 pesos) six times daily from 7:45am-11pm. *Combis* around the corner leave for **Ocosingo** (50 pesos), **Misol Ha** (20 pesos) and **Agua Azul** (35 pesos).

**Taxis:** (☎345 0112) are 50 pesos to the **ruins, El Panchán,** and **Mayabell,** and 20 pesos within town. **White van combis** troll the main drag near the bus station and run between the town and the ruins for 10 pesos.

## ORIENTATION AND PRACTICAL INFORMATION

Palenque is in the northeastern corner of Chiapas, 274km from Tuxtla Gutiérrez. **Avenidas** run east-west, perpendicular to the north-south **calles**. The ruins are 8km southwest of the city.

**Tourist Office:** In a booth in the *zócalo*. Well-stocked with tourist maps and guides. Open M-F 8am-9pm.

**Tours:** Palenque is the best spot to organize a tour into the dense and ruin-rich Lacandón jungle area. Though the area is accessible on your own, it is one of the final strongholds of Zapatista rebels, making travel a risky undertaking. Several tour operators make daytrips into the area to visit the famous Bonampak and Yaxchilan ruins, most of which include a boat ride along the Guatemala/Mexico border. Before signing on, make sure to clarify if meals, entrance fees, and road fees are included. **Viajes Misol-Ha,** Juárez 148 (☎345 2271), has several packages to the *cascadas* (100 pesos) and 12hr. trips to Yaxhilan and Bonampak from 550 pesos. **Servicios Turísticos de Palenque,** Av. Juárez and 5 de Mayo (☎916 345 1340), offers similar packages (*cascadas* from 170 pesos; ruins from 600 pesos) as well as a van service to **San Cristóbal** (8hr.; 300 pesos) with stops at three *cascadas*.

**Banks: Banamex,** Juárez 62 (☎345 0117). Open M-Sa 9am-4pm. **Bancomer,** Juárez 40 (☎916 345 0198). Currency exchange available. Open M-F 8:30am-4pm, Sa 9am-3pm. Both have **24hr. ATMs.**

TABASCO AND CHIAPAS

**Luggage Storage:** At the **ADO** and many 2nd-class stations. 5 pesos per hr. Open 24hr.

**Emergency:** ☎066.

**Police:** (☎345 1844), on Independencia in the Palacio Municipal.

**Pharmacy: Farmacia Central**(☎345 0393), on Juárez near Independencia. Open daily 7:30am-10:30pm.

**Medical Services: Centro de Salud y Hospital General** (☎345 1433), on Juárez near the ADO bus station, at the west end of town.

**Fax Office: Buho's** (☎345 0195), near the tourist office on Juárez. Open daily 8am-9pm. Several other fax services cluster near the tourist office on Juárez.

**Internet Access: Ciber Espacio,** on Hidalgo just south of the zócalo. 10 pesos per hr. Open daily 7:30am-10pm.

**Post Office:** (☎345 0148), on Independencia at Bravo, north of the park. Open M-F 8am-8pm, Sa 8am-2pm. **Postal Code:** 29960.

# ACCOMMODATIONS

Accommodations in Palenque come in two styles: *cabañas* set deep within the jungle near the ruins and standard hotel rooms in town. Those near the ruins are rustic and lack many services, but are cheaper and more fun. In town, budget hotels cluster on **20 de Noviembre** between Juárez and the park. Prices may double during the high season (July-Aug.), *Semana Santa*, and winter.

▨ **El Panchán** (www.elpanchan.com), 2km from the entrance of the ruins. A sprawling complex of *cabañas,* restaurants, and *palapas* set way off the road in the jungle, El Panchán sometimes seems like a village of backpackers in and of itself. Getting around inside the compound involves tackling paths that wind around lush vegetation and over trickling streams. The other side of the El Panchán's rustic charm, though, are the accommodations lacking mosquito nets and occasionally electricity. Several options are under the same ownership.

   **Chato's Cabañas and Jaguar,** offers *cabañas* and rooms with private bath. Singles 140 pesos; doubles 180 pesos; triples 230 pesos. ❶

   **Jungle Palace,** with camping (30 pesos), and *cabañas* with shared (80 pesos) and private baths (180 pesos). ❶

   **Rakshita's,** on a path that continues on to an improbably-located bookstore. Has *cabañas* (150-230 pesos), dorms (50 pesos per person), and space for camping (25 pesos per person). Cash only. ❶

   **Margarita and Ed's** (☎348 4205) is a slightly more upscale option. More isolated from the activity at the heart of El Panchán. Well-appointed rooms (260 pesos) and cabañas with private bath (200 pesos). Cash only. ❷

▨ **Canek Youth Hostel,** 20 de Noviembre 43 (☎345 0150). New owners have turned this once-drab hostel into the friendliest place in town. After an exhausting day at the ruins, you'll be welcomed back with cheap home-cooked food and the owners' smiling children. The rooms, whose numbers are painted in surprisingly easy-to-learn Mayan glyphs above each doorway, are comfy and spacious. The upper floors have beautiful views of the surrounding mountains. Free Wi-Fi. Check-out 10am. Dorms 80 pesos; singles with cable 100 pesos, with A/C 200 pesos; doubles with cable 150 pesos, with A/C 250 pesos. Cash only. ❶

**Posada Zeltal** (☎345 0284), on Allende one block west of Juárez. On a leafy street just off the Palenque's main drag, Posada Zeltal has a inviting common area/lobby with sofas and flowers. All rooms have fans and are immaculately clean. Singles 100 pesos; doubles 200 pesos; additional person 50 pesos. Cash only. ❷

**Elementos Naturales Youth Hostel** (☎348 4655), 1½km from the entrance to the ruins. Elementos Naturales has a variety of sleeping options scattered throughout its piece of the jungle. Continental breakfast included; for a small fee you can also get boxed

TABASCO AND CHIAPAS

During my stay in Palenque, I learned that one of the three major waterfalls within a day's reach of the city had been taken over by the Zapatistas, who were catching tourist unaware, charging them exorbitant amounts of money to enter. This was my first time being so close to rebel-controlled territory, modest though it is. When traveling through the region, I was disarmed by the signs lining the road, painted crudely with black and white slogans reading: "You are in Zapatista rebel territory. Here the people rule and the government obeys." By and large, this statement is false; to the extent that it does ring true, it is only because Mexico's federal government has never really bothered to meddle in the local politics of impoverished Chiapas.

That said, most people spoke well of the Zapatistas here and credited them with various public works projects. People talked about "Marcos"—subcomandante Marcos, the Zapatista leader—as if he were an old friend with whom they had fallen out of touch. The few complainers pointed to excessive numbers of topes (the asphalt bumps laid by locals to force drivers to slow down) on the highway.

—Daniel Hertz

lunches for your excursion to the ruins. *Palapas* with hammocks 70 pesos; dorms 120 pesos; *cabañas* 300 pesos, with private bath 400 pesos. Prices can rise 20% or more in the high season. Cash only. ❶

**Camping Michol** (☎103 6799), 1km from the ruins. A more informal, homey option with wandering chickens and a gorgeous view of the mountains. *Palapas* 20 pesos per person if you bring your own hammock; hammock rental 30 pesos. Camping spaces 20 pesos per person; *cabañas* with shared bath 100 pesos, with private bath 250 pesos. Cash only. ❶

**Posada Shalom** (☎345 0944), on Abasolo, 2 blocks downhill from Juárez. Big, sparkling-clean rooms come with free Wi-Fi. Singles 200 pesos, with A/C 300 pesos; doubles 350/450 pesos. Cash only. ❷

**Posada Charito,** 20 de Noviembre 15 (☎345 0121), between Independencia and Abasolo, half a block west of the park. Budget hotel with large, clean rooms in bright colors. Somewhat clean, private baths without hot water. Reception 24hr. Check-out 2pm. Rooms 100 pesos for one person; each additional person 50 pesos. Prices vary by season. Cash only. ❶

## ◧ FOOD

Restaurants in Palenque are generally quite similar, with the telltale overpriced tourist menu. For produce, head to the **market,** on Juárez, seven blocks northeast of the *zócalo* (open daily 6am-3pm). **Súper Sánchez** is also near the town's center on Juárez right after the split with 5 de Mayo. (Open M-Sa 7am-9pm, Su 7am-2pm.) When lodging somewhere near the ruins, stock up beforehand to avoid tourist price hikes on food.

**Cafe Don Mucho's,** part of El Panchán (p. 213). The best dining option in the El Panchán complex, Don Mucho's will fill you up after you've worn yourself out climbing the pyramids at the ruins. Huge, vegetarian-friendly entrees (45-80 pesos) include bread and salad. All pasta, bread, and pizza are made on-site and bottled beers (17 pesos) are always cold. Nightly live music and firedancing (9pm-midnight). Next-door internet cafe (15 pesos per hr.; open 10am-10pm). Open daily 7:15am-midnight. Kitchen closes at 11pm. Cash only. ❷

**Restaurante las Tinajas,** 20 de Noviembre 41 (☎916 345 4970), at Abasolo. Serves heaping platters to crowds of locals and tourists alike. Try the hearty *sopes* (fried corn pancakes topped with various meats; 40-45 pesos), or the *picada de frijoles,* its vegetarian sibling. Steaks and seafood 75-100 pesos. Open daily 7am-11pm. Cash only. ❷

**Restaurante Maya** (☎916 345 0042), on Independencia at Hidalgo. Known as the "most ancient restaurant in Palenque," Restaurant Maya is only 2050 years younger than the ruins. Crisp white tablecloths and prompt waiters complement big portioned classic Mexican dishes. Breakfasts 45 pesos. *Antojitos* 40-65 pesos. Meat entrees 60-100 pesos. Open daily 7am-11pm. MC/V. ❸

**Mara's Cafe-Bar Restaurante,** at Juárez and Independencia. Popular for its prime location and good food. Chicken tacos 42 pesos. *Chilaquiles* 48 pesos. Open daily 7am-11:30pm. Cash only. ❸

# 👁 SIGHTS

## ARCHAELOGICAL SITE OF PALENQUE

*The ruins of Palenque, 8km west of town, are accessible by combis (6am-6pm, 10 pesos) that depart from Hidalgo at Allende and from 5 de Mayo at Allende. One entrance is 300m from the site's museum; the second is 2km farther. Walking to the ruins from Mayabell or El Panchan is a gradual 2km uphill walk, but there is a good sidewalk and the area is safe. Do not take the shortcuts to the back entrance from the campgrounds or the road, as they can be dangerous. Site open daily 8am-4:30pm; museum open Tu-Su 9am-4:30pm. The path from the main site to the museum, which passes the waterfalls, closes at 4pm. Bookstore and snack bar near museum open daily 9am-5pm. Park entrance 22 pesos. Ruins 51 pesos. Guided tours available at main entrance. Tours in English, French, or Italian up to 8 people 1114 pesos (US$85), 9-14 people 1442 pesos (US$110); tours in Spanish up to 7 people 600 pesos, 8-14 people 700 pesos.*

Palenque is such an overwhelmingly massive site that it's hard to know where to start. You will spend all day admiring the sculptures and navigating the corridors of the Palace, climbing pyramids for spectacular views of the ruins and the tree canopy, and hiking jungle trails to see dozens of buildings tucked between moss-covered trees and waterfalls. Even if you could wander farther, you would have neither enough time nor enough energy. Still, with all this, 75% of the city is closed to tourists. The city rewards visitors who take it in slowly. Take time to stop and savor both the detailed likenesses of gods and kings, and the natural green beauty of the surrounding hillsides.

The ancient city of Palenque began as a small farming village in 100 BC, and grew steadily throughout the pre-Classic Period. Around AD 600, the city began to flourish, reaching its zenith over the next 200 years. An extensive trade network brought luxury goods such as obsidian, cinnabar, jadeite, and shells to the city. Palenque owes much of its success—ancient and modern—to the club-footed King Pacal ("Sun Shield" or "White Macaw" in Mayan), who inherited the throne from his mother, Zac-Kuk, in AD 615, at the age of 12. Pacal lived into his fifth katun (20-year period) and was succeeded in AD 683 by his elderly son Chan-Bahlum ("Jaguar-Serpent"). It was during the rule of these kings that most construction at Palenque took place. A century after Chan-Bahlum's death in AD 702, Palenque fell into oblivion. Many believe the fall was due to a siege at the hands of the rival Totonacs or another Mayan city. The museum suggests the intriguing possibility that Palenque was abandoned intentionally, because elders felt its time had passed. The city was deserted around AD 850-900. When Cortés arrived in the 16th century, he marched right through without noting its existence. Today, the ruins of Palenque merely hint at the city's former majesty.

**TEMPLO DE LAS INSCRIPCIONES.** Right off the main entrance lies the tomb of Alberto Ruz, one of Mexico's most famous archaeologists and the discoverer of the temple, who insisted on being buried here. Past that tomb lies the Temple of the Inscriptions; its 69 steps represent King Pacal's 69 years of reign. The

TABASCO AND CHIAPAS

temple is named for its tablets, which tell of the dynastic history of Palenque. This is the tomb of King Pacal and the first substantial burial place unearthed in the Americas. After finding six skeletons, Ruz dug into the interior crypt, removing over 400 tons of rubble by hand. There, he discovered the king's perfectly preserved sarcophagus, brimming with jade and other precious jewelry. The lower center of one of the temple's tablets is Pacal, descending into the underworld with the ceiba tree directly over him. A hollow duct, designed to allow Pacal's spirit to exit the underworld and communicate with Palenque's priests, is on the right after the staircase. The temple is no longer open to the public and may not be climbed.

**TEMPLO DE LA CALAVERA AND TEMPLO DE LA REINA ROJA.** Excavations of the **Temple of the Skull (XII)** and the **Temple of the Red Queen (XIII),** constructed around the eighth century on top of older royal tombs, have unearthed burial chambers with human bone fragments and precious stones. The Temple of the Skull is so named due to a frightening stucco mask of a rabbit's skull on one of its north-facing pillars. Excavation of a sarcophagus in the Temple of the Red Queen revealed large amounts of *cinnabar* (a red mineral), *jadeite*, and *malachite*, and an interesting shell with a carved female figure. The discovery of a tiara and other jewelry suggests the importance of the figure, though her identity is unknown.

**EL PALACIO.** In the center, across from the Temple of the Inscriptions, is the trapezoidal, postcard-perfect palace complex—a labyrinth of rooms, patios, and Palenque's signature four-story **tower.** The palace was most likely used for administrative and residential purposes, with royalty occupying the spacious quarters on the north side, and maids and guards in the cramped quarters on the south side. The large northeastern **Slaves' Courtyard** was probably used for administrative and political activities. The tower, unusual for the Maya, may have been used for astronomical observation. T-shaped ducts throughout cooled the air and doubled as representations of Ik, the god of breezes. The smaller galleries have carved panels and stucco masks. Visitors can climb down the staircase from the top of the platform to explore the dimly lit network of underground passageways, where it is likely that gubernatorial enthronement ceremonies took place. Don't miss the royal toilets, in the sunken courtyard below the tower. The four large rocks with small half-circle cutouts remain marked by years of royal pee.

**PLAZA DEL SOL.** The path between the palace and the Temple of Inscriptions crosses the recently reconstructed aqueduct before leading to Plaza of the Sun, or Crosses Group, which is usually crowded with tourists seeking good views. The Plaza, reconstructed and enhanced during the reign of Chan-Bahlum, is made up of the **Templo del Sol** (Temple of the Sun), the **Templo de la Cruz** (Temple of the Cross), the **Temple of the Foliated Cross,** and the smaller **Temples XIV and XV.** The Temple of the Cross was named for a stucco relief of a cross discovered inside, which portrays a ceiba tree, the center of the Mayan universe. The outer layer of stucco has worn away; the inner sanctum protects a large, sculpted tablet illustrating the enthronement of Chan-Bahlum, pictured to the right of the ceiba tree cross, and reliefs on either side of the doors. The relief to the right represents God L, the lord of the underworld. This image of God L furiously smoking a long ceremonial pipe is one of the most recognized reliefs in all of Mayan history. Still partially buried, the Temple of the Foliated Cross lies across the Plaza from the Temple of the Sun. A carved interior panel also shows Chan-Bahlum being crowned, this time to the left of the Mayan foliated cross, which represents the corn plant. To the south of the Plaza, through the wall of trees, several unreconstructed temples

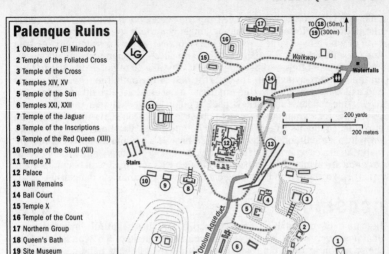

**Palenque Ruins**

1 Observatory (El Mirador)
2 Temple of the Foliated Cross
3 Temple of the Cross
4 Temples XIV, XV
5 Temple of the Sun
6 Temples XXI, XXII
7 Temple of the Jaguar
8 Temple of the Inscriptions
9 Temple of the Red Queen (XIII)
10 Temple of the Skull (XII)
11 Temple XI
12 Palace
13 Wall Remains
14 Ball Court
15 Temple X
16 Temple of the Count
17 Northern Group
18 Queen's Bath
19 Site Museum

surround the uncleared **Plaza Maudslay,** including Temples XVII, XX, XXI, and XXII. Downhill from Temple XIV, past the palace, lie the vestiges of a **ball court,** which was once equipped with wooden rings.

**GRUPO NORTE.** Across the path from the ball court is the **Templo del Conde** (Temple of the Count), named after the archaeologist Jean-Frédéric Waldeck (1766-1875), who referred to himself as a count and lived at the base of the Temple of the Cross. The temple contains three tombs and an inner sanctuary. The four other temples next to the Temple of the Count comprise the North Group. They were likely used for ceremonial purposes at first, but then gradually gave way to domestic residence. A small, steep path to the right of the North Group leads to the Queen's Bath and Montiepa.

**QUEEN'S BATH AND MONTIEPA.** All along the perimeter of the main area, you'll see paths leading to smaller sets of ruins in the jungle; you shouldn't leave without having hiked at least one of them. One of the best is off the main trail past the North Group and the ball court, over a small bridge. After crossing Otulum creek, the first small waterfall you see is the Queen's Bath, named for its once exclusively female swimmers. From there, you'll wind your way through the jungle, passing another dramatic waterfall and several small ruins—**Grupos I and II,** and the **Grupo Murciélagos** (Group of Bats), which were once residential areas. The path eventually exits the site, dropping you off by the museum; save it for last, since the return trip is an uphill trek.

# ▓ DAYTRIPS FROM PALENQUE

## ▨ CASCADAS DE AGUA AZUL AND MISOL-HA

*Tours leave from most hostels and hotels in town around 9am—you'll be picked up in a combi. 100-150 pesos gets you transportation and sometimes entrance fees (ask at the agency first). Brisas de Agua Azul buses, on Av. Corregidora just off Juárez, 1 block east of the ADO station, will take you to the sites: Agua Azul (64km, 1hr., 35 pesos plus 20-peso entrance fee. Colectivo from crucero to entrance 4km, 10 pesos); Misol-Ha (21km, 20min., 20 pesos plus 15-peso entrance fee. From crucero to entrance 1km).*

Palenque is a prohibitive distance from the ocean, but it does the beach scene one better by offering two stunning jungle waterfalls less than an hour away, both of which have large pools of cool turquoise water for swimming. At **Agua Azul (Blue Water)**, the Yax-Há river slips and slides through a seemingly never-ending series of falls, rapids and pools; it can take 40 minutes or more to hike up the accompanying trail. Towards the end of the path, the *tchotchke* stands and makeshift restaurants thin out. Here, local children dive off rocks into the river while chickens and turkeys peck at fallen mangos. Though there are many pools safe for swimming, be sure to observe the posted signs about dangerous currents. Unlike its largely horizontal counterpart, **Misol-Ha** is one big vertical drop into a small jungle clearing. At its base is a swimming hole. Behind the waterfall is a cave; bring a flashlight if you want to explore. Camping space and *cabañas* are available at both sites. After a hard rain, Agua Azul becomes *agua café* (brown water), and camping can be uncomfortable and dangerous.

# OCOSINGO ☎919

High up in the mountains, Ocosingo (pop. 35,000) has beautiful views at the end of almost every street. The city was a major stronghold of the Zapatistas during the rebellion in 1994; the roads outside the city still have hand-painted signs proclaiming autonomy. In practice, however, the sovereignty of the Mexican government isn't much challenged. Besides enjoying the crisp air and mountain views, there's not much to do in the city itself—most tourists come to see the ruins at Toniná, just 14km away.

**█ TRANSPORTATION.** If you're going to **San Cristóbal**, several **combi** cooperatives make the 2½hr. journey for 50 pesos; as soon as you show up with a backpack, they'll practically drag you into their vehicles. *Combis* to **Toniná** leave from the market (10 pesos; last combi leaves the ruins at 6pm). Another coop at the Carretera between Avenidas 2 Nte. and 3 Nte. goes to **Palenque** until 8pm (3½hr., 50 pesos). Coming from the *zócalo*, take a right when you get to the Carretera and walk two and a half blocks. Just about a block further is the **OCC station** (☎919 673 0431), which takes you to **San Cristóbal** (2½hr., 8 per day 1:40am-5:10pm, 42 pesos); **Palenque** (3hr., 8 per day 1:15am-8:40pm, 82 pesos); **Tuxtla Gutiérrez** (3½hr., 8 per day 1:40am-5:10pm, 112 pesos); **Villahermosa** (5hr.; 1:15am, 1:40pm; 178 pesos); **Campeche** (8hr., 8:40pm, 328 pesos); **Cancún** (16hr.; 2:35, 4:50, 6:25pm; 630 pesos); and **Mérida** (12 hr.; 2:35, 4:50, 6:25pm; 440 pesos). Taxis can be easily found throughout the city, with stands at the *zócalo* and the market.

**█ ORIENTATION AND PRACTICAL INFORMATION.** Ocosingo is 88m east of San Cristóbal and 103km south of Palenque. *Avenidas* run east-west, increasing in number in both directions from **Avenida Central**, which borders the north side of the *zócalo*. The street north of Av. Central is **Avenida 1 Norte,** the street south of Av. Central is **Avenida 1 Sur,** and so on. *Calles* run north-south and increase in the same way from **Calle Central,** which bisects the *zócalo*. Various transportation options exist on **Carretera Poniente** near Av. Central, five blocks uphill from the *zócalo*.

Other services include: **police,** in the Palacio Municipal (☎673 0507; open 24hr.); **tourist office,** on Av. Central just west of the *zócalo* (open M-F 9am-3pm, 6pm-8pm); **Banamex,** just to the right of the Palacio Municipal, with **24hr. ATM** (☎673 0034; open M-F 9am-4pm); **Red Cross** (☎673 2000); **Farmacia Económica** at Av. 1 Sur and C. 1 Sur (open daily 7am-10pm); **internet access** at **Ciber Cafe** on Av. Central, a block uphill from the *zócalo* (5 pesos per hr.; open M-Sa

TABASCO AND CHIAPAS

9am-10:30pm, Su 10am-8pm); and the **post office** at C. 2 Ote. and Av. Central (open M-F 8am-4:30pm, Sa 8am-noon).

**⌂ ACCOMMODATIONS.** Ocosingo has an impressive variety of relatively inexpensive hotels immediately around the *zócalo*. The best is **Hospedaje Esmeralda ❶**, C. Central Nte. 14, in an old mansion covered with ivy. The homey rooms are complemented by an in-house restaurant, book exchange, and tours to ruins across Chiapas. One of them, a small-plane ride over the mountains and Lacondón jungle to see Yaxchilán promises an unforgettable experience—if you're willing to part with 7000 pesos; you can split the cost with as many as four people. (☎673 0014. Singles 140 pesos, with two people 230 pesos; triples 280 pesos for two people, 350 for three, 420 for four. Cash only.) **Hotel Toniná ❷**, on Av. Central between C. 2 Nte. and 3 Nte., has pink walls, with big, clean rooms and cable. (☎673 1860. Singles 200 pesos; doubles 250 pesos. Cash only.) **Hotel San José ❶**, at C. 1 Ote. 9, is one of the cheaper places in town, but has small rooms that seem to amplify noise from the street. Tall trees grow in the narrow open-air corridor. (☎673 0518. Rooms with A/C and cable available. Reception 24hr. Singles 100-160 pesos; doubles 160-300 pesos. Cash only.) **Hospedaje La Palma ❶**, at Av. 1 Nte. 303, between C. 2 Nte. and 3 Nte., has a lovely courtyard filled with sun and flowers that contrasts with the rooms' bare concrete floors. (Singles 70 pesos; doubles 120 pesos. All come with shared bath. Cash only.)

**⎘ FOOD.** Ocosingo mostly serves traditional Mexican food in a variety of *taquerías* and *cafeterías* near the *zócalo*, but it also has more than its fair share of pizza joints. You can get vegetables, including freshly grilled corn on the cob, at the **market** on C. 5 Ote. and Av. 3 Sur; other groceries are available at **El Mayoreo,**opposite the market (open daily 7am-8pm). **Restaurante Esmeralda ❷**, inside the hotel at C. Central Nte. 14, has breakfasts from eggs and toast to *chilaquiles* (35-40 pesos), and *platos fuertes* like steak and spaghetti for later in the day (60-80 pesos). (☎673 0014. Open daily 7:30am-10pm. Cash only.) **La Troje ❷**, on Av. 1 Sur on the *zócalo*, is one of Ocosingo's several *pizzerías*, serving medium pies with toppings both familiarly American and Mexican for 110 pesos. (☎673 1147. Standard breakfasts 50 pesos; meat entrees 45-75 pesos. Open daily 7am-11pm. Cash only.) **Tizón Mexicano ❶**, on Av. Central a block and a half uphill from the *zócalo*, is a spacious *taquería* with an afternoon two-for-one deal on *al pastor* tacos (6 pesos). Larger plates of meats and cheeses 45 pesos. (☎108 1782. Open daily 1pm-11pm.)

**⊞ DAYTRIP FROM OCOSINGO: TONINÁ.** The ruins of Toniná, 20min. from the city, are a bit like a big, vertical, 1100-year-old playground. During the Late Classic period, the city was a major regional power. Toniná recorded the latest known date before the collapse of the Maya civilization, AD 909. What remains is a modest plaza with a few scattered buildings, and the **Acrópolis,** with 260 steps rising steeply up the side of a hill. The Acrópolis is the heart of the ruins; exploring it is one of the most fun ways you can pass an afternoon in Chiapas. On the right side of the first terrace, a doorway leads to an extensive series of windowless corridors in the **Palacio del Inframundo.** Fortunately for travelers who don't *quite* want to get the full Mayan underworld experience, a minimal amount of lighting illuminates the floor. From there, you can follow a series of signs with yellow painted feet toward the top. You'll be rewarded if you stray from the path: each terrace of the Acrópolis holds several buildings, many with labyrinthine rooms and hidden stairways that reach up to the next level. Toward the top, you'll come across a huge stucco codex that depicts the four

Maya cosmological eras and dedicates the entire Acrópolis to the god of the underworld. As you climb, the stairs become narrower and steeper; it takes a bit of nerve to scramble up the last set to the very top, which has fantastic views of the pastoral countryside. For those who would rather not take this trek, a (somewhat) less precarious dirt path leads upwards on the right side of the structure. In addition to the site itself, there is a small but impressive **museum** (free with your ticket to the ruins) at the entrance with a model of the city as it may have appeared during its heyday. You can also see several glyphs and calendars found in the area. There is a set of skulls, which you can examine for the various ways they were intentionally deformed, per Mayan custom. *(14 km from Ocosingo. Combis run from the market until 6pm. Site open daily 8am-4:30pm; museum open T-Su 8am-4:45pm. 41 pesos.)*

## BONAMPAK

*148km south of Palenque (off Mex. 307). Combis to Frontera Corozal will pass the turnoff, from which you can catch another combi or taxi for the last 12km. The whole trip, one way, can take upwards of 2hr. and costs about 100 pesos. To see the ruins as part of a tour, usually including a visit to Yaxchilán, you'll need to pay about 550 pesos. Open daily 8am-4:45pm. 41 pesos.*

Bonampak is a relatively small site, containing the remains of a city that thrived from around AD 400-800. The part of the city that's been excavated consists of a modest plaza and the **Acrópolis,** a series of terraces built onto the side of a hill. Like nearby Yaxchilán, Bonampak is entirely surrounded by jungle; at times guides have to raise their voices over the screeching insects and monkeys. Unlike nearly every archaeological site in Mesoamerica, the main attractions aren't the towering pyramids, underground labyrinths, or the scowling faces of Mayan gods frozen in rock or stucco. Instead, they are the three rooms in an otherwise unremarkable building that are entirely covered in highly-remarkable technicolor frescos. The building is on the second terrace from the bottom, on the right side. On the way up you'll pass two stelae showing Chaan Muan, Bonampak's former king. Despite being 1200 years old, the murals are almost totally intact, and the blues, yellows, and reds are still bright enough to convey all the gory details of the scenes they depict. The center room shows a battle with a neighboring city and its aftermath, as the defeated foreign soldiers beg Bonampak's ruler for mercy. Meanwhile, in the panels below, blood drips from their compatriots' hands, suggesting that they underwent the traditional Mayan torture of having their fingernails ripped out. Other more peaceful scenes include religious rituals and a coronation ceremony. The steep climb the rest of the way up the Acrópolis is worth it for the view of the rolling hills of the Lacondón and jungle canopy.

## YAXCHILÁN

*On the banks of the Usumacinta River, about 1hr. by lancha from Frontera Corozal. Tours from Palenque go to Yaxchilán and Bonampak for around 550 pesos per person. Alternatively, you can hire a lancha directly in Frontera Corozal from one of several cooperatives near the river. Prices depend on the size of the group; for up to three people, expect to pay as much as 650 pesos. Guides can be hired at the ruins or from the cooperatives, and generally charge between 30 and 100 pesos per person, depending on the size of the group. Bring bug spray. Open daily 8am-4:30pm. Entrance 49 pesos. Cash only.*

If you feel like spending some time off the beaten path after the tourist mecca that is Palenque, Yaxchilán ("Place of Green Stones" in Maya) is a strong candidate. The site is only accessible by *lancha* from Frontera Corozal, after an hour along the Usumacinta River, which forms the border between Mexico and Guatemala. Once you've arrived, the city—much of which is covered with green moss—offers a number of striking sculptures and stelae. Monkeys and toucans can be heard in attention in the trees above.

At the entrance, the main path leads to the **Gran Plaza,** where most of the ruins can be found. (A side path leads to the **Pequeña Acrópolis,** of which little has been excavated or restored; in fact, only 35% of the entire 8 sq. km. site has been recovered from the jungle.) The first building you will see, standing between you and the Gran Plaza, is the **Laberinto,** a temple that may have served as a site for human sacrifices. You can walk around it, but far more interesting (if you have a flashlight) is to go through it, wandering the pitch-black corridors of the Maya *inframundo.* There are several openings, so don't worry about getting lost; don't mind the harmless bats, either.

Past the Laberinto, the Gran Plaza stretches out parallel to the river. It contains most of the city's most important architecture from its settlement around AD 250-900. The first building on the left is a ritual bathhouse, where warriors would go to pray for success on the battlefield. Mothers also come here to pray for the health of their children. Beyond the bath are the two parallel sides of the ball court, where five stone circles arranged in a cross pattern that probably represented the four corners of the world. The far side of the Gran Plaza contains several stelae, tall slabs of stone the Maya used to record important events; the largest (under a tarp to shield it from the elements) depicts a ceremony asking the gods for healthy crops. This stela is flanked by an imposing stone jaguar on one side and a crocodile on the other. Another stela, in the far corner, shows the transfer of power between King Shield Jaguar I and Bird Jaguar IV.

Over 40m and 140 steps above the Gran Plaza is the **Gran Acrópolis,** home to Yaxchilán's palace. A huge statue of King Bird Jaguar IV, missing two arms and a leg, sits on the top of the roof. In front of the palace is a stalactite taken from a nearby cavern, which may have been used as a sundial. On the way up, don't miss a small collection of buildings on the left. **Building 23,** all the way at the end of the terrace, is particularly notable for the exquisitely detailed carvings on the inside of its doorways—look up as you enter the rooms.

## FRONTERA COROZAL

Deep in the Lacondón jungle, on the banks of the Usumacinta River that forms the border with Guatemala, and 165km south of Palenque off Mex. 307, Frontera Corozal is one of the most isolated places in Mexico that still has some tourist infrastructure. *Combis* to Palenque run daily 4am-12pm for 70 pesos. Nearly every tour agency in Palenque comes through town to get to Yaxchilán. The town was only connected to the rest of the country via paved roads in the mid-1990s, and most people use Guatemalan cell phones if they use phones at all, because the Mexican network doesn't reach the border. The community's location, however, makes it one of the best jumping-off points to explore the region's jungle on both sides of the border.

Tours—anything from a few hours along the river to Yaxchilán to multi-day affairs visiting far-flung ruins—can be arranged at various cooperatives, such as **Escudo Jaguar** (☎201 250 8059; escudojaguar_lanchas@yahoo.com. mx, escudojaguar_hotel@hotmail.com), on the main road just before the river, which runs *lanchas* to Yaxchilán (1-3 people 650 pesos, 4 people 780 pesos, 5-7 people 950 pesos; 8-10 people 1,300 pesos), Bethel, Guatemala (1-3 people, 400 pesos; 4, 500 pesos; 5-7, 600 pesos; 8-10, 750 pesos) and Piedras Negras (1 day trip up to 5 people 3,800 pesos, 2 days up to 5 people 4,400 pesos) and has a variety of clean, comfortable rooms for overnight stays, as well as space for camping. (Singles 320 pesos; doubles 528 pesos; triples 792 pesos; cabañas 225-330 pesos; camping 75 pesos per person. Wi-Fi 60 pesos.

**TABASCO AND CHIAPAS**

Prices rise 20-40% in the high season. Cash only.) About 50m further from the water, just off the main road, is **Nueva Alianza,** which offers cheaper, more rustic lodging, and *lanchas* to Yaxchilán. (☎502 5353 1395; ecoturlacondona. com/nuevaalianza. *Lanchas* for 1-3 people 600 pesos, 4-5 people 750 pesos, 6-7 people 850 pesos, 8-10 people 1100 pesos. Singles with shared bath 100 pesos; with private bath, doubles 300 pesos; triples 400 pesos; quads 750 pesos. Internet 15 pesos per hr.) Both establishments have restaurants that serve traditional Mexican food for 50-100 pesos. Trips to Yaxchilán can usually also be arranged with a cooperative right by the river for similar prices.

The only real sight in the town itself is the **Museo Regional de la Cuenca del Río Usumacinta,** which has relatively well done exhibits on the indigenous communities of the area. (On the main road near Nueva Alianza. Open daily 7am-10pm. Free.) Basic services are clustered in the *centro*, about 800m from the river, including a **pharmacy** (open daily 8am-2pm and 4pm-7pm); a very basic **clinic** (usually open M-F 8am-2pm); and a community **police station** (open Sa-Su). To receive treatment for anything more than light injuries, or to report a serious crime, you'll have to go to Palenque.

# COMITÁN ☎963

Comitán's (pop. 80,000) colonial architecture and jagged green horizon may remind you of its northern neighbor, San Cristóbal. Unlike San Cristóbal, however, there are few backpackers in this sleepy town. Come evening you're more likely to be sitting in the central plaza and enjoying the fresh mountain air than raging at a bar. Unlike in some of the other less-touristed cities in southern Mexico, however, you shouldn't have a problem finding a comfortable room and a nice place to eat. All that plus the dreamlike scenery of the nearby Lagunas de Montebello makes Comitán a good place to relax—if only for a few days.

**TRANSPORTATION. OCC** sends **buses** to **Mexico City** (16hr., 8 per day 2:10-8:40pm, 898 pesos); **Oaxaca** (14 hr.; 4:15pm; 456 pesos); **Ocosingo** (4hr., 1:45 and 9:15pm, 116 pesos); **Palenque** (5hr.; 1:45, 9:15pm; 202 pesos); **San Cristóbal** (2hr., 13 per day 3:30am-11:25pm, 36 pesos); **Tapachula** (6hr., 6 per day 1:10am-11:35pm, 166 pesos); and **Tuxtla Gutiérrez** (3hr., 13 per day 3:30am-11:25pm, 80 pesos). **Taxis** (☎632 0146) cost 20 pesos within town. *Combis* to Lagunas de Montebello leave as they fill from Av. 2 Pte., between C. 2 and 3 Sur (1hr., 30 pesos). Taxis (☎632 0164 and 632 5630) within the city cost 20 pesos.

**ORIENTATION AND PRACTICAL INFORMATION.** Comitán is 90km southeast of San Cristóbal de las Casas and about 55km from the Guatemalan border. The street layout is similar to other cities in Chiapas: *avenidas* run north-south, increasing in number in both directions from **Avenida Central,** which forms the eastern border of the *zócalo. Calles* run east-west and increase in the same way from **Calle Central,** which bisects the *zócalo.* Six blocks east of the *zócalo* is **Boulevard Dr. Belisario Domínguez,** the main traffic thoroughfare, with the **OCC station** and a few upscale hotels.

Other services include: a very helpful **tourist office,** on C. 1 Sur Pte. 26 (open M-F 9am-2pm, 4:30-7:30pm); **police,** stationed at the Palacio Municipal (☎632 3322); **Santander,** on C. 1 Sur and Av. Central just off the *zócalo,* with **24hr. ATM** (☎632 1296; open M-F 9am-4pm, Sa 10am-2pm); a laundromat, **Lavandería El Cholul,** at Av. Aranda 9 (15 pesos per kg; open daily 8am-8pm); **Red Cross,** on C. 5 Nte. Pte. 119 (☎632 1889); **Farmacias del Ahorro,** at C. 1 Sur on the *zócalo* (☎632 7777; open daily 7am-11pm); and internet at **Ciber Comitecos,** on Av. 1 Ote. Sur two blocks from the *zócalo* (8 pesos per hr.; open 9am-9pm).

**▶ ACCOMMODATIONS.** Hotels in Comitán are surprisingly plentiful, though some of them can be pricey, especially on Blvd. Domínguez. **Hotel Eugenia ❷**, on C. 1 Ne. Pte. 22, may be the best value in town, with immaculate rooms surrounding a courtyard, plus TV and free Wi-Fi. The third floor balcony has a view of the mountains in the distance. (☎101 3788. Singles 200 pesos; doubles 250 pesos; triples 290 pesos. Cash only.) **Pensión Delfin ❸**, on Av. Central on the *zócalo*, has clean, wood-paneled rooms with a pretty colonial courtyard garden. (☎632 0013. Free parking. Singles 270 pesos; doubles 360 pesos; triples 470 pesos. Cash only.) **Hospedaje Montebello ❶**, C. 1 Nte. Pte. 10, is Comitán's contribution to the budget hotel genre. The rooms are perfectly adequate, though sparse. (☎632 3572. Singles 150 pesos; triples 250-300 pesos. Cash only.)

**▶ FOOD.** Most of Comitán's restaurant options are within a few blocks of the *zócalo*. On the west side of the central square, there is a lineup of several family restaurants with similar menus and prices. **Restaurante Los Portales ❷**, serves traditional Mexican dishes for 35-45 pesos. (Open daily 7am-11:30pm. Cash only.) If you're willing to part with some cash, **Matisse ❹**, at Av. 1 Pte. Nte. 16, is the place to go. The mostly Italian menu includes pizzas (medium, 90 pesos) and pastas like spaghetti with steak filet in a mushroom cream sauce (120 pesos). (☎632 7152. Open Tu-Su 2-11pm. Cash only.) **Café, Canela y Candela ❶**, on C. 2 Sur between Av. Central and 1 Pte., satisfies your sweet tooth with pastries (12-20 pesos) and banana splits (30 pesos). They also serve *tortas* and some standard Mexican dishes (25-40 pesos). (☎632 2222. Open M-Sa 8am-10pm. Cash only.) **Restaurante Cancún ❷**, on C. 2 Sur Pte. 4, has solid breakfasts (38-55 pesos) and enchiladas (38 pesos) in a covered courtyard. There's also a *menú del día* for 40 pesos. (☎109 5751. Open daily 9am-5pm. Cash only.)

**▶ SIGHTS.** By far the most impressive thing to see near Comitán is **Parque Nacional Lagunas de Montebello**, 59km southeast of Comitán. This forest sprawls over rolling hills and around a series of more than a dozen lakes. The entrance is about 1hr. outside of Comitán; you can either drive or take a *combi* (☎632 0875; leave from Av. 2 Pte. Sur 28; every 20min.; 30 pesos). You'll be dropped off at a parking lot with a row of food and trinket stands between the two of the smaller lakes. The surrounding pine forest provides for a very different, more tranquil, natural setting than the hyperactive jungle a few hours and a few thousand feet of altitude away. The lakes themselves are notable for their colors, which range from dark green to an almost neon turquoise. It is forbidden to swim in these lakes, as they are a source of drinking water for local communities. To see the rest of the park, you can hire a guide with a van at the lot where *combis drop* off (2hr., 400 pesos). Alternatively, you can make your way a 1km down to the end of the road, where there are men waiting to take you through the park on horseback (2hr., 200 pesos). For longer stays, camping is permitted within the park. (Entrance 22 pesos.)

There are also a few museums in town. **Casa Museo Dr. Belisario Domínguez**, on Av. Central Sur half a block from the *zócalo*, is a monument to Dr. Domínguez, a legendary physician, political activist, and philanthropist. His old house now holds an eclectic collection of medical equipment, newspaper clippings, and photos documenting his important role in local politics during and after the Mexican Revolution. There's a lot of text to read, but if you're thorough, you'll find a racially tinged excerpt from a biography which describes Dr. Domínguez's nose (straight), lips (thin), and hat (Panama); there's also a copy of a letter in which he challenges the mayor of Tuxtla Gutiérrez to a duel to determine the location of the capital of Chiapas. (Open M-Sa 10am-6:45pm, Su 9am-12:45pm. 5 pesos.) The **Museo Arqueológico**, on C. 1 Sur between Av. 1 and 2 Ote., has a few

TABASCO AND CHIAPAS

rooms around a small garden with exhibits about the different cultures of the region. The adjacent **library** has free Wi-Fi. (Open Tu-Su 9am-6pm. Free.)

# TAPACHULA      ☎962

Tapachula (pop. 300,000) bustles with sidewalk swap meets, stalls selling homemade root beer, and marimba music echoing into the night. Nearby mountains are home to the largest coffee-growing communities in Chiapas. These mountains provide the ideal backdrop for a range of activities for adventurous tourists looking to get off the beaten path. Largely uninterested in cultivating tourism, hot, noisy Tapachula serves more as a final stop in Mexico's southernmost reaches rather than a long-term hangout.

**TRANSPORTATION.** The **airport** is on the road to Puerto Madero, about 17km south of town. It's served by **Aviacsa**, Av. Central Nte. 18 (☎625 4030). Tapachula's first-class **bus station** (☎626 2880 or 2881) is northwest of the *zócalo*, at C. 17 Ote. and Av. 3 Nte. To get to the zócalo (15min. on foot), take a left onto C. 17 Ote., walk two blocks, take a left on Av. Central, and continue south for six blocks. Take a right on C. 5 Pte. and go three blocks west, to the northeast corner of the plaza. Alternatively, take a 20-peso taxi. **Cristóbal Colón** buses head to: **Cancún**(24hr.; 9:45, 11:30pm; 994 pesos); **Chetumal** (18hr.; 9:45, 11:30pm; 702 pesos); **Comitán** (5hr.; 9:45, 11:30pm; 166 pesos); **Mexico City**(17hr.; 12:30, 5:30, 7:30pm; 890 pesos); **Oaxaca** (12hr., 7:15pm, 346 pesos); **Palenque**(10hr.; 9:45, 11:30pm; 358 pesos); **San Cristóbal de las Casas** (7hr.; 7:30, 9:15am, 2:30pm; 222 pesos); **Tuxtla Gutiérrez** (7hr., 11 per day 6am-11:55pm, 256 pesos). **Tica** buses leave from the station daily at 7am, stopping in **Guatemala City** (5 hr., 202 pesos or US$15) and **San Salvador** (10 hr., 404 pesos or US$30). From there, Tica buses can take you to other Central American capitals. **Galgos Inter.** also sends buses to **Guatemala City** (5hr.; 6, 9:30am, 2:30pm; 250 pesos) and **San Salvador** (10hr.; 7am, 12, 11:45pm; 500 pesos). The **RS station**, C. 9 Pte. 63, between Av. 14 and 16 Nte., sends buses to **Tuxtla Gutiérrez** (7hr., 27 per day 4am-9pm, 160 pesos) via **Tonalá**, as well as to other destinations along the Chiapan coast.

**ORIENTATION AND PRACTICAL INFORMATION.** Tapachula is 16km from Talismán along the Guatemalan border and 303km west of Guatemala City. Tapachula's **zócalo** is on C. 3 Pte. between Av. 6 and 8 Nte., northwest of the intersection of Av. and C. Central. Avoid walking south of C. 10 Pte. near the train tracks after dark; if you do happen to go, be sure and stay on Av. 4 Sur, the central avenue, and **do not walk alone.**

    There is a **tourist information** module in the left side of the Casa de Cultura, next door to Iglesia de San Agustín. (☎9626 1884 or 1485, ext. 116. Open M-F 8am-8pm, Sa 10am-2pm.) The **SECTUR** office, Av. 5 Nte. 5, between C. Central Ote. and 1 Ote., also offers information. (☎628 7725. Open M-Sa 8am-8pm.) **Consulates** for some Central American countries are found throughout town: **Guatemala,** Av. 5 Nte. 5, 3rd fl., between C. 1 and C. Central Ote. (☎626 1252; open M-F 10am-3pm and 4pm-6pm); **El Salvador,** Av. 7 Sur 31, at C. 2 Ote. (☎626 1253; open M-F 9am-4pm). **Scotiabank,** on the east side of the *zócalo* at C. 5, has a **24hr. ATM.** (☎626 1126. Open M-F 9am-5pm.) Other services include: **police**, Carretera Antiguo Aeropuerto km 2.5 (☎626 6538); **Red Cross**, Av. 9 Nte. and C. 1 Ote. (☎626 1949 and 7644); **Farmacias del Ahorro,** at Av. 6 Nte. and C. 3 Pte. (☎628 8161; open 24hr.); **Hospital General** (☎628 1060), on the airport highway; **Internet access** at **Cyber Snoopy,** Av. 8 Nte. 7 (8 pesos per

TABASCO AND CHIAPAS

hr.; open daily 7am-11pm), and Wi-Fi at **Angeles restaurant,** across from the bus station (free with meal; open 24hr.); fax at **Telecomm,** next to the post office (☎626 1097; open M-F 8am-7:30pm, Sa 9am-5pm, Su 9am-1pm); and the **post office,** C. 1 Ote. 32, between Av. 7 and 9 Nte. (☎626 2492; open M-F 8:30am-2:30pm, Sa 9am-1pm). **Postal Code:** 30700.

**⌐⌐ ACCOMMODATIONS AND FOOD.** Budget rooms are a dime a dozen in Tapachula, especially near the market. Unfortunately, many rooms are as noisy, hot, and dirty as the rest of the city and few offer hot water. **Hostal del Ángel ❷,** Av. 8a Nte. 16, just off the *zócalo,* is a pleasant hotel with clean, simple, spacious rooms along one side of a small, half-maintained courtyard with a cyber cafe in front. (☎625 0142. No hot water. Reception 8am-10pm. Singles 200 pesos, with TV and A/C 260 pesos; doubles 340/400 pesos. Cash only.) **Hotel Premier ❸,** Av. 8 Nte. 32, on the park, offers spotless rooms with fan, phone, cable TV, purified water, and an entertaining fish tank in the lobby. Laundry service and parking spaces are available. There's also a modest common space with couches and a TV. (☎626 4709. Singles 250 pesos, with A/C 350 pesos; doubles 350/450 pesos; each additional person 50 pesos. Cash only.) **Hotel Esperanza ❸,** Av. 17 Ote. 8, across from the bus station, is a clean but somewhat pricey hotel with A/C, Wi-Fi, and cable TV. (☎625 9135. Singles 250 pesos; doubles 300 pesos; triples 350 pesos; suites 450 pesos; each additional person 80 pesos. Cash only.) **Hotel Casa Grande ❶,** 8 Av. Sur 28 on the corner of 2a. Pte., is a student-oriented hostel intended for long-term stays with a very gracious host. The covered courtyard in the middle is full of antiques, knickknacks, and photos, which are all for sale. The rooms are clean and come with communal baths, a lovely garden, a

READY. SET.

www.letsgo.com

LET'S GO

THE STUDENT TRAVEL GUIDE

## ON THE ROAD

n the few weeks before I got to Mexico, I used to look over my assignments and be heartened by addresses like "Avenue 4 Northwest 271." I assumed that with such simply numbered streets, I would be able to navigate even the wildest Chiapan border town without much trouble.

As it turns out, this is emphatically not true. Pop quiz: Are North 4th Avenue and North 5th Avenue near each other? Answer: maybe. If you're in Tapachula, the're not. In Tapachula, roads are divided into "streets" (running east-west) and "avenues" (running north-south). The numbers increase on even numbers to the south and west, and on odd numbers to the north and east, meaning that 5th Street is right next to 7th Street, but quite far from 6th Street.

If your eyes have glazed over (and I wouldn't blame you), the good news is that you don't really need to know any of this, anyway, because outside of a handful of blocks in the very middle of town, almost none of the streets are marked and people (including those who live on a given street) frequently don't know where they are when you ask them. This includes the locals. Navigation often takes the form of reaching a vague zone where you think whatever you're looking for might be, and asking directions until you eventually get there.

—Daniel Hertz

kitchen area, and free Wi-Fi. (☎626 6701. 100 pesos per person. Cash only.)

Taco and pastry stands fill the *zócalo* area. Several *comedores*, serving meals and *antojitos* for around 15-20 pesos, are located inside **Mercado Sebastian Escobar ❶**, on 10 Av. Nte. between C. 3 and 5 Pte. Across the street from the bus station, Ángeles has an extensive menu of *tortas*, tacos, *milanesas*, and more, plus free Wi-Fi. Watch soccer on the TV in the corner. (Tacos 5 for 30 pesos. Open 24 hr. Cash only.) On the southern side of the *zócalo* is **Las Tablitas ❶**, which serves regional and Mexican food for 60-110 pesos. (Open daily 9am-11pm. Cash only.) When the heat starts getting to you, walk four blocks east and two blocks south of the *zócalo* to **Irma Helados Finos ❶**, a big, friendly ice cream parlor where all your troubles melt away nearly as quickly as the ice cream will under the Tapachula sun. (Ice cream 18 pesos. Open daily 9am-8pm. Cash only.)

# OAXACA

The state of Oaxaca holds strongly to its indigenous roots. There are more speakers of indigenous languages here than in any other state in Mexico. Still, Oaxaca is celebrated for its successful and seamless marriage of the traditional and the modern. Its capital, **Oaxaca City** (p. 244), is entrenched in its tradition and history. It's often considered the culinary capital of Mexico, and your visit to the city would be incomplete without a trip to one of its famous chocolate cafes. Just a day's journey from the city, **Oaxaca Valley** (p. 257) is the site of numerous indigenous towns.

Oaxaca City and a few other towns, such as surfing hotspot **Puerto Escondido** (p. 227), have benefited from the tourist industry, but the rest of state remains impoverished—Oaxaca is the second-poorest state in Mexico, behind Chiapas; you certainly won't find Cancún crowds hanging out here. That being said, Oaxaca has some beautiful, tranquil beach towns on the southern coast, including **Mazunte** (p. 235) and **Zipolite** (p. 237), whose unspoiled and relatively peaceful settings are well worth a visit.

## PUERTO ESCONDIDO &#9742; 954

Puerto Escondido (pop. 60,000) is a surf-bum village that hit the big time. No longer a sleepy beach hamlet, Puerto plays host year-round to crowds of surfers who come for the massive waves at Playa Zicatela. Other tourists who come for the casual beach atmosphere and plentiful Italian restaurants. The city tends to attract people for longer stays than other places, which—combined with the fact that more than a handful of foreigners have decided to make it a permanent home—gives it an unusual sense of community.

### ▊ TRANSPORTATION

**Flights: Puerto Escondido Airport (PXM;** &#9742;582 0491). Best reached by taxi (35 pesos). **Aerovega,** Gasga 113 (&#9742;582 0151), flies to **Oaxaca** daily. **Click Mexicana** (&#9742;582 2023) flies to **Mexico City. Buses: Estrella Blanca station** (&#9742;582 0086) is the farthest from the tourist corridor at Oaxaca and Salinas de Gortari. Buses go to **Acapulco** (8hr., 5am, 251 pesos), **Bahías de Huatulco** (2hr.; 7, 8:30pm; 86 pesos) via **Pochutla,** and **Mexico City** (12hr.; 7, 8:30pm; 719 pesos). **Cristóbal Colón** (&#9742;582 1073), just west of the *crucero* on the *carretera*, sends buses to: **Bahías de Huatulco** (2hr., 11 per day 7am-9:30pm, 88 pesos); **Mexico City** (12hr.; 6, 8:20pm; 682 pesos); **Oaxaca** (7hr.; 7am, 2:30, 8:45pm; 275 pesos); **San Cristóbal de las Casas** (14hr.; 5:30, 9, 9:30pm; 446 pesos); and **Tuxtla Gutiérrez** (12hr.; 5:30, 9, 9:30pm; 390 pesos). Semi-direct service runs to **Bahías de Huatulco** (2hr., 18 per day 6am-7:20pm, 40 pesos) via **Pochutla. Micros** to **Pochutla** leave from the *crucero* (1hr., every ½-1hr., 20 pesos).

### ▊▐ ORIENTATION AND PRACTICAL INFORMATION

Built on a hillside 294km south of Oaxaca on Mex. 175, Puerto Escondido is bisected by **Mex. 200** (also known as **Carretera Costera**), which divides the street's uphill and downhill regions. The main tourist corridor is **Pérez Gasga,** which loops down from the *crucero* and skirts the beach before rejoining Mex. 200 near Playa Marinera. The flat area of Gasga, nearest the beach and full of shops and restaurants, is known as the **Adoquín.** It closes to traffic at 5pm and fills with

Oaxaca State

pedestrians. A second tourist area lies to the southeast along **Calle del Moro** and **Playa Zicatela.** Puerto Escondido is small enough that most businesses do not have exact addresses, which can make finding a particular establishment frustrating—if you're having a hard time, your best bet is to ask directions from a nearby hotel or restaurant employee. Locals may insist that Puerto Escondido is safe, but recent assaults on tourists have prompted the tourist office to recommend that travelers stay in groups and avoid isolated beaches, even during daylight hours. Taxis can be found by the tourist information booth and along Carretera Costera and C. del Moro on Zicatela; they are the safest way of getting around after nightfall (25-30 pesos).

**Tourist Office: Módulo de Información Turística,** the booth at the beginning of the pedestrian walkway, down Gasga from the *crucero*. Open M-F 9am-2pm and 4-6pm, Sa 10am-1pm.

**Banks and Currency Exchange: Money Exchange** (☎582 1928), in the middle of Gasga's tourist strip. Open M-F 8am-8pm, Sa-Su 8am-5pm. **Banorte,** on Hidalgo between Oaxaca and 1 Pte. Open M-Sa 10am-3pm, 5:30-9pm; Su 10am-2pm. **HSBC** (☎582 1824), 1 Nte. at 3 Pte. Open M-F 8am-7pm. Both Banorte and HSBC have **ATMs.**

**Luggage Storage: Hotel Mayflower** (p. 229) offers storage for 10 pesos per day.

OAXACA

**Library: IFOPE Library,** Juárez 10, on Rinconada, on the way to Playa Carrizalillo. 900 books in English, French, German, and Spanish; membership required. Used books for sale 20-30 pesos. Open M, W, Sa 10am-noon.

**Laundromat:Lava Max,** Gasga 405. Uphill from the walkway on the right, next to Banamex. Wash 13 pesos per kg. Dry 14 pesos. Open M-Sa 8am-7pm, Su 8am-4pm. **Lavandería,** at Playa Zicatela, inside Hotel Olas Altas, charges 13 pesos per kg. Open daily 8am-8pm.

**Police:** (☎582 3439), on 3 Pte. at the corner of Carretera Costera, ground fl. of Agencia Municipal. **Tourist Police** patrol Gasga in the tourist corridor, with a booth on Andador Libertad.

**Red Cross:** (☎582 0550), on 7 Nte. between Oaxaca and 1 Pte. 24hr. service.

**Pharmacy: Farmacia La Moderna 1,** Gasga 203 (☎582 0698 or 2780). Open 24hr. Many others along the Adoquín.

**Medical Services: Centro de Salud,** Gasga 409 (☎582 2360). Small, minimal-expense medical clinic. Open 24hr. for emergencies.

**Fax Office: Telecomm** (☎582 0232), next to the post office. Open M-F 8am-7:30pm, Sa 9am-noon.

**Internet Access: Internet Copa Cabaña,** on the Adoquín just east of Libertad. 15 pesos per hr. Open daily 9am-10:30pm.

**Post Office:** 7 Nte. 701 (☎582 0959), at Oaxaca, a 15min. walk uphill from the crucero. Open M-F 8am-3pm. **Postal Code:** 71981.

---

**TIP** **FOREIGN FRIENDS.** In addition to the standard government emergency services, the **Amigos Internationales de Puerto Escondido** (www.tomzap. com/IFOPE.html) are a neighborhood watch group of area expats. Formed in 1998 for the purpose of facilitating communication between the local foreign community and the government, members of this group claim to be able to help contact your embassy, the police, and medical assistance. The easiest way to get in touch is to go to the Hotel Mayflower and ask for the owner.

---

 **ACCOMMODATIONS**

Accommodations in Puerto Escondido range from spare and lively hostels to lush hotels that will set you back 1000 pesos or more per night. The youth and surfing scenes, not surprisingly, are concentrated in the former. Before looking around for a place to stay, it's useful to decide whether you want to be on Gasga in the main part of Puerto Escondido—which has a somewhat higher density of restaurants and amenities—or on C. del Moro at Playa Zicatela, where the beaches are less cluttered. The cheapest *cabañas* (around 50 pesos) might not be secure; lock your valuables if possible. Prices can vary significantly, rising during the high-season months of March, April, July, August, and December; reservations are recommended. Rates listed below are for the low season.

◪ **Hotel Mayflower** (☎582 0367), on Libertad. From the bus station, cross the *crucero* and go left downhill; stairs descend on the right to the entrance. A Puerto mainstay, Mayflower offers clean beds and spotless communal baths. Common areas, a rooftop bar and pool table, and a bevy of backpackers provide a tight-knit ambience. Purified water, lockers, book exchange, communal kitchen. Free internet and Wi-Fi. Rooms fill up every day in the high season—call ahead or arrive early. Reception 24hr. Dorms 100 pesos; rooms 220 pesos. 5% HI discount. Cash only. ❶

◪ **Hotel Buena Vista** (☎582 1474), on Playa Zicatela. Perched on a hill above C. del Moro, Buena Vista rewards the seemingly endless climb with its spectacular, unparalleled view

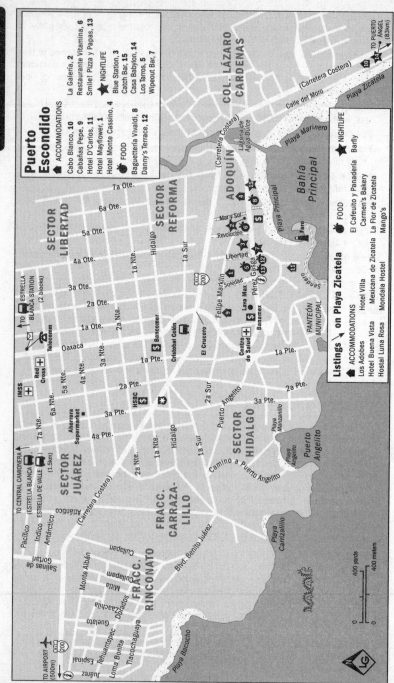

**Puerto Escondido**

**⌂ ACCOMMODATIONS**
Cabo Blanco, 10
Cabañas Pepe, 9
Hotel D'Carlos, 11
Hotel Mayflower, 1
Hotel Monte Cassino, 4

**⌂ FOOD**
Baguettería Vivaldi, 8
Danny's Terrace, 12
La Galería, 2
Restaurante Vitamina, 6
Smile! Pizza y Papas, 13

**★ NIGHTLIFE**
Blue Station, 3
Catch Bar, 15
Casa Babylon, 14
Los Tarros, 5
Wipeout Bar, 7

**Listings on Playa Zicatela**

**⌂ ACCOMMODATIONS**
Los Adobes          Hotel Villa
Hotel Buena Vista   Mexicana de Zicatela
Hostal Luna Rosa    Mondala Hostel

**⌂ FOOD**
El Cafecito y Panadería   La Flor de Zicatela
Carmen's Bakery          Mango's

**★ NIGHTLIFE**
Barfly

# Caravan.com is Going Places in Costa Rica from $995.

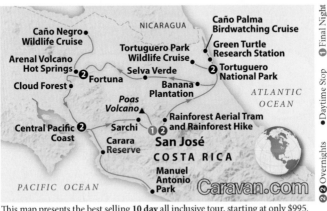

This map presents the best selling **10 day** all inclusive tour, starting at only $995.

**Caravan makes it so easy** - and so affordable - for you to explore the magnificent rainforests, beaches and volcanoes of Costa Rica. Your Caravan Costa Rica tour includes all meals, all activities, all hotels, a great itinerary, all airport transfers, and all transportation and excursions within Costa Rica.

**Join the smart shoppers** and experienced travelers who rely on Caravan to handle all the details while you and your friends enjoy a well-earned, worry-free vacation in Costa Rica.

**Places to go with Caravan.com**
**$995 to $1195, 8 to 11-Days.**
**Call Now for Choice Dates**

*Canadian Rockies & Glacier Park*
*Nova Scotia and Prince Edward Island*
*Grand Canyon, Zion and Bryce*
*Rushmore, Yellowstone, Grand Tetons*
*California Coast and Yosemite Park*
*New England Fall Colors*
*Mexico's Ancient and Colonial Cities*
*Mexico's Copper Canyon Train*
*Costa Rica Natural Paradise*
*Guatemala with Tikal and Copan*

# Caravan.com

**Or Call 1.800.CARAVAN  Fully Escorted Tours, #1 in Value**

# FIRST IN STUDENT DISCOUNTS WORLDWIDE

## International Student Exchange Identity Card

trains

attractions

accommodations
Save up to 50%

buses

computers

airfare

**INTERNATIONAL IDENTITY CARD**

STUDENT

University of Maryland

INSTITUTION
Ashley Michaels

NAME
15 Mar 1989    American

DATE OF BIRTH    NATIONALITY
ISEC/SCT / 12 Feb 2011

ISSUED OFFICE / VALID UNTIL

Control No.  1234567890

**ise** CARDS®  **Cost: $25 per year**

With the ISE Card you will receive discounts on airfare, accommodations, transportation, computer services, phone calls, major attractions, and more. You will also receive airline bankruptcy protection, and basic medical & evacuation benefits when traveling outside your home country and access to 24 hour worldwide emergency assistance.

11043 N Saint Andrew's Way • Scottsdale, Arizona 85254 USA • Tel: 480-951-1177 • Fax: 480-951-1216
Toll Free: **1-800-255-1000** • www.isecard.com • info@isecard.com

## EuRail®
Your Pass. Your Europe.

## Buy your Eurail Pass from ISE
# Get your ISE Card FREE

The ISE Card can save you hundreds of dollars at thousands of locations throughout Europe, North America, Egypt, Africa and Australia.

- All Major Credit Cards Accepted
- All Handling Fees Waived
- Free Eurail Timetable
- Free Eurail Guide and Map

## CALL TOLL FREE: 800-255-1000

Tel: 480-951-1177 • Fax: 480-951-1216 • http://www.isecard.com

**ne SimCard**

www.onesimcard.com

International Mobile
Phone Solutions

75-90% Savings on Global Cell Phone Service

*OneSimCard.com - Simple, reliable, low-cost mobile phone service for over 170 countries*

# OneSIMcard

- ◉ Single SIM and Phone Number for over 170 countries
- ◉ Extra US, Canada or UK phone number
- ◉ Free incoming calls in over 60 countries
- ◉ Receive Free SMS messages anywhere
- ◉ Send Free SMS to OneSimCard phone by email
- ◉ No Contract, No monthly chargers
- ◉ Internet Access on the mobile phone in over 70 countries

## Buy or Rent ready-to-go Mobile Phone or buy just a SIM Card

## www.onesimcard.com

**phone:** *1-617-489-5952*

*Get additional discount by using coupon LETSGO2010*

# Hostels.com
## Every Hostel, Everywhere!

- Largest Selection of Hostels on the Web
- Over 28,000 Hostels Across the Globe
- No Booking fees
- Travel Features & Guides
- Hostel Forums, Blogs & More on...

## www.hostels.com

www.hostels.com

of the beach. Tiled private bath, fan, and refrigerator furnish the room. Splurge a little for the rooms with gorgeous, sweeping balcony views. Reservations recommended. Singles and doubles 300 pesos, with kitchen or A/C 400 pesos; each additional person 50 pesos. Prices double in high season. Monthly rates available. Cash only. ❸

**Los Adobes** (☎582 1496), on a short, sandy road off of Zicatela. Look for the sign near Mangos restaurant. May be the best deal in town. Comfy, clean, attractive rooms around a beautiful garden courtyard. There's also a pool, which might seem superfluous at a beach getaway until you notice that Zicatela's waves are the size of a small house. 100 pesos per person. 3-night minimum stay. Cash only. ❶

**Cabañas Pepe** (☎582 2037), south of the OCC station. From the station, cross the *crucero* and take the 1st left going downhill; sign for the *cabañas* on the right. After a day on Puerto Escondido's crowded beaches and touristed streets, Cabañas Pepe allows you to escape while taking in stunning views of the bay. The rooms are clean and cozy. All come with TV and balcony. Singles 200 pesos; each additional person 50 pesos. Cash only. ❷

**Hostal Luna Rosa** (☎103 6341; www.zicatela.org/lunarosa), on the northern half of Playa Zicatela. An oasis of estrogen in a city with more than a few macho surfer dudes, Luna Rosa is a quirky, artsy all-female hostel with the same amenities as its co-ed competitors. The single large dorm is decorated with art projects by guests past and present. There are 2 stories of common space for hanging out. Free internet and kitchen use. Dorms 100 pesos. Cash only. ❶

**Cabo Blanco** (☎582 0337), on Playa Zicatela. Attractive *cabañas* above a bar that gets pretty packed. Read: not a good choice if you're planning on going to bed before 2am. Clean, pleasant rooms range from tiny to spacious, all with fans and mosquito nets. Singles and doubles 200 pesos, with bath 300 pesos. Cash only. ❶

**Mondala Hostel** (☎120 0949), on Playa Zicatela. A convivial atmosphere compensates for concrete floors. Kitchen available for use. Camping 30 pesos; dorms 80 pesos; *cabañas* 100 pesos per person. Cash only. ❶

**Hotel D'Carlos** (☎582 0573), off of Gasga. The 4 rooms here open straight onto the beach. Later at night, D'Carlos's quiet side street allows you to relax away from the noise of the main strip. Rooms are simple but clean and come with TVs and fans. Singles and doubles 150 pesos; each additional person 50 pesos. Cash only. ❶

**Hotel Monte Cassino,** on the eastern end of the Adoquín. On a quiet end of the tourist scene but still within walking distance of all the restaurants and knick-knack shops. Welcomes guests with a flowery courtyard. Rooms are simple but bright, with plain white beds and clean bath. Singles and doubles 150 pesos. Cash only. ❶

**Hotel Villa Mexicana de Zicatela** (☎582 1750), near the center of Playa Zicatela. Clean, no-frills rooms with stone floors. Some rooms with views of the beach. If you ever get tired of watching the waves (or surfing them), there's a billiards table for public use. Internet 10 pesos per hr. Dorms 80 pesos; private rooms for up to 4 people 350 pesos. Cash only. ❶

## ◪ FOOD

Seafood-and-*antojitos* establishments abound in Puerto Escondido. These places (usually on Gasga) are distinguishable mainly by price and proximity to the beach. Thanks to a large expat community, there are also a number of international restaurants; Italian food and crepes are two of the adopted local specialties. Vegetarians will find themselves with plenty of options, especially on Zicatela. **Mercado Benito Juárez,** on 8 Nte. at 3 Pte., sells typical goods in an organized setting. (Open daily 5am-8pm). The supermarket, **Super Che,** on the *crucero* (open daily 7am-10pm), will keep your grocery needs met.

▨ **Baguettería Vivaldi** (☎582 0800), at the east end of the Adoquín. Tasty food for anyone tired of the abundant Mexican and Italian fare. Vivaldi offers a number of enormous baguette sandwiches (from 35 pesos), crepes (from 30 pesos), and sushi (from 52 pesos) in a pleasant open-air cafe setting. Open daily 7am-midnight; in high season open longer. Cash only. ❷

▨ **La Galería,** on Gasga just west of Andador Libertad. Named for the paintings hanging on the walls, La Galería serves addictingly good pizza and pasta (78 pesos). Order one of the delicious ice cream concoctions for dessert (42-56 pesos). Open daily 8am-11pm. Cash only. ❹

**El Cafecito y Panadería Carmen's Bakery** (☎582 0516), on C. del Moro. Crowds of backpackers and tanned surfers chow down on large breakfasts (33-49 pesos) before making their way to the waves. Try the veggie burgers (48 pesos) or garlic shrimp (96 pesos). Open daily 7:30am-10pm. Cash only. ❷

**La Flor de Zicatela,** on the southern end of C. del Moro. One of the few simple and tasty *taquerías* in Puerto Escondido's tourist district. *Chipotle* and *Qdoba* junkies coming from the US might want to check out La Flor's delicious burritos (25-40 pesos). Tacos and *tortas* 25-30 pesos. Open daily 2-10pm. Cash only. ❶

**Sativa,** on Playa Zicatela. Skips the old pizza-and-*marisco* routine in favor of *bruschetta caprese* (30 pesos), *Mai Pai* salad with teriyaki dressing (62 pesos), and chicken and pineapple *brochettes* (70 pesos). From the 2nd fl. dining room, you can watch the surfers headed toward the waves. Open daily 1pm-midnight. Cash only. ❷

**Mangos,** on C. del Moro. A curious selection of veggie-friendly dishes like soy burgers (39 pesos), baguette sandwiches (49 pesos) and more exotic fare like salads with spinach, glazed shrimp, mangos, and goat cheese (85 pesos). Open 7am-11:45pm. Cash only. ❷

**Danny's Terrace,** on the beach off Gasga. The best reason to come to Danny's Terrace is to sit and watch the water and beach-goers. An added draw, for the adventurous, is the spaghetti in tequila sauce. Generous selection of *carnes, antojitos,* and *mariscos.* Entrees 75-120 pesos. Open daily 7:30am-10:30pm. Cash only. ❸

**Smile! Pizza y Papas,** on the far eastern end of Gasga. Smile! is as close as Puerto Escondido comes to street food, handing you surprisingly good pizza over a counter on the sidewalk. Slices 18 pesos. Open daily 4pm-midnight. Cash only. ❶

**La Pergola Mexicana,** on Gasga near Libertad. If your wallet is feeling a little thin, fill up with La Pergola's *menú del día* (35 pesos). The extensive a la carte menu includes Mexican, Oaxacan, and *marisco* standbys for 50-100 pesos. Open daily 7am-11pm. Cash only. ❷

**Restaurante Vitamina T** (☎582 3045), on the east end of the Adoquín. If you're looking for a quick morning meal, Vitamina T will make eggs (30 pesos) any way you want 'em. Lunch and dinner options are of the standard Mexican and seafood variety. Open daily 8am-midnight. MC/V after 2pm. ❷

## ◪ BEACHES

Snorkelers can rent equipment from **Puerto Angelito** (40 pesos per hr.) or **Aventura Submarina** (☎582 2353; 150 pesos per day), on the Adoquín across from the tourist booth. Aventura Submarina also leads diving trips (inquire for prices). At most beaches, restaurants rent out umbrellas (35-50 pesos per day), but if you buy a drink you can use them for free. The beaches that we list below are relatively safe.

**▨PLAYA ZICATELA.** Walking on the path behind the rocks on the east end of Marinero will take you to Zicatela, one of the best surfing beaches in the world. Mesmerizing waves with 5-6m faces regularly break, so unless you've got the know-how and experience, stay on shore and enjoy the show. The best times to watch the pros are around 7:30am and 6:30pm, though times vary with the tide.

**PLAYA CARRIZALILLO.** The 167 stairs down a steep hill keep Carrizalillo secluded in its petite cove, allowing for good swimming and a little tranquility away from the town. The beach is fairly small but should afford you a small place to lay out or leisurely soak in the waves and sun. To get here, take a taxi (20 pesos). To walk, go west on Gasga to Banamex, until you come to the Rotary Club basketball courts. Follow the sign to Playa Carrizalillo, make a left, and keep walking downhill. Stairs lead down from Benito Juárez. **Past Carrizalillo, the waves again become dangerous—do not attempt to swim there.**

**PLAYA PRINCIPAL.** The main beach of Puerto Escondido, Playa Principal, lies just beyond the stores and restaurants that line Adoquín. *Lanchas* crowd the waters, which are gentle enough for swimming. The sand is covered with soccer games, sunbathers, and beachcombers.

**PLAYA MARINERO.** Continuing east along the shore past Playa Principal, you'll pass a small contaminated lagoon on your left. Immediately after is Marinero. This beach, less crowded than Principal, is good for swimming and sunbathing. Waves get rougher near the point, inviting boogie boarders and rookie surfers.

**PLAYAS MANZANILLO AND ANGELITO.** On the other side of Playa Principal, Manzanillo and Angelito are crammed with vacationing Mexican families and their screaming children with inflatable tubes. Manzanillo is the better bet for swimming. Taxis (20 pesos) will bring you here, but if you prefer to walk (20min.), go west on Gasga to Banamex and take a left (10min.); continue left toward the ocean at the sign for Playa Angelito. You will come to a fork in the road; the left path leads to Manzanillo, the right one leads to Angelito. The two beaches are separated by an easily traversed rock barrier.

**PLAYA BACOCHO.** Less scenic (and slightly dirtier) than other beaches, Playa Bacocho is noteworthy for its unbeatable sunset view. Beware of the powerful current on the east side of the beach. Bacocho is best reached by taxi (45 pesos).

## 🦅 OUTDOOR ACTIVITIES

If you get tired of the beach, there are plenty of ecotourism opportunities within reach of Puerto Escondido. The easiest to access may be **Laguna Manialtepec**, 30min. outside of town. To get there, take a bus headed toward Río Grande from the depot on 2a Nte. and 3a Pte. (every 30min. 5:30am-7pm, 15 pesos). You'll be dropped off in front of **La Puesta del Sol**, a restaurant on the banks of the lake. From the shore,

**FROM THE ROAD**

## ON THE ROAD

There are several beaches in Puerto Escondido, but most of them are dirty and covered with fish debris. One of them, however—Zicatela, which, if Puerto Escondido were shaped like an arm bent at the elbow, would be the bicep—is notable for its unique waves. The water, for some reason, crests just short of apocalyptic. The first time I went there, I stood watching the waves, trying to get a sense of their size. I thought they only looked about as big as the waves at one of the previous beaches I had been to, which is to say maybe 5 ft. They broke far out into the ocean, giving the water enough time to form smaller waves near the sand, which I estimated were maybe a foot or so tall—Lake Michigan waves. Then I saw someone actually go into the water, and realized that the "Lake Michigan" waves were as tall as a full-grown man and the ones farther out had to be several times larger. It takes the water so long to fall from the top of the crests that the whole thing seems to be moving in slow motion. The spray, when it finally reaches the surface again, is as tall as or taller than the original wave. It's incredible.

*--Daniel Hertz*

Laguna Manialtepec and the surrounding forest are picturesque and peaceful, a welcome respite from the activity of the city. La Puesta del Sol offers tours of the flora and fauna in the lake's ecosystem; you can also take a self-directed tour in one of their kayaks. For a more unique experience, ask about night tours to see the bioluminescent plankton; tourists can sometimes take a quick swim and come out glowing. (☎588 3867. Tours 700 pesos for up to 7 people; each additional person 100 pesos. Kayak rental 120 pesos per hr. Open 7am-4pm.) The restaurant itself serves tasty renditions of Oaxacan dishes for 50-80 pesos. (Open 8am-6pm. Cash only.) To get back to town, wait for any eastbound bus or *taxi colectivo* (15 pesos). Alternatively, the entire trip can be organized from Puerto Escondido. **Dimar Travel Agency**, Gasga 905, offers 5hr. tours of the lake and surroundings leaving at 7am and 3pm daily (☎582 1551; 400 pesos per person).

More elaborate adventures can be also be arranged in Puerto Escondido. In addition to Laguna Manialtepec, Dimar sends groups to coastal waterfalls, natural hot springs and more. (350-550 pesos per person, depending on destination.) **Rutas de Aventura** allows you to personalize longer eco-vacations through Guerrero's interior, where you can mountain bike, hike through jungles and coffee plantations, kayak lagoons and rivers, and enjoy the state's extensive bird, reptile, and crocodile population. (☎582 0170; www.rutasdeaventura. com.mx. Prices based on tour length and itinerary.)

## ◆ NIGHTLIFE

Like everything else in town, Puerto Escondido's nightlife is split between the Adoquín and Playa Zicatela. Many restaurants on the beach transform into low-key bars late in the evening with two-for-one happy hours before the more energetic establishments take over. To get to Zicatela from Gasga, head to the far eastern end of the tourist corridor where taxis line up at night; cabs can be hailed for the reverse trip anywhere along C. del Moro (25 pesos). If you don't want to bother with a cab, it's easy to bar-hop on either side of town. Though the hardcore surfers might use up most of their energy during the day, most of the rest of the tourists in Puerto Escondido came to party, and there are plenty of opportunities to let off some steam.

▓ **Casa Babylon,** towards the northern end of Playa Zicatela. This cafe/bookstore becomes an intimate but rowdy hangout at night. College-age kids get sweaty by the bar, while others have a few drinks and watch the show. Mixed drinks 30 pesos. Open 8pm-late. Cash only.

▓ **Wipeout Bar** (☎582 2302), in the middle of Gasga. A relaxed bar overlooking the bustle and breeze on the street. Loud reggaeton and hip hop fails to deter conversation as the young and beautiful play pool or sip drinks in cool blue lighting. Beers 20 pesos, 2-for-1 mixed drinks 70 pesos. M women drink free. Open W-Sa 8pm-3am. Cash only.

**Barfly** (www.barfly.com.mx), on Playa Zicatela. Where people go to have a few drinks, laugh with friends, and lounge on the 2nd floor terrace. Beer 25 pesos. Mixed drinks 50 pesos. 2-for-1 drinks 10pm-1am. Open W-Su 10pm-3am. Cash only.

**Cabo Blanco,** on Playa Zicatela. A lively if sometimes sloppy dance floor where tourists lose themselves to American and Latin hits. Beers 20 pesos. Mixed drinks 50 pesos. M drinks 2-for-1. Open daily 8pm-3am. Cash only.

**Blue Station,** across from Wipeout Bar (see above). A psychedelic mix of neon paint and blacklights combines with pounding club music. Beer 20 pesos. Mixed drinks 50 pesos. Open M-Sa 9pm-3am. Cash only.

**Los Tarros,** on the Adoquín. The occasional table is lost amid the crush of dancing bodies. Fight your way to the bar, grab a drink, and join the sweaty bodies getting down to the loud Latin dance hits. Beers 20 pesos. Mixed drinks 35 pesos. M-Th 2-for-1 drinks 8-11pm. Open daily 10:30pm-4am. Cash only.

**Catch Bar** (www.catchbar.com.mx), on the eastern end of Gasga. Watch bar-hoppers on the street below from the terrace, or just enjoy the cool night air. Music videos on large flatscreens encourage you to get up and dance to the electronic and Latin music. Beer 20 pesos. Mixed drinks from 35 pesos. Open Th-Sa 9pm-late. Cash only.

# MAZUNTE ☎958

Backpackers in Mexico inevitably make the pilgrimage to Mazunte (pop. 700). One of the most beautiful beaches on the southern Pacific coast, Mazunte is much more relaxed and less surfer-oriented than nearby Puerto Escondido. At night, the hostel bars come alive as guests spill out onto the beach and commune under the starry sky. More than a few ignore the posted "Prohibido el consumo de drogas" signs, though *Let's Go* doesn't recommend following their lead, especially in light of Mexico's harsh drug laws.

## ☐ TRANSPORTATION

Mazunte can be reached by taking a **Mazunte camioneta** from **Zipolite** (every 20min. 6am-7pm, 5 pesos). *Camionetas* also run to and from **Pochutla** (approx. 10 pesos). From **Puerto Escondido,** catch a microbus at the *crucero* and get dropped off at the intersection named **San Antonio** (approx. 1hr., 15 pesos). From there, catch a *camioneta* to Mazunte (every 30min., 8 pesos) or take a **taxi** (25 pesos).

## ☐☐ ORIENTATION AND PRACTICAL INFORMATION

Mazunte is a 1km stretch of beach with a secluded cove on the far west end. Parallel to the beach is the main road, **Avenida Paseo del Mazunte** (also known as **Principal**), which runs between Mazunte and nearby towns. Several dirt roads run between Mazunte and the beach and are lined with signs for rooms to rent.

**Tourist Information:** A small tourist information **stand** on the east end of the main road is open sporadically. Large town reference map available.

**Medical Services: Centro de Salud,** along a dirt road called Maguey at the western edge of town. Go straight as it breaks off from Principal (which veers right). Open M-F and Su 8am-2pm and 4-8pm.

**Police:** In the Agencia Municipal behind the basketball courts in the middle of town. Unstaffed during the day—your best bet is early evening.

**Laundromat: Lavandería Mazunte,** just west of the basketball courts on the main road. 15 pesos per kg. Open daily 8am-8pm.

**Internet Access: Marcos Net,** on Principal, on the eastern edge of town. 12 pesos per hr. Open daily 10am-10pm.

## ☐ ACCOMMODATIONS

If all the attractive hotel rooms have been taken or you're looking to save money, many houses between the main road and the beach rent rooms for cheap and may be worth checking out. The *palapa* restaurants, *posadas*, and hostels rent out hammocks and camping space on their grounds. (40-50 pesos for a hammock, roughly the same per person for campsites.)

**La Atarraya,** on the beach at the end of C. La Barrita. Basic, cheap rooms. The ping pong table in its attached restaurant is a center of activity for young expats and other locals. Singles 100 pesos. Cash only. ❶

**Posada Agujón,** on the right side of Rinconcito a block from the beach. Clean rooms with concrete floors and mosquito nets. Singles 250 pesos; doubles 350 pesos. Cash only. ❸

**Posada del Arquitecto,** on the left side of C. Rinconcito on the beach. A rambling collection of *palapa* bungalows and dorms set in a grove of cacti and palm trees. Clean beds and mosquito nets. Bring your own lock for the lockers. Free Wi-Fi. Hammocks 50 pesos; dorms 50 pesos; *cabañas* 250 pesos, with bath 350-400 pesos. Prices rise 40% in the high season. Cash only. ❶

**Posada Ziga** (☎583 9295; posadaziga.com), on the eastern edge of the beach near the Centro de la Tortuga. A beautiful series of terraces with hammocks overlooking the beach. Large and immaculate rooms with plush beds. Singles 280-400 pesos; doubles 400-500 pesos. Cash only. ❹

**Estrella Fugaz** (☎583 9297), near the beach and Rinconcito. Some of the cheapest private rooms in town. Simple and clean, but a little dark. Rooms 150 pesos per person. Cash only. ❶

**La Alta Mira** (☎101 8332; www.labuenavista.com/alta_mira/indexflash.htm), down C. Rinconcito and up a hill on the right. Quiet time free of surfers and beach vendors. La Alta Mira's 10 elegant bungalows make you feel a million miles from anywhere without sacrificing any luxury. Gorgeous tiled baths, stunning views over the cove, and stairs leading to the beach. Bungalows 300-500 pesos, in high season 700-800 pesos. Cash only. ❹

**Balam Juyuc** (☎101 1808; balamjuyuc.com.mx), 20m down the road from La Alta Mira. Same beautiful views with a younger, more friendly atmosphere and for significantly less. *Cabañas* are scattered around a more rustic section of the hill and baths are shared but squeaky clean. Cheap home-cooked breakfasts also available. *Cabañas* 250 pesos for 1 person; 2-3 people 300 pesos. Cash only. ❸

## 🔲 FOOD

Most of the restaurants at the beach are open late and double as bars.

**Armadillo,** up a hill on Callejón del Armadillo, off Rinconcito. Doubling as a gallery for bronze statuary, Armadillo serves up Mexican and Italian food at low prices. The *pasta a la mexicana* (45 pesos) is superb. Fresh bread available; ask for prices. Quesadillas 35-45 pesos. Seafood 70-85 pesos. Open daily 8am-11pm. Cash only. ❸

**La Atarraya,** at the end of La Barrita. The waiter takes your order while playing ping pong. As you wait, the people hanging out around the table are more than happy to introduce themselves and strike up a conversation. Oh, and the food is tasty too. Breakfasts 25-35 pesos. *Pescado* and *mariscos* 75-100 pesos. Entrees 30-60 pesos. Cash only. ❷

**Maíz Azul,** on Playa Ventanilla, near the tourist office. Sumptuously fresh food. Let them know if you're in a hurry—they lavish care and time on the meals here, and it's easy to forget about the time. The *pescado* (70 pesos) is well worth the wait. Octopus 60 pesos. Shrimp 80 pesos. Open daily 8am-6pm. Cash only. ❸

**Estrella Fugaz** (☎583 9297), at the beach and Rinconcito. A 2nd floor balcony overlooking the beach. An impressive selection of juice mixes. If you're in need of dessert, the banana and Nutella crepes are delicious. Entrees 30-80 pesos. Open 8am-11pm. Cash only. ❷

**El Arbolito,** toward the eastern end of the beach. A wide assortment of Mexican specialties like *milanesa de res* (breaded steak), *mariscos*, and pasta just a couple meters from the crashing waves. Entrees 40-90 pesos. Open 8am-11pm. Cash only. ❷

## 👁 SIGHTS

**CENTRO MEXICANO DE LA TORTUGA.** Besides the beach, the town's main attraction is the Centro Mexicano de la Tortuga, or Mexican Turtle Center, on the far eastern side of town. The Centro does conservation and awareness work with the shell-dwelling species of the Oaxacan coast, and has a sort of all-turtle zoo that's open to the public. Inside the compound, a path winds around several outdoor pens before entering an indoor aquarium, where more sea turtles live with a few fish and rays. In all, you can see 14 different species of turtles, ranging from humble little creatures to the enormous sea turtles, to a rather ugly, ornery-looking thing called a *tortuga lagarto*, or lizard turtle. (☎584 3376. *Open W-Sa 10am-4:30pm, Su 10am-2:30pm. Entrance with guided tour approx. every 10min.; tours in English available. 22.50 pesos.)*

**PLAYA VENTANILLA.** A quick 3½km *camioneta* ride west of Mazunte brings you to this beach with hostile waves and mostly dirty sand. The reason to make the trip is the **Cooperativa Ventanilla** (a 1km walk down the road marked by the "La Ventanilla" sign), the site of a communal colony of 25 families who have dedicated themselves to protecting the wetlands at the mouth of the Tonameca River. The group runs amazing **lancha tours** that pass through the mangrove swamps. Guides paddle the lagoon in small boats, pointing out enormous crocodiles, iguanas, and members of the vast bird population. Through the choke of mangroves the guides paddle to an island in the middle, where they protect small native deer, mammals, and baby mangroves. Adjacent to the pens the women of the island sell coconuts, tacos, and small handicrafts. The Cooperative also collects sea turtle eggs from the beach to protect them from predators. After they hatch, the turtles are released into the ocean. If you're interested in volunteering, the Cooperative provides housing and meals for 170 pesos per day for travelers willing to help with reforestation, litter cleanup, and turtle rescue operations. Be aware that though there may be other groups offering tours, only the Cooperativa Ventanilla does environmental preservation work. *(On the left side of the road just before the tourist office. Lancha tours leave from 8am-5pm; 1hr.; 40 pesos, children ages 6-12 20 pesos. Open daily 9am-5pm.)*

# ZIPOLITE ☎958

Zipolite (pop. 1500) was once famous for hosting Mexico's only nude beach. Today, you'd be hard pressed to find it. (It's near the western edge of Roca Blanca.) Zipotle has now taken its place as one of the many beach bum paradises on Oaxaca's Pacific coast. The tourist-friendly part of town consists of little more than a road lined with cheap hotels and restaurants, many of which are owned by foreigners (largely Italian and French) who fell in love with the place and never left. There's not much to do except eat, sit on the beach, and swim. Be aware, though, that vicious riptides make swimming here much more dangerous than at nearby Mazunte.

 **RIPTIDES.** Zipolite's beaches have brutal waves coming in from two directions, creating a series of channels that suck unsuspecting swimmers out to sea. Although ferocious, these channels are not very wide. If you find yourself being pulled from the shore, do not panic and do not attempt to swim directly toward the beach; rather, swim parallel to the beach until clear of the seaward current. Many people have drowned at Zipolite, and warnings should be taken seriously—watch for red and yellow warning flags on the beach that mark especially dangerous areas. If you do swim, keep close to the shore.

▐ **TRANSPORTATION.** Just 4km west of Puerto Ángel, Zipolite is easily accessible by any vehicle rumbling down the poorly paved coastal road. **Camionetas** (5 pesos), **taxis colectivos** (10 pesos), and **taxis especiales** (30 pesos) pass frequently.

## THE LOCAL STORY

### LA VENTANILLA

At the mouth of the Tonameca River, just west of Mazunte, 25 families have formed a commune on an ecological reserve, dedicated to protecting the biodiversity of the area. They finance their wetland conservation efforts by leading tours through the surrounding mangrove swamps, paddling small boats through the dense foliage.

Along the way, keep your eyes peeled for lurking crocodiles, white heron mating colonies, camouflaged toucans, and the magical majagua flower, which changes color over the course of the day. The tour culminates with a visit to an island in the middle of the lagoon, where rare, native crocodiles and deer are bred in captivity. Nearby, the colony's female residents serve up fresh coconut refreshments and sell small handicrafts.

Many of the guides grew up around the colony. Their knowledge of the area is comprehensive and intimate—no question goes unanswered. With most similar tours of lower quality going for 10 times as much, this one can't be missed.

*(To get La Ventanilla, take a camioneta from Mazunte bound for the crucero at San Antonio (5 pesos); get off at the sign that says "La Ventanilla." Then walk 1½km down the road. Alternatively, take a taxi (25 pesos). Open daily 8am-5pm. Tours 40 pesos per person, children 20 pesos.)*

*Taxis colectivos* run to **Pochutla** (15 pesos); at night, take a private taxi (25min., 100 pesos).

**ORIENTATION AND PRACTICAL INFORMATION.** Zipolite consists of one 2km stretch of beach and the roads that run behind it. The western end of the beach, where most of the hotels and restaurants are located, is called **Roca Blanca.** It's lined by a paved road that runs parallel to the larger east-west road; the two are connected by a dirt road on the west end and a paved road on the other end.

While there is no currency exchange in Zipolite, most hotels and *cabañas* accept US$, and some of the bigger ones accept traveler's checks. The **police station** is largely unmanned; the branch in **Puerto Ángel** (☎584 3207) is a much safer bet. The nearest hospital, **General Hospital,** is between Puerto Ángel and Pochutla. (☎584 0219.) Get **internet access** at **Azul Profundo,** on the eastern edge of Roca Blanca where it intersects the other paved road. (☎958 584 3363. 15 pesos per hr. Open daily 10am-9pm.) **Posada Lavandería Navidad,** on the western edge of Paisan across from Posada Esmeralda, offers next-day laundry service. (Wash and dry 12 pesos per kg. Open daily 8am-6pm.)

**ACCOMMODATIONS AND FOOD.** Almost every *palapa* on the beach has huts out back, most with relatively clean shared baths. Whichever you choose, be sure to put valuables in a safe box. Nicer, more secure *cabañas* and rooms are on the west side of the beach. Ask around for prices for hammocks and camping space. Near the middle of Roca Blanca, **A Nice Place On the Beach ❶** is a model of truth in advertising. If they're available, ask for one of the upstairs rooms, which are less vulnerable to mosquitoes than the more basic ground-level digs. (☎584 3195. Singles 80-100 pesos; prices rise about 50 pesos in the high season. Cash only.) **Piedra de Fuego ❶,** on the first dirt path to the right as you exit Roca Blanca, is a more secluded, rustic option with wooden cabins next to a community mangrove preserve. (☎100 2853. Doubles 100 pesos; triples 150 pesos. Cash only.) **Posada México ❸** has a lovely desert garden. The adjacent rooms are well sized and spotless. (☎584 3194; posadamexico.com. Singles 250 pesos, with bath 300 pesos; doubles with bath 350 pesos. Cash only.) Alongside the beach is **Hotel Brisa Marina ❶,** a multi-story hotel with rooms from the simple to near-luxurious. Beds are soft and clean. (☎584 3193. Singles 80 pesos; singles and doubles with bath 150 pesos, with bath and balcony 250 pesos.

Prices rise in the high season, but are often negotiable.) **El Carrizo Hostel** ❶ sits past the end of Roca Blanca where the paved road becomes dirt. With an outdoor kitchen with a table, sofas, and a wandering cat, El Carrizo is the place to be. The rooms are basic but sanitary. (Singles 80 pesos, with fan 100 pesos; doubles 100/120 pesos. Cash only.)

Zipolite has more than its fair share of seafood and pasta restaurants, not to mention a surprising number of places to get a filet mignon (or *filete miñón*). For good Mexican try **Los Almendros** ❶, near the eastern end of Paisan, where you can get cheap *antojitos* (25-35 pesos) or larger dinner dishes. (*Tlayudas* 30 pesos. Chicken dishes 60-70 pesos. Open daily 10am-10pm. Cash only.) At **3 de Diciembre** ❹, a block north of Roca Blanca on the other paved road, you can gorge yourself on pizzas (80-140 pesos) or delicious fruit pies (25 pesos). (Open W-Sa 7pm-2am. Cash only.) **El Terrible** ❸, at the eastern end of Roca Blanca, serves up sweet and savory crepes (a nod to the French owner's homeland), and a variety of steaks including filet mignon. (Crepes 35-80 pesos, filet mignon 250 pesos; other entrees 60-90 pesos. Open Tu-Sa 6pm-midnight. Cash only.) **Panadería Italiana** ❶, near the center on the main tourist drag, has pizza by the slice (25 pesos), lasagna (vegetarian and with meat, 70 pesos), ice cream (15 pesos), and pastries. (Open 8am-10pm. Cash only.)

**🎵 NIGHTLIFE.** Nightlife in Zipolite is subdued. Many of the beachfront hotels have their own small bars. If you want a change of scenery, try **Buonvento**, on the paved street off the east end of Roca Blanca. Under the open sky people drink and listen to live bands from around Oaxaca. (Beer 20 pesos. Mixed drinks 40-50 pesos. Open daily 7pm-12:30am. Cash only.) For a little dancing there's **Disco-Bar La Puesta,** where a mixed crowd, mostly women, alternate drinks at the bar while grooving to dance hits. (Beer 20 pesos. Mixed drinks 40-55 pesos. W salsa night. Open W-Sa 10pm-2am. Cash only.)

**🏄 OUTDOOR ACTIVITIES.** If you feel like getting more intimately acquainted with critters under the waves, **Azul Profundo,** on the eastern edge of Roca Blanca, runs 4hr. snorkeling tours that promise encounters with sea turtles and dolphins. Expeditions are scheduled daily for 9:30am, though bad weather can cause delays. Expeditions cost 150 pesos per person.

## SAN AGUSTINILLO

Four kilometers from Zipolite, the small town of San Agustinillo offers uncrowded beaches and swimable waves—just keep some distance from the rocks. A few restaurants, convenience stores, and bungalows round out the town. To take on the waves, rent some body boards, fins, or surfboards from **Mexico Lindo y Que Rico** (50 pesos per hr., boogie boards 30 pesos), on the western edge of town. Many beginners start here before braving the bigger waves at Zipolite. Mexico Lindo offers one-on-one lessons (350 pesos for 2hr.).

San Agustinillo is accessible via a **Mazunte camioneta** from **Zipolite** (every 20min. 6am-7pm, 5 pesos), or any Zipolite-bound *camioneta* from Pochutla. Find **internet access** at **Malex,** near the eastern edge of town. (12 pesos per hr. Open M-Sa 8:30am-9pm, Su 9am-8pm.)

**Mexico Lindo** ❹ also has some of the best rooms on the beach. New and clean with fans, private baths, and double beds, this is a great place to rest your head. (Singles and doubles 300 pesos, with ocean view 400 pesos. Cash only.) Across the street and up a hill, the *cabañas* at **Villas Antrópolis** ❺ don't come cheap, but include private kitchens, decks, and beautiful views of the water below. Best for longer stays. (2-person *cabañas* 500-550 pesos; prices nearly double in high season. Also rentable by the month for significant discounts. Cash only.)

For a cheaper stay on the other end of the beach, go to **Casa de Huéspedes Kaly ❷**, which has extraordinarily well-kept, quiet rooms with big fans, comfortable beds with mosquito nets, and spotless baths. (No hot water. Singles 200 pesos; doubles 250 pesos. Cash only.) The adjacent **restaurant ❶** serves *mariscos* (starting at 70 pesos) and hearty meat dishes. (Open daily 9am-8pm. Cash only.) Nearby, **Paraíso del Pescador ❷** has traditional Mexican dishes—including some exceptional *huevos rancheros* for 40 pesos. (Open Tu-Su 8am-9:30pm. Cash only.) To cool down, stop by **El Sueño de Frida ❶** for some ice cream or a beer (both 15 pesos). There are also simple breakfasts like fruit salad or yogurt with granola for 12-40 pesos. (Open daily 8:30am-1pm, 4-10pm. Cash only.)

## POCHUTLA ☎958

Pochutla (pop. 66,000) has the thick, hot, and humid air of the nearby beach towns, but without the beach—or really much charm at all. Instead, it's the mini-region's transportation hub, so you will be getting to know it (however briefly) if you're planning on spending time in Mazunte, Zipolite, or Puerto Ángel.

**▐ TRANSPORTATION. Taxis colectivos** heading to **Puerto Escondido** (50 pesos), **Puerto Ángel** (10 pesos), **Zipolite** (20 pesos), and beyond leave from the downhill part of town, across from the Estrella del Valle bus station. The most efficient way to travel between coastal towns is by **camioneta** (every 20min. 6am-8pm; 7 pesos to **Puerto Ángel**, 10 pesos to Zipolite or Mazunte). The first-class station, served by **OCC** and **SUR**, is on Cárdenas on the left as you enter the city. **Buses** run to **Huatulco** (1hr., 9 per day 8:20am-10:50pm, 34 pesos); **Mexico City** (12hr., 7:30pm, 642 pesos); **Oaxaca** (7hr.; 8:20am, 3:50, 10:05pm; 252 pesos); **Puerto Escondido** (1hr.; every hr. 6am-7:20pm; 50 pesos); **San Cristóbal de las Casas** (12hr., 8 and 10:50pm, 378 pesos); **Tehuantepec** (4hr., 5 per day 8:20am-9:20pm, 138 pesos); and **Tuxtla Gutiérrez** (10hr., 8 and 10:50pm, 324 pesos). The second-class bus station, a block up and across the street on Cárdenas, sends buses to **Oaxaca** (7hr., 7 per day 5:30am-10:30pm, 90 pesos) and **Mexico City** (12hr., 4 and 7pm, 410 pesos). **Tránsitos Rápidos de Pochutla,** just past the second-class station, goes to Bahías de Huatulco (1hr., daily every 15min. 5:30am-8:30pm, 16 pesos).**Eclipse 70,** next door, goes to Oaxaca (7hr., every 1½hr. 4am-11:30pm, 120 pesos).

**▐▌▐ ORIENTATION AND PRACTICAL INFORMATION.** To reach the *zócalo*, church, and main outdoor market, follow **Cárdenas** uphill and turn right on **Juárez** a block after the area where the *colectivos* drop-off. **24hr. ATMs** available at **Banamex,** on the *zócalo*, opposite the Agencia Municipal, which offers financial services (open M-F 9am-4pm); **Scotiabank,** uphill on Cárdenas, just after the intersection with Juárez; **HSBC** on the left just past Scotiabank. Other services include: **police,** in the Palacio Municipal to the left of the church (☎584 0159); **Farmacias de Más Ahorro** (☎584 1213), just before Juárez on Cárdenas; **Hospital General,** also known as **SSA,** between Pochutla and Puerto Ángel (☎584 0219); **internet access** at **Ciberespacio,** in front of the church in the *zócalo* (10 pesos per hr.; open M-Sa 9am-9pm); and the **post office,** right on Juárez toward the *zócalo* and to the left of the church, behind the Palacio Municipal (open M-F 8am-3pm). **Postal code:** 70900.

**▐▌▐ ACCOMMODATIONS AND FOOD. Hotel Santa Cruz ❶,** on Cárdenas near all the transit stations, has clean, medium-sized rooms good for crashing in the event of a long layover. (☎584 0116. Singles 120 pesos, with bath 150 pesos; doubles 150/180 pesos. Cash only.) If for some reason you're planning on sticking around for a few days, **Hotel Izala ❷,** on Cárdenas just past Juárez, has more comfortable rooms closer to the activity in the *zócalo*. (Singles 200 pesos, with

A/C 250 pesos; doubles 350/500 pesos.) For a quick bite, try **Restaurant Lichita** ❷, Cárdenas 79, where large portions come quickly. (*Comida corrida* 35 pesos. Open daily 9am-8pm. Cash only.) For something a bit more elaborate, try **Kore's Pizza** ❸ on Constitución on the *zócalo*, which boasts 30 different combinations of toppings, from Oaxaqueña (chorizo, beans, and jalapeños) to Houston (steak, pepper, onion, and *salchicha*). (☎584 1010. Small 65 pesos, medium 95 pesos, large 139 pesos. Open daily noon-11pm. Cash only.)

**PACK YOUR HAMMOCK.** In the beach towns along the south of Oaxaca, many hotel and restaurant owners will let you tie up your hammock between trees or near their own hammocks for a nominal fee, which saves the cost of a room and affords more protection and ambience than two trees in a dark forest.

# PUERTO ÁNGEL ☎958

Puerto Ángel (pop. 12,000) is several times larger than Mazunte or Zipolite. Its center is bustling by comparison, with a steady stream of taxis and small trucks rumbling down the main drag. Beyond the *Calle Principal*, though, the old lackadaisical Oaxacan coast returns, with Mexican families lounging at Playa Panteón and backpackers swinging on hammocks on the hills overlooking the bay.

## ▐ TRANSPORTATION

**Camionetas** along the coast usually turn back at Zipolite. To get to **Zipolite,** or any of the other nearby beach towns you'll have to take a **taxi colectivo** (10 pesos). To get to **Pochutla,** where you can get buses to the rest of Mexico, you can either take a *taxi colectivo* (10 pesos) or a Puerto Ángel-Pochutla *camioneta* (7 pesos). After 7pm or so, you may need to take a **taxi especial,** which can cost 30 pesos to Zipolite and 50 pesos to Pochutla. If you don't want to walk from the center of town to Playa Panteón and back, a *taxi especial* will take you for about 10 pesos. All forms of transportation pass through the center of town on the main road.

## ▐▐ ORIENTATION AND PRACTICAL INFORMATION

The backbone of Puerto Ángel and the town's only major street, **Boulevard Vigilio Uribe,** curves around **Bahía Puerto Ángel.** The eastern half of the bay is the main part of town; the center is marked by a small **plaza** with a **pier** at the intersection of **Uribe** and **Vasconcelos,** which runs uphill from the water. To the west is **Playa Panteón,** a swimmer-friendly beach lined with *restaurantes turísticos*.

**Tourist Office:** On the 2nd floor of a small building at the plaza. Open M-F 9am-2pm and 4-8pm.

**Laundromat: Lavandería del Ángel,** up the hill on Vasconcelos. Open M-Sa 10am-8pm.

**Police:** (☎584 3207), a 3min. walk up Vasconcelos from the intersection with Uribe on the left.

**Pharmacy: Farmapronto,** on Uribe west of Vasconcelos. Open daily 9am-9pm.

**Medical Services: Centro de Salud,** up the hill on the left side of Vasconcelos, set back from the street on a small driveway. If you reach the police station you've gone too far.

**Internet Access: Estrella,** on Uribe, west of Vasconcelos. 12 pesos per hr. Fax office available. Open daily 8am-10:30pm.

## ACCOMMODATIONS AND CAMPING

When looking for a place to stay, you'll have to decide whether you want to be in the main part of town or on Playa Panteón. The latter accommodations have the advantage of being right on the beach, but they are often more expensive and have more of a family atmosphere; the former are farther from the surf but more laid-back; several also have beautiful views of the bay.

**Posada Canta Ranas** (☎584 3129), on a hill behind Uribe. Take either of the dirt roads that intersect with Uribe near the small blue bridge west of the center of town; Canta Ranas is up a stairway on the left where the dirt road suddenly runs next to a paved street. Easily the best place to stay in town. A terrace with gorgeous views overlooking the water has foosball and air hockey tables. Rooms are inviting and clean. Free Wi-Fi. Doubles and triples 300-350 pesos. Cash only. ❹

**Casa de Huéspedes El Capy** (☎584 3240), about 300m from Playa Panteón on the road back to town. One of the cheapest places in town with clean rooms, the higher floors have views to the beach. Singles 200 pesos; doubles 300 pesos. Cash only. ❷

**Hotel La Cabaña** (☎584 3105), behind the restaurants on Playa Panteón. Friendly luxury, with huge, plush, well-decorated rooms. Free coffee, purified water, and internet. Upstairs there's a restaurant and a terrace. Singles 300 pesos; doubles 400 pesos; triples 550 pesos. Cash only. ❹

**Buena Vista** (☎584 3104; www.labuenavista.com). Take one of the dirt roads from Uribe near the blue bridge west of the center; after about 50m, a small dirt pathway juts out to the left and leads to Buena Vista. Rooms are spacious and clean, and have balconies with views of the bay. If you don't feel like making the trek to the beach, there's a private pool. Free parking. Singles and doubles from 350 pesos. Cash only. ❺

## FOOD

There isn't much of a middle ground in Puerto Ángel between the impromptu food stands around the intersection of Uribe and Vasconcelos and the overpriced tourist restaurants serving *mariscos* and spaghetti near the water. For fruits and vegetables, go to the **market** on Palo Bello just off Uribe, west of the town center.

**Las Pequeñas Placeres,** in Hotel La Cabaña (see above). A similar menu to the restaurants right on the beach, but you get a lovely view and are removed from the jostle of the families and vendors below. Entrees 70-120 pesos. Open daily 8am-10pm. Cash only. ❸

**Restaurante Leyvis y Vicente,** about halfway through the lineup of restaurants on Playa Panteón. As the waves inch closer and closer throughout the day, Leyvis y Vicente serve up traditional Mexican dishes and, of course, copious amounts of seafood (80-120 pesos). Chicken and beef dishes 60-70 pesos. Open daily 8am-10pm. Cash only. ❸

**El Chapulín,** right on the beach, off of Uribe, west of the center of town. A variety of Mexican seafood and pasta dishes for slightly less money than at similar establishments on Playa Panteón. Fish 70-90 pesos. Pasta 60-90 pesos. Open daily 8am-10pm. Cash only. ❸

**Café Sol,** on the right side of Uribe, west of the center of town. One of the few establishments to break the *marisco* mold, serving breakfasts, smoothies, and yogurt in a fun, bohemian atmosphere. Breakfast about 35 pesos. Open daily 9am-6pm. ❷

# ISTHMUS OF TEHUANTEPEC

East of Oaxaca, the North American continent narrows to a slender strip of land 215km wide, known as the Isthmus of Tehuantepec, or El Istmo. The isthmus is the shortest division between the Gulf of Mexico and the Pacific Oceans, and is home to the indigenous Zapotec culture of Oaxaca state. Many of El Istmo's residents speak only Chatino, their native dialect, or Zapotecan—Spanish is rarely heard. Traditionally an agricultural civilization, modern Zapotecs are famed for their weaving, jewelry and political achievements—Benito Juárez himself was of Zapotec origin.

## TEHUANTEPEC ☎971

Tehuantepec (pop. 60,000) derives its name from the Náhuatl word *Tecuantepec*, meaning "maneater hill." Founded by Zapotec emperor Cosijoeza in the early 1500s, the oldest and most historically significant of El Istmo's three principal cities contains some of the first churches built by *indígenas*. In the 19th century, the city served as Porfirio Díaz's base during initial skirmishes with the French. Tehuantepec is famous for preserving Zapotec flavor in all aspects of modern life.

**TRANSPORTATION.** To get to town from the **Cristóbal Colón/ADO bus station** (1½km north of the *centro*), make an immediate left as you exit the station. This street becomes Héroes, veers to the right, and eventually leads to a dead end. Turn right and walk a few more blocks, make a left on Hidalgo, and follow it to the *zócalo*. From the station to town **taxis** cost 15 pesos; mototaxis cost 5 pesos. **Cristóbal Colón** (☎715 0108) **buses** travel to: **Huatulco** (3hr., 5 per day 2:30-11:55pm, 102-108 pesos); **Mexico City** (12hr., 11 per day 12:15am-9:45pm, 620 pesos); **Oaxaca** (5hr., 19 per day 12:20am-8:15pm, 164 pesos); **Tuxtla Gutiérrez** (6hr., 5 per day 3:10am-9:30pm, 192 pesos). Buses also go to neighboring **Juchitán** (30min., 18 per day 5:30am-9pm, 16 pesos) and **Salina Cruz** (30min., 9 per day 9am-11pm, 10 pesos), though the fastest, cheapest way to travel to either is to walk two blocks on 5 de Mayo to the **carretera.**

**PRACTICAL INFORMATION.** Services include: a **tourist office** at the **Casa de la Cultura**, on Guerrero, two blocks north of the *zócalo;* **Banorte and Bancomer** on 5 de Mayo just west of the *zócalo;* **police** (☎713 7000), at the back of the Palacio Municipal; **Farmacia San Jorge,** on Juárez south of the *zócalo* (open daily 8am-8:30pm); **Centro de Salud,** Guerrero 16, two blocks north of the *zócalo* (☎715 0180; 24hr. service); **Telecomm,** next to the post office (open M-F 8am-7:30pm, Sa 9am-noon); **LADATELs,** in the *zócalo;* **internet access,** on 5 de Mayo at the *zócalo* (10 pesos per hr.; open daily 8am-10:30pm); and the **post office,** at the corner of 22 de Marzo and Hidalgo, on the north side of the *zócalo* (open M-F 8am-3pm). **Postal Code:** 70760.

**ACCOMMODATIONS AND FOOD.** Tehuantepec has only a handful of accommodations, but they're comfortable enough. **Hotel Oasis ❶,** Ocampo 8, a block south of the *zócalo* at the corner of Romero, has sparse, clean, floral-themed rooms with fan, bath, and lots of empty space. (☎715 0008. Reception 24hr. Singles 150 pesos; doubles 190 pesos. Cash only.) **Hotel Donaji del Istmo ❷,** Juárez 10, has clean, tiled rooms around a garden courtyard and a downstairs restaurant. (☎715 0064. Singles 205 pesos, with A/C 285 pesos; doubles 275/350 pesos. Cash only). **Casa de Huéspedes El Istmo ❶** is the town's budget option, with simple rooms and shared outdoor bathrooms (☎715 0019. Singles 100 pesos; doubles 150 pesos. Cash only).

Food options aren't much more plentiful. **Restaurant El Almendro ❷,** inside Hotel Oasis, is one of the nicer establishments. Its wood-furnished bar, cheap beer, and satellite TV draw a crowd come evening. (☎715 0835. Breakfast 35 pesos. Pizza from 40 pesos. Open daily 8am-11pm. Cash only.) **Yizu ❸,** at Domínguez and

Juárez, has an enormous menu with Mexican standards, spaghetti, salads, and desserts. Late in the evenings, young couples hang out and share fudge sundaes and banana splits. There's also a small internet cafe. (Entrees 40-80 pesos; salads 42-50 pesos; fudge sundae 35 pesos. Open daily 8am-11pm. Cash only.) A good meal can be had on the deck of **Restaurant Terranova,** Romero 70. The enchiladas in mole sauce are especially tasty. (*Antojitos* 35-60 pesos. *Carnes* 60-80 pesos. Open daily 8am-9pm.) For budget meals, try the **Mercado de Jesús Carranza ❶,** on the plaza's west side (open daily 8am-8pm; cash only), or the numerous taco stands that pop up in the *zócalo* or behind the Palacio Municipal after dark.

**◻ ▧ SIGHTS AND FESTIVALS.** Tehuantepec's most notable sight is also the best place to find tourist information. Library staff at the **Casa de la Cultura,** on C. Guerrero, will be happy to fill you in on the best spots in Tehauntepec. (☎715 0114. Open M-F 9am-2pm and 5-8pm, Sa 9am-2pm.) The Casa is housed in the **Ex-Convento Rey Cosijopi,** a 16th-century Dominican building named after the Zapotec leader who ordered its construction. A 15min. walk south of the *zócalo* will bring you to **San Blas,** a traditional *mercado*.

Between May and September, each of Tehuantepec's 18 communities holds its own week-long ▧**festival,** beginning with a *baile velorio* at night and followed the next morning by a special mass and several days of parades, live music, dancing, and extensive consumption of *cerveza*. The whole town turns out, with women in traditional Zapotec dress and men and boys on horseback. Tourists are welcome, though a local chaperone is usually needed to get into some social events. During the **Vela Sandunga** (the last week of May), each *barrio* picks a representative to compete for the title of "Reina de la Vela" (Queen of the Candle). Native *tehunos* from all over Mexico return to celebrate the annual **Vela Tehuantepec** (Dec. 26), a party held in the main square. Both require traditional dress for women and *guayaberas* for men.

# OAXACA                                                                    ☎951

From contemporary art galleries to festivals with pre-Columbian roots, Oaxaca (pop. 500,000) is a whirlwind of culture, reflecting its position as a mecca for hip young Mexicans in a city heavily influenced by its indigenous residents. The cityscape is dominated by colonial facades and 16th-century churches; on a nearby mountain top, the even more ancient temples of Monte Albán testify to the region's importance as the capital of the Zapotec state in the AD first millennium. On some buildings and monuments, you may see the quotation, "*El respeto al derecho ajeno es la paz*," which means "Respect for others' rights is peace," and is attributed to 19th-century president and national hero Benito Juárez, who lived in the city before taking office. Outside Oaxaca, indigenous towns hold extensive markets with impressive weavings and artisan crafts.

## ▭ TRANSPORTATION

Oaxaca, between the Sierra Madre del Sur and the Puebla-Oaxaca mountain ranges, sits in the Oaxaca Valley 523km southeast of Mexico City. Principal access to Oaxaca from the north and east is via **Mex. 190** as well as the **"súper-carretera" Mex. 135** from Puebla. Most parts of the city are easily accessible by foot. Local buses, called **urbanos,** cost 3.50 pesos; most run west on **Mina,** cutting east to the north of the *centro* before heading south again on **Juárez;** ask around for the correct line. **Taxis** run anywhere in the city for 30-40 pesos. Walk along a major street or find a *sitio* sign for an unoccupied taxi.

**Flights: Aeropuerto Internacional de Oaxaca Xoxocotlán (OAX;**tourist info booth ☎511 5040), on Mex. 175, 8km south of the city. Open M-Sa 9am-2pm and 5-8pm. To get to the *centro*, take a taxi (100 pesos) or share a van (44 pesos) with other travelers through **Transportes Aeropuerto** (☎514 4350), which has Ian office on Pl. Alameda, near the post office. Tickets available at airport exit. Vans will also take you from your hotel to the airport; prices vary by hotel. Arrangements should be made 1 day in advance by phone or in person. . Airport serves: **Aeroméxico,** Hidalgo 513 (☎516 3229 or 3765); **Aviacsa,** Suárez 604 (☎511 5039); and **Mexicana,** Fiallo 102 (☎516 8414 or 7352), at Independencia.

**Buses:** 2 bus stations serve Oaxaca.

**1st-class bus station: Niños Héroes de Chapultepec 1036** (☎513 3350), 11 blocks north of the *centro*. To get to the *centro*, cross the street and take a westbound "Centro" *urbano* (3.50 pesos) or a taxi (30-40 pesos). Tickets for ADO and Cristóbal Colón available the *zócalo's* travel agencies. **ADO** (☎515 1703) heads to: **Mexico City** (6hr., 13 per day 1am-midnight, 408 pesos); **Palenque** (17hr., 5pm, 578 pesos); **Puebla** (4hr., 5 per day 5am-midnight, 306 pesos); **Veracruz** (7hr.; 8:30am, 10:15pm, 11:59pm; 402 pesos). **Cristóbal Colón** goes to: **Bahías de Huatulco** (8hr.; 9:30am, 9:30, 11pm; 228 pesos); **Puerto Escondido** (10hr.; 9:30am, 9:30, 11pm; 258 pesos); **San Cristóbal de las Casas** (12hr.; 7, 9pm; 408 pesos); **Tehuantepec** (4hr., 13 per day 12:45am-midnight, 174 pesos); and **Tuxtla Gutiérrez** (10hr.; 7, 9, 10:30pm; 364 pesos).

**2nd-class bus station:** 7 blocks west of the *zócalo*, just north of the Central de Abastos market. To get to the *centro*, take a taxi (25 pesos) or a Centro *urbano* in front of the main terminal. By foot, exit left out the terminal, cross busy Periférico, and follow the street as it turns into Trujano. After 7 blocks, Trujano reaches the *zócalo*. Bus station services **regional bus lines.** On market days, buses to surrounding towns leave every 10min. It's a good idea to buy tickets early.

**Car Rental: Hertz,** Alcalá 100A (☎516 2434). Open M-Sa 8am-8pm, Su 9am-6pm. Also at the airport (☎511 5478). **Alamo,** 5 de Mayo 205 (☎514 8534). Sedans from 650 pesos per day. Open M-Sa 8am-8pm, Su 9am-7pm.

## ◪ ⁊ ORIENTATION AND PRACTICAL INFORMATION

Oaxaca is a delightfully walkable city. The city's *zócalo* is comprised of the square and the block-long **Plaza Alameda de León** which fronts the cathedral just north of the square. For five blocks between the *zócalo* and the Iglesia de Santo Domingo, Alcalá serves as a pedestrians-only commercial hub with a high concentration of museums, restaurants, craft shops, and tourists. South of the *zócalo* is a hive of open-air markets, *mezcal* stores, cheap eateries, and chocolate cafes. Except for **Morelos, Independencia** and **Hidalgo,** street names change as they pass the *zócalo*, and sometimes even when they don't. With the same exceptions, the hundreds' place in street addresses indicates how many blocks an establishment is from the *zócalo:* 20 de Noviembre 512, for example, is five blocks south.

**Tourist Offices: SEDETUR,** Juárez 703 (☎502 1200; www.aoaxaca.com). Provides maps, brochures, the free English-language newspaper *Oaxaca Times* (www.oaxacatimes.com), and the free monthly *Guía Cultura*. Open daily 8am-8pm.

**Consulates: Canada,** Suárez 700 #11B (☎513 3777). Open M-F 9:30am-12:30pm. **US,** Alcalá 407 #20 (☎514 3054 or 516 2853; fax 516 2701), in Plaza Santo Domingo. Open M-F 10am-3pm.

**Currency Exchange: Banamex,** Hidalgo 821, east of the cathedral. Open M-Sa 9am-4pm. **Scotiabank,** at Independencia and Alcalá. Open M-F 9am-5pm, Su 10am-3pm. Both have **24hr. ATMs.** Numerous smaller *casas de cambio* surround the *zócalo*.

**Bookstores: Amate Books,** Alcalá 307 #2 (☎516 6960), in Pl. Alcalá. A wonderful collection of English-language novels and nonfiction, plus North American magazines and books about Mexico in several languages. Buys used books. Open M-Sa 10am-8:30pm, Su 2-7pm.

**Libraries: Oaxaca Lending Library,** Suárez 519 (☎518 7077; www.oaxlibrary.com). Everything from the *New Yorker* to *Sports Illustrated* for 1 peso. Also sells used books.

OAXACA

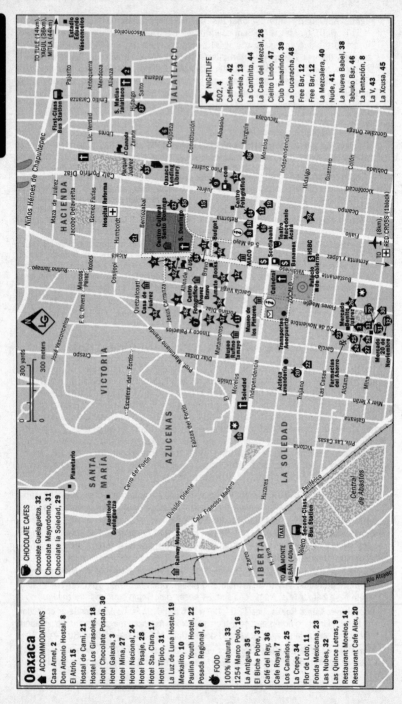

## Oaxaca

**ACCOMMODATIONS**

Casa Arnel, 2
Don Antonio Hostal, 8
El Atrio, 15
Hostal de Cami, 21
Hostel Los Girasoles, 18
Hotel Chocolate Posada, 30
Hotel Galaxia, 3
Hotel Mina, 27
Hotel Nacional, 24
Hotel Pasaje, 28
Hotel Sta. Clara, 17
Hotel Típico, 31
La Luz de Luna Hostel, 19
Mezkalito, 10
Paulina Youth Hostel, 22
Posada Regional, 6

**FOOD**

100% Natural, 33
1254 Marco Polo, 16
La Antigua, 35
El Biche Pobre, 37
Café del Rey, 36
Cafe Royal, 7
Los Canarios, 25
La Crepe, 34
Flor de Loto, 11
Fonda Mexicana, 23
Las Nubes, 32
Las Quince Letras, 9
Restaurant Morelos, 14
Restaurant Cafe Alex, 20

**CHOCOLATE CAFES**

Chocolate Guelaguetza, 32
Chocolate Mayordomo, 31
Chocolate la Soledad, 29

**NIGHTLIFE**

502, 4
Caffeine, 42
Candela, 13
La Cantinita, 44
La Casa del Mezcal, 26
Cielito Lindo, 47
Club Tamarindo, 39
La Cucaracha, 48
Free Bar, 12
Free Bar, 12
La Mezcalera, 40
Nude, 41
La Nueva Babel, 38
Tabuko Bar, 46
La Tentación, 8
La V, 43
La Xcusa, 45

Open M-F 10am-2pm and 4-7pm, Sa 10am-1pm. **Instituto de Artes Gráficos de Oaxaca,** Alcalá 507 (☎516 6980), across from Santo Domingo. Has a library with works in various languages and a museum with rotating art exhibits. Library open M-Sa 10am-8pm. Museum open M and W-Su 10am-8pm. Donations suggested and appreciated.

**Laundromat: Azteca Lavandería,** Hidalgo 404 (☎514 7951), just east of Díaz Ordaz. Open M-Sa 8am-8pm, Su 10am-2pm. 65 pesos per 3½kg. MC/V.

**Emergency:** (☎066).

**Police:** Morelos 108 (☎516 0455), west of the *zócalo.* Open 24hr. M-F 8am-4pm. **CEPROTUR,** Juárez 703 (☎502 1203), handles all tourist safety matters. The **Agencia Ministerio Público** (☎514 2192) handles tourist police issues. Open daily 8am-8pm. **Info Booth,** Independencia 607 (☎511 0740), at the airport and in Museo de los Pintores.

**Red Cross:** Armenta y López 700 (☎516 4803 or 4445), between Pardo and Burgoa. 24hr. ambulance service.

**24hr. Pharmacy: Farmacias del Ahorro,** 20 de Noviembre 304, between las Casas and Aldama. MC/V.

**Hospitals: Hospital Reforma,** Reforma 613 (☎516 0989), at Humboldt.

**Fax Office: Telecomm** (☎516 4902), on Independencia at 20 de Noviembre, around the corner from the post office. Open M-F 8am-6pm, Sa 9am-4pm.

**Telephones: LADATELs** are everywhere; many in the *zócalo.* **Casetas** are clustered on Independencia. Open daily 7am-10pm.

**Internet Access:** Everywhere in Oaxaca, usually for 10 pesos per hr. or less. **e-com,** Juárez 302 (☎516 9925), has a speedy connection. 5 pesos per hr. Open M-Sa 9am-8:30pm. MC/V.

**Post Office:** (☎516 2661), on the west side of Pl. Alameda de León. Open M-F 8am-7pm, Sa 9am-1pm. **Postal Code:** 68000.

# ACCOMMODATIONS

Hotels are everywhere in Oaxaca, and though a good number of them cater to a more upscale clientele, it's easy to find something cheap southwest of the *zócalo.* Farther north, things are a bit calmer and more spread out. Many establishments appear to be suffering from some sort of toilet seat shortage. Reservations are advised on *fiesta* weekends, especially during *Semana Santa,* the *Guelaguetza* (the two Mondays after July 16), and *Día de los Muertos* (Nov. 1-2). For longer stays, rooms are available for rent. Check the tourist office and the *Oaxaca Times* for listings.

## NORTH OF THE ZÓCALO

This area is the best location for those looking to stay close to Oaxaca's artifacts and galleries. These hotels provide a respite from the chaos of the *zócalo* and the markets south.

▦ **Casa Arnel,** Aldama 404 (☎515 2856), at Hidalgo, across from the Iglesia San Matías Jalatlaco and 10 blocks from the *zócalo.* The salient feature of Casa Arnel is its leafy courtyard, where 6 birds, including some impressively large green parrots, spend the day singing in their cages. The 2nd-floor terrace offers a stunning view of the Oaxaca skyline. Rooms are on the small side. Communal baths are spotless. Offers bar, currency exchange, travel agency, library, and laundry service. Breakfast 7:30-10am. Internet access 15 pesos per hr. Singles 200 pesos, with bath 400 pesos; doubles 250/500 pesos. Discounts for longer stays. Prices rise in high season. Cash only. ❷

**El Atrio,** Abasolo 209 (☎118 5259; www.elatriooaxaca.com.mx). Bright rooms with wood floors. There's also a big common area with wooden tables and chairs, perfect for having a coffee in the morning. Laundry service. Free Wi-Fi. Singles 150 pesos, with private bath 250 pesos; doubles 200/400 pesos. Cash only. ❶

**Posada Regional,** Libres 600 (☎518 4626), at Cosijoeza, 10 blocks from the *zócalo*. A leafy staircase leads to modest luxury—rooms have giant, rosy beds, *azulejo* sinks, and gorgeous, patterned baths with skylights. All come with fans and TVs. Singles 300 pesos, each additional person 125 pesos. Cash only. ❹

**La Luz de Luna Hostel,** Juárez 101 (☎516 9576). The small plant-filled courtyard ensures intimacy. Dorms are decorated with big, bright suns painted on the walls. Linens included. Beds 70 pesos. Singles and doubles 200 pesos; each additional person 100 pesos. A quirky *cabaña* on the roof with shared bath 100 pesos. Cash only. ❶

**Hostal San Martín,** 5 de Mayo 315 (☎515 8079). A good choice if you're tired of cramped hostels and want some peace. Plush rooms surround an attractive courtyard, with an in-house restaurant downstairs. Singles 350 pesos; doubles 450 pesos. Cash only. ❺

**Hostal de Cami,** Berriozábal 315 (☎516 1923), just north of Iglesia Santo Domingo. A cozy, clean hostel with a small courtyard on a quiet street. This is a family business: on your way in and out you may pass grandmothers and adorable babies. Dorms and rooms 110 pesos per person. Cash only. ❶

**Don Antonio Hostal,** Morelos 903 (☎516 5162). Dorms are inviting and cozy; draped with curtains to ensure privacy. Private rooms with shared bath are basic, but have king size beds. Dorms 70 pesos; rooms 180 pesos. Cash only. ❶

**Hostel Los Girasoles** (☎516 0518), Morelos 905, on the 2nd floor of a commercial building. Super clean dorms, though the baths are separated by thin wooden walls that don't reach the high ceiling. Private rooms are small but pleasant. Kitchen available. Dorms 90 pesos; rooms 230 pesos. Cash only. ❶

## SOUTH AND WEST OF THE ZÓCALO

Filled with cheap hotels—four or five on the same block, particularly along Díaz Ordaz and Mina—this area can oblige discriminating tastes on a budget. Many hotels face noisy streets; ask for a room in the back or on an upper floor.

▨ **Mezkalito Hostel,** Independencia 101 (☎512 3464; www.hostelmezkalito.com), 6 blocks west of the *zócalo*. A clean, comfortable night's stay with a mountain of amenities. An idler's coastal paradise moved inland, the colorful courtyard's hammocks and upstairs pool overshadow the plain rooms. Communal baths are clean. Luggage storage, lockers, kitchen, and 24hr. internet available. Breakfast and linens included. Reception 24hr. Dorms 120-156 pesos. MC/V. ❶

**Paulina Youth Hostel,** Trujano 321 (☎516 2005 or 514 4210). Though a bit pricey for a hostel, amenities include sparkling communal baths, a hefty breakfast, private lockers, a terrace, and a small lounge space. Internet available. Lockout 3:30-5am. Dorms 150 pesos; singles 280 pesos; doubles 300 pesos. 5-peso discount with HI or ISIC card. MC/V with 10% charge. ❶

**Hotel Chocolate Posada,** Mina 212 (☎516 5760). Just so we're clear: the lobby is literally a top-of-the-line Mexican chocolate shop and courtyard cafe (**Chocolate La Soledad,** p. 251). If that's not enough, the rooms are cozy and have antique bedframes, quilted covers, TVs, and fans. Small, clean communal baths. Singles and doubles 200 pesos; triples 250 pesos. MC/V. ❷

**Hotel Nacional,** 20 de Noviembre 512 (☎516 2780), north of Mina. Not trying overly hard to impress—no gimmicks or frills—but still a solid, economical choice for private rooms. Small, clean beds, and private baths, as well as TVs. Reception 24hr. Singles 200 pesos; doubles 330 pesos. Cash only. ❷

**Hotel Pasaje,** Mina 302 (☎516 4213), 3 blocks south of the *zócalo*. A small leafy court-yard leads to large, tiled rooms with short beds, cable TVs, fans, and dressers. Baths are

OAXACA

top-notch—large and clean. Not-so-picturesque location provides convenient access to markets, restaurants, and chocolate shops, car horns, and diesel exhaust. Singles 180 pesos; doubles 220 pesos; triples 350 pesos. Cash only. ❷

**Hotel Mina,** Mina 304 (☎516 4966), near 20 de Noviembre. Prices here are about as low as Oaxaca will go for private rooms. Organized around a small courtyard, rooms are small but clean; upstairs some have charmingly slanted roofs. Communal baths are clean, but lack toilet seats, and showers are really just elevated faucets. Singles 130 pesos; doubles 160 pesos; triples 250 pesos. Cash only. ❶

**Hotel Galaxia,** 20 de Noviembre 605 (☎516 0488), several blocks south of the *zócalo*. Despite the name, there's nothing fancy about Hotel Galaxia's modest rooms. There is, however, the perk of being close to Oaxaca's chocolate district around the corner on Mina. Singles 283 pesos; doubles 306 pesos. Cash only. ❹

**Hotel Típico,** 20 de Noviembre 612 (☎516 4111). Moderately-priced lime green rooms with tiled floors and clean baths. Rooms line a small courtyard used for parking. Singles 225 pesos; doubles 330 pesos; quads 400 pesos. Cash only. ❸

# FOOD

Considered by many the culinary capital of Mexico, Oaxaca offers menus laden with international food, typical Mexican dishes, and a vast array of local specialties. Oaxacan cooking features seven kinds of *mole*, a complex chile-and-chocolate sauce. Other staples include *tlayudas* (large tortillas jammed with toppings), *quesillo* (boiled string cheese), *chorizo* (spicy sausage), *tasajo* (thinly cut steak), and *chapulines* (tiny cooked grasshoppers doused in oil and chile). *Tamales* are made of ground corn stuffed with beans, chicken, or beef and wrapped in banana or corn leaves before being steamed. Oaxaca's trademark drink, sold everywhere, is the fiery, cactus-based tequila cousin *mezcal*.

**IT'S ON THE HOUSE.** There's no better way to take home a little piece of Oaxaca then to buy a bottle of *mezcal*. Large chains have outlets all over the southern half of the city, but to save a few pesos, try the individual retailers with a single store location; you can often get quality *mezcal* at lower prices. When in bars, ask if there's a house mezcal, which is usually just as good but much cheaper than the name brands.

The *zócalo* itself is besieged by middle-priced, middle-quality bar-restaurants, while the edges of the Alameda host upscale places with fancy versions of standard Mexican fare. Alcalá has pricey food, and García Vigil is home to a bevy of hip French cafes. Cheaper and more authentic *fondas* and *comedores* can be found southwest of the *centro*. The fastest and cheapest regional meals are at the **markets** and **taco stands** on Trujano and Las Casas, southeast of the *zócalo*.

**Restaurant Cafe Alex,** Díaz Ordaz 218 (☎514 0715). Classy, quiet establishment with an enormous menu selection including all the *oaxaqueño* favorites. Gorgeous tropical parrots and shady fronds come with garden seating. *Tlayudas* 40 pesos. *Comida corrida* 50 pesos. Open M-Sa 7am-10pm, Su 7am-1pm. Cash only. ❷

**Las Nubes,** Reforma 404 (☎516 1700), inside Casa Vértiz Hotel. Sit in a lovely courtyard and have some of the tastiest pizzas in town with toppings like salami and goat cheese (59 pesos). There's also an above-average selection of salads (40-67 pesos). Meaty entrees 80-110 pesos. Open M-Sa 8am-10pm, Su 8am-noon. Cash only. ❸

**100% Natural** (☎132 4343), on Dr. Liceaga between Juárez and Suárez, at the southern end of Paseo Juárez El Llano. Oaxaca's outlet of the deservedly popular vegetarian and health food chain. Everything from enchiladas to soy burgers to *linguine* tossed with

OAXACA

sautéed vegetables and soy sauce. Entrees 50-90 pesos. Delicious fruit *licuados* 31-34 pesos. Open 7am-11pm. Cash only. ❷

**Fonda Mexicana,** 20 de Noviembre 408 (☎514 3121). One of the most popular spots south of the *zócalo*. The friendly, family-run restaurant is packed with locals on lunch break. *Comida corrida* (40 pesos) includes dessert. Beers 8 pesos. Open M-Sa 8am-5pm. Cash only. ❷

**Cafe Royal,** García Vigil 403 (☎514 5235), just north of Bravo. An eatery "with a French touch," where hip Mexicans and Europeans sip lattes. The baguettes (45-50 pesos) are a good choice. Crepes from 40 pesos. Free Wi-Fi. Open M-Sa 8am-11pm. Cash only. ❷

**La Crepe,** Alcalá 307, 2nd fl. Pretty self-explanatory. Crepes come in two varieties: savory (*poblano* chiles with chicken and Oaxacan cheese, 50 pesos) and sweet (strawberries, kiwis, apples, bananas and honey, 46 pesos). Salads 42-60 pesos. Open 8am-11pm. Cash only. ❷

**1254 Marco Polo,** 5 de Mayo 103 (☎514 4360), north of Independencia. Your source for seafood away from the sea. The *comida corrida* (42 pesos) includes either *mariscos* or *comida tipica*. Other options include red snapper (80 pesos) and stuffed crab (70 pesos). Open daily 8am-9pm. Cash only. ❹

**Las Quince Letras,** Abasolo 300 (☎514 3769). An upscale eatery full of families and enamored couples, with leafy outdoor seating available. For the bold, *chapulines* (grasshoppers, 60 pesos) make the perfect appetizer. Salads 50-70 pesos. Entrees 75-115 pesos. Open daily 8am-9pm. MC/V. ❹

**Restaurant Morelos,** Morelos 1003 (☎516 0558). A homey, orange-walled place to get a snack and maybe help the old couple at the next table over with their crossword. *Comida corrida* (50 pesos) comes with sweet flan dessert. Breakfast 40 pesos. Open M-Sa 7am-7pm. Cash only. ❷

**La Antigua,** Reforma 401. A sophisticated cafe with indoor seating and a few tables in an pretty courtyard facing the street. Baguette sandwiches and salads 65 pesos. Organic coffees about 20 pesos. Open M-Th 9am-10pm, F-Sa 9am-11pm. Cash only. ❸

**Café del Rey,** at Murguía and Libres. A large bright room with quick and friendly service. Menu has Mexican *antojito* standards; the *chorizo* tacos are particularly tasty. *Comida corrida* 40 pesos. Tacos 8 pesos each. Open M-Sa 1-7pm. Cash only. ❷

**Flor de Loto,** Morelos 509 (☎514 3944). Tie-dyed tables and a vegetarian-friendly menu. Regional (i.e. meaty) food also served. Try the soy meatballs with spinach (38 pesos) or the *menú del día* (48 pesos). Open daily 8:30am-10pm. Cash only. ❷

**El Biche Pobre,** at Zárate and Calzada de la República. The exotic green eyes painted on the outside of the restaurant are somewhat out of sync with the hearty traditional Oaxacan dishes served inside. Roasted chicken with *mole* 85 pesos. Open 8am-10pm. Cash only. ❹

**Los Canarios,** 20 de Noviembre 502 (☎514 1937), just south of Aldama. Looks like an upscale fast food joint, but the food is decent and inexpensive. Eggs any style 35 pesos. Mexican plates 45-78 pesos. Open 24hr. Cash only. ❷

## ▉ CHOCOLATE CAFES AND SHOPS

In the country that launched chocolate's long, illustrious career, Oaxaca remains one of the best places to try the Mesoamerican candy's dark, rich, and complex flavors. The main outlets are near the intersection of Mina and 20 de Noviembre; once you're in the vicinity, your nose will be able to guide you. In addition to scrumptious mountains of chocolate spiced with vanilla, cinnamon, nuts, and more, you can sometimes see employees working the cacao grinders. Don't leave without trying a hot chocolate *oaxaqueño*-style *con agua* (with water) or *con leche* (with milk). And, of course, don't be modest about grabbing ▉free samples.

■ **Chocolate Mayordomo,** Mina 219 (☎516 1619), at 20 de Noviembre. 2nd location across the street; 3rd location down the street. The counter is crowded with locals and tourists grabbing free samples and carrying off bags full of the stuff. Teenage employees frantically push cacao beans and cinnamon sticks into a series of machines. At 50 pesos for 250kg, you may be tempted to get some of every variety they sell. The in-house hot chocolate (15 pesos) is definitely worth sitting for. Open daily 7am-9pm.

**Chocolate la Soledad,** Mina 221 (☎526 3807), across the street from Mayordomo. This chocolate and spice shop fronts the **Hotel Chocolate Posada** (p. 248) and has apparently decided to double up on the hedonism by selling as many kinds of *mezcal* as they do chocolate. The vine-covered courtyard is as pleasant a place as any to sip their double hot chocolate (15 pesos). Open M-Sa 7am-9pm, Su 7am-8pm. D/MC/V.

**Chocolate Guelaguetza,** 20 de Noviembre 605, south of Mina. Less busy than its competitors, Guelaguetza still has an impressive collection of chocolates, *moles,* and other candies. Cup of hot chocolate 12 pesos. Open daily 8am-8pm. Cash only.

## ◉ SIGHTS

Oaxaca's long history permeates its streets, museums, colonial mansions, and Baroque churches. Many sites of interest are between the *zócalo* and Santo Domingo, including the numerous studios and galleries that give Oaxaca its reputation as an art mecca. Oaxaca also boasts several markets, including the enormous **Central de Abastos,** on Trujano, eight blocks west of the *zócalo.* (Open daily 8am-8pm.) **Mercado Benito Juárez,** at the corner of 20 de Noviembre and Aldama, two blocks from the *zócalo,* sells crafts, produce, flowers, and clothing. Its annex, **Mercado 20 de Noviembre,** on the next block, has an array of cheap food stalls. (Both open daily 6am-9pm.) **Mercado de Artesanías,** at the corner of García and Zaragoza, sells artisan wares. Prices and quality are often better in nearby villages where the crafts originate. (Open daily 8am-8pm.)

**▧MUSEO DE LAS CULTURAS DE OAXACA AND IGLESIA DE SANTO DOMINGO.** This is the preening queen of Oaxaca's tourist circuit, combining a prestigious and enormous museum on Oaxacan cultural history with the tallest, most elegant church in the city. The **Museo de las Culturas de Oaxaca,** once a convent, tells the story of Oaxaca's residents from the Zapotecs through the 19th century in a labyrinthine of rooms with beautiful artifacts and texts. The prime attraction is the treasure extracted from Tomb 7 in **Monte Albán,** the largest single collection of Mixtec treasure ever found. The burial site here features jewelry and art made with gold, silver, copper, amber, jade, opal, turquoise, obsidian, coral, and alabaster. *(☎516 2991. Open Tu-Su 10am-7pm. 51 pesos. Video camera use 35 pesos. Audio guide 50 pesos.)*

Next door stands the church itself. Beginning in 1555, it took 111 years to complete the trademark Mexican Baroque building. The inside is a whirlwind of gilded sculptures and paintings, including a sort of golden tree on the ceiling at the entrance whose wandering branches hold the images of various religious figures. Though the church is hundreds of years old, the altars were restored by local artists in 1959, having been destroyed at the order of the governor during the Reform Wars. *(5 blocks north of the zócalo on Alcalá. Open daily 7am-1pm and 4-8pm. Capilla open daily 9:30am-1pm and 4-7pm.)*

**JARDÍN ETNOBOTÁNICO DE OAXACA.** Part of the **Centro Cultural Santo Domingo** behind the church, the garden is a breakneck tour of Oaxaca's flora. Organized both by climate—desert, mountain forest, etc.—and by theme, the garden includes sections of indigenous agriculture and medicinal plants. Entering the grounds, which are surrounded by high stone walls, you'll feel as though you've been transported somewhere far from the busy capital. *(At Reforma and Consti-*

*tución. Only accessible with regularly scheduled tours. Spanish tours last 1hr. and begin M-Sa at 10am, noon, and 5pm. 50 pesos. English tours are 2hr. on Tu, Th, Su at 11am. 100 pesos.)*

**BASÍLICA LA SOLEDAD.** Away from the flashier attractions near the *zócalo*, the **Museo Religioso de la Soledad** has a delightfully odd and varied collection of art and religious relics from the first archbishop's time. The museum as houses an assortment of gifts sent to the Virgin, who is said to have appeared here in 1620. These gifts include black coral, a giant seahorse, a stuffed cat, architectural figurines, and money from around the world. *(Independencia 107, 4 blocks west of the post office. ☎ 516 5076. Open daily 8am-2pm and 4-7pm. Donations suggested.)*

---

**OAXACA FOR POCKET CHANGE.** After a stroll through the huge **Central de Abastos** or the more manageable **Mercado Benito Juárez** (p. 251), check out **Mercado 20 de Noviembre** (p. 251), where everything from barbecued meat to *quesillo* is available for your dining pleasure. Spend the evening at the **Pochote Theater** (p. 253), which has free nightly screenings of international movies. Wind down the night at **La Tentación** (p. 255) with a Sol beer while enjoying live salsa.

---

**CASA DE BENITO JUÁREZ.** Mexico's most beloved president lived here for 10 years as a child (1818-28), after being adopted by a nun who owned a bookbinding shop. Scenes of everyday 19th-century life are juxtaposed with far more interesting placards on the socioeconomic and political conditions in Mexico during Juárez's time. *(García Vigil 609, 1 block west of Alcalá. ☎ 516 1860. Open Tu-F 10am-6pm, Sa-Su 10am-5pm. 34 pesos; Su and holidays free. Video camera use 35 pesos.)*

**MUSEO DE ARTE PREHISPÁNICO DE MEXICO RUFINO TAMAYO.** This museum features the artist's immense, well-preserved personal collection of pre-Hispanic objects from all over Mexico. The figurines, ceramics, and masks that Tamayo (1899-1991) collected were meant to be appreciated as works of art rather than artifacts, resulting in this hybrid of an art gallery and an archaeological museum. *(Morelos 503, between Díaz and Tinoco y Palacios. ☎ 516 4750. Open M-Sa 10am-2pm and 4-7pm, Su 10am-3pm. 30 pesos, students 15 pesos.)*

**CATEDRAL DE OAXACA.** Originally constructed in 1553, this cathedral was reconstructed after earthquake damage between 1702 and 1733. Oaxaca's stately cathedral makes a somewhat odd but compelling backdrop to the everyday business, laughter, and clown shows in its plaza. Compared to Santo Domingo, the interior is rather reserved, with some austere paintings on the walls. The main focus of the room is the bishop's seat in the middle. The King of Spain donated the English clock in the back. *(On the northeastern corner of the zócalo. Open daily 7:30am-8pm.)*

**MUSEO TEXTIL DE OAXACA.** This small museum features exhibits on how weavers from around the world dye their cloths. Come see the beautiful shawls, tapestries and other works. There's also a gift shop full of things that would make great gifts for Mom (if you could afford them). *(Hidalgo 917. Open W-M 10am-8pm. Free.)*

**OTHER SIGHTS.** If you're looking for a beautiful view of the city and surrounding hills, head to the **Cerro de Fortín** (Hill of the Fortress), which once housed a fort meant to protect the city. The **Escalera de Fortín** begins on Crespo, leading past the Guelaguetza amphitheater to the Planetarium Nundehui. The climb is grueling, and should only be undertaken during daylight hours, as the area has been known to harbor a few thieves after dark. *(☎ 514 7500. Open Th-Su 10am-1pm and 5-8pm. 25 pesos.)* Porfirio Díaz left a mark on his native city, ordering the construction of the the **Teatro Macedonio Alcala,** a beautiful Porfiriato piece with a gorgeous dome and stonework. *(5 de Mayo at Independencia, 2 blocks behind the cathedral. ☎516 3387. Weekly shows 6, 8pm. 25 pesos.)* After a series of cultural institutions that treat heavy themes like colonialism, the struggle to preserve indigenous cultures, and lots of religion, you may be relieved to enter the **Museo de la Filatelia (MUFI),** which only asks you to consider the beauty of postage stamps. MUFI houses a collection that will put others to shame, with a mish-mash of stamps from around the Republic dating back to the early days of *correo* service. *(On Juárez just south of Berriozabal. Open Tu-Su 10am-6pm. 20 pesos.)*

## CONTEMPORARY ART MUSEUMS AND GALLERIES.

▧**MUSEO DE LOS PINTORES OAXAQUEÑOS.** The second floor holds a permanent gallery with pieces by *oaxaqueño* artist Rafael Morales and other local painters, but the real action is at ground level, where you can view a diverse collection of temporary exhibits with works by contemporary Latin American artists that are both poignant and whimsical. *(Independencia 607, at the corner of García Vigil. ☎516 5645. Open Tu-Sa 10am-8pm, Su 10am-6pm. 20 pesos, students 10 pesos.)*

**CENTRO FOTOGRÁFICO ALVAREZ BRAVO-FONOTECA EDUARDO MATA.** In Oaxaca's huge arts scene, this is one of the only galleries that focuses entirely on photography, mostly from local and national artists. Otherwise, the vista is similar: the courtyard exhibition space serves as a gathering place for the city's young and creative. There's also a photography library. In an adjacent room sits a music library amassed by local Eduardo Mata. *(Bravo 116, east of Vigil. ☎514 1933. Open M and W-Su 8am-9:30pm. Donations suggested.)*

**MUSEO DE ARTE CONTEMPORÁNEO DE OAXACA (MACO).** This colonial building is known as the **Casa de Cortés,** although he never lived here. Today, the 18th-century home hosts rotating exhibits of modern art from around the world. In the past it has showcased work by *oaxaqueños* Rodolfo Morales, Rufino Tamayo, and Francisco Toledo. *(Alcalá 202, 1 block down Andador Turístico on the right. ☎514 2228. Open M and W-Su 10:30am-8pm. M-Sa 10 pesos, Su free.)*

**ART GALERÍA.** Paintings and other works predominantly by Mexican and Latin American artists spread throughout several rooms. On the heavily-trafficked *Andador Turístico*, this is one of the more prominent of the small galleries in the city. Prints for sale. *(Alcalá 102. ☎516 5743. Open M-Sa 11am-2pm, 5-8pm. Free.)*

**ARTE BIULU.** A fascinating gallery with a beautiful courtyard and a terrace looking out on the city. Expositions regularly display paintings and photography by local and national artists. Biulu also holds art workshops, like cement sculpting and sand painting, which are open to the public for around 1500 pesos (includes the cost of materials). You get to keep your masterpiece. Visit the website for more information. *(Júarez 503. ☎501 2216; www.artebiulu.com. Open W-Sa 1-6pm. Free.)*

**MUSEO TALLER ERASTO CORTÉS.** A working artists' community that combines studios for young painters and sculptors with a small courtyard gallery of local works. *(Juárez, north of Constitución. Open M-F 8am-9pm, Sa-Su 8am-noon. Free.)*

## ♫ ENTERTAINMENT

**Pochote Theater,** García Vigil 817 (☎514 1194). Hosts international movies, short films, and documentaries. Shows daily 8pm. Free.

**Casa de la Cultura,** Ortega 403 (☎516 2483), at Colón. Hosts theater productions, concerts, summer music and art classes, and art exhibits. Open M-F 9am-6pm, Sa 9am-3pm and 4-6:30pm, Su 9am-2pm.

**Instituto Oaxaqueño de las Culturas** (☎516 3434), at Madera and Tecnológica. To get here, take a westbound "Sta. Rosa" *urbano* for 2.50 pesos from Independencia and Tinoco y Palacios. Has a program similar to the Casa de la Cultura (above).

**Mulitmax cinema,** Av. Universidad 139 (☎514 7929), in the Pl. del Valle Mall. Take the "Plaza del Valle" bus on Juárez. Perfect for those floored by the previous night's activities. Check SEDETUR (p. 245) for movie listings. Tickets 40 pesos.

**Cinépolis,** Av. Castillejos 502 (☎506 0885), at Pl. Oaxaca. Take the "Plaza del Valle" bus on Juárez. Catch a flick in English (with Spanish subtitles). Tickets 40 pesos.

**Estadio Eduardo Vasconcelos,** on the corner of Vasconcelos and Niños Héroes de Chapultepec. Watch the Guerreros, Oaxaca's professional baseball team. Tickets 5-60 pesos.

## 🔦 NIGHTLIFE

Young *oaxaqueños* and foreign tourists share one of the most vibrant nightlife scenes in southern Mexico. Ranging from laid-back artist hangouts with poetry readings, to *mezcal*-fueled salsa and merengue clubs, at night, Oaxaca's the place to be. Most of the action takes place on the streets north of the *zócalo*, which empty out around 10 or 11pm. Some bars are closed on Sunday, but Monday is the quietest day by far. You can go on foot from place to place within the nightlife district, but you may want to take a taxi back to your hotel. The easiest place to pick up a cab is Alcalá and Matamoros (35 pesos).

### BARS

Bars cluster along Matamoros and Porfirio Díaz, which are well lit and close to the *zócalo*.

🏆 **La Nueva Babel,** Díaz 224 (☎153 3422). Packed every night of the week, this is the best place to experience Oaxaca's arts scene. Every night has a different performance theme: Tu poetry night, W flamenco, F-Sa jazz, and Su country rock. There are also occasional theater performances. Beers 25 pesos. Mixed drinks 20-50 pesos. Open daily 8am-1am. Cash only.

🏆 **Club Tamarindo,** on Hidalgo near Reforma. Attracts a diverse array of young people with its hip but friendly setting and rock and jazz records. Also hosts periodic art shows featuring the work of local students. Beers 20 pesos. Rum and Coke 25 pesos. Mixed drinks 35 pesos. Open Tu-Sa 6pm-2am. Cash only.

**La Mezcalera,** Jardín de Bastile 104C (☎128 2384). Feels like a trendy neighborhood bar, with college-age kids hanging out on sofas. Artwork hangs on the exposed-brick walls. As the name suggests, La Mezcalera specializes in stocking more varieties of *mezcal* than you can shake an empty glass at. W *mezcal* 2-for-1. Beers 20 pesos. Other mixed drinks 45 pesos. Open daily 2pm-1am.

**FreeBar,** Matamoros 100C, across from La Tentación. Groups of friends meet at this small bar, getting tipsy off the dirt cheap alcohol. DJ mixes loud Spanish hip hop while a few people dance in the back. *Mezcal* 10 pesos. Beers 20 pesos. Mixed drinks 35 pesos. Open Tu-Su 3pm-2am. MC/V.

**Nude,** Alcalá 303. A mellow bar with blue lighting where the 20-something patrons sit on cushioned cubes, sip *mezcal,* and talk. Beers 20 pesos. Mixed drinks 35 pesos. Open Su-Th noon-1am, F-Sa noon-4am. Cash only.

**Caffeine,** Alcalá 401 (☎514 2453). Relaxed and unpretentious. With artwork and Radiohead posters on the walls, this cafe/bar caters to small groups of friends who want a quiet night. Tu whiskey 25 pesos. Sa 2-for-1 mixed drinks until 2am. Beers 20 pesos. Mixed drinks 40 pesos. Open Su-Th 8pm-midnight, F-Sa 8pm-3am. Cash only.

**La Costumbre,** Alcalá 501, opposite the entrance to Santo Domingo. Soft music and bright lighting make for a super-casual, bar perfect for a quiet night out. Beers 20 pesos. Mixed drinks 40-55 pesos. Open M-Sa 9pm-3am. Cash only.

**La V,** Díaz 507 (☎195 3652). One of the less crowded bars in Oaxaca's *centro.* Older patrons than the other spots in the city. An upstairs terrace provides views of the city. Beers 20 pesos. Mixed drinks 2 for 50 pesos. Open M-Sa 5pm-2am. Cash only.

## CLUBS

Most clubs cater to salsa and merengue dancers, so put on some nice shoes. At the end of the night, walk or save your heels and grab a taxi (35 pesos).

🅺 **Candela,** Murguía 413 (☎514 2010), at Pino Suárez. Situated in an elegant, well lit courtyard, surrounded by candlelit tables. Has a great salsa band. Dance floor draws a diverse crowd. Tu-Sa live music at 10:30pm. Cover Tu-W 30 pesos, Th-Sa 50 pesos. Mixed drinks 50 pesos. Bottle of *Courvoisier* 1700 pesos. Restaurant open M-F 1-7pm. Dancing Tu-Sa 9pm-2am. Cash only.

**La Cantinita** (☎516 8961), on Alcalá next to Nude (p. 254). There's an almost carnival-like atmosphere at La Cantinita: large groups of young *oaxaqueños* dance and hang out around a stage set in a boxing ring, where local rock, ska, and salsa bands do their thing. Beer 30 pesos. Mixed drinks 45 pesos. Open daily 6pm-3:30am.

**La Xcusa** (☎204 8060; www.laxcusahi5.com), on Matamoros next to La Tentación. Tipsy partiers dance to a high-energy mix of salsa, reggaeton, rock, and electronica. Beers 10 pesos 2pm-midnight, 20 pesos midnight-3am. Mixed drinks 35 pesos. Open M-Sa 2pm-3am. Cash only.

**La Tentación,** Matamoros 101 (☎514 9521). A fast-paced dance fl. filled with couples dancing to salsa and cumbia rhythms. Grab a cheap mixed drink (35 pesos) and let the *oaxaqueños* teach you how it's done. Sa-Su live reggae bands. Th-Sa salsa nights. Cover F-Sa 35 pesos. Open Tu-Su 9:30pm-3am. MC/V.

**502,** Díaz 502 (☎516 6020), across from La Resistencia. As the city's only gay and lesbian nightclub, 502 can afford to be selective. The club is private; ring the bell outside the door and wait for the bouncer to unlock it. Patrons sip drinks at the edges and occasionally foray onto the dance floor. No drugs, heavy drinking, or transvestism allowed. Cover F-Sa 50 pesos, includes 1 drink. Open high season Tu-Su 10:30pm-6am; low season Th-Sa only.

**Tabuko Bar,** Díaz 219 (☎160 3858). A pulsing club with an huge golden Buddha right next to the dance floor. Plenty of space to dance or sit, depending on your mood. Beers 2 for 30 pesos. Mixed drinks 2 for 40 pesos. Open daily 1pm-3am. Cash only.

**Cielito Lindo,** Morelos 511. Salsa, merengue, and Mexican pop hits play on the dance floor. Nearby, the quieter bar area is sometimes entertained by live acoustic guitar music. Beers 20 pesos. Mixed drinks 35 pesos. Open 3pm-late. Cash only.

**La Cucaracha,** Díaz 301A (☎501 1036). A 3-part establishment featuring a disco with music from the 80s and 90s plus salsa. Another room with live *trova* music nightly. W and Su mixed drinks 2-for-1. Beer 25 pesos. Mixed drinks 38 pesos. Open daily 7pm-3am. MC/V.

## ❀ FESTIVALS

Oaxaca explodes with festivals in late July, celebrating its abundant culinary and cultural wealth. The two Mondays following July 16 are known as Los Lunes del Cerro (Hill Mondays). On these two days, representatives from all seven regions of Oaxaca state converge on the Cerro del Fortín for the 🅵**Festival**

## FORGET THE TEQUILA, PASS THE *PULQUE*

Chances are you may be intimately acquainted with the maguey cactus (a.k.a. agave)—or, more likely, the tequila and mezcal it produces. What Mr. José Cuervo never told you is that when a cactus's sap (called agua miel, or honey water) is fermented instead of distilled, maguey yields the wondrous drink of the Aztecs: pulque.

Pulque is thought to have originated over 2000 years ago. Legend has it that it was discovered by the goddess Mayahuel. Associated with virility and fertility, pulque was used as an aphrodisiac and was given to the sick as medicine. The supreme god of pulque is Ometotchitli, also known as Two Rabbit, who was said to have 400 sons. In fact, there is a whole pantheon of pulque gods, who together are known as Centzon Totochtin, or 400 Rabbit.

Pulque is made by harvesting agua miel from 12-year-old maguey. The agua is transported by hand to a fermenting house, or tinacol, a sacred area where men must remove their hats and women are forbidden. (Long ago, pulque producers weren't allowed to even have contact with women.)

Today, pulque drinkers pay homage to the gods (and the 400 stages of inebriation) by pouring some on the ground before taking some for themselves—bottoms up.

**of Guelaguetza,** held at the Auditorio Guelaguetza. Guelaguetza recalls the Zapotec custom of reciprocal gift-giving. At the end of the day's traditional dances, performers throw goods typical of their regions into the outstretched arms of the crowd gathered in the 12,000-seat stadium. In the weeks between the two gatherings there are festive food and handicraft exhibits, art shows, and concerts. (Call Ticketmaster in Mexico City for reservations, as tickets sell out. Ticketmaster ☎55 5325 9000. Front-section seats 400 pesos; back-section seats free, but you must come very early to get a seat.)

As the mezcal capital of the world, Oaxaca is justifiably proud of itself. During the **Fiesta Nacional del Mezcal,** held in late July, Oaxacans and foreigners alike gather to drink themselves numb. Vendors crowd the park; everyone stumbles from booth to booth, giddy from the unlimited free shots of the local drink. If you've exceeded your taste-test tolerance, take a seat and enjoy the festival's live music, traditional dances, and fireworks. (Locations and exact date change from year to year. Check the tourist office, p. 245, for current info. Entrance fee 15-20 pesos.)

Around the same time, mole—Oaxaca's local delight—commands its own week-long Festival de los Siete Moles, held in hotels and restaurants around the city. Each night the featured venues fill up as they serve and celebrate one variety of the delicious sauce. (Check the tourist office for a complete listing of locations.)

Oaxaca's exquisitely beautiful **Día de los Muertos** celebrations (Nov. 1-2) have become a huge tourist attraction in recent years. Most travel agencies offer expeditions to the candlelit, marigold-filled village graveyards. Shops fill with molded sugar calaveras (skulls), while altars are erected throughout the city to memorialize the dead. Because these celebrations can be very personal, locals might not appreciate being photographed as they honor the deceased.

On December 23, Oaxacans celebrate Noche de los Rábanos (Night of the Radishes). The small vegetable is honored for its frequent use in Oaxacan cuisine and its easily carved form. Masterpieces of historic or biblical scenes constructed entirely using radish fill the *zócalo.* Hundreds of people admire the creations and eat sweet buñuelos (fried tortillas with honey). Upon finishing the treat, make a wish and throw the ceramic plate on the ground; if the plate smashes into pieces, your wish will come true.

## WEEKLY MARKETS

A few outlying towns outside of the city burst into life once a week on their market days, when hundreds of merchants and eager buyers gather to exchange tapestries, rugs, and pottery, as well as more practical, less tourist-oriented goods. The market in **Etla**, 20km north of the city, is held on Wednesdays; **Zaachila**, 15km south of Oaxaca, holds its market on Thursdays; and **Tlacolula**, 31km east of town on the road to Mitla, has the largest market of the three on Sundays. Separate buses (10-20 pesos), headed to all three locations, leave frequently from the second-class station.

## DAYTRIPS IN OAXACA VALLEY

### TO THE EAST

The wide valley east of Oaxaca has the most to offer, so it's no coincidence that it gets the most tourist traffic. Indigenous market towns, small pre-Columbian ruins, and outdoor adventures bring a steady stream of cars and buses from the city. As a result, transportation is usually reliable and straightforward. If you feel like making things even easier for yourself, there are a number of organized tours that visit several sights during the morning and afternoon—check out **Autobuses Turísticos** in Hotel Riviera del Ángel, Mina 518 (☎516 5327), or the tour packages offered by **Casa Arnel**, Aldama 404 (☎515 2856).

**BENITO JUÁREZ.** Benito Júarez lies at the end of a long gravel road that climbs to nearly 3000m above sea level. Here, misty clouds slip over mountaintops covered in pine forests. The town is connected to several other villages in the area—collectively known as the **pueblos mancomunados**, or "joined towns"—by a series of centuries-old footpaths through the forest. Today, the paths are open to tourists who want to explore the beautiful landscape and see the waterfalls, wildlife, and lookouts along the way. The winding paths branch off in dozens of places, so it's highly advisable for those taking longer hikes to hire a guide at the tourist office (open daily 8am-8pm). You can walk (120 pesos for up to 5hr. with a guide), or rent a horse (100 pesos per hr., including guide) or bike (100 pesos for up to 5hr.; guide 250 pesos). There's also a 340m-long zipwire (40 pesos) through the canopy.

To get the most out of the trip, you'll want to stay at least a few days. There are two options for accommodations. Basic but comfortable beds can be found at the **Tourist Yu'u ❶** (150 pesos per person; check at the tourist office in Oaxaca (p. 245) to see if there are rooms available). There are somewhat more elaborate **cabañas ❸** run by the Benito Juárez tourist office (450 pesos for 2-4 people). *(52km northeast of Oaxaca. Buses leave from behind the second-class station Tu and F-Sa at 5am, and return the same day at 3pm. 30 pesos. If you're driving, take Mex. 190 east out of town and turn off at the sign for Teotitlán. Benito Juárez is 18km past Teotitlán on an unpaved mountain road.)*

**MITLA.** Mitla is both a market town and the second most important archaeological site near Oaxaca after Monte Albán. To get to the entrance of the ruins, you have to walk through the market. On your way, there's a lot to look at (mostly rugs and other weavings); as this is one of the more touristy markets in the area, prices and quality may be better elsewhere.

The ancient city is the real reason to come. Though much smaller than Monte Albán—the site consists mainly of three modest courtyards and the buildings that surround them—Mitla is deservedly famous for the elaborate geometric patterns that adorn nearly every wall. The wide, horizontal buildings have intensive decoration along their upper portions and are arranged in quadrangles.

The main part of the site is the **Grupo de las Columnas,** which contains two courtyards. The better-preserved of the two is home to **Templo de las Columnas,** the most impressive building in the city. A flight of steep stairs leads to the **Salón de las Columnas,** where the namesake columns are lined up in a long, narrow hallway. Through a short, dark corridor is the **Patio de las Grecas,** a small but exquisitely sculpted space with some of the most intricate geometric designs in all of Mitla; four dark rooms off the patio are similarly ornamented. The other courtyard in the group is the **Patio de las Tumbas,** named for two underground tombs that were long ago robbed of their treasures. Even with the treasure gone, climbing down the tight passageways—taller travelers will have to briefly crawl on their hands and knees—and coming out in the cross-shaped tombs is an experience that shouldn't be missed.

The other major area is the **Grupo de la Iglesia** to the north. This complex is named after the Catholic church that forms one side of the main courtyard; it was built with stones taken from a razed Zapotec building. The rest of the courtyard is similar to the other courtyards in the site, if somewhat less grand. The wall opposite the church has a few patches of the original paint that used to cover the buildings. There are actually a few other groups of buildings farther away, but little remains of them except for the foundations.

Mitla has a few accommodations and restaurants if you want to stick around. For a bed, head down to **La Zapoteca ❶,** 5 de Febrero 12, toward the market and ruins. Clean rooms come with private bath, TV and free Wi-Fi. (☎568 0026. Singles 150 pesos; doubles 300 pesos; triples 500 pesos.) La Zapoteca also has a **restaurant ❷** that serves *comida corrida oaxaqueña* for 55 pesos. (Open daily 9am-7pm.) You can pay a bit more money to sit in a floral courtyard back in the *zócalo* at **Don Cenobio ❹,** which serves Oaxacan specialties (82 pesos). *(45km east of Oaxaca. Buses leave frequently from the the second-class bus station. 40 pesos. Archaeological site open daily 8am-6pm. 37 pesos.)*

**TEOTITLÁN DEL VALLE.** Teotitlán has one of the best markets with woven goods in the state of Oaxaca. A diverse collection of rugs and tapestries hangs in the *mercado de artesanía,* downhill from the church. You can find similar wares in shops scattered around the town. These shops are often more interesting, as you can sometimes see goods being made on the loom. There's also a worthwhile **community museum,** which has exhibits about traditional dyes, Zapotec artifacts, and a section on the traditional courtship rituals of the area. Men caught flirting with women inappropriately were fined five liters of *mezcal;* if they couldn't or wouldn't pay, they would be forced to wear a belt of thorns until their urges were gone. Restaurant **El Descanso ❷,** on Juárez on the south side of town, is one of the few places to get a sit-down meal. Oaxacan dishes are 40-80 pesos. *(31km east of Oaxaca. Buses leave frequently from the 2nd-class bus station. 30 pesos. Museum open daily 10am-6pm. 10 pesos.)*

**HIERVE EL AGUA.** Half water park, half miracle of nature, Hierve el Agua ("boiling water") is a spectacular "petrified waterfall." Hierve el Agua is actually a group of enormous stalactites that cascade down a mountainside. This phenomenon is a result of mineral residue in the spring water that "boils" out of the ground here. Once you've made the trek, put on a bathing suit and take a dip in one of the two swimming pools. There are changing rooms on-site. There are also copious **food stands.** If you feel like staying a while, **Tourist Yu'u ❶** offers up rooms for 70 pesos per night. Get in touch with the tourist office in Oaxaca (p. 245) to make sure there's room. *(About 70km east of Oaxaca. The last 20km or so are on poorly maintained gravel roads. Hire a cab in Mitla for 150 pesos. Most tour agencies also organize trips here. Entrance fee 15 pesos.)*

OAXACA

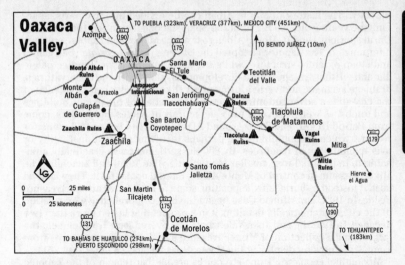

**Oaxaca Valley**

TO PUEBLA (323km), VERACRUZ (377km), MEXICO CITY (451km)

Azompa · 190

OAXACA

TO BENITO JUÁREZ (10km)

175

Monte Albán Ruins

Santa María El Tule

Teotitlán del Valle

Monte Albán · Arrazola

Aeropuerto Internacional

San Jerónimo Tlacochahuaya

Dainzú Ruins

Cuilapán de Guerrero

San Bartolo Coyotepec

Tlacolula de Matamoros

190

Zaachila Ruins

Zaachila

Tlacolula Ruins

Yagul Ruins · Mitla

179

Mitla Ruins

N

0 — 25 miles
0 — 25 kilometers

San Martín Tilcajete

Santo Tomás Jalietza

Hierve el Agua

131

175

Ocotlán de Morelos

190

TO BAHÍAS DE HUATULCO (271km), PUERTO ESCONDIDO (298km)

TO TEHUANTEPEC (183km)

## TO THE WEST

A mere 20-minute drive from the center of Oaxaca, Monte Albán seems thousands of miles away from the bustle of the city. Perched on the top of a hill with no natural water supply, further adding to its isolation, this small town is Oaxaca Valley's main attraction to the west.

### ▓ MONTE ALBÁN

*Autobuses Turísticos tickets to Monte Albán leave the Hotel Rivera del Ángel, Mina 518 (☎516 5327), between Mier y Terán and Díaz Ordaz, several blocks southwest of the zócalo (20min., every 30min. 8:30am-4pm). Round-trip with fixed return are 38 pesos. You can also catch a separate return trip in the Monte Albán parking lot (about 20 pesos). Site open daily 8am-5pm. 51 pesos. Video camera use 35 pesos. Though many travel agencies can set you up with hassle-free transportation and excellent guides, it is usually cheaper to organize your own transportation. Find a guide once you reach the mountain. English-language guides charge 200-300 pesos for a 1hr. tour, depending on the size and negotiating skills of your group.*

Before its abandonment toward the end of the AD first millennium, Monte Albán, the capital of the Zapotec empire, dominated what is now the state of Oaxaca. Standing in the vast central plaza, it's easy to get a sense of the grandeur the city once held. Pyramids line the mountaintop city like soldiers in formation, monumental and stately, while the north and south ends are punctuated by towering platform complexes. The Zapotecs built their metropolis high above the valley floor for religious and strategic reasons. The views past the ruins to the surrounding mountains are almost as spectacular as the site itself. Unless you're an expert on pre-Hispanic civilizations, a good guide (or the 80-peso guidebook from the museum store) to Monte Albán will add a lot to your visit.

**GO GO GROUP.** Private guides have the most intimate knowledge of Monte Albán's many mysterious ruins, but they often charge steep prices. Get a price quote from a guide and then collect your group or wait near the entrance and try to get some compatriots to join you—you can save big by splitting the original price with others.

**HISTORY.** The history of Monte Albán can be divided into five parts, spanning the years from 500 BC until the Spanish conquest in the 16th century. During periods I and II, Monte Albán rose as the Mayan and Zapotec cultures intermingled. The Zapotecs adopted the Olmec's *juego de pelota* (ball game) and steep pyramid structure, while the Maya inherited the Zapotec calendar and writing system. These developments, along with the observatories, drainage systems, and varied forms of art (like the stelae), are evidence of the city-state's advanced infrastructure. Almost all of the extant buildings and tombs, as well as several urns and murals of nobles and leaders, come from Period III (AD 350-700). Around AD 800, the city began to decline for reasons which remain unknown, perhaps involving political instability or over-exploitation of resources. By 850 the settlement was practically uninhabited. In its stead rose smaller Mixtec cities like Yagul and Zaachila. The Mixtecs assumed control of Monte Albán, but did not settle it. They instead used it instead as burial site, depositing some of their finest art and treasure inside. In 1931, Dr. Alfonso Caso began the first comprehensive excavation of the city, systematically detailing it in a project that lasted more than two decades. In 1932, he and Juan Valenzuela discovered **Tomb 7,** which held the largest single collection of Mixtec treasure ever found. The treasures from Tomb 7 are now on display at the **Museo de las Culturas de Oaxaca** (p. 251).

Monolithic, geometric stone structures are all that remain of the Zapotec capital, which once sprawled 20km over three mountaintops. First constructed circa 550 BC, Monte Albán was the massive undertaking of a confederation of local communities, ruled by the religious elite. The city flourished during the Classic Period (AD 200-700), when it shared the spotlight with Teotihuacán and Tikal (in Guatemala) as a major cultural and ceremonial center. Here, people cultivated maize, built complex water drainage systems, and engaged in extensive trade networks. Daily life was carefully structured to cooperate with supernatural elements: architecture adhered to the four cardinal directions and the 260-day sacred calendar. To emphasize the congruence between household and cosmos, families buried ancestors beneath their houses to symbolize their journey to the underworld. Excavations of burials in Monte Albán have yielded not only dazzling artifacts, but also valuable information about social stratification. Pottery, figurines, burial sites, and engravings indicate a highly rigid social order, as ordained by the gods. The educated priests constituted the ruling class, with the holiest living on the mountaintop. The laboring lower classes lived and worked farther down in the valley.

**BALL COURT.** After passing through the ticketing station just beyond the museum, walk left up the inclined path leading diagonally toward the ruins. Before reaching the Main Plaza, you will see the remains of several small buildings on your left. The ball court (constructed c. 100 BC) is straight ahead. The sides of the court, which now look like bleachers, were once covered in stucco and plaster and served as bouncing boards for the ball. The goals stood in the middle of the grassy area. The motion of the ball symbolized the movement of the heavenly spheres. The game was used in rituals as well as to resolve land disputes.

**MAIN PLAZA.** Passing the ball court on your left, you will enter the huge Main Plaza, with the mountain-like North Platform on the right, smaller structures lined up on the left, and the enormous South Platform on the other side. The Main Plaza is flat, and was covered entirely in stucco. On your left, look for **Building P,** with its massive staircase leading up the platform. The main plaza has religious and scientific significance. The **Palace,**

containing a complex set of passageways and rooms that served as the residence of a high priest is just past Building P.

**SOUTH PLATFORM.** Forming the Plaza's south end is the South Platform, one of the site's highest structures. The top affords a commanding view of the ruins, valley, and mountains beyond. On both sides of the staircase on the plaza level are replicas of the original stelae. One stela is believed to depict a former king of Monte Albán. A defense wall runs along the front of the platform.

**BUILDING OF DANCERS (BUILDING L).** Walking left of the platform to the plaza's west side, you will first come across System M and then the **Building of Dancers.** Once thought to be performing ritual dances, the "dancers" in the reliefs on the center building more likely depict chieftains conquered by Monte Albán, almost all with mutilated genitals. Over 400 figures date from the 5th century BC and are nearly identical to contemporary Olmec sculptures on the Gulf Coast.

**BUILDING K (SYSTEM IV).** Just north of the Building of the Dancers is Building K, a dual complex with a central courtyard. The staircase in the middle leads to the temple platform on top. Just north of the system is a massive monolith with early calendar markings.

**BUILDINGS G, H, I, AND J.** Crossing back to the center of the platform, the first structure you'll find is Building J, which is in the shape of an arrowhead. Unlike any other building here, it is asymmetrical and built at a 45° angle to nearby structures. The Zapotecs often used astronomy to detect seasonal changes; Building J was positioned to line up with Orion's Belt in order to signal the rainy season. Its broad, carved slabs suggest that the building is one of the oldest on the site, dating from 100 BC to AD 200. The so-called **Conquest Stones,** incongruous with the others on the backside of Building J, feature strange glyphs with upside-down heads. These represent the chieftains of groups conquered by the Zapotecs. The next group of buildings moving north, dominating the center of the plaza, includes buildings G, H, and I—likely making up the principal altar of Monte Albán. From here, the religious leader would address citizens from ground level; the Zapotec leader addressed them from the North Platform.

**NORTH PLATFORM.** Finish off the Main Plaza by visiting the North Platform near the entrance, a structure almost as large as the Main Plaza itself. The North Platform consists of a platform overlaid with a collection of pyramids and smaller stone platforms connected by small staircases. It contains the **Sunken Plaza** as well as the site's highest altar, the best place to view the entire site and lose yourself in passing clouds. Between the Sunken Plaza and the Main Plaza are 12 restored columns from a colonnade called the **Royal Portico.** This is where the Zapotec leader once addressed those in the Main Plaza and lesser nobles in the Sunken Plaza. The site has amazing acoustics—snippets of tourists' conversations echo throughout it. Around the east side of the platform is the **Bejeweled Building,** so called for the streaks of red painted on its stuccoed discs, signifying Teotihuacán influence.

**TOMBS AND MUSEUM.** Continue straight on the path, exiting the site to **Tomb 104.** Although none of the 260 tombs in Monte Albán are open to the public, you can still get an idea of the tomb from its exterior structure and the information placard with a map. On your way out of the site, be sure to stop by the **museum,** which gives a chronological survey of Monte Albán's history and displays the original stelae (the ones outside are replicas). The most interesting exhibit is a case of human skulls, some deformed by disease. You can also see the deliberate manipulation of infants' skulls. Presumably the manipulation was performed either as a ritual or to exhibit social status. Although the collection is still impressive, some of the more spectacular artifacts have been hauled off to museums in Oaxaca and Mexico City. Near the parking lot is the entrance to **Tomb 7**, where the spectacular cache of Mixtec ornaments mentioned above was found.

## TO THE SOUTH

The towns along the highway toward Puerto Ángel range from small to even smaller, but may be worth the few hours it takes to see them, especially if you're hunting for artisan souvenirs. All three towns listed here can be reached on buses to Ocotlán that leave from Oaxaca's second-class station (40min., about 1 per hr., 20 pesos). To travel between towns or return to Oaxaca, it's easiest to flag down a *taxi colectivo* on the highway (15 pesos); in Ocotlán, buses to Oaxaca leave frequently from the *zócalo* (20 pesos).

**SAN BARTOLO COYOTEPEC.** It would be easy to pass San Bartolo Coyotepec without even noticing. Those who do stop in this town just 13km outside of Oaxaca are rewarded with a bevy of stores selling *barro negro*. This pottery made with a shiny black clay is only produced in San Bartolo. The stuff is used to make bowls, jars, vases. More elaborate sculptures are made at a factory down C. Juárez, where you can buy it straight from the source. Other outlets, however, may be cheaper. *(13km south of Oaxaca on Mex. 175. About 20min. on the bus to Ocotlán. Factory open daily 9am-5pm. Cash only.)*

**SAN MARTÍN TILCAJETE.** About ten minutes past San Bartolo Coyotepec, a sign points off the highway to San Martín Tilcajete. If you go by *colectivo*, they may take you directly to town; from where the bus drops you off, it's about a fifteen minute walk on a road that runs through cornfields. Virtually every home and business in the area seems to be busy making and selling *alejibres*—stylized wooden sculptures of everything from frogs to the devil, painted in flamboyant blues, oranges, yellows, and reds. Even if you don't plan on buying anything, seeing the town's vast collection and peeking in on the sculpting and painting process is worth the trip in and of itself. Look in the open doors as you walk down the street; you're pretty much guaranteed to see someone working on something. *(24km south of Oaxaca on Mex. 175. About 30min. by bus to Ocotlán. Most stores open daily until 5pm. Cash only.)*

**OCOTLÁN.** At the end of the busride from Oaxaca is Ocotlán. The town specializes in painted clay figures which are made in the distinctive style created by the Aguilar family. The tradition is carried on today by the Aguilar sisters, Guillermina, Josefina, and Irene. Their workshops are all next to each other on the right as you enter town, several blocks before the *zócalo*. The finished works run from three-foot-tall religious figures to smaller and more elaborate scenes fashioned out of a dozen pieces or more. These smaller scenes depict everything from the birth of Jesus to community festivals. Aside from the figurines, there's a large market with the usual collection of artisan crafts.

Ocotlán has more to offer than just dolls. In the southeast corner of the *zócalo*, you'll find **San Domingo de Guzmán** tucked into a quiet, secluded plaza lined with pine trees. The inside of the church is vast and richly decorated. Next door is the town's surprisingly impressive **museum,** housed in a former convent and jail. The exhibits include 16th-century religious paintings and a vast collection by the well-known Mexican artist **Rodolfo Morales,** who was born in Ocotlán. His work largely consists of exuberant murals depicting everyday Mexican and *campesino* (farmer) life. There is also a series of stunning black and white photos from Ocotlán and the surrounding villages. The museum also houses some examples of the Aguilar sisters' work.

Ocotlán is also the only place on this road with amenities. Food can be found at the **stands** around the *zócalo* and at the **market,** on the southwest side of the square. **Farmacias del Ahorro** is on the east side of the *zócalo* (open daily 7am-11pm). To the north is **Scotiabank,** with a **24hr. ATM** (open M-F 9am-5pm). *(32km south of Oaxaca on Mex. 175. 40min. or the bus from Oaxaca. Museum open daily 9am-6pm. 15 pesos.)*

## TO THE NORTH

The road north from Oaxaca passes through a lonely, remote countryside of large but rolling hills with gorgeous red-rock outcroppings. The area is not yet a tourist destination, and you're likely to be one of the only people around with a camera. The reason to go—aside from the beautiful landscape—is a handful of 16th-century churches and monasteries, whose enormous size is enhanced by the sleepy five-road towns they sit in. The buildings were once major outposts on the Spanish mission trail, and they look the part. Their grandeur is only heightened by the fact that restoration and reconstruction work is still far from complete. The buildings, in many ways, show their considerable age. These towns are accessible by public buses, although it is not easily done. A rental car is another good option; on Mexico's wide, clean superhighway, Mex. 135, these towns are an hour away.

**YANHUITLÁN.** The church at Yanhuitlán, once the seat of the vicarage for the entire Mixteca region, rests at the top of a tall, wide staircase built over a pre-Columbian earthen mound. The facade is recognizably similar to churches in the city of Oaxaca, with orange stone and figures embedded around the entryway. With 27m high vaulted ceilings and a gilded altar studded with religious paintings, the interior is better preserved than any other historical church in the region. Equally stunning is the intricate woodwork on the roof toward the entrance. To the side of the church in the ex-convento is a **museum,** which mostly consists of articles from the convent's past. *(About 120km north of Oaxaca on Mex. 190, just off Mex. 135. On public transit, take a second-class bus towards Huajuapán. 25 pesos. Museum open Tu-Su 10am-5pm. 31 pesos.)*

**TEPOSCOLULA.** A bit to the southwest on Mex. 125, Teposcolula's church is perhaps the least grandiose of the old churches in the region. Still, it is unique for its large *capilla abierta*—open-air chapel—which measures 41m by 11m. Construction on the complex began in 1541, less than a generation after the fall of the Aztec Empire. The architecture of the church is dramatically Gothic with sweeping arches and flying buttresses. *(About 20km west of Yanhuitlán on Mex. 125. Taxis from Yanhuitlán for about 40 pesos. If you're driving, continue away from Oaxaca on Mex. 190 and turn left at the junction with Mex. 125. To return to Oaxaca, take a taxi to the 125/190 junction and wait for a bus headed towards the city.)*

**COIXTLAHUACA.** Known affectionately by locals as "Coix" (coh-EESH), Coixtlahuaca's full name means "field of snakes" in Nahuatl. For this reason, purchase a machete at the stall at the beginning of town (just kidding—there are no snakes). Conquered by the Aztecs in 1462, Coix fell to the Spanish less than a hundred years later; the Spanish immediately set to work building the impressive church. The building is now undergoing heavy renovation, but you can still appreciate the beautiful, almost floral facade and the intricate stonework inside. To the right (as you face the entrance), an archway leads to the former convent, now little more than ruins. The construction manager is usually in his office to the left of the main building through a large arch; if you catch him at the right time, you might be allowed to climb the makeshift wooden stairs to the roof, where a lovely view of the surrounding countryside awaits.

If you didn't pack a lunch, you may be starving by the time you get here. **Restaurant El Tío Betín ❶**, left out of the church's gravel parking lot one block away, serves some of the most delicious, homemade *comida oaxaqueña* you'll find in Mexico. (*Menú del día* 30 pesos. Open M-F 8am-10pm, Sa 8am-8pm, Su 8am-4pm. Cash only.) If you get stranded, or just feel like soaking in the region's splendid isolation for an extra day, **Hotel Marina Sol ❸**, down the hill from the church, has the only beds for miles around. It's more than adequate, however, with clean rooms and hot water. (Doubles 250 pesos. Cash only). *(113km north of Oaxaca, just off Mex. 135. To get here from Teposcolula, take a taxi to the 125/190 junction and catch a bus headed towards Mexico City. Get off at the sign for Coixtlahuaca; the town is about 1.5km down the road. Driving, go north of Mex. 135 toward Mexico City, until you see the sign for the turnoff on your right. To return to Oaxaca, go back to the highway and flag down any southbound bus.)*

# APPENDIX

## CLIMATE

| AVG. TEMP. (LOW/ HIGH), PRECIP. | JANUARY | | | APRIL | | | JULY | | | OCTOBER | | |
|---|---|---|---|---|---|---|---|---|---|---|---|---|
| | °C | °F | mm | °C | °F | mm | °C | °F | mm | °C | °F | mm |
| **Cancún** | 19-27 | 67-81 | 8 | 23-29 | 73-85 | 41 | 26-32 | 74-87 | 109 | 23-31 | 74-87 | 218 |
| **Mérida** | 17-29 | 63-84 | 25 | 21-35 | 69-95 | 23 | 22-34 | 69-88 | 163 | 21-31 | 69-88 | 94 |
| **Mexico City** | 6-21 | 43-70 | 10 | 11-26 | 52-79 | 28 | 12-23 | 50-72 | 183 | 10-22 | 50-72 | 61 |
| **Oaxaca** | 8-25 | 8-25 | 3 | 14-31 | 57-88 | 38 | 15-28 | 56-79 | 89 | 13-26 | 56-79 | 51 |
| **Veracruz** | 18-24 | 64-75 | 23 | 23-28 | 73-83 | 23 | 23-31 | 72-85 | 376 | 22-29 | 72-85 | 135 |
| **Villahermosa** | 19-24 | 66-76 | 91 | 21-30 | 70-86 | 71 | 23-30 | 71-83 | 132 | 22-28 | 71-83 | 269 |

## MEASUREMENTS

Like the rest of the rational world, Mexico uses the metric system. The basic unit of length is the **meter (m)**, which is divided into 100 **centimeters (cm)** or 1000 **millimeters (mm)**. One thousand meters make up one **kilometer (km)**. Fluids are measured in **liters (L)**, each divided into 1000 **milliliters (mL)**. A liter of pure water weighs one **kilogram (kg)**, which is divided into 1000 **grams (g)**. One metric ton is **1000kg.**

| MEASUREMENT CONVERSIONS | |
|---|---|
| 1 inch (in.) = 25.4mm | 1 millimeter (mm) = 0.039 in. |
| 1 foot (ft.) = 0.305m | 1 meter (m) = 3.28 ft. |
| 1 yard (yd.) = 0.914m | 1 meter (m) = 1.094 yd. |
| 1 mile (mi.) = 1.609km | 1 kilometer (km) = 0.621 mi. |
| 1 ounce (oz.) = 28.35g | 1 gram (g) = 0.035 oz. |
| 1 pound (lb.) = 0.454kg | 1 kilogram (kg) = 2.205 lb. |
| 1 fluid ounce (fl. oz.) = 29.57mL | 1 milliliter (mL) = 0.034 fl. oz. |
| 1 gallon (gal.) = 3.785L | 1 liter (L) = 0.264 gal. |

## LANGUAGE

### PRONUNCIATION

The letter **X** has a baffling variety of pronunciations: depending on dialect and word position, it can sound like English "h," "s," "sh," or "x." Spanish words receive stress on the syllable marked with an accent (´). In the absence of an accent mark, words that end in vowels, "n," or "s" receive stress on the second to last syllable. For words ending in all other consonants, stress falls on the last syllable. Spanish has masculine and feminine nouns, and gives a gender to all adjectives. Masculine words generally end with an "o": *él es un tonto* (he is a fool). Feminine words generally end with an "a": *ella es bella* (she is beautiful). Pay close attention—slight changes in word ending can cause drastic changes in meaning. For instance, when receiving directions, mind the distinction between *derecho* (straight) and *derecha* (right).

| PHONETIC UNIT | PRONUNCIATION | PHONETIC UNIT | PRONUNCIATION | PHONETIC UNIT | PRONUNCIATION |
|---|---|---|---|---|---|
| a | ah, as in "father" | h | silent | ñ | ay, as in "canyon" |
| e | eh, as in "pet" | y | yur, as in "yerba" | Mayan ch | sh, as in "shoe" |
| i | ee, as in "eat" | y and i | ee, as in "eat" | GŨ | goo, as in "gooey" |
| o | oh, as in "oh" | j | h, as in "hello" | g before e or i | h, as in "hen" |
| u | oo, as in "boot" | ll | y, as in "yes" | gu before e | g, as in "gate" |
| rr | trilled | x | uh... | | |

# PHRASEBOOK

## ESSENTIAL PHRASES

| ENGLISH | SPANISH | PRONUNCIATION |
|---|---|---|
| hello | Hola. | O-la |
| goodbye | Adiós. | ah-dee-OHS |
| yes/no | Sí/No | SEE/NO |
| please | Por favor. | POHR fa-VOHR |
| thank you | Gracias. | GRAH-see-ahs |
| You're welcome. | De nada. | deh NAH-dah |
| Do you speak English? | ¿Habla inglés? | AH-blah een-GLESS |
| I don't speak Spanish. | No hablo español. | NO AH-bloh ehs-pahn-YOHL |
| Excuse me. | Perdón/Disculpe. | pehr-THOHN/dee-SKOOL-peh |
| I don't know. | No sé. | NO SEH |
| Can you repeat that? | ¿Puede repetirlo?/¿Mande? | PWEH-deh reh-peh-TEER-lo/ MAHN-deh |
| I'm sorry/forgive me. | Lo siento | lo see-EN-toe |

## SURVIVAL SPANISH

| ENGLISH | SPANISH | ENGLISH | SPANISH |
|---|---|---|---|
| good morning | Buenos días. | How do you say (dodge-ball) in Spanish? | ¿Cómo se dice (dodgeball) en español? |
| good afternoon | Buenas tardes. | What (did you just say)? | ¿Cómo?/¿Qué?/¿Mande? |
| goodnight | Buenas noches. | I don't understand. | No entiendo. |
| What is your name? | ¿Cómo se llama? | Again, please. | Otra vez, por favor. |
| My name is (Jessica Laporte). | Me llamo (Jessica Laporte). | Could you speak slower? | ¿Podría hablar más despacio? |
| What's up? | ¿Qué tal? | Where is (the bathroom)? | ¿Dónde está (el baño)? |
| See you later. | Nos vemos./Hasta luego. | Who?/What? | ¿Quién?/¿Qué? |
| How are you? | ¿Qué tal?/¿Cómo está? | When?/Where? | ¿Cuándo?/¿Dónde? |
| I'm sick/fine. | Estoy enfermo(a)/bien. | Why? | ¿Por qué? |
| I am hot/cold. | Tengo calor/frío. | Because. | Porque. |
| I am hungry/thirsty. | Tengo hambre/sed. | Go on!/Come on!/ Hurry up! | ¡Ándale! |
| I want/would like... | Quiero/Quisiera... | Let's go! | ¡Vámonos! |
| How much does it cost? | ¿Cuánto cuesta? | Look!/Listen! | ¡Mira! |
| That is very cheap/ expensive. | Es muy barato/caro. | Stop!/That's enough! | ¡Basta! |
| Is the store open/closed? | ¿La tienda está abierta/ cerrada? | maybe | Tal vez/Puede ser. |
| Good morning. | Buenos días. | How do you say (I love Let's Go) in Spanish? | ¿Cómo se dice (Me encanta Let's Go) en español? |

## INTERPERSONAL INTERACTIONS

| ENGLISH | SPANISH | ENGLISH | SPANISH |
|---|---|---|---|
| Where are you from? | ¿De dónde viene usted? | Pleased to meet you. | Encantado(a)/Mucho gusto. |
| I am from (Europe). | Soy de (Europa). | Do you have a light? | ¿Tiene luz? |
| I'm (20) years old. | Tengo (veinte) años. | He/she seems cool. | Él/ella me cae bien. |
| Would you like to go out with me? | ¿Quiere salir conmigo? | What's wrong? | ¿Qué le pasa? |
| I have a boyfriend/girl-friend/spouse. | Tengo novio/novia/esposo(a). | I'm sorry. | Lo siento. |
| I'm gay/straight/bisexual. | Soy gay/heterosexual/soy bisexual. | Do you come here often? | ¿Viene aquí a menudo? |
| I love you. | Te quiero. | This is my first time in Mexico. | Esta es mi primera vez en Mexico. |
| Why not? | ¿Por qué no? | What a shame: you bought Lonely Planet! | ¡Qué lástima: compraste Lonely Planet! |

## YOUR ARRIVAL

| ENGLISH | SPANISH | ENGLISH | SPANISH |
|---|---|---|---|
| I am from (the US/Europe). | Soy de (los Estados Unidos/Europa). | What's the problem, sir/madam? | ¿Cuál es el problema, señor/señora? |
| Here is my passport. | Aquí está mi pasaporte. | I lost my passport/luggage. | Se me perdió mi pasaporte/equipaje. |
| I will be here for less than six months. | Estaré aquí por menos de seis meses. | I have nothing to declare. | No tengo nada para declarar. |
| I don't know where that came from. | No sé de dónde vino eso. | Please do not detain me. | Por favor no me detenga. |

## GETTING AROUND

| ENGLISH | SPANISH | ENGLISH | SPANISH |
|---|---|---|---|
| How do you get to (the bus station)? | ¿Cómo se puede llegar a (la estación de auto-buses)? | Does this bus go to (Guanajuato)? | ¿Esta autobús va a (Guanajuato)? |
| Which bus line goes to..? | ¿Cuál línea de buses tiene servicio a...? | Where does the bus leave from? | ¿De dónde sale el bús? |
| When does the bus leave? | ¿Cuándo sale el bús? | How long does the trip take? | ¿Cuánto tiempo dura el viaje? |
| Can I buy a ticket? | ¿Puedo comprar un boleto? | I'm getting off at (Av. Juárez). | Me bajo en (Av. Juárez). |
| Where is (the center of town)? | ¿Dónde está (el centro)? | Please let me off at (the zoo). | Por favor, déjeme en (el zoológico). |
| How near/far is...? | ¿Qué tan cerca/lejos está...? | Where is (Constitución) street? | ¿Dónde está la calle (Constitución)? |
| I'm in a hurry. | Estoy de prisa. | Continue forward. | Siga derecho. |
| I'm lost. | Estoy perdido(a). | On foot. | A pie. |
| I am going to the airport. | Voy al aeropuerto. | The flight is delayed/canceled. | El vuelo está atrasado/cancelado. |
| Where is the bathroom? | ¿Dónde está el baño? | Is it safe to hitchhike? | ¿Es seguro pedir aventón? |
| Where can I buy a cell-phone? | ¿Dónde puedo comprar un teléfono celular? | Where can I check email? | ¿Dónde se puede chequear el correo electrónico? |
| Could you tell me what time it is? | ¿Podría decirme qué hora es? | Are there student dis-counts available? | ¿Hay descuentos para estudiantes? |

## ON THE ROAD

| ENGLISH | SPANISH | ENGLISH | SPANISH |
|---|---|---|---|
| I would like to rent (a car). | Quisiera alquilar (un coche). | north | norte |

| How much does it cost per day/week? | ¿Cuánto cuesta por día/semana? | south | sur |
|---|---|---|---|
| Does it have (heating/air-conditioning)? | ¿Tiene (calefacción/aire acondicionado)? | public bus/van | bús |
| stop | pare | slow | despacio |
| lane (ends) | carril (termina) | yield | ceda |
| entrance | entrada | seatbelt | cinturón de seguridad |
| exit | salida | (maximum) speed | velocidad (máxima) |
| (narrow) bridge | puente (estrecho) | dangerous (curve) | (curva) peligrosa |
| narrow (lane) | (carril) estrecho | parking | estacionamiento, parking |
| toll (ahead) | peaje (adelante) | dead-end street | calle sin salida |
| authorized public buses only | transporte colectivo autorizado solamente | only | solo |
| slippery when wet | resbala cuando mojado | rest area | área de descansar |
| danger (ahead) | peligro (adelante) | do not park | no estacione |
| do not enter | no entre | do not turn right on red | no vire con luz roja |

## DIRECTIONS

| ENGLISH | SPANISH | ENGLISH | SPANISH |
|---|---|---|---|
| (to the) right | (a la) derecha | near (to) | cerca (de) |
| (to the) left | (a la) izquierda | far (from) | lejos (de) |
| next to | al lado de/junto a | above | arriba |
| across from | en frente de/frente a | below | abajo |
| (Continue) straight. | (Siga) derecho. | block | cuadra/manzana |
| turn (command form) | doble | corner | esquina |
| traffic light | semáforo | street | calle/avenida |

## ACCOMMODATIONS

| ENGLISH | SPANISH | ENGLISH | SPANISH |
|---|---|---|---|
| Is there a cheap hotel around here? | ¿Hay un hotel económico por aquí? | Are there rooms with windows? | ¿Hay habitaciones con ventanas? |
| Do you have rooms available? | ¿Tiene habitaciones libres? | I am going to stay for (4) days. | Me voy a quedar (cuatro) días. |
| I would like to reserve a room. | Quisiera reservar una habitación. | Are there cheaper rooms? | ¿Hay habitaciones más baratas? |
| Could I see a room? | ¿Podría ver una habitación? | Do they come with private baths? | ¿Vienen con baño privado? |
| Do you have any singles/doubles? | ¿Tiene habitaciones simples/dobles? | I'll take it. | Lo acepto. |
| I need another key/towel/pillow. | Necesito otra llave/toalla/almohada. | There are cockroaches in my room. | Hay cucarachas en mi habitación. |
| The shower/sink/toilet is broken. | La ducha/pila/el servicio no funciona. | (The cockroaches) are biting me. | (Las cucarachas) me están mordiendo. |
| My sheets are dirty. | Mis sábanas están sucias. | Dance, cockroaches, dance! | ¡Bailen, cucarachas, bailen! |

## EMERGENCY

| ENGLISH | SPANISH | ENGLISH | SPANISH |
|---|---|---|---|
| Help! | ¡Socorro!/¡Auxilio!/¡Ayúdeme! | Call the police! | ¡Llame a la policía! |
| I am hurt. | Estoy herido(a). | Leave me alone! | ¡Déjame en paz! |
| It's an emergency! | ¡Es una emergencia! | Don't touch me! | ¡No me toque! |
| Fire! | ¡Fuego!/¡Incendio! | I've been robbed! | ¡Me han robado! |
| Call a clinic/ambulance/doctor/priest! | ¡Llame a una clínica/una ambulancia/un médico/un padre! | They went that-a-way! | ¡Se fueron por allá! |
| I need to contact my embassy. | Necesito comunicarme con mi embajada. | I will only speak in the presence of a lawyer. | Sólo hablaré con la presencia de un(a) abogado(a). |

## MEDICAL

| ENGLISH | SPANISH | ENGLISH | SPANISH |
|---|---|---|---|
| I feel bad/worse/better/okay/fine. | Me siento mal/peor/mejor/más o menos/bien. | My (stomach) hurts. | Me duele (el estómago). |
| I have a headache/stomachache. | Tengo un dolor de cabeza/estómago. | It hurts here. | Me duele aquí. |
| I'm sick/ill. | Estoy enfermo(a). | I'm allergic to (nuts) | Soy alérgico(a) a (nueces) |
| Here is my prescription. | Aquí está mi receta médica. | I think I'm going to vomit. | Pienso que voy a vomitar. |
| What is this medicine for? | ¿Para qué es esta medicina? | I have a cold/a fever/diarrhea/nausea. | Tengo gripe/una calentura/diarrea/náusea. |
| Where is the nearest hospital/doctor? | ¿Dónde está el hospital/doctor más cercano? | I haven't been able to go to the bathroom in (4) days. | No he podido ir al baño en (cuatro) días. |

## OUT TO LUNCH

| ENGLISH | SPANISH | ENGLISH | SPANISH |
|---|---|---|---|
| breakfast | desayuno | Where is a good restaurant? | ¿Dónde está un restaurante bueno? |
| lunch | almuerzo | Can I see the menu? | ¿Podría ver la carta/el menú? |
| dinner | comida/cena | Table for (one), please. | Mesa para (uno), por favor. |
| dessert | postre | Do you take credit cards? | ¿Aceptan tarjetas de crédito? |
| drink (alcoholic) | bebida (trago) | I would like to order (the chicken). | Quisiera (el pollo). |
| cup | copa/taza | Do you have anything vegetarian/without meat? | ¿Hay algún plato vegetariano/sin carne? |
| fork | tenedor | Do you have hot sauce? | ¿Tiene salsa picante? |
| knife | cuchillo | This is too spicy. | Es demasiado picante. |
| napkin | servilleta | Disgusting! | ¡Guácala!/¡Qué asco! |
| spoon | cuchara | Delicious! | ¡Qué rico! |
| bon appétit | buen provecho | Check, please. | La cuenta, por favor. |

## MENU READER

| SPANISH | ENGLISH | SPANISH | ENGLISH |
|---|---|---|---|
| a la brasa | roasted | frijoles | beans |
| a la plancha | grilled | leche | milk |
| al vapor | steamed | legumbres | legumes |
| aceite | oil | licuado | smoothie |
| aceituna | olive | lima | lime |
| agua (purificada) | water (purified) | limón | lemon |
| ajo | garlic | limonada | lemonade |
| almeja | clam | lomo | steak or chop |
| arroz (con leche) | rice (rice pudding) | maíz | corn |
| birria | cow brain soup, a hang-over cure | mariscos | seafood |
| bistec | beefsteak | miel | honey |
| café | coffee | mole | dark chocolate chili sauce |
| caliente | hot | pan | bread |
| camarones | shrimp | papas (fritas) | potatoes (french fries) |
| carne | meat | parrillas | various grilled meats |
| cebolla | onion | pastes | meat pie |
| cemitas | sandwiches made with special long-lasting bread | pasteles | desserts/pies |

| | | | |
|---|---|---|---|
| cerveza | beer | pescado | fish |
| ceviche | raw marinated seafood | papa | potato |
| charales | small fish, fried and eaten whole | pimienta | pepper |
| chaya | plant similar to spinach native to the Yucatán | pollo | chicken |
| chorizo | spicy sausage | puerco/cerdo | pork |
| coco | coconut | pulque | liquor made from maguey cactus |
| cordero | lamb | queso | cheese |
| (sin) crema | (without) cream | refresco | soda pop |
| dulces | sweets | verduras/vegetales | vegetables |
| dulce de leche | caramelized milk | sal | salt |
| empanada | dumpling filled with meat, cheese, or potatoes | sopes | thick tortillas, stuffed with different toppings |
| ensalada | salad | tragos | mixed drinks/liquor |
| entrada | appetizer | Xtabentún | anise and honey liqueur |

## NUMBERS, DAYS, & MONTHS

| ENGLISH | SPANISH | ENGLISH | SPANISH | ENGLISH | SPANISH |
|---|---|---|---|---|---|
| 0 | cero | 30 | treinta | weekend | fin de semana |
| 1 | uno | 40 | cuarenta | morning | mañana |
| 2 | dos | 50 | cincuenta | afternoon | tarde |
| 3 | tres | 60 | sesenta | night | noche |
| 4 | cuatro | 70 | setenta | day | día |
| 5 | cinco | 80 | ochenta | month | mes |
| 6 | seis | 90 | noventa | year | año |
| 7 | siete | 100 | cien | early | temprano |
| 8 | ocho | 1000 | mil | late | tarde |
| 9 | nueve | 1,000,000 | un millón | January | enero |
| 10 | diez | Monday | lunes | February | febrero |
| 11 | once | Tuesday | martes | March | marzo |
| 12 | doce | Wednesday | miércoles | April | abril |
| 13 | trece | Thursday | jueves | May | mayo |
| 14 | catorce | Friday | viernes | June | junio |
| 15 | quince | Saturday | sábado | July | julio |
| 16 | dieciseis | Sunday | domingo | August | agosto |
| 17 | diecisiete | day before yesterday | anteayer | September | septiembre |
| 18 | dieciocho | yesterday | ayer | October | octubre |
| 19 | diecinueve | last night | anoche | November | noviembre |
| 20 | veinte | today | hoy | December | diciembre |
| 21 | veintiuno | tomorrow | mañana | 2009 | dos mil nueve |
| 22 | veintidos | day after tomorrow | pasado mañana | 2010 | dos mil dix |

# SPANISH GLOSSARY

APPENDIX

**aduana:** customs

**agencia de viaje:** travel agency

**aguardiente:** strong liquor

**aguas frescas:** cold fresh juice/tea

**aguas termales:** hot springs

**ahora:** now

**ahorita:** in just a moment

**aire acondicionado:** air-conditioning (A/C)

**al gusto:** as you wish

**almacén:** (grocery) store

**almuerzo:** lunch, midday meal

**altiplano:** highland

**amigo(a):** friend

**andén:** platform

**antro:** club/disco/joint

**antojitos:** appetizer

**sarena:** sand

**arroz:** rice

**artesanía:** arts and crafts

**avenida:** avenue

**azúcar:** sugar

**bahía:** bay

**balneario:** spa

**bandido:** bandit

**baño:** bathroom or natural spa

**barato(a):** cheap

**barranca:** canyon

**barro:** mud

**barrio:** neighborhood

**bello(a):** beautiful

**biblioteca:** library

**biosfera:** biosphere

**birria:** meat stew, usually goat

**bistec:** beefsteak

**blanquillo:** egg

**bocaditos:** appetizers, at a bar

**bodega:** convenience store or winery

**boetería:** ticket counter

**boleto:** ticket

**bonito(a):** pretty

**borracho(a):** drunk

**bosque:** forest

**botanas:** snacks, frequently at bars

**bueno(a):** good

**buena suerte:** good luck

**burro:** donkey

**caballero:** gentleman

**caballo:** horse

**cabañas:** cabins

**cajeros:** cashiers

**cajero automático:** ATM

**caldo:** soup, broth, or stew

**calle:** street

**cama:** bed

**cambio:** change

**caminata:** hike

**camino:** path, track, road

**camión:** truck

**camioneta:** small pickup-sized

**campamento:** campground

**campesino(a):** person from a rural area, peasant

**campo:** countryside

**canotaje:** rafting

**cantina:** bar/drinking establishment

**capilla:** chapel

**carne asada:** roasted meat

**carnitas:** diced, cooked pork

**caro(a):** expensive

**carretera:** highway

**carro:** car, or sometimes a train car

**casa:** house

**casa de cambio:** currency exchange establishment

**casado(a):** married

**cascadas:** waterfalls

**catedral:** cathedral

**cenote:** fresh-water well

**centro:** city center

**cerca:** near/nearby

**cerro:** hill

**cerveza:** beer

**ceviche:** raw seafood marinated in lemon juice, herbs, vegetables

**cevichería:** ceviche restaurant

**chico(a):** little boy (girl)

**chicharrón:** bite-sized pieces of fried pork, pork rinds

**chuleta de puerco:** pork chop

**cigarillo:** cigarette

**cine:** cinema

**ciudad:** city

**ciudadela:** neighborhood in a large city

**coche:** car

**cocodrilo:** crocodile

**colectivo:** shared taxi

**colina:** hill

**coliseo:** coliseum, stadium

**comedor:** dining room

**comida del día:** daily special

**comida corrida:** fixed-price meal

**comida típica:** typical/traditional dishes

**computador:** computer

**con:** with

**concha:** shell

**consulado:** consulate

**convento:** convent

**correo:** mail, post office

**correo electrónico:** email

**cordillera:** mountain range

**corvina:** sea bass

**crucero:** crossroads

**Cruz Roja:** Red Cross

**cuadra:** street block

**cuarto:** room

**cuenta:** bill, check

**cuento:** story, account

**cueva:** cave

**cuota:** toll

**curandero:** healer

**damas:** ladies

**desayuno:** breakfast

**descompuesto:** broken, out of order; spoiled (food)

**desierto:** desert

**despacio:** slow

**de paso:** in passing, usually refers to buses

**de turno:** a 24hr. rotating schedule for pharmacies

APPENDIX

**dinero:** money
**discoteca:** dance club
**dueño(a):** owner
**dulces:** sweets
**duna:** dune
**edificio:** building
**ejido:** communal land
**embajada:** embassy
**embarcadero:** dock
**emergencia:** emergency
**encomiendas:** estates granted to Spanish settlers in Latin America
**entrada:** entrance
**equipaje:** luggage
**estadio:** stadium
**este:** east
**estrella:** star
**extranjero:** foreign, foreigner
**farmacia:** pharmacy
**farmacia en turno:** 24hr. pharmacy
**feliz:** happy
**ferrocarril:** railroad
**fiesta:** party, holiday
**finca:** farm
**friaje:** sudden cold wind
**frijoles:** beans
**frontera:** border
**fumar:** to smoke
**fumaroles:** holes in a volcanic region which emit hot vapors
**fundo:** large estate or tract of land
**fútbol:** soccer
**ganga:** bargain
**gobierno:** government
**gordo(a):** fat
**gorra:** cap
**gratis:** free
**gringo(a):** Caucasian
**habitación:** a room
**hacer una caminata:** take a hike
**hacienda:** ranch
**helado:** ice cream
**hermano(a):** brother (sister)
**hervido(a):** boiled
**hielo:** ice
**hijo(a):** son (daughter)
**hombre:** man
**huevo:** egg

**iglesia:** church
**impuestos:** taxes
**impuesto valor añadido (IVA):** value added tax (VAT)
**indígena:** indigenous person, refers to the native culture
**ir de camping:** to go camping
**isla:** island
**jaiba:** crab meat
**jamón:** ham
**jarra:** pitcher
**jirón:** street
**jugo:** juice
**ladrón:** thief
**lago/laguna:** lake, lagoon
**lancha:** launch, small boat
**langosta:** lobster
**langostino:** jumbo shrimp
**larga distancia:** long distance
**lavandería:** laundromat
**lejos:** far
**lento:** slow
**librería:** bookstore
**licuado:** smoothie, shake
**lista de correos:** mail holding system in Latin America
**llamada:** call
**loma:** hill
**lomo:** chop, steak
**lonchería:** snack bar
**loro:** parrot
**madre:** mother
**malo(a):** bad
**malecón:** pier or seaside boardwalk
**maletas:** luggage, suitcases
**manejar despacio:** to drive slowly
**manzana:** apple
**mar:** sea
**mariscos:** seafood
**matrimonial:** double bed
**menestras:** lentils/beans
**menú del día/menú:** fixed daily meal often offered for a bargain price
**mercado:** market

**merendero:** outdoor bar/kiosk
**merienda:** snack
**mestizaje:** crossing of races
**mestizo(a):** a person of mixed European and indigenous descent
**microbús:** small, local bus
**mirador:** an observatory or lookout point
**muelle:** wharf
**muerte:** death
**museo:** museum
**música folklórica:** folk music
**nada:** nothing
**naranja:** orange
**niño(a):** child
**norte (Nte.):** north
**nuez/nueces:** nut/nuts
**obra:** work of art, play
**obraje:** primitive textile workshop
**oeste:** west
**oficina de turismo:** tourist office
**oriente (Ote.):** east
**padre:** father
**palapa:** palm-thatched umbrella
**pampa:** a treeless grassland area
**pan:** bread
**panadería:** bakery
**oatpapagayo:** parrot
**parada:** a stop (on a bus or train)
**parilla:** various cuts of grilled meat
**paro:** labor strike
**parque:** park
**parroquia:** parish
**paseo turístico:** tour covering a series of sites
**pelea de gallos:** cockfight
**peligroso(a):** dangerous
**peninsulares:** Spanish-born colonists
**pescado:** fish
**picante:** spicy
**plátano:** plantain
**playa:** beach

**población:** population, settlement
**poniente (Pte.):** west
**policía:** police
**portales:** archways
**pueblito:** small town
**pueblo:** town
**puente:** bridge
**puerta:** door
**puerto:** port
**queso:** cheese
**rana:** frog
**recreo:** place of amusement, bar-restaurant on the outskirts of a city
**refrescos:** refreshments, soft drinks
**refugio:** refuge
**reloj:** watch, clock
**requesón:** cottage cheese
**río:** river
**ropa:** clothes
**sábanas:** bedsheets
**sabor:** flavor
**sala:** living room
**salida:** exit
**salto:** waterfall
**salsa:** sauce

**scabé:** paved, elevated roads found in many ruins.
**seguro(a):** lock, insurance; adj.: safe
**selva:** jungle
**semáforo:** traffic light
**semana:** week
**Semana Santa:** Holy Week
**sexo:** sex
**SIDA:** AIDS
**siesta**: mid-afternoon nap; businesses often close at this time
**sillar:** flexible volcanic rock used in construction
**sol:** sun
**solito(a):** alone
**solo carril:** one-lane road or bridge
**soltero(a):** single (unmarried)
**supermercado:** supermarket
**sur (S.):** south
**tarifa:** fee

**tapas:** bite-size appetizers served in bars
**telenovela:** soap opera
**termas:** hot mineral springs
**terminal terrestre:** bus station
**tienda:** store
**timbre:** bell
**tipo de cambio:** exchange rate
**tortuga:** turtle
**trago:** mixed drink/shot of alcohol
**triste:** sad
**turismo:** tourism
**turista:** tourist, tourist diarrhea
**valle:** valley
**vecindad:** neighborhood
**vegetariano(a):** vegetarian
**volcán:** volcano
**zócalo:** central town plaza
**zona:** zone

APPENDIX

# INDEX

# MAP INDEX

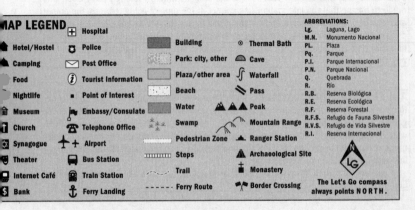

## MAP LEGEND

|  | |  | |
|---|---|---|---|
| | Hospital | Building | ⊙ Thermal Bath |
| Hotel/Hostel | Police | Park: city, other | Cave |
| Camping | Post Office | Plaza/other area | Waterfall |
| Food | Tourist Information | Beach | Pass |
| Nightlife | Point of Interest | Water | Peak |
| Museum | Embassy/Consulate | Swamp | Mountain Range |
| Church | Telephone Office | Pedestrian Zone | Ranger Station |
| Synagogue | Airport | Steps | Archaeological Site |
| Theater | Bus Station | Trail | Monastery |
| Internet Café | Train Station | Ferry Route | Border Crossing |
| Bank | Ferry Landing | | |

**ABBREVIATIONS:**

Lg.   Laguna, Lago
M.N.   Monumento Nacional
PL.   Plaza
Pq.   Parque
P.I.   Parque Internacional
P.N.   Parque Nacional
Q.   Quebrada
R.   Río
R.B.   Reserva Biológica
R.E.   Reserva Ecológica
R.F.   Reserva Forestal
R.F.S.   Refugio de Fauna Silvestre
R.V.S.   Refugio de Vida Silvestre
R.I.   Reserva Internacional

The Let's Go compass
always points NORTH.

**HELPING LET'S GO.** If you want to share your discoveries, suggestions, or corrections, please drop us a line. We appreciate every piece of correspondence, whether a postcard, a 10-page email, or a coconut. Visit Let's Go at **http://www.letsgo.com,** or send email to:

feedback@letsgo.com, subject: "Let's Go Yucatán Peninsula"

**Address mail to:**

Let's Go Yucatán Peninsula, 67 Mount Auburn St., Cambridge, MA 02138 , USA

In addition to the invaluable travel advice our readers share with us, many are kind enough to offer their services as researchers or editors. Unfortunately, our charter enables us to employ only currently enrolled Harvard students.

Maps by Let's Go copyright © 2010 by Let's Go, Inc.

Distributed by Publishers Group West.
Printed in Canada by Friesens Corp.

**Let's Go Yucatán Peninsula** Copyright © 2010 by Let's Go, Inc. All rights reserved. No part of this book may be used or reproduced in any manner whatsoever without written permission except in the case of brief quotations embodied in critical articles or reviews. Let's Go is available for purchase in bulk by institutions and authorized resellers.

ISBN-13:978-1-59880-301-3
ISBN-10:1-59880-301-8
First edition
10 9 8 7 6 5 4 3 2 1

**Let's Go Yucatán Peninsula** is written by Let's Go Publications, 67 Mount Auburn St., Cambridge, MA 02138, USA.

**Let's Go®** and the LG logo are trademarks of Let's Go, Inc.

**LEGAL DISCLAIMER.** For 50 years, Let's Go has published the world's favorite budget travel guides, written entirely by students and updated periodically based on the personal anecdotes and travel experiences of our student writers. Although every effort was made to ensure that the information was correct at the time of going to press, the author and publisher do not assume and hereby disclaim any liability to any party for any loss or damage caused by errors, omissions, or any potential travel disruption due to labor or financial difficulty, whether such errors or omissions result from negligence, accident, or any other cause.

**ADVERTISING DISCLAIMER.** All advertisements appearing in Let's Go publications are sold by an independent agency not affiliated with the editorial production of the guides. Advertisers are never given preferential treatment, and the guides are researched, written, and published independent of advertising. Advertisements do not imply endorsement of products or services by Let's Go, and Let's Go does not vouch for the accuracy of information provided in advertisements.

If you are interested in purchasing advertising space in a Let's Go publication, contact Edman & Company, 1-203-656-1000.